SUMNER COUNTY TENNESSEE COURT MINUTES

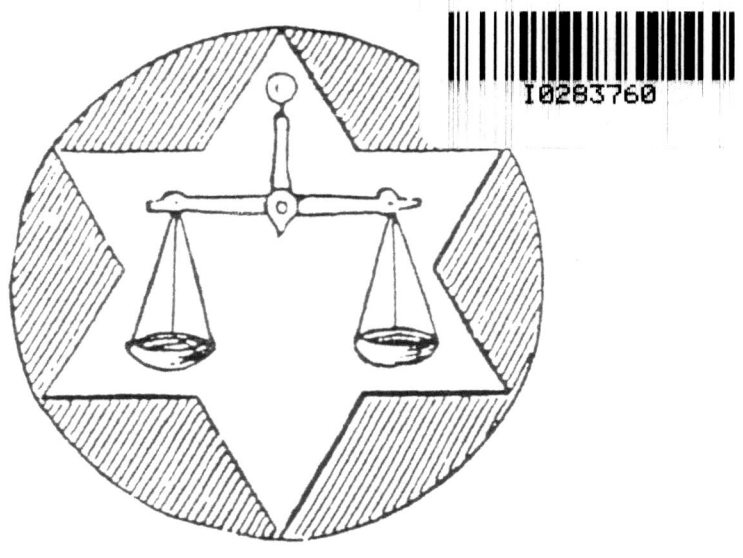

1787-1805 *and* 1808-1810

Carol Wells

HERITAGE BOOKS
2008

HERITAGE BOOKS
AN IMPRINT OF HERITAGE BOOKS, INC.

Books, CDs, and more—Worldwide

For our listing of thousands of titles see our website
at
www.HeritageBooks.com

Published 2008 by
HERITAGE BOOKS, INC.
Publishing Division
100 Railroad Ave. #104
Westminster, Maryland 21157

Copyright © 1995 Carol Wells

All rights reserved. No part of this book may be reproduced or
transmitted in any form or by any means, electronic or mechanical,
including photocopying, recording or by any information storage
and retrieval system without written permission from the author,
except for the inclusion of brief quotations in a review.

International Standard Book Numbers
Paperbound: 978-0-7884-0295-1
Clothbound: 978-0-7884-7279-4

TABLE OF CONTENTS

Part 1. 1797-1805:

Foreword vii

Abbreviations viii

Court Minutes:
1787
    April 1
    July 1
    October 2

1788
    January 3
    April 4
    July 5
    October 6

1789
    January 8
    April 9
    July 10
    October 11

1790
    January 12
    April 13
    July 15
    October 17

1791
    January 18
    April 20
    July 22
    October 24

1792
    January 26
    April 28
    July 30
    October 32

1793
    January 32
    April 33
    July 35
    October 37

1794
    January 39
    April 41
    July 43
    October 46

1795
    January 47
    April 50
    July 52
    October 53

1796
- January 56
- April 58
- July 61
- October 64

1797
- January 67
- April 70
- July 74
- October 77

1798
- January 80
- April 83
- July 89
- October 91

1799
- January 97
- April 102
- July 108
- October 113

1800
- January 119
- April 124
- July 129
- October 133

1801
- January 137
- April 141
- July 145
- October 150

1802
- January 156
- April 157
- July 161
- October 165

1803
- January 171
- April 175
- July 179
- October 185

1804
- March 190
- June 199
- September 205
- December 212

1805
- March 218
- June 226

Index to Part 1 234

Part 2, 1808-1810:

1808
    June 1
    September 5
    December 15

1809
    March 23
    June 36
    September 46
    December 55

1810
    March 63

Index to Part 2 68

FOREWORD

Cut from Davidson County in 1786, Sumner was the fastest growing county in central Tennessee. Sumner covered a large area now divided into many other counties. When Indian troubles ended, Sumner was a hive of activity: ferries and mills were established, new roads laid out, old roads were altered to follow more convenient ways. Town lots were sold; courthouse, prison and stocks were constructed. The larger population created other situations for the county court to deal with. Inheritances of orphans were protected, widows' dowers laid off, conditions such as poverty, insanity, and illegitimacy were dealt with. Court justices ruled on lawsuits over matters from debt and conflicting land claims to Sabbath breaking and profane swearing. Lawbreakers were fined, sold out, flogged, or imprisoned.

In the flood of new settlers were those who found themselves overextended and hopelessly in debt. Still the population grew. For the years from 1786 to 1805 covered by this book, nearly 4300 names are listed on 38 index pages. Since the first surviving Federal census for Sumner is 1820, Court minutes are important in determining who was present as well as what they were doing. In minutes are found names of witnesses, bondsmen, adjoining landowners, county officials, and others. Heirs, children, remarried widows, and transients may all appear in minutes and nowhere else.

This book was abstracted from microfilm of handwritten minutes. Names are printed as they appeared on these pages. The reader will please allow for the clerks' curious spelling, and for the abstractor's misinterpretation of the penmanship. Please consult the original when verification is needed.

Carol Wells

ABBREVIATIONS

A&B	Assault & Battery
ac	acres
ackd	acknowledged
addl	additional
admr	administrator
agt	against
appt	appoint
atty	attorney
compy	company
cr	creek
CSC	Clerk Sumner County
dam	damages
decd	deceased
depo	deposition
dft	defendant
D/G	deed of gift
DS	deputy sheriff
exd	excused
exn	execution
exr	executor
judgt	judgment
P/A	power of attorney
plf	plaintiff
rd	road
recd	received
retd	returned
sec	security
secy	security
shff	sheriff
TAB	trespass assault & battery
will	last will and testament
wit	witness

APRIL 1787

NOTE: Many names in the early minutes are obscured by a material used to mend frayed and torn pages. Missing names are indicated by [].

Agreeable to an Act of Assembly for the establishment of Sumner County...John Hambleton, Daniel Smith, Isaac Bledsoe, Isaac Lindsey, D[ ], Joseph Kuykendall, William Hall & George Winchester, Esqrs, Justices of the Peace.
Appoint David Shelby Clerk of Court.
Appt John Hardin Jr Sheriff,[] Kuykendall, Benjn [], Edward Douglass, Securities. Isaiah [] apptd Ranger.
[] Kuykendall records his stock mark.
Richard Searcy minor orphan bound to James McKain to age 21; sd McKain guardian.
William Price minor orphan bound to John Hardin till age 21; Hardin promises to make sd orphan a title to 200 acres exclusive of his freedom dues when he is free.
Grant admn on estate of William Price decd to [] Hardin.
John Searcy and Reuben Searcy minor orphans bound unto Thomas [] to age 21.
Court adjourned till tomorrow ten oclock.

April the 10th 1787. Present Isaac Bledsoe John [], [ ].
Jurors nominated for ensuing Term: William Bowan, Kasper Mansker, William [], Stephen Montgomery, James Sanders, Zachariah Green, William McNeely, George Mansker, [ ], James Franklin, James McKain, Elmore Douglass.

p.-   Court of Pleas & Quarter Sessions at the house of John Hardin Monday July 1787. Present Isaac Bledsoe, Isaac Lindsey, John Harden, Joseph Kuykendall, George Winchester.
Francis Hainey v Thomas Spencer, dft not appearing, judgt by default agt him.
Appt Charles Morgan to take list of inhabitants in Lynns district; James Douglass for Capt Elmore Douglass Compy; Ezekiel Norris, Kuykendalls Compy; Capt William Walton for Capt S Kuykendalls Compy.
David Shelby v John & Saml Campbell. Suit dismissed, dfts paying costs.
Order a road cleared sufficient for pack horses to pass, from Bledsoes to State line, most convenient way to Blue Spring. Major Isaac Bledsoe, James Harrison, Charles Morgan, James Wilson, James Wilson, George Mansco, Capt Elmore Douglass, James Franklin, Ephm Payton, Abner Bush, James Hays, George Winchester, Obediah Terrell, James [] to mark the road from Major Bledsoes to State Line; Robert Desha apptd to oversee sd road; Capt Lynns & Capt Douglass companies to work on sd road.
Order road cleared from Capt Kuykendalls to Capt Winchesters mill. Jos Kuykendall William Hacker Thomas Hamilton Jesse Summers Ezekiel Norris Philip [] [] Sutton Thomas Kilgore Zebulon Hubbard John Morgan John Hicks & John Desha to mark sd road; William Maxwell to oversee sd road from Capt Kuykendalls to head of Deshas fork of Bledsoes creek; Thomas Patton to oversee from thence to Winchester mill.
Grand Jurors: William Walton foreman, Kasper Mansker, Wm Montgomery Jr, Zachariah Green, George Mansker, John Norris, James Franklin, James McKain, [] ---lass, John John Brigham, Peter Looney, Harmon, John Steel, Benjamin Kuykendall, William [],

1

JULY 1787

Richard Caveat, Charles Arrington, William Hacker, William Snoddy.
Anthony Bledsoe chairman qualified.
Following militia officers produced commissions: Anthony Bledsoe Lieut Colonel commandant, Isaac Bledsoe 1st major, [ ] 2nd Major, James Lynn, Elmore Douglass, Joseph Kuykendall Captains; Abner [], [] Manscoe, James Frazer Lieuts, John Hickison, Joseph McElwrath & Zachariah [].
John Hardin returned inventory of late William Price.
Stock mark & brands recorded by Thomas Billen, Doke Hannah, Ezekiel Douglass, Peter
p.4   Looney, William Hacker, Anthony Bledsoe, Isaac Bledsoe, Daniel Smith, James McKain, David Shelby, Peter Looney (Harmon), Charles Morgan.
Jurors to October 1787 Session: James Hannah, Charles Morgan, John Hicks, Robert Bell, William Bowman, Henry Rule, John Roberts, George Ridley, Robert Looney, Matthew Kuykendall, James Douglass, James McKain Junr, Ephraim Payton, Alexr Dever, William Thompson, Laurence Thompson, Francis Catron, Richard Carr, Reuben Douglass, Robert Brigance, John Hambleton, Ezekiel Norris, Zebulon Hubbard, Thomas Kilgore, Uriah Anderson, Joseph Dixon, Thomas Hampton, James Wilson, William [].
Appt Thomas Martin[Masten?] sheriff; Elmore Douglass & James Lynn securities.
Appoint to take lists of taxable property: C Smith in Capt Simon Kuykendalls district; Capt Hardin in Capt Elmore Douglass's dist; Joseph Kuykendall in his own district; George Winchester in Capt Lynns district.
Charles Carter records his stock mark.
Appt Thomas Kilgore to oversee road in room of William Maxwell.
Order Capt Kuykendalls compy clear the road from Capt Kuykendalls to top of ridge; Capt Lynns Compy from ridge to Capt Winchesters mill.
The party to clear road from Major Bledsoes to Blue Spring go on [] 2th inst.
Philip Trammell, Joshua Campbell & David Brigham constables gave bond.
Court adjourned until Court in Course.   Anthony Bledsoe.

p.   Court of Pleas & Quarter Sessions, house of John Hamilton, second Monday, October 1787. Present Isaac Bledsoe, David Wilson, John Hardin, George Winchester.
Ephraim Payton security on bond of John Hardin as admr instead of Jos McElwrath.
Bill/sale Joseph Dixon to Robert Desha ackd.
Joseph Kuykendall Esqr appeared and took his seat.
Nuncupative will of Abner Bush proven by Uriah Anderson Richard [], James Hannah and William Baldwin; he apptd his wife Elinder Bush extx, John Hamilton security.
Grand jurors: Chas Morgan foreman, Robt Bell, John Roberts, Jas Douglass, James McKain Jr, Ephraim Payton, Laurence Thompson, Reuben Douglass, John [], Thomas Hampton, Joseph Dixon, James Hannah, James Wilson.
Jurors to January 1788 Session: William Bow[], Henry Rule, Thomas Thompson, Richd Carr, Isaac Walton, Ezekiel Norris, Thomas Kilgore, Zebulon [], David Beard, John Sutton, John Kuykendall, John Brigham, Robert Looney, Alexr Dever, Wm Montgomery, James Franklin, Hugh Crawford, Lewis Crane, John Payton, William Clary, Charles Carter, Ezekiel Douglass, Richard Hogin, Edward Hogin, James Hays, William Wilson, Jas Wilson Jr, Robert Desha, Joseph Morgan, Henry Ramsey, James Harrison, John Du[], John Hicks, William Frazer, John Cravens, Isaac Lowel.
John Dunahoo records his stock mark and brand.

2

OCTOBER 1787

Admn on estate of William Hall decd granted to Thankful Hall; bond 200 pounds with David Wilson and George Winchester securities. Appoint Isaac Bledsoe, Robert Desha & Alexr Neely to appraise estate of Wm Hall decd.
Ordered that John and Saml Campbell serve two years three months & an half inclusive indented time which includes time for the expences of their imprisonment. Court adjourns till tomorrow 10 oClock.

Tuesday October 9th 1787. Present Anthony Bledsoe, Daniel Smith, Isaac Bledsoe, David Wilson, John Hardin, George Winchester Esqrs.
Order County Tax 1/ on every Poll, 4d on every 100 acres; also 1/ on every Poll & 4d on every 100 acres for building Courthouse prison & stocks.
Order Corn received in Taxes at 2/8 pr bushel; Beef at 3d pr lb; pork 4d pr lb for good fat Bear meat if delivered at the place where the troops are; 3d pr lb for prime Buffaloe beef; 1d pr lf for good venison if delivered as afsd 9d pr lb; 6d pr lb for dried beef; 1/4 pr lb for salt; each person to pay in proportion as follows: one fourth in corn; one half in meat; eighth part in salt and eighth part in money.
p. Capt Kukendall to receive tax in his district; Capt Walton in Capt Simon Kukendalls dist; Capt Winchester in Capt Morgans dist; Capt Douglass his own dist.
Order Thomas Martin[Masten?] superintend removal of special tax from the places at which it may be collected to the places where troops are staying.
Capt George Winchester apptd register; Anthony Bledsoe & Capt Isaac Bledsoe sec.
Court adjourned till Court in Course to meet at Elmore Douglasses.   A. Bledsoe

Court of Pleas & Quarter Sessions, Sumner County, house of Elmore Douglass, second Monday in January 1788. Present Daniel Smith, Isaac Bledsoe, Isaac Lindsey, David Wilson, George Winchester Esqrs.
Inventory of goods of Wm Hall decd rendered into Court by admx.
Court adjourned till Tomorrow.

Tuesday January 15th 1788. Present Daniel Smith, Isaac Bledsoe, Isaac Lindsey, David Wilson, George Winchester Esqrs.
Bill/sale Wm Harrison to Robert Desha proved by Thomas Jimason.
Grant admn/estate of William Starr decd to Jesse Summers, bond £500, Phi Trammell and Richard Hogin securities.
Grand Jurors: David Beard, Henry Rule, Wm Montgomery, Thos Thompson, Alexr Dever, Rd Carr, Jno Sutton, Jno Brigance, Rob Looney, Jas Franklin, Hugh Crawford, Lewis Crane, John Payton, Wm Clary, Chas Carter, Ezekl Douglas, Richd Hogin, Edwd Hogin.
Jurors April Ct: Wm Bowan, Kasper Mansker, Simon Kuykendall, Jas Alexander, Alex Montgomery, Elisha Ogelsby, Laurence Thompson, Capt Jas Frazer, Jos Thompson Thos Jones, Wm [], Richd Caveat, Ezekiel Norris, John Minor, Saml Gragg, David Hainey, Jas McKain, Zachariah Green, Peter Looney, P, John Norris, Jas Hays, Benjn Kuykendall, Peter Kuykendall, Elmore Douglass, Doak Hannah, Jas Clendening, Chas Morgan.
fined for profane swearing and Sabbath breaking: Ephraim Payton, Bazel Fry.
John Hardin Jr for Sabbath breaking.

JANUARY 1788

John Boles to appear at next Court to answer presentment [bottom line cut off].
p.   John Hardin Jr paid his fine 10 shillings.
George Winchester fined 5 shillings for breach of peace. Paid fine.
Bazel Fry to appear at next Court: living in unlawful manner with Jane Mansker.
Jane Kendrick fined 25 shillings for having a base born child.
Court adjourned till Court in Course to meet at Capt Elmores.   Danl Smith

Court of pleas & quarter Sessions, house of Elmore Douglass, second Monday, April 1788. Present Isaac Lindsey John Hardin George Winchester Esquires.
Will of Charles Morgan decd proved by [ ] Morgan.
Deed Nicholas Long to William Bowan proved by Anthony Bledsoe.
Deed Robert Desha to Joseph Dixon ackd.
Grand Jurors: Wm Bowan, Kasper Mansker, Simon Kuykendall, Jas Alexander, Ezekiel Norris, James McKain, David Hainey, Zachariah Green, Peter Looney (Harmon), John Norris, James Hays, Benjamin Kuykendall. Philip Trammell to attend Grand Jury.
Grand Jury present William Clary for keeping Nancy Hicks unlawfully.
Deed William Snoddy to Joseph McElwrath ackd.
State vs John Watts Crunk. Dismissed by parties. Dft pays costs.
Fi fa vs Ephraim Payton returned with fine & costs. Also vs Bazel Fry; likewise fi fa vs Jane Kendrick executed with fines & costs.
John Bolie submitted to Court; fined 12 shillings 6 pence with costs.
Court adjourned till Tomorrow 9 oClock.   Isaac [ ].

Tuesday April 15th 1788.
Jurors to Superior Court: Isaac [ ], William Bowan, Kasper Mansker, Thomas Egnew, David Beard, John Hardin, Elmore Douglass, John Minor, Robert Looney, John Wilson, James Clendening, Robert Desha, Alexr [ ], Richard Cavit, Joseph Kuykendall.
Motion by James Harrison James Odam & Roger Gibson, order [ ] Bledsoe Isaac Bledsoe & Geo Winchester divide personal estate of late [ ] into four equal parts.
Order Sheriff make returns to Col A Bledsoe of [ ] by him collected; also that Col [ ] settle with officer commanding the troops for disposition of the provisions.
p.   Appointments to take lists of taxable property: [ ] in formerly Capt Simon Kuykendalls; Isaac Lindsey in Capt Douglasses; Joseph Kuykendall in his own dist; Geo Winchester in late Capt Morgans.
Jane Kendrick made oath George Winchester is father of her bastard child.
King Carr vs Mattw Kuykendall. Jury Uriah Anderson, James Clendening, Lewis Crane, John Hardin, Edward Hogin, David Crady, David Hainey, Richard Hogin, David [ ], Alexander Montgomery, Peter Looney, James McKain. Plf recovers damages & costs.
Inventory goods of Wm Starr decd rendered by admr.

State of North Carolina Sumner County April Sessions 1788.
James Cook vs John Kuykendall. At Jany 1788 plf by atty E Douglass; dft in proper person. April: dft by Jas Cole Mountflorence pleads Not Guilty. Jury Jas Hamilton,

APRIL 1788

Reuben Douglass, James Frazier, Joseph Dixon, Isaac Walton, Isaac Lowel, Joseph Hardin, Saml Findley, James Harrison, Francis Hainey, Wm Brigham, John Payton. Plf recovers damages and costs.
State vs Bazel Fry. Stealing a pair of leather leggins. Dft reprimanded, acquited on his paying Costs.
Jurors to July Court: Jas Frazier, Elisha Ogelsby, Alexr Montgomery, Jno Cravins, Geo Mansker, Henry Rule, Geo Martin, Jas Hamilton, Thos Kilgore, James Yates, Mathw Kuykendall, Saml Gragg, Hugh Crawford, John Steel, James Douglass, Reuben Douglass, James Bone, John Brigham, Wm Brigham, Robt Brigham, Richd Hogan, Simon Kuykendall, Jos McElwrath, Jas Lynn, Jas Franklin, Elisha Clary, Wm Clary, John Norris, Ezekiel Douglass, Jno Roberts, Elmore Douglass, Geo Blackmore, James Harrison, Lewis Crane.
Isaac Bledsoe qualified a Lieut Colonel for Sumner County.
Appoint inspectors Thomas Martin David Wilson & David Shelby to inspect the paper currency in circulation and deface such as they think Counterfeit.
Court adjourned till Court in Course to meet at the same place. Anthony Bledsoe.

p. Second Monday in July 1788. House of []. Present Anthony Bledsoe, Isaac Bledsoe, Isaac Lindsey, David Wilson, Joseph Kuykendall, Esquires.
Deed James Franklin to John Norris ackd.
Power/atty John Latham to Isaac Bledsoe proved by David Hay.
Deed John Latham to John Province ackd by Isaac Bledsoe for sd Latham.
Negro Cuff property of Dr Minor is infirm, ordered him exempted from taxation. Anthony Bledsoe absent.
Grand Jurors: Jas Frazor, Elisha Ogelsby, Jas Yates, Saml Gragg, Hugh Crawford, John Steel, Jas Douglass, Reuben Douglass, Jas Bone, Jno Bryance, Richd Hogan, [] Clary. Presentments Joshua Baldwin for [ ] his name to Joshua Campbell & for profane swearing; also [] Payton for taking away by force a man from Joshua Campbell.
Nicholas Conrod vs Philip Trammell. Jury John Roberts, Elmore Douglass, George Blackimore, James [], David Beard, Wm Frazier, Jesse Sumner, Wm Baldwin, Robert Looney, Obediah [], [] Right, Peter Looney. Plf recovers of dft his damages and costs. Dft granted appeal, security Richd Hogin, Jesse Sumner.
William Blackimore vs Edmund Jennings. AB. Plf by Edward Douglass. Jury Edwd Hogin, Wm Brigham, Wm Snoddy, Jos [], Wm Hacker, Chas Harrington, Doke Hannah, James Hays, Chas Cailer, [] Cross, Jas Clendening, Wm Clary. Plf recovers damages & cost.
Deed Col Daniel Smith to Thomas Masten ackd.
Court Adjourned till Tomorrow 10 oClock.

Tuesday July 15th 1788. Present Anthony Bledsoe, Daniel Smith, Isaac Lindsey, David Wilson Esquires.
Joshua Campbell vs William McNeely. Jury Peter Looney, Robert Brigham, King Carr, George Blackemore, Lewis Crane, Geo D Blackmore, James [], Wm Snoddy, Jesse Sumner, Robert Looney, James Wilson, Simon Kuykendall. Find for plaintiff.
[Top line cut off] Dft by atty James Cole Mountflorence. Jury Wm Clary, Chas Harrington, Elmore Douglass, Wm Hacker, John Sutton, Wm Brigham, Wm Frazier, David Crady, Thos Lemaster, [] Willingham, Zachariah Greer, James Brigham. Find for plf

5

JULY 1788

his damages & costs. Plf appeals, S Kuykendall and Matthew Anderson his security.

Jane Kendrick vs George Winchester. Trespass A&B. Dft by Edwd Douglass; plf by James Cole Mountflorence. Jury Peter Looney, Robt Brigham, King Carr, Geo Blackmore, Lewis Crane, Geo D Blackmore, Jas Right, Wm Snoddy, Jesse Sumner, [] Looney, James Wilson, Simon Kuykendall. Plf recovers damages and costs.

Ephraim Payton vs Thos Mastin. Plf to take depositions of Col James Robinson, Thomas Inglish James Keith Reuben Keith Wm Bucknell W[] Charles Neel Henry McGuffee, Thomas Alley, Wm Thompson, James Turmon, Capt Israel Lin[], Wm Spurlock, Edmund Vansel, John Spurlock.

Order Clerk/Court advertise for nonresidents to pay taxes.

Order Ezekiel Norris Wm Maxwell Richd Cavit repair to plantation of late [] Starr, view cleared land & cabbin built by Jethro Sumner, make inquiry the trouble sd Sumner has been at in taking care of sd Starr in his Illness & make report.

Deed Elmore Douglass to Charles Carter ackd.

Order road laid off from upper settlements on Red River to place fixed on for Courthouse; James Yates, [] Sumner, Ezekiel Norris, David Hughes, Thos Hampton, Wm Hacker, Jas Wilson, Wm [], Robt Looney, Robt Brigham, John Hardin, Matthew Kuykendall to lay off sd road.

Stock marks recorded by Geo D Blackemore, David Wilson.

Allow inhabitants until 4th August to make return of taxable property.

Capeas issued vs Wm Clary for living with Nancey Hicks in unlawful way.

Nancy Hicks to answer presentment of Grand Jury.

Shff allowed £10 for exofficio services; Clerk allowed same.

[The next two pages are out of order on the microfilm; here arranged correctly]
p.   Appointments of constables: []Masten, []Douglass & Chas Carter sec; E[] Hogan in Capt Douglass Dist, Ephraim Payton & Robt Brigance sec; George D Blackmore in Capt Hicksons Dist, Isaac Bledsoe securities.

Jurors to October Term: Robert B[], []Hamilton, Isaac Walton, James Frazier, David Beard, Wm Bowan, Geo Mansker, John Cravins, Wm Maxwell, Ezekiel Norris, Richd Cavit, Wm Hacker, Thomas E[], Thos Hampton, Peter Looney P John Norris, Ephraim Payton, John Payton, James McKain, James McKain Sr, James Franklin, Wm McNeely, James Bone, Chas Carter, Jam[], Thomas Jamison, Joseph Dickison, Alexr Neely, John Hickerson, John Morgan.

Court adjourns till Court in Course.   Anthony Bledsoe

Court of Pleas & Quarter Sessions, Sumner County, place appointed by Commissioners for establishment of the Courthouse, Second Monday in October 1788. Present Daniel Smith, Isaac Bledsoe, David Wilson, John Hardin, George Winchester.

Will of Anthony Bledsoe decd proved by Thos Murry & Hugh Rogan.

Deed Benjn Kuykendall to David Shelby ackd.

Deed Peter Looney to John & James Wilson ackd.

Court adjourned till to morrow 10 OClock to meet at Simon Kuykendalls Station.

October 14th 1788. Present Daniel Smith, David Wilson, John Hardin, Geo Winchester.

OCTOBER 1788

[ ] produced license as atty at law and took oath.

Grand jurors: Geo Mansker, Chas Carter, Wm Maxwell, Richd Cavit, [ ] Johnson, Ephraim Payton, John Norris, James McKain, James McKain Jr, James Hay, [ ] Curly, [Carty?], James Lynn, James Wilson Smoaky.

State vs Joshua Campbell; submitted; fined 2/6.

Order from Davidson County. Order Daniel Smith, David Wilson, & George Winchester to meet three Davidson commissioners.

p.   Deed John Hamilton to [ ] Kuykendall proved by [ ].

Deed Simon Kuykendall to John Hamilton ackd.

James McKain appellee vs James Douglass appellant. Jury Peter Looney Wm Baldwin Sampson Williams Henry Houdeshell Wm Clary Elisha Clary Wm Brigham Thos Patton Jesse Sumner Jos McElwrath David Looney Simon Kuykendall. Juror withdrawn. Continued.

Jurors to Superior Court: Isaac Walton, Wm Bowen Saml Hay Jno Hardin Elmore Douglass Robert Looney John Wilson Robt Desha Alexr Neely Jas Winchester Peter Looney (Harmon) Richd Hogan Wm Maxwell Simon Kuykendall Adam Laurence David Beard.

Order tax 1/ on every poll; 4d every 100 acres for building courthouse prison & stocks; 1/ every poll, 4d every 100 acres to defray county expenses.

Order where any person furnished rations for Cumberland Battalion & produces a certificate from comdg officer, that he be allowed 11d per ration.

Court adjourns till tomorrow 8 OClock.

Wednesday October 15th 1788. Present Daniel Smith, Isaac Bledsoe, Isaac Lindsey, David Wilson, George Winchester, Esquires.

Ephraim Payton vs Joshua Campbell. Malicious prosecution. Dft by Edwd Douglass, plf by Jas Cole Mountflorence. Jury Peter Looney Henry Houdeshell Uriah Anderson Elisha Clary W Brigham Thos Patton Jesse Sumner Joseph McElwrath Simon Kuykendall John [ ] Chas Harrington John Ervin. Plf recovers damages & costs.

Order Ephraim Payton make his tax on lands for 1787 equal [ ].

Henry Houdeshell appearance bond to give testimony behalf State vs John Robinson.

James Wilson Joseph McElwrath & Thomas Patton appeared & Qualified [ ].

Tavern and Ordinary rates [omitted].

p.   Appoint [ ][ ], David Wilson & George Winchester to divide the estate of Anthony Bledsoe deceased.

Jurors to next Court: Robt Bell, [ ] [ ], John Hamilton, Elisha Ogelsby, Richard Carr, Wm Wilson, Henry Houdeshell, John [ ], [ ] Fair, John Morgan, Ben Kuykendall, Jas Odom, Geo Ridley, James Lynn, [ ] [ ], Hugh Crawford, James Franklin, John Payton, Ezekiel Douglass, Wm S[ ], John Steel, Robt Brigham, Alexr Dever, Jas Hamilton, Thos Hamilton, Chas [ ], [ ] Kilgore, Thos Hampton, Michael Sheffer, mason, Capt Jos Dixon, Jos Desha, Saml Gragg, Joseph [ ].

Appt George Ridley oversee road from Croft mill to [ ] sufficient for waggons to pass; inhabitants on Indian Crk (Deshas Station excepted) work thereon.

Appt John Hamilton to oversee road from Simon Kuykendall; people residing at Kuykendalls and John Wilsons Stations work thereon.

Appt Thomas Patton to oversee road from Majr Wilson; people at Deshas & Majr Wilsons Stations work thereon.

Appt Chas Harrington to oversee road from Wm Maxwells to McKains & Bens Creeks.

Appt Wm Baldwin to oversee road to Majr Wilson...from Kaspers to Douglass and from McKains Crk and Snoddies inclusive work on sd road.

Appt Robt Bell to oversee road from Kaspers Creek to [ ].

JANUARY 1789

Road overseers appointed: George Mansker, from Drakes Creek, Col Smiths Station, & adjacent persons. John Norris from George Manskers to [] Station, people from McKain down creek to road []. James Wilson east fork of Station Camp Cr; inhabitants south of road from Capt Douglass to []. Obediah Terrell from Indian Crk to []. James [] plf; [] Hamilton to take deposition of Thomas Hendricks.
Court adjourned till Court in Course.

Court of Pleas & Quarter Sessions, house of Simon Kuykendall, second Monday in January 1789. Present Daniel Smith, Isaac Bledsoe, John Hardin, Joseph Kuykendall.
Appt Bennet Searcy esqr Solicitor for the County.
Recorded stock marks of George Ridley, Thankful Hall, James Adam.
Grand Jurors: William Bowan foreman, John Cravins, John Hamilton, Richard Carr, Henry Houdeshall, Ephm Fair, John Morgan, Ben Kuykendall, James[], Reuben Douglass, Hugh Crawford, James Franklin, John Payton, William Sn[], Samuel Mason.
Andrew Jackson Esqr produced licence to practice as atty at law; took the oaths.
Bill/Indictment vs Margery Robinson for fornication is quashed. John Robinson and Margery Robinson fined twenty five shillings each for fornication.
Adjourned till tomorrow 10 oClock.

Tuesday January 13th 1789. Present Danl Smith, Isaac Bledsoe, David Wilson, John Hardin, Joseph Kuykendall.
Jethro Sumner allowed £129.16 & public & county tax...estate of late William Stair[Starr?] for two preceding years.
Deed David Wilson to George McWhirter ackd.
Inventory estate of Anthony Bledsoe decd rendered by exrs.
Capt Wm Bowman exempted from double tax.
State vs Bazil Fry. Fornn. Jury Thomas Kilgore, Charles Harrington, Joseph Dixon, Joseph Desha, Joseph Hardin, Ezekiel Douglass, William [], David Milburn, Joseph McElwrath, James McKain, Charles Carter, David Hainy find dft not guilty.
p. Simon Kuykendall's bond for indemnification of County of charges of supporting a child of Jane Mansker.
James McKain Junr v James Douglass. At Octr Term 1788 jury: Peter Looney, William Baldwin, Sampson Williams, Henry Houdeshell, Wm Clary, Elisha Clary, Wm Brigham, Thos Patton, [] Sumner, Joseph McElwrath, David Looney, Simon Kuykendall; cause continued. Jury: Thos Kilgore, Chas Harrington, Jos Dixon, Jos Desha, Jos Hardin, John Kuykendall, Wm [], David Milburn, Jos McElwrath, Ezekiel Norris, Chas Harrington, David Hainey. Verdict for dft.
Jane Mansker fined 25 shillings for having a base born child.
Wm Bowman v John Sutton. Jury Jesse Hughes, Ezkl Douglass, Jacob Sanders, Thos Lemaster, Ben Dickeson, Abraham L[], John Payton, James Hays, Elisha Herndon, Peter Looney, Ephm Payton, James Maxwell. Plf recovers of deft.
Court adjourned till tomorrow 8 oClock.

Wednesday January 14th 1789. Present David Wilson, John Hardin, Joseph Kuykendall.

APRIL 1789

Andrew Davis v Edmund Jennings. Trover. Dft by Josiah Love Esqr. Plf by Edward Douglass. Jury George Wills, John Kuykendall, Jacob Landers, Thomas Lemaster, Ben Dickeson, Chas Harrington, John Hamilton, Elias McBee, Elisha Herndon, Thomas Jimason, Wm Tate, James Maxwell find for deft.

Jurors to April Session: Robert Bell, Henry Rule, [] Mansker, Laurence Thompson, Andrew Steel, Francis Catron, Ezekiel Norris, Thomas Hamilton Senr, [] Maxwell, Wm Hacker, David Beard, George Mansker, John Norris, Peter Looney, Pitman, Elmore Douglass, John Brigham, Peter Looney, Harman, Robert Looney, John Steel, Samuel Gragg, [] Doctor, Thomas Jimason, Joseph McElwrath, Elisha Herndon, Archibald Fisher, Simon Kuykendall, [] Sanders, Charles Carter, James Wilson Jr, William Wilson, Ephraim Pharr, Matthew Alexander, [] Hickison, Joseph Morgan, James Harrison, John Doke Hannah.

Order John Bartley, Daniel McGooden, Henry Houdeshell assist John Hamilton on road for which sd Hamilton is overseer.

Order Daniel Smith & David Wilson settle with Shff for tax.

Court adjourned till Court in Course.

Court of Pleas & Quarter Sessions, house of Simon Kuykendall, Second Monday in April 1789. Present Danl Smith, Isaac Bledsoe, David Wilson, Joseph Kuykendall.

Deeds ackd: Isaac Bledsoe to Alexr Neely. Henry Houdeshell to Thos Patton. Richard Hogan to Henry Houdeshell; John Minor dismissed from atty[].

Jurors to Superior Court: David Wilson, John Wil[], Alexander Neely, Robert Desha, Robert Looney, Peter Looney, Harmon, Elmore Douglass, James Franklin, J[] Kilgore, Thomas Hamilton.

Grand Jurors Abraham Landers Wm Wilson Francis Catron Jas Wilson John Norris Peter Looney Elmore Douglass Peter Looney(Harmon), Robt Looney John Steel Thos Jimason Joseph McElwrath, Elisha Herndon Archd Fisher Chas Carter found agt John Hardin Esqr for not making a true return of all money arising from sale of [] property of William Price decd.

Appt John Wilson guardian for William Price orphan of William Price decd.

Order road laid off from Maddisons Lick to Major Wilsons by John Harpole Elmore Douglass Elisha Ogelsby Wm Snoddy; appt John Harpole to oversee from Maddisons Lick to ridge between Drakes Cr & Station Camp. Polls on Drakes from Capt Laurence Thompsons incl him and Jas & Wm Frazier work on sd road; Elmore Douglass apptd overseer of remainder of sd road from ridge to Majr Wilsons; polls on Station Camp above McKains inclusive of them work thereon. John Steel & Hugh Crawford are exempted from working sd road.

Heirs of Wm Starr decd to shew cause why order of sale not go agt real estate of decedent to satisfy demand of Jethro Sumner.

Ephraim Payton v Thomas Martin[Masten?]. Slander. Dft by Edwd Douglass at Octr 1788; cause contd. Deft by John Overton & Andrew Jackson. Jury James Harrison Wm Snoddy Saml Mason Adam Lynn Robt Bell Jas Wilson Jas Hays Jas Reese Joseph Morgan Robt Looney Jos Dixon Stephen Cantrel find for plf his damage one shilling. Plf granted appeal; security Richard Hogin & John Payton.

Court adjourned till tomorrow 8 OClock.

JULY 1789

Tuesday April 14th 1789.
Bill/sale James Bosley to David Shelby proved by George Blackemore.
Recording stock marks & brands: John Hickeson, Abraham Sanders.
p.   Jurors to July Session: James Clendening, William [], William Beard, Ben Kuykendall, Roger Gibson, Thos Patton, Matthew Alexander, James Wilson, Jam[] [], Thos Jimason, Uriah Anderson, Joseph McElwrath, Chas Carter, James Douglass, Reuben Douglass, Wm Brigham, David Hainey, Richd Hogin, Wm Maxwell, Ezekiel Norris, Wm Hacker, David Beard, Thos Hambleton Jr, Jas Hambleton, Saml Mason, Matthew Kuykendall, Wm Frazier, Elisha Ogelsby, Thos Egnew, John Rule, Saml Hays, Cornelius Glasgow, Thos Simpson, Laurence Thompson, Alexr Montgomery, Richd Carr, King Carr.
Deed Kasper Mansker to Thomas Hambleton ackd.
Joseph Dixon records his stock mark.
Report of David Wilson & Danl Smith who settled with Sheriff [omitted]; provisions furnished Capt Martins company of Cumberland battalion.
Property tax laid for purpose of paying guard & road cutters to Clinch Mountain.
Order Danl Smith David Wilson & Thos Masten procure a copy of entries in military land office.
Order Wm Walton or Danl Smith take list of taxable property in Capt F[] company; Isaac Lindsey in Capt McKelwraths Compy; Joseph Kuykendall his own compy; David Wilson for Capt Wilsons Compy.
Ephraim Payton exempted from tax on caveated land.
Deed James McKain to Peter Looney ackd.
Order Each private who served as road cutters & guard to lower end of Clinch Mountain allowed 6/ pr day & officers in proportion.
James Winchester is appointed County Trustee.
Court adjourned till Court in Course; meet at Capt Elmore Douglass's. Danl Smith

Court of Pleas & Quarter Sessions, house of Elmore Douglass second Monday July 1789. Present Danl Smith Isaac Bledsoe Isaac Lindsey David Wilson esquires.
Deed Edwin Hickman to Wm Minor proven by Josiah Love.
Deed Philip Trammell to Moses Moore ackd.
Thomas Masten allowed 20 lbs for exofficio services as sheriff.
David Shelby allowed 20 lbs for exofficio serves as clerk.
Howel Tatum produced license to practice as attorney & took oath.
Deed Philip Trammell to Eneas Hannah ackd.
Grand Jurors, David Beard foreman, Matthew Alexander, Wm Beard, Jas Hays, Chas Carter, Jas Douglass, Reuben Douglass, Wm Brigham, David Hainey, Richd Hogin, Saml Mason, Jas Hamilton, Wm Frazier, Elisha Ogelsby, Alexr Montgomery, Richd Carr return bill agt Robert Espy for profane swearing, bill agt overseer of road from Simon Kuykendalls to courthouse, likewise of road from ridge of Drakes Crk.
Deed Mary Hunter to Isaac Penelton proved by Andrew Jackson.
Deed Elijah Robinson to John McNairy proved by Andrew Jackson.
Thos Murry v Thomas White. Attacht. Dft came not; judgt agt dft; land to be sold.
James McKain v John Roberts & Lewis Crane. Trover. Apl. Plf by John Overton; dft by Andw Jackson. Jury King Carr, John Morgan, Archibald Fisher, John Norris, Peter Looney,H, Ben Dickison, Alexander Neely, Ezekiel Douglass, Stephen Cantril, Hugh

OCTOBER 1789

Crawford, Joseph Desha, Adam Laurence find for defendant who recovers costs.
George Pain proved attendance as witness in suit McKain v Roberts & Crane.
John Roberts records stock mark. Lewis Crane records stock mark.
Court adjourned till tomorrow 8 oClock.

Tuesday July 14th 1789.
p.   Deed Trammell to Glaves ackd.
Deed Edward Hogin to Adam Laurence ackd.
Allow Philip Trammell to erect a mill on middle fork Red River where he lives.
Allow Jas McKain to erect a mill on west fk Station Cr ¼ mile of where he lives.
Edmund Gambell v Thomas White. Attacht. Decree land to be sold by sheriff.
Addl inventory estate of Wm Price decd rendered by Jno Hardin admr.
Appt Mary Bledsoe gdn for Thos Bledsoe, Anthony Bledsoe, Isaac Bledsoe, Polly Bledsoe, Abraham Bledsoe, Henry Bledsoe, Prudence Bledsoe, orphans of Anthony Bledsoe decd; bond 10,000 lbs, Josiah Love Alexr [ ], Robt Looney Thos Masten sec.
Sheriff allowed for delinquent taxes & Ephm Paytons caveated land.
Order road from Col Manskers to Virginia line to pass by Cave Spring be laid off by Joseph Kuykendall, John Kuykendall, Ezekiel Norris. Polls by Gaspers Crk Maddisons Crk with Isaac Walton overeer work thereon to ridge; polls in Capt Kuykendalls with Richard Caveat overeer work on remainder of sd road.
Deed Elmore Douglass to Reuben Douglass ackd.
Sheriff allowed settlement of tax.
Joseph Morgan nominated constable for Capt Wilsons company.
John Hardin bound over to next Superior Court for Mero Dist to answer presentment of Grand Jury for not making true return of property of late Wm Price decd.
John Smith Dennis Griffin & George Ridley delinquent tax payers.
James Douglass apptd Sheriff & Collector; bond 5000 lbs, with Joshua Hadly, Elmore Dougass, Charles Carter, Edwd Douglass, Robt Montgomery securities.
Order Clerk furnish Collector with list for collecting tax.
Court adjourned till Court in Course & meet at same place.   Daniel Smith.

Court of Pleas & Quarter Sessions, house of Elmore Douglass, 2d Monday in October 1789. Present Isaac Bledsoe, Isaac Lindsey, Joseph Kuykendall, George Winchester.
Jurors, Superior Ct: Geo Blackmore, Archd Fisher, Jas Reese, Jas Wilson(shooting) Jas McKain, Pr Looney(Pitmon) Wm Bowman, Jos McElwrath, Wm Snoddy, Wm Walton, Robt Bell, Laurence Thompson, Capt, David Beard, Jas Hambleton, Wm Maxwell, Robt Sh[ ].
Road oveseers apptd: Hugh Crawford from ridge bet Bens Cr & McKains Cr to Majr Wilsons; James Hays from Simon Kuykendalls to Court house; James Hamilton, ridge bet Cumberland & Red R to Arringtons Cr; James McKain in place of Capt Douglass.
Grand Jurors James Hannah, Laurence Thompson, James Hamilton, James Bone, James Reese, Danl McGoodin, Richd Cavit, Robt Shaw, John Hardin Jr, Wm Bowman, Wm Snoddy, Jas Franklin; present Joseph Desha Robert Hardin John Cotton & Thos Simpson.
Order sale of half preemption of heirs of Wm Starr decd incl improvement made by sd Starr to satisfy demand of Jethro Sumner agt sd Starrs estate.
Robert Esspy vs heir of William Cooper. Attacht. Shff levied on tract entered for

11

OCTOBER 1789

Wm Cooper 2 mi above mouth of Kaspers lick cr entry 27 Decr 29 1783. Deft came not; judgt by default agt dft. At this Term plf prays damages be ascertained. Jury Elmore Douglass, James McKain, John Norris, Zachariah Cross, Zachariah Green, Peter Looney H Joseph Dixon, Henry Gambell, Joseph McElwrath, Robt Montgomery, Robt Brigance & Jethro Sumner find damages £100.3.7 and costs.
    State v Robert Esspy for profane swearing; dft fined two shillings six pence.
    State v Elmore Douglass: not performing duty as road overseer; fined six pence.
    State v John Hamilton: nonperformance of road overseer duty. Jury [above] find dft guilty; fined six pence.
p.   Bill/sale Thomas Henry[Kenny?] to Zachariah Green ackd.
    Order to sell property of heir of William Cooper on which attachment of Robert Esspy was levied.
    Hugh McGary v Justinian Cartwright; exceptions taken agt appearance bail.
    Court adjourned till Tomorrow 8 OClock.

Tuesday October 13th 1789. [Outer edges of pages have been cut and names lost.]
    William Blackmore v Joseph Desha. Case. Dft by Josiah Love. Plf by Andrew Jackson. Jury [] McKain Jr, Robt Brigance, Robert Montgomery Elmore Douglass Uriah Anderson Zachariah G[] Henry Gambell James McKain Joseph McElwrath Richard Hogin Elisha Ogelsby Thomas Jimason. Juror withdrawn; suit continued.
    Jurors to January Term: Robert Steel, John H[], James Odom, James Gambell, Roger Gibson, John Bartlet, Jas Wilson Curly, Charles Reese, W Snoddy, Simon Kuykendall, Jas Lynn, Geo Mansker, Lewis Crane, Robt Looney, John Bryance[Briganer?], Andw Steel, Thos Simpson, Samuel Hays, William Green, Robert Hambleton, [] Kuykendall, David Hughes, Anthony Sharp, Thos Hampton, John Kuykendall, James Yates, Ezekiel Norris, James Hambleton, Thomas Kilgore.
    James Wynn v Samuel Mason. Depositions of Jos Haycraft & Alexander McCowan to be taken at house of Joshua Ferguson in Nelson County Kentucky.
    William Crabtree v Robert Montgomery. Trover. At July Term plf by Andw Jackson. Jury Joseph McElwrath Uriah Anderson Wm Parmer David Hainey Ephrm Payton Joseph Desha Zachariah [] Henry Gambell Thos Jimason Elisha Ogelsby Richd Hogan Robt Brigance; non Suit ordered.
    Deed James Cole Mountflorence to Anthony Sharp proved by James Wilkison.
    State v Robert Hardin: breach/peace. Dft fined 16/.
    State v Joseph Desha: breach/peace. Deft fined 16/.
    Ordered Saml Hays Alexr Hambleton John Hickison James Odom Wm [] David Hughes Matthew Kuykendall Geo Martin fined each £5 for nonattendance as jurors.
    Court adjourned till Court in Course to meet at same place.   Isaac Bledsoe.

Court of Pleas & Quarter Sessions at house of Elmore Douglass, second Monday, January 1790. Present Isaac Bledsoe Isaac Lindsey Joseph Kuykendall.
    Deed William Sanders to Robert Motherall proved by Joseph Motherall.
    Order tax one shilling each poll; four pence every hundred acres for building Court house prison & stocks. Also tax one shilling each poll & four pence every hundred acres for defraying contingent charges.

JANUARY 1790

William Roan, attorney, took oath; at same time is apptd Solicitor for the State.
Grand Jurors: Jno Hickeson James Wilson Charles Reese Simon Kuykendall Lewis C--, John Brigance Wm Brigance Zachariah Green Elisha Clary John Steel Samuel Gragg William Frazier, Andrew Steel present John Gillaspy for profane swearing.
State v Jno Cotton. A&B. Jury Thos Simpson, David Hughes, Jas Lynn, Robt Hambleton, John Roberts, John Hardin, Peter Looney P, George Mansker, Thos Hambleton, Joseph Desha, James Bone, Thos Murry find dft guilty; fined 3 pounds & costs.
State v Thomas Simpson. Destroying Public property. Nolle prosequi.
Thomas Kinny v Jesse Hughes. Octr Term dft came not; judgt entered agt him. Plf by Howel Tatum prays damages be ascertained. Jury [above except Sion Perry for Jos Desha]. Plf recovers of dft damages and costs.
Power/attorney Arthur Galbreath to Thomas Sgharp proven by Robert Stuart.
Court adjourned till tomorrow 8 oclock.

Tuesday January 12th 1790. Present Isaac Bledsoe, Isaac Lindsey, Joseph Kuykendall.
Deed John Weathers to Isaac Bledsoe proved by John Jones & James McD[].
Alexr Montgomery fined 25/ for begetting a base born child with Jenny Dyal.
Jenny Dyal fined 25/ for committing act/adultery with Alexr Montgomery.
Joseph Arnold Setgraves produced license as attorney; took prescribed oath.
Deed Thomas Masten Sheriff to Jethro Sumner ackd.
David Shelby v Eusebius Bushnell. Debt. Octr 1789 Plf by Josiah Love; dft by Andw p.   Jackson. Jury: James Lynn, Wm Bowman, David Hughes, John Wilson, James Odom, Richard Hogin, Josh Hadley, Thomas Hamilton, John Roberts, Charles Carter, Reuben Douglass, Jos McElwrath. Plf recovers of dft his debt and costs.
James Bone qualified as constable; James McKain Jr security.
Money arising from fines to be applied to Clerks & Sheriffs exofficio services.
Deed Eusebius Bushnell & Wm Dobbins to Wm Frazier proved by Laurence Thompson.
Grant admn/estate of Joshua Baldwin decd to Sarah Baldwin; Thos Masten security.
Jurors to Superior Ct: Alexr Neely [] Anderson James Harrison Roger Gibson Ben Kuykendall Zebulon Hubbard James Yates Thomas Kilgore Wm Hacker Matthew Kuykendall Wm Young Christopher Funkhauser John Young Peter Looney H Reuben Douglass David Brigance Elmore Douglass James McKain Sr James Franklin Sion Perry John Norris John Jones Jacob Sanders Ephraim Payton J[] Wallace John Roberts Edward Hogin William Wyer Elisha Ogelsby King Carr James Frazier John [] Kasper Mansker William Bowan Richard Jones Thos Hamilton.
Court adjourned till Court in Course.   Isaac Bledsoe

Court of Pleas & Quarter Sessions, house of Elmore Douglass, first Monday April 1790. Present Daniel Smith, Isaac Lindsey, David Wilson, Esquires.
Inventory goods of Joshua Campbell decd returned by admr.
Deeds: Isaac Bledsoe to Pearce Wall ackd. Edward Douglass to Joseph Wallace & James Wilson ackd. Peter Looney (Pitman) to John Hamilton ackd.
Isaac Lindsey Esqr deposited 17 shillings 6 pence of fines.
James Wilson apptd Deputy Ranger at request of Isaac Lindsey, Ranger.
John Overton produced license as attorney; took oath.

APRIL 1790

Daniel Smith Isaac Bledsoe Isaac Lindsey David Wilson David Shelby Esqrs took oath required of justices/peace.

Grand Jury: James Harrison foreman, Ben Kuykendall, Zebulon Hubbard, James Yates, [] Kilgore, Wm Hacker, John Young, Wm Young, Peter Looney (harmon), Reuben Douglass,[] Waller, Edward Hogan, Wm Wyn, Ephraim Peyton present agt Pheba McNeely for A&B; agt Jesse Maxey for A&B & profane swearing; William Totevine for profane swearing; & agt James Hannah for profane swearing.

State v John Gillaspie. Profane Swearing. Fined 40 shillings and costs.

p. Kasper Mansker, James McKain, Joseph McElwrath, John White, Elisha Clary, Peter Looney Pitmon officers of militia took oath prescribed by law.

James Cole Mountflorence atty produced license to practice in Court; took oath.

William Walton took oath of Justice/Peace.

Tuesday April 6th 1790. Present Daniel Smith Isaac Bledsoe, David Wilson.

Matthew Alexander apptd overseer/road in place of Obediah Terrell.

William Blackmore v Joseph Desha. July 1789 dft by Josiah Love; Octr 1789 plf by Andw Jackson. Jury withdrawn, cause continued. April 1790 jury Obediah Terrell, Francis Hainey, Peter Looney P, King Carr, Joseph Dickson, Joseph McElwrath, Joseph Beard, James Fair, Peter Fisher, Wm Neely, James McKain Senr, Zachariah Green find for deft who recovers of plf his costs of suit.

John Steel v James Lynn. Jury [above except John Harpole & James Wilson for James McKain and Zachariah Green]. Plf recovers of dft his damages 75 pounds and costs.

James Bosley v George Winchester. Dft at Jany 1790 by Josiah Love. At April Session dft waived plea and confessed judgt. Plf recovers of £19.18 with costs.

Edward Douglass took oath of Justice/peace.

State v James Hannah. Profane swearing. Dft fined 5 shillings; fine remitted.

David Briganer allowed £4.0.0 for services as Constable.

Jurors to next Superior Court: George Blackemore Archd Fisher James Reese James Wilson shooting, James McKain Peter Looney (Pitman) Wm Bowan Joseph McElwrath Wm Snoddy Capt Laurence Thompson David Beard Michael Cavit Wm Maxwell George Martin Wm Bowman John Whitsitt.

Lease Edward Hogan to John Cotton proved by William Wyer.

p. Deed Isaac Bledsoe & Mary Bledsoe exr & exx of Anthony Bledsoe decd to William Bowman ackd.

Court adjourns for one hour. Met accordingly.

David Brigance & Ephraim Payton having failed to return taxable property make return upon paying tax.

[Paragraph that clarifies sheriff's duties in collecting taxes is here omitted.]

Appointments to take lists of taxable property: Wm Walton in Capt Fraz[] company. Edward Douglass in Capt McKains & Capt McElwraths companies. Isaac Bledsoe in Capt M[] compy. Joseph Kuykendall in Capt Shaws company.

Order polls on west fork Station Camp Cr down to McKains, below Elmore Douglass to Major Wilsons to [] Andersons inclusive of Brigance & Perry work on road from ridge of Drakes Creek to Red River Road.

Jurors to July session: Joshua Hadley, Anthony Graves, James McKain Jr, Volentine Shoat, Robt Looney, John Steel, Alexr Dever, Abraham Bird, John Hambleton, Laurence Thompson (weaver) Andrew Steel, Wm Frazier, Richard Carr, Wm McNeely, Thos Cubbins, [] Wilson, Robt Desha, Abraham Sanders, John Wilson, John Dunihoo, John Morgan, Peter Furney, Joseph [], Joseph McElwrath, Pearce Wall, Wm Edwards, Uriah Anderson,

JULY 1790

Aaron Perry, John Hickison, [] Kuykendall, Adam Kuykendall, Chrisr Funkhower, Thomas Hamilton John Hughes Francis Hainey Thomas Viningham.

David Wilson & Edward Douglass commrs for selling land adj salt licks enter bond with Thomas Martin David Shelby Josiah Love securities.

Edward Douglass took the oath of a Sheriff.

David Shelby v Philip Shackler. Jany 1790 dft came not; judgt agt him. Apl Term dft confesses judgt. Plf recovers 30 pds 13 shillings with costs.

Court adjourns till Court in Course.   Danl Smith

p.   Court of Pleas & Quarter Sessions, Courthouse, first Monday, July 1790. Present Daniel Smith, Isaac Bledsoe, William Walton, Esquires.

Venire facias Anthony Graves James McKain Jr Laurence Thompson Volentine Shoat Abraham Bird John Hamilton William Frazier William McNeely William Wilson Robert Desha Abraham Sanders John Wilson John Dunahoo John Morgan Joseph Wallace Joseph McElwrath Peter Turney William Edwards Uriah Anderson John Hickison Adam Kuykendall Christopher Funkhower Thos Hamilton John Hughes Francis Hainey.

Grand jurors: John Wilson foreman, Laurence Thompson, Volentine Shoat, Abraham Bird, Wm Frazier, Wm McNeely, Wm Wilson, Robert Desha, Abraham Sanders, John Dunahoo, John Morgan, Joseph Wallace, Anthony Graves.

Lease from Edward Hogin to William Wyer is proved by John Cotton.

Will of Henry Rule decd proved by Edward Jones; Catharine Rule & John Rule exexutor and executrix therein named appeared and qualified.

Hopkins Lacy produced his license as an attorney; took the oath of office.

William Edwards records his stock mark.

Deed Robert Desha to Abraham Sanders proved by David Wilson Esqr.

Lazarus Cotton vs John Butler. April 1790 plf by John Overton. July 1790 dft by Josiah Love. Jury Wm Snoddy, Peter Turney, Uriah Anderson, Adam Kuykendall, Thos Hamilton, Francis Hainey, Thos Cubbins, Joseph McElwrath, John Hickison, Chrisr Funkhouser, John Hughes, John D Hannah. Plf recovers of dft 20 pds and costs.

Edward Hogin fined 10/ for quarrelling, which fine sd Hogin paid.

State vs Jesse Maxey profane swearing. Paid 2/6 fine.

State vs Jesse Maxey A&B. Paid 2/6 fine.

Court adjourns till tomorrow 8 o clock.

Tuesday July 6th 1790. Present Danl Smith Isaac Bledsoe William Walton Esquires.

Alexr Dever, Richard Carr, Pearce Wall, Aaron Perry, Matthew Kuykendall, Thos Viningham, jurors for present Term having failed to appear are fined.

Clerk & Sheriff allowed arrears of exofficio services for 1787 and 1788.

Admn on estate of Henry Ramsey granted to Hetty Ramsey; bond 500 pds, Peter Looney & John Morgan her securities.

Mistake in tax payment of Anthony Sharp rectified.

Anthony Sharp qualified as justice of the peace.

William Cage apptd Sheriff; James McKain, Elmore Douglass, Peter Turney secs.

Additional inventory of Anthony Bledsoe decd rendered by executors.

p.   James Douglass allowed £17 for exofficio survices as sheriff.

JULY 1790

William Cage bond £2000 [as tax collector; securities as on sheriff's bond].
Joel Rice a commissioner for disposing of public lands adj salt licks bond £2000 with William Cage, Howel Tatum his securities, and took oath.
Court adjourns for one hour & an half. Met according to adjournment.
James Douglass & Wilson Cage qualified as deputy sheriffs.
Lists of taxable property returned by Edward Douglass in Capt McKains & Captain McElwraths Compys; Isaac Bledsoe in Capt Morgans compy; Wm Walton in Capt Fraziers Company; Joseph Kuykendall in Capt Shaws company.
Sheriff allowed £29.19.11 from comdg officer, Cumberland battalion, for furnishing rations & other necessities.
Grand Jury present agt John Steel for making false & malicious []; Robert Montgomery for profane swearing; William Totevine for profane swearing.
State vs Phebe McNeely. A&B. Dft by Josiah Love. Jury Uriah Anderson, Francis Hainey, Thos Cribbins, John Hikison, Chrisr Funkhouser, Jo[][] Ezekiel Douglass, Richd Hogin, Robt Brigham, Joseph McElwrath, David Hughes; juror withdrawn; contd.
Deed Charles Carter to John Agin ackd.
State v William Totevine. Profane swearing. Jury Hugh Crawford, David Brigance, [] Montgomery, David Hainey, David Hardin, Wm Grimsly, John Butler, Elisha Eerndon, [] Steel, Wm Davis, Charles Carter find dft not guilty.
Benjn Ganes[Garris?] v Wm McNeely. Allow deposition/John Cotton, benefit dft.
Stock marks recorded: John Cotton, Joseph Kuykendall, Anthony Sharp.
Benjn Garris[Ganes?] Allow deposition of [].
Joshua Scott v Hardins. Deposition of [] to be taken.
Court adjourns till tomorrow []

Wednesday July 7th 1790.
Appt Thomas Conyer overseer of road from Kaspers Cr to dividing ridge [].
Appt Christopher Funkhouser overseer/road in place of Rich[]
Fine Peter Turney Uriah Anderson John Hickison Adam Kuykendall Christopher [] Thos Hamilton John Hughes Francis Hainey each 10/ for nonattendance as jurors.
p.   Bill/sale Abraham Sanders to Robert Desha proved by David Wilson.
Recording of stock marks & brands by William Cage, Robt Desha, David Wilson.
State vs James Hannah. Profane swearing. Jury Joseph McElwrath, Richd Hogin, Thos Cribbins, [] Wilson, Wm Brigance, Wm Snoddy, Leonard West, Robt Brigance, William Grimsly, Thos [], David Brigance, Wm Bowman find dft []
Joseph McElwrath records his stock mark.
Jurors to October Term: Wm Bond, John Johnston, Charles [], Wm Oarr, Elisha Ogelsby, Archd Buchannon, Robt Steel, Joseph Morgan, David [], Joseph Dixon, Joseph Desha, Ephraim Payton, Ephraim Fair, James Wilson Senr, John Kuykendall, [] []oung (Irishman), Wm Young, Adam Flenor, Benjn Smith, John Norris, Richard Hogin, [] Bowyer, Saml Gragg, David Bryance, James McKain jr, Thomas Smith, Charles Carter, John D [], John White, Thomas Jimason, Robert Jones.
Appt [] Wilson and Edward Douglass guardians for William Price orphan of late William []; bond, David Shelby & James Harrison securities,2000 pounds.
Payment of Jurors to Superior Court arranged. Payment of Clerk arranged.
Power/atty Alexr Dever to Joseph McElwrath ackd.
David Shelby v Robert Esspy. Jany 1790 dft by Howel Tatum. July dft confesses judgt. Plf recovers £38.2.3 & costs less price of fire shovel & tongs.
David Shelby v Laurence Thompson. David Shelby recovered £83.13 in suit vs

OCTOBER 1790

Eusebius Bushnell, Laurence Thompson, Bushnells security, to appear at Court at Elmore Douglass's; dft confesses judgt; plf recovers.
Court adjourns till Court in course.
                                                                     Danl Smith

First Monday in October 1790. Present Edward Douglass Joseph Kuykendall and Anthony Sharp Esquires.
John Norris exempted from serving as a Juror this Term.
Hopkins Lacy apptd solicitor for Sumner County; took oath.
Grand Jury: James Wilson foreman, Wm Oarr Elisha Ogelsbie Richard [], Reason Bowyer, John White, Joseph Morgan, Samuel Gragg, David Bryance, James McKain Jr, [] Smith, Thomas Jimason, William Bird. Benjn Williams apptd to attend Grand Jury.
Licenses to keep ordinaries at dwelling houses: [] Douglass, [] Douglass security. [] McKain, James Lynn & Joseph Kuykendall, securities.
Deed [] Payton to Roger Gibson ackd.
Exempted from fine for failure to attend as Juror this Term: [] Wall, [] Turney, [] Hickison. Last Term: [] Kuykendall, [] Karr, [] Kuykendall.
Failing to appear this Term, to be fined: John Johnston, Charles Harriman, Archd Buchannon, [] [], David Hainey, Joseph Dixon, Joseph Desha, John Kuykendall, John Young, Wm Young, Adam [], Benja Smith, Charles Carter, Robt Jones.
Will of Simpson Hart decd proved by Man Philips & John Whitsett.
Court adjourned till Tomorrow 9 oClock.

Tuesday 5th October 1790. Present Daniel Smith David Wilson Edward Douglass, Esq.
Deed Thomas Johnston atty for John Elliott to John Drake ackd.
Robert Hays v Thomas Smith. Covt. Plf by Josiah Love. Jury John Butler, Isaac Lowel, John Cotton, Henry Robinson, Wm Baldwin, James Frazier, Wm Snoddy, Edwd Hogin, Robt Brigance, Peter Looney, John Sutton, John Ross. Plf recovers agt dft.
Appt Benjamin Williams constable; James Wilson security.
Benjamin Garris v William McNeely. Trespass. Plf by John Overton; Dft by Josiah [lines at bottom of this page are cut off].
p.-- Inventory/estate of Henry Ramsey decd rendered by admx.
Bill/sale Wm Edwards to Elmore Douglass proved by Reuben Douglass.
Bill/sale John Williams & Benjn Williams to Elmore Douglass for Negro man proved by Edward Douglass Esq.
Power/atty Nathl Parker to Elmore Douglass proved by Edward Douglass Esqr.
Further inventory of Joshua Campbell decd rendered into Court by admx.
John Butler v Lazarus Cotton. Appeal. Jury Wm Wyn, Isaac Lowel, Henry Robertson, James Frazier, Wm Brigance, Peter Looney, John Sutton, Geo Mansker, Ephm Farr, Robt Bell, James Brigance. Dft recovers of plf.

Wednesday 6 Octr 1790. Present Danl Smith David Wilson Edwd Douglass Wm Walton.
Bill/sale Hugh McGary to Kasper Mansker Negro [] proved by Andrew Jackson Esqr.
Jurors to Superior Court: Alexr Robertson, Stephen Cantrel, Wm Bird, Hugh Crawford, Saml Gragg, James McKain Jr, Joseph Wallace, James Reese Abraham [], Robert

JANUARY 1791

Shaw, James Yates.
Benja Garris v Wm McNeely, parties pay their own witnesses, Atty John Overton [].
Alexr Dever exempted from fine for nonattendance as a juror last Term.
State v Phebe McNeely. A&B. Dft by Josiah Love. Jury Henry Robertson, Fredk Barns, Dennis Graves, Silas McBee, John Morrison, Thomas Egnew, Samuel Bell, John Kindrick, Thos Kindricks, Alexr Dever, Geo Hamilton find dft not guilty.
Anthony Sharp v James Wilkison. Order/sale of attachment levied on.
Delinquent jurors this Term John Johnston, Charles Harriman, John Kuykendall, Wm Young, Benja Smith, Adam Fliner, Robt Jones to be fined.
Allow John Hardin 31 pds 10 shillings of estate of Wm Price, orphan of Wm Price decd, for keeping sd orphan 3½ years, sd Hardin to give up sd orphan to guardians.
John Hardin allowed 3 pds for administering estate of Wm Price.
Jurors to January Term: John Steel, Peter Looney, Abraham [], John Bryance, Reuben Douglass, Zach Green, John Wilson, Abraham Sanders, John Hamilton John Williams, Roger Gibson, James Harrison, Lewis Crane, Isaac Walton, Charles Harriman, Stephen Wright, Edwd [], Robert Hamilton, John Kuykendall, Ben Smith, John Young, Thos Hamilton, John Johnston, John Rule, Thomas Agnew, Richard Cavit.
Deed James [] to [] proved by Edward Douglass Esqr.
[Last item cut off page]

p.   Territory of United States South of the river Ohio., Sumner County, first Monday in January 1791. Present George Winchester Edward Douglass Anthony Sharp who produced their several commissions as Justices under hand & seal of William Blount Esqr apptd governor and commander in Chief over Territory, which commissions bear date 15 December 1790. David Wilson unanimously apptd chairman of Court.
Appt David Shelby Clerk of Court, George Winchester & Edward Douglass securities.
Appt Wm Cage Shff until July term, took oath, gave bond, James Douglass & Edward Douglass his securities.
Appt George Winchester register; David Wilson and David Shelby securities.
Appt Isaac Walton coroner; James Bone & Simon Kuykendall securities.
Constables apptd: James Bond; John Harpool security. Benja Williams; Wm Newton security. Philip Trammell; Zebulon Hubbard, security.
Approve Wilson Cage as a deputy sheriff.
Appt Thomas Hendricks admr of John Hendricks decd; bond $1000, Simon Kuykendall & Robert Jones securities.
Appt James McColgin admr of James Gillaspie decd; bond $1000, Joseph Waller sec.
David Wilson, Thomas Masten, Joseph Kuykendall produced commissions as Justices under hand and seal of William Blount.
Bills/sale proven: Thankful Hall admx of William Hall decd to Isaac Bledsoe Negro boy proved by John Neely. Pearce Wall to Isaac Bledsoe, Negro man & girl, proved by James Winchester. Alexr Cromwill to Joseph Desha, Negro girl, proven by John Neely.
p.   Jas D Hannah to Isaac Bledsoe, Negro girl, proved by Peter Looney.
Deeds proved: Isaac Bledsoe to Pearce Wall 320 acres on Station Camp proved by James Winchester. Isaac Bledsoe to heirs/Wm Hall decd 640 acres by Jas Winchester.
Will of Edward Turner decd proved by Wm Newton; Elizabeth Turner admx qualified.
Grand Jury: John Wilson foreman, Alexander Dever Reuben Douglass Zach Green John

JANUARY 1791

Hamilton Roger Gibson Lewis Crane Isaac Walton Charles Harriman John Rule Thomas Egnew Stephen Right Edward Jones Peter Looney Robert Hamilton.
Robert Jones exempted from fine for nonattendance as a Juror at last Term.
Court adjourns till tomorrow 9 oClock

Tuesday 4th January 1791. Present David Wilson George Winchester Anthony Sharp.
Mortgage Laurence Thompson to Jno Whitsitt & Azariah Thompson proven by Jas Bone.
Joshua Scot v John Hardin. Plf by John Overton; dft by Hopkins Lacy. Jury James Odam John Kuykendall Leonard West Sion Perry Robert Montgomery Wm Brazil Ephraim Payton David Beard Ben Garris Joseph McElwrath Ezekiel Douglass John Butler. Dft recovers of plf. Plf obtained appeal. Securities [blank].
George Martin apptd road overseer in place of James Hamilton.
Territory v Thos Doil. A&B. Dft fined one shilling.
Adam Flener exempted from fine for nonattendance as a juror last Term.
Deed Elmore Douglass to John Williams 320 acres ackd.
Deed Elmore Douglass to Benja Williams 320 acres ackd.
James Odam v Elisha Rolls. Sheriff's return at Octr 1790 he levied on 640 acres p.33 on Desha Creek; dft came not; plf by atty John Overton. Jury [above except Wm Bartlet for James Odam] find plf's damages 400 pounds. Plf recovers of dft also costs; land to be sold by sheriff.
Henry Robinson v Joseph Beard. Shff returned at Octr 1790 he levied on a mare; dft came not. Jury Dennis Graves John Hardin Wm Wier Robert Bryance Lazarus Cotton Silas McBee John Ross Geo Mansker Robt Sharp Wm McAdams Jas Sheppard John Morgan ascertain plfs damages 9 pds; plf recovers; property attached to be sold by shff.
Order waggon road to be laid off & cleared from Bledsoes Lick to a convenient ford on Cumberland River; Capt Hubbard apptd one of overseers, together with his militia company to work 3 days on sd road; Capt Frazier apptd overseer, his company to work 3 days from where Hubbard terminates; Capt McKain apptd overseer, militia company to work at end of Fraziers road 3 days; Capt McElwrath apptd overseer, company to work 3 days; Capt Morgan apptd overseer, company work in same manner.
John Steel exempted from attending as Juror for present term. Court adjourns.

Wednesday 5 January 1791. Present David Wilson Geo Winchester Edwd Douglass Esqrs.
James White, Josiah Love, John Overton, Howel Tatum, Bennet Searcy produced licenses to practice as attornies; took oaths for qualification.
Thomas Simpson v John Sutton. Octr 1790 Shff executed; dft came not; Jury Thos Spencer Jas Shaw Benjn Garris Zachariah Cross Jas Franklin Robt Montgomery Henry Woodwert Lazarus Cotton Stuart Briganer Robt Jones John Kuykendall Simon Kuykendall find plfs damages 12 pds; Plf recovers of dft with costs.
Jonathan Oneal v John Sutton. Octr Term, dft came not. Plf by atty John Overton prays damages be ascertained. Jury [above except Thos Simpson for Jas Shaw] find damages 18 pds. Plf recovers.
Bill/sale John Dawson to Elmore Douglass 3 Negroes proved by Edward Douglass Esq.
Territory v Basil Fry. Z&B. Jury [above] find dft guilty; fined 30 shillings.
Zachariah Cross fined 10 shillings for withdrawing himself from jury on trial between Territory and Basil Fry; sd Cross paid the fine.
Territory v Benja Garris. A&B. Jury [above except John Young & John Hickison for Benj Garris and Zach Cross] find deft not guilty.

APRIL 1791

Summon Wm Edwards to next Court to show cause, if any, why David Cooper & John Cooper shall not be released from their apprenticeship on acct illegal treatment.
Order Thomas Edwards John Hardin Jr William Totwine Reason Bower & Richard Hogin be summoned in behalf of the Justices vs William Edwards.
William Dobbins apptd County Surveyor; Josiah Love & Edward Douglass securities.
Sampson Williams vs John Scott's attorney. Sampson Williams garnishee. Dft came not, judgt by default. Plf by John Overton esq prays damages be ascertained. Jury James McKain Silas McBee George Hamilton Henry Robinson Wm Brigance John Hardin Robert Brigance Thomas Hampton Elisha Clary John Young John Carr John Cotton find damage 52 pds 10 shillings; plf recovers of dft afsd sum with costs.
Thomas S Spencer deputized to execute a writ John Cummins v Thomas Hall maketh oath that sd writ after coming to his hands through misfortune was left.
Jury to April Term: Zebulon Hubbard James Yates G D Blackmore Abraham Sanders James Harrison James Clendening James Reese John Cotton James McKain Silas McBee George Hamilton Henry Robinson Wm Brigance John Hardin Thomas Williams William Hacker Adam Laurence Adam Clap Robert Desha James Vinson Thos Patton Robert Brigance Thos Hampton Elisha Clary John Young John Carr David Brigance Robt Looney Hugh Crawford James McKain Sr Stephen Cantrel Richd Carr Jas Frazor Elisha Ogelsby Kasper Mansker Robt Bell Alexr Robinson.
p.35   Jurors agt whom Si fa issued & who failed to appear are fined £5.
William Pryor v John Cotton. On behalf dft, deposition of Jos Jones of Lincoln Co Kentucky to be taken.
Grant Capt S Williams privilege of keeping a ferry for one year at upper end of first bluff on Cumberland R above Salt lick; rate 8/for man & horse and in proportion; bond of Williams $1000, Peter Land John Boyd & James Shaw securities.
County tax one shilling on each poll, four pence on every 100 acres.
Overseer of road from Col Manskers to Cave Spring straighten sd road so as to avoid bad places; polls in Hubbards compy work from Cave Spring to Virginia line.
William Bird apptd overseer/road in place of Isaac Walton.
Order Thos Mastin Esqr contract for building of a gaol with logs, 12 feet square.
Court adjourns till Court in Course.   David Wilson

Court of Pleas & quarter Sessions at Courthouse on first Monday in April 1791.
Present George Winchester Joseph Kuykendall Anthony Sharp Thomas Mastin Esquires.
Venire: Zebulon Hubbard James Yates George D Blackmore James Harrison John Cotton James McKain Silas McBee George Hamilton Henry Robinson Wm Brigance John Hardin Jr Thos Williams Wm Hacker Jas Frazier Elisha Ogelsby Jas Clendening Adam Laurence Adam Clap Robt Desha Jas Vincent Robt Brigance Thos Hampton John Carr David Brigance Robt Looney Hugh Crawford James McKain Sr Stephen Cantrel Richd Carr Kasper Mansker Alexander Robinson Abraham Sanders James Reese.
John Young & Thomas Patton exempted for serving as Jurors for present Term.
Stock marks recorded: Robert Payton. William Neely.
Appt Margaret Neely admx of Alexr Neely decd; bond 1000 pds with Isaac Bledsoe & George D Blackmore securities.
Suppl inventory/Henry Ramsey decd rendered by admx.
Elisha Clary exempted attending as Juror present term for reasons offered by Ed-

APRIL 1791

ward Douglass, also Thomas Williams on affidavit of Zebulon Hubbard & James Yates.
   Grand jurors: Abraham Sanders foreman, John Cotton Adam Laurence Silas McBee George Hamilton James Frazier Kasper Mansker James McKain Sr Henry Robinson Geo D Blackmore Robert Brigance Alexr Robinson James Reese David Bryance James Vincent.
   Jurors to Superior Court: Anthony Sharp Joseph Kuykendall Thos Martin David Beard James Wilson(Curly) Richard Waller Thomas Simpson James McKain Jr Zebulon Hubbard William Wyer Benj Kuykendall John Dawson.
   Deed Thomas Denton to Robert Cambell proved by Philip Trammel & Ezekiel Norris.
   Deed William Turnbull to David Shannon proved by Joseph Shannon.
   John Cravins exempted from double tax for 1789.
   p.36 Hopkins Lacy Esq produced license, qualified as an attorney at law.
   John Johnston released from execution issued agt him for fine for nonattendance as Juror Octr last provided he pay costs.
   George Mansker apptd overseer/road from Drakes Crk to Manskers house; polls below sd road and at Montgomerys plantation work thereon.
   Thos Simpson & Jonathan Oneal v John Sutton. Dfts bail Thos Smith delivered him.
   Thos Hendricks v John Sutton. Dfts bail Wm Hacker delivered dft to Court.
   Silas McBee v John Sutton. Dfts bail Robert Shaw delivered sd deft to Court.
   Isaac Bledsoe produced commission/Peace from hand & seal of Wm Blount; qualified.
   James Cole Mountflorence produced license as atty; took oath of office.
   Uriah Anderson v Wm Totevine. Sion Perry, dfts bail, delivered Wm Totevine.
   Anthony Sharp v James Wilkeson. Sheriff Octr 1790 levied on corn crop growing in field; John Sutton garnishee; deft came not. Plf by atty John Overton prays damage be ascertained. Jury James Harrison James McKain Jr Wm Brigance James Yates John Hardin Jr Wm Hacker Elisha Ogelsby James Clendening Adam Clap Robt Desha Thos Hampton Zebulon Hubbard find damages 107 pds 12 shillings 9 pence halfpenny. Plf recovers afsd verdict with costs; attached property to be sold by Sheriff.
   Wm McAdams fined 10/ for profane swearing in hearing of Court; paid fine.
   James Vinson & James Clendening exempted from attending as Jurors for present Term.
   Court adjourned till tomorrow 10 OClock.

Tuesday 5th April 1791. Present David Wilson Isaac Bledsoe George Winchester Esqrs.
   James Wilson ranger, bond 1000 pds; Benjn Williams security.
   Persons charged county tax on lands out of County released.
   Ezekiel Norris garnishee in suit between him & James McCollister sayeth he is not indebted neither has any property of sd McCollister.
   Deed Elmore Douglass to John Dawson ackd.
   Matthew & Adam Kuykendall exempted for nonattendance as Jurors last July.
   p.37 Edwd Douglass deposited 25/ recd of Susannah Bone for being pregnant with illegitimate child; likewise deposited for Isaac Lindsey 17/6 sd Lindsey recd of James Bone for profane swearing & breach of the Sabbath.
   Justinian Cartwright v Laurence Thompson. Plf by John Overton; dft by Howel Tatum. Jury [above except Robt Looney & Richd Carr for John Hardin & Jas Clendening] assess plfs damage 134 pds 8 shillings; Plf recovers of dft with costs.
   Allow Isaac Pearce Jr to keep a ferry on Cumberland river for one year on land formerly property of James Esspy; charge for crossing, man & horse one shilling, sixpence for man or horse.
   Benjamin Williams records his stock mark.
   Justices v William Edwards, illegal treatment to orphans David & John Cooper;

APRIL 1791

after investigation, sd Edwards exculpated from charge & costs arising thereon.
John Hardin Jr fined 40 shillings for breach/Peace; David Hainey & David Hardin each 20 shillings, same offense; kept in custody of sheriff until paid with costs.
Court committed error in apptg overseers/roads that were not legally laid off by a jury of 12 men; all former overseer appointments declared void.
Thomas Hendricks admr/Jno Hendricks decd rendered inventory.
Deed James McKain to James Frazier ackd.
Thomas Hendricks v John Sutton. Plf by Josiah Love, deft by Andrew Jackson. Jury James Yates James Harrison James McKain Jr Wm Hacker Elisha Clary Adam Clap Robt Desha Zebulon Hubbard Robt Looney Richd Cair Geo D Blackmore Joshua Scott; plf not appearing, non suit entered; plf liable for full costs.
Wm Edwards v Wm Tolwine. Appeal. Jury [above] find for dft; plf liable for costs.
Wm McDanold apptd constable; gave bond, George Mansker security.
Release Charles Harriman from fine for nonattendance as juror last October.
Court adjourns 'till tomorrow 10 0 Clock.

p.38   Wednesday April 6th 1791.
Jurors to July Term: Richard Hogin, Ezekiel Douglass, Joseph McElwrath, Simon Kuykendall, Wm Edwards, Reason Bowyer, Thos Spencer, Chas Carter, Reuben Douglass, Ephraim Payton, James Franklin, John Williams, Joseph Wallace, Samuel Gragg, Robert Shaw, Thos Kilgore, Jas Ewing, John Hacker, John Huse, John Laurence, John Bartlet, John Hicks, Wm Beard, Jas Odam, James White, Daniel McGooden, Henry Vincent, James Cambell, Wm Miller, Thos Eqnew, John Harpool, Wm Bowan, James Hays, Richard Jones, Jno Cravins, John Hamilton Genl.
On motion of John Cotton, subpoena issues to Sheriff of Tennessee County to summons John Pryor to appear at this Court next Term and to bring a horse mentioned in a suit by him agt sd Cotton, under penalty of £100.
John Pryor v Jno Cotton; motion of Howel Tatum esq, deposition of Joseph Damril Amos Googe Isaac Baker John Baker to be taken in Green County behalf of plf. Also to Sumner County to take depositions of Frederick Barns James Barns and Wm Davis, also to Sheriff to summon Isaac Lindsey William Davis Geo Mansker & Jno Mansker.
Appointments to take lists of taxable property: Majr Geo Winchester in Capt Morgans Compy; Thos Masten for Capt Frazers Compy; Anthony Sharp for Capt Hubbards Compy; Edward Douglass for Capt McKains & Capt McElwraths districts.
Bill/sale Joseph Wallace to Edward Douglass proven by George Hamilton.
Deed Jacob Zeigler to Joseph Wilson ackd.
Anthony Sharp v John Sutton. Octr, Anthy Sharp obtained conditional judgt vs John Sutton a garnishee in his suit agt James Wilkeson for 50 pds. Executed by Wilson Cage, D.S. Deft obtained appeal but gave no security.
Ezekiel Norris v James McCallester. Philip Trammel constable executed on 100 acres on Arringtons Cr property of James McCollister. April Ct dft failed to appear to replevy property attached; sd land to be sold by sheriff.

p.39 Court of Pleas and quarter Sessions, first Monday July 1791. Present George Winchester and Edward Douglass. Adjourned till tomorrow 8 0 Clock.

JULY 1791

Tuesday July 6th 1791. Present George Winchester & Edwd Douglass. Adjourned till tomorrow 8 O Clock.

Wednesday July 7th 1791. Present David Wilson Geo Winchester Edwd Douglass Esqrs.

Margaret Neely returned Inventory of Alexander Neely.

Allowances for attendance as jurors at Superior Court: James McKain £3.16.8; Wm Wyer £3.14; David Beard £3.3.4.

Grand Jury: Reuben Douglass foreman, Ezekiel Douglass, Joseph McElwrath, William Edwards, Reason Bowyer, Thos Spencer, Charles Carter, James Franklin, Jno Williams, Robert Shaw, Thomas Kilgore, James Ewing, John Hughes, John Hicks.

Grant Patsey Hickison ltrs/admn on estate of John Hickison; bond 300 pds with Wm Cage & Richard Hogan securities.

Deeds ackd & proven: Simon Kuykendall to George McWhirter ackd. John Hamilton to Geo McWhirter proven by Simon Kuykendall. Ephm Payton to David Shelby ackd.

Deposition to be taken of Sarah Childers otherwise Sarah Green, Nelson County, KY behalf plf in suit J C Mountflorence agt Adam Kuykendall.

John Callen v George Mansker. Octr 1790 plf by John Overton; dft by Andw Jackson. July Jury Richard Hogan Simon Kuykendall Saml Gragg John Laurence Thos Egnew John Harpool Jas Odam Henry Vinson James Hays Richd Jones John Cravins Jas McKain; assess plfs damages to 8 pds. Plf recovers verdict with costs.

Deed Wm Cage Sheriff to James Odam ackd.

Stock marks and brands recorded: James Clendening, James How[Han?]

p.40   William Cage unanimously apptd Sheriff; bond, Josiah Love & David Shelby securities; also bond as collector for 1791.

Wilson Cage & Reuben Cage took oaths for qualification as deputy sheriffs.

Deed William Gillaspie to James McGavock proved by Howel Tatum.

James Odam excused from attending as Juror present term.

Peter Looney v Thomas Hendricks. Octr 1790 plf by John Overton; dft by Josiah Love. Jury William Brigance, Thos Christmass, Ephraim Payton, Jas Wilson, Stephen Jones, Andw Steel, Wm Baldwin, Abraham Bird, Francis Hainey, David Hardin, Robert Brigance, Wm Montgomery find for plf damage 8 pds 10 shillings. Verdict with costs.

Wm Cage Sheriff enters protest against gaol by reason of insufficiency thereof.

Grant admn estate of Benjn Kuykendall to June Kuykendall; bond 1000 pds, Richard Hogan Peter Looney Ephraim Payton securities, and took prescribed oath.

Justinian Cartwright v James Shaw. Jany 1791 plf by John Overton; dft by Andw Jackson. Dft confesses judgt 56 pds 18 shillings sixpence; stay of execution six months on David Shelby assuming himself security for dft.

Adam Hampton v James Shaw. Jany 1791 plf by Jno Overton; dft by Josiah Love. Dft in proper person confesses judgt £27.10.3; Plf recovers accordingly with costs.

Joseph Head v Andrew Jackson. Jury Richard Hogan Simon Kuykendall Saml Gragg John Laurence Thos Egnew John Harpool Henry Vincent Richd Jones John Cravins Jas McKain James Hays Dennis Graves, find for plf damages £300.0.0 & costs, or delivery to plf a negro specified in declaration; negro delivered by dft to Turner Williams attorney in fact for sd plf.

p.41   Thomas Kilgore exempted from attending as juror by reason of old age.

Edwd Douglass retd lists/taxable property in McElwraths & McKains companies.

George Winchester retd list of taxable property in Capt Morgans Company.

Territory v William McAdams. A&B. Jury [above] find dft guilty, also pays costs.

Deed Elmore Douglass to Reuben Douglass ackd.

Court adjourns till tomorrow 7 oclock.

OCTOBER 1791

Thursday July 7th. Present David Wilson George Winchester Edward Douglass Esqrs.

Cotton ads Pryor. Deposition of Joseph Jones Lincoln County Kentucky also Buton Smith Hawkins County Holston.

Jurors to Octr Term: Jos Wallace John Bartlet Jas Campbell Wm Miller James White John Hamilton(Genl) Abraham Bird William Snoddy Thos Edwards James Douglass Robert Looney David Brigance Thos Christmass James Wilson Jr Wm Wilson Joseph Wilson John Morgan James Herndon John Dunihoo Thomas Patton Robt Bell Isaac Pearce Kasper Mansker Stephen Cantrel Zebulon Hubbard Geo McWharton John Payton Isaac Walton Hugh Tinnon Thomas Simpson Elisha Ogelsby Wm Montgomery Richard Cair Jason Thompson.

Clerk & Sheriff each allowed £20 for exofficio services for preceding year.

Bill/sale Silas McBee to Thomas Hendricks proved by Edward Hogin.

John Dawson comes & agrees Courthouse shall continue as it now stands.

Admr/Edwin Hickman decd agt Francis Fordner, attacht levied on 428 acres 1½ miles from Salt lick on Cumberland R, order to sell half of sd tract issues.

John Baly v Wm McDanold. Dft in proper person confesses judgt £20 to be discharged by dft delivering to plf or his atty three cows & calves of a second rate and a two yr old Heifer agt 15 Augt next.

Court adjourns till Court in Course.   David Wilson

p.42   Court of Pleas & Quarter Sessions at Courthouse first Monday in October 1791. Present David Wilson, Anthony Sharp, and Thomas Masten Esquires.

Jurors: Joseph Wallace John Bartlet James Campbell James White John Hamilton Abraham Bird Wm Snoddy Thos Edwards Jas Douglass Robt Looney David Brigance Thomas Christmas James Wilson Jr Wm Wilson Jos Wilson John Morgan Jas Herndon John Dunihoo Thos Patton Robt Bell Isaac Pearce Kasper Mansker Stephen Cantrill Zebulon Hubbard George McWhirter John Payton Isaac Walton Hugh Tinnon Thomas Simpson Elisha Ogelsby Wm Montgomery Richard Cair Azariah Thompson.

Joseph Wallace John Bartlet James Campbell Abraham Bird Wm Snoddy Robt Looney Wm Wilson John Dunihoo Isaac Pearce Zebulon Hubbard Isaac Walton Hugh Tinnor exempted from serving as jurors for present session.

Thomas Christmas Wm Miller & James Herndon fined for nonattendance as jurors.

Deeds ackd: Robert Ewing to Francis Catron; Richard Caveat to Wm Maxwell; Richard Caveat to Michael Caveat ackd; George McWhirter to David Wilson.

Order waggon road cleared from Davidson County line through Geo McWhirters land.

Richard Caveat produced commission as Justice/Peace, hand & seal of Wm Blount.

Will of Alexander Robinson decd proved by John McCauly and James Whitsett; Mary Robinson James McCollister & Azariah Thompson exrs therein named, qualified.

Bill/sale John Sadler to Joseph McElwrath proved by James Hays.

Grand Jury: Kasper Mansker foreman, James White John Hamilton Thos Edwards James Douglass David Brigance James Wilson Joseph Wilson John Morgan Thomas Patton Robert Bell Stephen Cantril George McWhirter John Payton Thomas Simpson.

Deed Simon Kuykendall to James McKinsey proved by Robert Ellis.

Inventory of Benjamin Kuykendall decd rendered by admx.

Constable Wm McDanold, bond with Ephm Payton security in lieu of George Mansker.

Motion on collection of tax on deeds resolved in negative.

Robert Shaw records his stock mark.

OCTOBER 1791

On motion of Mrs Kuykendall: order James Winchester & David Wilson appraise the estate of Benjamin Kuykendall decd.
Release Thomas Hamilton from fine for not attending as juror at preceding Term.

p.41   Tuesday October 4th 1791. Present David Wilson Jos Kuykendall Anthy Sharp.
Deed George Mansker to William Gillaspie ackd.
Jurors to Superior Court Joseph Kuykendall Robert Shaw J[] [], Azariah Thompson, William Orr, George McWhirter, James Frazier, William Bowman, Sion Perry, James Franklin, Reason Bowyer, William Frazor.
James Cole Mountflorence v Adam Kuykendall. July 1790 plf by Josiah Love; dft by Andrew Jackson. Octr 1791 jury: Richd Hogan Jno Cotton Elisha Ogelsby R[][], James Frazier, Alexr Montgomery, Thos Hamilton, Dennis Graves, Henry Robinson, [] McElwrath, William Gillaspie, Sion Perry. Plf not appearing is nonsuited.
Allowances for attendance as jurors to Superior Court: Simon Kuykendall £2.15.4; Peter Looney £2.19.8.
Deed William Cage Shff to Ezekiel Norris proved by Stephen Anderson.
Admn on estate of Robert Jones decd granted to Agnus Jones & William Jones; bond 500 pds, Isaac Lindsey & James Hays securities.
Anthony Sharp esq records his stock mark.
Deed Ephraim Payton to Joel Echols ackd.
James McKain, fined 8 shillings for breach/peace, paid same to Clerk.
Order David Brigance fined 8 shillings for breach/peace; 20 shillings for nonattendance as a Grand Juror. Peter Looney, Pitmon, James McKain Jr & Wm Brigance fined 8 shillings each for breach/peace. David Brigance paid 8 shillings fine.
Bill/sale Page Billen to Peter Looney, stud horse proved by James Fr[].
Two bills/sale Ruffin Deloach to Michael Shanon, negro each, ackd.
Bill/sale Richard Strother to Michael Shanon ackd.
Order county tax one shilling on each poll, fourpence each 100 acres.
Peter Looney paid 5 shillings, part of his fine for breach/peace.
Anthony Sharp Esq returns list/taxable property Capt Hubbard's company.
p.42   Jurors to January Term: Elijah Ewing James Ewing Adam Flinor, Christopher Funkhouser, John Laurence, Conrod Strader, Moses Stevenson, Wm Bird, Volentine Shoat, Joseph Waller, John Rule, Martin Harpool, Wm Donely, Philip Myars, Thomas Conyer, James Hays, Thomas Cribbins, Thomas Strain, Hugh Crawford, Joseph Latimer, Nathl Latimer, John Steel, James Steel, Robt Brigance, Amos Smith, James McKinsey, Pearce Wall, Zacheus Wilson, Uriah Anderson, Robert Ellis, Henry Houdeshell, Wm Wilson, James Vinson, Jos Desha.

Wednesday 5th October 1791. Present David Wilson Anthony Sharp Thomas Masten.
William Lemar exempted from double tax for 1789.
David Brigance credited for fine 8 shillings for breach/peace; order it deducted from his acct agt County for service as constable; also 20/ for fine for nonattendance as a juror; likewise he is credited for Peter Loonys fine of 8/.
Charles Carter v Page Billen. Plf summons John Gillaspie & Silas McBee.
Order waggon road from Col Manskers to Virginia be laid off by Joseph Kuykendall Ezekiel Norris John Kuykendall Elmore Douglass Robt Looney Zach Green Wm Brigance James Hamilton King Carr William Maxwell Michael Caveat Robt Brigance John Steel James Ewing Matthew Kuykendall & George Martin. Order William Bird oversee afsd

OCTOBER 1791

road to ridge top; polls who formerly worked with Isaac Walton work thereon. King Carr to oversee to Arringtons Crk; James Ewing to oversee from Arringtons Creek to the Virginia line.

Order road to be laid off from Courthouse at John Dawsons to Cave Spring by above jury; appt Peter Looney, Harmon, overseer from Dawsons to ridge top. Wm Maxwell to oversee to Cave Spring; polls in Hubbards company to work thereon.

Order a road from Bledsoes Lick to Captain William Gillaspies and the upper road from Courthouse at Dawsons to junction be laid off by Ephraim Payton Simon Kuykendall James Hays Ruffin Deloach Joseph McElwrath Richard Hogin Esekiel Douglass Wm Snoddy Abraham Sanders James Harrison Samuel Wilson David Wilson John Wilson Mattw Alexander Sion Perry, any 12. Appt Ephraim Payton overseer from Capt Gillaspies to East fork Station Camp Cr; James Hays to oversee from Station Camp to Indian Creek; Matthew Alexander to oversee from Indian Creek to Bledsoes Lick.

Order a road from Station Camp Creek below Capt Wm Gillaspies to Kaspers Creek be laid off by Kasper Mansker Wm Gillaspie, Isaac Lindsey, Lewis Crane, Robert Bell, Joseph Waller, James Hannah, Thos Masten, Stephen Cantrill, Jas Frazor, Thos Simpson, Elisha Ogelsby, Peter Looney P, Thos Egnew, Wm Montgomery, W Steel, John Rule. Appt Wm Gillaspie to oversee from Station Camp to Drakes Crk. Samuel Bell to overp.45 see from Drakes Crk to Kaspers Crk.

Ordered a road laid off from Col Manskers to John Dawsons by Kasper Mansker Wm Gillaspie Isaac Lindsey Lewis Crane Robt Bell Joseph Waller Jas Hannah Thos Masten Stephen Cantrell James Frazor Thomas Simpson Elisha Ogelsby Peter Looney P Thomas Egnew William Montgomery Andrew Steel John Rule. Appt Andrew Steel to oversee from Manskers Creek to Drakes Cr; Thomas Egnew to oversee from Drakes to Station Camp.

Order Ezekiel Douglass oversee road from Courthouse at John Dawsons to East fork Station Camp Crk; Pearce Wall to oversee from East fork Station Camp to junction with road from Bledsoes Lick to Nashville.

Allow Benjamin Williams constable for attendance 6 days at 8/ pr day.

William Brigance credited for fine of 8/ for breach/peace, sum to be deducted out of David Brigances acct for services as constable.

Bay mare taken up as stray by Anthony Sharp was stolen from him; he is released from demands which county may have in consequence of entering stray with ranger.

Order Saml Gragg Saml Bell & Thos Smith to estimate value of gaol & clerks table.

James Douglass sheriff for 1789 allowed £2.4 pr Cumberland battalion voucher.

James Douglass Esqr returns list of supernumeraries for year 1789.

Clerk allowed Ten pounds for exofficio services.

James Douglass lost an order from Court to Joshua Hadley for rations to amount of £57.7.9 order that [] issue alias transcript to Hadley for sd amount.

Sheriff credited for tax on nine insolvent polls for taxes of 1789.

Court adjourns till Court in Course. David Wilson

p.46 Court of Pleas & Quarter Sessions first Monday in January 1792. Present Edward Douglass Esquire. Court adjourns till Tomorrow 9 OClock.

Tuesday January 3d 1792. Present Edwd Douglass Thomas Masten Richard Caveat Esqrs
Jurors: William Bird Volentine Shoat John Ruyle Martin Harpool Wm Donely Philip Myars Thomas Conyers James Hays Thomas Cribbins Thomas Strain Hugh Crawford Joseph

JANUARY 1792

Latimer Nathaniel Latimer John Steel James Steel Robert Brigance Amos Smith James McKinsey Pearce Wall Zacheus Wilson Robert Ellis Henry Houdeshell Wm Wilson.
Grand Jurors William Donely foreman Wm Wilson Henry Houdeshell James McKinsey James Steel Thos Cribbins Philip Myars Nathaniel Latimer James Hays Robt Brigance Thomas Strain Amos Smith William Bird.
Inventory/goods & chattels of James Gillaspie decd rendered by admr.
Ephraim Payton v Josiah Love. Apl 1791 plf by John Overton; dft by Andw Jackson. Jan 1792 jury John Steel Volentine Shoat Robt Ellis John Ruyle Jos Latimer Martin Harpool Zacheus Wilson Thos Conyers Hugh Crawford James Farr Wm Montgomery Abraham Bird assess plfs damage 40 pds. Plf recovers with costs.
Inventory of Robert Jones decd rendered by admx & admr.
Inventory of John Hickison decd rendered by admx.
Deeds ackd & proved: Thos Jennings to Wm Walton by Jesse Glasgow. Wm Walton to Isaac Walton ackd. John Hamilton to Moore Stephenson by Isaac Walton. Lewis Crane to Elmore Douglass ackd. Wm Walton to Moore Stephenson ackd. Wm Cage to Wm Douglass proved by Wm Dobbins. Wm Cage to Elmore Douglass ackd. Anthony Sharp to John Spurgin proved by Saml Gragg.
Stock marks & brands recorded: William Primer. George Blackmore.
Grant admn on estate of Lewis Melone decd to Lydia Melone; bond 500 pounds with Henry Vinson and James Vinson securities.
p.47   Andw Jackson v Josias Adams. Wm Bowan garnishee oath he is not indebted to Adams nor has any of Adams property.
William Dillard records his stock mark and brand.
Appt Jas Reese John Wilson & Jas Wilson to appraise estate of Lewis Melone decd.
Deed James Hays to Thomas Smith ackd.
Charles Carter v Page Bellen. July 1791 dft by Josiah Love. Plf by Andw Jackson. Jan 1792 Jury: Isaac Lowel Robt Looney Wm McAdam John Hamilton Thos Payton Henry Robinson Jas Frazier Sion Perry Thos Smith William Brigance James Vinson Wm Frazor. Plf recovers of dft with costs.
Amos Heaton v Thomas Woodard. July 1791 Shff levied on preemption 337; dft came not. Jany 1792 plf by John Overton prays damage ascertained. Jury Martin Harpool Thos Conyer Hugh Crawford Jos Latimer John Steel John Rule Volentine Shoat Robt Ellis Jas Farr Wm Montgomery Zacheus Wilson Abraham Bird fine damages £47.6.11 & costs. Attached land to be sold to satisfy judgment & costs.
Amos Heaton v Simm Woodard. July 1791 Sheriff levied on preemption 340 dated 10 March 1784. Dft came not. Jan 1792 plf by John Overton prays damage be ascertained. Jury Isaac Towel Robt Looney Wm McAdams John Hamilton Henry Robertson David Beard James Frazor Sion Perry Wm Brigance Wm Frazor James Vinson Peter Turney find plfs damages £40.8.3. Attached land to be sold to satisfy judgment & costs.

Wednesday January 4th 1792. Present Edwd Douglass Thos Masten Richd Caveat Esqrs.
p.48   Deeds ackd: James McKain to John Dawson. Wm Cage to Wm Cage Junr.
John McCumsey v James McKain. Jan 1791 plf by John Overton; dft by Josiah Love. Jan 1792 Jury Abraham Bird Zacheus Wilson James Fair John Steel Jos Latimer Robert Looney John Hamilton Volentine Shoat Hugh Crawford James Vinson Sion Perry David Beard assess plfs damage £18.16. Dft obtains appeal, Jno Dawson & Zach Green sec.
Supplemental inventory Ben Kuykendall decd rendered by admr.
Jurors to April Term: David Beard Thomas Egnew Elisha Ogelsby Reuben Douglass Ruffin Deloach Peter Looney Samuel Gragg Wm Edwards Jos Wallace Zachariah Green Wm

APRIL 1792

Gillaspie Jas Franklin Jas McKain Chas Carter John Dawson Hugh Crawford Thos Smith Ezekiel Norris James Ewing David Hughes Bostic Martin Wm Bowan Wm Reed Wm Green Geo D Blackmore James Reese John Wilson John Williams Peter Looney P Thomas Spencer Jno Weathers James Harrison James White John White Francis Catron Alexander Montgomery.
 Ltrs/admn on estate of Joseph Dixon granted to David Beard; Robt Looney security.
 Deed Hardy Murfree to Lemuel Laurance proven by James Norfield.
 Territory v Robt Brigance. breach/peace. Submitted; fined 8 shillings.
 Stock marks recorded: Lazarus Cotton. Sion Perry. Wm Brigance. Hugh Crawford. Amos Smith
 Motion of Mrs Hickison; James Wilson Curley, Pearce Wall, Jos McElwrath apptd to appraise personal estate of John Hickison decd.
 Appt Adam Beard constable in Capt Frazors Compy; Edwd Douglass & David Beard sec.
 Motion of David Beard admr of Jos Dixon decd, order Jas Reese Jas White Jno White appraise personal estate of Joseph Dixon decd.
 Order Adam Beard & Philip Trammel attend ensuing Court as constables.
 Edward Douglass records his brand.
 Mark & brand recorded for Richd Caveat. John Steel. Jos Latimer. Nathl Latimer.
 Road orders made at last Term are to continue until next ensuing Term.
 p.49   Justinian Cartwright v John Whitsett. Cartwright recovered £134.8 in suit agt Laurence Thompson with £4.8.4 costs. Whitsett was Thompsons special bail to surrender Thompson but failed. Whitsett to show cause if any why execution ought not be agt him. Dated first Monday Octr 1791, D Shelby Clerk. William Cage made return to Jany 1792 Term "Made known before Edward Douglass Esq & James Bone" whereupon dft being called, judgt entered agt him.
 Court adjourns till Court in Course.   Edward Douglass

Court of Pleas & Quarter Sessions first Monday in April 1792. Present Isaac Bledsoe David Wilson George Winchester Joseph Kuykendall Edward Douglass Thomas Masten.
 Jurors: David Beard Elisha Ogelsby Reuben Douglass Ruffin Deloach Peter Looney Samuel Gragg William Edwards Zachariah Green Wm Gillaspie James Franklin Jas McKain Charles Carter Hugh Crawford Thomas Smith Ezekiel Norris David Hughes Bostic Martin William Bowan Wm Reed Wm Green Geo D Blackmore Jas Reese John Wilson John Williams Peter Looney Thomas Spencer John Weathers James Harrison James White John White Francis Catron Alexander Montgomery.
 Grand Jury: William Gillaspie foreman, Wm Edwards Peter Looney H Chas Carter Jas McKain John Williams Wm Reed Zachariah Green Saml Gragg Ezekl Norris Geo Blackmore Francis Catron James Franklin.
 Exempted from attending as juror this Term: Jas White. Jas Reese.
 David Wilson Esq deposited with Clerk 25 shillings being fine of Elizabeth Manry for having a base born child.
 Allowances for attendance as jurors: Wm Orr £2/8. Thos Masten £2.19.6. Jas Franklin £2.14.
 Deeds proved & ackd: James Clendening to James Vinson by David Wilson. Isaac Bledsoe to James Reese ackd. Isaac Bledsoe to Matthew Alexander ackd. Reuben Douglass to Wm Brazil ackd. James Clendening to Henry Vinson by David Wilson.
 Inventory of Lewis Malone decd rendered by admx.

APRIL 1792

p.50   Order John Wilson & Geo D Blackmore apptd in lieu of Jas Reese & Jas White to estimate value of residue of estate of Joseph Dixon decd.
Deeds ackd & proved: Isaac Bledsoe to Obediah Terrell ackd. Jno Boyd Sr to Levise Simpson proved by John Boyd. Jas Wilson Curly to Chas Dement ackd.
Jurors to Superior Court: Robt Desha John Buckly Jas White Kasper Mansker Hugh Tinnan Simon Elliot Chas Carter Adam Laurence Wm Hacker Thos Hamilton John Cummins Ruffin Deloach.
Appearance bond: James Wilson Carly[Caily?]
Motion of Mrs Melone, order Lewis Melone orphan of Lewis Melone decd bound to Thomas Payton to learn hatting trade.

Tuesday 3d April 1792. Present Isaac Bledsoe David Wilson George Winchester Joseph Kuykendall Richard Caveat.
Jury to lay off road from Bledsoes Lick to Station Camp Cr below Capt Gillaspies, upper road from forks sd rd above Maj Wilsons to John Dawsons report they met 10 Feb 1792 and marked sd road.
Supplemental inventory Benjn Kuykendall rendered by admx.
Order Sheriff make settlement for money arising from strays at next Court.
Matthew Pain records his stock mark.
Order overseers of road from Bledsoes Lick to Manskers Cr, thence by Court house to above Major Wilsons allowed untill July Term to clear out sd road 20 ft wide and sign posts set up at forks of roads with indexes pointing each way, the near end to begin at Bledsoes Lick and number of miles thence marked at end of every mile.
Order for road from Col Manskers to Cave Spring to be received next Term
Bills of sale: Henry Vinson & James Vinson to James Clendening each for a negro proved by David Wilson. Charles Carter to Elmore Douglass ackd.
Robt Shaw allowed £2.14 for attendance as juror last Superior Court.
Assignment of grant from Isaac Linton & Silas Linton to Joshua Campbell proved by John Burgess.
James Douglass v William Bowman. Jan 1792 Shff levied on 640 acres joining heirs of Anthony Bledsoe & Wm Neely decd; dft came not; judgt by default. Apl 1792 plf by atty Andw Jackson prays damage be ascertained. Jury David Beard Elisha Ogelsby Ruffin Deloach Peter Looney Hugh Crawford Thos Smith John Wilson Thos Spencer John Weathers Jas Harrison John White Alexr Montgomery find damages £100. Plf recovers
p.51   of dft afsd verdict & costs. Property levied on condemned to use of judgt.
Deeds ackd & proved: John Williams to Edwd Williams ackd. Wm Shaw to Simon Spring by Bennet Searcy.
Stock marks recorded. Edward Williams. Richard Strother. William Gillaspie & his brand. John Williams.
Motion of Major Martin. Order Anthony Sharp Esq pay sd Martin £4.6.8 being ¼ the appraisement of stray H taken up by Anthony Sharp; sum allowed sd D Martin for his services as sheriff 1787 and 1788.
Order Daniel Smith Esq pay sd Martin ¼ value of stray stear taken up by sd Smith.
John Thompson exempted from County demands for ¼ value of mair taken up by him.
Jabus Fisher John Butler Justinian Cartwright Richard Bruff each fined 10/ for disobeying order of officer apptd to guard Jail.
David Shelby v Robert Espy. Shelby recovered £38.2.3 in suit agt Robt Espy & 12 shillings fourpence costs. Espy hath discharged £13.6. D Shelby Clerk. Apl 1792 Dft by John Overton & Andw Jackson tendered cattle. Plf failed to attend to receive

JULY 1792

them. Dft prays judgt whether he should be charged with debt. Jury David Beard Elisha Ogelsby Ruffin Deloach Peter Looney Hugh Crawford Thos Smith John Wilson Thos Spencer John Weathers James Harrison John White Alexr Montgomery find for plf damage £25.8.7. Therefore plf to recover verdict and costs.

p.52   John white exempted from attending as a juror for present Term.

Wednesday 4th April 1792. Present Isaac Bledsoe David Wilson Edward Douglass Thomas Masten.

Inventory goods & chattels of Joseph Dixon decd rendered by admr.

Will of John Shaver decd proved by Thomas Larimore.

Justices apptd to take lists of Taxable property: David Wilson for Capt Moyars & Capt McElwraths districts. Edward Douglass for McKains & Frazers. Thos Masten for Cantrils district. Anthony Sharp for Hubbards district.

John Butler released from fine for noncompliance with officer guarding gaol.

Deed John Agin to Robert Sharp proved by Peter Looney P.

Territory v Nathl Holley. Petit Larceny. Jury David Beard Elisha Ogelsby Ruffin Deloach Peter Looney Hugh Crawford Thos Smith Jas Harrison Alexr Montgomery Bostick Martin Jos Wallace Robt Shaw Mattw Kuykendall find dft guilty. Culprit to be taken to public whipping post and there receive 39 lashes on bare back well laid on.

Robt Espy & Wm McAdams paid fines 2 shillings sixpence each for profane swearing.

Philip Trammel allowed for attendance on Court 33 days at 8/ pr day.

Release Saml Fair from ½ value of stray horse posted by him, stolen by Indians.

Peter Looney v Thomas S Spencer. Looney recovered £8.10 & £4.13.6 agt Thos Hendricks. Spencer was Hendricks special bail, failed to surrender him. Apl 1792 Sheriff's return before Simon Ellis & Hugh []. Judgt agt dft.

Jurors to July Term: Roger Gibson Joseph Desha Robt Steel Wm Bird Wm Beard Thomas Spencer Hugh Elliott Wm Newton Chas Reese Isaac Pearce Robt Bell Robt Shannon Mattw McCormack Smith Hambrough Michael Caveat John Young(blacksmith) John Young (Irish) John Hughes Joseph Taylor Edwd Hogin Thomas Strain Robt Looney Abraham Bird George Wolwood Stephen Cantril Ezra Thompson John Hamilton (Genl) John Gatlin John Deloach David Bryance John Boyd Robt Bryance Lewis Crane Thomas Jimason.

Office of Sumner v James Cole Mountflorence. Scire facias to Jany 1792 & scire facias to April 1792 "Not found"; dft liable to full costs in suit James Berry v Laurence Thompson.   Court adjourns till Court in Course. Isaac Bledsoe

p.53   Court of Pleas & quarter Sessions first Monday July 1792. Present Joseph Kuykendall Anthony Sharp Thomas Masten Esquires.

Jurors Roger Gibson Jos Desha Robt Steel Wm Bird Wm Beard Thos Spencer Hugh Elliot Wm Newton Chas Reese Isaac Pearce Robt Bell Robt Shannon Mattw McCormack Smith Hambrough Michael Cavit John Young(black) John Young (Irish) John Hughes Joseph Taylor Edwd Hogin Thos Strain Robt Looney Abraham Bird Geo Wolwood Stephen Cantril Azariah Thompson John Hamilton John Deloach David Brigance John Boyd Robt Brigance Lewis Crane Thos Jimason.

Grand Jurors: Robt Bell foreman Matthew McCormack Thos Strain Roger Gibson Thos Spencer Jos Taylor John Boyd John Hamilton Wm Bird Isaac Pearce John Deloach Robt

JULY 1792

Looney Abraham Bird Edward Hogin.
    Deeds ackd & proved: John Topp to Peter Turney by Obediah Smith. Peter Turney to Obediah Terrell ackd. Josiah Love to Joseph Barnes by Bennet Searcy. Geo Payne to Justinian Cartwright by Mattw Payne. James Espy to Isaac Pearce ackd. Samuel Mosby by Squire Grant atty in fact to heirs of Hugh Henry decd proved by Andrew Jackson.
    Lewis Crane is exempted from attending as juror for the present term.
    Motion of Mrs Askins. Appoint Philip Trammell guardian for Nicholas Trammell son of sd Mrs Askins; David Beard and John Young his securities, bond 500 pounds.
    Appt John Williams admr of Benjamin Williams decd; bond, Reuben Douglass and Edward Williams securities.

Tuesday 3d July 1792. Present Edward Douglass Joseph Kuykendall Anthony Sharp.
    Deed George A Sugg to William White proved by Andrew Jackson.
    Bill/sale Thomas Hampton to Robert Desha proved by David Hainey.
    Thomas Hendricks v John Sutton. Deposition of Adam Kuykendall directed to [blank] Barnet at Mason Town on the Ohio behalf deft.
    John Sadler v William Gillaspie. Jury: Michael Cavit Stephen Cantril John Young Richard Hogin Wm Snoddy Alexr Montgomery Joshua Scott Thomas Jimeson Wm Anderson Wm Frazor James Frazor David Hainey; juror withdrawn, suit continued.
    Deeds ackd: Adam Laurence to Wm Wyer 160 acres Drakes Crk. Deed/gift Robt Cartwright to daughter Elizabeth Rutherford 200 ac Station Camp Creek. James McKain to Zachariah Green.
    Bill/sale Michael Shaver decd to Roger Gibson; witnesses thereto are both wounded and unable to attend. George Winchester & Isaac Bledsoe esqrs to take depositions of sd witnessess respecting execution of sd bill/sale.
    Allow John Cummins £2.10 for attendance as juror at Superior Court May 1792.
    Allow Sheriff £2.3.6 for finding Page Billen whilst in confinement.
p.54   Deeds ackd: James Crabtree to David Purvoyner. Ruffin Deloach to Richard Strother. Joseph Kuykendall to John Young. Joseph Kuykendall to William Young.
    Wm Cage apptd Sheriff; Elmore Douglass & David Shelby securities, William Cage is also apptd Collector, same securities.
    Lists/taxable property retd: Thomas Masten in Captain Cantrells Company. Anthony Sharp in Captain Hubbards. Edward Douglass in Capt Frazer & Capt Loonies dists.
    Deed Mussenden Matthews to William Snoddy proved by Simon West.
    John Young recorded his stock mark and brand.
    Sadler v Gillaspie. Deposition of Ivy McPherson to be taken on behalf of the dft.
    Order Thomas Christmas fined 40 for contempt/court; fine remitted.

Wednesday 4th July 1792. Present Edward Douglass Anthy Sharp Jos Kuykendall Esqrs.
    Order Sheriff receive of Clerk 30 shillings fines agt Cartwright Fisher & Brough for disobedience of orders of officer apptd to guard gaol.
    William Cage & Reuben Cage Esqrs took oath of office of Sheriff.
    Jurors to Octr Term: Reuben Douglass Archd Martin John Patterson Peter Looney H Jas Franklin Ephm Payton Isaac Towel Wm Dillard Jas Winchester Geo D Blackmore Elmore Douglass John Dobbins Robt Looney Thos Simpson John Whitsitt Azariah Thompson Wm Bowan Moore Stephenson Wm Keneday Isaac Lindsey Thos Hendricks Geo Martin Robert Shaw Thos Hamelton Jr Jacob Sanders Matthew Kuykendall Wm Maxwell Jas Yates Chrisr Funkhouser Richd Strother Robt Brigance John Steel Sion Perry Chas Carter William

JANUARY 1793

Edwards Jos Wallace Phdy Alton.
Jury to lay off road from Manskers to Cave Spring at Maj Sharps thence to Virginia line: Kasper Mansker Hugh Tennon Isaac Walton Thos Simpson John Johnston Jos Kuykendall John Kuykendall Wm Maxwell Ezekiel Norris King Cair Robt Shaw Thos Hamilton Jr Jas Hamilton Geo Martin Matthew Kuykendall Richd Caveat.
Deeds ackd: Justinian Cartwright to Adam Harpool. Justinian Cartwright to Prudence Farrier.
Appt Wm Hacker overseer/road from Arringtons Creek to Virginia line.
Order Sion Perry Richd Hogin Wm Snoddy work on road Courthouse to East fork Station Camp under Ezekiel Douglass overseer/road.
Appt Wm Dillard & David Hay to estimate value of Jail. Edwd Douglass

p.55   Court/Pleas & Quarter Sessions, Courthouse 1st Monday Octr 1792. Present: Isaac Bledsoe David Wilson Edwd Douglass esq. Court adjourned till Court in Course.

Court of Pleas & Quarter Sessions at plantation of John Dawson 1st Monday January 1793. Present Isaac Bledsoe David Wilson Geo Winchester Thomas Masten, Esquires.
Deeds ackd & proved: Joshua Campbell to Thos Masten by Wm Green. John Donelson to Danl Smith by Thos Masten & Wm Green. Joshua Campbell to Wm Green by Thos Masten. Thos Masten to Robt Green ackd. Sampson Williams to John Scott by Jason Thompson. Jas Clendening to Lewis Melone by Wm Wilson. Geo Leeper to Robt King by Wm Wilson. Abraham Hargis to Jas Yates by Thos Yates. Isaac Shelby to Jas Whitsitt by John Whitsitt & Azariah Thompson. Joseph Kuykendall to Thos Smith by Anthony Sharp.
Bill/sale John Hynes to Anthony Sharp proved by Richard Caveat.
Deeds ackd & proved. Reason Bowyer to Wm Edwards by Wm Dobbins. Thos S Spencer to Zacheus Wilson by Saml Wilson. Isaac Pearce to Isaac Pearce Jr ackd. Isaac Pearce to Jonathan Pearce ackd.
Will/Michael Shaver decd proved by Wm Wilson; David Wilson & John Wilson exrs.
Thomas Egnew records his stock mark.
Joel Echols & Gabriel Black made oath 7 Sept 1792 to Isaac Bledsoe & Geo Winchester Esqrs that they saw Michael Shaver sign bill/sale day & date therein specified.
Grant admn on estate of Jacob Zeigler decd to Mrs Christina Zeigler; James Wilson & Peter Turney securities.
Appearance bond John Kuykendall Jr. Simon Kuykendall John Dawson Reason Bower Matthew Kuykendall securities.
p.56 Road overseers apptd: Peter Turney in place of Matthew Alexander. John Dobbins in place of King Cair. Also Edwd Williams in place of Pearce Wall.
Bill/sale Jesse Maxey to Wm Maxey Loving & Edwd Maxey Loving. Another, Jesse Maxey to to Wm Maxey Loving & Edwd Maxey Loving proved by John Organ.
Obligation Elizabeth Maxey to Wm & Edward Loving proved by Wm Wilson.
Obligation Wm & Edwd Maxey to Elizabeth Loving otherwise Elizabeth Maxey proved by William Wilson.

APRIL 1793

Deed James McKinsey to Thomas Payton proved by David Wilson.
Grant admn on estate of John Purvoiner decd granted to Richard King. William Thomas & William Wilson securities.
Jury apptd to lay off road from Col Manskers to Cave Spring to Virginia line report same agreeable to former road except for shunning bad hills, also David Hughes shall make a lain through his field. Mathw Kuykendall, Michael Caveat.
Jurors apptd last July Term continued to ensuing Term except Geo Martin Robt Shaw Thos Hamilton Jacob Sanders Matw Kuykendall in whose places are Adam Laurence Thos Woodard John Hardin Jr Adam Clap & John Young blacksmith.
Appt Wm Hacker overseer/road Arringtons Creek to Virginia line.
Bill/sale Henry Vinson to James Clendening proved by George Winchester.
Bill/sale William Penny[Perry?] to David Shelby proved by Wm Brigance.
Court adjourns till Court in Course to meet at Pearce Walls.   Isaac Bledsoe.

Court of Pleas & Quarter Sessions at house of Pearce Wall first Monday in April 1793. Present David Wilson Thomas Masten Edward Douglass Esqrs.
Allow Wm Dillard to keep a ferry one year on Cumberland R. at Dillards landing.
John Williams returned inventory/sales of estate of Benjamin Williams decd.
Deeds ackd & proved: James Frazer to Francis Catron. Justinian Cartwright to Jonathan Latimer by Joseph Latimer. Moore Stephenson to Isaac Walton. Justinian Cartwright to John Robertson by James Gambling. John Robertson to Daniel Rogers by James Gambling.
Richard King returned inventory/sales of estate of John Purvoince decd.
Christina Zeigler returned inventory/estate of Jacob Zeigler. Order Matthew Alexander & James Reese to appraise personal estate of Jacob Zeigler decd.
p.57   Mrs Hickison retd supplemental inventory of goods of John Hickison decd.
Grand jurors: William Dillard foreman, Moore Stephenson John Steel Charles Carter Robert Brigance John Dobbins John Whitsitt James Franklin Richard Strother Azariah Thompson Archibald Martin Reuben Douglass Joseph Wallace.
Bill/sale Lydia Melone to James Clendening proved by David Wilson.
Appt John Burgess constable; John Weathers & Thomas Edwards his securities.
Grant to John Morgan the admn on estate of Armstead Morgan decd; bond $250, with James White and George D Blackimore securities.
John Hamilton appointed constable; John Wilson his security.
Deeds ackd & proved. Thomas Hamilton to Rowland Hughes. Justinian Cartwright to James Gambling by Peter Loony. Joseph Kuykendall to John Young.
Inventory estate of Michael Shaver decd rendered by executors.
Motion of David Wilson, order Geo D Blackmore James Reese & John Barckly appraise estate of Michael Shaver decd.
Bond of Edward Douglass $200 to indemnify County of expenses in consequence of Margaret Nelson having a base born child; he paid 50 shillings for her fine, she refusing to come forward & swear the said child.
Allow Thomas Hamelton £2.16 for attendance as juror to Superior Court.
Bond of Nancy Mercer $200, James Vinson security, to indemnify County of expenses in consequence of her having a base born child; she paid her fine 50 shillings.
Court adjourns to meet Tomorrow at 9 oclock at house of Ezekiel Douglass.

APRIL 1793

Tuesday April 2d 1793. Present David Wilson Edward Douglass Thomas Masten esquires.
Obligation from Hugh Crawford to William Cage proved by Edward Douglass.
Motion of Mr Barnet, allow Thomas Bailey the appraised value of stray horse taken up by Edward Hogin, horse being property of Bailey.
Robert Steel records his stock mark.
Deed: James McNair to Henry Wiggins proved by William Donelson.
Charles Carter v John Hardin Silas McBee John Dawson David Brigance. Jury Isaac Towel Peter Looney H, Wm Kennedy Sion Perry Wm Edwards Rody Allon Ruffin Deloach John McCarty Richd Hogin Jas Wilson Jas Hays Thos Smith find for dfts. Plf granted a new trial.
Deed Obediah Terrell to Peter Fisher proved by George Winchester Esqr.
Archibald Fisher records his stock mark and brand.
p.58   Thomas Hendricks v John Sutton. Refered to Thomas Mastin Joseph Kuykendall & Sampson Williams.
License Geo D Blackmore to keep an ordinary at his dwelling, Reuben Douglass sec.
Ferry rates at Wm Dillards: boating man & horse 12½ cent; man or horse 6 cts; bond 50 pounds with Edward Douglass security.
Wm Nash v Wm Dobbins. Jany 1792 plf by Howel Tatum; dft by John Overton. April Jury [above except Thos Edwards for Wm Edwards] assess plfs damage £33.15.9.
Thos Hendricks v John Sutton. July 1791 Shff executed on dft. Apl 1792 plf by atty Josiah Love; dft by Andw Jackson. Apl 1793 cause refered to Thos Mastin Jos Kuykendall & Sampson Williams, return award: Jno Sutton indebted 16 pds & costs.
William Douglass records ear mark & brand.
Grant admn on estate of Dianah Jones decd to Wm Jones; bond $500, Ruffin Deloach & Peter Turney securities.
William Lusk v Nathaniel Holly. July 1792 Shff executed on dft. Apl 1793 plf by Howel Tatum prays damages be ascertained. Jury Thos Patton John Payton Thos Edwards Saml Wilson Robt Sharp Peter Turney John Williams Jeremiah Doxey Wm Snoddy Joshua Scott Ephm Payton Francis Catron find damages one penny. Also costs.
p.59   Arthur Gilbreath v James McKain. Debt. July 1792 plf by Andw Jackson; dft by John Overton. Apl 1793 Jury Isaac Towel Peter Looney H Wm Kennedy Sion Perry Wm Edwards Rody Allon Ruffin Deloach John McCarty Richd Hogan Jas Wilson Jas Hays Thos Smith find for plf 75 pds. Plf recovers accordingly with costs.
Wm Quarter v James McKain. Debt. Jan 1793 Shff executed. April 1793 dft came not. Judgt by default agt him £2 7 4 pence with costs.
Thos Spencer v Thos Hendricks.. Jany 1793 Shff levied on horse & filly. Apl 1793 dft came not. Judgt by default £16.2.4 with costs.
Wm Gillaspie v James Cole Mountflorence. Debt. Shff Apl 1793 levied on 500 acres part of 1000 acres adj R Jones; dft came not. Judgt by default £41.4.10 & costs.
Allow Jos Wallace £6 for furnishing guard to Holston with beef & salt.
Allow Thos Edwards to erect mill on Station Camp above John Williams house; bond $250, Reuben Douglass & Wm Edwards securities.
Deeds ackd & proved: Thos Smith to James Hays. James Hays to John Purvoince. Michael Shaver to Ruffin Deloach by David Wilson. Anthony Hart to Howel Tatum by Andrew Jackson.

Wednesday April 3d 1793. Present David Wilson Edwd Douglass Thos Masten esquires.
Motion of Mr Jackson, order whereon attacht Thos S Spencer v Thos Hendricks was levied be condemned for use of judgt; property to be sold.

JULY 1793

Jurors to Superior Ct: Kasper Mansker John Cummins Thomas Waller Stephen Cantrel John Wilson Simon Kuykendall William Gillaspie John Whitsitt John Young Edward Gwin John Hamilton Genl & John Bryance.

Charles Carter v John Hardin. Wm Bryance Sarah Carr Sarah Douglass & John Kuykendall to be summoned in behalf of the defendant.

Simon Elliott to appear at next Court to show cause why the orphans of Thomas Fry shall not be legally bound.

p.60 Jurors to July Term: Elmore Douglass Charles Carter Richard Hogin Joseph McElwrath Simon Elliott Richd King Henry Vinson Wm Snoddy Thos Edwards James White John Williams Chas Dement Matthew Anderson Wm Frazer Thomas Egnew Wm McNeely Joseph Hendricks Thomas Simpson Wm Green Smith Hansbrough John Weathers Robert Bell Archd Buchanan Wm Bowan David Scoby Wm Maxwell Charles Latimer Zach Green John Norris Jas Harrison Jacob Scot Francis Catron Andrew Sug.

William Jones fined 50 shillings for neglect of duty in guarding John Kuykendall to the District Jail.

Francis Catron records his stock mark and brand.

Order tax one shilling on Poll and 4 pence on every hundred acres.

Clerk & Sheriff allowed each 15 pounds for exofficio services for 1791.

Justices apptd to take lists of taxable property: Isaac Bledsoe for Capt Morgans dist; George Winchester for Capt Kings dist; David Wilson for Capt McElwraths dist; Edward Douglass for Capt Lunas dist; Thomas Mastin for Capt Cantrills dist; Joseph Kuykendall for Capt Youngs dist; Edward Douglass for Capt Frazers district.

Court adjourns to meet Court in course at house of Ezkl Douglass.   David Wilson

Court of Pleas & Quarter Sessions at house of Ezekiel Douglass first Monday in July 1793. Present David Wilson George Winchester Thomas Masten Esquires.

James Doherty permitted to practice as an attorney at law during present Term.

Grand Jury: Thos Simpson foreman, Chas Carter Jno Norris Richd Hogan Thos Edwards Henry Vinson Chas Latimer Wm Frazor Francis Catron Zach Green Simon Elliott Charles Dement William Snoddy.

Appt Isbel Houdeshell admx of Henry Houdeshell decd; bond $1000, Thomas Patton & Joseph McElwrath securities. Griffith Rutherford James Wilson & John Wilson apptd to appraise the estate of Henry Houdeshell decd.

Deeds ackd & proved: Peter Turney to Jeremiah Morgan & Joseph Morgan. Peter Turney to George D Blackmore.   Abraham Sanders to James Blythe by Geo Winchester.

Will/Isaac Bledsoe decd proved by Jesse Hughes; codicil proved by Geo Winchester. Catharine Bledsoe & Geo Winchester exr & exx qualified.

Catharine Shaver widow of Michael Shaver decd enters dissent to will of deceased and claims her right of dower agreeable to law.

Grant admn on estate of Samuel Fair decd to Ephraim Fair; bond $500, John Hamilton & Simon Kuykendall securities. Appt Griffith Rutherford Thomas Donald & John Wilson appraisers of estate of late Samuel Fair.

Allow Kasper Mansker to keep a grist mill on Mansker Creek.

Deed Michael Glaves to Richard Waller proved by Andrew Jackson.

p.61 Deeds proved: David Purvoince to John Purvoince by Thomas Patton. Lewis Brown to Abraham Rogers by Elizabeth Rogers.

JULY 1793

Grant admn on estate of James Steel decd to Robert Steel; bond $1000 John Steel & David Beard securities.
John Morgan rendered inventory estate of Armistead Morgan decd.
William Jones rendered inventory estate of Dianah Jones.
Order Archibald Fisher & James Gambling appraise estate of Armstead Morgan decd.
Deeds ackd & proved. Isaac Bledsoe & Mary Parker exrs of Anthony Bledsoe decd to David Shelby by Wm Neely. Philip Shackler to David Shelby by Ruffin Deloach. James Odam to Robert McCorkle.
Bill/sale John Williams to David Shelby negro girl Annis proved by Jas Douglass.
On motion of Howel Tatum, deposition of Sampson Williams to be taken in Davidson County in suit Jason Thompson v James McKain.
William & Samuel Gillaspy v Joseph Waller. Debt. Apl 1793 plf by Andrew Jackson; pleaded condition of obligation is that James McColgin admr estate of Jas Gillaspy decd; covenant duly performed. July 1793 Jury Elmore Douglass Joseph McElwrath Jno Williams Mattw Anderson Wm McNeely Smith Hansbrough Jno Weathers Wm Bowan Wm Maxwell Jas Harrison Elisha Clary Jeremiah Doxey find for plfs £36.10.8.
Appt Hugh Crawford John Morgan Jas Gambell to appraise estate of James Steel dec.
Bill/sale John Williams to James Douglass negro boy proved by Thomas Edwards.
Rhody Allen records his stock mark.
Clerk & Register produced their bonds.

Tuesday 2d July 1793. Present David Wilson Edwd Douglass Thos Mastin esquires.
Deed James McKain to John Dawson ackd. Deed Jas McKain to James McKain Jr ackd.
Bond of Edward Douglass to indemnify county in consequence of Susannah Black having a base born child; he paid 50/ N.C. currency for her fine.
Order Thomas Mastin Esq call on James Douglass for £3.14 which sd Douglass is required to pay him out of public money in hands of sd Douglass.
p.62   William T Lewis v Wm Worldly. Apr 1793 plf by Bennet Searcy; dft by Andw Jackson. Manner of winning a horse. Jury Jos McElwrath Matw Anderson Wm McNeely Smith Hansbrough John Weathers David Scoby John Williams Wm Maxwell Jas Harrison Robt Bell Thos Patton John Neely. Find for deft, and costs. Plf obtains appeal to Superior Court, Robt Edmanston & Bennet Searcy securities.
Deed Thos Patton to Griffith Rutherford ackd.
Bill/sale Griffith Rutherford to Thos Patton ackd.
Thomas Jimason v William Crafford. Jury [above] find plf his damages $320.
David Shelby v John Whitsitt & Azariah Thompson; Jury above; juror withdrawn.
Subpoena to Davidson County to summon John Lancaster to bring agreement between Anthony Crutcher & James McKain date 13 February 1790 to next Court.
Order Nancy Fryat continue to live with Mr Latimer until next Term likewise Peggy Fryat live with Zacheus Wilson. Polly Fryat live with Samuel Wilson unless she should board with Mr Harrison to go to school.
License Ezekiel Douglass to keep an ordinary at his dwelling; Wm Cage security.
Appt Wm Cage sheriff for ensuing year; David Shelby & Edwd Douglass securities.
Order James Douglass Esq give receipts on certificates issued for services in guarding families.
Wm Cage apptd Collector/taxes for ensuing year; Edwd Douglass & David Shelby sec.
Allow Sheriff & Clerk 15 pds each for exofficio services for 1792.
Thos Masten retd list/taxable property in Capt Cantrills dist; Edwd Douglass of Frazors & Looneys dists; David Wilson of Kings; George Winchester of Morgans dist.

OCTOBER 1793

Jurors Octr term: Richard Hogin Reuben Douglass Jas Douglass Wm Montgomery Ruffin Deloach Robt Looney Jas Gwin Thos Hamilton Peter Lemon Henry Robertson Wm Gillaspie Wm Douglass Wm Edwards Wm Wilson Lazarus Cotton Jonathan Latimore Wm Maxwell Wm Beard John Berkley Robt Desha David Beard Rhody Allon Peter Turney John Roberts Jas White James Vinson James Campbell John Rule Jos Waller Isaac Pearce Wm Green.
Patrollers apptd: Ruffin Deloach & Wm Gillaspie of Capt Looneys district; David Shelby & Robt Jones for Capt McElwraths district; to qualify before Edwd Douglass.
p.63   Jno Irwin v Elisha P Chambers. Plf recovers of dft in proper person £9.12.
Court adjourns till Court in course to meet at same place.   David Wilson

Court of Pleas & quarter Sessions at house of Ezekiel Douglass first Monday October 1793. Present David Wilson Thomas Masten Richard Caveat esquires.
Deeds ackd & proved: Squire Grant to Thos Donnell by John Overton. Adam Laurence to John Roberts by Peter Turney. Peter Looney to Elisha Clary. Mary Parker to Wm Neely by Henry Hicks. Wm Crafford to Thos Jimason by David Wilson. Wm Crafford to John Laurence by David Wilson. Richard Thomas to Geo Walker. Philip Shackler two tracts each 640 in one deed to John Young by Robert Johnston.
Bills/sale ackd & proved: Robert Fryat to Reason Bowyer. James McKain to James Leatherdale proved by Wm Leatherdale. James McKain to James McKain Jr by Ruffin Deloach. James McKain to Zachariah Green by James Leatherdale Jr.
Grand Jurors: Ruffin Deloach foreman, William Maxey Peter Lemon William Wilson Jonathan Latimer James Dougan Thomas Hamilton Richd King William Douglass Jas White Henry Robinson William Edwards Isaac Pearce Peter Turney John Rule.
Inventory & acct/sales chattels of Saml Fair decd proved by admr.
Supplement inventory chattels of Jacob Zeigler proved by admx.
Inventory of late Henry Houdeshell exhibited by admx.
Christina Zeigler records age of her children: Mary Zeigler born 1st March 1785; Elizabeth Zeigler born 7th April 1787; Hannah Zeigler born 4th April 1789, John Zeigler born 20th February 1791.
Ltr/atty James McCallister to John Robinson ackd in Mercer county Kentucky & certified is admitted and ordered to be registered.
Richard Cavit returns list of taxable property in Capt Youngs district.
Appearance bond of Andrew Hays to appear this Term, John Overton security.
p.64   John Carr records his stock mark.

Tuesday Octr 8th 1793. Present David Wilson Anthony Sharp Richd Caveat Thos Masten.
Appt Wm Kennedy to oversee road in place of William Bird.
Thos Mastin allowed £5.13 for service as sheriff out of which he is paid 50 shillings it being the fine of Thomas Christian & Betsy Strain for fornication.
David Wilson & Simon Elliott apptd guardians for Nancy Peggy & Polly Fryit; bond $1000 with Thomas Mastin security.
Deed Mary Parker to James Clendening proved by Robert Steel.
Deed Robert Steel to Archibald Fisher ackd.
Charles Carter v John Hardin Silas McBee David Brigance John Dawson. Chas Carter had recovered £42.15 agt Page Billen with £6.10.8 costs. Dfts were Billens special

OCTOBER 1793

bail...Sheriff to summon dfts to appear before July 1792 Court to shew cause if any why plf afsd might not have execution agt them for his damages & costs. July 1792 Sheriff returned: D Brigance cited before Charles Latimer & Joseph Latimer. Silas McBee cited before Wm Frazor and Martin Harpool. John Hardin cited before Jeremiah Doxey & Thomas Davis. Alias scire facias to issue agt John Dawson returned to Octr 1792 term: executed in presents of Wm Wilson and Ezekiel Douglass. Cause continued. April 1793 Term John Dawson by Bennet Searcy. Jury Isaac Towel Peter Looney H Wm Kennedy Sion Perry Wm Edwards Rhody Allor[Allon?] Ruffin Deloach John McCarty Richd Hogin Jas Wilson Jas Hays Thos Smith found for defts. Plf by Andrew Jackson granted new trial. Oct 1793 Jury Lazarus Cotton John Roberts Thomas Patton Wm Snoddy Edward Hogin Jas Roberts John Wilson Henry Bradford Cornelius Herndon Robert Ellis William Montgomery John Whitsitt find for plf. Plf recovers of defts. Dfts obtain appeal, Peter Turney & Ruffin Deloach securities.

Deed William Cage Sheriff to James Douglass ackd.
Extrs of Isaac Bledsoe decd rendered inventory of chattels of decedent.
Inventory/chattels late James Steel decd rendered by admr.
p.65   David Shelby v John Whitsitt & Azariah Thompson. July 1793 Plf by Howel Tatum; contd. Octr 1793 Jury [above except Chas Carter Edwd Williams Robt Ellis for Jas Douglass Lazarus Cotton Jno Cummins] assess plf damages £5.8 and costs.

James Douglass v Ephraim Payton. July 1793 plf by Andw Jackson; dft by Howel Tatum. Octr 1793 jury Jno Roberts Edwd Hogin Jas Roberts Pearce Wall John Wilson Cornelius Herndon Wm Montgomery Henry Bradford James Frazor Chas Carter Edwd Williams Robt Ellis assess plfs damage £5.8. and costs.

Deed Thomas Payton to John Payton proved by Elizabeth Payton.
Bill/sale William Jones to Ruffin Deloach proved by John Payton.
Order land on which attachment Gillaspie v Mountflorence was levied be condemned and exposed to sale by Sheriff.
Ltr/atty Catharine Shelby to David Shelby authenticated by Sullivan County by sd Catharine Shelby and admitted to record.

Wednesday October 9th 1793. Present David Wilson Geo Winchester Edwd Douglass.
Stock marks recorded: William Wilson, James Wilson.
Jurors to Superior Court Abraham Sanders Robert Wilson Thos Simpson Hugh Tinnon Thomas Strain Peter Looney H William Gillaspie Richard King Charles Carter Thomas Smith Thomas Waller Azariah Thompson.
Jurors to January Term: Zacheus Wilson John Weathers James Odam James Harrison Reason Bowyer Chas Dement Rhody Allon Joseph Steel Robt Jones Richard Hogin Reuben Douglass James Franklin James Hays Wm Haynes Adam Class Wm Armstrong Abraham Young Wm Wills Kasper Mansker Wm Bowan Jas Frazer Elisha Ogelsby Amos Balch John Harpool Jas Whitsitt Henry Bradford Smith Hansbrough Wm Wyer Elisha Clary Wm Thomas Joseph McElwrath William Frazor John Boyd George Wolwood Thomas Edwards.
Order Clerk advertise for persons with claims agt County for escorting families through the wilderness or furnishing provisions for Guard to attend at next Term.
Peace bond, Wm Wyer keep peace towards John Cummins & family, Silas McBee secy.
Peace bond, John Butler toward Elizabeth Jones & family, Silas McBee security.
p.66   George Wotwood to appear at next Court & bring orphan Welham Winters to shew how he came to possession of said boy.
William Maxey records his stock mark.
Grant admn/estate of James McKain decd to James McKain, bond $1000, Wm Douglass

JANUARY 1794

Elijah P Chambers and James White securities.
Subpoena issues behalf Territory v Robert Desha & Paul Overfield to James Wilson son of D.
William Cage & John Dawson bond $200 for indemnification of County in consequence of Jane McKain having a base born child.
Court adjourns till Court in Course to meet at the same place.   David Wilson

Court of Pleas & quarter Sessions at house of Ezekiel Douglass first Monday January 1794. Present David Wilson Edward Douglass Thomas Masten esquires.
Grand Jury: Henry Bradford foreman George Wotwood Joseph McElwrath Joseph Steel John Whitsitt Amos Balch James Harrison Wm Fry Thomas Edwards James Odam Zacheus Wilson James Hays Reuben Douglass. John Hamilton apptd to attend Grand Jury.
Deeds ackd & proved: Isaac Shelby to John Withers by John Roberts. Joseph Kuykendall to Abraham Sanders by John Young. Joseph Kuykendall to John Young by Abraham Landers. William Young to Abraham Young by Robert Johnston. John Young to Abraham Young. Lewis Crane to Wm Dillard. David Allison to John Dawson by Sampson Williams. Robert Campbell to David Hughes by Philip Trammell. David Hughes to Thomas Clark.
Abraham Sanders & Stephen Cantrill produced commissions/Peace from Wm Blount date 29 Novr 1793 and took oaths for qualification and office.
Thomas Blackimore records his stock mark and brand.
Appt Katy Thompson & John Whitsitt admrs/estate of Azariah Thompson decd; bond $2500, Hugh Tinnon and Thomas Perry securities.
Appt Esther Scoby admx/estate of David Scoby decd; Robt Looney, Peter Looney sec.
Bill/sale Ruffin Deloach to Silas McBee for negro girl ackd.
Bill/sale Joseph Kuykendall to Simon Kuykendall 2 negroes proved by Silas McBee.
Allow Lewis Crane to erect & keep a grist mill on Cranes Crk adj Wm Dillard land. Sd Dillard agrees in Court to sustain damage that may accrue by erection of mill.
Sarah Smith paid fifty shillings fine for being pregnant with illegitimate child.
Lydia Young paid 25 shillings fine for having an illegitimate child.
Philip Trammell paid part of what County owes for his services as constable.
p.67   Thomas Smith & John Hurt bond $500 for maintenance of illegitimate child of which Sarah Smith is now pregnant.
Philip Trammell & John Young bond $500 for maintenance of child of Lydia Young.
Deeds ackd: Peter Turney to John Berkley. Matthew Kuykendall to John Dunahoo. Matthew Kuykendall to Archibald Mastin. Matthew Kuykendall to John Patterson.
Grant admn/estate of Richard Robinson decd to Elizabeth Robinson, bond $500, Thos Clark & Davis Hughes securities.

Tuesday Jany 7th 1794. Present David Wilson Anthony Sharp Richard Cavit Abraham Sanders esquires.
Appraisement/estate of Michael Shaver rendered by executors.
Inventory/sales of part of estate of Henry Houdeshell decd rendered by extx.
George D Blackemore v Henry Robinson. July 1793 plf by Howel Tatum, dft by Andrew Jackson. Jany jury John Withers Reason Bowyer Chas Dement Rhody Allon Adam Clap Wm Armstrong Abraham Young James Frazor Elisha Ogelsby John Harpool Wm Wyer Wm Thomas.

JANUARY 1794

Plf failed to appear; non suit agt plf; plf is liable for full costs.
Jason Thompson v James McKain. July 1792 Plf by John Overton; original dft by Andw Jackson. Admr/estate of deft at Jany 1794. [Same jury]. Plf recovers agt dft.
Supplement inventory/goods of James Steel rendered by admr.
Edward Douglass credited £7.10.8 by two certificates from Superior Court, one to James McKain, other to Wm Wyer, for fines.
John McFarland v Simon Kuykendall. Plf fails to appear; non suit agt him.
John Cordry witness behalf plf in McFarland v Kuykendall failed to appear. Fined.
Joseph McElwrath exempted from attending as a juror for present term.

p.68 Robert Desha v Nathaniel Parker. Octr 1793 plf by Jno Overton, dft by Andw Jackson. Jany [preceding jury]. Plf recovers damages £3.12.9 of dft.
Robert Desha v Nathaniel Parker. Dft confesses judgt £61.3 which plf recovers.
Deed James & George Winchester to Reason Bowyer proved by Edward Douglass.
Ltr/atty David Looney to Edwd Douglass proved by Hugh Crawford.
Order Henry Jinnings orphan of Joshua Jinnings apprenticed to Stephen Cantril till he arrives at full age to learn the art of hatting.
Deed John Williams to James Williams ackd.
James Williams records his stock mark.
Order William Brooks apprenticed to Zachariah Betts till age 21 to learn art of tanning and currying of leather.
James McKain v Joseph Hendricks. Depositions to be taken: Richard Brough & Obediah Gent[Gert?], Halifax County, VA, behalf of defendant.

Wednesday Jany 8th 1794. Present David Wilson Thos Mastin Richard Caveat Esquires.
Deed James Sanders by Danl Smith atty/fact to Thos Cotton proved by Thos Mastin.
Order road from Capt Gillaspie to George Payne be layed off by Daniel Smith Henry Bradford William Douglass Elmore Douglass Thomas Blackmore William Gillaspie William Cage Isaac Lindsey William Hankins Arthur Hankins Edward Jones Robert Bell Jas Hannah James Buchannon Isaac Pearce Smith Hansbrough.
Inventory of goods of James McKain decd rendered by admr.
Territory v Joseph Desha. Petit Larceny. [Preceding jury] Dft guilty.
Bill/sale William & Edward Maxey to Roger Gipsen proved by Walter Maxey.
Deed David Shelby to John, Benjamin, Jesse, Jonathan, James, Lewis & Robert Kuykendall heirs of Benja Kuykendall acknowledged.
Deed David Shelby to William Beard ackd.

p.69 Territory v Robert Desha. Opposing Jno Hamilton constable in execution of his office. [Preceding jury]. Dft guilty; fined £6 and costs.
Territory v Paul Overfield. Refusing to assist Jno Hamilton constable on taking Joseph Desha with a state warrant. Jury Wm Beard Jas Clendening Thos Patton Sion Perry Chas Carter Wm Neely Thos Smith Jas Roberts Elijah P Chambers Roger Gibson Lewis Crane Jeremiah Doxey. Dft guilty; fined £4; in custody/sheriff till paid.
Lewis Crane bond $500, Charles Carter security, for keeping a mill.
David Wilson esq returns list/taxable property Capt Jos McElwraths district.
Anthony Crutcher v Admrs of James McKain. Jury Thos Patton Sion Perry Chas Carter Thos Smith Jas Roberts Elijah P Chambers Roger Gibson Lewis Crane Jeremiah Doxey Wm McAdams Jas Dougan Jas Farr; Mistrial; cause continued.
James Whitsitt & John Perry apptd patrollers in Capt Cantrills District are to qualify before Stephen Cantril esqr.
Order Wm Gillaspie & Robt Bell oversee road from Capt Gillaspies to Geo Paynes.

APRIL 1794

Adam Clap & James Frazier exempted from attending as jurors for present Term.
Henry Vinson released one shilling of taxes for 1792.
Danl Smith esqr an extr nominated in will of Anthony Bledsoe appeared, qualified.

Thursday January 9th 1794. Present David Wilson Edward Douglass Richard Caveat.
Joseph Kuykendall agt John Nettles, plf failing to appear, dismissed at plf cost.
John Hamilton v Thomas Payton. Sheriff Octr 1793 levied on land where sd Payton lives; dft came not; judgment by default agt him. Jan 1794 writ/enquiry executed. Jury Reason Bowyer Charles Dement Rhody Alton Wm Armstrong Abraham Young Elisha Ogelsby John Harpool Wm Wyer Wm Thomas Wm Snoddy Roger Gibson Chas Carter find plfs damages 36 pounds hard money. Plf to recover sd verdict with costs.
Order/sale at instance Wm Gillaspie agt James Cole Mountflorence to sell 500 acres joining Robert Jones; land not sold by reason of land not belonging to sd Mountflorence. Order/sale agt goods & chattels of Mountflorence to satisfy judgt.
Appt David Shelby auditor for county to liquidate claims of guard for escorting families through wilderness from Holston to Cumberland; Edwd Douglass assist Shelby
p.70   Anthony Crutcher v James McKain admr. Order Wm Dobbins survey lands interfering with a tract located by Jas McKain decd for afsd Anthony Crutcher adj Benja Kuykendall on the north, and make return to next Court.
Appt John Sadler overseer of road in place of Ephraim Payton.
Jurors to April Term: John Hains Philip Trammel John Hardin John Laurence Matthew Kuykendall Jas Franklin Wm Dillard Wm Gillaspie John Dawson David Beard Wm Edwards Wm Snoddy Ruffin Deloach Robt Looney Hugh Crawford Joshua Scott Simon Ellis H Mathw Anderson Thos Simpson Thos Patton Robt Jones Jas McKinsey Isaac Landry Richd Hogin Edwd Gwin Alexr Braden Thos Jimason Jos Wallace Wm Neely Jas Clendening Jno Cummins
Order Edwd Douglass & David Wilson settle with Clerk for public money.
John Hamilton v Thomas Payton. Attached land condemned; order of sale to issue.
Constables certificates for attending Court to be received.
Mr Hall exempted in future from paying tax on Negro woman named Lucy.
Polls not clearing road near Capt Gillaspies work on road laid off this term from sd Gillaspies to George Paynes.
Thomas Hendricks v Peter Turney & Mattw Kuykendall. Thos Hendericks recovered 16 pds & costs in suit agt John Sutton; Peter Turney & Adam Kuykendall were Suttons special bail; shff to have sd bail appear at January Term held at house of Ezekiel Douglass; Shff returned writ was made known before Abraham Sanders, John Morgan, & Wilson Cage. Peter Turney pleads he surrendered the principle to Sheriff in discharge of himself, ackd by sheriff.
Court Adjourns till Court in Course.   David Wilson

p.71 Court of Pleas & Quarter Sessions at house of Ezekiel Douglass first Monday in April 1794. Present George Winchester Edward Douglass Thomas Masten esquires.
Deeds ackd & proved: John Williams to Wm Newton. John Williams to Rhody Allon. Robt King to Wm McCorkle. Edward Cox to Thomas Donnell 320 acres by Andw Jackson. Jonathan Latimer to Danl Rogers. Ephraim Payton to Adam Mosier. Joseph McElwrath to Geo Brown & Joel Echols. Thos Clark to Christopher Funkhouser. Jethro Sumner to Chrisr

APRIL 1794

Funkhouser by Jno Young. Jno Dawson to Reuben Douglass. Sion Perry to Henry Vinson.
  Grand Jury: Edwd Gwin foreman James Franklin David Beard Hugh Crawford Alexander Braden Wm Neely Ruffin Deloach Matthew Kuykendall Matthew Anderson John Cummins John Dawson William Edwards James McKinsey.
  Inventory goods of Azariah Thompson decd rendered by admr.
  Grant admn/estate of Nathl Latimer decd to Griswold Latimer; Jonathan Latimer sec Release from covenant of deed from Squire Grant to Thos Donnell ackd by Donnell.
  Inventory/goods of David Scoby decd rendered into Court.
  Jurors to Superior Court: Henry Bradford Robert Bell William Bowen Kasper Hansker William Gillaspie Elisha Ogelsby William Montgomery John Whitsitt Moore Stephens Robert Shaw Archibald Marlin James Wills.
  Supplement inventory/goods of Isaac Bledsoe decd by George Winchester an extr.
  Supplement inventory/goods of John Hickison decd by extx.
  Order Esther Scoby admx of David Scoby sell so much of goods of estate as be sufficient to discharge debts due from estate.

Tuesday April 8th 1794. Present Edward Douglass Thomas Mastin Stephen Cantrill.
  Deed Samuel Barton to James Green proved by Peter Luna.
  Deed Samuel Barton to Zachariah Green proved by Peter Luna.
  Anthony Crutcher v James McKains admrs. Jury Richd Hogin Chas Carter John Laurence Thomas Jimason Francis Bird John Hardin Uriah Anderson Michael Gilbert Jos Crabtree Thomas Waller John Williams Thomas Hamilton find for dfts. Mistrial.
  Power/atty Anthony Crutcher to David Shelby proved by Bennet Searcy.
  p.72   Francis Hainey v Thomas Spencer. Jury Sion Perry John Payton Jos McAdams Henry Potts Isaac Towell Saml Wilson Francis Catron Henry Vinson Zack Wilson Joshua Scott James Clendening Peter Luna; juror withdrawn; cause continued.
  John Cummins v Wm Wyer & wife. Slander. Octr 1793 plf by Andrew Jackson; dfts by John Overton. Apl 1794 jury Richd Hogan Charles Carter John Laurence Thomas Jimason Francis Bird John Hardin Uriah Anderson Michael Gilbert Joseph Crabtree Wm Brigance John Williams Thomas Hamilton find for dfts; each party pays half costs.
  Officers comdg guards to Holston escorting families through wilderness allowed pay pr day LtCol 16/ Majr 12/ Capt 10/ Lts & Ensigns 8/ noncommissioned 7/.
  Wm McLin & Rob Searcy v James McKain. Scire facias agt admr made known before John Dawson & Ruffin Deloach. Apl 1794 jury Sion Perry John Payton Joseph McAdams Henry Potts Isaac Towel Samuel Wilson Francis Catron Henry Vinson Joshua Scott James Clendening Jeremiah Doxey Smith Hansbrough find plfs damages 18 pds 4 shillings & also find admr fully administered agreeable to plea except inventory. Plfs recover of dft with costs. Dft died between exn/writ & Octr term.
  James McDanold v Wm & George Hacker. Jury [above]. New trial granted.
  Susannah Wyer proves attendance 5 days witness in Jno Cummins vs Wm Wyer & wife.
  Deed Howel Tatum to James McKinsey proved by Ezekiel Douglass.
  Deed Matthew Kuykendall to Abraham Sanders ackd.

Wed. April 9th 1794. Present Dd Wilson Edward Douglass Stephen Cantril Thos Mastin.
  Deed Thomas Spencer to Stephen Cantril proved by Edward Douglass.
  Jurors to July term: Wm Kennedy Jos McAdams John Payton Peter Luna P Chas Carter Sion Perry Elijah P Chambers Jacob Sanders Wm Wyer Henry Potts Francis Catron Peter Looney H Joseph McElwrath Zachariah Green Wm Snoddy Roger Gibson Thomas Potts Robt

JULY 1794

Looney Chas Latimer Wm Frazor Elisha Clary Thos Strain James Dougin William Hankins William Thomas Isaac Towel James Vinson John Harpool Thomas Simpson John Young Robt Wilson John Williamson Abram Young Thos Britton Robt Jones Reuben Douglass.
Deed Robert Nelson to John Overton proved by Bennet Searcy.
p.73   Lists/taxable property to be taken: Geo Winchester in Capt Morgans & Kings dists; David Wilson in Capt McElwraths; Edwd Douglass in Capt Lunas; Thos Masten in Capt Frazers dist; Stephen Cantril his own dist; Abraham Sanders in Capt Youngs.
Mortgage James McKain Sr to James Lauderdale proved by James Lauderdale Jr.
Wilson Cage records his stock mark.
Order James McKain admr expose to sale personal property of James McKain decd.
Michael Glaves v Robert Dougherty. Shff Jany 1794 levied on 640 acres; dft came not; judgt by default. April 1794 plf by atty Andw Jackson prays damages be ascertained. Jury James Clendening Richd Hogin Francis Catron John Hardin Thos Jimason Sion Perry Wm Snoddy Thos Clark Wm Brigance Jas Bone Chas Carter Jas McDanold find damages $160. Plf recovers verdict with costs.
On motion of Andrew Jackson esq., order judgt entered agt Sheriff of Tennessee County for detaining £2.15.8 recd by an execution of Wm Luck v Nathl Kelley.
On motion of Andrew Jackson esq, order John Cadry be released from fine for not attending as a witness in suit John McFarland v Simon Kuykendall.
Anthony Crutcher v James McKain. Plf granted new trial; plf pays accrued costs.
James McDanold v Wm & George Hacker. Order new trial be granted.
Barton v Hannah: deposition of Benj Estell & Peter Kerlin in Kentucky be taken.
Anthony Crutcher v James McKain, order for plf to pay costs rescinded.
Appt Henry Harrison constable in place of John Bayes; to qualify before Edward Douglass esqr.   Court adjourns till Court in Course. David Wilson.

p.74   Court of Pleas & Quarter Sessions at house of Ezekiel Douglass 1st Monday July 1794. Present David Wilson Geo Winchester Abraham Sanders Stephen Cantrell.
Deeds ackd & proved: David Wilson to Matthew Alexander. Joseph Hendricks to Robert Bell by Thos Masten. Robert Espy to Edward Jones by Wm Hankins. Robert Campbell to Joseph Payne by Phillip Trammell. John Hamilton to Peter Looney by Griswold Latimer. George McWhirter to William Walton by Jesse Glasgow. James Sanders to Joseph Hendricks by Daniel Smith atty/fact for Sanders. John Gatlin to Moore Stephenson by Isaac Walton. Reason Bowyer to John Neely by Cornelius Herndon. Reason Bower to Jas Odam by Cornelius Herndon. Reason Bower to James Harrison by Cornelius Herndon. Jno Withers to James Harrison by Cornelius Herndon. David Shelby to Robert Jones.
Allow of Wm Hankins to erect a grist mill on Drakes Crk on land he lives on within 100 yds of south boundary of Thos Spencers preemption; Hankins to be accountable for damages any persons may sustain by reason of erecting a dam & overflowing land.
Instrument/writing from Wm Whitsitt to James Whitsitt proved by George Blakes.
Inventory/goods Nathl Latimer decd rendered by admr.
Order Kasper Mansker Isaac Walton Amos Balch appraise goods/Azariah Thompson dec. Suppl inventory/goods of Jacob Zeigler decd rendered by admx.
Grand Jury: Thomas Simpson foreman Sion Perry Elijah P Chambers William Frazor Reuben Douglass Peter Looney H Robert Looney Roger Gibson Abraham Young Thomas Britton Thomas Patton Robert Jones Charles Carter.

JULY 1794

Bill/sale 3 negroes: Job, Rachel & Nanny from Robert Jones to David Shelby ackd.
Jos McElwrath Jno Young Chas Latimer exempted from attdg as jurors present Term.
Geo Winchester & Stephen Cantrill esqrs to settle with admr/Benjn Williams decd.
James McDanold v Wm & Geo Hacker. Trover. Jan 1794 plf by Jas Doherty; dft by Jno Overton. Apl Jury: Sion Perry Jno Payton Jos McAdams Henry Potts Isaac Towel Samuel Wilson Francis Catron Hy Vinson Joshua Scott Jas Clendening Jerh Doxey Smith Hansbrough assess plfs damage £10. New trial granted. July jury: Jacob Sanders Wm Wyer Peter Turney Archd Masten Jno McCarty Jno Williams Lazarus Cotton Wm Snoddy James
p.75   Vincent Jno Harpole Ephm Farr Mattw Kuykendall for plf damages £10, costs.
John Young v Wm Beadle. Francis Bird garnishee says he is indebted to Beadle 14 shillings Virginia currency; likewise John Laurence garnishee indebted 32 shillings Va currency, Thomas Clark 10 gal & 1 qt of whiskey estimated at $10½; Geo Hacker 3 pounds nine shillings Virginia currency.
Inventory/sales of goods of David Scoby rendered by admx.
John Young v Wm Beadle. James McKain & Abraham Young garnishees. Sd McKain indebted to Beadle 8 shillings VA currency; Abm Young 18 shillings 6 pence Va money.
David Wilson released of value of horse taken up by him later stolen by Indians.
Mrs Kuykendall released of value of mare taken up by her later stolen by Indians.
Young v Beadle. Peter Turney declares he is indebted to Beadle 12 lbs of cotton.

Tuesday July 18th 1794. Present David Wilson Edward Douglass Thomas Masten Abraham Sanders.
Deed Ephraim Payton to John Dawson proved by Ruffin Deloach.
Bond of William Hankins 500 lbs for erecting mill with Thomas Masten security.
Bill/sale Thomas Hickman to Hugh Crawford proved by William Cage.
Court annulled guardianship of Mary Parker for ward of Anthony Bledsoe decd; appt Edwd Douglass & David Shelby guardians for Polly Bledsoe & Abraham Bledsoe; James Clendening & Thomas Mastin for Isaac & Henry Bledsoe; David Wilson & William Neely for Prudence Bledsoe.
Anthony Crutcher v James McKain. Covt. July 1793 plf by Howel Tatum; dft by Andw Jackson. Jany 1794 admr pleaded he had fully admrd chattles mentioned in inventory. Jury; juror withdrawn. April Jury Richd Hogin Chas Carter Jno Laurence Thos Jimason Francis Bird Jno Hardin Uriah Anderson Michael Gilbert Jos Crabtree Thos Waller Jno Williams Thomas Hamilton found for dft. New trial granted. July jury: Jacob Sanders Wm Wyer Francis Catron Jas Vinson Wm Snoddy John Harpole Henry Potts Ruffin Deloach Hugh Crawford Robt Dougan Wm Hankins Alexr Bredon find for plf; assess damage $576.
p.76   Grant Mary Bralon[Braton?] ltrs/admn on estate of Charles Bralon[Braton?], James White Edward Hogan securities.
Appt Jas White Jno White & Jos Wallace to appraise estate of Charles Bralon decd.
Deeds ackd & proved: James Taylor to Hugh Tinnon by William Kennedy. James Taylor to William Kennedy by Hugh Tinnon. Reason Bower to William Edwards by Thomas Edwards. Reason Bower to Thomas Edwards by William Newton.
Geo Winchester & Stephen Cantrill esqrs report estate of Benj Williams Decd is indebted to admr 65 pounds eight shillings three pence.
John Young ackg 12 lbs cotton which Peter Turney garnishee in his suit v William Beddle declared himself indebted to sd Beadle.
Francis Catron v Henry Wiggins. January 1794 plf by James Doherty; dft by Andrew Jackson. July jury: Jas Wilson Richard Hogin Peter Looney H Zach Green John Payton Griswold Latimer Peter Turney Robt Shaw Wm Brigance King Carr Wm Montgomery William

44

JULY 1794

Kennedy. Assess plfs damage $24. Plf recovers of dft according to verdict, & costs.
John Young ackd satisfaction with Abraham Young for 18 shillings 6 pence Virginia money which sd Abraham as garnishee declared he owned sd [Wm] Biddle.
Samuel Bailon[Bailor?] v James Hannah. Depositions to be taken of Thomas Smith Jonathan Skinner & others, Nelson County, KY, at instance of dft .
John Irwin v Richard Sutton. Debt. Apl term 1794 Sheriff had executed on dft; dft came not; judgt entered agt dft; July 17694 judgt agt dft £76.4.11.
John Young v Wm Biddle. Philip Trammell constable Apl 1794 executed attachment; summoned John Young blacksmith and Thomas Clark garnishees; dft came not; judgt by default agt him. July 1794 plf by John Overton prays damage ascertained. Jury James Wilson Richard Hogin Peter Looney P Zack Green John Payton Griswold Latimer Peter Turney Robt Shaw Wm Brigance King Carr Wm Montgomery Wm Kennedy find damages $75.
Wm Shaw v Silas McBee. Refered to Danl Young Nicholas Conrod Peter Looney Thomas Simpson John Harpool, their award to be rule of Court.
Order Robt Looney Peter Looney H Archd Mastin appraise estate/Nathl Latimer decd.
Appt Jas Handon Robt Jones Roger Gibson patrollers for Capt McElwraths district.
p.77   Wm Cage took oath as Sheriff & Collector for ensuing year; Edward Douglass & David Shelby securities.
John Young ackd satisfaction with James McKain for eight shillings VA money which he declared himself indebted to William Biddle.
John McFarland v Simon Kuykendall. April 1794 plf by John Overton; dft by Andrew Jackson. July 1794 Jury Jacob Sanders Wm Wyer Francis Catron James Vinson Wm Snoddy Ruffin Deloach Robt Dougan Wm Hankins Jas Harrison Zach Green Peter Turney Griswold Latimer find for plf damage $16, with costs.
James McKain admr rendered inventory/sale, Jas McKain decd. Remainder to be sold.
Admr/James McKain dec v Zach Green. Jury [above except Wm Edwards for Zach Green] Find issue in favour of the defendant.
Wetherall Latimer records his stock mark.

Wednesday July 9th 1794. Present David Wilson Abraham Sanders Stephen Cantrell.
Jurors to Octr Term: Thomas Cotton John Williams Robert Wilson Wm Brigance Conrod Strader John Laurence Elisha Clary Thos Strain Wm Crabtree Wm Thomas Isaac Towel Wm Wills Wm Neely Wm Wilson Jas Frazor Mathw Alexander Wm Gillaspie Jno Norris Richard King Jas Wilson(Smkg) Henry Vinson Thos Thompson Richard Jones Peter Looney H Abraham Rogers Jas Gambling Jno Cummins Jos Waller Isaac Pearce Jr Volentine Shoat John Tinnon Kasper Mansker William Bowan James Carton Richard Jones Zach Green.
Allow John Hamilton £2.9 for service as constable at Superior Court.
Reuben Cage took oath as Deputy Sheriff.
Glaves v Dougherty. Attached property to be sold.
Stephen Cantrill esq retd list/taxable property for his own district; Abraham Sanders returned list for Capt Youngs Company; Thos Mastin for Capt Frazors Compy.
Allow John Burges £4.16 for extra services as constable.
Thos Masten & James Clendening apptd gdns for Isaac Bledsoe & Henry Bledsoe gave bond; Ezekiel Douglass and William Cage securities.
Edward Douglass & David Shelby apptd gdns for Polly Bledsoe & Abraham Bledsoe entered bond with James Douglass & William Cage securities.
David Wilson & William Neely apptd gdn for Prudence Bledsoe entered bond; Geo D Blackmore security.
p.78   Appt Wm Gillaspie Wm Douglass Zach Green Ruffin Deloach patrollers for

OCTOBER 1794

Capt Looneys Company who are to be qualified before Edward Douglass Esqr.
Court adjourns till Court in course.   David Wilson

Court of Pleas & Quarter Sessions at house of Ezekiel Douglass 1st Monday October 1794. Present Edwd Douglass Thomas Masten Abraham Sanders Stephen Cantrill esqrs.
Appt James Yates overseer of road in place of William Hacker.
Deeds ackd & proved: Henry Vinson to Thos Patton. Matthew Kuykendall to William McWhirter by Robt Shaw. David Brigance to William McAdams by James Brigance. John Johnston to Thos Britain. John Young to Abraham Sanders. Thos Kilgore to Johnston Kilgore by John Williamson. Thomas Kilgore to Charles Kilgore by John Williamson.
Grand Jury: Kasper Mansker foreman, Peter Looney H, Volentine Shoat Thos Patton Isaac Pearce Jas Frazor Elisha Clary Robt Wilson Henry Vinson John Norris William Brigance Thos Thompson Wm Crabtree Wm Gillaspie. John Hamilton attends grand jury.
Thos Bledsoe v Jeremiah Rogers. Wm McDanold, bail, surrendered Jeremiah Rogers. Obligation for 174 acres Abraham Young to Thomas Smith proved by John Young.
Young v Biddle. John Hardin owed Biddle 6 shillings VA money which Hardin paid to plf in sd suit. Thomas Hamilton owed 2 gal 1 qt whiskey; settled with plf.
Wm Hacker released from value of stray mare posted by Hacker; proved to be property of Elenor Low and delivered to her by Hacker.
Nuncupative will of Thomas Bledsoe decd proved by Katy Bledsoe William Reed Joseph Evans. Admn granted to William Neely & David Shelby; bond $2000, James Clendening & Richard Hogin securities.
John Whitsitt an admr of Azariah Thompson decd rendered appraisement. Order personal property of Azariah Thompson except Negroes be sold by admr.
James Clendening last term apptd jointly with Major Mastin as guardians for Isaac Bledsoe & Henry Bledsoe gave bond with sd Mastin, Ezekiel Douglass & Wm Cage sec.

Tuesday Octr 7th 1794. Present Edward Douglass Thomas Masten Abraham Sanders Stephen Cantrell esquires.
Power/atty John Odam to James Odam proved by Thomas Nicholls.
p.79   Territory v Lazarus Cotton. A&B. Jury John Williamson Wm Thomas Wm Wills Wm Neely Richd King Richd Jones Abraham Rogers John Tinnon Jas Carson Thos Hamilton James Gambling David Hardin. Verdict dft guilty; fined sixpence.
Estate James McKain released from payment of ½ value appraisement stray steers.
Deed William Edwards to William Beakley ackd.
Grant admn/estate of Robert Brigance decd to Wm & James Brigance; bond $1000 with Thomas Cotton & Peter Looney H securities.
James Roberts v Lazarus Cotton. A&B. Jury John Williams Wm Thomas Wm Wills Wm Neely Richd King Richard Jones Abm Rogers Jno Tinnon Jas Carson Thos Hamilton James Gambling David Hardin; juror withdrawn; suit dismissed by plf who assumes costs.
Jurors to Superior Court: John Williamson John Cummins Thos Perry James Franklin Moore Stephenson Joseph McElwrath James Frazor John Harpole Wm Frazor Peter Looney Richard King Charles Carter.
Deed William Cage sheriff to Amos Heaton ackd.
Rescind former order; Wm McDanold remains security for Jeremiah Rogers.

JANUARY 1795

Balance due Thos Masten for exofficio services as sheriff 1787 & 1788, £3.3.4, is paid from money arising from strays.
Grant license to Ezekiel Douglass to keep an ordinary at his dwelling house; entered bond $500 with Wm Douglass security.
Appt John Walker admr/estate of Simon & Thomas Woodard decd; bond $1000 with Sampson Williams & Samuel Donelson securities.
For exofficio services for 1793, allow Clerk 15 pounds, sheriff 20 pounds.
Jurors to January term: Elmore Douglass Wm Parmer Joseph Wallace Edward Jones Jonathan Pearce John Ruyle Thomas Strain Edwd Hogin Griswold Latimer Hugh Crawford Thos Simpson Wm Parr Lazarus Cotton Henry Vinson Reubin Douglass Thomas Williamson Robt Looney Archd Martin Thos Hamilton Robert Steel Jas Clendening Wm Wilson James Wilson(shooting), James McKinsey James Douglass Wm Snoddy Wm Edwards Edwd Williams Joseph Waller James White Adam Clap Conrod Strader John Laurence (Red River) John Laurence James Brigance.
Court adjourns till Court in Course, at house of Ezekl Douglass. Edward Douglass

p.80   In pursuance of an Act ascertaining what property shall be deemed taxable property and the method of collecting taxes, Court met at house of Ezekiel Douglass 24 November 1794. Present Edward Douglass Thomas Mastin Abraham Sanders Stephen Cantrell esqrs.
Order Stephen Cantrill esq to take list of Taxable property in sd Cantrills Dist; Thos Masten of Capt Frazors dist; Edwd Douglass of Capt Loonies dist; Anthony Sharp of Capt McElwraths dist; David Wilson of Capt Kings & Morgans dist; Abraham Sanders of Capt Youngs district.   Court adjourns.   Edward Douglass

Court of Pleas & Quarter Sessions, house/Ezekiel Douglass, first Monday in January 1795. Present David Wilson Thomas Mastin Abraham Sanders Stephen Cantrell esqrs.
Grant admn/estate of William Ridley to Thankful Hall; bond $1250, Wm Cage sec.
Deeds ackd & proved: Ambrose Jones to William Rasco by Jesse Rasco. Robert Weakley to Philip Kiser by John Cummins. Thomas Hamilton to Robt Hamilton by King Carr. William Bowan to John Cummins by Daniel Smith. Thomas Donnell to James Farr. Robert Campbell to Daniel Holaman[Holdman?] by Abraham Sanders.
Inventory & appraisement goods of Charles Braton decd rendered by admx.
Inventory & appraisement goods of Nathaniel Latimer decd rendered by admr.
Excuse James White from attending as juror for present term.
Bond Anthony Bledsoe decd to Hugh Rogan.
Grand Jury: Hugh Crawford foreman, John Laurence James Douglass Wm Parmer William Snoddy Edwd Hogin Thos Williamson Edwd Williams James Wilson James Brigance Joseph Waller William Edwards Archibald Marlin. John Hamilton const attends grand jury.
Inventory/sales of goods of Azariah Thompson decd rendered by John Whitsitt admr.
Motion of Mr Jackson, order admn/estate of Thomas S Spencer decd granted to William Spencer; bond $2000, Griffith Rutherford security.

JANUARY 1795

Commission/Peace from William Bount, Thomas Donnell took necessary oaths/office.
Saml Donelson produced license from Wm Blount to practice as attorney; qualified.
Power/atty James Lauderdale to Peter Looney proved by James Lauderdale Jr.
Bennet Searcy resigns as solicitor; Court appt Samuel Donelson county solicitor.
p.81   Deeds ackd & proved: William Penny & wife Lushy to Nathaniel Parker by Nathl Parker Jr. David Briganer to Hugh Crawford. Wm Spencer to Obed Hendricks.
Order Robt King John Wilson David Shelby appraise estate of Thos S Spencer decd.
Inventory/goods of Thomas Bledsoe decd rendered by admrs. Order/sale issues.

Tuesday Jan 6th 1795. Present Thomas Mastin Abraham Sanders Thomas Donnell esqrs.
  Deeds ackd & proved: John Williams to Wm Maxey. James Sanders to Wm McWhirter by Joseph Motherall. James Sanders to Daniel Smith by Joseph Motherall. George Nevell special guardian for Tebiah & George Syms Elliott orphans of John Elliott decd to James McCarrell by Bennet Searcy. Robert Nelson to John Overton by Bennet Searcy. George Nevell sp gdn/heirs of John Elliott to Robert Nelson by Andrew Jackson esq.
  Bill/sale Thomas T Guy to John Shelby Jr sundry negroes proved by David Shelby.
  Bill/sale Joseph Richeson to John Shelby Jr negro boy Tom proved by David Shelby.
  Bill/sale James McKinsey & Thos Hendricks to Hugh Elliott proved by Thos Strain.
  Motion of Danl Smith esqr to renounce his executorship/estate of Anthony Bledsoe decd, declaring he had no assets of sd estate. Motion overruled.
  Edwd Douglass esq returns list of taxable property in Capt Looneys district.
  Bill/sale James McKinsey to Hugh Elliott proved by Pearce Wall.
  Appt Mrs Hickison gdn for William Isaac Tabitha & John Hickison orphans of John Hickison decd; bond $500, Henry Loving security.
p.82   David Wilson returns lists/taxable property, Capts King & Morgans dists.
  Abraham Sanders returns list/taxable property, Capt Youngs company.
  Bill/sale Silas McBee to Joseph Hendricks ackd.
  Appt Robert Desha & Wm Wilson patrollers for Capts King & Morgans districts.
  Appt James McKinsey & Lazarus Cotton patrollers for Capt Lunas company who are to qualify before Edward Douglass esq.
  John Williams admr/Benja Williams decd allowed 6 pds 19 shillings with heirs of decedant for sum paid William Newton & Robert Barnett as pr accts filed.
  Inventory/goods of Robert Brigance decd rendered by admrs.
  Jane Kuykendall admx/Ben Kuykendall decd allowed in settlement with Court in full of the share & parts of John Kuykendall & Jinny Kuykendall of estate of sd decd.
  Appt Hugh Crawford Thomas Cotton Joshua Scott appraise estate/Robt Brigance decd.
  Appt Simon Kuykendall gdn for Ben Kuykendall orphan of Ben Kuykendall decd; bond $1000 with Charles Carter security.
  Thomas Masten esq returns list/taxable property Capt Frazurs company.
  Stray mare taken up by Robert Hamilton was stolen by Indians.
  Allow Wm Gillaspie to keep a ferry on Cumberland R any place bet Cainy Fk & roaring R for one year; 25 cts each passenger with horse, 12½ cts man or horse; bond $500 with James Winchester & David Shelby securities.

Wednesday Jany 7th 1795. Present Anthony Sharp Thos Masten Stephen Cantrill esqrs.
  Deed/release Elizabeth Winchester Lydia Winchester Edward Hodgkiss John Roberts to James Winchester proven by William Cage Jr.
  Deed/release William Winchester Richd Winchester Stephen Winchester David

JANUARY 1795

Winchester to James Winchester ackd by David Shelby atty/fact for sd Wm Richard Stephen & David Winchester: Wm Richd Stephen & David Winchester all of Maryland & James Winchester of Sumner County. George Winchester late of Sumner at his death possessed real estate which descended to sd William Richard Stephen David & James Winchester who are brothers & heirs at law of sd George Winchester. Personal estate of George belongs by law to brothers & sisters of sd intestate, for love and $1 to brother James Winchester grant to James Winchester [omitted]. Witnesses
p.83   George Dicker John A Hamilton. 18 Sept 1794 Wm Winchester Richd Winchester Stephen Winchester & David Winchester ackd foregoing before Samuel Chase, Chief Justice of Maryland. Certification by Jno G...lth. Certification by John Kilty.
p.84   Certification by Samuel Harvey Howard Reglour.
Commission/Peace from Wm Blount esq 15 Decr 1790 to James Winchester who took oath of office.
Deed John Donelson to Jacob Pennington proved by Stephen Cantrill.
Anthony Sharp returns list/taxable property Capt McKelwraths company.
Stephen Cantrill returns list/taxable property in sd Cantrills Company.
Order David Wilson Edwd Douglass Thos Masten settle with sheriff & Clerk for public money in their hands & report thereof to ensuing Court.
Allow John Hamilton $11 for services as constable.
Allow Clerk/Court $10 for services of auditing the Guard claims.
Jurors to April Term: James McKinsey Thos Williamson Jas Hamilton Robt Shaw Abraham Young Smith Hansbro Wm Wyer John Roberts James Frazor John Harpole John Whitsitt Kasper Mansker William Kennedy Amos Balch John Gatling Robert Latimer Peter Looney Capt Thomas Cotton Charles Carter Sion Perry Wm Brigance Wm Neely James Odam Peter Turney John Williams Thomas Edwards Isreal Moore Jas Wilson Curly Ander Blythe Saml King Wm Bowan Jacob Thomas John Dawson Wm Douglass Robt Donelson Charles Dement.
John Williams admr/estate of B Williams decd allowed $22 of estate as per acct.
Grant David Wilson esq ltrs/admn on estate of Nathan Heral; John Williams sec.
Henry Vinson v Thomas Patton & John Wilson. Octr 1794 plf by Bennet Searcy; Jany 1795 dfts confess judgt $150, interest & costs.
James Douglass v Wm Bowman. James Douglass Apl 1792 recovered £100 agt William Bowman; property sold; shff retd that £65 of sd judgt was satisfied; therefore Wm Bowman to appear at ensuing Court at house of Ezekiel Douglass to shew cause why James Douglass ought not have execution agt him for balance & costs, D.Shelby
p.85   Clerk, July 1794. Octr 1794 Shff returned "Not found," Reuben Cage.
Wm Quarles & Co v James McKain admr of James McKain decd. Wm Quarles at Apl 1793 recovered £2.10.10 agt Jas McKain, also £3.13.10 costs/suit; dft died shortly after afsd recover agt him; judgt yet unsatisfied. Writ issued; retd "made known before James Wilson & Wm Wilson by me Reuben Cage." Judgt agt dft.
Admrs/James Steel v James McKinsey & James Vinson. Plf by Andw Jackson; dfts in proper person confess judgt $43.35; stay of exn until next Court.
David Hardin v Elijah P Chambers & Jno Rutherford. Debt. Plf by Andw Jackson; dfts in proper person confess judgt $25.37 with costs.
James Winchester an exr nominated in will of Isaac Bledsoe decd qualified.
Court adjourns till Court in Course.   David Wilson

APRIL 1795

Court of Pleas & quarter Sessions at house of Ezekiel Douglass first Monday April 1795. Present Edward Douglass Stephen Cantrill Thomas Donnell esquires.

Deeds ackd & proved. Robt Montgomery & wife Esther to Wm Montgomery proved by Jas Alexander. David Purvoince to Peter Fleming by John Knox. Robt Hays to John Johnston by John Overton. Jno Grant to Jno Sterns by Saml Harris. Charles Campbell to Samuel Harris by Jno Sterns. Robert Esspy to Thomas Cubbins[Cribbins?] by William Hankins. Thomas Cribbins to Abijah Millis. Thomas Jimason to Joseph Steel by John Hamilton. Abraham Sanders[Landers?] to Andrew Blythe. John Hamilton to Moore Stephenson by Peter Looney. Henry Turney to Michael Turney by Peter Turney. Peter Turney to James Winchester. Jacob Sanders to James Thomas by Robert Shaw. John Johnston to Volentine Shoat. Isaac Bledsoe to James & George Winchester by James Sanders. William Spencer to Elizabeth Spencer.

Inventory/goods of Wm Ridley decd rendered by admrs.

Will of Joseph Barns decd proved by John Deloach & John Roberts; Selah Barns & John Barns exx & exr qualified.

Suppl inventory/goods of Samuel Farr decd rendered by admr.

Grant admn/estate of Hugh Tinnon to Sibella Tinnon & John Tinnon; Bond $2000, Amos Balch and John Harpool securities.

Grant admn/estate of John Neely decd to Massey Neely; bond $500, James Odam & Henry Harrison securities.

Grant admn/estate of Robert Moore decd to John Moore; bond $2500, Kasper Mansker & William Hankins securities.

Grand Jurors: Kasper Mansker foreman Peter Looney John Whitsitt Jacob Thomas Isreal Moore Thomas Cotton Thomas Edwards James Wilson James Hamilton William Neely James Odam John Williamson Sion Perry Peter Turney.

Bond Lewis Malone to James Campbell proved by John Wilson.

Bond Isaac Bledsoe to James & George Winchester proved by James Sanders.

Bond Isaac Bledsoe to Edward Douglass proved by Thomas Donnell; sd Edwd Douglass hereby transfers land specified in sd bond be made to James Winchester.

Order Anthony Sharp & Stephen Cantrell settle with admrs of Jno Purvoince & Saml Farr for estates of sd decedants.

p.87   Deeds ackd & proved: John Deloach to Theophilus Allon. John Deloach to Henry Bloodworth. James Douglass Shff to Geo Martin. Simon Kuykendall to Jas Hays. Wynn Dixon to exrs of Isaac Bledsoe decd by Tilman Dixon.

Theophilus Allon records his stock mark.

Indenture between John Averett & Jno Young proved by Abraham Sanders.

Wm Cage collector entered bond $1570.64, David Shelby & Edwd Douglass securities.

Samuel Harris released from double tax on 300 ac, of Chas Campbells preemption.

Jurors to Superior Court: Peter Turney Witheral Latimer Thos Strain Wm Snoddy Wm Dobbins Wm Douglass Wm Wyer Peter Looney Capt Wm Montgomery Jno Payton Henry Vinson Matthew Kuykendall.

Bill/sale Ruffin Deloach to Henry Vinson proved by John Deloach.

Ambrose Maulding released from fine & double tax on 640 acres on Drakes Cr & 374 ac on middle fk Red River; Robert Ewing released from fine on 100 acres Red River.

Appt Thomas Smith (little) constable for Red River district.

Philip Trammell constable allowed $21 for services as constable.

Peter Turney released from fine & double tax on one white poll 3 black polls & 1000 acres, 640 in Davidson, balance in Sumner.

Admrs/Thomas Bledsoe decd rendered inventory of sales.

J Doherty produced license as attorney; took oaths & qualified.

APRIL 1795

Robert Robinson released from fine & double tax on one white poll.
Appt Richard King guardian for Jinny Purvoince orphan of John Purvoince decd; bond $500 with Thomas Donnell security.
Release Majr Tilman Dixon & Jas Sanders from fine & double tax on lands.
Wm Pryor v Thomas Hamilton. Dismissed by agreement.

Tuesday April 7th 1795.
Motion/Tilman Dixon; error in return of heirs of Henry Dixons 2300 acres; heirs released from tax for 1795.
Wm Wilson returns inventory/goods of Nathan Heral decd to be proved by David Wilson admr in future, sd David not being able to attend at this time.
Bill/sale Simon Kuykendall to Matthew Cowan proved by Elijah P Chambers.
Motion of James Right: order Danl Wheaton released from fine & double tax on 428 acres on Station Camp Creek.
p.88 Order road laid off from Ezekiel Douglass house to Kentucky line by Ezekl Douglass Wm Brigance Hugh Crawford Jas Brigance Thos Cotton Peter Loony Thos Williamson Richd Cavett Wm Armstrong Sr Matthew Kuykendall Jos Crabtree Danl Holdman.
Robert Latimer records his stock mark.
Deeds ackd & proved: John Withers to Stephen Cantrill. David Shelby to Wm Cage. Noah Sugg to Wm Standly & Chas Dement. Chas Campbell to Jno Deloach by Laz Cotton.
Appt Jas Vinson constable for Walnut field dist; Peter Turney & Sion Perry sec.
Allow Jas Douglass 15 shillings 9 pence in settlement of his accts as shff 1789.
Afsd settlement made by Edwd Douglass Thos Mastin & David Wilson.
Allow Thomas Masten £3.14 agreeable to former order.
Bill/sale John Morgan to Anthony Sharp proved by Roger Gibson.
Henry Wiggins released from fine & Double tax on 640 acres Bledsoes Creek.
Appraisement/goods of Robert Brigance decd rendered by Wm Brigance admr.
Motion of Mr Overton atty for Jas Sanders Jr. Depositions of Thos Dunihoo Alenson Trigg Jas Sanders to prove exn of agreement Wm Sanders & John Marshall of one part & James Sanders Jr of other, they being witnesses to sd agmt date 11th Novr 1785.
Bill/sale John Shelby Jr to David Shelby proved by Isaac Shelby.
Wm Spencer released from fine & double tax on 640 accres Harpeth River.
John Wilson released from fine & double tax on 640 acres Bledsoes Creek.
Jurors to July term: Elmore Douglass John Dawson Zach Green Jas Franklin George Wotwood Jas Clendening Francis Catron Edward Hogin Wm Hankins James Buchannon James Armstrong Danl Holdman Thos Yates Jos Payne Bostick Martin Wm Orr Thos Simpson Thos Harrison Thomas Britton Jno Perry Jas McKinsey Jas Douglass Jas Harrison Jas Wilson Sr Patton Chambers James Wilson son of David Wm Morrison Jas Wilson (shootg) David White Chas Carter Richd Hogin Jos McElwrath Wm Anderson Hugh Elliott Sion Perry.
Thos Smith little constable Red River Dist; bond, Robt Shaw & Abraham Young sec.
Appt Henry Harrison constable; John Burgess & James Odam securities.
Appt Thos Edwards Jno Williams James Douglass appraise estate of John Neely decd.
p.89 Deposition of Thomas Smith behalf dft in suit Hannah ads Barton be taken.
Barton v Hannah. Deposition of Benj Estill & Peter Kerlin behalf plf.
Lynn v Spencers admrs. Deposition of John Butler behalf plf.
James McKain records his stock mark.
Inventory of the goods of Thomas S Spencer decd rendered by the administrator.
Deposition of William Asby to be taken in behalf plf in suit Cummins v Pearce.
John Irwin v Edward Hogin. July 1794 John Irwin recovered £76.4.11 agt Richard

JULY 1795

Sutton & £3.12.7 costs; Edwd Hogin was Suttons special bail. Shff to summon Edward Hogin to April Court at home of Ezekiel Douglass. Shff returned "made known before Smith Hansbrough & Wm Hankins," but defendant came not; judgt by default agt him.
James Cosby v Thomas Walker. Debt. Defendant came not; judgt by default agt him.

p.90   Court of Pleas & Quarter Sessions held at house of Ezekiel Douglass first Monday July 1795. Present Edwd Douglass Stephen Cantrill Thomas Donnell esquires.
Deeds ackd & proved: Alexander Montgomery to Chamberlain Hutson proved by Garland Terrell. Moor Stephenson to Isaac Walton by Osman Allon. Elmore Douglass to William Edwards. William Dobbins to William Montgomery.
Inventory/goods of Hugh Tinnon decd proved by John Tinnon an admr.
Inventory/goods of Robert Moore decd rendered by admr.
Government v Jeremiah Doxey. A&B. Dft submits; fined one cent with costs.
Grand jury: James Clendening foreman, James Wilson (son of Majr) Elmore Douglass James Douglass Boston Martin James Buchannon Thomas Britton Wm Hankins John Perry Thomas Simpson David White James Harrison Joseph Payne.   Wm McDanold attends jury.
Grant admn/estate of John Edwards decd to William Edwards; bond $2000, Reuben Douglass & James Odam securities.
Motion of Mr Jackson, Wm Shelton released from fine & tax on 2394 acres.
Motion of Mr O Allon, Jno Williams released from fine & tax, 857 acres Goose Cr.
Francis Hainey v Thomas S Spencer. Covt. Octr 1793 plf by Andrew Jackson; dft by John Overton. April 1794 mistrial. Decease of dft; admn granted. July 1795 jury: James Wilson Chas Carter Jos McElwrath Wm Anderson Hugh Elliott George Wotwood Edwd Hogin Thos Edwards Jeremiah Doxey Jas Wilson C Robert Steel Jos Steel find for plf.
John Harvey, Davidson Co, proved stray horse taken up by Reason Bower was his.
Fined for contempt of Court: Simon Kuykendall $25, John Beson $5; John Dawson $2.
Government v James McKain. A&B. Dft submits; fined $3 which dft pays.
Robt Desha v Jane Kuykendall. Deposition of Jane Martin in Kentucky to be taken.
p.91   Ezekiel Douglass v Jno Gatlin. Take deposition of Peggy Payton behalf dft.
Deed Wm Cartwright to Danl Smith ackd. Deed Daniel Smith to Wm Cartwright ackd.
Thomas Masten & James Clendening return inventory/goods assigned to them in trust for Isaac & Henry Bledsoe orphans of Anthony Bledsoe decd.   Edward Douglass & David Shelby return inventory goods of Polly & Abraham Bledsoe, orphans of Anthy Bledsoe.

Tuesday July 7th 1795. Present Edwd Douglass Thos Masten Thos Donnell esqrs.
Deeds ackd & proved: Wm Cage Shff to Michael Glaves. Peter Looney to Patrick Mooney. Matthew Anderson to Chas Carter. David Wilson to Wm Wilson by Jas A Wilson.
Saml Barton v James Hannah. Debt. Jury Wm Anderson Jos McElwrath Chas Carter Edwd Hogin Jas Wilson Geo Wotwood Francis Catron Hugh Crawford Jeremiah Doxey Jno Tinnon Smith Hansbrough Jonathan Roser; mistrial.
Release Ephm Payton from fine & double tax on 2 black polls 2218 acres.
Barton v Hannah. Take depo of Ben Estill & Peter Kerlin, Maddison Co KY for plf.
Barton v Hannah. Take depositions of Thomas Smith Jonathan Skiner & others in Nelson County, KY.
John Cummins v Isaac Pearce. Take depo David Watkins behalf of the deft.

OCTOBER 1795

Deed/gift Andrew Jackson to Eneas Hannah for stock.

George Wotwood v Anthony Graves. Appearance bond of Anthony Graves, James Hays & Wm Brigance securities.

Hugh Rogan petitions for division of land called Greenfield tract among of heirs of Anthony Bledsoe so sd Rogan may obtain title to 640 acres agreeable to bond from sd Bledsoe to Rogan. George D Blackmore, James Reese & John Morgan apptd together with David Shelby surveyor.

Motion/Andw Jackson, order David Shelby apptd special guardian for heirs of Isaac Bledsoe decd for purpose of executing deed to James Winchester for 440 acres on Bledsoes Crk agreeable to bond from Isaac Bledsoe decd to Jas & Geo Winchester for title to sd land.

Wm Gillaspie released from fine & tax, land on Mill Crk, Harpeth, & Red River.

Lease Richard Hogan to Anthony Matcalf proved by Edward Matcalf.

p.92 Commission Reuben Cage sheriff for ensuing year, Wm Douglass & David Shelby securities.

Grant admn/estate of John Wyss[?] decd to William Gillaspie, Edward Douglass & Wm Frazor securities.

Inventory/goods of Joseph Barns decd proved by Jno Barns one of the executors.

Jurors to Octr Term: Robt Hamilton Amos Balch Jno Rule Jno Hamilton Jas Frazor Wm Montgomery Jas Franklin Wm Ore Edwd Gwin Wm Snoddy John Dunahoo Jr Smith Hansbrough Thos Walker Jno Sadler Wm Douglass Matthew Alexander Robt Desha Jos Wallace Zacheus Wilson Simon Kuykendall Pearce Wall Jno Cotton Robt Looney Jacob Houdeshell Jas Fry Simon Elliott Zach Green Richd Hogan William Donnell Hugh Crawford Volentine Shoat Abraham Young Joseph Crabtree James Yates Adam Clap Robert Bell.

Deed Edward Williams to Robert Ellis ackd.

Lazarus Cotton & Thomas Edwards indebted to James Montgomery $500 condition that Ephraim Payton deliver up property on which attachment was levied at instance of sd Montgomery agt sd Payton.

Motion/Mrs Scoby; Edwd Douglass, Thos Masten to settle with admrs of David Scoby.

Allow admrs of Hugh Tinnon decd to sell goods of decedant except Negroes.

Grant Clerk & Sheriff $50 each for exofficio services for preceding year.

Court adjourns till Court in Course.   Edward Douglass

Court of Pleas & Quarter Sessions at house of Ezkl Douglass first Monday Octr 1795. Present David Wilson Edward Douglass Abraham Landers[Sanders?] Thomas Masten Thomas Donnell.

Ltr/atty John Hamilton to William Hamilton ackd.

Ltr/atty John Payton to William Hamilton proved by Isaac Walton.

Appt Roger Gibson overseer/road in place of Edward Williams.

Inventory/goods of Robert Moore decd proved by admr.

Grand jurors: Matthew Alexander Jas Franklin Adam Clap Wm Donnell Zacheus Wilson John Sadler Robt Hamilton Jacob Houdeshell Pearce Wall Jas Frazer Richd Hogin Robt Desha John Rule John Cotton. Henry Harrison constable.

Wm Walton to keep ferry on Cumberland at mouth of Cainey fork. [rates omitted]

Inventory of goods of John Neely decd proved by admr.

Taxes laid [rates omitted in this abstract].

OCTOBER 1795

p.93   John Cummins v Isaac Pearce. January 1795 plf by Andrew Jackson; dft by Bennet Searcy. Octr Jury: John Dunihoo William Snoddy Edward Gwin James Hays John Seriker Francis Bird Sion Perry John Dawson Jas Wilson Isaac Towel Geo Hamilton Thos Patton find for dft. Plf obtains appeal; Wm Hankins security.

Deeds ackd & proved: Mary Gilmore & Laniford[Samford?] Long to Henry Hyde by Jos Eubank. John Young to Robt Johnston by Abraham Landers. Thos Kilgore to Thos Kilgore Jr by Wm Crabtree. Christopher Funkhouser to John Williamson & Ezekiel Cloyd by Wm Crabtree. Jas Frazor to Elisha Ogilsby. Matthew Anderson to Jeremiah Doxey. Tilmon Dixon atty for Charles Dixon to Catharine Bledsoe & James Winchester exrs of Isaac Bledsoe decd proved by David Shelby. William Fort & Howel Tatum to Wm Pryor by Andw Jackson. Wm Fort & Howel Tatum to Jno Hannah by Andw Jackson. Robt Esspy to James Buchannon by Archd Buchannon. Daniel Smith to Wm Hankins by Smith Hansbrough. Richd Thomas to Moor Stevenson by Isaac Walton. John Young to John Haynes. Matthew Kuykendall to Michael Shannon by Robt Shaw. George Alexander to James Dougherty by Abraham Landers. Wm Stanwell to Thos Williamson & David Cloyd by Abraham Sanders.

Seth Lewis produced license as an attorney and qualified.

Appt John Moore guardian for Francis Moore & Robert Moore orphans of Robert Moore decd; bond $750 with Isaac Walton and Jonathan Pearce securities.

Appt Andrew Jackson guardian for Saml Moore orphan of Robert Moore decd, Edwd Douglass sec.

Osman Allon records his stock mark and brand.

Deed/lease & release George Brown & Joel Achols to Joseph McElwrath ackd.

Ltr/atty Charles Reese to William Irwin ackd.

Will/Edward Douglass decd proved by John Dawson.

Bill/sale Jno Dawson atty for Ephraim Payton to James Clendening negro woman Rose proved by Edwd Douglass.

p.94   Tuesday Octobr 6th 1795. Present David Wilson Thomas Masten Thomas Donnell Edward Douglass.

William Edwards admr/estate of John Edwards decd took oath, rendered inventory.

Samuel Barton v James Hannah. Debt. Jury Zachariah Green Volentine Shoat Thos Walker Hugh Crawford Robt Looney Isaac Walton Thos Smith Jas Brigance Archd Marlin John Gatling Wm Spencer Peter Turney find special verdict "that in case dft can have recourse on Anthony Rogers they find for plf otherwise for dft" Case determined by parties, to Superior Court.

Motion of Howel Tatum, depo/Richard Fenner to prove exn of deed Andw Armstrong to John Gilmore of Halifax County North Carolina, deposition to be taken in Franklin County before Green Hill esqr. Also deposition of Daniel Anderson before John Jefferies of Dunwiddie County Virginia.

Deed Andrew Boyd to Isaac Patton proved by Joshua Dale.

Appt Robert Steel guardian for Rebecca & Mary Steel orphans of James Steel decd; Matthew Alexander security.

Supplementary inventory goods of Thomas Bledsoe decd rendered by admrs.

John Hamilton records his stock mark.

Grant admr/estate of Thos Jimason decd to Wm Gillaspie; bond, Jas Winchester sec.

Inventory/goods of John Myrs decd rendered by admr.

Bond Thomas Evans to James Douglass 428 acres proved by Edward Douglass.

Inventory/goods of Thomas Jimason decd proved by admr.

Deed David Shelby special gdn/heirs/Isaac Bledsoe decd to James Winchester ackd.

OCTOBER 1795

Deed John Williams to Perigan Taylor 50 acres proved by James Douglass.
Robt Desha v Jane Kuykendall. Trover. Jury John Dunihoo Wm Snoddy Edwd Gwin Jas Hays Sion Perry Jno Dawson Jos McAdams Thos Hamilton Peter Looney Wm Bruce Robt Shaw King Carr find for dft; New trial granted to plf.
License John Cummins to keep an ordinary at his dwelling house, Wm Hankins secy.
Deeds ackd & proved: Geo Walker to Howel Tatum by Bennet Searcy. Howel Tatum to George Walker. James Douglass Shff to Thomas Murry. James Douglass Shff to Thomas Murry. David Wilson to James A Wilson. James Winchester to Robert Wilson.
Bill/sale Jas & Geo Winchester to Isaac Bledsoe mulatoe boy Dan ackd by sd James.
p.95 Bill/sale Sarah Haynes to Jno Young negro woman Winny proved by Peter Turney.
Deed Jas Sanders by Danl Smith his atty/fact to Jacob Higgs proved by Wm Edwards.
Petition of Hugh Rogan; James Reese Geo D Blackmore John Morgan with David Shelby surveyor to lay off 640 acres due from estate/Anthony Bledsoe decd to Hugh Rogan.

Wednesday October 7th 1795. Present David Wilson Abraham Landers James Winchester.
Ltr/atty David Looney to Edward Douglass proved by Margaret Minor.
Appt Thos Masten & Stephen Cantrill to settle with admr of James McKain decd.
Allow James Carson to keep ferry on Cumberland River at end of Jones Bluff opposite John Bosleys plantation at place where sd Carson lives. [ferry rates omitted]
David Wilson & Wm Neely guardians/Prudy Bledsoe rendered inventory of sd ward.
Whereas non pros entered in suit Noah Sugg v Wm Standley & Chas Dement at July past, and whereas Dement on whom writ was executed waves non pros & errors, therefore order suit entered this term.
Ezekl Douglass v John Gatlin. July 1794 shff executed on dft; Octr 1794 dft came not; judgt by default. Jan 1795 dft by Andw Jackson. Octr 1795 plf by John Overton. Jury Wm Neely Wm Snoddy Edwd Gwin Jno Dunihoo Thos Walker Hugh Crawford Robt Looney Isaac Walton Thos Jimason Thos Patton Jno McCarty Volentine Shoat find for dft.
Deed David Looney by Edward Douglass atty-in-fact to Samuel Gragg ackd.
Jurors to Superior Court John Williams James Douglass William Edwards Joseph Wallace James White Joseph Crabtree Joseph Hopkins Thomas Edwards Isreal Moore James Wilson (Curly) Henry Bradford James Frazer.
Government v Richard Hogan. A&B. Dft submits; fined $5; reduced to one dollar.
Douglass v Gatlin; order plaintiff pay no more than two of dfts witnesses: Joseph McElwrath and James Hays.
Petition of James Winchester esq. Order James Reese John Morgan George D Blackmore with David Shelby surveyor to lay off 320 acres agreeable to bond from Isaac Bledsoe decd to Edward Douglass and by him transfered to sd Winchester.
p.96 Appt David Wilson special gdn for heirs of Isaac Bledsoe decd for purpose of executing a deed to James Winchester for 320 acres.
Robert Desha v Jane Kuykendall. Depo of Jenny Mastin to be taken behalf dft.
Robt Desha v Jane Kuykendall. Depo Thos Billen, Logan Co, KY, be taken for plf.
Elijah Robertson v Harrison Parsons. Continued untill next Court.
Jas Montgomery v Ephrm Payton. Cont by consent of plf & Lazarus Cotton plfs atty.
Geo Wotwood v Anthony Graves. Continued by consent.
David Wilson enters bond $5000, Edward Douglass security, for service as register; also bond $500, same security, for collection & payment of taxes on grants.
Thomas Bledsoe v Jeremiah Rogers. Shff Oct 1794 executed process on dft; plf died; suit revived; Apl 1795 write made known before Wm Ellis. July 1795 dft came not. Octr 1795 dft in proper person confesses judgt $22.50, also costs.

JANUARY 1796

Thursday October 8th 1795. Present David Wilson Abraham Sanders Thomas Donnell.
Writ by Noah Sugg agt Wm Standley & Chas Dement retd by shff executed on Dement; Standley not found. Motion of Mr Lewis, attacht agt estate of sd Standley.
Daniel James v Elijah P Chambers. Covt. Apl 1795 plf by Jno Overton; dft by Jas Doherty. Octr 1795 dft in proper person confesses judgt, $56.10.
James Synn[Lynn?] v admr/Thos S Spencer, two suits continued by consent.
Gdns of minor orphans of Anthony Bledsoe decd agt his exrs to draw out of their hands the proportional share of estate of minors. Summon exrs to next Court.
Appt Major Blackmore overseer/road from Majr Whites on Rockey Cr to Indian Crk.
Overseer/road from Indian Crk to W Station Camp Crk to straighten road through James Hays plantation with his approbation.
Jury to lay off road from Hankins mill on Drakes Crk to Carsons ferry on Cumberland R: John Cummins Isaac Pearce Jr Isaac Pearce Sr Joseph Waller William Walker Joseph Hendricks Robt Bell Thos Waller James Carson Robert Shannon James Buchannon William Hankins Arthur Hankins Richard Waller.
Jurors to January Term: Jas Wilson Sr Richd King Ebenezer Wilson John Welhams Jr James Harrison John Within William Gilbert Abraham Young Richard Cavit David Cloyd Jas A Wilson Wm Reed Jas Reese Jos Steel Andw Blythe Jos McElwrath Kasper Mansker Wm Bowan Jas Whitsitt Thomas Simpson Jno Cummins John Tennon James McKinsey Reuben Douglass Wm Douglass Wilson Cage Joshua Scott David Beard Thos Egnew Jas Franklin Richd Hogan Chas Carter Jacob Thomas Smith Hansbrough Jas Clendening Wm Cage.
p.97   Rates set for William Gillaspie's ferry on Cumberland R at Fort Blount.

Court of Pleas & Quarter Sessions house/ Ezkl Douglass on 1st Monday January 1795. Present David Wilson Thomas Masten Abraham Sanders Stephen Cantrill.
Deeds ackd & proved: Thos Masten to Peter Hansbrough. David Wilson to Jas Wilson. Jno Wilson to Jas Wilson by David Wilson. Wm Pryor to Thos Traves by Abraham Sanders. Adam Laurence to Conrod Strader by Abrm Sanders. Thos Donnell to Wm Morrison. Ephraim Payton to Geo Brown by Joel Achols. David Brigance to Wm Gibson. Wm Snoddy to Alexr Rasco. Anthony Sharp & wife Margaret to Alexander Rasco by John Williams.
Wm Edwards admr/John Edwards decd rendered account of sales.
Bond Jeremiah Morgan to John Morgan proven by William Morgan.
Inventory/goods of Hugh Tinnon decd rendered by John Tinnon one of admrs.
Bill/sale Hardy Murfree to Henry Vinson negro woman & child proved by Jas Vinson.
John Walker renders inventory of goods of Simon Woodard decd saying no goods or chattels have come to his hands or knowledge.
Allow Collector of taxes for 1795 to settle with treasury for same, 1440 acres, part of 7200 property of Silby Harney, 1440 acres returned by Hardy Murfree subsequent to that made by sd Harney for whole tract of 7200 acres.
Grand jurors: Smith Hansbrough Wm Gilbert Jos Steel Jas Wilson Jr John Tinnon Jos McElwrath Richd Hogin Richd King Richd Cavit Jacob Thomas Andw Blythe Jas Whitsitt Joshua Scott Abraham Young. Wm McDanold to attend the Grand Jury.
Court adjourns for one hour and met accordingly.
Isaac McNutt esq produced license to practice as atty at law; qualified.
Will of Charles Harrington decd proved by Ezekiel Cloyd; Elizabeth Harrington one/executors took oaths & qualified.

JANUARY 1796

Randolph McGavock & Robt Knox allowed to practice as attorneys for present Term.
Bill/sale Alexr Rasco to Wm Snoddy for negro woman ackd.
p.98   Appt Massey Neely gdn for James Neely & Alexr Neely orphans of John Neely decd; bond $250 with James Harrison & Thomas Edwards securities.
Order Jno Payton admr/estate of Robert Payton decd; Joel Achols & Jas Hays secys.

Tuesday Jany 5th 1796. Present Thos Masten Thos Donnell Abraham Landers[Sanders?].
Appt Catharin Thompson guardian for Sarah Joseph Laurence & Caty Thompson orphans of Azariah Thompson decd; bond $2000, Thomas Thompson & Thomas Perry securities.
Authorized Nathl Parker executor/Anthony Bledsoe decd to sell the stock/estate of sd decd by advertisement; Nathl Parker to settle with gdns for orphans of Anthony Bledsoe decd. Thomas Donnell & James Winchester apptd to settle with Nathl Parker.
License Ezekiel Douglass to keep ordinary at his house; James Douglass security.
Deed Martin Armstrong to Andrew Steel proved by William Dobbins.
Elijah Robertson v Harrison Parsons. Apl 1795 shff levied on 1000 acres Stones R; dft came not; judgt by default agt dft. Dft by Bennet Searcy his atty prays damages be ascertained. Jury Ebenezer Wilson Jas Harrison Jno Withers Jas A Wilson Wm Bowen Reuben Douglass Jas Franklin Thos Jimason Jas Hays George Wolwood Wm Snoddy Charles Dement find damages £9.8.9.
Deed Andrew Steel to John Harpool ackd.
James Lynn[Synn?] v Wm Spencer admr of Thomas S Spencer. Detinue. Apl 1795 plf by John Overton; dft by Jas Doherty. Jany 1796 jury [above except John Harpool & Peter Turney for Thomas Jimason & James Hays]. Assess plfs damage $74.54, with costs.
Appoint to take lists of taxable property: James Winchester in Capt Morgans district; David Wilson in Capt Kings; Thos Donnell in Capt Snoddees; Edwd Douglass in Capt Looneys; Thos Masten in Capt Hansbrough dist; Abraham Sanders in Capt Youngs dist; Stephen Cantrill in his own district.
Deed Andrew Steel to Daniel Ogelsby ackd.
p.99   Appt Thomas Donnell guardian for Elizabeth Dixon orphan of Joseph Dixon; bond $500 with William Cage security.
Nathl Parker executor/Anthony Bledsoe decd rendered supplemental inventory.
Deed Andrew Steel to Thomas Conyer ackd.
Order Stephen Cantrill & Thos Masten settle with Jas McKain admr/Jas McKain dec.
Bill/sale John Laurence to John Young proven by William Haynes.
County tax: 12½ on polls, 6¢ on each 100 acres for 1796.
Appt David Wilson Stephen Cantrill & Thos Mastin settle with Collector for 1794.
Order David Wilson & Thomas Donnell esqrs settle with admx of Lewis Melone decd.

Wednesday Jany 6th 1796. Present David Wilson Abraham Sanders Thomas Masten esqrs.
Tavern & Ferry rates at Fort Blount [omitted].
Taverns & Ferry rates, Ft Blount excepted [omitted].
James Lynn v admrs of Thos S Spencer decd. Jury Thos Patton George Wilwood John Hamilton Jas Desha Wm Hogan Ebenezer Wilson Jas Harrison John Withers Jas A Wilson Robt Desha Reuben Douglass Simon Kuykendall. Mistrial.
Lynn v Spencer admrs. Thomas Jimason & Robert Fryat witnesses behalf dft failed to appear.
Anthony Sharp v John Young. Refered to James Winchester David Wilson & James Reese; their award to be judgment of the Court.

JANUARY 1796

James Lynn v Wm Spencer admr of T S Spencer decd. Rule discharged.
Deed Howel Tatum to Micajah Barrow proved by Seth Lewis.
James Synn v Wm Spencer. If Wm Spencer enter sufficient security, appeal to Superior Court will be granted.
Jurors to April Term: John Williams Wm Reed Jas Reese Kasper Mansker John Cummins David Beard Thos Egnew Jas Clendening Jas Franklin Chas Carter David Cloyd Ezekiel Cloyd Wm Armstrong Jas Crabtree Jas Hamilton King Carr Conrod Strader Peter Looney P Lewis Crane John Tate Moore Stephenson Thomas Cotton Wm McNeely Elisha Clary Chas Latimer Richard Jones John Gatling John Moore Elisha Ogelsby Thomas Jimason William Montgomery Wm Douglass Thos Harrison David Stuart Thos Button John Payton.
Samuel Barton v James Hannah. Debt. Apl 1794 plf by John Overton; dft by Bennet
p.100   Searcy. Oct 1795 jury Zach Green Volentine Shoat Thos Walker Hugh Crawford Robt Looney Isaac Walton Thos Smith Jas Brigance Archd Martin John Gatling Wm Spencer Peter Turney found special verdict that in case dft can have recourse on Anthony Rogers, verdict for plf. To Superior Court; judgt for dft. Andw McNairy.
Charles Wheaton v Ruffin Deloach & Jno Dawson. Debt. Jany 1796 shff had executed on dfts; dfts came not; judgt by default $30.60 with costs.
Court adjourns until Court in Course.   David Wilson

Court of Pleas & Quarter Sessions at house of Ezekiel Douglass first Monday April 1796. Present David Wilson Abraham Sanders[Landers?] Thomas Donnell esquires.
Deed James McKain to Zachariah Green proved by Wm Lauderdale.
Wm Parmer exempted from serving as a juror for present term.
Stock marks & brands recorded: William Lauderdale. Christopher Cooper. James Wilson. Zacheus Wilson. Joseph Steel. James Trousdell. Samuel Wilson.
Deed Isaac Lindsey to Ezekiel Lindsey ackd.
Order Mrs Thankful Hall admx of Wm Ridley decd sell two warrants 400 acres each issued from Secy/state of No Carolina to sd Wm Ridley for services in battalion for protection of inhabitants of Davidson County, to discharge estate debts.
William Harrington an extr named in will of Charles Harrington decd qualified; sd Wm Harrington & Elizabeth Harrington, previously qualified, returned inventory.
Allow John Whitsitt $14 for administering estate of Azariah Thompson decd.
Grant admn/estate of Wm Black decd to Agnus Black; bond, Kasper Mansker security.
p.101   Appt Elizabeth Harrington guardian of Thomas Harrington orphan of Charles Harrington decd; bond; Samuel Gilbert security.
John Wilson records his stock mark.
Agreement, Pearce Wall & Roderick Jinkins ackd.
Benjamin Cooper fined $15 for A&B.
Pearce Wall fined $25 for Sabbath breaking, swearing, disturbing public worship, and insulting two Justices/Peace, with costs.
Grand jurors: Thomas Cotton James Franklin John Dawson Kasper Mansker William Reed William Newton William Douglass John Williams James Clendening James Hays William Gillaspie Edward Hogin Peter Looney John Hogan.
Government v Henry Hoover. A&B. Dft pleads guilty; fined one cent.
Permit Geo D Blackemore to turn great road between his house & John Banklers[?].
Andrew McClelan & Saml Moore bound as apprentices unto John Murphy until age

APRIL 1796

twenty one; John Murphy entered into indenture with David Wilson chairman.
Deeds ackd & proved: John Young to Robert Desha. Elisha Rice to Wm Blount by Bennet Searcy. Elisha Rice as exr of John Rice decd & as atty/fact for Wm H Rice Nathan Rice & Joel Rice to William Blount proved by Bennet Searcy. Bennet Searcy to James Jett. William Lytle to William McGee by Joshua Hadley. John Hannah to James Haynes by John Young. Robert Williams to James Kitching by Jno Garner. David Beard to William Byrd. David Beard to Thomas Byrd. Robert Hays to William Orr by John Perry. Howel Tatum to Joseph Pryor. Joseph Pryor to Richard Pryor by John Young. Wm Spencer & Elizabeth Spencer to Thomas Donnell part of 1000 acres granted to Thomas S Spencer, proved by James Farr. Thomas Oneal to Alexander McKee by Wm McKee. Robert Campbell to Alexr McKee by Wm McKee. David Shannon to Geo Donnell by James Farr. Robt Hays to John Perry by Wm Orr. Henry Loving to Wm Wilson by David Wilson. Geo D Blackmore to Stephen Alexander.
Bill/sale John Whitsitt to Laurence Whitsitt 2 negroes, household furniture ackd.
Bill/sale Jas Winchester to Jas Clendening negro Harry proved by Reuben Douglass.
Mortgage John Hamilton to Isaac Walton 108 acres ackd.
Edward Douglass returns list/taxable property in Capt Morgans district taken by James Winchester.
p.102   Deed Edward Gwin to Peter Simon[Lemon?] 160 acres ackd.
Lists of taxable property returned: David Wilson in Captain Kings company; Edward Douglass in Capt Looneys Co; Thomas Donnell in Capt Snoddees Co; Edward Douglass in Capt Cantrills taken by sd Cantrill.
Deed Anthony Sharp to Edward Williams 100 acres ackd.
Agreement between Thomas Donnell, guardian for Elizabeth Dixon, & Samuel King; to divide land of Joseph Dixon decd on Deshas Crk; Samuel King takes the improved part being part of Robert Deshas preemption; Betsey Dixon has the unimproved tract.
David Wilson Thomas Masten & Stephen Cantrill report they settled with Sheriff.

Tuesday April 5th 1796. Present Edward Douglass Thomas Masten Abraham Sanders.
Rates of ferry at Fort Blount set.
Edwd Douglass & Thos Masten report they settled with admx of David Scoby decd.
Thos Donnell & David Wilson report they settled with admx of Lewis Melone decd.
Permit Sampson Williams to keep a ferry on Cumberland River at Fort Blount for one year; bond $1250 with Andrew Jackson & Bennet Searcy securities.
James Lynn[Synn?] v admr of Thomas S Spencer decd. Apl 1795 plf by John Overton; dft by James Doherty. Jany 1796 mistrial. Apl 1796 jury James Reese Elisha Ogelsby Robt Steel Chas Carter Peter Simon Thos Hamilton James Armstrong Richd Jones Isaac Towel Ezekiel Lindsey James Wilson John Dunihoo. Plfs damage $52, with costs.
Deed Howel Tatum to Thomas Archer 300 acres proved by Bennet Searcy.
Deed Howel Tatum to William Moore 134 acres proved by Bennet Searcy.
Deed Peter Fisher to James Winchester 64 acres proved by William Hall.
Griffith Rutherford returned 1000 acres for 1795 taxation which lie within Indian boundary, not subject to taxation, order Griffith Rutherford exonerated from tax.
Abraham Sanders returns list/taxable property Captain Youngs company.
p.103   Taxable property retd by David Shelby as agent for John & Isaac Shelby for 1795 7000 acres was previously retd in Tennessee County & tax paid.
Bill/sale Wm Pearce[Roses?] to Anthony Sharp negro girl proved by David Shelby.
Deed Hugh Rogan to William Morgan 320 acres proved by Griffith Rutherford.
John Barkley v S Forkaid[?]. John Hamilton constable Apl 1795 levied on 2 cows &

APRIL 1796

calves; July 1795 dft came not; judgt by default agt him. Apl 1796 plf by Bennet Searcy prays damage be ascertained. Jury John Tate Thomas Cribbins James Douglass Gabriel Black Alexr Breden Hugh Crawford Anthony Matcalf Lazarus Cotton George Wotwood Thos Edwards Zach Green John Hamilton find damages $44 with costs.

Elijah Robertson v Harrison Parsons. Property to be sold for use of judgment.

Wm Douglass v John Lefouard[Sefocard?]. Apr 1795 shff levied on barge awning sails cow calfcalf, guns. July 1795 dft came not; judgt by default. Apl 1796 plf by Bennet Searcy prays damage be ascertained. Jury James Reese Elisha Ogelsby Robt Steel Chas Carter Peter Simon Thos Hamilton Jas Armstrong Richd Jones Isaac Towel Ezekiel Lindsey Thos Edwards John Dunihoo. Damages $43.83 with costs.

Edmund Gambell v Thomas White. Edmd Gambell at July term 1789 recovered £35.2 in attachment agt Thos White with costs. Octr 1789 Shff sold attached property, satisfying £20 of sd judgt & costs. Thomas White to appear at Jany 1790 court at Ezekiel Douglass's house, D.Shelby Clerk/Court. Jany 1796 Shff reported "Not Found." Order p.104 of sale issued. Dft did not appear; property to be sold.

Simon Kuykendall v Stephen Wright. July 1795 Shff levied on 274 acres; dft came not; judgt by default. Apl 1796 plf by Andw Jackson prays damage be ascertained. Jury John Tate Thomas Cribbins James Douglass Gabriel Black Hugh Crawford Anthony Metcalf Lazarus Cotton Geo Wolwood Zach Green Wm Neely Thos Jimason John Hamilton find plf's damage $45.83. Also costs.

Noah Sugg v Charles Dement & Wm Standley. Debt. July 1795 Shff executed on Chas Dement; Wm Standley was not found. Plf came not; non pros entered agt him. Oct 1795 Charles Dement revived sd suit. Attachment issued agt estate of Wm Standly whereon Sheriff levied on 500 acres main East fork Stones River; dfts came not. Judgment by default agt them. Apl 1796 plf by John Overton prays damage be ascertained. Jury [above except James Brigance for Zach Green] find plfs damages $307.25. Also costs.

Bill/sale Charles Carter to Hugh Crawford negro girl Sall ackd.

Deed Lazarus Cotton atty/fact for Ephraim Payton to John Gardner ackd by Cotton.

Government v Wm Gillaspie. Misdems in keepg a ferry. Jury Jas Reese Elisha Ogelsby Robt Steel Charles Carter Peter Lemon[Simon?] Thomas Hamilton Jas Armstrong Richd Jones Isaac Towel Ezekiel Lindsey Thos Jimason William Neely find dft guilty; Motion for arrest of judgt made by Andrew Jackson atty for deft; judgment arrested.

Simon Kuykendall v Stephen Wright. Order property attached to be sold.

Jurors to Superior Court: Anthony Sharp Sion Perry Wm Gillaspie Wm Armstrong Jr John Cummins Jas Wilson (smooky) Wm Kennedy Wm Dobbins Robert Desha Henry Bradford Wilson Cage John Payton.

Deed John Dever to Thos Sharp 228 acres proven by Peter Looney.

Inventory/sales of Thos Jimason decd rendered by admr.

p.105   John Barckley v Le Forkard & William Douglass v John Laforcard; property attached ordered to be sold.

Thomas Maston esq returns list/property in Capt Hansbrough's district.

Deed John Gordon to James Brigance 640 acres proved by Wm Gibson.

Deed James Brigance to Robert Patterson 100 acres ackd.

Wednesday April 6th 1796. Present Thos Masten Abraham Sanders Thomas Donnell.

Deed/gift Elizabeth Jones to Polly Patsey & Sarah Cotton daus of Jno Cotton ackd.

Deed Jas Sanders by Danl Smith his atty to John Veal 490 ac proven by Jno Dawson.

Thomas Patton v Thomas White. July 1795 Shff levied on 403 acres on Jennings Crk; dft came not; judgt by default agt him. April 1796 Plf by Andw Jackson prays damage

APRIL 1796

be ascertained. Jury Jas Reese Robt Steel Jas Douglass Chas Carter Peter Simon Thos Hamilton James Armstrong Richard Jones Isaac Towel Thomas Cribbins John McCarty Wm Edwards. Damages $84.62 & costs. Attached property to be sold.

James Douglass v Benjamin Mires. Jany 1796 Constable James Vinson levied on Thos Edwards, garnishee; dft came not; judgt by default agt him. Apl 1796 plf by Samuel Donelson prays damages be ascertained. Jury[above, except Ezekiel Lindsey for James Douglass]. Damages $37; also find value of property in hands of garnishee $31.16. Plf recovers afsd verdict with costs.

Petition to have road laid off & cleared from Courthouse at Ezekiel Douglass's to Nashville to Kentucky road at Caveats, thence to Kentucky and road to Logan Courthouse. Jury to lay off road: Hugh Crawford Wm Armstrong Junr Peter Looney H David Brigance John Dunihoo Andw Patterson Wm Snoddy Wm Dobbins Sion Perry Richard Caveat Thos Williamson John Young David Shelby Thos Cotton Wm Armstrong Jr.

Pearce Wall & Benjamin Cooper; Pearce Wall's fine reduced to $15 & Coopers to $5.

Appt Abraham Landers & Thos Donnell settle with exrs of Anthony Bledsoe decd.

Appt David Wilson & Thos Donnell to examine records of taxable property for lands still liable to fine & double tax.

p.106 Jurors to July Term: Isaac Pearce Jr Thos Waller Arthur Hankins Edwd Jones Wm Green Volentine Shoat John Harpole Osman Allin Robt Hamilton Robt Shaw Jas Gwin Adam Clap Thos Williamson Wm Crabtree James Yates Edwd Gwin Wm Brigance Wm Edwards Joseph Wallace Edwd Williams Jas Harrison Roger Gibson Wm Wilson Zacheus Wilson Jas Fair John Hamilton Jeremiah Doxey Jacob Thomas William Anderson Jas Snowden Lazarus Cotton Peter Looney P Saml Allen Andw Patterson Archd Martin Joseph McAdams.

Tavern rates set [here omitted].

Deed Philip Pipkin to Frederick Batts 640 acres proved by Daniel Woodard.

Admx of Samuel Hays decd v James Hannah & Josiah Hunter. Debt. Jany 1796 Sheriff executed on James Hannah, Josiah Hunter not found; dfts came not; judgt by default agt them, $23.25.

Court adjourns till Court in Course.   Edwd Douglass

July Term 1796. Commission/Peace by John Sevier governor: David Wilson Thos Donald James Winchester Jas Reese Edwd Douglass William Cage Stephen Cantril Isaac Walton Thomas Masten James Gwin Witheral Latimer James Douglass severally appeared at the house of Ezekiel Douglass first Monday in July 1796 and took oaths of office.

Appt David Shelby Clerk/Court; James Winchester & Edwd Douglass securities.

Appt Reuben Cage sheriff; Jas Winchester Edwd Douglass Stephen Cantrill sec.

Appt David Wilson register; James Winchester & James Reese securities.

Grand Jurors: Archibald Martin foreman, Edward Williams James Farr Zacheus Wilson Robert Hamilton Lazarus Cotton James Snowden William Crabtree Thomas Waller Jeremiah Doxey Peter Looney P Ormand Allen William Edwards.

David Wilson is appointed chairman of the Court.

James Farr records h is stock mark and brand.

Giddeon Davis Pendleton, Jno Brown & Thos Stuart permitted to practice as attys.

Release Archibald Lytle from tax on 7040 acres, same is within Indian boundary.

Deeds proved: David Looney to John Josy by Stephen Cantrill. Hugh Rogan to Nathl Parker by George D Blackemore. Ezekiel Norris to William Black by Reuben Cage.

JULY 1796

p.107   Deeds ackd & proved: Nathl Parker & Mary Parker exrs of Anthony Bledsoe decd to Hugh Rogan by Henry Lyon. Wm Brigance to Hugh McGee. Hance Hamilton by Andw McNairy atty/fact to John Slop[Sloss?] by Miles Wallace. Archibald Fisher to Hallery Melone by Stephen Cantrill. Adam Laurence to John Young by Robt Johnston. David Wilson to Matthew Brown. John Boyd to Richard Jones by Robt Donelson. Daniel Smith to Smith Hansbrough by Henry Bradford. William McGee to Alexander Anderson. Adam Laurence to Bartimus Pack by Robt Johnston. John Knox to William Gillaspie by Abraham Walker. Adam Laurence to George Laurence by Robt Johnston. James Winchester to Robert Caruthers. Jas Winchester to John White. John Knox to Mussendon Matthews by Abraham Walker. James Winchester to Patrick Morrison. Deed/lease John Deloach to Thomas Leach, Alexander Witherspoon, Saml Cross[Crop?] & Wm Leach by Wm Sadler.
   Bill/sale Peter Lyon to John Morgan, for negro Sam proved by John Lyon.

Tuesday July 5th 1796. Present Jas Winchester Jas Reese Witheral Latimer Jas Gwin.
   Spencer Mercer v Benjamin Cooper. Jury Isaac Pearce Edward Jones Edward Gwin Wm Brigance Jos Wallace Jas Harrison Roger Gibson Wm Wilson Jacob Thomas Thos Jimason Henry Vinson Jno McCarty find for plf. Dft granted a new trial.
   Appt Henry Harrison constable for Capt Snoddies District; Peter Turney security.
   Inventory/sales estate of Wm Ridley decd rendered by admx.
   Robert Desha v Jane Kuykendall. Apl 1795 plf by Jno Overton; dft by Jas Doherty. Oct 1795 jury: John Dunihoo Wm Snoddy Edwd Gwin Jas Hays Sion Perry Jno Dawson Jos McAdams Thos Hamilton Peter Looney Wm Bruce Robt Shaw King Carr found for dft. Plf granted new trial. July 1796 Jury Robt Dougan Saml Harris Jas Yates Jno Harpool Thos Williamson Wm Neely Henry Pots Robt Ellis Geo Wotwood John Laurence Elijah P
p.108   Chambers Henry Morris find for plf damages $80.
   Will of Thomas Cotton decd proved by Abraham Rogers & Isaac Walton; Isaac Walton Geo Perry & Moore Cotton exrs qualified. See p.136 for proof of another witness.
   Anthony Sharp v John Young. Oct 1795 plf by Andrew Jackson; dft by James Doherty. Jan 1796 cause refered to David Wilson Jas Winchester & Jas Reese; Plf recovers.
   Thomas Donnell records his stock mark and brand.
   Grant admn/estate of Isaac Swet to Isaac Lindsey; Richard Hogin security $25. Inventory returned; order of sale issued.
   Appt Henry Vinson constable for county; Sion Perry security.
   Appt King Carr constable, James Gwin & Witherall Latimer securities.
   Appt James Vinson constable, Peter Turney security.
   Nathl Parker v Lazarus Cotton. Apl 1796 dft by Jas Doherty. July 1796 jury Isaac Pearce Edwd Jones Edwd Gwin Wm Brigance Jos Wallace Jas Harrison Roger Gibson Wm Wilson Jacob Thomas Jno McCarty Thos Jimason Peter Turney find plf damages $16.25. Dft obtains appeal; bond, with Zach Green security.
   Power/attorney Simon Kuykendall to James Baker ackd.
   John Gordon v William Dobbins. Apl 1796 plf by Bennet Searcy; dft by Jas Doherty. July 1796 jury[above] find plfs damage $57.74 with costs.
   Deeds ackd & proved: Reubin Cage Sheriff to James Hamilton. John Lawrence to Wm Phipps by David Wilson. Richard Thomas to Moore Stephenson by Isaac Walton. James McKain to Jno Dawson. Robt King to Henry Potts by Thomas Donnell. Sinclair Pruit to Robert White by Thomas Patton. Richard Thomas to Moore Stephenson by Isaac Walton.
p.109   David Wilson special guardian for heirs of Isaac Bledsoe decd to Jas Winchester. Sinclair Pruit to David White by James White. Thomas Walker to Edmund Hall by Robert Collins. James Williams to Thomas Walker by Edward Williams.

JULY 1796

Bills of sale proved: Isaac Collier to James Douglass negro woman Esther and her children Aggy Candass & Delce proved by Robert Collier. Edmund Hall to James Douglass negro Isaac by Robt Collier. William Standly to Jas Douglass negro Hampton by Henry Bradford. Wm Sanders to Katharine Bledsoe negro girl Comfort by John Hogan.
Appt George D Blackmore gdn for Joseph Neely; David Shelby security $1000.
Appt Robert Dougan constable; Edwd Douglass security.
James Douglass v William Bowman. Jan 1795 Jas Douglass recovered £38.8.3 agt Wm Bowman & £1.3.3 costs. Shff levied on 640 acres sold for £5 each. Wm Bowman to appear at court at house of Ezekiel Douglass, D.Shelby Clerk/court. Jan 1796 Reuben Cage returned "Not found." July 1796 "Not found." Judgment against dft.

July 6th 1796. Present David Wilson William Cage & James Reese Esquires.
p.110   Deed Robert Esspy to Edward Jones 50 acres proved by William Hankins.
Suppl inventory sales/goods of Thomas Bledsoe decd rendered by Wm Neely an exr.
Bill/sale for negro man York from Isaac Pearce to Isaac Pearce Jr proved by Henry Allison.
Late treasurer/Mero Dist certified Sarah Ruthage paid tax in Davidson Co for 2560 acres which was reptd in Sumner 1795; Sheriff settles with treasurer.
Deed Hardy Murfree to James Moore 1000 acres proved by Hezekiah Oneill.
Appt Wm Hall guardian for John Hall and Robert Hall orphans of William Hall decd; bond $1000 with William Cage security.
Lease Mary Robinson to Stephen Cantrill 140 acres Maddisons Creek for one year proved by Willis Whitfield.
Deed Anthony Sharp to Thomas Howell 230 acres 50 perches proved by David Shelby.
Power of attorney Ephraim Payton to John Dawson ackd.
State v William Beard. A&B. Dft submits; fined 25¢.
State v William Beard. A&B. Dft submits; fined 25¢; pays 50¢ for fines.
Bond of Robt Hogin & Anthony Matcalf to William Galbreath, condition Robert Hogin performs sentence in suit Wm Galbreath v Robert Hogin.
Order James Winchester Matthew Alexander John Morgan William Wilson James Reese to divide the real estate of Alexander Neely deceased.
Witheral Latimer paid tax on property in Davidson which is since found to lie in Sumner, also Thomas Steuart in same situation. Order Clerk to certify to Court of Davidson of such returns so sd persons may be exonerated from paying taxes thereon.
Bond of Reubin Cage as Collector/taxes 1796, James Douglass & Wm Cage securities.
Jurors to october Term: Chamberlain Hutson Francis Catron John McMurtry Job Hicks Wm Smothers Joseph Summers Wm Green Joseph Wallace Nathl Parker Peter Lyon Jonathan Hannum Isaac Morgan Wm Reed James Beason Jas Wilson (Curley) Richd King Thos Patton Robt Wilson Robt Carithers James Trousdell Jno Wilson (son/Saml) Isreal Moore Rhody Allen Jno Withers Jas Odam Jno Williams Samuel Thornton Thomas Edwards Jno Whitsitt John Boyd John White John Ruyle John Payton John Cummins Chas Dement Josiah Howell.
Covenant John Hogan with Wm Dobbins for emancipation of negro man Demon at expiration of a period which commenced 29 Octr 1795 ackd by sd Hogan.
Appt Peter Turney overseer/road from Second Creek to Paytons Creek.
Appt James White overseer/road from Second Creek to Bledsoes Creek.
p.111   Appt George D Blackemore overseer/road Bledsoes Crk to Indian Creek.
Appt Richard King overseer/road from Indian Crk to big east fork of Station Creek & Maj Wilson is to furnish sd overseer with list/polls who are to work on sd road.
Appt William Thomas overseer/road east fk Station Camp Cr to Capt Gillaspies.

JULY 1796

Appt Wm Hankins overseer/road from his mill to Manskers Crk; Thomas Mastin Esq is to furnish list of polls who are to work on sd road.

Appt James Wilson curley overseer/road fork near Indian crk to east fork Station Camp Cr; Majr Wilson is to furnish sd overseer with list of polls to work thereon.

Appt Ezekiel Douglass overseer/road east fk Station Camp crk to west fork sd crk; Major Wilson is to furnish list of polls who are to work on sd road.

Appt James Frazor overseer/road from west fork Station Camp crk to Drakes Cr; Col Douglass is to furnish sd overseer with list of polls to work thereon.

Appt Andrew Steel overseer/road Drakes Creek to Manskers Crk; Capt Cantrill is to furnish sd overseer with list of polls who are to work thereon.

Appt Wm Beard & William Hall patrollers for Capt Morgans district. Roger Gibson & Gabriel Black for Snoddies. Wm Wilson & Geo D Blackimore for Kings. Robert Dougan & Griswold Latimer for Looneys. Isaac Towel & Bazaleel Wyer for Hansbroughs.

Appt James Gwin coroner; James Winchester and William Cage securities.

Appt James Wilson (shooting) Ranger for the County.

Clerk to receive returns/taxable property; enter same to Sheriff for collection.

Order Major Wilson & James Douglass to examine taxable property records for 1795.

Order Edwd Douglass and Witheral Latimer settle with admr of James McKain decd.

Power/atty William Kennedy to John Kennedy Jr of Green County ackd.

Shadrick Bird v Wm Gibson & John Bryance. Plf by Seth Lewis; Wm Gibson one of dfts confesses judgt for $24.87. Plf recovers sd sum with costs.

Court adjourns till Court in Course.   David Wilson

p.112 Court of Pleas & Quarter Sessions first Monday October 1796. Present David Wilson William Cage Isaac Walton James Gwin Esquires.

Motion of Alexr Ewing; he sent his return of taxable property to April term past which was handed by Major Bradford to David Shelby by by him to Col Douglass who failed to enter same on his return of taxable property. Order return received: 640 acres Cedar Lick, 640 Smiths fork, 274 Smiths fork; Ewing exonerated from fines.

Archibald Felts exonerated from tax on 1280 acres mistakenly charged to him.

Deed Thomas Masten to James Fugate 275 acres in Russell County Virginia ackd.

Will of Edward Howell decd proved by Matthew Scoby; his signature not legible so he wrote his name again & wrote another seal. Frances Howell extx qualified.

Deed Sinclair Pruit to James White Jr known as Major White proved by Archd White.

Mortgage Major James White to James Winchester 170 acres ackd.

Inventory goods of Thomas Cotton decd rendered by exrs of deceased.

Grant admn on estate of Thomas Egnew to Thomas Sharp; David Beard & Wm Bowen sec.

John Wilson Jr records his stock mark.

William Thomas records his stock mark.

Grand jury: Thos Edwards foreman, William Reed, Joseph Summer, John Boyd, Robert Wilson, Chamberlain Hutson, Francis Catron, Rhody Allon, Charles Dement, John Whitsitt, Thomas Patton, Robert Caruthers, John White. Henry Vinson, constable.

Bond of Wilson Cage, David Shelby, security; maintenance of child of Anne Strain, sd Wilson the reputed father; also his fine 25 shillings equal to $3.12½ paid.

Appoint James Lyons patroller for Captain Reeds company in place of William Hall.

Order personal estate of Charles Bratton decd to be sold by administrator.

OCTOBER 1796

Jurors to Superior Court: William Hankins, Smith Hansbrough, William Reed, John Morgan, Thos Simpson, Hugh Crawford, Wm Green, Thomas Britton, John Weathers, James Franklin, John Williams, James Douglass.

Jurors to January term: Thomas Blackemore Wm Parmer Elmore Douglass Christopher Cooper Lewis Crain William Douglass John Norris Cornelius Glasgow John Perry Reuben Douglass Willis Whitfield Zachariah Green Peter Looney P Moor Cotton David Brigance Wm Edwards Alexr Breden Wm Frazier Andw Steel David Beard Richd Caveatt Alexr Gwin John Dawson Alexr McKee Rhody Allin Moor Stevenson John White Daniel Rogers Abraham p.113 Rogers John Boyd William Bowen John Roberts James Odam Thomas Parker James Clendening Henry Lyons Henry Melone.

Deeds ackd & proved: Abraham Rogers to Wm Good by George McCormack. John Boyd to Willis Whitfield by Richd Jones. Catharine Bledsoe & James Winchester exrs of Isaac Bledsoe decd to Caleb Willis by Richard Willis. Willie Barrow to William Roark by Nathan Arnet. Saml Gragg to Wm Fisher by Wm Stalcup. Zachariah Green to Thos Egnew. Sampson Williams to Joseph Hendricks by Thomas Stuart. Henry Skinner to Jonathan Magness by Thos Hutchins. James Kerr to Jas Huston by James Reese. James Odam to William White by Wm Edwards. Robert Hays to Cornelius Glasgow by John Gatling. Stephen Cantrill to Matthew Cartwright. Thomas Edwards to Geo Wimbeldorf. Reuben Douglass to Hugh Elliott. Deed/lease: Roderick Jinkins to Thomas Willis.

Bill/sale Benjamin Hicks to Malachi Nicholas Bedgegood for negroes Tony Will Jim Sandy Caroline Kent Scipio Ralp[Ralf?] Tiner Cloe Milly Sue Sampho Doll Juda Venus Fosey Lucy Grace proved by Elizabeth Odam.

Bill/sale Henry Loving to Patrick Dunihoo negro George ackd.

Bill/sale Benjamin Hicks to James Odam for boy Plato proved by Elizabeth Odam.

Ltr/attorney Michael Caveatt to Richard Caveatt ackd before Edward Douglass Esq with attestation of Clerk & County Seal.

Tuesday October 4th 1796. Present David Wilson Edward Douglass William Cage.

Inventory/sales goods of Anthony Bledsoe decd rendered by Nathaniel Parker.

Edward Douglass & Witheral Latimer Esqrs rendered settlement with admr of James McKain decd.

Bennet Searcy esq produced his license to practice as an attorney; took oath.

William Snoddy released from tax on stud horse, tax paid by Wm Baul[Bant?].

James Winchester & James Reese esqrs appear and take their seats.

Deed James Winchester to William Robb 400 acres ackd.

Inventory/goods of Thomas Egnew decd rendered by admr.

p.114 Order admr of Thomas Egnew decd sell personal estate of deceased.

William Galbreath v Robert Hogin. July 1796 plf by Samuel Donelson; dft by Seth Lewis. Oct 1796 jury: John McMurtry, Job Hicks, Wm Smothers, Wm Green, Nathaniel Parker, Peter Lyon, Jonathan Hannum, Jas Trousdell, John Wilson, John Weathers, John Payton, Josiah Howell. Plf recovers with costs.

Jurors to lay off a road from Hankins mill to Montgomeries mill to Kentucky road: William Hankins Elisha Ogelsby William Montgomery(mercht) Edward Gwin James Gwin.

Jurors to lay off road from Capt Trousdells to Kentucky road between Maj Sharps & KY line: James Douglass Hugh Crawford Richard Cavette Anthony Sharp John Williams.

Jurors to lay off road from Croft mill up west fk Bledsoes Crk to KY line: James Wilson(shooting) Robert Steel William Wilson William Morgan Robert Desha.

Jurors to lay off a road from Fort Blount to Dixons Creek: Sampson Williams James Roberts James Desha Richard Jones Uriah Anderson Edmund Jinnings.

OCTOBER 1796

Jurors to lay off a road from Dixons Creek to Bledsoes Lick: George D Blackmore Peter Turney James Clendening James Wright David White.

Jurors to lay off a road from mouth of Cainey fk to road to Fort Blount: William Hall William Reed James McKinny Thomas Jimason Nicholas Davis.

State v John Pankey. Selling spiritous liquors contrary to law. Paid $1 fine.

License John Pankey to keep an ordinary at his dwelling house, John Murphy, sec.

Order James Winchester & James Douglass compleat settlement with exrs of Anthony Bledsoe deceased.

State v Benjamin Cooper. Profane swearing. Confessed. Fined $1; paid.

Polly Bledsoe orphan of Anthony Bledsoe decd chose David Shelby her guardian; bond $1000 with David Wilson security.

Bill/sale Joshua Coffee to Robert Desha for negro woman Phillis proved by James Winchester.

Deeds proved & ackd: Sion Perry to William Smothers. Jean Burton & Wm Ross exrs & heirs of William Burton decd to Lovick Ventress proved by James H Bryan. William Ray by James Billingsly atty/fact to Andrew Carnahan proved by Andrew Blair. Wm Ray by Jas Billingsly atty/fact to John Blair proved by Andrew Carnahan.

p.115 Deeds ackd: Nathaniel Parker to Thomas Parker. Nathaniel Parker to James Clendening. James Clendening to Nathaniel Parker. Ephraim Payton to John Gardner.

Bill/sale Ezekiel Douglass to Sampson Williams negro wench Peg ackd.

Ltr/atty William Martin to Edward Douglass ackd.

William Dobbins bond, Sion Perry security; maintenance of child of Agnus Jones; sd Dobbins, reputed father, paid his fine 25 shillings equal to $3.12.

Wednesday October 5th 1796. Present David Wilson James Winchester William Cage.

John Caffery v William Rasco. July 1796 plf by Saml Donelson; dft by Jas Doherty. Octr 1796 [yesterdays jury except Israel Moore for Josiah Howell]. Plf recovers with costs; dft obtains appeal, Alexander Rasco & Josiah Howell securities.

Henry Lyons v Nathl Parker. July 1796 plf by Seth Lewis; dft by Jas Doherty. Oct 1796 jury[above except Wm Neely & David Beard for Nathl Parker & Peter Lyon] assess plfs damage at $50. Plf recovers verdict with costs.

John Magness v Samuel Gilbert. Ejectmt. July 1796 plf by Samuel Donelson; dft by Isaac McNutt. Oct 1796 jury[above] find dft guilty of trespass; plfs damage 6¢.

p.116 Robert Hogin relinquishes title to a mare in declaration in suit William Galbreath v Robert Hogin.

Petition of James Winchester praying relief from errors committed by surveyor on plat of land; witnesses to be examined; David Wilson ackd notice of same.

Deed William Slade to Thomas Overton 1286 acres proved by Joshua Hadley.

Deed Reuben Cage Shff to Thomas Patton 403 acres ackd.

Deed David Beard to Henry Skinner 213½ acres proved by Samuel Donelson.

Jas Reese Mattw Alexander J Winchester apptd to divide real estate of Alexr Neely decd made return: Preemption 640 acres Goose cr granted decedant by NC 27 June 1793 divided to Wm Neely & heirs of John Neely decd. Tract of 289 acres on Bledsoes Crk conveyed to Alexander Neely decd by Isaac Bledsoe 28 Feb 1789 to Joseph Neely.

Thursday Oct 6th 1796. Present David Wilson James Winchester Stephen Cantrill James Reese William Cage Witherall Latimer James Gwin esquires.

Appt Andrew Hoover constable for Capt Hansbroughs district, Edward Hogin and John

OCTOBER 1796

White securities.
p.117   Allow Witheral Latimer 12 shillings 3 pence Virginia money equal to $2.04 for rations furnished guard who guarded Elisha Tarias[Favas?] from Lincoln County KY to this state agreeable to rect from Wm Bryant deputy shff of Lincoln County.
   Polly & Abraham Bledsoe by guardian v Nathaniel Parker. Jury Jno Withers Jno McMurtry Jno Wilson Rhody Allon Jas Trousdell Jno Wilson Jr Jno Payton Wm Snoddy Andw Hoover Isreal Moore Wm Green Jas Carson to try whether extrs of Anthony Bledsoe dec have sold lands and what amount. Seth Lewis for plf; J Doherty for dft. Jury found exrs of Anthy Bledsoe decd sold land on Holston called Gravelly ridge for £200 Virginia currency also on Holston for £216 Va currency. Order James Reese Jas Douglass Thomas Donnell esqrs meet first Monday in December to arrange proceedings.
   Deed Thomas Archer to William Moore proved by David Wilson.
   Allow Sheriff for exofficio services for 1795 $50.
   Allow Clerk for exofficio services for 1795 $40.
   Tavern rates set [omitted here].
   Allow Robert Dougin $4 for taking a prisoner to Nashville jail.
   Order Sheriff summon 2 constables to attend next term.
   James Reese esq apptd County trustee; David Shelby security.
   License John Cotton to keep an ordinary at his dwelling, John Pankey security.
   Order David Wilson & James Reese make settlement with admrs of Thos Bledsoe decd.
   Allow commissioners for dividing real estate of Alexr Neely decd $2 each.
   Appt Alexr McKee overseer/road from ridge between Red & Cumberland rivers to the Kentucky line; Stephen Cantrill to furnish list of polls.
   Appt Wm Kennedy overseer/road from ridge to Manskers Cr [as above].
   Wm Dobbins paid fine of Agnus Jones for having a base born child.
   Hugh Elliott v Elijah P Chambers & John Rutherford. Sheriff served on Chambers 29 August; not served on Rutherford. Chambers came not; judgt by default $33.33½.
   Court adjourns till Court in Course.   David Wilson

p.118   Court of Pleas & Quarter Sessions at house of Ezekiel Douglass first Monday in January 1797. Present Thomas Masten Thomas Donnell James Reese Isaac Walton Witheral Latimer, esquires.
   Grand Jury: James Clendening foreman Peter Looney P Henry Melone Zach Green Moore Stevenson Henry Lyon Abraham Rogers Alexander McKee Thomas Blackemore William Edwards Christopher Cooper John Dawson William Douglass.
   John Wilson & James Wilson record conditional line mutually agreed between them.
   John Hamilton & Ephraim Fair [as above]
   Grant ordinary license to Thomas Perry; Isaac Walton security.
   King Carr allowed $5 for keeping prisoner William Daniel in his charge.
   Appoint John Franklin constable for Captain Looneys dist; Zack Green security.
   Daniel Rogers records his ear mark.
   John Beeson allowed $4 for furnishing two pair of handcuffs for two culprits.
   Inventory of goods of William Black decd rendered by administratrix.
   Bond Hugh Crawford & Edward Douglass to William Cage proved by David Shelby.
   Bill/sale Benjamin Cooper to Ezekiel Able 30 acres, horse, household furniture, ackd.

JANUARY 1797

Bill/sale James Cotton to Wm Benthall negro man Simon proved by Laban Benthall.
Bill/sale Thomas Perry to Sibella Tennon for a named negro girl Ginne ackd.
Acct/sales of goods of Thomas Egnew decd rendered by admr.
Will of James Lauderdale decd with codicil thereto proved by John Wood James Lauderdale & John Mills. Wm Lauderdale, James Lauderdale & James Henry, exrs therein named, qualified.
Acct/sales of goods of Isaac Sweat decd and an acct of Isaac Lindsey, admr, agt estate, rendered.
Deeds ackd & proved: John Ingles by Anthony Crutcher atty/fact to William Bowan by James Franklin. David Looney by Edwd Douglass atty/fact to William Cage by Edwd Douglass. James Winchester to Robert Bratney by Samuel White. James Winchester to Abraham Sanders by William Beard. Ephraim Payton by Lazarus Cotton atty/fact to
p.119   Elmore Douglass proved by Thomas Blackemore. Michael Cavitt to Richard Cavitt. Ambrose Maulding to Michael Cavitt proved by Joseph Cavitt. Thomas Sharp to Maxwell Sharp. Ephraim Payton to Solomon Harpool proved by John Harpole. John Boyd & Wm Boyd to Peter Blair by proved John Boyd. Philip Philips & Michael Campbell by P Philips atty in fact to Nicholas Roof by Jo Herndon. Ephraim Payton to Peter Turney proved by Pearce Wall. Deed/gift John White to James White jr. John Haynes to John Young. Ambrose Mauldin to Alexander Witherspoon by William Dobbins. Martin Armstrong to David Shelby proved by Henry Bradford. John Knox to John Armstrong by David Shelby. John Knox to David Ireland proved by David Shelby. John Knox to Elijah Mitchell proved by David Shelby. John Brown to Jesse Womack proved by William Lowthar.
Permit Jo Herndon to practice as an attorney at law in this Court.
Bond of James Wilson as ranger, Jacob Houdeshell & Ephraim Farr securities.
Allow Sampson Williams to keep ordinary at Fort Blount, Bennet Searcy security.
Rates at Fort Blount ferry regulated [omitted here].
Pearce Wall records his ear mark and brand.

Tuesday January 3. Present Thomas Donnell Thomas Masten James Reese Isaac Walton.
Appearance bond of Richard Scott; Christopher Cooper & Benj Cooper securities.
Appearance bond of Margaret Douglass and Reuben Cage; to give testimony on behalf State v Richard Scott.
Edward Gwin William Hankins William Montgomery report they laid off a road from Hankins mill to Montgomerys up Drakes creek to the path by Hamilton Station to the Kentucky road near Hamiltons race paths.
p.120 Deed Michael Shannon to John Seraker proved by Alexander Gwin.
Commissioners report they settled with administrators of Thomas Bledsoe decd.
Appt Orman Allon constable for Captain Cantrills district, David Beard security.
In suits Martin v Travis and Lyon v Travis order property levied on to be sold.

Wednesday January 4th. Present James Douglass Witheral Latimer James Gwin.
Deed Thomas Hamilton to Joseph Summers proved by James Smothers.
Bill/sale Henry Ratcliff & William King to Hugh Elliott for a negro girl Nancy proved by Elijah P Chambers.
Acct/sales of goods of Thomas Bledsoe decd rendered by the administrators.
William Alexander records his ear mark and brand.
Henry Lyon records his ear mark and brand.

JANUARY 1797

Deed Reubin Cage Shff to Wilson Cage 1000 ac. Wilson Cage to Reubin Cage 1000 ac.
James Morrison records his ear mark & brand.   David White records his ear mark.
Bill/sale Jonathan Standley to James Hays, horse &c proved by David Shelby.
Appt James Lyon constable for Captain Reeds company; Henry Lyon security.
Motion of Mr Doherty: appraisement of the estate of Anthony Bledsoe decd reduced one third by reason of same being made in paper currency; executors stand chargable for no more than two thirds sd appraisement.
License Henry Lyon to keep an ordinary; David Shelby security.
Deeds proved and ackd: Wm Cage to Wm Parmer. Zachariah Green to David Beard. Wm Cage to Christopher Cooper. Wynn Dixon to Thomas Bradley by Wm Sanders & Wm Parr. Ephraim Payton to John Deloach by James Bodine.
Covenant between John Deloach and Ephraim Payton acknowledged by sd Deloach.
Bill/sale Ephm Payton to John Deloach 2 Negroes 3 mares 13 cattle 16 hogs household furniture and farming tools proved by James Bodine.
Grand Jury dismissed; Daniel Rogers a juror for this term is also dismissed.

Thursday January 5th 1797. Present Thomas Donnell Thomas Masten James Gwin Witheral Latimer esquires.
p.121   Deed Philip Philips & Michael Campbell by P Philips his atty/fact to John Sirney for 640 acres proved by Isaac McNutt.
Appointments to take lists of taxable property: James Reese in Capt Reeds company; Thos Donnell in Capt Wilsons; Jas Douglass in Capt Snoddies Co; Edwd Douglass in Capt Loonies Co; Thomas Masten in Capt Hansbroughs Co; Capt Cantrill in his own company; Witheral Latimer in Capt Hamiltons Company.
Appearance bond of William Bell; Thomas Donnell security.
Charles Dunihoo John Murphy Thomas Parker William Cosby appearance bond to give testimony on behalf state agt William Bell.
Order Nathaniel Parker be credited in his settlement with legatees of Anthony Bledsoe decd for appraisement of negro Philis, £80, which Negro was assigned to Anthony Bledsoe one of the legatees.
Henry Lyon, garnishee in suit Isaiah Boon v Thomas Traves, has in possession corn that grew on nine acres property of sd Traves except 35½ bushels sd Lyon's by contract between him & sd Traves.
Isaac & Henry Bledsoe by guardians v Nathaniel Parker. Petition for legatees. Jul 1796 dft by Jas Doherty; plfs by Bennet Searcy & Seth Lewis. Jan 1797 Isaac & Henry Bledsoe by gdns James Clendening & Thomas Masten v Nathl Parker exr in right of his wife of will of Anthony Bledsoe decd. Petition for legacy. Nathl Parker to pay sd gdns. Signed: Thos Donnell, With Latimer, J Douglass.
Prudy Bledsoe by gdn v Nathaniel Parker. Petition for legacy. July 1796; plfs by Bennett Searcy & Seth Lewis; dft by Jas Doherty. Jany 1797 Prudy Bledsoe by gdns Wm Neely & David Wilson v Nathaniel Parker exr in right of his wife of will of Anthony Bledsoe decd. Nathaniel Parker to pay Neely & Wilson gdns for use of Prudy Bledsoe $398.64, also costs of suit. Thomas Donnell Witheral Latimer J Douglass.
p.122   Polly and Abraham Bledsoe by guardians v Nathaniel Parker. Petition for legatees. Defendant by atty James Doherty. January 1797 plaintiff by Bennett Searcy and Seth Lewis. Polly and Abram Bledsoe by guardian David Shelby v Nathaniel Parker, executor, &c. Defendant pays David Shelby gdn for use of Polly and Abram $1304.29 and costs. Thomas Donnell Witheral Latimer. James Douglass.
Tavern rates altered respects brandy and whiskey per half pint 25 cents.

APRIL 1797

Jurors to April term: Chas Carter Wm Gillaspie Henry Bradford John Sadler Ezekiel Douglass Robert Barrow Wm Wier Matthew Cartwright Hugh Crawford Roger Gipson James Smothers Wm Bowen Wm Dillard Wm Hankins Richard Waller jr James Whitsitt Cornelius Glasgow Kasper Mansker Jno Perry Wm Reed John Morgan Robt Steel Robt Desha George D Blackmore Jas A Wilson Jas C Wilson Wm McKorkle Joseph Wallace Jas Harrison Michael Cavitt Thos Williams Jas Frazor Jas Franklin Sion Perry Jos McElwrath Thos Patton.
Court adjourns, meet at house of Wm Gillaspie at Court in Course.   Thos Donnell

p.123 Court of Pleas & Quarter Sessions at house of William Gillaspie on the first Monday in April. Present David Wilson Thomas Masten Thomas Donnell esqrs.

Thos Donnell esq deposited 62½¢ in hands of Clerk, it being a fine levied on Nathaniel Parker for profane swearing.

Isaac Dorris bond, Saml Dorris Senr & Saml Dorris Jr securities; maintenance of base born child of Mary Garrison; paid his fine $6.25.

Will of Danl Benthall decd proved by Laban Benthall & Mary Benthall; James Cryer an executor therein named appeared and qualified.

Will of Robert Hobdy proved by Moor Cotton; James Cryer & Telitha Hobdy exr & extx appeared and qualified.

Grand jury: John Morgan foreman James Smothers William Reed Robert Barrow William Bowan Robt Steel John Sadler Hugh Crawford Wm Hankins James A Wilson James Franklin Geo D Blackemore Sion Perry Cornelius Glasgow. James Lyon constable to attend jury.

James Warrnock v Elijah McKinny. Levied on horse & saddle; dft gives James Johnston security to replevy property attached.

Appt Matthew Cartwright Champ Madden & Jacob Woodram apptd patrollers for Capt Hansbroughs company, to qualify before Thomas Masten esquire.

Order orphan Jno Aflick bound to Wm Thomas to age 21; chmn security for sd Thos.

Deed John Bond to Edward Moore 640 acres proven by William Curl.

Order personal estate of John Neely decd be exposed to sale by admx.

Appt Thos Donnell special gdn for heirs of Jeremiah Morgan for purpose of executing a deed of conveyance for 250 acres to John Morgan.

Henry Bunn v Robert Bowman. Dfts bail surrendered dft to Sheriff; Jas Hays, bail.

Will of Sarah Douglass decd proved by Jas Cage; Reubin Douglass extr qualified.

William Bryance v Henry Webster. Dft brings to Court Thomas Edwards bail for dft.

Jurors to superior court: Wm Barrow Danl Smith Wm Hall Kasper Mansker Nathl Parker Hy Bradford John Dawson Thos Perry Robt Jones Edwd Gwin Wm Douglass Wm Saunders.

Deeds ackd & proved: Wm Cage to Reuben Cage. Charles Hardy and Jonathan Hardy to Benjn Bashaw proved by William Blackmore. George D Blackmore to Jesse Hainey. Geo p.124 D Blackmore to Arthur Davies. Thomas Jimason to John Wilson proved by James A Wilson. Matthew Kincannon to George D Blackmore proved by Daniel Smith. Dixon Marshall to Robert Barnett by Adam Young. Isaac Patton to Samuel Fleming by John Walker. Meady White to Josiah Howell by Nathaniel Harrison. Peter Blair to John Savely proved by John Boyd. James Montgomery to Alkenah Echols. John Payton to Robert Hobdy by Moore Cotton. Thomas Simpson to John Harpole proved by William Montgomery. Elisha Ogelsby to William Montgomery by Jas Frazor. William Saunders to Montgomery McConnel by Charles Dunihoo. Edward Gwin to John McMurtry by Francis Catron. William Parmer to William Dillard. Edward Gwin to Francis Catron proved by

APRIL 1797

John McMurtry. Jonathan Latimer to Chas Latimer. Jonathan Latimer to Griswold Latimer. Jonathan Latimer to Hannah Latimer William Latimer and Nathaniel Latimer. Jonathan Latimer to Robert Latimer. Robert Espy to Armstead Rogers proved by Thomas Cribbins. John Payton to John Carr. John Payton to Elisha Ogelsby. George Summers to Dennis Kelly by Lijah Loyd. Archibald Buchannon to John Golagher 200 acres in Mercer County Kentucky proved by Thomas Masten. Thomas Donnell special guardian for the heirs of Jeremiah Morgan to John Morgan ackd. John Morgan to Nathaniel Gilmore. Deed of lease David Shelby to John Plunket.
   Bill/sale John Payton to Robert Box for cattle ackd.
   Bill/sale Moses Echols to Joseph Hendrick for negro Daniel ackd.
   Bill/sale Henry McKinny to Thomas Patton for negro girl Juda proved by Nicholas Boyce.
   License William Gillaspie to keep ordinary at his dwelling; John Beson security.
   License James Cotton to keep ordinary; William Richards & Saml Loyd securities.
p.125   Appt James Gwin and John Gwin guardians for Hannah Latimer William Latimer Nathaniel Latimer orphans of Nathaniel Latimer decd; Jonathan Latimer and William Montgomery securities.
   Inventory/James Lauderdale decd proved by Wm & Jas Lauderdale, exrs of sd decd.
   Thomas Masten & Stephen Cantril esqrs return their lists of taxable property.

Tuesday April 4th 1797. Present David Wilson James Gwin & Witheral Latimer esqrs.
   Deed William Snoddy to Roderick Jinkins 100 acres proved by David Shelby.
   John Hamilton records his ear mark.
   Spencer Mercer v Benjamin Cooper. Apl 1796 plf by James Dohertie; dft came not; judgt by default. July 1796 jury: Isaac Pearce Edwd Jones Edwd Gwin Wm Bryance Jos Wallace Jas Harrison Roger Gibson Wm Wilson Jacob Thomas Thos Jimason Henry Vinson Jno McCarty assess plfs damage $50. Dft by Isaac McNutt granted new trial. Apl 1797 Apl 1797 jury: William McCorkle Joseph McElwrath Matthew Cartwright Thomas Patton Charles Carter James Whitsitt James C Wilson Richard Waller Thomas Williamson Wm Wyer John Hamilton Henry Lyon find plfs damage $45, with costs.
   Spencer Mercer v Benjamin Cooper. Peter Looney witness behalf/plaintiff came not.
   William Spencer admr of T S Spencer v John McCarty. July 1796 plaintiff by James Dohertie; dft by Isaac McNutt. April 1797 Jury Joseph Wallace William Dillard John Perry John Harpole William Brigance Peter Turney Charles Dement Jno Tait Robt Ellis John Beason William Parmer Joel Dillard find for the defendant.
   Deed Jesse Womack to William Montgomery 340 acres proved by Thomas Masten.
   Deed Richard Fenner to Thomas Stokes 3 tracts 640 acres each; Clerk of Court of Franklin County, N.C. certifies that deed was admitted to probate in that Court.
p.126   Deed James Cole Mountflorence to Thomas Stokes nine tracts of 6120 acres certified by the Clerk of Court of Franklin County, North Carolina, sd deed there admitted to probate.
   Deed Caleb Phifer to David Wilson 320 acres proved by Zacheus Wilson.
   Deed David Looney by attorney Edward Douglass to Margaret Minor, Hannah Turner Minor, and Daniel Looney Minor 320 acres proved by William Brigance.
   Deed Nathl McCann to Thos Overton & John Beck 2560 acres proved by Wm Dickson Jr.
   Deed John Beck to Wm Sullivan half of 2560 acres which sd Beck held as tenant in common with Thomas Overton was proved by Lee Sullivan.
   Ltr/atty Jas Vinson to Jas Vinson Jr authenticated agreeable to Act of Congress.
   Order John Riley oversee road from Hankins mill to road from Bledsoes Lick; road

APRIL 1797

from Hankins mill to Montgomeries mill; Thomas Masten to furnish list of Polls.
Appt John McMurtry overseer/part of road from Hankins mill to Montgomeries mill; James Gwin esqr to furnish him with a list of the Polls.
Appt Robert Hamilton to oversee part/road Hankins mill to Montgomeries mill; Witheral Latimer esqr to furnish him with a list of polls.
Petition of Thomas Stokes sets forth an error made by the surveyor on 1000 acres of land upon which grant 283 issued, stating north side of Cumberland River instead of south side. Clerk/Court to certify same to Secy/State of North Carolina.
Supplemental inventory of goods of Ben Kuykendall decd rendered into Court.
Ltr/atty James Deacon to Joshua Scott proved by John Scott.
Appoint Simon Kuykendall guardian for Jesse Kuykendall orphan of Ben Kuykendall decd; William Montgomery & William Douglass securities.
State v Samuel Snoddy. Appearance bond of defendant.
State v James Wornock. Appearance bond of defendant.
Sion Perry v William Smothers. Covt. July 1796 plaintiff by James Dohertie; dft
p.127 by Bennet Searcy. April 1797 Jury William McKorkle Joseph McElwrath Matthew Cartwright Thomas Patton Chas Carter Jas Whitsitt Jas C Wilson Richd Waller Thomas Williamson Wm Wyer Henry Lyon Jas Hays find for dft; plf granted appeal, James Gwin & Nathaniel Parker securities.
Witheral Latimer returns list of taxable property in Capt Hamiltons Company.

Wednesday April 5th 1797. Present David Wilson James Winchester Witheral Latimer William Cage James Reese James Douglass James Gwin Thomas Donnel Thomas Mastin.
Order taxes set on land and polls [omitted here].
Henry Lyon v Nathaniel Parker. Oct 1796 plf by Seth Lewis; dft by James Dohertie. April 1797 jury William McKorkle Joseph McElwrath Matthew Cartwright Thomas Patton Charles Carter Peter Seamon Joseph Wallace William Dillard John Perry Edward Hogin Gabriel Black Richard Hogin find for defendant.
Deed Griffith Rutherford to Charles Ready 214 acres ackd.
Deed Isaac Walton to Bryan Garner 230 acres proved by Willis Horton.
Lyon v Parker. Andrew Moore & John Harrison witnesses; no subpoena filed.
David Wilson deposited fines of Betsey Maxey and Peggy Hinson for fornication.
State v Richard Scott. A&B. Dft by Thomas Stuart. Jury Wm Montgomery Wm Dobbins Francis Martin Chas Dement John Mays Jas McKinsey Edward Hutson Isaac Pearce Saml Thornton Henry Huddleston James C Wilson Richd Waller find dft guilty; fined 1¢.
State v William Bell. Appearance bond of Wm Bell, William McKorkle security.
State v Wm Bell. John Murphy witness behalf State last term failed to appear and forfeits recognizance.
p.128 State v William Bell. State witnesses Charles Donihoo Thos Parker William Cosby, appearance bonds.
Reubin Douglass exr/Sarah Douglass decd rendered inventory of estate.
James Reese esq returns list of taxable property in Capt Reeds District.
Deed Wm Martin by Edwd Douglass atty/fact to Andw Jackson proved by Thos Stuart.
Deed Andrew Jackson to William Martin 840 acres ackd.
Deed Andrew Jackson to John Hays 640 acres proved by Thomas Stuart.
Ezekiel Ray v James Baker. James Lyon garnishee has between $30 & $40 of dft.
Ezekiel Ray v James Baker. John Cotton garnishee has no property of dft.
John Lyon v Thomas Traves. Jan 1797 Shff levied on 9 acres corn; judgt by default agt dft. Apl 1797 plf by Isaac McNutt. Jury[above except Wm Brigance & James Weath-

APRIL 1797

ered for Francis Martin & Jas C Wilson] find plf damage $26.52. With costs.
Francis Martin v Thomas Travis. Atta. Jan 1797 Shff levied on 9 acres corn; dft came not; judgt by default. Apl 1797 plf by Isaac McNutt prays damages be ascertained. Jury John Mays Chas Dement Wm Dobbins Wm Wyer Edwd Hutson Henry Huddleston Jas McKinsey Saml Thornton Wm Brigance Isaac Pearce Wm Montgomery Chas Carter find plaintiffs damage $50. With costs.
License Ezekiel Douglass to keep ordinary at his dwelling; John Cotton security.
Sheriff reports taxable property of persons as have no personal property.
Tavern rates [omitted here].
James Douglass & Thomas Donnell return lists of taxable property in Capt Snoddies & Capt Wilsons districts.
Jurors to July Term: William Edwards Solomon Barns Thomas Howel Robert Wilson Jno Quisenbury Christ Cooper William Parmer William Douglass Zachariah Dillard George
p.129 Cummins Thomas Watson Peter Lemons Armstead Rogers Peter Looney Moore Stevenson Richard Jones Willis Whitfield Volentine Shoat John Sterns Samuel Stuart Jas Wilson C Richard King Andrew Blythe Solomon Reese James Harrison Ezekiel Douglass James Hamilton Richd Fossit John Seroker Robert Latimer Francis Catron John Farrier David Lane James Adam Charles Dement John Williams.

p.129   Thursday April 6th 1797. Present David Wilson Thomas Donnell William Cage.
William Gillaspie v James Cole Mountflorence. Apl 1793 plf recovered £41.4.10 agt dft also £3.10.4 costs. Apl 1794 Shff levied on two tracts 640 acres each sold for £21.0.0 to Jonathan Latimer, leaves balance £23.15.2 equal to $59.39½. James Cole Mountflorence to appear at ensuing Court, house of Ezekiel Douglass. David Shelby. Jan 1797 Shff returned Not found. R.Cage. Apl 1797 Not found. R Cage. Court gives judgt agt sd dft for $59.39½ with costs of suit.

David Shelby v Philip Shackler. April 1790 plaintiff recovered £30.13 agt Philip Shackler, also £2.12.4 costs. Sheriff sold 640 acres on Paytons Creek warrant 1604 located 9 Decr 1785 for £10 purchased by David Shelby, leaving balance of £23.5.4 equal to $58.16; execution issued. Philip Shackler to appear at the ensuing County
p.130   Court, David Shelby. Jany 1797 "Not found." Philip Shackler to appear at ensuing Court. April 1797 Sheriff returns Not Found, R Cage. Judgment against the defendant $58.16 & costs.

Joseph Wallace v James Douglass. Oct 1796 plf by James Dohertie; dft by Bennet Searcy. Apl 1797 jury: Joseph McElwrath Matthew Cartwright Charles Carter Richard Waller William Wyer John Perry Henry Lyon Richard Hogin John Mays Sion Perry Carlton Atkinson Edward Hutson find for plaintiff his damages $30. Defendant obtains appeal, Seth Lewis & William Cage securities.

State v Richard Hogan. A&B. Deft submits; fined $1 and costs.

Allow Henry Lyon $12 for gathering Thos Travers corn last year at Greenfield.

Rates for Mr Dillards ferry man & horse 6½¢; man or horse 3¢.

Appt Jas Lyon Edwd Hudson Stephen Box patrollers for Capt Reeds Company; to qualify before Major Wilson.

Order all orders respecting roads made at last October Term be revived.

Order road laid off from Croft mill to Major Sharps by James Douglass Hugh Crawford Richard Cavett Anthony Sharp John Williams & Joseph Wallace.

Order a road be laid off from below Capt Gillaspies opposite Pilot Knob to near Major Sharps by Reubin Douglass William Gillaspie John Dawson Archibald Martin Peter Looney H Moore Stevenson James Franklin & John Dunihoo.

Matthew Cartwright records his ear mark.

JULY 1797

William Wyer records his stock mark.
Court adjourns till Court in Course to meet at this place.   David Wilson

p.131 Court of Pleas & quarter Sessions at house of Wm Gillaspie, first Monday in July 1797. Present David Wilson Edward Douglass Thomas Masten esqrs. Thos Donnell.
Jurors Charles Dement Christopher Cooper John Quisenberry George Cummins Ezekiel Douglass James Wilson Richard King exempted from attending for present Term.
Grand jury: Thos Watson foreman John Ferrier Peter Lemon Willis Whitfield Thomas Howell Richard Jones John Williams Volentine Shoat William Douglass James Hamilton Armstead Rogers David Lane Zachariah Dillard.
Release John Motheral from tax on 868 acres for 1796, same returned in 2 places.
Mary White formerly Mary Bratton rendered additional inventory & appraisement of goods of Charles Bratton decd.
Appt Edwd Douglass & Jas Gwin esqrs to settle with admr of Nathl Latimer decd.
State v Henry Webster. Slaughtering beef cattle in the woods and not bringing forward their ears agreeable to law. Jury Richd Fossit Peter Looney Wm Parmer Jas Harrison Jas Odam Francis Catron Solomon Barnes Wm Edwards Moore Stevenson Gabriel Black Thomas Cribbins William Spencer. Mistrial. Defendant pays all costs.
Release Wallace Estill from tax on 640 acres on Bledsoes Cr, twice returned.
Appt Tilmon Dixon William Sanders James Bradley Peter Turney Uriah Anderson Danl Mungle William Anderson James Roberts James Clendening Hezekiah Oneal to lay off a road from Fort Blount to Bledsoes Creek.
Bound Phebe Harris to Saml White until age 18; sd White's bond with chmn/Court.
James Wilson renders inventory/sales of goods of John Neely decd.
Appt Jacob Parks constable for Red River Dist; George Parks security.
John Wright v William Montgomery. Apl 1797 plf by James Dohertie; dft by Samuel Donelson. July 1797 refered to Henry Bradford and Samuel Thornton whose award shall be judgt of Court. Arbitrators chose Saml J Wilson as umpire. Award each party pays own lawyer; Montgomery pays clerk, sheriff, tax fees & is discharged from cause.
Thomas Stuart George Smith Robt Hamilton Francis Hall esqrs produced licenses to practice as attornies at law, took oaths and qualified.
Order Clerk receive all returns of taxable property.
Appearance bond of Samuel Snoddy, John Wright his security.
p.132 Deeds ackd & proved: Archibald Buchannon to John Golagher 200 acres in Mercer County Kentucky proved by oath of James Hays. Michael Kimberlin by Benjamin Hollidy atty-in-fact to Wallis Estill. James Winchester to John Anderson proved by James Mecklin. James Cole Mountflorence to Anthony Sharp proved by Edwd Douglass. Ambrose Porter to John Withers proved by Gabriel Black. Thomas Edwards to Cornelius Tinsley proved by James Odam. Abraham Sanders to Daniel Taylor proved by John Tripplet. James Wilson to William McCorkle. William Spencer to John West. John Scott Senr to John Scott Jr proved by Samuel Thornton. Perigan Taylor to Solomon Barnes proved by Edmund Hall. John Veal to William Benthall proved by Jesse Williams. Jno Ferrier to Daniel Rogers. Andrew Jackson to Joseph Hendrick. James McKinsey to John Reasons proved by John Mayes.
Ltr/atty Michael Kimberlin to Benjamin Hollidy & others.
Deed/gift Ambrose Porter to Mary Porter 160 acres proven by Gabriel Black.

JULY 1797

Bill/sale Francis Fonvill to Charlotte Ware negro girl Lock proved by Edmd Hall.
Bill/sale Armstead Rogers to Robt Esspy negro girl Chloe proved by Thos Cubbins.
Bill/sale Andw Jackson to Ezekl Douglass negro girl Suck proved by Hugh Crutcher.
Ltr/atty Arthur Hession to Capt Watris Alexander ackd.

Tuesday July 4th 1797. Present David Wilson Thomas Masten William Cage esqrs.
   Jury report they laid off a road from below Capt Gillaspies up Station Camp to the road from Cavits to Major Wilsons. Reubin Douglass William Gillaspie Archibald Maclin James Franklin Peter Luna John Dunihoo.
   Grant admn on estate of Simon Elliott decd to Hugh Elliott; bond $1500, Simon Kuykendall & William Cage securities.
   Order road from Croft mills up Bledsoes Creek to the Kentucky line be laid off by James Wilson shooting Robert Steel William Wilson William Morgan Robert Desha John Morgan David Baird.
   Appt James Franklin overseer/road from below Captain Gillaspies to road by John Dawsons; William Cage esqr to furnish sd overseer with a list of Polls.
   Appt Peter Looney overseer/road from John Dawsons to west fk Station Camp Creek; Edward Douglass esqr to furnish a list of Polls to work on said road.
   p.133 State v James Wornock. Retailing spiritous liquors by the smalls contrary to law. Jury John Cotton Jas Clendening Henry Bunn Richard Strother James McKinsey John Mayes John Payton Samuel Stuart John Norris John Deloach Peter Looney P Samuel Harris find deft not guilty as charged. Dft pays costs.
   State v Wm Bell. Petit larceny. Jury[above except Jas Harrison & Robt Ellis for Peter Looney & Jas Clendening] find dft not guilty; prosecutor pays all costs.
   William Hall William Reed Henry McKinny Thomas Jimason Nicholas Davis report they laid off road from the mouth of Cany Fork to road to Dixons Springs to Fort Blount.
   State v William Bell; order prosecution pay all costs thereon.
   Appt Robt Bates constable for Capt Hansbroughs Company; Thos Cribbins security.
   Appt John Fisher admr of Joshua Fisher decd; Wm Hall & James McKain securities.
   Appt Jeremiah Watson admr of Nicodemus Watson decd; Wm Hall & Robert Steel sec.
   Order admr of Nicodemus Watson decd sell the personal estate of deceased.
   Robert Ellis v Ephraim Payton. Attachment. Lazarus Cotton garnishee declares he is not indebted to dft. John Deloach declares he is not indebted to him unless considered so in consequence of covenant formerly entered into with sd Payton.
   Deeds ackd & proved: George Chandler & wife Mary to Jesse Wilkinson proved by Wm Smith. James Whitsitt to heirs of Azariah Thompson decd proved by Elisha Bernard. Elisha Rice for himself as executor of John Rice decd and as attorney for Nathan Rice, William H Rice, and Joel Rice to Andrew Jackson proved by Samuel Donelson. Thomas Murry to Stephen Peters. Robert Dobbins to William Montgomery proved by William Dobbins. Andrew Bowman to John Russell proved by James Douglass. Robert Orr to Thomas Dunihoo proved by George Smith. Thomas Shute to William White proved by Isaac Totewine. Zacheus Wilson to Robert White proved by David Wilson. Robert White to Charles Ready proved by John Shaver.
   Deeds of Release: Andrew Bowman to James Douglass proved by John Russell. James Douglass to Andrew Bowman. Robert Collier to Andrew Bowman proved by Jas Douglass.
   Bill/sale Nathan Allen to James Douglass for a negro woman Nan.
   Bill/sale Fergus Sloan to John Morgan for three negroes: Priscilla, Peter, Fan proved by William Lyon.
   Articles of agreement William Sanders John Marshal and James Sanders Junr proved

JULY 1797

by Thomas Doniho.
Ltr/atty Thomas Harris to David Wilson proved by James Hart.

Wednesday July 5th 1797. Present David Wilson William Cage Isaac Walton esquires.
p.134   State v Mary Turner. Fornication. Jury: James Harrison James Odam John Wright Robert Bowman Andrew Blythe Peter Turney Richard Hogin Richard Fossit Solomon Barnes Moore Stevenson Thomas Cubbins Uriah Anderson find the defendant not guilty; defendant pays costs.
Deed Abraham Sanders to William Anderson 100 acres proved by David Wilson.
Deed Ephraim Farr to Joseph Wilson 20 acres proved by Jacob Houdeshell.
Deed William Gillaspie to Job Bass 320 acres ackd.
State v Hugh Elliott. Fornication. Jury Peter Luna Wm Parmer Francis Catron Wm Edwards Edwd Gwin Wm Dobbins Jno Gatlin Jno Wright Jno Mays Jno Gwin Jno Morgan Nathaniel Parker find dft not guilty. Dft pays all costs.
State Solicitor in suit State v Hugh Elliott interrogated a witness in behalf of the state thus: What do [you] know respecting Hugh Elliott & Margaret Cowins [Coweny?] living in fornication which Question was objected to by the defence attorney; Court decided in favour of the question.
Order road laid off from Donohoos mill to Montgomeries mill by Robert Latimer Adam Harpool John Donihoo Archibald Martin James Gwin.
Deed William Benthall to Elizabeth Benthall Charlotte Benthall Francis Benthall Mary Benthall & Susannah Benthall heirs of Danl Benthall decd 163½ acres ackd.
Inventory/goods of Daniel Benthall decd rendered by executor.
State v Stephen Cantrill. Fornication. Jury Peter Luna Wm Parmer Francis Catron Wm Edwards John Gatlin John Wright John Mays Robt Ellis John Gwin Nathl Parker Elisha Clary Andrew Blythe find dft not guilty as charged.
Elijah Hedgcock v Wm Richards. Dismissed. Each party pays own atty & half costs.
Wm Williams v Sion Perry. Covt. Oct 1796 plf by Samuel Donelson; dft by Isham A Parker. July 1797 jury Wm Parmer Francis Catron Wm Edwards Henry Bunn Jas Harrison Jas Odam Moore Stevenson Wm Bryance Hugh Crawford Henry Hill Andrew Blythe Robert Bowman assess plfs damages $51.95. Dft obtains appeal.
Deed Samuel Barton to Andrew McCasland 400 acres proved by Bennet Searcy.
Jurors to Oct Term: James Farr Robert Anderson Robert Carothers John Wilson Thos Patton John Sterns Thomas Reese George D Blackmore Robert Wilson Henry Loving William Alexander (Greenfield), Thomas Hamilton Junr John Curica John Tripplet Isaac Towell William Frazor Bryant Gardner Thomas Perry Thomas Simpson James Whitfield Robert Barrow Joshua Hadley Rhod Rowlings William Montgomery (Nuntl?) John Dawson Robert Looney Joel Dillard Christopher Cooper Owen Dillard Lewis Crane John Baker Ezekiel Lindsey William Green Captain Hansbrough Captain R Bell Thomas Waller.

Thursday July 6th 1797. Present Isaac Walton James Gwin Witheral Latimer.
p.135   Reuben Cage is apptd Collector of taxes; Wm Edwards Peter Looney security.
John & Ephraim Payton v Thomas Cribbins. July 1796 plf by James Doherty; dft by Saml Donelson & Isaac McNutt. July 1797 jury Andw Blythe Richd Fossit Peter Looney H Jas Harrison Jas Odam Solomon Barnes Wm Edwards Moore Stevenson Jas Wornock Edwd Hogin Peter Luna P Wm Clary find plf damages $31.25.
Bond: Reubin Cage, collecting County Tax, Henry Bradford & Moore Stevenson sec.
Wm Williams v Sion Perry. Dft's bond for appeal, James Gwin & Wm Montgomery sec.

OCTOBER 1797

Timothy Chandler v Stephen Anderson. Jury Francis Catron John Payton Joseph Wilson Thomas Cribbins Henry Hill John Beson Henry Bunn John Cotton Richard Hogin Sion Perry Alexander Gwin John Mayes. Mistrial.
Deed Samuel Barton to Andrew McCasland 400 acres ackd.
Anthony Foster v Edward Hogin. Covt. Oct 1796 plf by Bennet Searcy; dft by Isaac McNutt. July 1797 jury James Odam James Harrison William Edwards Peter Luna P Moore Stevenson Richard Fossit Solomon Barnes Robert Ellis Peter Looney H William Clary Hugh Elliott Andrew Blythe find plaintiffs damage $28.32. Also costs.
Appt Thomas Howell constable for Capt Snoddies dist; Solomon Barnes security.

Friday July 7th 1797. Present Edward Douglass Thomas Donnell William Cage Esqrs.
Inventory of goods of Sarah Douglass decd returned by executor.
Order Thomas Donnell & James Reese Esqrs settle with admx of Jacob Zeigler decd.
Appt William Bruce Griswold Latimer Rhodam Rowlings patrollers for Capt Lunas and Captain Stevensons companies; to qualify before Edward Douglass esquire.
Appt Archibald Martin overseer/road west fork Station Camp cr to Kentucky road; Edwd Douglass to furnish a list of polls to work on sd road.
Payton v Cubbins. Motion for arrest of judgt; motion overruled; judgt confirmed.
Deed John & George M Deaderick to Henry Bunn 228 acres proved by Wm Curl.
Allow Clerk $30 for stationery.
Court adjourns till Court in Course.   Edward Douglass.

p.136 First Monday in October 1797 at the house of William Gillaspie. Present: James Reese Thomas Masten Witheral Latimer Esquires.
Will of Robert Hobdy decd exhibited to April Court and proved by Moore Cotton is exhibited again this Term and proved by William Carr, another subscribing witness.
Grant admn on estate of Benjamin Mires decd granted to Dicy Mires, Wm Brazil sec.
Grant admn on estate of Ephraim Farr dec to Jennet Farr; Joseph Wallace sec.
Order Richd Caveat Thos Williamson & Wm Armstrong keep orphan boy Harris Grisham at school until April next, then bring boy to Court to be dealt with by law.
State v Harman Hensly. Fornication. Dft bond, Elisha Ogelsby security for maintenance of base begotten child of Betsey Meekly now pregnant; also paid his fine.
Andrew Blythe records his ear mark.   James Blythe records his ear mark.
Jonathan Hannum records his ear mark.
Edwd Douglass & Co v Robert Dobbins. Dft appearance bond, Sion Perry security.
Grand Jury: Robert Barrow foreman William Green Thomas Waller Wm Frazor Lewis Crane John Serrica Owen Dillard Joel Dillard John Wilson Christopher Cooper Thomas Hamilton James Farr Thomas Reese.
Appt James Winchester and William Maxey admrs of Henry Loving decd; bond $4000, Thomas Masten & James Douglass securities; inventory returned.
Archibald Martin witness to will of Thomas Cotton decd signed will in presence of Isaac Walton another witness to sd will.
License William Kennedy to keep ordinary; Orman Allon security.
License John Pankey to keep ordinary; Smith Hansbrough security.
Jury apptd in July report road laid off from Fort Blount, crossing Goose Creek

OCTOBER 1797

below Donoho mill to William Whites to Bledsoes Creek. T Dixon, James Bradley, P Turney, W Sanders, Daniel Mungle.

Appt Sampson Williams overseer/road Ft Blount to Defeated Crk; Capt Reese to furnish a list of polls.

Appt Wm Young overseer/road from Defeated Creek to Dixons Creek; Capt Reese to furnish overseer with a list of polls.

Appt Tilmon Dixon overseer/road from Dixons Creek to east fork Goose Creek, Capt Reese to furnish sd overseer with list of polls.

p.137   Appt Thos Stubblefield overseer/road from east Goose Crk to second Crk, Capt Reese to furnish sd overseer with a list of polls.

Appt Wm Neely overseer/road from Second Crk to Bledsoes Crk; Capt Reese to furnish sd overseer with list of polls.

Deeds ackd & proved. John Savely to Jorden Barnes proved by Henry Bunn. Charles Moore to Thomas Harmon Sr proved by Thomas Harmon Jr. John Wilson to James Wilson. Bradley Gambell to Benjamin Smith proved by Daniel Frazor. James Wilson to Francis Fonvielle proved by Matthew Brown. Joseph Wilson to Francis Fonvielle proved by Matthew Brown. Ebenezer Alexander to Joseph Wallace proved by Israel Moore. Daniel Wilburn to John Dillard proved by James Womack. Isaac Pearce Senr to Isaac Pearce Junr and Thomas Waller proved by John Young. David Wilson to Joseph Wilson proved by James A Wilson. Robert Hays to Robert Moore proved by John Moore. Robert Green to Michael Black. William Spencer to Joseph Hendrick proved by Lewis Crane. John Scott to John Roberts proved by Robert Hogin. David Caldwell to William Wherry. James Winchester to Isreal Moore. James Winchester to William Newton. William Montgomery to Robert Wadkins. Elisha Clary to James Montgomery. Henry Lovin to David Caldwell proved by John Rutherford. Thomas Donoho to William Roper proved by Arthur Exum.

Deed/gift Richard Waller to Joseph Waller 104 acres ackd.

Deed/lease Theophilus Allon to Milley Bloodworth for four years ackd.

Inventory/goods of Robert Hobdy decd proved by executors of sd deceased.

Inventory/goods of Simon Elliott decd rendered by admr.

Commissioners apptd to settle with admx of Jacob Zeigler decd report settlement.

Commrs apptd to settle with admr/Nathl Latimer decd report settlement.

Admx of Benjamin Mires decd rendered inventory/goods of sd decd.

Samuel L Crawford produced license as atty at law; qualified.

p.138   Jno Mitchel esq, Hawkins Co, to take deposition of Lewis Cox or Richard Mitchell to prove execution of deed Peter Turney atty in fact for Michael Turney to Samuel Mitchell.

Tuesday Oct 3d 1797. Present James Winchester Thomas Donnell James Reese William Cage Witheral Latimer esquires.

Robert Searcy produced license to practice as atty; certified by Clerk of Davidson County Court that he had taken necessary oaths; admitted to practice in Sumner.

Jurors to Superior Court: Alexander Gwin Alexr Braden Jas Frazor William Edwards Tilmon Dixon Moore Stevenson William Gillaspie Jno Williams James Douglass George D Blackemore James Clendening Rhodham Rowlings.

Deed Edward Gwin to John Harpole 320 acres ackd.

Deed John Barkley to George D Blackmore 100 acres ackd.

John Dorris v Peter Lemon. Covt. Jan 1797 plf by Samuel Donelson; dft by Isham A Parker. Oct 1797 jury: Solomon Reese James Franklin Joseph McElwrath Richd Strother

OCTOBER 1797

Robert Steel John Dawson Adam Turner John Baker Ezekiel Lindsey Robert Anderson Edward Gwin John Sadler find for dft. Plaintiff to pay full costs of suit.

Jurors to January Term: Thomas Simpson John McMurtry John Garrison William Montgomery farmer[?] Job Hicks Jas Odam Robt Egnew Boston Martin Solomon Barnes Edmund Hall George Brown Robert Steel Wm Penny Jr Thomas Jimason James Graham Peter Turney Jeremiah Watson Isaac Towel Hugh Crawford Joshua Scott Wm Brigance Philip Howel Geo Tittle Reubin Douglass Zachariah Green Jas Franklin Smith Hansbrough Sion Perry Wm Maxey James Harrison Jno Gillaspie Isaac Pearis John More Richard Foster Capt James Wilson Robert Caruthers.

Deed Griffith Rutherford to Thomas Walker 110 acres ackd.

Deed Arthur Davis to Jonathan Hannum 120 acres proved by William Penny.

Order James Gwin & John Gwin guardians for Hannah Latimer William Latimer & Nathl Latimer expose to sale the personal estate of their wards afsd.

Order admrs of Benjamin Mires decd sell personal estate of sd deceased.

Joel Pate v Edward Hudson. Judgment that the defendant shall answer over--

Deed Thomas Donoho to Champness Mading 150 acres proved by James Sanders.

Hugh Elliott v James & John White. Jonathan Hannum, bail for Jno White surrenders him to Court; David White bail for defendant.

Deed Thomas Edwards to Nathan Edwards 100 acres ackd.

Deed Josiah Howel to Joel Holland 118 acres ackd.

p.139 Tavern Rates [omitted]. Court adjourns.

Wednesday Oct 4th 1797. Present Thomas Donnell William Cage Witheral Latimer Esqrs.

Robert Ellis v Ephraim Payton. Plea in abatement for want of bond.

Deed Edward Gwin to Nathan Allon 100 acres proven by Theophilus Allon.

State v Dempsey Kennedy. A&B. Jury William Montgomery Jas Watson William Maxey Laurence Zeigler Chas Carter Robert Anderson Robt Wilson John Dawson John Baker Jas McKinsey Jno Hamilton Lazarus Cotton find dft guilty. Fined ten cents.

Charles Harriman v Moses Moore. January 1797 sheriff levied on 200 acres joining James Hannah & Richard Waller; dft came not; judgment by default. Oct 1797 plf by Samuel Donelson prays his damage be ascertained. Jury Ezekiel Lindsey Robert Ellis Elisha Clary John Josey John Miller Jeremiah Dickins William Norris William Cartwright James Wornock John Looney Gabriel Black John Gardner find plaintiffs damages $800. Plaintiff recovers of defendant.

John Murphy v George Sheibly & Andrew Hoover. Archibald Hatcher delivers Sheibly. William Cartwright records his ear mark.

State v Joseph Benthall. For transporting free negroes to this State. Appearance bond $1500 to appear and to bring Anthony and London, suggested to be free, who were taken from Virginia without their consent, and by Benthall made slaves. William Benthall and James Cryer securities.

p.140 Thursday Oct 5th 1797. Present James Reese James Douglass William Cage and Witheral Latimer esquires. James Winchester, Thomas Mastin esquires.

Order admrs of Henry Loving decd sell personal estate of decedant.

Appt Jas Douglass & William Maxey guardians for Walter Loving Mary Loving William Loving Elizabeth Loving; bond $4000, James Winchester security.

Report of James Wilson William Wilson William Morgan John Morgan Robert Desha and Robert Shute who laid off road from Genl Winchester up Deshas Crk to Bledsoes Creek

JANUARY 1798

crossing the forks of Drakes Creek to the Kentucky line.
Appt Jno Morgan oversee/road from Croft mills; Jas Winchester furnish list/polls.
Appt Jno Sterns overseer/road from fork of Bledsoe Creek to the Kentucky line; James Winchester to furnish a list of polls to work on said road.
Appt Alexander McKee overseer/road by Col Manskers to middle fork of Red River; Witheral Latimer to furnish sd overseer with list of polls to work on sd road.
John Murphy v George Sheibly and Andrew Hoover. July 1797 plf by George Smith; dft by James Dohertie. Oct 1797 jury: Robert Bell John Baker Jeremiah Doxey Philip Howel Laurence Zeigler John Dawson Charles Carter Edward Gwin Peter Looney William Clary William Maxey James McKinsey assess plaintiffs damages to $58.81, also costs.
John Murphy v George Sheibly and Andrew Hoover. William Cartwright appearance bail for George Sheibly having failed to bring sd Sheibly, order Cartwright special bail. Wm Cartwright brings to Court sd Sheibly and surrenders him to Court.
Motion whether Ephraim Payton is resident of this State determined in negative.
Sheriff enters protest against insufficiency of the Jail.
Order Clerk to receive returns of taxable property.
Robert Ellis v Ephraim Payton. Dft by atty replevies personal property levied on by attachment; brings to Court William Gillaspie and Charles Carter bound to deliver into next Court afsd property, two negroes named Peter and Hannah and two pewter plates.
p.141 Financial statement of Reuben Cage, collector of public & County taxes for 1796 [omitted here, except that the following names appear in this statement: David Carson, Wm Atmore, Allon Jones, Benjamin Smith, William T Hughett, James Kitchen, Frederick Edwards, Thomas Harris, Dixon Marshall, Wm Jimason heirs.]
Court adjourns till Court in Course.   Thos Mastin

p.142 Court of Pleas & quarter Sessions first Monday January 1798 at house of Wm Gillaspie. Present William Cage Thomas Mastin Isaac Walton Esquires. Edwd Douglass.
Bond Kasper Mansker to Wm Montgomery to support title to 128 acres.
Bill/sale Elijah Hendrick to Obediah Hendrick & Jeremiah Hendrick two Negro boys named Dragon James and Jim Dragon James proved by Moses Echols.
Francis Fonvielle records a conditional line between him & James Wilson. Witness Jacob Houdeshell.
Appt Joel Blackwell constable, Capt Hansbroughs district, Thomas Mastin security.
Grand Jury: Reuben Douglass foreman William Montgomery Jeremiah Watson Smith Hansbrough Boston Martin William Maxey John Garrison Robert Steel William Brigance Job Hicks George Tittle Edmund Hall Zachariah Green.
Inventory/goods of Nicodemus Watson decd rendered by admr.
Acct/sales, estate of Chas Bratney decd proved by Saml White & Mary White admrs.
Grant admn/estate of Abijah Millins decd to Mary Millins relict/decd, bond $2000, Thomas Cribbins and Armstead Rogers securities.
Jacob Pickerel bond $500, Joseph Summers security to indemnify County of expenses of maintaining base born child of Mary Summers; paid his fine 50 shillings.
Inventory/sales of goods of Ephraim Farr decd rendered by admx.
Acct/sales of Benjamin Mears decd rendered by admx.
Authorize Joseph Bishop keep ferry on Cumberland River at mouth of Falling Creek,

JANUARY 1798

to be rated agreeable to ferries at Ft Blount & Cainey fork; Martin Douglass sec.
Thomas Draper v John Murphy. John Tait garnishee has articles, list filed.
Authorize Sampson Williams to keep ferry on Cumberland at Ft Blount; Henry Bradford security; ferry rates to be same as last year.
License Sampson Williams to keep an ordinary at his house at Fort Blount, Edward Jinnings security.
John Patterson records his ear mark.
Ltr/atty Obed Hendrick of Hallifax County Virginia to Jeremiah Hendrick to convey 440 acres Drakes Crk to Thomas S Spencer proved by Moses Achols & David Allon.
Deed James Wilson Sr to Jacob Houdeshell 182 acres proved by Francis Fonvielle.
Deed Samuel Fleming to Jacob Lewis 320 acres proved by James McNight.
p.143 Deeds ackd & proved: William Morgan to Henry Gambell. Roderick Jinkins to James Cryer proved by Stephen Brown. Robert Marley to William Donnell proved by John Foster. Robert Marley to William Donnell proved by Robert Foster. Robert Marley to John Foster proved by Robert Foster. Robert Marley to Alexander Foster proved by Robert Foster. Joseph & John Fleming to John Foster and William McClain proved by Robert Foster. Joseph Hendrick to John Hays. Edward Gwin to John Garrison. Edward Gwin to Joab Hicks. John Hays to Joseph Hendrick. Thomas Donoho to Benjamin Ellis proved by James Ellis. Henry Turney to John Looney proved by Peter Turney. James Douglass to James Morrison. Thomas Donoho to David Ventura proved by John Hargis. William Walton to Isaac Walton proved by Jesse Sheen. James Douglass to Henry Lyon.
Bills/sale: Uridice Mears admx of Ben Mears decd to Humphry Mears two Negroes James & Tom ackd. James Cryer to Roderick Jinkins two Negro girls, Marriam & Rose, ackd. Uridice Myars admx Ben Myars decd to Anthony Sharp negro girl Sarah proved by David Shelby. Joseph Penrice to Moore Cotton Negro girl Lucy proved by Stephen Brown.
Ltr/atty John Grant of Kentucky to Robert Hays to convey moiety of Henry Doughertys preemption to John Morgan proved by Hallery Melone.
Ltr/atty Hen Dougherty to John Grant to convey 320 acres part of sd Doughertys preemption to John Morgan proved by William Morgan.
Report of jury apptd to lay off road from Fort Blount to Bledsoe Crk thence to Nashville road. Road ought to go from Fort Blount to William Youngs plantation on Paytons Crk, leaving old road & passing between his house & corn crib and thence through the gap to intersect old road at John Bostons plantation, old road to Peter Turneys passing through old Hessions field and assess damage $6, at Turneys leave old road, go to Bellews on Dixons Creek to Dixons lick, up same to where Mungles trace crosses, to Goose crk, to the bluff above Hickisons branch to Donohos North p.144 boundary near widow Hickesons field to road from Greenfield to Goose Crk to where McConnells live, to Gipsons trace to Deshas ford on Bledsoes Crk to Deshas fork below Mr Blythes plantation, thence Kuykendalls field to Caruthers plantation to path to meeting house to Nashville road at Curley Wilsons. The new road is at least three miles shorter than the old road and the ground is entirely above the back water. Sampson Williams Andrew Blythe James Clendening James Morrison Hallery Melone Uriah Anderson.
James Winchester to furnish lists of polls to work on sd road to following road overseers: Robert Caruthers, James Clendening, Montgomery McConnell, Peter Turney.
Bond Francis Graves to Edmund Jinnings proven by Sampson Williams.
Appt James Winchester & James Reese esqrs to settle with admn of Jas Steel decd.
Rules of doing business in this Court established.

JANUARY 1798

Tuesday January 2d 1798. Present Thos Donnell Wm Cage Jas Reese Isaac Walton Esqr.
Deed Samuel Mitchell to Richard Alexander & William Lock Alexander 640 acres proven by William Alexander.
Deed Tilmon Dixon to Jeremiah Thacker 50 acres proven by Larkin Thacker.
Jesse Carter v Joel Thornton. Wm Alexander dfts bail surrenderes dft to Court.
Appt John Berkley overseer/Cany fork road from Dixons spring to Paytons creek, Davis, Oneel, & Robt Bowman and all below road & above Dixons Creek work thereon.
Deed Henry Loving to Alexander Graham 180 acres proved by Walter Maxey.
James Winchester Edwd Douglass Witheral Latimer & Jas Douglass take their seats.
County tax laid [omitted].
State v Joseph Benthall. Dft failing to appear, forfeits recognizance.
State v William Benthall & James Cryer. Joseph Benthall failing to appear, his
p.145 securities forfeit their bond.
State v Dempsey Kennedy. A&B. Jury James Odam Thomas Jimason James Graham Peter Turney Isaac Towell Hugh Crawford Philip Howel James Franklin Sion Perry James Harrison Isaac Pearce John Moore find dft not guilty.
Joel Pate v Edward Hudson. Jan 1797 plf by Jas Dohertie; dft by Seth Lewis. Jan 1798 Jury[above] assess plfs damage $4. Also costs.
Whereas Zachariah Betts to whom orphan Wm Brooks was bound as apprentice 9 Jan 1794 has made it appear sd apprentice is not capable of learning the trade to which he was bound or to read write & figure agreeable to sd indenture, order Betts be released from sd obligation.
Deeds ackd & proved: James Douglass to Albert Holmes. Samuel Barton to Robert Johnston by proved John Walker. James Sanders to John Laurence. Matthew McCormack to Isaac Lindsey proved by Isaac Green. Nathaniel Parker to James Douglass.
Court lays tax for defraying a debt to North Carolina contracted in escorting families through the wilderness [omitted].

Wednesday January 3d 1798. Present James Winchester James Reese William Cage Esqrs.
Under seal of Gov. John Sevier, Thomas Blackmore apptd justice/peace; took oaths.
Bill/sale John Wood to Wilson Cage for negro man Ned proved by Seth Lewis.
Deed Theopholus Allon to Thomas Bloodworth 50 acres proved by Wm Bloodworth.
John Hamilton exhibited license, took oaths as an attorney at law.
Timothy Chandler v Stephen Anderson. Jury Peter Turney Isaac Fonviell James Harrison James Franklin Hugh Crawford James Odam Philip Howel Nathaniel Parker James Billew James Graham Thomas Jimason Wm Snoddy. Mistrial.
p.146 Appointments to take lists/taxable property: James Winchester in Capt Williams & Capt Murrys Compy. James Reese in Capt Reeds Compy. David Wilson in Capt Wilsons compy. James Douglass in Capt Snoddies Compy. Wm Cage in Capt Lunas Compy. Stephen Cantrill in Capt Cantrills compy. Witheral Latimer in Capt Hamiltons Compy. Thomas Mastin in Capt Hansbroughs Compy. Edward Douglass in Capt Stevensons Compy.
William Beard records his ear mark.
James Winchester records his ear mark.
Allow $10 to Jacob Parkes, William Stringfield, & Simon Kuykendall for guarding prisoners to the district Jail.
Appt Richard Hogin gdn for Jonathan Kuykendall, bond $500, Sion Perry security.

Thursday January 4th 1798. Present James Winchester James Reese Edward Douglass

JANUARY 1798

Witheral Latimer, Esquires. Wm Cage, Thomas Masten Thomas Donnell James Douglass.
Ambrose Porter v Abraham Hardin. Dft failing to appear, Judgt by default entered agt him; court orders property whereon attachment was levied to be sold.
Isaac Towell records his ear mark.
Lazarus Cotton v George Norris. Apl 1797 plf by Seth Lewis; dft by James Dohertie. Jan 1798 jury: James Odam James Graham Peter Turney Isaac Towell Hugh Crawford Philip Howell James Harrison Isaac Pearce James Wornock Richard Hogin Wm Snoddy Jno Gillaspie. No declaration filed; dft recovers of plf his full costs of suit.
David Beard v Hezekiah Oneill. Debt. Oct 1797 plf by Saml Donelson; dft by George Smith. Jan 1798 jury[above] find for plf $130.45. With costs.
Edward Douglass v David White. Oct 1797 plf by Saml Donelson; dft came not. Judgt by default agt dft. Jan 1798 jury[above] find plfs damage $27.93½. With costs.
p.147 Deed Joseph Hendrick to David Shelby 322 acres.
Deed/gift: William Phipps to James Lain 50 acres proved by Isaac Lain.
Deed/gift: William Phipps to Isaac Lain 50 acres proved by James Lain.
Robert Ellis v Ephraim Payton. David Shelby garnishee has $15.62½ of dft, being half of judgment obtained by John & Ephraim Payton v Thomas Cribbins.
Petition by Edmund Jinnings to have land of Francis Graves decd divided. Appoint Peter Turney Jas Balen Christian Boston with Sampson Williams Surveyor for purpose.
Jurors for April Term: William McCorkle Zach Wilson Robert Desha Samuel Harris John Sadler Will Alexander Greenfield William Reed Ezekiel Douglass William Lauderdale Nathaniel Gilmore Lewis Crane William Douglass Robert Shaw Robert Duggan Michael Caveatt William Montgomery (Ment[?]) Joseph McElwarath Christopher Cooper Owan Dillard Thomas Waller William Sanders (Dixon Crk) Matthew Cartwright Edward Gwin William Nowlin William Wier James Whitsitt John Withers William Bowan James Franklin Thomas Edwards Robert Ellis William Barrow David Lane James Wilson (Capt) Jacob Thomas Thomas Harris.
Robt Ellis v Ephraim Payton. Bond of John Deloach Sion Perry James McKinsey to plf Robert Ellis condition they produce to next Court two negroes Peter & Hannah.
Deed Thomas Edwards to Robert Ellis two acres proved by James Douglass.
Two deeds Elisha Rice for himself & as executor of John Rice decd and as atty in fact for Nathan Rice William H Rice & Joel Rice, 320 acres and 426½ acres to David Shelby ackd by sd Elisha Rice.
Charles Harriman v Moses Moore. Property attached to be sold.
Allow Sheriff $50 for exofficio services from 1st July 1796 to same 1797.
Allow Clerk $40 for exofficio services from 1st July 1796 to same 1797.
Deed Edward Douglass to James Winchester one moiety of 640 acres ackd.
Release Charles Petigrew from 1797 tax on 800 acres lying in Indian bounds.
State v John Jones & Elizabeth Jones. Selling spiritous liquors without license. Defendants submit; fined £50. Reconsidered; fine remitted.
Court adjourns till Court in Course.   Edward Douglass

p.148 Court of Pleas & Quarter Sessions at house of William Gallaspie first Monday in April 1798. Present William Cage Thomas Masten James Gwin Witheral Latimer.
Inventory of sales of goods of Nathaniel Latimer decd returned by James Gwin.
Jacob Thomas records his ear mark.

APRIL 1798

Allow James Gwin coroner receive $4 for holding inquest on body of negro Peter, property of Charles Carter.

State v Matthew Cowan. Trespass A&B. Dft submits; fined 25¢ and costs.

State v Matthew Cowan. Trespass A&B. Dft submits; fined 25¢ and costs.

Deeds acknowledged & proved: William Cage to Reubin Cage. Roger Gibson to John Withers proved by Gabriel Black. William Brigance to William Stalcup proved by Samuel Stalcup. John Withers to George Gabriel Black. William Benthall to Laban Benthall proved by James Cryer. Robert Sharp to Jacob Thomas proved by Joseph McElwrath.

Lease Wallis Estill of one part & Henry Truitt & Elijah Truett by Robert Steel.

Deed of Laban Benthall to Wm Benthall, Rhody Benthall, Enos Benthall & Mary Benthall for stock household furniture &c and 150 acres land ackd.

Deed/gift Robert Espey to John Espey and Alexander Espey land whereon sd Robert liveth proved by Drury Milam.

Deed/gift Robert Espey to John Espey & Alexander Espey personal estate of sd Robert proved by Drury Milam.

Allow James Morrison keep ferry on Cumberland River opposite Station Camp Crk; bond $1250 with Samuel Snoddy security.

License James Cryer to keep ordinary at his dwelling, John Josey security.

Tuesday April 3d 1798. Present Edwd Douglass Thos Mastin Witheral Latimer Esqrs.

Deed Tilmon Dixon to Joseph & Wm Clark 640 acres proved by Larkin Thacker.

Deed Tilmon Dixon to Joseph & Wm Clark 403½ acres proved by Larkin Thacker.

Deed Robert Looney to Hugh Elliott 224 acres ackd.

Grand Jury: William Douglass foreman Joseph McElwrath William Wier William McCorcle John Sadler Edward Gwin Matthew Cartwright Samuel Harris Robert Desha John Withers Ezekiel Douglass Thomas Edwards Robert Shaw. James Vinson constable apptd to attend grand jury.

Samuel Donelson Esq resigned his appointment as county solicitor; at same time George Smith is appointed solicitor for the County in his stead.

p.149 Will of Mary Hellin decd proved by Paul Harpole; Jas Winchester exr qualified; retd inventory of goods &c of sd decd. Order horses of estate to be sold.

Acct/sales & supplemental inventory of Henry Loving decd rendered by admr.

State v Thomas Sharp admr/Egnew v William McMann & Alexr Dobbins. Debt. Dft in proper person confessed judgment $25.97 and costs.

James Wornock v Elijah McKinny. April 1797 Sheriff levied on horse & saddle; dft by atty Isham A Parker replevied property. Apr 1798 jury William Alexander William Reed Lewis Crain Christopher Cooper James Cryer Robert Looney William Bruce Thomas Draper Montgomery McConnell Richard King Elisha Clary Andrew Blythe who find plfs damage $32.25. With costs.

Thomas Donnell Esq deposited in Clerks office $3.12½ collected as fine of Polly Taylor for having a base born child.

James Lane records his ear mark.

William Reed records his ear mark & brand.

Lists/taxable property retd by David Wilson James Winchester Witheral Latimer.

Commissioners report they settled with admrs of James Steel decd.

William Lowther v James Cooper & Edwd Bradley. Debt. Dfts in proper person confessed judgment $60.76 and costs of suit.

David Wilson Jas Winchester Wm Cage Jas Reese & James Douglass took their Seats.

APRIL 1798

Appt Milly Edwards James Douglass & Charles Dement guardians for Clarissa Edwards John Edwards, William Edwards, & Benjamin Edwards orphans of John Edwards deceased.
Charles Donoho & John Morgan commissioned justices/peace by Gov John Sevier.
Deeds acknowledged & proved: Elisha Davis to Samuel Gray 274 acres. William Green to James Mason 227 acres proved by Thomas Mastin. John Roberts to Samuel Cross 320 acres. James Winchester to William Alexander 25 acres 30 poles proved by George D
p.150   Blackmore. Matthew Alexander to William Alexander 50 acres proved by George D Blackmore. David Wilson to Zacheus Wilson. James Winchester to Samuel White 100 acres. Obediah Terrell to Paul Harpole 136 acres proved by George Stout. David Wilson to Perigan Taylor 120 acres. Joseph Motheral to David Wilson 50 acres proved by James A Wilson. William Wilson to Zebulon Brevard 100 acres proved by James A Wilson. Thomas Donoho to James Hartt proved by Wm Alexander. Thomas Harris by atty in fact David Wilson to James Hart. James Winchester to James Blythe. John Payton to William Crabtree. Robert Dobbins to Whitehead Joiner. Robert Dobbins to George Wotwood. Henry Turney to John Barnes by Peter Turney.
Bill/sale Thos Cocke to Wm Beard negro boy Charles proved by George D Blackmore.
Release Ephraim Payton to John Payton proved by Charles Blalock.
Bill/sale Uridice Mears admx/Benjn Mears decd to Nathan Edwards two Negroes Esther and Frank proved by James Douglass.
Bond Ananias McCoy to Peter Turney 500 acres proved by John Roberts.
Commrs & surveyor apptd Jan 1798 on petition of Edmund Jinnings to divide land of Francis Graves decd report proceedings and plat of tract.
Supplement/acct of sales of John Edwards decd rendered by admx.
James Reese returns list/taxable property in Capt Reeds Company.
Deed John Hinds to Wm Campbell sundry tracts/land certified by Thomas Bodley clerk of Lexington District Kentucky.

Wednesday April 4th 1798. Present David Wilson James Winchester James Douglass Esq.
Deeds proved: Thomas Donoho to Patrick Donoho 100 acres Charles Donoho. Hardy Royall & Rachel Royall to Charles Hays 640 acres proved by Ann McLendon.
Deed/lease William Pryor to Henry Newby 200 acres proved by Tomson Newby.
James Douglass esq rendered list of taxable property in Capt Snoddies Compy.
Order Edwd Douglass & Stephen Cantrill esqrs settle with admrs/John Edwards decd.
p.151   Deed Thomas Donoho to Arthur Exum 476 acres proved by William Cathy.
William Cage esq returns list/taxable property in Capt Lunas Company.
Deed Thomas Donoho to Charles Donoho 360 acres 36 poles proved by Wm Cathy.
Deed Thomas Donoho to William Sanders 790 acres proved by William Cathy.
State v Edward Bradley. A&B. Defendant submits; fined $1 and costs.
Thomas Sharp admr/Egnew agt John Beson & Edward Hogin, sd Beson surrendered.
Tavern rates set [omitted here].
Deed Thomas Donoho to William Cathy 300 acres proved by Thomas Walker.
Deed Thomas Donoho to John Cathy 200 acres proved by Thomas Walker.
Bill/sale Joel Holland to Charles Dement negro boy Virgil proved by Jas Douglass.
Deed Thomas Mairy[Many?] to Francis Hollinshead 240 acres ackd.
State v John Pankey. Retailing liquors higher than rates. Jury Wm Alexander Wm Reed Lewis Crane Wm Montgomery Chrisr Cooper Owan Dillard Wm Nolen Robt Ellis Joshua Scott Jeremiah Doxey Jas Billew Peter Looney find dft guilty.
Deed John Gatlin to John Payton 228 acres ackd.
Deed George Cummins to Philip Kiser 600 acres ackd.

APRIL 1798

Bill/sale Philip Kiser to George Cummins negro girl Winny ackd.
Bill/sale William Nowlin to Philip Kiser negro girl Winny ackd.
State v John Stamps. Retailing spirits without license. Dft submits; fined $1.
Inventory/goods of Abijah Millins decd proved by admx.
License John Stamps to keep ordinary at his dwelling, Thomas Edwards security.
p.152 State v Joseph Benthall. Dft files affidavit; released from forfeiture of his recognizance and is discharged from custody of the sheriff on paying costs.
State v James Cryer & Wm Benthall. Dfts released from forfeiture/recognizance.
Order road laid off by James Gwin Wm Carr John Carr Elisha Ogelsby Richd Brittain Daniel Mangle & Andrew Green between Dixons Creek and Goose Creek to Kentucky line.
State v Henry Morris. Branding a heifer not his own. Jury William Alexander Lewis Crain Wm Reed Wm Nolin Owan Dillard Richd Hogin Jas Cryer Peter Turney Wilson Cage Wm Anderson Thos Draper Gabriel Black return special verdict: heifer is not proven to be property of any other person. Charge not supported by law; acquits dft.
David Wilson esq deposited fine of Polly Ward for having base born child $6.25; also fine of Henry Morris for profane swearing 92¢.
Samuel Barton assignee of Robt Dean who was assignee of Anthony Rogers agt James Hannah, note/hand 10 July 1792; suit determined agt sd Barton who comes into Court; prays Clerk deliver sd note to him, & is bound in penalty $500.
State v Henry Lyon. Retailing spirits higher than rates. Dft submits; fined.
State v Henry Lyon. [as above]
Commrs report they settled with admrs of John Edwards decd.

Thurs April 5th 1798. Present Jas Winchester David Wilson Thos Masten Isaac Walton.
Deed Josiah Watson by Charles J Love his atty in fact to John Caffery & George M Deaderick 1428 acres proved by Archibald Lewis.
Deed Josiah Watson by Chas J Love his atty in fact to John Caffery & George M Deaderick ten 640 acre tracts of land proved by Archibald Lewis.
Tyre Harris v James McKain. Debt. Dft in proper person confesses judgt $25 with interest; stay of execution four months.
p.153 License Shadrick Nye & Co keep ordinary at their dwelling, Geo Smith sec.
Executors of Isaac Bledsoe decd report division made by Daniel Smith & James Winchester of land divised by decedant to his two daughters Salley Bledsoe now Sally Gibson & Catey Bledsoe [land description here omitted].
William Bowan v William Dobbins. July 1797 plf by Francis Hall; dft by Seth Lewis. Apl 1798 jury Wm Alexander Wm Reed Lewis Crane Chrisr Cooper Owan Dillard Wm Nolin Robert Ellis Thos Walker John DeLoach Jas Baker Edmund Jinnings Wm Montgomery find for dft; deft recovers of plf the full costs of sd suit.
Jurors to Superior Court: James Wilson Jr Sampson Williams James Harrison Gabriel Black James Sanders Jno Payton James Watson Andrew Green Jr Richard Caveatt William Montgomery (mercht) Hugh Crawford Thomas Simpson.
Deed William Smothers to James Roads 108½ acres proved by Shadrick Nyes.
Edward Douglass & Co v Robert Dobbins. Covt. Octr 1797 plf by Saml Donelson; dft by James Dohertie. April 1798 jury: David Lain Robert Jones Peter Looney Rhodeham Rowlings Edwd Hudson John Orr Wm Montgomery Edwd Hogin Richd Hogin Jno Payton James Billens Zachariah Green assess plfs damage $26.01½. With costs.
Thomas Sharp admr of Egnew v Terry Poe & James McKain. Debt. Dfts failing to appear, judgt by default for $37.50.
Thomas Sharp admr/Egnew v William Walton. Debt. Dft failing to appear, judgt by

APRIL 1798

default debt with interest $19.99.
Edward Douglass & Thomas Mastin esqrs return lists/taxable property by them taken for Captain Stevensons and Hansbroughs companies.
p.154   Charles Dement v William Standley. July 1797 Shff levied on 500 ac. Jan 1798 judgt by default. Apl 1798 plf by Seth Lewis prays damage be ascertained. Jury [above] find damage $356.42½. With costs.
Aquilla Dolerhide for meritorious acts has been legally liberated by his master Laurence Thompson, and is in future a free man of color.
Ezekiel Douglass v Richard Hogin. Oct 1797 plf by Robt Hamilton; dft by Seth Lewis. Apl 1798 jury Wm Reed Lewis Crane Chrisr Cooper Owan Dillard Wm Nolin Robt Ellis Thos Walker John Deloach Edmund Jinnings Alexr Braden Chas Dement John Gardner assess plfs damage $7.33. With costs.
License Wm Gillaspie to keep ordinary at his dwelling, William Cage security.
Jurors to July Term: Richard Alexander Thomas Jimason John Shelton William Sanders Junr [illegible] William Lauderdale Daniel Mungle William Hall Thomas Parker son of Nathaniel William Morgan David Beard Samuel King William Morrison Junr John Anderson James McKlin James Caruthers Robert Wilson Robert Pearson John Hamilton Jr William Thomas James Whitts William Perry John Perry Richard Jones Laurence Turning Nathaniel Gilmore Matthew Alexander James Espey William Anderson Alancon Trigg Jonathan Pearce John Railey Armstead Rogers Isaac Towel James Montgomery John McMurtry Alexander Graham.
Patrollers apptd: Reubin Douglass Robert Looney Moore Cotton for Capt Stevensons company to qualify before Edward Douglass Esqr. Zachariah Green James Norris John Gardner for Capt Loonas Company; to qualify before Edward Douglass Esqr.
Appt James Winchester & David Wilson to settle with admr of Benjamin Kuykendall.
Deed Francis Hall to Jesse Scheen 274 acres proved by Isaac Walton.
Deed Anthony Sharp to Elmore Douglass 250 acres proved by William Cage.
Commissioners report they settled with admr of Benjamin Kuykendall decd.
p.155   Hugh Elliott admr/Simon Ellis decd v James White & John White. Oct 1797 plf by Seth Lewis; Jan 1798 defendant came not; judgment by default. Apl 1798 jury [above] find plfs damage $219.16. With costs.
Unpaid taxes for 1796; judgment against David Carson, William Atmore, Allon Jones, Benjamin Smith, William T Hughett, James Kitchen, Frederick Edwards, Thomas Harris, Dixon Marshall, William Jimasons heirs; order sheriff sell so much of properties as will satisfy debts.

Friday April 6th 1798. Present David Wilson Thos Mastin Jas Reese Thos Donnell.
Suspend order for road Deshas Crk to Nashville rd, part of Ft Blount road.
State v Henry Lyon. Retailing spirits without license. Dft fined $1 and costs.
Appt Reubin Cage collector of taxes for 1798; Edwd Douglass & Saml Donelson sec.
Jesse Carter v Joel Thornton. Covt. Jan 1798 plaintiff by George Smith; dft came not; judgt by default. Jury to ascertain damages Ezekiel Lindsey Peter Luna Robert Steel Lazarus Cotton Lewis Crain Christopher Cooper Owan Dillard William Nolin William Alexander Isaac Lindsey Rhodeham Rowlings John Payton find plaintiffs damage $54.85. With costs.
Edward Douglass appears and takes his seat.
Ephraim Payton v Lazarus Cotton. Dft bond $500, Edward Douglass & William Cage securities, condition sd Cotton deliver negro girl Nann to next Court.
p.156   Joseph Fanning v William Sanders. Jan 1798 plf by Randal McGavock; dft by

APRIL 1798

Thos Stuart. Apl 1798 jury Ezekiel Lindsey Peter Looney Robt Steel Lazarus Cotton Lewis Crain Christopher Cooper Owan Dillard Wm Nolin Wm Alexander Isaac Lindsey Rhodeham Rowlings John Payton find for dft. Plf obtains appeal, William P Anderson and Isaac McNutt his securities.

James Winchester v John Murphy. Jan 1798 Shff levied on land where John Tait now lives; dft came not; judgt by default. Apl 1798 plf by Geo Smith; jury to ascertain damage: Robert Ellis David Lain Sion Perry Robert Dobbins Edward Hogin Michael Ward Richd Hogin William Norris William Hoge William Neville John Gallaspie Joseph T Williams find damage $22.66. With costs.

William Par v John Murphy. Jan 1798 Shff levied on allotment in hands of Thomas Draper garnishee. Apl 1798 plf by George Smith; jury to ascertain damages: Robert Ellis David Lain Sion Perry Robert Dobbins Edward Hogin Michael Ward Richard Hogan William Norris William Hoge William Nevill John Gallaspie Joseph T Williams find plaintiffs damage $27.75. With costs.

Edward Settle v John Murphy. Jan 1798 sheriff levied on land whereon John Tait now lives. Apl 1798 plf by Samuel Donelson; jury to ascertain damages Robert Ellis David Lain Sion Perry Robt Dobbins Edward Hogin Michael Ward Richard Hogin William Norris William Hoge William Nevills Jno Gallaspie Joseph T Williams find plaintiffs damage $65.70. With costs.

Ambrose Porter v Abraham Hardin. Jan 1798 sheriff levied on a horse. April 1798 jury: Robt Ellis David Lane Sion Perry Robt Dobbins Edwd Hogin Michael Ward Richard Hogin William Norris William Hoge William Nevill John Gillaspie Joseph T Williams find damage $124.80. With costs.

p.157 Thomas Draper v John Murphy. Jan 1798 shff levied in hands of John Tait summoned as garnishee, also on 400 acres Bledsoes Crk, and summoned Anthony Pate a garnishee; dft came not; judgment by default. Apl 1798 plf by George Smith; jury to ascertain damages Robt Ellis David Lain Sion Perry Robt Dobbins Edwd Hogin Michael Ward Richd Hogin Wm Norris Wm Hoge William Nevill John Gallaspie Joseph T Williams find plaintiffs damage $147.10. With costs.

William Nevells v Isaac Lindsey. Appeal. Plf by Geo Smith; dft by Saml Donelson. Jury Wm Alexander John Payton Wm Nolen Robt Looney Rhodeham Rollings Robt Ellis Peter Looney John Deloach Lazarus Cotton Chrisr Cooper Owan Dillard Adam Harpole find for dft; defendant recovers of plf the full costs expended.

Nevills v Lindsey. Dfts atty motion to admit Martin Nevells as witness overruled.

Jos Fanning v Wm Sanders; Clerk to deliver note to plf.

State v John Pankey. Continued.

William Nevells v Isaac Lindsey. New trial not granted.

Saturday April 7th 1798. Present David Wilson Edward Douglass Wm Cage Thos Mastin.

Clerk to give shff writ at instance of Thomas Sharp admr of Egnew decd v Henry Stajner[Stazner?] & John White, previous writ having been lost.

Order D Shelby Clerk receive $25 to purchase books for the use of his office.

Order Sheriff sell property attached by Ezekiel Douglass of John Murphy.

Thomas Sharp admr of Egnew decd v John Beson & Edward Hogin. Debt. Apr 1798 plf by Saml Donelson; dfts failed to appear. Judgment by default $98.88 agt them. Court decrees that plaintiff recover of dfts afsd sum with costs.

John Plunkit v Benjamin Kuykendall. Debt. Jan 1798 plf by Saml Donelson; alias writ issued against Reuben Martin; retd April 1798 non est inventus; judgt $56.65.

Court adjourns till Court in Course.   David Wilson

JULY 1798

p.158 Court of Pleas & Quarter Sessions at house of Wm Gallaspie first Monday in July 1798. Present Thomas Donnell Thomas Masten Isaac Walton James Gwin Esquires.

Grand Jury William Sanders foreman Nathl Gilmore Richard Jones William Perry Thomas Jimason John Perry John Anderson Armstead Rogers William Morrison James Whitsitt James Montgomery Thomas Parker William Hall.

Charles Elliott v John Withers. Debt. Dft in proper person confesses judgt $80.

Ltr/atty William Benthall to James Cryer proved by David Shelby.

Clerk to receive returns of taxable property.

John Carr Wm Carr Elisha Ogelsby Andw Green Richd Britton James Gwin report they laid off a road between Dixons Creek & Goose Creek to Kentucky line.

Release heirs of Charles Gerard from tax on 3000 acres twice listed.

James McKain v David Adams. Zachariah Green, bail, surrenders Adams to sheriff.

Bind John Witt White, orphan, unto James Rather until age 21.

Shadrick Nye records his ear mark.

Alexander Piper bond $500 with Samuel Piper security for maintenance of base born child of Sally Norton; paid his fine $3.12½.

Appt Jesse Hainey overseer/road from Maj Jas White to Second crk; Thos Blackmore to furnish list of polls to work with sd overseer.

Appt Jas White overseer/road Bledsoe crk to his own house; Thos Blackemore to furnish overseer with list of polls to work with sd overseer.

Appt Jas Hart overseer/road lately layd off between Dixons crk & Goose crk to KY line, from sd line to second fork; James Gwin to furnish list of polls.

Appt Danl Mungle overseer on middle section of above road; Jas Gwin furnish list.

p.159 Appt Wm Carr overseer/sd rd from Jas Gwins; Jas Gwin furnish list/polls.

Order Saml Barton John Harpole Elmore Douglass Thos George & Martin Harpole lay road from mouth of Cany fork to Davidson line south of Cumberland River.

Deeds acknowledged & proved: David Beard to William Barrow. Richard Gordon and Susannah Gordon admrs of William Fork decd to Matthew Payne proved by David Beard. William Morrison to William Bell. Robert Weakley to Thomas Simpson proved by Peter Luna. Thomas Simpson to William Perry proved by Josiah Perry. Hardy Jones to Aaron Lambert proved by Avery Lambert. Benjamin Sheppard to Robert Taylor proved by Robt Taylor Junr. Samuel White to Robert Bratney. Samuel Gray to Joseph Peyton. Oliver Williams admr of Francis Graves decd to Edmund Jinnings proved by George Smith. Jane Kuykendall to Patrick Gibson proved by Reubin Cage. Charles Dungworth to William Stone proved by William Burk. John Sloss to Elias Morrison by Joseph McAdams. George Purtle to Daniel Alexander. Andrew Steel to Shadrick Nye proved by John Turner. Samuel Barton to Wilie Cherry proved by Thomas Seawell. John Baker to James Maxcey by Cordall Norfleet. Thomas Hoffler to John Baker proved by Cordall Norfleet. Thomas Hoffler to John Baker by Cordall Norfleet. James Godfrey to Joseph Latimer proved by Alexander Gwin. James Godfrey to Witheral Latimer proved by Alexander Gwin.

Deed/lease Moses Echols to James C Hodges land on Bartons Creek ackd.

Bill/sale John Carter to John Mills negro boy Jacob proved by Zachariah Green.

Bill/sale John White to James A Wilson horned cattle proved by David Wilson.

Bill/sale John White to Wm Wilson one man & two cows proved by David Wilson.

Deed/gift Susannah Benthall to Elizabeth Benthall Charlotte Benthall Frances Benthall Mary Benthall Susannah Benthall 3 negroes Darkess Sall & Ross, three beds and furniture and one colt proved by James Cryer.

JULY 1798

p.160 Tuesday July 3d 1798. Present David Wilson James Reese Thomas Donnell Isaac Walton Esquires.

Release Jeremiah Watson from tax on 260 acres & 2 black polls listed twice.

Order Tilman Dixon Peter Turney Andw Green Robt Loony James Billen Thos Jimason mark a road from Dixons Spring to Mongles Gap.

Tilmon Dixon commissioned Justice/peace took oaths for qualification.

Allow James Hart to keep ferry north side Cumberland River below mouth of Goose Creek; bond $1250 with Charles Dunoho security.

Release William T Lewis from tax on 2560 acres listed in name of Francis Graves.

Appt John Sterns guardian for Robert Steel George Steel & Joseph Steel orphans of James Steel decd; bond $500, Richard Alexander and Hallery Malone securities.

Order Chas Donoho Richd Brittain Danl Mungle Jas Hart Jno Carr Danl Alexander to mark road from Harts ferry to road lately laid off.

Order property whereon attachment at instance of Charles Dement agt Wm Standley was levied be condemned for use of judgment and to be exposed to sale.

Deed Demcy Moore to Benjamin Fowlar 260 acres proved by Richard Cooke.

Appt Hallery Malone constable for Capt Reeds company; John Sterns & Wm Hall sec.

Appt Alexander Cathy constable for Capt Bradleys compy; Wm Hall & Wm Sanders sec.

Jesse Wharton produced license to practice as atty; took oaths for qualification.

State v Thomas Adams. Trespass A&B. Dft submits to law; fine $50, reduced to $25.

Appt Reubin Cage sheriff; Henry Bradford & Thomas Blackmore securities.

Appt James Gwin coroner, Wm Cage & James Reese securities.

p.161 License Henry Lyon to keep ordinary at his dwelling, Edward Gwin and James Hart securities.

Appt James Whitsitt Richd Jones Robt Perry patrollers for Capt Cantrills company; they are to qualify before Isaac Walton esquire.

Appt William Alexander Jr Champ Madden & Thos Walker patrollers for Capt Bradleys district; they are to qualify before Charles Donoho esquire.

Deeds proved: Wallace Estill to Hugh Barr proved by John Morgan. Abraham Kennedy to John K Wynne proved by John Brown. Frederick Ward to John Brown proved by John K Wynne. Thomas Donoho to Edward Donoho proved by Charles Donoho. Thomas Isbell to John Martin proved by Randall Miller. Matthew Anderson to James McKnight proved by John Deloach. Peter Hansbrough to James Dix proved by James Sanders.

Mortgage Jane Kuykendall to Peter Luna P for 274 acres proved by Reuben Cage.

Deed/gift Jno Wright to James Wright personal property proved by Elmore Douglass.

Bill/sale William White to William Snoddy negro boy Stephen ackd.

Ltr/attorney Abram Swett to Rhoadham Rowlings proved by Joshua White.

Edward Settle v John Murphy. Property levied on whereon John Tait then lived condemned for use of the judgment and ordered to be sold by the sheriff.

James Kelly v Nathaniel Parker. Thomas Parker special bail for defendant.

Two Certificates issued to Robert Edmunston as witness in suit Jason Thompson v James McKain were destroyed by fire before the amount was applyed to benefit of sd Edmunston, Clerk to issue duplicates of said certificates.

Appt Robert Wilson constable for Captain Vinsons company; bond $625, with David Wilson security.

Jurors to October Term: William Orr Thomas Britton Laurence Tenning Laurence Whitsitt Matthew Alexander William Beard Thomas Cocke William Par Joshua Hadley Thomas Murry James Rankin John Dawson Frederick Miller Peter Looney H Archibald Marlin Hugh Crawford John Josey James Frazor Griswold Latimer John Norris James Watson Charles Blalock William Parmer George Gallaspie Lewis Crain William

OCTOBER 1798

Harrington Joseph Crabtree Michael Sweetman, James A Wilson Robert Wilson Robert Carithers Thomas Patton William Thomas Josiah Hewitt Isaac Lain John Golston.
Order William Montgomery overseer/road Drakes Cr to 20 mile tree; Edward Douglass esquire to furnish sd overseer with a list of polls to work with sd overseer.
Order Richard Jones overseer of road from 20 mile tree to Mansker Creek; Stephen Cantrill esq to furnish list of polls to work on said road.
p.162   Appt Henry Vinson constable for Capt Stevensons Compy; James McKinsey sec.
Thos Masten, Edwd Douglass, Jas Gwin, Stephen Cantrill, Thomas Blackmore, James Douglass, Chas Donoho, Wm Cage esquires appear & take their seats.
Allow Sheriff for ex officio services July 1797 to present $40.
Allow Clerk for ex officio services from July 1797 to present $20.
Allow Clerk $40 for recording tax lists and other tax services.
James Dohertie v Wm Hammond & Isaac Pearce. Permit Sheriff to amend his return.
Order William Montgomery mercht, James Sanders, & Zacheus Wilson Senr settle with Collector of County Taxes and other holders of public money.

p.163   Court of Pleas & Quarter Sessions at house of William Gallaspie first Monday in October 1798. Present David Wilson James Reese William Cage Thomas Donnell Thomas Blackemore John Morgan Esquires.
Two deeds Jno Craddock to Edward Harris 1340 & 523 acres ackd by James McCafferty atty in fact for sd Craddock.
Excuse George Gallaspie & Thomas Britton for attending as jurors at present Term.
Allow William Walton to keep ferry at mouth of Caney fork, Isaac Walton security.
Permit Henry Harrison alter road between Wm Whites plantation & Maj Whites lain.
Grand Jury: Matthew Alexander foreman, Griswold Latimer, Peter Looney H, John Josey, Lewis Crane, Laurence Whitsitt, William Thomas, James Rankin, John Dawson, James A Wilson, Charles Blalock, Thomas Patton, William Orr.
Will of Pierce Wall decd proved by Hugh Elliott & Richard Bradley; James Cryer & John Withers qualified as executors.
Jacob Parks v Henry & John Robinson. George Parks security for prosecution released; Robert Shaw bound for prosecution.
Appt James Blackimore constable for Capt Murrys district, Thomas Blackemore and William Cage, securities.
James Jones v William Muckleyea. Debt. Chamblin Hudson bail for dft surrenders him to sheriff.   James Jones assee of Taylor v William Muckleyea. Debt. William Montgomery & Robert Shaw appearance bond for dft.
Simon Totevine v Hardy Sanders. Depositions of witnesses for plf to be taken.
Hardy Sanders ads Simon Totevine. Depositions of witnesses for dft to be taken.
Robert Ellis v Ephraim Payton. Judgt by default set aside. Dfts bond, John Payton and Lazarus Cotton, to perform decree of Court in sd suit.
George Brisco v John McDaniel. David Stuart garnishee declares he is indebted to dft payable 25 Decr 1801 $300, knows of no other effects of defendant.
p.164   James Douglass v Henry Lyon. Debt. Bail surrenders dft; Edward Gwin, bond.
Daniel Richardson v Henry Lyon. Debt. Bail surrenders dft; Edwd Gwin, bond.
Thomas Masterson v Andrew Hoover. Bail surrenders dft; Wm Hankins bond.
Grant ltrs/admn on estate of Jenny Sanders decd to Stephen Ward; bond $500, with

OCTOBER 1798

George Ross security.
Original certificate lost, duplicate issued to John Dunihoo for £10.16 for guard claims; also certificate to William Morgan for £9. Also certificate to James Reese for £10.16 he having produced vouchers; also to Archibald Fisher for £13.11.
Bill/sale William Penny to Jas Winchester for negroes stock &c proved by Wm Cage.
Mortgage Nathaniel Parker to George D Blackmore & Thomas Parker; Nathaniel mortgages 10 negroes, proved by James Clendening.
Deeds acknowledged & proved: Ebenezer Alexander to James Morrison 1000 acres proved by James A Wilson. David Shelton to John Shelton & John Miles 640 acres proved by David Cochran. James Powers to Wilie Cherry proved by Dennis Kennedy. Robert White to Archibald White. Peter Looney H to John Sadler. John Blackemore to James Rankins 320 acres. Stockley Donelson to Alexander McMillen 640 acres proved by Isaac McNutt. Joseph Nuty to James Harrison 13 acres proved by Nathaniel Harrison. William Hall to James Harrison 21 acres proved by Nathaniel Harrison. Matthew Brown to William Farr 200 acres proved by James A Wilson.
Deed/gift Simon Kuykendall to Edward Hogin 146 acres proved by David Shelby.
Deed/gift George Parker to William Parker 640 acres ackd.
p.165   Deeds acknowledged & proved: Lemuel Laurence to Matthew Figures proved by John Hays. Mann Philips to Hardy Sanders 1280 ac proved by Henry Tooley. James Boals to David Boals half quarter acre lot #40 in Shelbyville Kentucky ackd. James Hart to Harris Bradford proved by John Tuggle. Robert Heaton to Thomas Harmon proved by Richard Harmon. Robert Heaton to Richard Harmon 160 ac proved by Thomas Harmon. Thomas Harmon Senr to Richard Harmon proved by Thomas Harmon Junr. Montgomery McConnell to James Graham proved by Daniel McConnell. Samuel Barton to John Mitchell proved by William Edwards. James Godfree to Benjamin Rainey proved by Wm Rainey Junr. John Overton to Wilson Cage two tracts proved by Benjamin Rowlings. Samuel Patterson to Aaron Wilson proved by Samuel Wilson. William King to John Hassell & Abraham Hassell proved by John Hassell. Abraham Hassell and John Hassell to Asa & Jessee Hassell 220 acres proved by John Hassell. John West to David Shelby 90 ac. Obed Hendrick by Jeremiah Hendrick his atty in fact to David Shelby 220 acres proved by Matthew Scobey.
Deeds of gift proved: Richard Graham to Jane Graham, negro Mary & mare proved by John Cathey. Richard Graham to James Graham for Negro Jack, proved by John Cathey. Simon Kuykendall to Rebecca Hogin, three Negroes Jim, Poll, and Moses, proved by James Cryer. Simon Kuykendall to Martha Kuykendall four Negroes, Duke Doll Rachel & Rhody, proved by James Cryer.
Bill/sale Roderick Jenkins to Wm Snoddy two negroes Jim & Rose by Stephen Parmer.
Articles/agreemt Moses Caveatt Michl Caveatt Richd Caveatt proved by Robt Jones.
Ltr/atty Gideon Denison to Joshua B Bond with certificate of mayor of the city of Philadelphia [Pennsylvania] with seal annexed thereto, ordered to be recorded.
James Winchester returns a list of taxable inhabitants in districts of Captains Williams, Bradley, Carr, Murry, & Harpole.
David Wilson returns list/taxable inhabitants in Capt Vinsons company.
p.166   Lists of taxable inhabitants returned: William Cage in Capt Looneys & Capt Harpoles districts. Edward Douglass in Captain Moore Stevensons district.
Appt David Orr constable for Capt Vinsons company; James Vinson security.
Amelia Edwards widow of John Edwards decd allowed £13.3.8 Virginia money of value $43.94 agreeable to her account agt estate of her late husband.
Allow Charles Dement one of guardians for orphans of John Edwards decd allowed in settlement of wards estate 18 shillings Virginia money value $3.

OCTOBER 1798

Order Elmore Douglass Richd Banks Thos George John Ward Willis Jones John Harpole John Brown mark a road from Bledsoesborough toward Nashville.
Order Edmund Jinnings Silas Rolls John Harpole Martin Harpole Thomas George Arthur Hogin Willis Jones mark a road from mouth Cany fork to Davidson line.

Tuesday October 2d 1798. Present David Wilson James Reese William Cage Witheral Latimer Thomas Blackemore.
Deed Thos Donoho to Montgomery McConnell 129 ac 108 poles proved by Arthur Exum.
Deed Thos Donoho to George Wilson 103 acres proved by Arthur Exum.
Witheral Latimer renders list/taxable inhabitants in Capt Hamiltons district.
Deed William Sanders & Charles Donoho to Henry McKinney proved by Tilmon Dixon.
Appt Peter Turney overseer/road Dixons Spring to Mungles Gap; all polls in Capt Williams' company below Paytons creek to work with sd overseer in clearing road.
Deed Frederick Davis to William Gray 100 acres proved by Samuel Gray.
P Turney James Below Thomas Jimason Andrew Green T Dixon report they laid out a road from Dixons Spring to Frederick Debows to Mungles Gap, 26 Sept 1798.
Chas Donoho Danl Mungle Danl Alexander Richard Britton John Kerr Jas Hart report p.167 they laid off a road from Harts ferry to Donohos mill dam to near Wm Cathys to Clendenings branch Kentucky rd near Richard Brittons house.
Appt James Hart overseer/road from Harts ferry to Hickisons br; Charles Donoho esqr to furnish list of Polls to be taken from Capt Bradleys & Capt Kerrs compys.
Appt Richard Britton overseer/road Hickisons br to road to KY line; Chas Donoho esq to furnish list of polls from Capt Bradleys & Capt Kerrs companies.
Deed Thomas Donoho to William Haynie 400 acres proved by George Wilson.
Appt Stephen Cantrill James Frazor John Harpole appraisers of the personal estate of William Black deceased.
Appt Amos Lacey constable for Capt Williams District; William Sanders & Peter Turney securities.
Deed Joshua Knowlton by atty in fact Peter Turney to John Patterson 100 ac ackd.
Simon Bell v John Pankey. Debt. Oct 1797 plf by Samuel Donelson; dft by James Dohertie. Oct 1798 jury Laurence Tinning, Frederick Miller, Archibald Marlin, Hugh Crawford, John Norris, Wm Parmer, Robert Wilson, Josiah Howell, Stephen Anderson, Christly Catron, James Balen, James McKinsey find for plf $48.04. With costs.
Deed Edmund Hall to Devereux Wynne 50 acres ackd.
Appt Edmund Hall gdn for Dolly Hall; bond $600 with William Edwards security.
Deed Jacob Shores to Samuel Shannon 320 acres proved by Shadrick Nye.
Deed Thomas Conyers to Shadrick Nye 100 acres proved by Samuel McBride.
Deed Ephraim Payton to William McWhirter moiety of 10 acres ackd.
Apprentice Thomas Miers to George Wynne to learn the trade of bricklayer.
Sloo & Broderick v John Mansco. Debt. Apl 1798 plf by Isaac McNutt; dft by John C p.168 Hamilton. Oct 1798 jury Laurence Tinning James Lauderdale Frederick Miller Archd Marlin Hugh Crafford John Norris Josiah Howell Stephen Anderson James Balow John Plunket Adonijah Edwards William Stayner find for plf $27.55. With costs.
Apprentice Harris Grisham to William Kennedy to learn trade of wheelwright.
Deed John Payton to Jeremiah Dickin 100 acres ackd.
Appt Uridice Miers guardian for Thomas Miers Miles Miers Patsey Miers orphans of Benjamin Miers decd; bond $2000 with Devereux Wynne security.
Deed John Williams to James Douglass 137½ acres proved by Humphrey Miers.
Jurors to Superior Court: Peter Luna P, Peter Luna H, Thomas Patton, John Wilson,

OCTOBER 1798

James Wilson (shooting), James Rankin, William Edwards, Thomas Edwards, Griswold Latimer, Richard Britton, Robert Shaw, Ezekiel Douglass.

Wednesday Oct 3d 1798. Present David Wilson, Witheral Latimer, Thomas Blackemore.
William Phipps Senr records his stock mark. Isaac Lane records his stock mark.
Receipt Richard Hogin to Jane Kuykendall $98.15½ being Jonathan Kuykendalls share of his fathers personal estate proven by David Shelby. Receipt Simon Kuykendall to Jane Kuykendall for Benjamin Kuykendalls proportional share of personal estate of his deceased father proved by John Hamilton.
Edward Hudson records his ear mark and brand.
State v John Pankey. Retailing liquors higher than rates. Apl 1798 jury found dft guilty; cause continued. Oct 1798 dft submits; fined $3 and pay costs.
James Reese & Stephen Cantrill esqrs appear and take their seats.
Deed Frederick Davis to James McKain 367 acres proved by Thomas Isbell.
State v Adonijah Edwards. Trespass A&B. Jury Wm Parmer Fredk Miller Josiah Howell Jas Watson Isaac Lane John Norris Jno Plunket Laurence Tinning Wm White Edwd Hudson p.169 Hugh Crafford Pleasant Smith; dft guilty; fined $1 and costs.
Deed Griffith Rutherford to Henry Rutherford 3000 acres ackd.
Will of Samuel Lemmon decd proved by Joseph McAdam & Wm Moorhed. Executor therein named, William Montgomery, appeared and qualified.
State v Drury Smith. Retailing spirituous liquors without license; Dft submits; fined 25¢ and pay all costs.
Deed William Sanders to William Trigg 640 acres ackd.
Wilson Cage v William Dobbins. Joshua Hadley garnishee owes nothing, knows of two two warrants 400 acres each property of John Covenant claimed by dft.
Deed Joseph Neeley to William Hall 19 acres 20 poles proved by John Allcorn.
Deed James Harrison to William Hall 31½ acres proved by John Allcorn.
Order Henry McKinney Daniel McFarland Richd Alexander Champness Madding Benjamin Ellis Thos Bowman John Patterson mark a road from Waltons ferry through Bledsoesborough to Bledsoes lick.
John Kidd v Samuel Barton. Debt. April 1798 plf by Samuel Donelson; dft by Seth Lewis. Oct 1798 jury Devereux Wynne Frederick Miller John Rutherford Hardy Sanders Laurence Tinning James Watson Stephen Brown James Simpson Josiah Howell Wm Parmer Robert Ellis Isaac Lane find for plf $82. With costs.
Admrx of Benjamin Kuykendall decd released from interest of money arising from appraisement of personal estate of decedant for supporting orphans of sd decd.
John Wilcocks v William McDonold. Judgt by default is set aside on condition dft bring into Court special bail & pleads to issue.
Allow Wm Sanders to keep ferry on Cumberland at Bledsoesborough; Geo Smith sec.
Order William Huston constable for late Capt Reeds company; James Reese sec.
Allow David Shelby clerk $1.80 for furnishing treasurer of Mero Dist duplicate return of taxable property for year 1797.

p.170   Thursday Oct 4th 1798. Present David Wilson James Reese Thomas Blackemore.
Appt Jas Harrison Roger Gibson Wm Reed patrollers for late Capt Reeds company; to qualify before James Reese esquire.
Grant admn/estate of Joseph Beard decd to Hannah Beard & Wm Beard; bond $1000 with William Parmer security.

OCTOBER 1798

James Reese returns list/taxable inhabitants in Capts Love & Reeds districts.
John Irwin v Samuel Barton. Permit sheriff to amend return "committed to jail."
Deed James Brigance to Henry Pitt 60 acres proved by Wm Harrison.
Appt Joshua Cherry overseer/road Capt Trousdells to middle fk Station Camp creek; David Wilson esqr to furnish list of polls to work on sd road.
Ezekiel Ray v James Backer. Apl 1797 John Cotton garnishee owed nothing; James Lyon garnishee had between $30 & $40 of dft. July 1797 proceedings stayed for six mos. Jan 1798 judgt by default agt dft. Oct 1798 plf by Seth Lewis; jury to ascertain plfs damage: Wm Parmer Fredk Miller Stephen Brown Robt Ellis Geo Parks Robert Steel Robt Stuart Robt Caruthers Isaac Lain Archd Marlin Jno Norris Hugh Crafford find plf damages $29.48. With costs. Condemn amount of James Lyon as garnishee.
Edwd Douglass & Witheral Latimer appear and take their seats.
George Norris v Lazarus Cotton. Debt. Motion for more time overruled.
Inventory/goods of Pearce Wall decd rendered by executrix. To be sold.
George Norris v Lazarus Cotton. Argument waved by dfts attorney.
Appt George D Blackemore guardian for James Hellin orphan and son of present wife of George Martin; Bond $500, Matthew Alexander security.
p.171 Deed Stockley Donelson to David Walker 640 acres proved by John Walker.
State v Ezekiel Douglass. Neglect of duty as overseer/road. Bill quashed.
Appt Ezekiel Douglass overseer/road from John Dawsons to middle fork Station Camp Creek; James Douglass Esqr to furnish list of polls to work on road.
State v Hugh Bradshaw. Profane swearing. Fined 62½ cents and costs.
James Hays v Ezekiel Douglass. Apl 1798 plf by Samuel Donelson. Oct 1798 dft by Seth Lewis. Jury[above except Robt Wilson & Laurence Tinning for Robert Ellis & Geo Parks] find for plf damages $18. With costs.
Appt John Manning constable in Capt Hankins dist; Saml Donelson & Wm Hankins sec.
Appt Alexr McKee overseer/road head of Manskers crk to new road; Witheral Latimer esqr to furnish a list of polls to work with sd overseer.
Appt Robert Hamilton overseer/road from new road to middle fork Red River; Witheral Latimer to furnish overseer with list of polls to work on sd road.
Robert Wilson v George D Blackmore. Debt. April 1798 plf by John Hamilton. July 1798 dft by George Smith. Oct 1798 jury[above except Joel Blackwell Wm White Edward Hudson for Robt Wilson Hugh Crafford Archibald Marlin] find for plf $105.50. With costs. Stay of execution three months.

Friday Oct 5th 1798. Present David Wilson James Reese John Morgan esqrs.
John Overton v Thomas Murry. Debt. Depositions of James Hall & Wm Mairs in Logan County, Kentucky, to be taken behalf plf.
George Norris v Lazarus Cotton. Debt. Jan 1798 plf by Jas Dohertie. Dft by Bob
p.172 Hamilton. Oct 1798 jury Hugh Crafford Isreal Moore Fredk Miller Laurence Tinning Jno Rutherford Robt Stuart Jno Plunket Jno Sadler Archd Marlin Wm Haynie Stephen Brown Joel Blackwell find for plf $86.80. Dft obtains appeal to Superior Court, Reuben Douglass & Edwd Douglass securities.
Edward Douglass esqr takes his seat.
List/taxable inhabitants of late Capt Hansbroughs dist, now Capt Hankins & Capt McBrides districts rendered by Thomas Mastin esqr.
Samuel Elliott v John Pankey. Debt. Apl 1798 plf by Samuel Donelson; judgment by default agt dft. Oct 1798 jury Geo Parks Robert Caruthers Isaac Lane Wm Norris John Norris Robt Wilson Isreal Ambrose Thomas Murry Wm White Armstreet Stubblefield John

OCTOBER 1798

Mills John Gatling find for plf $4.40 & eight mills. With costs. Plf obtains appeal, William Cage & Seth Lewis securities.

Benjamin Cooper v John Pankey. Deposition of John Giffin of Virginia to be taken, benefit of plaintiff.

James Douglass appears and takes his seat.

James Kelly v Nathaniel Parker. Refered by consent of parties to James Reese, Matthew Alexander, George Ross, and John Stamps, the referees to appoint an umpire if necessary, whose award shall be the judgment of the Court.

Samuel Moore by his next friend Isreal Moore v Robert Hays. TA&B. Non suit.

Jacob Parker v Henry Robertson. July 1798 plf by Samuel Donelson; dft by Isaac McNutt. Oct 1798 jury Fredk Miller Robt Caruthers John Norris Hugh Crafford Robert Wilson Stephen Brown Isaac Lane Jno Rutherford Thos Murry Isreal Ambrose Armstreet Stubblefield Wm Parmer find for dft.

p.173 Order Reuben Douglass William Brigance William McAdams Samuel Cotton John Josey lay off a road leaving out the place where Robt Looney is now erecting a mill and also the place where he intends to dig the Race.

Saturday October 6th 1798. Present David Wilson William Cage James Reese Esquires.

John Wilcocks v William McDanold. Appearance bond, Henry Sadler security.

List/taxables in Capt Cantrills district returned by Stephen Cantrill Esqr.

John Wilcocks v William McDanold. Covt. July 1798 plf by Samuel Donelson; judgt by default against defendant. Oct 1798 jury Hugh Crafford, Frederick Miller, Robt Caruthers, Jno Norris, Isaac Lane, William Parmer, Stephen Brown, Archibald Marlin, Armstreet Stubblefield, Isreal Ambrose, John Plunket, Edward Hudson find for the plf and assess his damage $26.40. With costs.

John Wilcocks v William McDanold. Performance bond, Henry Sadler security.

John Wilcocks v William McDanold. Covt. July 1798 plf by Saml Donelson; dft failed to appear; judgt by default agt dft. Oct 1798 judgt set aside; dft pleads covenant performed. Jury[above] find plfs damage $26.37½. With costs.

John Rutherford v Elijah P Chambers. Debt. July 1798 plf by John C Hamilton; dft p.174 by James Dohertie. Oct 1798 Jury[above] find $25.75 for plf. With costs.

John Rutherford v Elijah P Chambers. Debt. July 1798 plf by John C Hamilton; dft by James Dohertie. Oct 1798 Jury[above] find for plf $50.47. With costs.

Robert Boyd v William Blackburn. Debt. July 1798 plf by George Smith; dft by Saml Donelson. Oct 1798 Jury[above] find for plf $73.15. With costs.

Jno Gatlin v Anthony Garn. July 1798 plf by Jno C Hamilton; dft by Saml Donelson. Oct 1798 Jury[above]. Plf failed to appear; non suit.

William Gallaspie released from obligation of his ordinary license, he intending to decline keeping tavern for the balance of the year.

Edward Douglass Esq appears & takes his seat.

John Cooper v Henry Sadler. Trover. Dft to take depositions of James Snowden and Samuel Hays in Kentucky.

List/taxables in Capt Snoddies District rendered by James Douglass Esqr.

Jurors to January Term: Christopher Cooper, Joseph Crabtree, Michael Sweetman, Wm Arrington, James Womack, Robt Foster, Owen Dillard, Jno Quisenbury, James Morrison, David Love, Peter Lyon, William Hubert, John Cothern, William Brown, Joshua Hadley, Charles Latimer, Robt Hamilton, Robt Shaw, Edwd Gwin, Peter Lemon, Jno Donoho, John Hassell, Robert Collier, Solomon Barns, Edmund Hall, James Odam, William Smith, Jno p.175 Stern, Fergus Sloan, Charles Ready, Jas Espy, John Lyon, Mattw Cartwright,

OCTOBER 1798

Armstead Rogers, Isaac Pearce, Charles McMurry.
Personal estate of Joseph Beard decd to be exposed to sale by admrs.
Auditors to issue duplicate certificate to Samuel Findley for guard claim agreeable to voucher, the original certificate being lost.
Simon Totwine v Hardy Sanders. Nonsuit entered.
Appt John Patterson overseer/road in place of Archibald Marlin.
John Murphy ads Ezekiel Douglass. Murphy to summon John Tate, his books & papers.
State v Randal Webster. Slaughtering beef cattle in woods without bringing forward the ears. July 1797 dft came not; judgt against him $150 and costs.
Personal estate/Abijah Millus decd to be appraised by Thomas Martin, William Hankins & James Sanders.
Timothy Chandler v Stephen Anderson. Oct 1796 plf by Bennet Searcy & Saml Donelson; dft by James Dohertie. July 1797 jury Francis Catron, John Payton, Jos Wilson, Thos Cribbins, Henry Hill, John Beson, Henry Bunn, John Cotton, Richard Hogin, Sion Perry, Alexr Gwin, John Mayes. Mistrial. Jan 1798 Jury Peter Turney, Isaac Towell, Jas Harrison, Jas Franklin, Hugh Crafford, Jas Odam, Philip Howell, Nathaniel Parker, James Bollew, James Graham, Thomas Jimason, Wm Snoddy. Mistrial. Continued.
p.176 Dft by counsel moves for abatement/suit; dft recovers of plf his costs.
Nicholas Boyce v Drury Milam. Debt. Plf by Saml Donelson; judgt by default $26.
Andrew Snoddy v James Carson. Debt. Plf by Saml Donelson; judgt by default $26.

p.177 Court of Pleas & Quarter Sessions at house of Wm Gallaspie first Monday January 1799. Present William Cage James Douglass Thomas Blackemore Esquires.
Will of Thomas Cummins decd proved by John Anderson who made oath Jane Anderson another witness; Robert Anderson one of the executors qualified.
Bond John Williams to Stephen Ward 25 acres proved by Wm Fletcher.
Inventory/goods of Jane Saunders decd proved by admr.
Personal estate of Jenny Saunders to be sold.
Inventory/goods of Joseph Baird decd proved by Wm Baird one of the admrs.
James Jones assee of Taylor v Wm Muckleyea. Debt. Robert Shaw & Wm Montgomery, bail, surrender defendant to custody of sheriff.
Grand Jury: Michael C Sweetman foreman, Owen Dillard, James Odam, John Donoho Jr, Wm Hubbard, Robt Collier, John Quisenberry, Armstead Rogers, John Lyon, Christopher Cooper, John Hassell, Robert Shaw, John Sterns, Matthew Cartwright.
James Blackemore constable apptd to attend sd Jury.
Order Henry Bradford, Isaac Towel, Wm Hankins, Wm Montgomery, Armstead Rogers, Philip Kerrs(?), John Roberts to view road from Hankins mill to Montgomerys mill.
John Dawson v William Totevine & Sion Perry. Debt. Appearance bond of Sion Perry, William McAdams security.
Appt Christopher Cooper admr of Wm Parmer decd; bond $1000, Wm Cage security.
Personal estate of Wm Parmer decd to be exposed to sale by admr.
Bill/sale Francis Fonveille & Wm Wherry to James Vinson negro boy Ebe proved by Joseph Weatherly.
Deeds ackd & proved: Asaph Alexander to Elijah Nicholson by William Steel. Geo G Black to Francis Willis by Thomas Willis. Jacob Higgs to John Cryer by James Cryer. Tilmon Dixon to William Sanders by James Bradley. William Sanders to James Bradley.

JANUARY 1799

P.178　Job Bass to Silas Rowles. Samuel Barton to Andrew Steel by James Buchanan. Roger Gibson to John Trousdell by James Trousdell Jr. George Brown to Wm Brown. Francis Catron to George Garrett by William Garrett. Paul Harpole to Patrick Gibson. Joseph Barnes to William King by John Hassell.

Deed/gift Henry Lyon to James Lyon & John Lyon 200 acres, 10 Negroes namely Nick, Buk, Tiblen, Dina, Moses, Rose, Peter, Deley, Molly, David, furniture, billiard table, stock, waggon & gears, tools, &c proved by James Weatherred.

Deed James McKain to William Gray 50 acres proved by James Douglass.

Deed Addison B Armstead by Andrew Jackson his atty in fact to William P Anderson 640 acres proved by Samuel Donelson.

Bill/sale Roderick Jenkins to James Cryer negro girl Rose proved by David Shelby.

Number of free taxable inhabitants in Sumner County October Term 1798: 333 list by James Winchester; 164 by James Reese; 116 by David Wilson; 169 by Jas Douglass; 163 by William Cage; 121 by Thomas Masten; 82 by Edward Douglass; 67 by Stephen Cantrill; 64 by Witheral Latimer. Total 1279. David Wilson P J; David Shelby C S C.

Report of Henry McKinny Danl McFarland Thos Bowman Benjn Ellis Champness Mading: marked road from Waltons ferry to Robt Bowmans to Danl McFarlins to Bledsoesborough by Wm Pennys along Water St of sd town to Dixons Crk at Indian old Fort, Capt Grant Allens to left, striking main road between Sheltons & Stalcups, to Bledsoes lick.

Appt Wm Sanders overseer/road marked from Waltons ferry to junction with old road; Tilmon Dixon Esquire to furnish a list of polls to work on said road.

Tuesday January 8th 1799. Present William Cage James Douglass Witheral Latimer Thomas Donnell, Charles Donoho, Esquires.

p.179　Benjamin Seawell presented his license to practice as atty; took oaths.

John Mills v James Collins. Refered to Edward Douglass, Moore Stephenson and Rhodeham Rowlings whose award to be judgment of the Court.

Appt Chas Ready Wm White Jas Rankin Chas McMurry & Jonathan Hannum mark road between Wm Whites plantation & Major Whites lain.

State v Jonathan Hannum. TA&B. Quashed.

James Elder & Co v John Mayes. Dft in proper person confesses judgt $21.69 with stay of execution till next Court. With costs.

John Tate witness in suit Ezekiel Douglass v John Murphy brings into Court the books & papers belonging to sd Murphy.

Apprentice Simon Wall to Alexander McKnight to learn the trade of Blacksmith; McKnight entered indenture with Thomas Donnell, chairman, for his performance.

Apprenticed Hugh Wall to Thomas Wilson to learn the business of farming; Wilson entered into indenture with Thomas Donnell chmn for performance of conditions.

Permit Joel Echols to keep ferry on Cumberland River half mile below Bledsoes Creek; bond $1250 with George Brown security.

Indenture between Wm Sample & Samuel McAdams with consent of his father Joseph McAdams proved by William Montgomery.

Bill/sale Edwin Perry to John Chloe household implements proved by Wm Cage.

Deeds ackd & proved: Jacob Higgs to Roderick Jinkins by David Shelby. James Winchester to Samuel Stuart by Charles Donoho. Elmore Douglass to Lewis Crane. James Sanders to William McGready. James Sanders to John Donnell. Edmund Gambol to Isaac Braken by Shadrack Nye. Griffith Rutherford to Francis Locke by Elijah P Chambers. Reuben Cage sheriff to Thomas Hardiman. Reuben Cage to Thomas Hardiman & Seth Lewis. William Morgan to William Hubart. David Brigance to Hugh Crafford by

JANUARY 1799

James Strother. John Cook to Frederick Davis proved by James Davis. George G Boswell & Demse Carrell to John Stern proved by by Joseph Bowman.
p.180   Appt Henry Bradford admr of Polley Fowler decd; Edward Douglass security.
Deed/gift for personal property John Pankey to Joseph Pankey ackd.
Release James Morrison from attending as a juror for present term.
William Houston v Thomas Adams. TAB. Dismissed at dfts cost.
John Overton v David Allison. Death of dft; si fa issues agt representative/dft.
Thos Hickman v James Cole Mountflorence. Discontinued by Seth Lewis atty for plf.
Thos Hickman v James Cole Mountflorence. Discontinued by Seth Lewis atty for plf.
Thos Adams v William Houston. Debt. Dismissed; plf assumes costs.
Order auditor issue certificate to Reuben Searcy for guard claims in escorting families through the wilderness; original certificate lost.

Wednesday January 9th 1799. Present Thomas Mastin William Cage John Morgan Esqrs.
Deed Hallory Malone & wife Caty to Patrick Barr 190 acres proved by John Morgan.
State v Wm Nolin. Profane swearing. Bill of presentment quashed.
State v James Tatum. Profane swearing. Bill of presentment quashed.
James Douglass esqr & James Winchester esqr appear & take their seats.
James Kelly v Nathaniel Parker. Case. July 1798 plf by Howel Tatum; dft by John C Hamilton. Referees Jas Reese Mattw Alexander Geo Ross Jno Stamps find for plf $90.
State v John Cummins. TAB. Jury Wm Maxey John Plunket Jas Vinson Edwd Hudson Jas Harrison Francis Catron Fergus Sloan Wm Smith Jas Esspy Solomon Barnes Chas McMurry Peter Simon find dft guilty; fined $2 and costs.
p.181   Deed Obed Hendrick by Jeremiah Hendrick atty/fact to Henry Bradford 220 acres proved by David Shelby.
Mortgage Jonathan Borns to Elizabeth Spencer negroes Simon & Jude proved by David Shelby.
Inventory goods of Polley Fowler decd proved by admr.
Howell Tatum v William Haynie. Debt. Oct 1798 plf by Isaac McNutt; dft by George Smith. Jan 1799 dft in proper person confesses judgt $24; stay/exn to next Term.
Lists of taxable property to be taken: John Morgan in Capt David Loves district; James Douglass in Capt Snoddies dist; Witheral Latimer in Capt Hamiltons dist; Thos Blackemore in Capt Murries dist; David Wilson in Capt Vinsons dist; James Reese in Capt Neeleys district; Tilmon Dixon in Capt Williams dist; Stephen Cantrill in Capt Cantrills district; Edward Douglass in Capt Stephensons dist; Thomas Masten in Capt Hansbroughs dist; Wm Cage in Capt Looneys & Capt Harpoles dists; James Winchester in Capt Martin Harpoles dist; Charles Donoho in Capt Carrs & Capt Bradleys dists.
John Den on demise/Maxwell Sharp v Uridice Heirs. Ejectmt. Proceedings stayed by injunction from Court of Equity for Mero district.
Deed Sampson Williams to William White 110 acres ackd.
Inventory goods/Samuel Limmon decd proved by executor.
Deed Thomas Walker to Basil Shaw 83 acres ackd.

Thursday January 10th 1799. Present Jas Winchester Jas Reese Wm Cage Thos Donnell.
State v Arthur Hankins. TAB. Dft submits; fined $10 with costs; paid.
p.182   H Bradford P Kiser Armstead Rogers Wm Hankins John Roberts report alteration to road between Hankins Mill & Montgomeries mill to turn & go by Cartwrights house.
State v Wm Hankins. TAB. Jury Solomon Barnes Fergus Sloan Charles McMurry Francis

JANUARY 1799

Catron Peter Lemmon Wm Smith Thos Draper Geo Bradley Henry McKinny Shadrach Nye Joshua Hadley John Payton find dft guilty; fined $3 & costs; paid.
Deed David Shelby to William Henderson 220 acres ackd.
Order Uriah Anderson Richard Anderson James Blackburn Elijah Hedgcock Sampson Williams Benjamin Blackburn to mark a road from Fort Blount to Indian boundary.
Appt James Billen overseer/road between Goose & Dixons crks at Mungles Gap to ridge between Dixons & Paytons creeks.
Appt Jacob Bowerman overseer/road from between Paytons & Defeated crks to between Defeated & Salt Lick creek.
Appt Christian Boston overseer/road between Dixons & Paytons creeks to between Paytons & Defeated creeks.
State v Archibald White. Appearance Bond.
State v Peter Turney & Thomas Walker. Appearance bond.
State v James Harrison & James Hibbits. Appearance bond to give evidence agt Archibald White.
Order Anthony Pate & Richard Kirby overseers/road between Defeated Creek & Salt lick creek to Fort Blount.
Ezekiel Douglass v John Murphy. Defendants appearance bond; Wm Hankins & Nicholas Boyce securities.
p.183   State v Jesse Bails. TAB. Appearance bond Joel Pate & John Andrews witnesses for the state.
State v John Cummins. TAB. Dft fined $2; paid.
Daniel Richardson v Henry Lyon. Debt. Oct 1798 plf by George Smith; dft by Isaac McNutt. Jan 1799 dft in proper person confesses judgt $79.70 with costs.
Reuben Cage Collector of taxes for 1797 reports unpaid taxes: [amounts omitted] William Asten, Daniel Anderson, John Brothers, Wm Brandon, Sherwood Barrow, Betsey Barrow, Henry Barrow, James Barrow, Matthew Barrow, Edwd B Dillon, John Dickson, Samuel Gwins, Henry Hyde, Jacob Houst[Hourt?], Selby Harney, Harney and Bledsoes
p.184   heirs, Jno Love, Robt McCorcle, Jas & John Morrow, Wm Porter, John Porter, Cornelius Ruddle heirs per James Mulherin, John Smith, Josiah Watson, John Wright by James McCuiston, Bryan Whitfield. List to be published in Knoxville Gazette.

Friday January 11th 1799. Present James Winchester William Cage John Morgan Esqrs.
John Farrier v John Josey. Jury Charles McMurry, Peter Lemmon, James Esspy, Fergus Sloan, Ezekiel Douglass, Robt Barnett, William Bowen, Solomon Barnes, John Payton, George Gallaspie, Francis Catron, John Plunket. Mistrial.
Order dfts in State v Wm & Arthur Hankins & John Cummins to pay Andrew Hoover & Richard Boyce for attendance as witnesses for state.
James Reese esqr appears & takes his seat.
James Douglass v Henry Lyon. Debt. Oct 1798 plf by Saml Donelson; dft by Isaac McNutt. Jan 1799 dft by atty confesses judgt $80.98 with stay of execution until next Court. Plf to recover with costs.
Release Wm Woods from tax on 1280 acres, it having been listed twice.
John Franklin assee of Kennedy v Sion Perry. Debt. Apl 1798 plf by John C Hamilton; dft by Geo Smith. Jan 1799 dft in proper person confesses judgt $84.80.
John Edgar & Co v Jas Johnston. Apl 1798 plf by Bennet Searcy; judgt by default.
p.185   Jan 1799 jury to ascertain plfs damages: Wm Smith Joshua Hadley Bazaleel Weir(Wier?) Wm Weir Henry Sadler Andrew Patterson John Robertson Lazarus Cotton Joseph McAdams James Brigance Robt Boyce Daniel Wilburn find plfs damages $89.50.

JANUARY 1799

Wilson Cage v William Dobbins. Att. Sion Perry garnishee owes dft nothing; John Stoss informed garnishee he would make title for 320 acres south side Cumberland R nearly opposite Bledsoes creek to anyone who would bring ltr/atty from sd dft for that purpose & pay his account against said dft.

James Winchester v William Murry. Debt. July 1798 plf by Geo Smith; dft by James Dohertie. January 1799 jury William Smith Joshua Hadley Bazaleel Weir William Wier Henry Sadler Andrew Patterson John Robertson Lazarus Cotton Joseph McAdams James Brigance Robert Boyce Daniel Wilburn find for plf $52.45. With costs.

Ezekiel Ray v James Lyon garnishee of James Backer. Ezekiel Ray recovered by attachment agt Jas Backer judgt $29.58 & costs. James Lyon garnishee declares he had between $30 & $40 of dfts a sum sufficient to satisfy sd judgt & costs. Lyon is notified by sheriff R Cage before Francis(?) Wethered and John Bailey to appear at Court at house of Wm Gallaspie. Jan 1799 Court enters judgt agt Lyon for $30.01.

Bill/sale Joel Dyer to Wm Brigance stock furniture & corn proved by Isaac West.

Ezekiel Douglass v John Murphy. Dft's move for abatement overruled by Court.

p.186 Reuben Cage Collector/Taxes for 1798 reports unpaid taxes [amounts omitted]: George Alexander, Frederick Aust, John Boyd, Sherwood Barrow, Matthew Barrow, Henry Barrow, James Barrow, Betsey Barrow, George Henry Barye, Matthew Brooks, Richard Caveatt atty for Watkins, William Falkner, Archibald Felts, Everard Garrett James Gadray, James Gibbons pr Jos Hannah, James Houston, Henry Hyde, Thomas Harris Richard Harmon, Thomas Harney, Robert Johnston pr Jno Walker

p.187 Matthew Kincannon, Isam Kittrel, James Lee, James Lee, George Laurence, Samuel Marsh, Hugh Mairs, William Porter, Morning Pryor, John & Morris Rayford, Hardy Royal exr of Saml Buchannon, Oliver Smith, John Scott pr Jas Morrison, Daniel McKesick, Benj McCullochs heirs, Thomas Smith, Jesse Shout, John Sheppard, Jesse Taunt, James Watson. To be published in Knoxville Gazette and the land sold.

Saturday January 12th 1799. Present James Winchester William Cage John Morgan.

p.188 Appt James Billen James Bradley & Anthony Samuel patrollers for Captain Billens district. They are to qualify before Tilmon Dixon Esquire.

Appt Champness Madding overseer/road from Second to Goose Creeks.

Appt Thomas Parker overseer/road from Goose Creek to Wm Stalcups house; Tilmon Dixon furnish list of polls to work on said road.

Ezekiel Douglass v John Murphy. Apl 1798 shff levied on feather bed & furniture bedstead chest hinges sheep shears candlesticks chears(sic) inkstand steelyard razors & hone. Judgt by default. Jan 1799 dft property giving Wm Hankins & Nicholas Boyce securities & his atty Thomas Stuart pleads abatement; overruled. Jury Joshua Hadley James Esspy Solomon Barnes Peter Lemmon Fergus Sloan Chas McMurry John Young Peter Turney William Smith Danl Burford John Payton Wm Morrison find for dft.

Release Frederick Edwards from taxes on 640 acres; taxes paid by Jos Motherall.

Thomas Masten Witheral Latimer & James Douglass Esqrs appear & take their seats.

Order road marked from Bledsoesborough to Davidson line by Elmore Douglass Solomon Harpole Richd Banks Thos George John Ward Willis Jones John Harpole John Brown.

Jurors to April Term: Jas Johnston Isaac Parker John Hawkins James Lauderdale Wm Edwards James McMurry David Love Peter Looney Capt John Clary Lewis Crane Wm Roarke Zachariah Green Rhodeham Rowlings Jesse Womack Jas McLin Wm Wilson Jas Wilson smoky Andrew Blythe Isaac Bratcher Jos Caveatt Isaac Stalcup Geo Michy Jno Dawson Wm Harrington Adam Hunter Archd Marlin Hugh Crafford Peter Looney H Robt Jones Thos Farmer Jno Allcorn Sion Perry Wm Donnell Thos Edwards Charles Dement Sr Chas Dement Jr.

APRIL 1799

John Cooper v Henry Sadler. Trover. July 1798 plf by Seth Lewis; dft by John C Hamilton. Jan 1799 jury: Joshua Hadley Jas Esspy Solomon Barnes Peter Lemmon Fergus Sloan Chas McMurry Jno Young Peter Turney Wm Smith Danl Burford Jno Payton William Morrison assess plfs damage $50. With Costs.

p.189 Thomas Donnell Esqr and Edward Douglass Esqr appear & take their seats.

John Cooper v Henry Sadler. Joseph Bishop witness for plf failed to appear; is fined; scire facias to issue against him. Simon Kuykendall witness for dft failed to appear; is fined; scire facias to issue against him.

Permit William Sullivan to keep ferry on South side Cumberland R below Hurricane Creek; bond $1250 with Edward Douglass & Joshua Hadley securities.

Order tax levied for present year [amounts omitted].

Agreeable to Act/Assembly by North Carolina in 1787, Court lays tax for purpose of redeeming certificates issued for services performed in escorting families through the wilderness and furnishing guard with provisions [amounts omitted].

Order tax for destruction of squirrels & crows [amounts omitted].

Order each person holding wolf scalps allowed $2 on complying with Act/Assembly.

Cooper v Sadler. Defendant to pay witnesses for plaintiff.

p.190 Court of Pleas & Quarter Sessions at House of William Galespie on first Monday in April 1799. Present James Winchester David Wilson Thomas Blackemore.

License John Stuart to keep ordinary at his dwelling, Jas White & Robt White sec.

James Brown records his stock mark. James Harrison records his ear mark.

Will of Borden Hawkins decd proved by James Lauderdale and Sarah Lauderdale; John Hawkins an executor therein named appeared and qualified.

Grant Ltrs/admn on estate of Robert Clark decd to Rachel Clark; bond $1000, Richard Clark and James Lauderdale securities.

Grand Jury: Robt Jones foreman, John Dawson, Lewis Crane, William Edwards, James Macklin, Jesse Womack, Jas McMurry, Joseph Caveatt, Peter Looney C, William Roark, David Love, George Mickey, Rhodeham Rowlings, Thomas Edwards.

Appt John Manning to attend the Grand Jury.

Appraisement/personal estate of Abijah Millens decd rendered into Court.

Grant ltrs/admn to John Douglass on estate of Martin Douglass; bond $500, James White, Chas McMurry sec; took oath; returned inventory; personal estate to be sold.

Grant ltrs/admn on the estate of Simon Kuykendall decd to Edward Hogin Jr; bond $4000, Henry Sadler & Richard Hogin securities.

Peter Ruyle orphan of Henry Ruyle decd chose John Ruyle guardian; bond $1000, George Smith and Thomas Masten securities.

Appt Francis Catron overseer/road in place of John McMurtry.

Samuel Elliot records his stock mark.

Order Wm Kennedy Cornelius Glasgow Laurence Tinning Thos Tinning & Thos Perry to mark a road from where road to Manskers cr to Major Sharps old place intersects Orman Allons clearing to William Kennedys plantation.

Order Clerk mark alteration in ltrs/admn granted on estate of Polley Fowler decd at last term to read "late of [blank] County in State of Virginia."

p.191 Admr estate of Polley Fowler sell personal property of decedant.

Permit Roderick Jenkins to keep an ordinary at his dwelling house; bond $2500

APRIL 1799

with John Donihoo & Sion Perry securities.
John Mills v James Collins. Jan 1799 cause referred to Edwd Douglass Moore Stevenson Rhodeham Rowlings who assess plfs damages $12.
Order Thomas Bradley William Parr Solomon Harpole Joseph Bishop Elmore Douglass Thomas George & William Smith mark road from Round lick to Bledsoes lick crossing Cumberland River at Harpole & Parrs landing.
Permit James Sanders to keep a ferry on North side Cumberland R below Drakes Crk; bond $1250, Tilmon Dixon security.
Order Danl Smith Wm Hankins Wm Trigg Wm Henderson Saml Donelson Thos Masten Edwd Jones mark road from Hankins mill to Sanders ferry on Cumberland below Drakes Crk.
Deeds ackd & proved: James White to James Winchester. James Winchester to James Macklin. John Withers to Richard Bradley. Samuel Cotton to Absolam Hall. Saml White to Robert Bratney by James Bratton. James Sanders to Thomas Stubblefield. James Sanders to Armstead Stubblefield. William Neely to John Brevard by James Hibbits. Tilmon Dixon to John McGee. Tilmon Dixon to Grant Allen. Tilmon Dixon to John Shelton. Griffith Rutherford to Henry R Chambers by Elijah P Chambers. Edward Gwin to Shadrack Nye & Co by Isaac Walton. David Beard Senr to William Anderson by Andrew Blythe. Samuel King to William Anderson by Andrew Blythe. Jacob Thomas to Malachia Hereford by John Withers.
Bill/sale Adam Hunter to Anthony Sharp Negroes Rachael & Violett ackd.
p.192 Permit Jacob Thomas to build a mill on Spencers Creek on his own property; bond $1000 with William Thomas security.
Appt John Franklin constable for Capt Lunas Dist, Peter Luna security.
John Edgar & Co v James Johnston. James Johnston took oath of insolvency; his property 1 plow 1 hoe 1 ax 1 rifle gun; released from custody of sheriff.

Tuesday April 2d 1799. Present David Wilson James Winchester Thomas Blackemore.
William Walton commissioned Justice/Peace, took oaths and took seat.
Deed of gift Samuel Barton to Elizabeth Stephen, Joseph & Gabriel Barton for personal property was proved by Arthur Hankins.
Hugh Wardlaw v Samuel McBride. Apl 1798 plf by Robt Hamilton; dft by Isaac McNut. Apl 1799 Jury Sion Perry Jas Lauderdale John Clairy Chas Dement Jr Andw Blythe Thos Farmer Robert Page Robert White Archibald Reed James Hibbits Wm Hall Peter Looney assess plfs damage $20. With costs.
Peter Turney v Armstreet Stubblefield. Debt. Discontinued by atty for plf; plf to pay sheriffs & attornies fees and dft the law tax & clerks fees. Pd by dft.
Deed Elizabeth Spencer to David Shelby 209 acres proved by Matthew Scobey.
Deed James McKinsey to William Dixon 112 acres proved by Edmund Crutcher.
Deed Charles Kilgore to Thomas Conyers 300 acres proved by Shadrach Nye.
Stephen Cantrill William Cage James Gwin Tilmon Dixon Isaac Walton Charles Donoho Esqrs appear and take their seats.
Amt/sales goods of Joseph Baird decd rendered by Wm Baird an administrator.
Supplement/sales & inventory/goods of Sarah Douglass decd proved by exr.
John Brown & Elmore Douglass commissioned as Justices/Peace, took oaths.
Lists/taxables retd by Tilmon Dixon Charles Donoho Thomas Blackemore.
p.193 Acct/sales of goods of Wm Parmer decd rendered by admr.
John Ferrier v John Josey. Apl 1798 plf by Saml Donelson; dft by John Hamilton. Jan 1799 Jury made mistrial. April 1799 jury: James Wilson smoky, Adam Hunter, John Donohoo, Anthony Metcalf, Wm Morgan, John Rutherford, James Harrison, Thos Murry,

APRIL 1799

Richd Clark, Jacob Thomas, Wm Gray, John Clairy assess plfs damage $35. Dft obtains appeal, bond $200 with Sion Perry & Henry Vinson securities.

Ltr/atty Eusebius Bushnell to his son Ezra Bushnell proven by a witness thereto before notary public for City of Charleston South Carolina.

License Shadrack Nye to keep ordinary, Samuel Donelson security.

Appt William Allon constable for Capt John Harpoles dist; Andrew Steel security.

Edward Douglass and James Reese Esqrs appear and take their seats.

John Overton v Thomas Murry. Oct 1798 plf by Jesse Wharton; judgt by default agt dft. Apr 1799 dft in proper person confesses judgt $25; stay/execution six months.

Isaac Walton v John Young. Debt. Jan 1799 plf by John C Hamilton; dft by Samuel Donelson. Dft in proper person confesses judgt $34.

Inventory/goods of Thomas Cummins decd proved by executor.

Bill/sale John Harpole to Robert Wynne negro boy Demarcus ackd.

Deed Reuben Cage shff to Charles Dement 500 acres ackd.

p.194 John Harpole John Brown Elmore Douglass Thomas George Willis Jones John Ward Solomon Harpole Richard Banks report they marked a road from Bledsoesborough from near Maj Figueres on little Cedar Crk to Browns mill on Bartons creek to John Hays on Cedar lick creek to Davidson line at Nashville road.

James McKain v John Mansker & William Hankins. Manskers appearance bond; Isaac Walton and Wm McWhirter securities.

James Douglass esqr appeared and took his seat.

Bill/sale Uridice Meirs to Reuben Douglass negro woman Sylva proved by Reub Cage.

Stephen Cantrill & Witherall Latimer return lists/taxable property.

Deed Simon Kuykendall to Seth Mabry 100 acres proved by Edward Hogin Jr.

Appoint John Shelton overseer/road east fork Goose creek to Dixons Creek; Tilmon Dixon to furnish list of hands to work on said road.

Appt John Ward overseer/road Bledsoesborough to Cedar Creek.

Appt Thomas Seawell overseer/road Cedar creek to John Harpoles house.

Appt John Hays overseer/road John Harpoles to Davidson line.

John Crawford v Richard Clark. Samuel Piper, bail for dft, surrenders him into custody of the sheriff.

Sampson Williams v Thomas Morris. John Roberts garnishee had dfts £5.6.6 Virginia money in gold two crowns & 12½ cents and 35 bushels corn; also half dollar in hands of Mr Gray on south side of Cumberland River as garnishee was informed by deft.

Sampson Williams v Thomas Morris. Elisha Clary bail for deft to replevy property levied on by attachment in hands of John Roberts a garnishee in sd suit.

Adam Hunter is excused from attending as a juror for present term.

Appt Isaac Donohoo constable for Capt Stevensons dist; John Donohoo Jr security.

Acct/sales goods of Jane Sanders decd rendered by admr.

p.195 Petition of Wm Sanders to build a mill on Dixons Cr 200 yards above blue spring; land on west side of creek is property of Tilmon Dixon Esqr; site is within two miles of a mill on sd creek belonging to sd Dixon; summon Dixon to shew cause if any why order shall not be granted agreeable to sd petition.

Clerk in docketing suit James Stringfield v Jno & James Hawkins made error by writing John instead of James Stringfield; error to be corrected.

David Wilson returns list/taxable property for Capt Vinsons Company.

Wednesday April 3d 1799. Present David Wilson Thomas Donnell James Reese Wm Walton.

John Cooper v Joseph Bishop. Dft makes oath he was unable to attend at last Court

APRIL 1799

by reason of his being lame; released from fine upon his paying all costs.
Peter Turney nominated as a deputy sheriff took the prescribed oath.
State v Archibald White. Petit larceny. Jury: Zachariah Green John Clairy James Wilson(Ss) Andrew Blythe Archd Marlin Hugh Crafford Thomas Farmer William Hall Sion Perry Charles Dement William Hankins William Haynie find dft not guilty.
Jonathan & Isaiah Boone v William Haynie. Covt. July 1798 plf by Samuel Donelson; dft by Thomas Stuart. Apr 1799 deft confesses judgt $59.40.
Release Frederick Edwards from taxes on 640 acres for 1798 same being listed for taxation by Joseph Motheral and by him paid.
Wm Cage Esq returns lists/taxable property, Capt Lunas & Capt Harpoles companies.
State v Jesse Bails. TA&B. Dft submits; fined $2 and costs.
Edward Douglass & Co v Joshua Hadley. July 1798 plf by Samuel Donelson; judgt by default. Apr 1799 jury[above except Chas Dement Jr for Wm Haynie] assess plfs damage $47.26½. With costs.
p.196 Will of John Brigance decd proved by Richard Strother & Joel Dyer. James Brigance qualified as an executor.
Appt Edward Bradley overseer/road in place of Thomas Stubblefield.
Benjamin Cooper v John Pankey. Oct 1798 plf by Saml Donelson; dft by Isaac McNutt. Apr 1799 jury[above except Nathl Scudder for Wm Hankins] assess plfs damage $60. New trial granted defendant.
Amt/sales goods of Pearce Wall decd proved by John Withers one of executors.
Deed James Odam to Thomas Edwards 3 acres ackd.
State v Archibald White. PL. Costs in case to be paid by County.
Thomas Johnston v William Gipson. Debt. Oct 1798 plf by Geo Smith; dft by John Hamilton. Apr 1799 jury[above except Jonathan Peirce Henry McKinney Robt Pearce for Zach Green Andw Blythe Wm Hankins] find for plf $121.32. With costs.
Jurors to Superior Court: Charles Donoho William Edwards Matthew Alexander James Wilson Senr James Harrison George Mickey Thomas Blackemore Wilson Cage Shadrach Nye Wm Hankins James Clendening Thomas Farmer.
Thomas Donnell & Wm Cage Esqrs take their seats.
Thomas Hickman v Edwin Perry. Oct 1798 plf by Seth Lewis; dft by Isaac McNutt. Jury John Clairy James Wilson Robert Pearce Hugh Crawford Zachariah Green Joel Dyer John Tinning John Robertson Thomas Farmer Wm Boyd Chas Dement Jr Sion Perry assess plfs damages $37.67½ and costs.
p.197 Appt Samuel Carrothers overseer/road in place of James Hart.
Appt John Barr overseer/road in place of Daniel Mungle.
Appt James Gwin overseer/road in place of William Carr.
Robert Pierce v Edward Gwin. Oct 1798 plf by Saml Donelson; dft by John C Hamilton. Apr 1799 Jury: Andw Blythe Stuart Brigance Archd Marlin John Donohoo John Bush John Gardner William Clairy Gabriel Black Chas Dement John Robertson Isaac Towell Chas Dement Jr assess plfs damage $80 & costs; plf gives credit $17.60½.
John Irwin v Samuel Barton. Oct 1798 plf by Saml Donelson; dft by Wm P Anderson. Apr 1799 jury[above except John Robinson for John Robertson] assess plfs damage $800 with costs.
Appt James Trousdale constable, Capt Vinsons district; David Orr & Wm Cage sec.
Will of William Beakley decd proved by Thomas Edwards & Richard Hogin.
Deed Frederick Ward to John Quisenberry 213½ acres ackd.
Deed Frederick Ward to Aaron Perry 306¼ acres ackd.
Deed Frederick Ward to Aaron Perry 240 acres ackd.
James Dohertie v Isaac Pearce & William Hammonds. Debt. Dismissed by George Smith

APRIL 1799

atty for plf. Costs in full were paid by Jonathan Pearce.
Hezekiah Oneill v Henry McKinny. TA&B. Discontd by plf; each pays half costs.
Deed Philip Shackler by Wm Galaspie atty/fact to Zachariah Green 640 acres ackd.

Thursday April 4th 1799. Present David Wilson Edwd Douglass Wm Cage Esqrs.
Motion of William Hall; order John Morgan be special guardian for John Hall and Robert Hall orphans of William Hall decd for purpose of division of real estate.
p.198 John & Ephraim Payton v James Morgan. July 1798 plf by John C Hamilton; dft by Saml Donelson. Apr 1799 jury James Wilson Hugh Crawford Sion Perry Zach Green Thos Farmer John Clairy Chas Dement Chas Dement Jr Wm Hall Andrew Blythe Gabriel Black Archibald Marlin assess plfs damage $10.84. New trial granted.
James Winchester & Thomas Masten Esqrs take their seats.
James Winchester renders list/taxable property for Capt Solomon Harpoles dist.
James Jones v Wm Muckleyea. Debt. Wm Montgomery & Benj Rowlings special bail.
Deed James Sanders to Thomas Donnell 228 acres ackd.
Grant admn on estate of Wm Young decd to Elizabeth Young & William Marchbanks; bond $10,000 with Sampson Williams & James Winchester securities & took oath.
Grant admn on estate of David Holliday decd to Sarah Holliday; bond $500, Sampson Williams security; & took oath.
Ltr/atty Philip Shackler to William Gallaspie to convey 640 acres on Patons Cr proved by David Rohrer who made oath ltr was executed in Spanish Territory on the Mississippi & person named altho name spelled wrong is William Galaspie of Sumner.
Matthew Locke v Richard Graham. Debt. Oct 1798 plf by Seth Lewis; dft by Samuel Donelson. Apr 1799 judgt agt dft $47 and costs.
Matthew Locke v Richard Graham. Debt. [item worded exactly as above item].
Matthew Locke v Richard Graham. Debt. [item worded as above].
p.199 Matthew Locke v Richard Graham. Debt. [item worded as above].
Sampson Williams commissioned justice/Peace, takes oath and takes his seat.
Order fi fa issue, instance of Chas Harriman v Moses Moore for balance of judgt.
Thomas Masten renders list/taxable property in Capt Hankins district.
Fi fa issues agt James Lyon garnishee in Ezekiel Ray v James Backer for atty fee.
John & Ephraim Payton v John Gambell. July 1798 plf by John C Hamilton; dft by Saml Donelson. Apr 1799 jury Hugh Crafford Sion Perry Zachariah Green Thos Farmer John Clairy Chas Dement Chas Dement Jr Wm Hall Andw Blythe Archd Marlin Alexr Graham Wm Maxey find for dft. Dft recovers full costs expended.
Inventory/goods of Simon Kuykendall decd proved by admr. Order/sale issued.
Order a road laid off from James Trousdells to Richard Cavetts on Red R, by Hugh Crafford John Withers John Donohoo Jr James Brigance Richard Caveatt Robert Jones & Richard Strother.

Friday April 5th 1799. Present David Wilson James Winchester Sampson Williams John Morgan James Reece William Cage Esquires.
Appt James Harrison Roger Gibson William Neeley William Reed & James White to divide real estate of late William Hall decd agreeable to law & petition of Wm Hall.
John Morgan renders list/taxable property for Capt Loves district.
p.200 John & Ephraim Payton v Joseph McAdams. July 1798 plf by John C Hamilton; dft by Saml Donelson. Apr 1799 Jury Zachariah Green John Clairy James Wilson Andrew Blythe Archd Marlin Hugh Crafford Thos Farmer Sion Perry Chas Dement Chas Dement Jr

APRIL 1799

Wm Clairy Chas Reese assess plfs damage $83.33½. With costs.
John & Ephraim Payton v Joseph McAdams. Bazaleel Wyer witness behalf plfs failing to appear, is fined, scire facias issues agt him.
Thomas Donnell & Isaac Walton Esqrs take their seats.
Ltr/atty David Stephenson to James Douglass proved by Robert Cock(?).
James Reese Esqr renders list/taxable property in Capt Neeleys company.
Benjamin Cooper v John Pankey. New trial granted.
James Douglass & John Morgan return settlement with exr of Mary Hellen decd.
John Crawford v Richard Clark. Jan 1799 plf by Geo Smith; dft by Jas Dohertie. Apr 1799 jury Zachariah Green John Clairy James Wilson Archd Marlin Thos Farmer Sion Perry Chas Dement Chas Dement Jr Henry Harrison John Ferrier Joseph McElwrath John Robinson assess plfs damage $41.20 and costs.
John Williams v Simon Totevine. Oct 1798 plf by Saml Donelson; dft by Seth Lewis. Apr 1799 jury[above except John Mills William Gibson James Harrison for Jno Ferrier Jos McElwrath Sion Perry] assess plfs damage $64 and costs.
p.201   Deed Daniel Miles to Thomas Edwards 640 acres in Wilkes County Georgia proved by Benjamin Seawell.
William Cage v Stockely Donelson. Attachment. April 1798 shff levied on 640 acres Pond lick cr. Jan 1799 judgt by default. Apr 1799 plf by atty Saml Donelson prays damages be ascertained. Jury[above] find damages $399 & costs.
John Ferrier v John Josey. Motion for a new trial.

Saturday April 6th 1799. Present David Wilson James Winchester John Morgan Thomas Donnell James Reese Esquires.
John Ferrier v Jno Josey. Dft obtains appeal, Sion Perry & Henry Vinson sec.
Wm Cage v Stokely Donelson. Attacht property condemned for use/judgt; order/sale.
Jas Reese deposits fine collected of Nancey Fryatt for having a base born child.
James Douglass renders list/taxable property in Capt Snoddies district.
John & Ephraim Payton v Jas Morgan. New trial granted.
Jas Winchester deposits 25 shillings equal $3.12½ being fine of Polley Stout for being pregnant with an illegitimate issue.
Grant Robert Looney leave to build a mill on west fork Station Camp Cr whereon he now dwells; bond $2500 with Edward Douglass security.
John & Ephraim Payton v John Gambell. New trial argued; not granted.
Edward Douglass esqr renders list/taxable property in Capt Stevensons district.
Jurors to July Term: James Clendening Samuel King Thomas Parker James Watson John
p.202   Hawkins John Lyons Wm Anderson (BS) David McMurry James Steel William Wilson Joseph Motheral James Trousdell Andrew Gun Isaac Lane James Hart Kasper Mansker Elisha Pruitt John Payton Henry Bunn Patrick Donoho Wm Hankins James Hamilton Isaac Braken Danl Taylor Isaac Guys Charles Blalock Saml Elliott Elisha Clary James Cartwright James Baker William Frazor John Josey Moore Stevenson Griswold Latimer John Donoho Senr William Brigance.
John Dawson v Ephraim Payton. Covt. Grant dft leave to amend his plea upon paying all costs which have accrued to present date.
Summon holders of public monies to appear at next term.
Clerk in making tax list for present year shall not include taxes due by those who failed to kill their quota of squirrels or crow scalps until after next Term.
Appt Reuben Cage Collector/public taxes; bond $10,000 with Wm Galespie Edward Douglass & Wm Cage securities, and took oath prescribed by law.

JULY 1799

Appt Reuben Cage Collector/County Taxes [worded as above].
Appt John Franklin John Gardner & Martin Young patrollers for Capt Lunas company; they are to qualify before Edward Douglass esquire.
Robert Wilson oversee/road Ashers cr to Bledsoes Cr in place of Geo D Blackmore.
David Shelby executor/will of William Beakley decd took oath & qualified.
Appt Nathan Edwards Adonijah Edwards & Isaac Baker patrollers for Capt Snoddies company; to qualify before James Douglass esqr.
Court adjourns till Court in Course to meet at house of William Gilaspie.

David Wilson

p.203   Court of Pleas & Quarter Sessions at house of William Gillaspie first Monday in July 1799. Present James Winchester Thomas Masten Thomas Donnell James Gwin Stephen Cantrill Thomas Blackemore Esquires.
Will of Francis Willis decd proved by Wm Snoddy & Chas Elliott. Mary Willis extx.
Inventory goods of Robert Clack[Clark?] decd proved by admr. Order to be sold.
Grand Jury: Elisha Pruitt foreman, Jos Motherall, Jno Donoho Sr, Chas Blalock, Wm Frazor, Jas Hamilton, John Payton, Jas Cartwright, Saml Elliott, Jas Baker, Patrick Donoho, William Hankins, Griswold Latimer, Andrew Gun. Jas Trousdale attends Jury.
John Hall & Robt Hall orphans of Wm Hall decd choose for guardian their brother William Hall; bond $1500, John Allcorn & John Doke Hannah securities.
John Hall orphan of Wm Hall decd chooses John Allcorn for special gdn for purpose of superintending division of real estate of decedant. Robt Hall orphan of Wm Hall decd chooses John Doke Hannah for special gdn for division of real estate.
Order James Winchester James Reese John Hawkins James Clendening George D Blackemore divide real estate of Wm Hall decd between heirs.
James Gwin Esq renders into Court $6.25 equal to 50 shillings, fine of Crusy Kennedy for having an illegitimate child.
Appt George Wilson overseer of road from Waltons ferry through Bledsoesborough between Wm Stalcups house & Goose creek to Bledsoes lick; Chas Donoho to furnish list of polls to work on said road.
Appt Richard Browning constable for Capt Harpoles dist; bond $625 with Elmore Douglass & Thomas Blackemore his securities.
Inventory/goods of David Holliday decd rendered into Court by the admx.
Tax lists to be returned without penalty.
p.204   Order road marked by James White John Bradley Job Bass Newit Drew Joseph Wilson Thos George Silas Rowley, Caney fork to road Bledsoesborough to Nashville.
Deeds ackd & proved: Thos Curtis to Fredk Turner by Chas Thomson. Fredk Turner to Adam Tooley by Henry Tooley. Adam Tooley to Frederick Turner by Henry Tooley. William Clack[Clark?] to William Draper by Larken Thacker. Reuben Cage shff to William Walton. Howel Tatum to Stephen Cantrill. John Gwin to Robert Davis by Robert Reed. Saml Barton to Andrew Goff by Benjamin Kavanaugh. Thomas Bradley to William Parr by Elmore Douglass & Andw Goff. Saml Gragg to Lemuel Cotton by Griswold Latimer. John Blackemore to Thos Blackemore by Saml Thompson. John Trousdale to James Winchester & William Cage Junr by Joel Eckols.
Bill of sale Richard Clack[Clark?] to Andrew Clack[Clark?] mare, cattle, hogs, household furniture proved by John Clack[Clark?].

JULY 1799

License Henry Lyon to keep Tavern at his dwelling near Bledsoes lick, Thos Parmer & Peter Turney securities.

Order James Wilson (shooting) Henry Belote Wm Reed Wm Morgan Wm Hubert Wm Cochran Jno Davison Jas Bradly to mark a road from ford of Bledsoes crk crossing Cumberland between Buffalo run & bluff below Caney fork road between Bartons & Spring Creek.

Order James Reese Joel Eckols Thos Reese Matthw Alexander Geo D Blackemore Caner [Canu?]Echols Ebenezer Wilson mark a road from Croft mills to Cairo thence across the river to Caney fork road near Moses Echols.

Jury report they marked a road from where Sanders ferry is proposed to be kept p.205 along James Sanders towards Hankins mill as far as George Cummins branch to Saml Donelsons lane to fork on Drakes cr below Wm Hankins plantation to Hankins saw mill. Road neither the nighest nor best way but will answer convenience of the settlement. To make it straight would pass through plantations. Daniel Smith Will Henderson William Trigg Thomas Masten Edward Jones William Hankins Samuel Donelson.

Inventory/goods of Wm Beakley decd rendered by exr.

Lists/squirrell scalps returned by James Reese Thomas Masten Stephen Cantrill Elmore Douglass Thomas Blackemore & Witheral Latimer Esquires.

Tuesday July 2d 1799. Present Isaac Walton Witheral Latimer Thomas Blackemore Elmore Douglass Esquires.

Deed Enoch Heaton to Pleasant Kirby 320 acres proved by William Condry.

Deed Moore Cotton to Anthony Garner 48 acres proved by John Cotton.

James & John Gwin heretofore apptd gdns for William Hannah & Nathl Latimer orphans of Nathl Latimer decd. John Gwin has wasted part of orphans estate & removed himself from them; order gdnship of sd John Gwin set aside, and James Gwin remain sole guardian for orphans afsd.

Acct/sales goods of Martin Douglass decd proved by admr.

Thos Perry Thos Tinnon[Tinning] Wm Kennedy Laurence Tinnon[Tinning] Cornelius Glasgow report they agree a road that Orman Allon has turned from above Wm Kennedys house to lower end of sd Canadys plantation shall stand as turned.

Edward Douglass James Douglass James Winchester James Gwin esqs take their seats.

James McKain v David Adams. Order Shff to bring David Adams to Court at house of Wm Gillaspie to answer James McKain on plea of trespass signed by David Shelby Clk. p.206 July 1798 command executed by John Franklin DS, but dft failed to appear; judgt by default. Oct 1798 plf by Saml Donelson declaration: messuage & 8½ acres, dft promised to pay to plf 10 bushels corn per acre equal to $45.50; not paid. July 1799 damages to be ascertained. July jury: John Josey Henry Bunn Isaac George Isaac Braken Elisha Clary Wm Brigance Jas Brigance Gabriel Black James Harrison Jeremiah Still Humphrey Miers Thos Parker find damages $25.50 & costs. Dft by Jas Dohertie.

Deed Wm Totevine & Simon Totevine to Sion Perry 640 acres proved by James Cryer.

Deed Fredk Ward to Saml Wilson Sherel 200 acres proved by Wm Minor Qusenberry.

Edward Douglass returns a list of squirrell scalps.

Robert Stothart v John Murphy. Probate made by John Boyd Jr before any Justice of peace for Davidson Co in support of plf shall make admissable testimony.

John & Ephraim Payton v James Morgan. Trespass. Jury[above except Wm Muckleyea James Cryer for Gabriel Black Thos Parker] find for dft. New trial granted.

Bill/sale Isaac Braken to Anthony Sharp negro girl Kity ackd.

p.207 John & Ephraim Payton v James Morgan. James Wilson witness/plf failed to appear; scire facias to issue against him.

JULY 1799

John & Ephraim Payton v James Morgan. Dfts atty moved for nonsuit; overruled.
Bill of sale James Wilson to William Price for four negroes: Sid Todd Feeb Lewis proved by David Wilson.
Deed Andrew Bowman to Jacob Blume 960 acres proved by Nathaniel Lash.
Inventory/goods of Wm Young decd proved by William Marchbanks one of admrs.
David Wilson esqr appears and takes his seat.
William Gillaspie v Henry Lyon. Debt. Dfts appearance bond, Joel Dyer and James McKain special bail.
Lewis Crain released from value of mare taken up by him.
Wilson Cage v William Dobbins. John Stofz garnishee has verbal agreement to convey to dft 320 acres at the mouth of Bledsoes creek upon dfts paying him $9.
John Parmer orphan of William Parmer decd age 14 makes choice of Christopher Cooper for his guardian; bond $500 with James McKain & Ezekiel Douglass securities.
Order Daniel Parmer & Wilson Lee Parmer bound as apprentices to Christopher Cooper until age 21 to learn trade of blacksmith.
Benjamin Cooper v John Pankey. Apl 1798 Order from David Shelby Clerk to sheriff to bring John Pankey to Court. R Cage endorsed that dft is not found. Order to find p.208 & hold Jno Pankey executed 3 July 1798. Plf by Saml Donelson. Dft by Isaac McNutt. Apr 1799 jury Zachariah Green John Clairy James Wilson Andrew Blythe Archd Martin Hugh Crawford Thos Farmer Wm Hall Sion Perry Charles Dement Chas Dement Jr Nathl Scudder assessed plfs damage $60. New trial granted dft. July 1799 jury: Wm Wyer Elisha Clairy Chas Reese Fredk Miller Jas Brigance Joel Dyer Thos Parker Robt Ellis Peter Turney Henry Harrison Gabriel Black Hezekiah Oneill find plfs damage $20 & costs.
Deed William Benthall to David Shelby 217 acres proved by James Cryer.
Order William Marchbanks one/admrs of William Young decd sell personal estate of decedant, Negroes excepted. William Martin Charles Donoho & Grant Allon to appraise the negroes belonging to estate of Wm Young decd.
James Gwin Esqr returns a list of squirrel scalps.
Elmore Douglass William Parr Solomon Harpole Joseph Bishop Thomas Bradley William Smith Thomas George report they marked a road from Bledsoes lick to Round lick.
Grand jury dismissed.

Wednesday July 3d 1799. Present David Wilson Thomas Donnell Witheral Latimer Esqrs.
Deed Robert Johnston to John Donohoo 182½ acres proved by Isaac Donohoo.
p.209 Thomas Masterson v Andrew Hoover. Debt. April 1798 order shff bring dft to court. R Cage reports dft not found. Plf by Bennet Searcy. July 1799 jury Elisha Clary Jas Clendening Isaac Braken Isaac George Henry Bunn Nathl Giles Gabriel Black Wm Morgan Isaac Donohoo Joseph Gibson Arthur Hankins Wm Muckleyea find for plf $105.28 & costs.
Reuben Cage presented to Court three Knoxville papers containing admertisements of reported lands in Sumner County for 1797 and 1798.
James Jones assee of Taylor v Wm Muckleyea. Debt. Aug 1798 D Shelby orders shff bring Wm Muckleyea to Court. Oct 1798 Dft by Saml Donelson; July 1799 nonsuit.
James Elder & Co v John Davidson. Sept 1798 D Shelby orders sheriff to bring dft p.210 to Court. Plf by Bennet Searcy. Dft came not; judgt by default. July 1799 jury[above] to ascertain damage, find damages $21.91½ & costs.
Deed John Hamilton Sr to John Hamilton Jr 120 acres ackd.
James Feland v John Philips. Atta. James Feland by his agent Sampson Williams

JULY 1799

complained to Wm Cage JP that Jno Philips owed him £64 specie certificates of No Carolina currency equal to $160 also 10 shillings eight pence. Shff levied on 640 acres above mouth of Bledsoes creek running down Cumberland including improvement made by dft. June 1798. Execution stayed six months. Dft came not; judgt by default agt dft. July 1799 plf by Saml Donelson; jury to ascertain damages Elisha Clary Jas
p.211 Clendening Isaac Braken Isaac George Henry Bunn Nathl Giles James Harrison Thomas Parker Wm Morgan Isaac Donohoo Arthur Hankins Wm Muckleyea find plfs damages $197.33½, with costs.

James Winchester Edward Douglass James Reese Tilmon Dixon take their seats.

James Byrum v Redmond D Barry. Covt. Judgt by default agt deft is set aside.

Inventory/goods of John Brigance decd proved by executor of decd.

William Gibson v Joel Dyer. TAB. Jury Jas Vinson William Snoddy Jno Murphy Henry McKinny Thomas Bowman John Deloach Lazarus Cotton Humphrey Miers Henry Sadler Devereux Wynne Wm Morgan Thos Parker. Mistrial.

William Standley v Blake Rutland & wife Patsey Rutland. TAB. Dec 1798 plf by John J Hamilton. Dfts by Isaac McNutt. July 1799 suit abates; dfts recover full costs.

Simon Wall orphan of Pearce Wall decd being 14 yrs of age chooses James Cryer for guardian; Court appts James Cryer gdn for Hugh Wall brother of sd Simon Wall; bond $1000 with Ezekiel Douglass & Henry Vinson securities.

License James Cryer to keep ordinary at his dwelling; Henry Vinson security.
p.212 James Hopkins v James Parsons. James Hopkins complaint to Isaac Walton J P that James Parsons in indebted to him in penal sum £1000 North Carolina currency value $2500, bonds dated 9 April 1787, void on conveying to Hopkins two tracts 1640 acres. Sd Hopkins is resident of No Carolina. R Cage Shff levied on 1000 acres on Cripple Creek of Stones River Dec 1798. Jan 1798 dft came not; judgt by default agt him; exn stayed for 6 mos. July 1799 plf by Saml Donelson; jury[above] to ascertain damage, find plfs damages $546.33 and costs.

David Wilson & James Douglass return lists of squirrel scalps.

Appt Jas Winchester Thos Donnell Jas Douglass to settle with David Shelby guardian for Polley Bledsoe for the estate of sd Polley Bledsoe.

Thursday July 4th 1799. Present Edward Douglass James Winchester David Wilson, James Reese Esqrs.

Robt Jones John Withers Hugh Crawford John Denehew Jas Bryance Richd Strother Richd Caveatt report they met at Capt Jas Trousdales to lay off road from Trousdales to Richd Caveatts upon Red River, following old road, shortening meanders.

Wm Tait v James Robertson. Trespass. R Cage executed writ Mar 1799. Plf by Ben-
p.213 net Searcy. July 1799 dft in proper person confesses judgt $29.36 & costs.

James McKain v David Adams. Dft prays appeal.

John Dawson v Michael C Sweetman. Jan 1799 plf by Seth Lewis. Dft by Samuel Donelson. Jury Wm Bryance Jas Clendening Thos Parker Nathl Giles Devereux Wynne Gabriel Black Robt Wynne Henry Bunn Isaac George Elisha Clary Jas Vinson Elijah
p.214 Hays find for plf damages $141.29 & costs.

John Dawson v William Totevine & Sion Perry. Debt. Dec 1798 Plf by Thomas Stuart, Dfts by Benjamin Seawell. Jury Wm Brigance Jas Clendening Thomas Parker Nathl Giles Devereux Wynne Gabriel Black Robt Wynne Henry Bunn Isaac George Elisha Clary James Vinson Elijah Hays find for plf $36.05 & costs.

James Douglass v James Smith. Jury Wm Bryance James Clendening Thos Parker Nathl Giles Devereux Wynne Gabriel Black Robt Wynne Henry Bunn Isaac George Elisha Clairy

JULY 1799

Jas Vinson Elijah Hays find dft to shew cause why new trial should not be granted.
Deed Howell Tatum to Elisha Bernard 320 acres proved by Stephen Cantrill.
Allow Tilmon Dixon to keep a mill on his own land on Dixon creek; bond, $2500 with David Wilson security.
Acct/sales goods of Polley Fowler decd proved by admr.
John Byrum v Redmond D Barry. Continued.
Benjamin Seawell v James Cole Mountflorence & Augustin Cuaty exrs of Andrew Armstrong decd. Dfts failed to appear; judgt by default agt them.
[Second item, worded as above].
Robert Boyce v Robert Page. Jan 1799 shff executed writ. Plf by Samuel Donelson.
p.215 Dft by Thomas Stuart. July 1799 jury Isaac Braken Wm Maxey Humphrey Miers Josiah Howell Hezekiah Oneill Robert Collier Edmund Smith Robert Ellis Wm Hankins William Montgomery Thomas Parker James Harrison assess plfs damage $65 & costs.
State v Richard Hogin. Dfts appearance bond, David Shelby & Isaac McNutt, sec.
Appt Wm Montgomery Jas Clendening & John Payton to settle with Collectors of County Taxes; bond $100 with James Reese security.

Friday July 5th 1799. Present David Wilson James Winchester Thomas Blackemore.
On affidavit of Simon Totevine taken before Elmore Douglass Esqr, Simon Totevine is released from taxes on 329 acres for present year.
John & Ephraim Payton v James Morgan. New trial awarded.
William T Gardner & Co v John Standley. Jan 1799 J Cage retd "Not found." Apl 1799 D Orr D S retd "John Standley arrested & afterwards broke custody." Plfs by
p.216 John Hamilton; Apr 1799 dft came not; Jury James Clendening Thomas Parker Elijah Hays Robt Wynne Henry Bloodworth Theopholus Allon Isaac George Elisha Clairy Wm Bryance Wiley Skinner John Payton Wm Snoddy assess plfs damage $45.90 & costs.
Benjamin Seawell v James Cole Mountflorence & Augustin Cuaty exrs of Andrew Armstrong decd. Seawell complained to Jas Douglass J P that estate of Andw Armstrong decd is indebted to him by a judgt £148.16 currency of No Carolina also £5.13.7 costs/suit obtained in Court/Franklin County No Carolina June 1790. Also James Cole Mountflorence & Augustin Cuaty are not residents of Tennessee or absconded or concealed themselves so process of law cannot be served upon them. Jan 1799 shff levied on 640 acres estate of sd Armstrong on Goose Creek joining land of
p.217 Charles Dixon. Stay of exn six mos. July 1799 dfts came not. Jury[above] find damages $594.57 & costs. Attached property to be sold.
James Reese Thomas Masten Witheral Latimer Jno Morgan Esqrs take their seats.
Benjn Seawell v James Cole Mountflorence & Augustin Cuaty exrs of Andrew Armstrong. Debt £47.16.5¼ currency of No Carolina and £6.10.1 like currency cost of suit [worded as above].
p.218 Benjamin Seawell v James Cole Mountflorence & Augustin Cuaty exrs of Andrew Armstrong. Property condemned for use of judgment, to be sold.
Benjamin Seawell v James Cole Mountflorence & Augustin Cuaty exrs of Andrew Armstrong. Property whereon attachment was levied condemned for use of judgt.
State v Richard Hogin. Dft appearance bond, Edward Hogin Jr security.
State v Richard Hogin. Witnesses James Douglass & Edmund Crutcher appearance bond to give testimony against sd Richard Hogin.
Ezekiel Douglass v William Plunket. Appeal. Summons for William Plunket to appear from John Morgan. Dft appeals giving George Cathey security. April 1799 plaintiff by Samuel Donelson; defendant by Isaac McNutt. Jury James Clendening Elijah Hays

JULY 1799

Robert Wynne Henry Bloodworth Theopholus Allon Elisha Clary Isaac George Wm Brigance Wiley Skinner Isaac Braken John Payton Wm Snoddy find for plf $3 & costs.

Ezekiel Douglass v Anthony Metcalf. Debt. J Cage executed writ 6 March. Apr 1799 plf by Saml Donelson complains of Anthony Metcalf in custody that he render to him
p.219   33 silver dollars which he promised to pay Elizabeth Jones or her assigns; Elizabeth Jones assigned contents of sd note be paid to John Cotton; sd John by endorsement Oct 1797 ordered contents of note paid to Ezekiel Douglass. Dft by John C Hamilton. Jury James Clendening Elijah Hays Robert Wynne Henry Bloodworth Theopholus Allon Elisha Clairy Isaac George Wm Bryance Wiley Skinner Isaac Braken John Payton Wm Snoddy find for plf $36.13 & costs.

Order personal estate of Abijah Millens decd exposed to sale by admrs.

Thomas Millens & Crotia Millens minor orphans of Abijah Millens decd made choice of Thomas Cribbins for their guardian; no bond; guardian could not give security.

Appt James Winchester Thomas Donnell & James Douglass Esqrs to settle with admr of Nathan Herrall decd; also with David Wilson one of the guardians for the heirs of Thomas Fryatt decd.

Robert Stothart v John Murphy. Deposition of Daniel Richardson of Kentucky Garrett County to be taken on behalf defendant.

Anthony Metcalf v Ezekiel Douglass. Depositions of James Brown & Charles Kilgore in Kentucky to be taken in behalf of the defendant.

Deed John Caffery to Benjamin Rowlings 214 acres proved by George Smith.

Settlement with David Wilson as admr of Nathan Harrell decd, also with him as guardian for heirs of Thomas Fryatt decd returned by commissioners.

Inventory/sales of goods of Simon Kuykendall decd, also supplemental inventory returned and proved by administrator.

Elmore Douglass Edward Douglass & Thomas Blackemore appear & take their seats.

Lazarus Cotton v Seth Lewis. Continued to next Term.

Jurors to Oct Term: Robert Desha, Thomas Cocke, Jas Espy, William Cochran, James Watson, David McMurry, Jno Doke Hannah, Patk Barr, James Weatherred, James Lauderdale, Joshua Hadley, John Dawson, Reuben Douglass, Archd Marlin, Moore Stevenson, Zachariah Green, Wm Sample, David Lane, Robert Barrow, Lewis Crain, Peter Turney, Joel Dyer, George Wynne, Charles Dement Jr, Solomon Barnes, Thomas Edwards, James Odam, Robt Motherall, Thomas Patton, Wm Anderson (Carpenter), Wm Hubbard, Wm Trigg Senr, Matthew Cartwright, William Montgomery (farmer), James Frazer, William Parr.
p.220   William Sanders v Tilmon Dixon. On petition to build a mill. Deft objects to sd mill; not granted. Plf obtains appeal, Thomas Masten & Thomas Stuart sec.

James Douglass v James Smith. Appeal granted, Edwd Douglass & David Shelby sec.

Ferry rates published [omitted].

Appt Humphrey Miers & Edward Williams patrollers for Capt Snoddy's Company; they to qualify before James Douglass Esquire.

John Morgan Esqr returns a list of squirrell scalps.

Commrs apptd to settle with David Shelby gdn of Polley Bledsoe return settlement.

Court adjourns to first Monday in October next in Course.   Edwd Douglass.

p.221   Court of pleas & quarter Sessions, house of Wm Gilespie, first Monday in October 1799. Present Thomas Donnell, James Douglass, John Morgan, Esquires.

OCTOBER 1799

Inventory/goods of Francis Willis decd proved by executrix.
Acct/sales of goods of William Young decd proved by admrs.
Appt Simon Totevine administrator on estate of William Totevine decd; bond $1000, Malachia Hereford security.
Motion of admrs of Wm Young decd; order Wm Alexander, Wm Martin, Chas Donoho, Grant Allen & Thomas Stubblefield divide the Negro property between heirs.
Release Richard Carr from tax on 576 acres & one black poll; charged by mistake.
Release George Wynne from attending as a juror for present Term.
Robert Latimer v James Bryance. Deposition of Milley Rowlin of Kentucky to be taken, behalf of plaintiff.
Isaac Philips v Richard Willis. Dft surrendered to custody of the sheriff.
Grant admn/estate of Andrew Clark decd to Mary Clark & George Clark; bond $3000, James McKain Samuel Allen & William Armstrong securities.
Grand jury: William Trigg foreman, Zachariah Green, Solomon Barnes, Archibald Marlin, Wm Sample, Matthew Cartwright, Moore Stevenson, Jas Weathered, Thos Patton, David Lane, Robert Barrow, Lewis Crane, Joel Dyer. Constable Browning to attend.
Appraisement/Negroes estate of Wm Young decd rendered into Court.
Isaac Philips v Richard Willis. Henry Bunn security for prosecution released; James Frazor stands security in his place for said prosecution.
Edward Douglass Esquire appears & takes his seat.
License James Steel to keep Tavern at his dwelling; James A Wilson security.
Robert Dobbins v Burrell Perry. Covt. July 1799 plf by John C Hamilton; dft by Benjamin Seawell. Oct 1799 dft in proper person confesses judgt $62.80 & costs; stay/execution to first March 1800, Nathaniel Perry & Josiah Skinner securities.
p.222   Road from where Green Town road in Kentucky intersects state line to the Nashville road near Daniel Taylors to be laid out by Bright Herren, John Russell, James Stuart, James Ferrell, Reuben Searcy. Appt Bright Herron overseer with hands Robt Taylor Jesse Sheen Herren Taylor Jonathan Wallace Wm Suiter Benj Suiter John Dennen Robert Selley[Lilley?] Joseph McGloughlin William Osborn to work thereon.
Appt Anthony Sharp overseer from where road from Green Town KY intersects state line to Nashville road between Danl Taylors & Summers branch; hands Anthony Sharps, Thos Smith, Ezekiel Norman, Reuben Searcy, Jas Terrell, Eli Stalcup, John Russell, Jesse Starkey, -- Groves, Joseph Weatherspoon, Richd Clark, Jas Stuart, Thos Lloyd, George Clack, Richard Caveatt, Michael Caveatt, Danl Taylor, Morgan & Samuel Piper.
Burrell Perry v Joseph McAdams. John Smith & Wm McAdams special bail for dft.
Allow Robert Shaw $7.40 for attendance as juror at Superior Court November last.
Isaac Philips v Richard Willis. Malachia Hereford special bail for deft.
Ltr/atty Anthony Pate to his nephew Capt John Pate of Bedford County, Virginia, to convey to his son John Pate of Franklin County, VA, 140 acres and his other lands in Franklin County to be sold ackd by sd Anthony Pate.
Appt Jacob Parkes constable for Capt Hamiltons district; George Parkes security.
Appt Adam Beard constable for Capt Loves dist; David Beard & James Frazor sec.
Deeds ackd & proved: William Stalcup Senr to Wm Stalcup jr by Basil Shaw.
Zachariah Green to Ephraim Beasley. Wm Prior to James C Wilson. Thomas Murry to David King by Thos Stubblefield. John Gardner to Jeremiah Doxey. James Lauderdale to John Lauderdale by John Wood.
p.223   Joshua Hadley to John Thermond by John Wood. Thomas Harney to Jacob Jenkins by Armstreet Stubblefield. Robert Fenner by Wm Christmass atty in fact to Reuben Cage by Reuben Douglass. George Wotwood to Benjamin Rowlings by Wm Bruce. Robert Johnston to Peter Looney by Archd Marlin. Howell Tatum to Zachariah Green by

OCTOBER 1799

Reuben Douglass. James McKain to Jacob Thomas. Reuben Cage shff to Thomas Patton. Noah Woodard to Thomas George by Witheral Latimer. John Russell to Norman Peck by Reuben Searcy. Wm Sanders to Joel Dyer by Anthony Metcalf. Henry McKenny to Isham Beasley by Joel Dyer. David Bryance to Frederick Miller by Ruffin Deloach. William Sanders to Thomas Bowman by Anthony Metcalf. William Sanders to Anthony Metcalf by Joel Dyer. Nathaniel Parker to Isaac Parker. Thomas Williamson & David Cloyd to Samuel Piper by William Armstrong.

Lease Griffith Rutherford to James Wright Elizabeth Wright John Wright Ann Wright proved by Joseph Teneson.

Articles of agreement William Christmass as atty/fact for Robert Fenner & Reuben Cage proved by Reuben Douglass.

Order James Douglass Thomas Donnell & David Wilson esqrs to settle with admr of Jenny Sanders decd.

Tuesday Oct 8th 1799. Present Thomas Donnell James Gwin Charles Donoho Esqrs.
Samuel Jackson released from tax on 428 acres.
Bill/sale Wm Swearingon to Reuben Cage negro boy Sam proved by Reuben Douglass.
Deed Wm Spencer to Samuel Wilson 500 acres proved by Griffith Rutherford.
Deed Samuel Marsh to James Braken 640 acres proved by Edward Gwin.
Thomas Sharp admr/Egnew v Benjamin E Bartlett. Debt. Apr 1798 plf by Saml Donelson; dft by John C Hamilton. Oct 1799 jury: James Frazor, Reuben Douglass, John Dawson, Robert Jones, Henry McKinney, Moses Cummins, John Mayes, Elisha Clary, Wm Wyer, Thos Draper, Jacob Thompson, Richd Boy[binding] find for plf $33.81½ & costs.
p.224   Appt Joseph Motheral James C Wilson Seth Mabry Alexander Anderson & Thomas Patton to appraise & divide negro property of estate of John Purviance decd.
Deed Andrew Hamilton & James Hart to John Caplinger ackd by James Hart only.
Deed James Hart to Joseph Priest ackd by J Hart.
John & Ephraim Payton v James Morgan. Trespass. July 1798 plf by John C Hamilton; dft by Samuel Donelson. Apr 1799 jury Jas Wilson Hugh Crafford Sion Perry Zachariah Green Thos Farmer John Clairy Chas Dement Chas Dement Jr William Hall Andrew Blythe Gabriel Black Archibald Marlin find dft guilty of trespass as charged; assess plfs damages $10.84. New trial awarded. July 1799 Jury: John Josey Henry Bunn Isaac George Isaac Braken Elisha Clary Wm Brigance James Harrison James Brigance Jeremiah Still Humphrey Meirs Wm Muckleyea James Cryer found dft not guilty of trespass. New trial awarded. Oct 1799 Jury: James Frazor Reuben Douglass John Dawson Robert Jones Henry McKinny Moses Cummins John Mayes Elisha Clary William Wyer Thos Draper Jacob Thompson Richd Boyce find dft not guilty of trespass as charged. Plf granted appeal and gives William McWhirter and Edward Gwin securities.
Supplementary inventory goods of John Purviance decd rendered by admr.
Samuel Blythe v Joseph Gibson. TAB. July 1799 plf by Saml Donelson; dft judgt by default. Oct 1799 plf in proper person dismisses suit at cost of the dft; dft paid.
Deed Samuel Barton to Willie Cherry 400 acres proved by William Edwards.
Deed Wm Edwards to heirs of John Edwards decd 51 acres ackd.
p.225   Articles/agreement Wm Waters & John Nichols proved by Thomas Farmer.
Order a road from James Morrisons fording on Cumberland river above Station Camp Creek to John Browns on Bartons Creek be laid off by John Harpole David Caldwell Alexander Bird Matthew Brown William Leach.
Grant Wm Douglass ltrs/admn on estate of Fanny Howell decd; bond $500; Elmore Douglass & Chas Blalock sec; took oath; retd inventory of her goods & chattels.

OCTOBER 1799

    Deed Nathan Allen to Walter Maxey 30 acres 100 perches proved by Wm Maxey.
    John & Ephraim Payton v James Morgan. Plfs appeal; Wm McWhirter & Edwd Gwin sec.
    Robert Latimer v James Brigance. Dismissed by plf who pays tax and clerks fees.
    Acct/sales goods of Robert Clark decd; supplementary inventory proved by admx.
    Robert Barrow v Joseph Shaw. Debt. Plf by Geo Smith; dft in proper person confessed judgt $62.70 & costs; stay of execution till January first next.
    State v John Wright. John Dawson dfts bail surrenders him to Court.
    State v John Wright. John Deloach & Ruffin Deloach dfts appearance bond.
    Order admx of Robt Clack decd sell articles contained in supplementary inventory.
    James Feland v John Philips. Property whereon attachment was levied to be sold.
    Appt John Josey overseer/road in place of Peter Looney H.
    Appt James Billen overseer/road Mungles Gap to ridge, Dixons & Paytons Creeks.
    Deed Richard Cook to Stephen Winham 200 acres proved by John Willis.
    John Young v James & Eneas Hannah. Eneas Hannah one of dfts is a minor. Plf continues suit agt James Hannah.
    Bill/sale James M Lewis to David Shelby negro girl Charity proved by Jos Herndon; p.226 sd Shelby ackd assignment on bill/sale to Jas Weathered & Polley his wife.
    Deed David Shelby to Wm Christmass 120 acres ackd.
    Deed William Christmass to James Douglass 120 acres proved by David Shelby.
    James Wilson (shooting) Henry Belote Wm Reed Wm Morgan Wm Hubert Wm Cochran John Davyson Jas Bradley report they laid off road Bledsoes Creek crossing Cumberland R between Buffaloe run & bluff below Cany fork road between Bartons & Spring creeks.
    Appt Wm Parr overseer/road Bledsoes lick to Cumberland R; Joseph Bishop from sd river to Round lick; Thos Blackemore to furnish list of hands for Wm Parr; Elmore Douglass to furnish list of hands for Joseph Bishop.

Wednesday Oct 9th 1799. Present Thomas Donnell James Reese Witheral Latimer.
    Motion of Mr Seawell, order writ in suit Geo Gabriel Black v Amos Lacey & others amended by inserting in sd writ the word & name George.
    Joseph Harrison v John Pankey. Debt. Oct 1798 plf by Saml Donelson; dft by Isaac McNutt. Oct 1799 jury Wm Montgomery James Watson Reuben Douglass John Dawson James Bradley Jas Wright Jas Collins Burrell Perry John Hamilton John Robertson Wm Roark William Wyer find for dft. New trial granted.
    Edward Douglass Esqr appears & takes his seat.
    David Wilson & Jas Reese to settle with Thos Donnell gdn for Miss Betsey Dixon.
    John Young v James Hannah. Dfts bail surrenders him into custody of sheriff.
    James Byrum v Redmond D Barry. Continued until Friday next.
    David Cannon v John Bradley. Appeal. June 1799 writ by Elmore Douglass. Judgt for plf 150 cents with 100 cents costs. Dft appeals giving John Bradley security. Oct 1799 dft failed to appear; judgt agt dft $2.50.
    p.227 William Gibson v Joel Dyer. TAB. Jan 1799 plf by John C Hamilton; dft by Seth Lewis. July 1799 jury; James Vinson Wm Snoddy John Murphy Henry McKenny Thos Bowman John Deloach Lazarus Cotton Humphrey Miers Henry Sadler Devereux Wynn Thos Parker Wm Morgan: mistrial. Oct 1799 jury: Wm Montgomery Jas Watson Reuben Douglass John Dawson James Wright James Collins Burrell Perry John Hamilton John Robertson Wm Roark Wm Wyer Jas Odam find dft guilty of A&B, plfs damage 8½¢ & costs.
    Wm Gibson v Joel Dyer. TAB. John Berkley plfs witness came not; si fa issues.
    Jurors to Superior Court: James Ranken William Edwards Robert Collier James Wilson(shooting) James Odam John Wynne Jr Solomon Barnes Wilson Cage George Mickey

116

OCTOBER 1799

Orman Allon John Byrns John Gatlin.

George M Deaderick v William Haynie. Debt. Jan 1799 plf by Seth Lewis; dft by Isaac McNutt. Oct 1799 jury James Lauderdale John Roberts Henry McKenny Thos Bowman Jas Bradley Wm Maxey Hezekiah Oneill John Orr John Hodge Thomas Howell George Ross Joseph McElwrath find for plf $30.70 & costs.

Ephraim Payton v John Deloach. Covt. Jan 1799 plf by John C Hamilton & Saml Donelson; dft came not; judgt by default. Oct 1799 cause dismissed by John Hamilton one of plfs attornies; plf liable for full costs expended.

Nicholas Boyce v John Mayes. Apl 1799 plf by Saml Donelson; dft by John C Hamil-
p.228   ton & Isaac McNutt. Oct 1799 dft proper person confesses judgt $34 & cost.

John Tucker v John & James Robertson. Covt. Apr 1799 plf by Saml Donelson. Oct 1799 jury Wm Montgomery Jas Watson Reuben Douglass John Dawson Burrell Perry John Hamilton Wm Roark Wm Wyer Jas Odam John Roberts Jas Lauderdale John Allen assess plfs damages to $33 and costs.

Deed John Berkley to Henry Tooley 700 acres proved by Alexander Graham.

Deed Adam Tooley to Henry Tooley 714 acres proved by Charles Thompson.

Deed Redmond D Barry to James Daughety 640 acres ackd by Barry; Wm Gilespie ackd execution of writing on back of deed guaranteeing premises mentioned in sd deed.

Thursday Oct 10th 1799. Present Edward Douglass James Winchester James Reese.

Release Wm Porter from taxes on 1040 acres; same land returned on two lists.

State v John Wright. Recognizance; to appear at Superior Court.

State v Matthew Cowan. TAB. Dft pleads guilty; fined $2 & costs.

James Douglass Esquire takes his seat. John Brown Esqr appears & takes his seat.

State v Joseph Skinner. TAB. Nolle prosequi.

Robert Stothart v John Murphy. Jan 1799 plf by Wm P Anderson; dft by Saml Donelson. Oct 1799 jury James Lauderdale James Odam John Dawson James Watson Reuben Douglass Wm Montgomery John Mills Wm Roark John Payton Robt Looney Chas Blalock Jas Bradley assess plfs damage $28.22 & costs. Plf by Thos Stuart obtains appeal; bond p.229   with Thomas Stuart and John Hamilton securities.

Two Negroes Danl & Bob property of Sion Perry on commitment from Edwd Douglass esq for concealing death of Wm Totevine are discharged from custody of sheriff.

Lazarus Cotton v Seth Lewis. Jan 1799 plf by John C Hamilton. Seth in proper person & Saml Donelson pro dft. Isaac McNutt pro dft. Oct 1799 dft overruled. Dft obtains appeal with Saml Donelson & Thos Stuart securities.

Motion of George Hamilton; admx/Ephraim Farr decd to bring orphans to next Court; and also summons Wm Orman Jane Orman & John Hamilton Sr as witnesses.

Motion of James Weathered at request of Nathl Parker acting exr/estate of Anthony Bledsoe decd, order Wm Hall Jas Winchester John Morgan David Love & Jas Reese lay off to Jas Weathered the land devised to his wife Polley a legatee of sd decd.

John Overton v David Allisons exr. Att. July 1798 shff levied on 15760 acres Obeds River[descriptions omitted] sd land conveyed to Andrew Jackson by Martin Armstrong & Stockley Donelson by John Hackett 9 May 1796; by sd Jackson to David Allison the dft. R Cage. Jan 1799 death of dft Allison; representatives not found by R Cage shff. Scire facias to shff of Knox County retd "not found." Wm Blount exr of decedent to appear at next Court at house of Wm Gilespie; D Shelby clerk. p.230   June 1799 made known to Wm Blount in presents of H S White & Andw White; H Breazeale DS. July 1799 Wm Blount exr came not; judgt by default. Oct 1799 plf by Jesse Wharton prays damages be ascertained. Jury James Lauderdale James Odam John

OCTOBER 1799

Dawson James Watson Reuben Douglass Wm Montgomery John Mills Wm Roark John Payton Robert Looney Chas Blalock Jas Bradley find damages $920.14, with costs.
Order Joshua Cherry oversee road from Mr Trousdales to Shelbys Creek; James Douglass Esq to furnish list of hands. Appt Hugh Crawford overseer/road Shelbys Crk to John Hassells; Jas Douglass Esqr to furnish list/hands. Appt John Hassell overseer of road from Hassells to Richd Caveatts; Edward Douglass to furnish list of hands.

Friday October 11th 1799. Present David Wilson James Reese John Morgan Esquires.
Deed James C Wilson to Zacheus Wilson 242 acres proved by David Wilson.
Inventory/goods of Andrew Clark decd proved by George Clark one of the admrs.
Ordered Geo Clark an admr of Andw Clark decd sell personal estate of sd decd.
James Byrum v Redmond D Barry. Covt. Oct 1798 plf by John C Hamilton; dft came not; judgt by default agt dft. July 1799 dft by Isaac McNutt pleaded 2 July 1799 he tendered to George G Black assignee of Jas Byrum a deed for 100 acres on Martins Cr which Geo G Black refused to accept, dft saith sd 100 acres was equal in quality to p.231 land called for by sd obligation. Plf saith dft never made tender of land until nine months after suit was instituted agt dft. Oct 1799 jury Reuben Douglass John Dawson James Watson Jas Bradley William Wyer Jas Wright Wm Montgomery Nicholas Boyce Jno Roberts Seth Mabry Burrell Perry Thos Bowman; plfs damages $100 & costs.
Bill/sale Humphrey Meirs to Edwd Williams negro boy Tom proved by James Douglass.
James Douglass & Thomas Masten esqrs take their seats.
Thomas Cooke Alexr Graham Robt Caruthers Andw Blythe Robt Desha Jas Clendening Wm Morgan to mark a road from Cairo to Croft mills; John Morgan Esq to qualify jury.
Thomas Bowman v William Gibson. TAB. July 1799 plf by Thos Stuart; dft by John C Hamilton. Oct 1799 jury James Odam John Payton Malachia Hereford John Mayes Rhodeham Rowlings Edmund Hatch Isreal Ambrose Richard Boyce Edwd Gwin Drury Milam Silas Alexander Moses Cummins assess plfs damages 8½ cents and costs.
Jurors to January Term: William Anderson blacksmith, Jas Caruthers, Zacheus Wilson Jr, Jas Wilson sr, Thos Hamilton Jr, John Russell, Isaac Stalcup, Jas Morrison, James Esspy, John Gibson, Joshua Cherry, Geo Wynne, Chas Dement, Isaac Baker, Patk Barr, Wm Steel, Edmd Brown, Jos Burton, Richard Alexander, Jas Bradley, Wm Martin, John Beasley, Grant Allon, Jonathan Hannum, Jesse Haney, James Stuart, Nathl Harrison, Joseph Neeley, Gasper Mansker, Smith Hansberry, Edward Gwin, Moore Stevenson, Arthur Hankins, Griswold Latimer, James Frazer, Shadrach Nye.
Joseph Harrison v John Pankey. Depositions allowed to be taken.
License Elisha Pruitt to keep ordinary, Henry McKenny security.

p.232 Saturday October 12th 1799. Present David Wilson James Reese John Morgan Thomas Masten, Esquires.
James Winchester v Samuel White. Permit plfs atty to amend writ.
Release Benijah Morgan from tax on black poll entered by mistake.
Deed John Payton to Moses Cummins 66 acres ackd.
Release Henry Tooley agent for James & Adam Tooley from tax on 640 acres listed twice for 1798.
Charles Harriman v Moses Moore. Charles Harriman at Oct 1797 recovered agt Moses Moore judgt $800 & $24.12½ costs; $700 & costs were satisfied. Shff to summon Moses Moore to July Court at house of Wm Gilaspie; July 1799 return "Not found. J Cage." Oct 1799 judgt agt dft for $124.12½ & costs.

118

OCTOBER 1799

Ltr/atty Nicholas Boyce & Sarah Boyer exr & extx of Richard Boyer decd to Daniel Richardson to sell in fee simple 1000 acres in Virginia, Ohio County, proved by p.233   John C Hamilton.

Ezekiel Douglass v John Mayes. Oct 1798 plf by Saml Donelson; dft came not; judgt agt him. Cont to Oct 1799. Dft in proper person confesses judgt $19.16 & costs.

State v William Astin. Judgt agt dft $4.23 taxes for 1797 & costs; shff to sell so much of land of sd defendant as will satisfy sd judgt and costs.

[Similar suits with varying taxes due entered agt: Sherwood Barrow, Betsey Barrow, Henry Barrow, James Barrow, Matthew Barrow, Edward B Dillon, Samuel Givins, Jacob Houst, Selby Harney, Harney & Bledsoe Heirs, John Love, Robert McCorcle, p.234   James & John Morrow, John Smith.]

James McKain v John Mansker & William Hankins. Apr 1799 plf by Samuel Donelson; dfts by John C Hamilton. Oct 1799 jury Reuben Douglass Geo Mickey Seth Mabry Robt Ellis Wm Wier John Mills James Lauderdale Edwd Gwin John Mayes John Deloach Henry Bloodworth Richd Boyer assess plfs damages $60 & costs.

State v Josiah Watson. Judgt $4.23 & costs; Sheriff sale to satisfy judgt.

State v John Wright. Judgt $4.23 & costs. Sheriff sale to satisfy judgt.

William Gillaspie v Henry Lyon. Debt. July 1799 plf by Saml Donelson; dft by Isaac McNutt. Oct 1799 jury[above] find for plf $91 & costs.

p.235   State v Sherwood Barrow. Judgt for $5.75 taxes for 1798 & costs. Sheriff to sell so much of land as will satisfy sd judgment and costs.

[Similar suits with varying taxes due entered agt: Matthew Barrow, Henry Barrow, Jas Barrow, Betsey Barrow, Matthew Brooks, Richard Caveatt as atty for Watkins, Wm Falkner, James Gadray, Jas Gibbons, Thos Harris, Richd Harman, Thos Harney, Robert p.236   Johnston, Isam Kittrell, James Lee, John Love, Hugh Mairs, John & Morris Rayford, Oliver Smith, John Scott, Danl McKesik, Benjamin McCulloch, Thomas Smith, Jesse Shoat, John Sheppard, James Watson.]

George G Black v Amos Lacey Peter Turney Thos Lacey Jr Thomas Lacey Sr. Debt. Oct 1799 plf by Benjamin Seawell; dfts by Thomas Stuart & John C Hamilton. Amos Lacey in proper person confesses judgt for $130 & costs.

Motion/Benjn Davis personal property of Abijah Millens decd to be sold by admr.

Release Wm Cage from two thirds value of stray mare & cost taken up by him.

Lazarus Cotton v Seth Lewis. Appeal granted dft, Saml Donelson & Thos Stuart sec.

Robt Stothart v John Murphey. Appeal, Thos Stuart & John C Hamilton securities.

p.237   Moses Echols v Samuel Barton. Appt John Payton to survey land in dispute.

Release Daniel Anderson from taxes; paid more than liable for last year.

Court adjourns till Court in Course to meet at this place.   David Wilson

p.238   Court of pleas & Quarter Sessions at house of William Gillaspie on first Monday January 1800. Present James Winchester Stephen Cantrell Thomas Donnell.

Deed Wm Polk to Robert Henderson 567 acres proved by James Wallace.

Deed Wm Polk to Joseph Wallace 433 acres proved by James Wallace.

Deed George Parkes to Jacob Parkes 258 acres ackd.

Deed Wm Christmass atty in fact for Robert Fenner to Thomas Hamilton Senr 640 acres proved by Benjamin Seawell.

Arthur Hogin v James C Mountflorence. Thirty acres whereon attachment was levied

JANUARY 1800

to be condemned for use of judgmt agt sd Mountflorence obtained before Wm Walton J P. for twelve dollars. Order rescinded.

Grand jury: Wm Martin foreman, Smith Hansbrough, Jas Morrison, Thos Hamilton, Jos Neeley, Zacheus Wilson Jr, Patrick Barr, Shadrack Nye, Isaac Baker, Arthur Hankins, Kasper Mansker, James Esspy, William Steel.

Agreeable to Commission/Peace by John Sevier 26th Oct 1799 following persons took oath: Reuben Searcy, James Cryer, Benjamin Rowlings, John McMurtry, David Love.

State v Wm Penny. Recognizance taken by Justices of Davidson County; dismissed.

Grant admn/estate of Wm Story to Ann Storey; Mark Richman & Nathan Richman sec.

Appt Andrew Hoover constable; William Hankins & James Frazor securities.

Appt Patrick Gibson constable; William Henderson & Edward Hudson securities.

Appt George Campbell constable; John Young & James Kirkpatrick securities.

Appt John Cryer constable; James Cryer & Rhodeham Rowlings securities.

State v Jabus Fisher. PL. Appearance bond.

State v William Neeley. Bond, security for Jabus Fisher.

p.239 Appraisement of Negro property/estate of John Purviance decd retd.

Acct/sales personal estate of Andrew Clack decd proved by George Clack admr.

Appt commissioners to settle with admrs of Jenny Sanders decd.

Appt commissioners who settled with Thomas Donnell as guardian for Betsey alias Elizabeth Dixon dau of Joseph Dixon decd, who return settlement.

Deeds ackd & proved: Will Sanders to Daniel Trigg by Danl Smith. Robert Desha to George Stout by James Winchester. George Stout to Robert Desha by James Winchester. William Alexander to William Trigg Senr by Wm Trigg Jr. John Knox to John Barclay, probate taken in Iredell County, North Carolina. John Knox to James Barclay certified probate in Iredell County, North Carolina. John Sterns to John Bunton proved by Joseph Bunton. John Sterns to William Foster by Joseph Bunton. John Laurence to James Chapman. Murfree Knight to William Cowper by James Cryer. William Cowper to William Rea by James Vinson. Nathan Arnett to William Stalcup by James Gambling. William Roark to Nathan Arnett by James Gambling. William Gibson to Peter Looney by James Cage. Reuben Cage sheriff to Edmund Crutcher by sd Cage.

Order exr of William Beckley decd expose to sale personal property of decedant.

Supplemental inventory goods of William Beckley decd rendered by executor.

Appt William Cathy constable to attend Grand Jury.

Tuesday January 7th 1800. Present James Winchester Thomas Donnell John McMurtry.

Inventory/goods of William Storey decd proved by administratrix; to be sold.

Order Thomas Donnell & Thomas Masten settle with admr of Thomas Egnew decd.

p.240 Supplement acct/sales of goods of Robt Clack[Clark?] decd proved by admr.

Thomas Cocke, Alex Graham, Robert Caruthers, Andrew Blythe, James Clendening, William Morgan report they marked a road from Cairo to Croft mills: begin at end of Oak St to William Browns plantation to Capt Reeses to near William Alexanders plantation. Assess damage sustained by George Brown $17; by Capt James Reese $5.

Benjamin Seawell v Executors of Andrew Armstrong decd. On motion of plf order scire facias issue agt heirs & devisees of sd decd.

Benjamin Seawell v Exrs of Andrew Armstrong decd. Scire facias issue agt heirs & devisees of sd decd.

Witheral Latimer, James Reese, James Douglass, John McMurtrie take their seats.

Joseph Harrison v John Pankey. Debt. Oct 1798 plf by Saml Donelson; dft by Isaac McNutt. Oct 1799 jury Wm Montgomery James Watson Reuben Douglass John Dawson James

JANUARY 1800

Bradley, Jas Wright, Jas Collins, Burrell Perry, John Hamilton, John Robertson, Wm Roark, Wm Wyer. New trial granted. Jan 1800 jury James Stuart, Jas Caruthers, Chas Dement, Joseph Bunton, Richard Willis, Bazaleel Wyer, James Lauderdale, Hezekiah Oneill, Jas Robertson, Jas Wilson(smoking), John Roberts, William Sizemore, assess plfs damage $140 & costs.

State v Benjamin Kuykendall. Securities surrender defendant.

Edward Gwin commissioned a Justice/Peace by governor takes oath.

State v Ben Kuykendall. Dft reputed father of illegitimate child of Priscilla Bloodworth; bond $500, James McKain & George Brown securities; fine $6.25.

Arthur Hogan v James Cole Mountflorence. Yesterdays order to sell land rescinded.

William Howel orphan of Edwd Howell decd bound to John Gilespie till age 21 to learn cabinet trade.

Edward Douglass takes his seat.

p.241 Amos Bailey v Elijah P Chambers. Debt. Apr 1799 plf by Samuel Donelson; dft by John C Hamilton. Jan 1800 jury[above except William Maxey for James Wilson] assess plaintiffs damage $25.20 & costs.

Receipt from Reuben Martin to Jane Kuykendall $98.15 part of personal estate of Benjamin Kuykendall decd was proved by Wm Brigance.

Appt Thomas Howell constable; Isaac Baker security.

Appt Samuel Donelson guardian for Jenny, George, Nelley, Jesse Egnew orphans of Thomas Egnew decd; bond $10,000, Edwd Douglass & Bennet Searcy securities.

Commissioners apptd to settle with admrs of Thomas Egnew decd make report.

Archibald Marlin commissioned Justice/peace by governor, took oath.

On petition of George Brown & James Reese, order estimate of damage sustained by a road laid off from Cairo to Croft mill be made by Wm Reece, Robt Desha, Wm Neely, Jas Morrison, Patrick Gibson, Edward Hudson, Nathl Gilmore, James Esspy, Wm Hubert, Robt Wilson, Thos Parker, Robert Steel, Hillery Malone, Joseph Wilson, Nathl Giles.

Deeds ackd & proved: Robt Weakley to Nathan Barnes by Henry Bunn. Jas Hair[Haw?] to James Frazor. James Frazor to James Haw. Charles Masterson to James Haw, certificate of Justice & Clerk of Hardin County, Kentucky. Thomas Hickman to Orman Allon by Bennet Searcy. William Lytle Jr to Thomas Murry by James Cotton.

Deed/gift Jeremiah Watson to son Jeremiah Watson three negroes Darkes Ephraim & Toney; also to his daughter Elizabeth Watson three negroes Patsey Esther Kit ackd.

Addl inventory/goods of William Beakley decd rendered by exr.

Order Wm Beard oversee road laid off from Cairo to Croft mills; James Winchester to furnish list of hands. Order James Esspy to oversee road from Bledsoes creek to Cumberland River near Buffaloe run; James Winchester to furnish list of hands.

p.242 Wednesday Jan 8th 1800. James Reese Witheral Latimer James Cryer.

Deed John Withers to Joshua Cherry 112 acres proved by William Snoddy.

Anthony Metcalf v Ezekiel Douglass. Apr 1799 plf by John C Hamilton; dft by Saml Donelson. Jury Chas Dement Peter Looney P Edmund Hatch Wm Wyer Robt Collier Elisha Edwards Jas White Thos Murry Jos McAdams Mattw Anderson Jabus Fisher Wm Snoddy assess plfs damage $37.50. New trial granted.

Edwd Douglass Isaac Walton Edwd Gwin Witheral Latimer Jno McMurtree take seats.

Appt James Sanders overseer/road from Sanders ferry to Hankins mill; Thos Masten to furnish list of hands to work on sd road.

Appt John Stuart overseer/road in place of Jesse Hainey from Major Whites house to Second Creek, and Thomas Blackemore to furnish list of hands.

JANUARY 1800

Sampson Williams v Thomas Morris. Apr 1799 J Cage summons John Roberts garnishee who has £5.6.6 Virginia money in gold, 2 crowns, 12½¢, 35 bushels corn, half dollar in hands of Mr Gray south of Cumberland River; property replevied by dfts atty Saml Donelson. Jan 1800 jury James Caruthers James Stuart Robt Hogin Jesse Womack Drury Milam Joseph Bunton James McKinsey John Gardner George Stuart Brigance Alexr Gordon Joseph McElwrath John Roberts assess plfs damage to $20 and costs.

Sampson Williams v James Comyn. Oct 1798 J Cage levied on 640 acs Flynns Cr. July 1799 dft came not; judgt by default. Jan 1800 plf by Saml Donelson. Jury[above except John Payton for Jos McElwrath] assess plfs damages $72.50. Plf obtains appeal, Samuel Donelson and David Shelby securities.

Sampson Williams v Thomas Morris. Plf obtains appeal, Henry Bradford and Thomas Stuart securities.

Thursday Jany 9th 1800. Present Thomas Donnell Edward Gwin John McMurtrey.

Release heirs of Anthony Bledsoe from 1797 taxes on 2200 acres, the same returned with 2200 acres more in name of Selby Harney; heirs of Bledsoe by Thos Harney agent for sd Selby not knowing same had been previously listed by guardians of sd heirs.

John & Ephraim Payton v Bazaleel Wyer. Jury Chas Dement Jos Bunton James Stuart John Young Nicholas Boyer John Ferrier Alexr Gordon Mattw Anderson John Boyce Caleb Impson Drury Milam Moses Echols; not agreeing, juror withdrawn by consent.

Jas Winchester Jas Douglass Jas Reese Wm Cage David Wilson Edwd Douglass Benjamin Rowlings John McMurtry Witheral Latimer & Archd Marlin Esqrs take their seats.

Allow Clerk $40 for exofficio services July 1798 to July 1799.

John Gordon v William Dobbins. 1799 D Shelby ordered sheriff to summon Dobbins. Dft came not; judgt by Court $65.76½ and costs of suit.

Reuben Searcy & Isaac Walton take their seats.

Taxes laid [omitted].

Allow $1 for wolf scalps. Act/Assembly for destruction of squirrels crows wolves.

Appt George Reeves constable, Red River Dist; Reuben Searcy & Bright Herren sec.

Deed Thomas Perry to William Hamilton 8 acres proved by Isaac Walton.

Deed John Hamilton Senr to Thomas Perry 16 acres proved by Isaac Walton.

Lists of taxable property to be taken: Isaac Walton in Capt Cantrills Dist; John McMurtrie in Capt McBrides dist; Thos Masten in Capt Hankins dist; Benjn Rowlings in Capt Lunas dist; Archibald Marlin in Capt Stevensons; Jas Cryer in Capt Snoddies dist; Thomas Donnell in Capt Vinsons; David Love in Capt Loves & Capt Carrs; James Reese in Capt Neelys dist; Thos Blackemore in Capt Haineys; Charles Donoho in Capt Bradleys; Witheral Latimer in Capt Hamiltons dist; Edward Gwin in Capt Gwins Dist.

Sheriff allowed $40 for exofficio services from 1 July 1798 to same in 1799.

Release Charles Petegrew from 1796 tax on 1000 acres within Indian boundary.

Reuben Cage collector of public taxes for 1796 reports unpaid taxes of persons having no personal property within county whereon to levy: [amounts omitted] John Boyd, John Derden, Jacob Shoer, Charles Dixon, Wynn Dixon, Wm Matcalf, Wm Anderson, Robert Ewing. Order tracts to be advertised in Knoxville Gazette.

Reuben Cage collector of 1797 public taxes reports unpaid taxes of persons with no personal property within county whereon to levy: John Dobbins, George Green, Wm Head, Wm Hays, Wm Harrington, Daniel James, Benjamin McNair, John Rains. Order Clerk transmit a copy hereof to Knoxville Gazette agreeably to Law.

Reuben Cage collector of 1798 public taxes reports unpaid taxes of personas with no personal property in County whereon to levy: James Crabtree, John Draper, Elisha

JANUARY 1800

p.246   Davis, Charles Eaton, George Green, Daniel Hunter, Magness McDanold, John Rains, Wm Whitehead, Wm Totevine, Philips heirs & Michael Campbell. Ordered published in Knoxville Gazette agreeably to law.

Friday January 10th. Present David Wilson James Winchester Reuben Searcy Edwd Gwin.
Order Bright Herrin James Stuart James Ferrell Reuben Searcy Anthony Sharp Ezekiel Norman John Hail to lay off a road from where Green Town KY road intersects state line to near Daniel Taylors.
State v Jabus Fisher. Dft failing to appear forfeits recognizance.
State v Wm Neeley. Security for Jabus Fisher forfeits recognizance.
State v John Williams. Retailing whiskey without license. Jury James Wilson James Caruthers Chas Dement Danl Hylton James Stuart Isaac Towell Peter Luna P Robt Hogin James Orr Wm Allen George G Black Nathaniel Hughes find dft not guilty as charged; prosecutor Hezekiah Oneill to pay costs.
Appt John McMurtrie coroner; bond $2500, Edwd Gwin & James Cryer securities.
Wm Cage Witheral Latimer Jas Cryer make their seats.
Geo G Black v Amos Lacey & others. Amos Lacey having confessed judgt at last term
p.247   with stay of execution 5 mos; trial agt other defts.
Deed James Sanders to Robert Campbell 228 acres ackd.
Ltr/atty Thomas Sanders of Buckingham County Virginia to Miles Wels Conway of Mason County Kentuckey ackd by sd Thomas Sanders.
Deed Joel Echols to Jas Winchester & Wm Cage 50 acres proved by Geo D Blackemore.
State v James Cage. TAB. Jury John Henderson Robert Campbell John Payton James Caruthers Jas Orr Nathaniel Hughes Matthew Anderson Jas Stuart Peter Looney P Henry Bloodworth Matthew Scobey Thos Bloodworth find dft guilty. Dfts atty Saml Donelson moves arrest/judgt; assault on James Cage Esqr; dft pays costs.
Exempt Capt Joshua Hadley from taxes on Negro Guy who has been rendered in great measure incapacitated for service.
Acct/sales goods of Frances Howell decd proved by admr.
Motion of Geo D Blackemore, order James Winchester & James Reese settle with guardian of James Hellen.
George Mickey Boswell Johnston Jno Deloach Samuel Harris Edwd Hogin Jr Laban Benthall Wm McCorcle to lay off a road from near Mr Mabrys to Capt Kings plantation.
State v Richard Hogin. TAB. Jury Joshua Hadley Jos McAdam Jos Bunton Seth Mabry Drury Milam Wm Sample Smith Hansbrough Daniel Hylton Alexr Gordon Edmond Smith John Gardner Jas McKinsey find dft guilty of assault only. Arrest/judgt. Dft pays costs.

Saturday Jan 11th 1800. Present David Wilson James Winchester Benjamin Rowlings John Morgan Edward Gwin esquires.
p.248   Deed/gift Wm Dixon to Edmond Smith negro Charlotte proved by Jeremh Doxey.
Jurors to April Term: Thos Cocke Andw Blythe Robt Desha Robt Anderson Jos Wallace Geo Gallispie Jno Hawkins Wm Smith Thos Murry Jas Bradley John Cathey Sr John Rutherford John Carr John Sterns Wm Wherry Robt Motheral Wm Reed Thos Patton Jas Vinson Richd King Reuben Douglass Griswold Latimer Peter Looney H Wm Gilespie Wm Douglass Danl Ogelsby Jno Denning Wm Gwin Menoa Taylor Stephen Montgomery Peter Kyser Thomas Simpson Thomas Perry William Bowan Joseph Caveatt Michael Shannon.
Moses Eckols v Samuel Barton. Covt. Oct 1799 plf by Benjn Seawell; dft by Samuel Donelson. Jan 1800 Jury Chas Dement Jas Caruthers Jas Stuart Jeremiah Doxey James

JANUARY 1800

Wilson Jno Young Isaac Towell Wm Hankins Jas Orr Jos Russell Jno Payton Nathl Hughes assess plfs damages $689. With costs. Attached property condemned.
   Sampson Williams v James Comyn. Plf appeals, Samuel Donelson & David Shelby sec.
   James Winchester v William Penny. Oct 1799 plf by Geo Smith; dft came not; judgt by default. Jan 1800 [previous jury] find plfs damages $204.30 & costs.
   James Winchester v William Penny. [as above; damages $58.69 & costs].
   James Winchester v William Penny. [as above; damages $241.10 & costs].
p.249   State v John Williams. Retailing whiskey &c. Motion to tax prosecutor with costs; exn issues agt Hezekiah Oneill prosecutor; Jas Orr proved attendance for $1.
   State v James Cage. TAB. Judgment is arrested; defendant pays costs.
   Supplement to acct/sales goods of Wm Parmer decd proved before Edward Douglass.
   James Reese & Reuben Searcy Esqrs take their seats.
   State v Richard Hogin. TAB. Judgt is arrested; dft pays costs.
   Release Geo Smith from tax on 640 acres listed in name Jno Donelson & taxes paid.
   Road overseers appointed: Solomon Barnes, Trousdales to Shelbys Crk in place of Joshua Cherry; James Douglass to furnish list of hands. Jonathan Buyet, Bledsoes lick to Bishops ferry in place of Wm Parr; Thomas Blackemore to furnish list/hands. Robt Steel from Croft mills to ridge; Jas Winchester to furnish list/hands. Howel Smith from ridge to KY line; Edward Gwin to furnish list of hands to work sd road.
   Moses Eckols v Samuel Barton. Covt. Attached property condemned & to be sold.
   Order that the surveyors chain carriers & markers for surveying & ascertaining limits of Sumner County be entitled to draw $189 from county treasury to pay same.
   Edward Gwin v Michael Plaster. Cow & calf levied on to be sold for use of judgt.
   State v Jane Farr. George Hamilton pay dfts costs, no default agt her.
   Guns or fire arms taken by patrollers in Capt Snoddys company to be returned to owners of negroes from whom they were taken.
   Appt Capt Geo Mickey overseer/road in place of William Thomas.
   Appt Wm Neeley Wm Hall Jno Hawkins Jas Cary Roger Gibson Cornelius Herndon to view road from Bledsoes lick to Second Crk.
   Court adjourns until Court in Course at Town of Cairo first Monday in April.
                                                                         David Wilson.

p.250   Court of Pleas & Quarter Sessions Town of Cairo first Monday April 1800. Present David Wilson James Winchester John Morgan Esquires.
   Jonathan Hannum commissioned in the Peace by his Excellency John Sevier 26 Oct 1799 takes oaths to qualify.
   Grand jury: George Gillespie foreman, Griswold Latimer, Robert Motherall, John Sterns, Robert Desha, John Cathey, Thomas Patton, Michael Shannon, Joseph Wallace, William Smith, Peter Looney, Andrew Blythe, Wm Wherry.
   Deed Joshua Scott to Micajah House 182 acres proved by Hugh Crafford.
   Deed Daniel Ogelsby to Shadrach Nye 10 acres ackd.
   Deed Alexander Graham to Wm Wherry 15 acres ackd.
   Deed Stephen Wynham to Jesse Spradling 200 acres proved by James Cryer.
   Grant admn/estate of Wm S Carson decd to Rachel Carson & Richard Alexander; bond $2000, Matthew Alexander & Alexander Graham securities; took oaths.
   James Frazor v James Richmond. Debt. Robert Shannon dfts bail surrenders him.

APRIL 1800

James Frazor v James Richmond. Debt. Robert Motherall special bail for dft.
License Henry Lyon to keep ordinary at his dwelling in Cairo, bond $2500 with William Neely and Alexander Graham securities.
Daniel Ogelsby excused from attending as juror for present Term.
Inventory of goods of Burden Hawkins decd proved by executor.
Will of Ruffin Barrow decd proved by David Lane.
Jury report damages sustained by George Brown & James Reese on account of road passing through their plantations: James Reese $12.50, Geo Brown $25. Certified by William Hubbart Robt Desha Nat Giles Jas Esspy Robt Steel Patrick Gibson Nathaniel Gilmore Jas Morrison Thomas Malone William Parker William Reed William Neely.
Deed Jas Winchester & Wm Cage Jr to Wm Scott lot in Cairo proved by Jno Borough.
Thomas Blackemore Esqr takes his seat.
Supplement inventory goods of Andrew Clark decd proved by George Clark an admr.
p.251 Appt Wm White overseer/road in place of John Stuart from Maj Whites house to 2d Creek; Jonathan Hannum Esqr to furnish list of hands to work on sd road.
Deed William Haynie to William Trigg Senr 400 acres ackd.
Acct/sales goods of William Storey decd proved by admx.
David Echols records his ear mark. John Echols records his ear mark.
Deed William Lauderdale to William Storey 50 acres proved by John Cathey.
Wm Morgan reputed father of child of Elizabeth Giles enters bond for maintainance of child, John Morgan security; pays fine 50 shilllings equal to $6.25.
Deed Richard Cook to Jesse Johnston 274 acres ackd.
Deed Richard Cook to Hance Shaw 120 acres ackd.
Witheral Latimer Esqr returns list/taxable property in Capt Shaws company.
James Hart Esqr commissioned in Peace by John Sevier takes oaths of office.
Thomas Willis makes oath that Stephen Wynham is only surviving heir to Obediah Wynham a soldier in continental line of North Carolina; Willis swears he saw said Stephen Wynham sign annexed assignment to Richard Cook for 640 acres 13th Nov 1798; David Wilson J P believes Thomas Willis to be a man of credibility.
Deed Obed Hendrick to David Shelby 220 acres proved by Richard Hogin.
Acct/sales goods of Wm Beakley decd rendered by exr of sd decd.

Tuesday April 8th 1800. Present David Wilson Charles Donohoo James Hart David Love.
Charles Donohoo esqr returns list of taxable property in Capt Bradleys dist.
Acct/sales/goods of Abijah Millens decd proved by Benjamin Davis admr in right of his wife Mary.
Bill/sale Richard Graham to Alexr Graham mulatto girl Sal proved by John Cathey.
Exempt patrollers from paying taxes for years they served if no more than $5.
Thomas Perry exempted from attending as juror for present Term.
p.252 John Overton v heirs & devisees of David Allison decd. Oct 1799 John Overton recovered agt dfts $920.14 & costs. David Shelby ordered sheriff to levy on dfts land. Apr 1800 dfts came not; judgt by default. Land condemned for judgment.
Appt Thomas Donnell & James Reese to settle with admrs of Abijah Millens decd.
Anthony Metcalf v Ezekiel Douglass. Wm Snoddy witness for plf failed to appear.
Thomas Masten returns list of taxable property in Capt Hankins company.
Promissory note Geo Parks to John McNairy transfered to Robt Stothart & Co proved by David Moore who also proved the assignment; to be admitted in suit agt Parks.
p.253 Anthony Metcalf v Ezekiel Douglass. Apr 1799 plf by John C Hamilton; dft by Saml Donelson. Jan 1800 jury Charles Dement Peter Looney P Edmund Hatch Wm Wier

125

APRIL 1800

Robt Collier Elisha Edwards Jas White Thos Murry Joseph McAdam Mattw Anderson Jabus Fisher Wm Snoddy assess plfs damages $37.50. New trial granted dft. April 1800 jury Wm Bowen James Vinson Henry Parr Isaac Towell Jno Savely Jas Morrison Solomon Reese Henry Belote Joseph McAdam Robert Caruthers Burrell Perry Eneas Hannah assess plfs damage $50. Dft granted appeal to Superior Court, Wm Snoddy & James McKinsey sec.
Jno Lancaster v Jas Coglin & Thomas Farmer. Debt. Robt Jones bail for dft Farmer.
Ltr/atty Charles Harrington of Logan County Kentuckey to Robert Jones of Sumner TN authorises sd Robert to apply to secretaries office in North Carolina for grant of land in Chatham County No Carolina 440 acres & to dispose of sd land, was proved by John C Hamilton.
Ltr/atty Malachi Fike of Logan County Kentucky to Robert Jones of Sumner, sd Robert to draw out of Treasury of No Carolina money due sd Malachi for military services performed in or for No Carolina proved by John C Hamilton.
James Lauderdale brings John Hawkins & John Allcorn who make oath that sd James on 29 March last did loose part of his left ear in a fight that same day.
William Hankins v John Young. Appeal. 21 Jan 1800 Wm Hankins made oath to Thomas Masten J P that John Young is indebted to him $50 for rent of house & lot; sd Young is about to remove from State. Andrew Hoover levied on horse cow & trunk of wearing apparel 29 Jan 1800. Feb 1800 plf & dft before Thomas Masten Esq but plfs witnesses p.254 failed to appear; judgt entered favour of dft. Plf appeals, Saml Donelson sec. Apr 1800 plf by Saml Donelson; dft by Isaac McNutt. Jury[above except Caleb Simpson & Eneas Herrall for Jas Morrison & Eneas Hannah]; plfs damages $10 & costs.
William Henderson named in Commission/Peace by John Sevier takes oaths of office.
George Mickey John B Johnson John Deloach Wm McKorcle Edward Hogin Laban Benthall report they laid off a road from Capt Richard Kings plantation to new cut way made by Capt King to Little East fork.
Anthy Metcalf v Ezekl Douglass. Dft obtains appeal, Wm Snoddy & Jas McKinsey sec.
Deed Zebulon Brevard to Nathl Thompson 100 acres proved by David Edmunston.
Bill/sale Henry Vinson to Simon Totevine negro boy Dick ackd.
David Wilson esq county register made oath that Richard Cooke delivered deed to be recorded from Stephen Merritt to John R Eaton 640 acres in military boundary; afsd deed taken out of his office without his knowledge before it was recorded.
William Read recovered agt John Dobbins by attachment before Witheral Latimer esqr $46.36 in several suits incl constables fees for each attachment; all were levied on 640 acres middle fork Red River; 106 acres ordered to be sold.
Commission apptd by act of Assembly to purchase land for a court house & prison & stocks, James Wilson David Beard Edward Gwin James Cryer David Shelby; bond $500, William Montgomery security.
Wm Montgomery named in Commission/Peace by John Sevier takes oaths & qualifies.

Wednesday April 9th 1800. Present David Wilson Isaac Walton Wm Henderson David Love John Morgan William Montgomery Esquires.
State v Matthew Cowan. TAB. Jury Wm Bowen James Vinson Wm Sample Wm Hankins Smith Hansbrough Arthur Exum Wm Read Wm Henderson Peter Dagner Drury Milam Mark Rickmon Enos Harrell find dft not guilty. Prosecutor Adonijah Edwards taxed with costs. Plf p.255 prays appeal to Superior Court, Thomas Edwards & George Smith securities.
Lists/taxable property returned: David Love in Capt Loves & Capt Carrs companies; Isaac Walton in Capt Whitsitts district; Edward Gwin in Capt Gwins district.
Deed James Winchester & William Cage to Joseph McElwrath lot #22 in Cairo proved

APRIL 1800

by Ambrose Porter.
  Deed William Cage to Thomas Blackemore 236 acres ackd.
  State v Joyce Jones. Presentment agt her children being in state of sufferance; dft submits; children not in state of sufferance; dft dismissed.
  State v John Sterns. Presentment, neglect/duty as overseer/road; fined 1¢ & cost. [Similar presentments agt James Clendening, James Franklin, & John Morgan.]
  Order Peter Looney be overseer/road in place of James Franklin.
  James Morrison apptd overseer/road in place of James Clendening.
  John Murphey v George Sheibly & Andrew Hoover. Oct 1797 John Murphey recovered agt George Sheibly & Andw Hoover judgt for $58.81 & costs, part remains unpaid; si p.256 fa issued by David Shelby. J Cage returned: Made known before Arthur Hankins & John Young to Andrew Hoover, Geo Sheibly not found. Apr 1800 Hoover by Samuel Donelson. Jury Wm Bowen James Vinson Arthur Exum Wm Reed Wm Henderson Peter Dagner Mark Rickmon Eneas Harrall Wm Snoddy Robt Wynne Matthew Anderson Robert Pearce find for dft who recover full costs of sd suit expended.
  Jacob Garrett v Jno Bradley. TAB. July 1799 plf by John C Hamilton; dft by Samuel Donelson & George Smith. Apr 1800 jury[above] find for plf damages $40. With costs.
  Deed Hugh Bradshaw to William Bradshaw 320 acres proved by J Bradshaw Jr.
  Order Wm Smith Jas Espie Joel Echols Wm Hubbart Thos Bradley Thos Murry lay off a road from Cairo to Second Creek where great road intersects sd creek.
  Release Robt Desha from ½ value of stray cow, sd cow being lost again.
  Edmund Hatch v Eneas Harrell. July 1799 Plf by Benjn Seawell; dft by Geo Smith. Apr 1800 jury Wm Bowen Jas Vinson Arthur Exum Wm Reed Wm Henderson Mark Rickmon Wm Snoddy Mattw Anderson Thos Edwards Drury Milam Adonijah Edwards Joseph McAdams find for dft. Plf granted appeal to Superior Court, Benjn Seawell & James Trousdale sec.
p.257 List/taxable property in Capt Kirkpatricks district retd by John McMurtry.

Thursday April 10th 1800. Present Edward Douglass Wm Cage John Morgan James Cryer David Wilson Isaac Walton Edwd Gwin Esquires.
  Bill/sale Richard Graham to Elizabeth Graham for a mare proved by James Wilson.
  State v Matthew Cowan. TAB. New trial is not granted.
  State v Henry Morris. Petit Larceny. Henry Morris on 11 Feb 1800 with force and arms being seduced by the instigation of the Devil did steal about a bushel & half of wheat, value six pence property of David Wilson. Witnesses James A Wilson David Wilson & Z Wilson sworn before D Shelby clk, true bill, Geo Gillespie foreman. Jury Wm Bowen Wm Reed Joseph McAdam Wm Douglass Joel Echols John Deloach Isaac Towell Robt Pearce John Boyce Drury Milam John Young James Rankin find dft guilty.
  Deed David Looney to Daniel Looney Miner 106½ acres proved by Richard Britton.
  Deed David Looney to Margaret Miner 106½ acres proved by Richard Britton.
  Deed David Looney to James Brigance 106½ acres proved by Richard Britton.
  Writ of enquiry issues to sheriff to summon a jury to ascertain degree of lunacy attached to William Cathey.
  Jurors to Superior Court: William Edwards Thomas Edwards Lewis Crain James Wilson (shooting) John Payton Moore Stevenson William Maxey.
  James Winchester Esqr takes his seat.
  Jury summoned to enquire into state of William Cathey's mind report he is in every degree to be considered a lunatic: Wm Bowen W Douglass John Deloach Wm Maxey Joseph McAdam Wm R Wier John Boyer[Boyce?] George Mansker Isaac Towell Robert Ellis Roger Gibson Joel Echols.

APRIL 1800

Appt Alexander Cathey guardian to Wm Cathey lunatic; bond $2000, John Cathey sec. Reuben Cage gives bond for collection/public taxes, Saml Donelson Edwd Gwin James
p.258 Winchester securities. Also bond for county taxes, same securities.
John Young v James Hannah. Jul 1799 plf by Saml Donelson; dft by Geo Smith. Alias writ agt Enos Hannah. Atty for dft suggests Enos was a minor; discharged. Apr 1800 jury William Bowen William Douglass John Boyce Jno Deloach Roger Gibson Joel Echols Robt Ellis Isaac Towel Russell Wyer Geo Mansker Jos McAdam William Reed assess plfs damage $40 & costs.
State v Joyce Jones. Order dft pay all costs.
Matthew Alexander surrenders Henry Morris into custody of the sheriff.

Friday April 11th 1800. Present David Wilson Thomas Donnell Jonathan Hannum James Winchester Wm Montgomery Ben Rawlings Esqrs.
Thomas Donnell returns list of taxable property in Capt Vinsons Company.
Robert Stothart & Co v George Parks. Oct 1799 plf by Joseph Herndon and Thomas Stuart; dft by Saml Donelson. Apr 1800 jury William Bowen Wm Douglass Wm Reed Robt Pearce Isaac Towell Jos Moore John Savely Drury Milam Elisha Taylor John Stevenson Geo Mansker Burrell Perry assess plfs damage $51.89. With cost.
Kasper Mansker v John Mansker. Oct 1799 plf by Saml Donelson & Geo Smith. Dft by John C Hamilton. Apr 1800 jury Wm Douglass John Barr Thos Edwards Isaac Towell Wm Reed Burrell Perry Jas Wilson (smkg) John Saveley Elisha Taylor Drury Milam Wm Dixon Jas A Wilson assess plfs damage $1 and cost.
Deed James Rhodes to John Wylls 108½ acres proved by Isaac Walton.
State v John Josey. Neglect of duty as overseer of road. Fined $1 and costs.
p.259 John Wright v Joseph McAdams. Attachment. Sept 1799 J Cage levied on three horses 3 cows. Plf by John C Hamilton; dft by Saml Donelson. Apr 1800 jury William Douglass John Barr Thos Edwards Wm Reed Jas A Wilson Jos Wilson Mattw Anderson John Mansker Wm Neely John Stevenson Jas Weatherred James Morrison find for plf damages $101. Dft granted appeal to Superior Court, Benjamin Rawlings & Wm Montgomery sec.
Appoint Shadrach Nye overseer/road in place of William Montgomery.
Jurors to July Term: Laurence Whitsitt Elisha Pruett Wm McGready William Bell Wm Anderson (carpt) James Frazor David Eckols James Weathered John Lauderdale Stephen Middleton Isaac Baker Adam Hunter Gabriel Black Jas Harrison Nathaniel Giles James Brown Matthew Alexander William Hubbard Jas Clendening Jeremiah Watson Fergus Sloan James Vinson Joseph Wilson John Mills John Carr Isaac Lane Robert Hamilton James Sanders William Trigg William Gwin William Gillespie Seth Mabry Robt Jones William Anderson (blacks) Richard King James Kirkpatrick.
Appt Robt Forrester Wm Brown & Jas Caruthers patrolers for Capt Vinsons district, to qualify before James Winchester Esqr.
Appt Wm McCorcle overseer of the road in place of Richard King.
Burrell Perry v Joseph McAdams. Attachment. Oct 1799 J Cage levied on waggon & two iron kettles. Plf by Benjn Seawell; dft by Saml Donelson replevyed property. April 1800 dft in proper person confesseth judgt $37.50.
Deed Howell Tatum to James McKinsey 43½ acres proved by Edward Douglass.
Benjamin Rawlings Esqr returns list of taxable property in Capt Greens district.

Saturday April 12th 1800. Present David Wilson James Winchester James Reese Isaac Walton Benjn Rawlings James Hart John Morgan Jonathan Hannum Esquires.

APRIL 1800

p.260   Commissioners report division of Negroes of estate of William Young decd.
Appt James Reese & Thomas Donnell to settle with admrs of Henry Loving decd.
John Wright v Joseph McAdams. New trial not granted.
Appt Francis Locke overseer/road Harts ferry by Harts mill to line between Sumner & Smith counties. Charles Donoho to furnish list of hands to work on sd road.
Appt Wm Exum overseer/road Harts mill to Dixon Spring to line between Sumner & Smith counties; Charles Donohoo to furnish list of hands to work on sd road.
George G Black v Peter Turney Thomas Lacey Sr & Thomas Lacey Jr. Dfts originally in joint action with Amos Lacey who confessed judgt. Dfts atty may add new plea.
Wilson Cage v William Dobbins. Attachment. Jury William Douglass William Reed Thomas Parker John Mansker Russell Wier Joseph McAdam Joseph Wallace James Lyon Isaac McNutt Robert Ellis Reuben Pruett William Penny. Mistrial.
Thomas Edwards v William Edwards. Attacht. July 1799 J Cage levied on 640 acres where Stuart Brigance & others are now living. Jan 1800 dft came not; judgt by default. Apr 1800 jury[above] find plfs damages $500. With costs. Condemn 200 acres for use of judgment; to be sold by sheriff.
Robert Ellis v Benjamin Kuykendall. Attachment. Jan 1800 J Cage levied on Benjn Kuykendalls part of 200 acres joining James Reese on Bledsoes Cr. Plf by Geo Smith; dft came not; judgt by default. Apr 1800 jury[above except Thomas Edwards for Robt
p.261   Ellis] find for dft; Condemn 20 acres to be sold by sheriff.
Clerk to pay $10 to the person who may erect a pound for strays.
Appt George D Blackemore guardian for Polley Betsey Hannah & John Zeigler orphans of Jacob Zeigler decd; bond $1000, James Reese & James Winchester securities.
State v Matthew Cowan. TAB. Verdict for deft; prosecutor Adonijah Edwards granted appeal; bond $500 with Thomas Edwards & George Smith securities.
Order James Winchester William Hall James Reese John Morgan & David Love to lay off to Polley Weathered & Prudence Bledsoe their part of real estate of their deceased father Anthony Bledsoe agreeable to his will.
Appt Wilcher Bandy Richard Hankins and Jesse Page patrollers for Captain Hankins district; they are to qualify before William Henderson esquire.
James Reese returns list/taxable property in Capt Neelys district.
John Wright v Joseph McAdams. Att. Dft obtains appeal, bond $500 with Benjamin Rawlings & William Montgomery securities.
Reuben Cage collector/ Public taxes takes oath prescribed by law.
Court adjourns till Court in Course to meet at the town of Cairo.   David Wilson

p.262 Court of Pleas & Quarter Sessions first Monday in July 1800. Present Thomas Donnell John Morgan Jonathan Hannum Esqrs.
Deed Mary Porter to Francis Fonvielle 60 acres proved by John Withers.
Persons who make returns/taxable property this term released from double tax.
Deed Henry Lyon to Francis Weatherred 96 acres ackd.
Grant admn/estate of William Bentley decd granted to James Bentley & Henry Belote in sum $2000 with William Hall & James Vinson securities.
James Winchester James Reese & William Montgomery Esqrs take their seats.
Grand Jury: Seth Mabry foreman, Isaac Lane Fergus Sloan James Weatherred Joseph Wilson John Kerr James Harrison James Clendening Richard King Wm Anderson carp,

JULY 1800

Nathaniel Giles Wm McGready John Lauderdale. Isaac Donohoo to attend Grand Jury.
Deeds ackd & proved: James Morrison & Elenor Morrison to Francis Weatherred 15 acres 59 perches proved by Henry Lyon. James Harrison to James Williams 43 acres. James Harrison to Cornelius Herndon 100 ac. James Harrison to Henry Harrison 58 ac.
Ephraim Payton v John Dawson. George Mickey bail for defendant.
Bill/sale John Deloach to William Fort 3 Negroes Ginney Edy Isaac ackd.
John Dickinson Esq presented license to practice as atty certified by Clerk of Superior Court of Mero District; took oath of an attorney and admitted.
Lemuel Henry Esqr presented license to practice as atty with certificate of clerk of Smith County; admitted to practice as an attorney in this Court.
State v James White. Neglect of duty as overseer of road. Failing to appear at April Term, defendant forfeited recognizance. July 1800 dft submits; released from forfeiture, fined one cent and to pay cost.
Deed Valentine Shoat to James Richmond 100 acres proved by David Stuart.
p.263 Deeds ackd & proved: James Richmond to David Stuart 100 ac. James Cary to Henry Harrison 43 acres by Cornelius Herndon. James McKain to Frederick Miller 16¼ acres. Benjamin Menees to John Dening 640 acres.
James Winchester & Wm Cage Jr lots in Cairo sold to: George D Blackmore(3 deeds). David Wilson(4 deeds). James Vinson(3 deeds). Matthew Alexander. George Brown.
Grant admr/estate of Simon Totevine decd to Heli Herring; bond $1000, John Deloach & Thomas Farmer securities.

Tuesday July 8th 1800. Present James Reese David Wilson Thomas Blackemore David Love Jonathan Hannum James Winchester William Montgomery.
Deed Samuel Stuart to John Goudy 125 acres ackd.
Deed James Winchester & Wm Cage Jr to Ebenezer Flin lot 11 in Cairo ackd.
Deed James Winchester & Wm Cage Jr to James Reese lot 19 in Cairo ackd.
George Gabriel Black v Peter Turney Thomas Lacy Jr Thomas Lacy Sr. Debt. Oct 1799 dfts by Thomas Stuart & John C Hamilton pleaded abatement. Judgt confessed by Amos
p.264 Lacy. July 1800 plf proceeds agt dfts notwithstanding recovery being had agt Amos Lacy by confession. Jury Elisha Pruitt David Echols Stephen Middleton Isaac Baker Mathew Alexander Wm Hubbard Wm White James Edwards George Logan Joseph George Hugh McGee John Gardner find for plf $145.75. Plf stays execution 2 months.
Appt James McKinsey overseer/road in place of John Josey.
Deed Lazarus Jones to Rencher McDaniel 337 acres proved by Turner Temple.
Deed Thomas Smith to Rencher McDaniel 274 acres proved by Turner Temple.
Deed Charles Dixon by Tilmon Dixon his attorney in fact to John Trousdale 165 acres proved by James Hart.
Court adjourns until 2 oclock PM. Court meets. Present David Wilson, James Winchester, Edward Douglass, James Reese, Thomas Mastin, William Cage, James Douglass, John Morgan, James Hart, David Love, Archibald Marlin, Reuben Searcy, Benj Rawlings, Wm Henderson, Jonathan Hannum, James Cryer, Edward Gwin, William Montgomery, Thomas Donnell, John McMurtry, Witheral Latimer, Thomas Blackemore.
Appt James Cage sheriff; bond $12,500, Edward Douglass George D Blackmore John Morgan securities.
John B Johnson esq presented license to practice as atty at law; took oath.
State v David Love. Dfts appearance bond, Smith Hansbrough security.
p.265 James McKain representative & heir of James McKain decd ack scire facias at instance of Anthony Crutcher to review judgt obtained by Crutcher agt decedant.

JULY 1800

Appt Jane Kuykendall guardian for Lewis Kuykendall & Robert Kuykendall orphans of Benjamin Kuykendall, bond $500 with John D Hannah security.
Release Henry Vinson from attending as a juror for present Term.
Inventory/goods of Wm S Carson decd proved by Richard Alexander one of the admrs.
State v John Young. Defts appearance bond. Edward Gwin security.
Appoint Robert White constable for Capt Haineys district, bond $625 with Matthew Alexander & Nathl Giles securities.
Order personal property, except Negroes, belonging to estate of William S Carson decd be exposed to sale by the administrator.
Edward Gwin v Michael Plaster. Attachment. Oct 1799 Jacob Parks DS levied on cow calf sundry articles. Oct 1799 plf by John C Hamilton. Dft came not; judgment by default. Jan 1800 order part of property attached to be sold. Continued. July 1800 jury Elisha Pruett David Echols Stephen Middleton James Harrison Richard Boyce Wm White John Mays John Deloach Moses Cummins Joseph T Williams William Hubbard Daniel Alexander find plfs damages $28.73 & 1 mill & costs.
Appt Francis Locke constable for Capt Bradleys dist; James Hart security.
Wilson Cage v William Dobbins. Attacht. Apr 1798 R Cage levied on 320 acres between Edward Douglass & Wm Frazor on south side Cumberland opposite Bledsoes creek near Jean Kuykendall whereon Robt Dobbins formerly lived; levied on 640 adj Witherall Latimer. Plf by Saml Donelson. Alexander McKee, garnishee. John Franklin, shff.
p.266   Summon Sion Perry & Joshua Hadley garnishees. July 1799 John Sloss would make title 320 acres to anyone who would bring ltr/ atty from dft for that purpose. Jan 1800 dft came not; judgt by default. April 1800 jury Wm Douglass Wm Reed Thomas Parker Jno Mansker Russell Wyer Jos McAdams Jos Wallace Jas Lyons Isaac McNutt Robt Ellis Reuben Pruett Wm Penny. Mistrial. July 1800 jury Elisha Pruit David Echols Stephen Middleton Jas Harrison Richd Boyce John Young John Mays John Deloach Moses Cummins Jos T Williams Wm Hubbard Danl Alexander find plfs damage $800 with costs.
Three deeds James Winchester & Wm Cage Jr lots in Cairo to James McKnight proved by Eli Giles.
p.267   Supplement acct/sales goods of Andrew Clark decd proved by George Clark.
Deed John Caffery to Reuben Searcy 640 acres proved by Samuel Donelson.
Ltr/atty Simon Spring to Elisha Cheek proved by Reuben Searcy.

Wednesday July 9th 1800. Present David Wilson James Winchester James Reese Jonathan Hannum Esquires.
Three deeds James Winchester & Wm Cage Jr to Daniel Alexander lots in Cairo ackd.
Inventory/goods of Wm Bentley decd proved by admrs.
Sion Perry v Daniel Richardson. Jury Elisha Pruett David Echols Stephen Middleton Matthew Alexander Wm Hubbard Joseph Neely Wm Neely Wm Sample Solomon Duty Henry Belote Jonathan Boone Wm Bell find for dft. Motion for a new trial.
William Moorhead acknowledges writ agt him at instance of William Philips.
Henry Harrison records his ear mark.
Deed James Winchester & Wm Cage Jr to Thomas Campbell lot 92 in Cairo ackd.
Robert Ellis v Benjn Kuykendall. Attached 8½ acres to be sold to satisfy judgt.
State v Jabus Fisher. Release dft from forfeiture/recognizance on paying costs.
Benjamin Seawell v heirs & devisees of Andrew Armstrong decd. Seawell recovered p.268   agt dfts; summon dfts. July 1800 dfts came not; judgment by default for $188.31½ and costs of suit.
Benjamin Seawell v heirs & devisees of Andrew Armstrong decd. [as above] judgt

JULY 1800

for $541.84 and costs of suit.

p.269   Office of Sumner v John Rutherford. Suit by John Rutherford agt Elijah P Chambers was nonsuited. D Shelby orders sheriff to summon sd Rutherford. John L Martin made summons known in presence of Henry Huddleston & Leonard Billens. July 1800 dft came not; judgt agt dft for costs of suit afsd.

Office of Sumner v John Murphey. Murphey was sued by Jas Winchester Wm Carr Thos Draper Thos Bradley; three former recovered judgts agt sd Murphey; latter dismissed his suit upon defts agreeing to pay cost $26.26 of which $7.50 settled by Murphey. J Cage made summons known to dft before Elisha Pruett & Isaac Walton.

Agreement between John Deloach William Gillespie & Redmond D Barry proved by James Daughety.

Ezekiel Douglass v Anthony Hogin & Matthew Cowan. Apr 1800 plf by Jno C Hamilton; dft by Saml Donelson. July 1800 jury Isaac Baker Robert Patton Wm Reed Robert Ellis Stephen Montgomery Joel Wilson John White Moses Cummins Daniel Alexander John Mays Moses Teague Wm Milligan find for plf damages $15 & costs agt Anthony Hogin. Mat-
p.270   thew Cowan not guilty. Defendant granted arrest of judgment.

Edwd Douglass Esqr deposits 62½ cents, a fine on John Young for profane swearing.

Appt Henry Belote guardian for John Bentley orphan of John Bentley decd; bond $2000 with James Bentley and Matthew Alexander securities.

Order admrs of Wm Bentley decd sell personal estate of decd except Negroes.

Reuben Cage esqr collector of public taxes for 1799 reports persons who failed to pay and who have no personal property within the county whereon to destrain: [amounts omitted]   Samuel Parker, W Jones agent. Moses Wilkerson. Joseph Woodfork. George Swingley. William Harrington. Samuel Marsh. Hugh Patrick. Hardy Sanders. Samuel Thornton. William Darhada. William Parker. James Woodard. Micajah Barrow. James Crockett. John Greenaway. Samuel Mitchell.

p.271   Richard Mitchell. James Watson. Will Henry per Thos Bedford. James Stuart. Robert Anderson heir of John. John Dobbins. Joseph Prior. John Blackemore. Elisha Davis. John Farland. Elias Fort. William Hay. Daniel McKisick. Frederick Ward. William Harrington. William Brandon. George Green. Edward Harris and John Grey Blount.   Thomas Love. Alexander McCaul.

p.272   Matthew Moore. John Shute. John White. John P Williams. To be published in the Knoxville Gazette agreeably to law.

Deed James Winchester & Wm Cage Jr to Daniel Alexander town lot in Cairo ackd.

Thursday July 10th 1800. Present James Winchester Edward Douglass James Reese Thomas Donnell William Montgomery Esquires.

Thomas Sharp admr of Egnew v Edward Hogin. Debt. Apr 1800 plf by Saml Donelson; dft by George Smith. July 1800 Jury Isaac Baker Wm Bell Elisha Pruett David Echols Stephen Middleton Matthew Alexander John White Saml Wilson Moses Wilson Robt Patton Jesse Johnson James Clark find for plf $126.86.

John Braly v John Troy. Attachmt. Apr 1800 J Cage levied on mare & saddle. Plf by John C Hamilton; dft came not; judgt by default. July 1800 jury[above except John Boyce for Robert Patton] find plfs damage $367.50 & costs.

Appt Thomas Masten & Isaac Walton to settle with admrs of Abijah Millens decd.

Appt James Reese & Thomas Donnell to settle with admrs of Henry Loving decd.

Order Bills/Indictment agt persons in other counties be directed to sheriffs.

p.273   Jesse Berryman v Nathan Jackson & Daniel Hylton. Debt. Plf by S Donelson. July 1800 dfts by Benjn Seawell. Jury Wm Hubbard Joel Pate Howell Pate Thos Farmer

JULY 1800

Danl Melton John Gibson Ephraim Alexander Moses Cummins Thos Bradley Henry Bloodworth Chas Forrester Owen Dillard find for plf $94.88.
　Anthony Crutcher v James McKain representative & heir of James McKain decd. Scire facias. Judgment $389.25 and costs of suit.
　Sion Perry v Daniel Richardson. New trial granted.
　State v Elijah Hendrick. Appearance bond Moses Cummins & Wm Donohoo state wits.
　Deed James Winchester & Wm Cage Jr to James Steel lot 10 in Cairo ackd.
　Sion Perry v Daniel Richardson. Parties permitted to amend declaration & pleas.
　Jurors to Oct Term: Adam Hunter Chas Reedy Cornelius Herndon Thomas Wherry Henry Belote Samuel Gibson Richard Parker Robert Desha Joel Eckols George Brown William Reed Nathaniel Thompson Thos Reese Paul Harpole James Morrison Thos Cocke Armstreet Stubblefield John Trousdale Wm Sanders Senr William Anderson B John Gardner Thomas Patton James Vinson Zacheus Wilson Jr Joseph Motherall Hugh Caruthers John Hamilton Jr Laurence Whitsitt James Kirkpatrick James Sanders William Trigg Junr John Dawson Hugh Crafford Cap William Reed Joseph Wallace Joshua Hadley.
　Ezekiel Douglass v Anthony Hogin & Matthew Cowan. New trial argued; overruled.
p.274　State v Robert Patton. TAB. Dft pleads guilty; fined $2 and costs.
　Ezekiel Douglass v Anthony Hogin & Matthew Cowan. Order arrest of judgment.
　Order Zacheus Wilson Jr commissioner in place of Wm Montgomery for settling with sheriff and other holders of public monies.
　Order execution agt estate of Henry Morris for costs in suit State v sd Morris.
　Thomas Edwards v William Edwards. Order two hundred more acres of land attached be condemned for use of balance of judgment obtained in sd suit.
　Deed Wm Sanders to John Seawell 110 acres ackd.
　Deed James Bradley to Owen Dillard 110 acres ackd.
　Deed James Bradley to Hardy Hunt 110 acres ackd.
　Bond Will Sanders & James Bradley to John Seawell support title of 110 ac ackd.
　Court adjourns half an hour. Met. Present Jas Winchester Jas Reese Wm Montgomery.
　License Seth Mabry to keep tavern at his dwelling, James Harrison security.
　State v Joel Dyer. TAB. Dft failed to appear, forfeits recognizance.
　State v Andrew Greer. Dyer's security forfeits his recognizance.
　William Brazil v Stephen Conger. Plf failing to appear, non suit entered agt him.
　Six deeds, 640 ac each, Reuben Cage shff to John Irwin proved by Samuel Donelson.

p.275　Court of Pleas & Quarter Sessions, first Monday in October at Town of Cairo. Present David Wilson Thomas Donnell & James Cryer Esquires.
　Appt James Sanders overseer of road in place of Edward Bradley.
　Grant ltrs/admn on estate of Martha Johnson decd to Jesse Johnson, bond $600 with James Vinson security.
　Bill/sale Catey Shaver to James Harrison household furniture stock and wearing apparel proved by Henry Harrison.
　Acct/sales goods of Wm S Carson decd proved by Rachel Carson one of admrs.
　Grand Jury: Hugh Crawford foreman, Charles Reedy, Joseph Wallace, Laurence Whitsitt, Cornelius Herndon, Henry Belote, James Vinson, John Gardner, John Trousdale, Thomas Cocke, William Anderson, John Dawson, John Hamilton Jr, Hugh Caruthers.
　Wm Reed Wm Sanders Wm Wherry Saml Gibson Paul Harpole exempted from attending as

OCTOBER 1800

jurors for the present Term.
Ltr/atty Matthew Kincannon to Daniel Smith one moiety of 640 acres to James Dysart proved by Samuel Meek.
Ltrs/admn on estate of William Cathey decd granted to Alexander Cathey son of the decedent, the widow of decd having relinquished her right; bond $5000 with William Sanders and John Cathey securities; took oath & received ltrs/admn.
Order Elizabeth Cathey orphan of Wm Cathey decd be committed to care & tuition of her mother Alice Cathey who is apptd her guardian; bond $1000, Wm Sanders security.
James Cathey, orphan of Wm Cathey decd, having attained age 14 makes choice of Wm Cathey his guardian; bond $1000, Montgomery McConnell security.
Wilson Cage v William Dobbins. Att. Order 320 acres property of dft agreeable to oath of John Sloss garnishee condemend for use of judgt; to be sold.
Sarah Storey orphan of Wm Storey decd having attained age 14 made choice of James Sanders to be her guardian; bond $600 with Wm Sanders security.
Order James Hart Charles Donohoo & John Cathey divide Negro property of estate of William Storey decd between heirs of sd decd.
Appt Mark Rickmon guardian for James B Storey Elizabeth S Storey & Ann R Storey orphans of William Storey decd; bond $2000, Joseph Mallard security.
State v Joseph Russell. Peace bond; towards Sarah Parks for a year & a day.
Recognizance of Richard Hogin, condition Joseph Russell keeps peace.
p.276   Inventory/goods of Simon Totevine decd proved by administrator.
Appt Edward Bradley James Sanders & Abraham Ellis patrollers, Bradleys company.
Appt James Franklin constable for Capt Greens company, Peter Looney security.
Order personal estate of Simon Totevine decd to be sold by admr.
Joel Dyer reputed father of bastard child of Susanna Morgan enters bond for expences of sd child $500, William Hall security.
License John Stuart to keep ordinary at his dwelling house, bond $2500 with Wm White & Henry Harrison securities.
Deeds ackd & proved: James Trousdale to James Wilson Curley by James Trousdale Jr. Marshall Stroud to Joseph Mallard by Mark Rickmon. Marshall Stroud to David Henry by Mark Rickmon. Robert Wilson to Eli Giles by David Wilson. Zacheus Wilson Jr to David Shelby. David Shelby to Zacheus Wilson. Richard Hogin to David Shelby.
Mortgage Simon Totevine to Jesse Hereford 3 cows 4 yearlings & 13 hogs & two fields of corn proved by Malachi Hereford.

Tuesday October 7th 1800. Present James Reese, James Cryer, David Love, Esquires.
Deed Thomas Jeffreys & wife Mildred to William Flournoy Booker 520 acres admitted to record on certificate of Clerk of Caswell County North Carolina.
Nicholas Perkins esqr exhibited license to practice as atty & is admitted.
Deed Chas Dixon by Tilmon Dixon atty in fact to Peter Lyons proved by James Hart.
Bill/sale John D Hannah to Katey Bledsoe negro girl Agg proved by William Cage.
George Parks v John Mansker. Debt. Oct 1799 plf by Saml Donelson; dft by John C Hamilton. Oct 1800 jury Robt Desha, Zacheus Wilson, Jos Motherall, Bryant Gardner,
p.277   George Mickey, Solomon Reese, James Wilson Sr, Laban Benthall, John Withers, James Lyon, James Simpson, Robert Steel find $30.60 for plf. And costs.
Thomas Owings v Rachel Clark admx of Robt Clark decd. Debt. Jan 1800 plf by Thos Stuart. Oct 1800 dft by Saml Donelson. Jury[above] except James Rankins & William Daniel for Jas Wilson Sr & Laban Benthall find for plf $41.04. & costs.
Deed William Hankins to William Henderson 150 acres proved by John Henderson.

JULY 1800

License James Steel to keep ordinary at his dwelling in Cairo, Jas A Wilson sec.
Bill/sale John Orr to Joseph McElwrath negro girl Mary proved by David Shelby.
Deed Reuben Cage to Robert Fenner 577 acres proved by Reuben Douglass.
Bill/sale James Daughety to Henry Bradford negro boy named TomTom boy proved by Reuben Douglass.
Jesse Johnson admr/Martha Johnson decd took oath prescribed by law for an admr.
Laban Benthall v Anthony Hogin. TAB. William Sadler bail for dft surrenders him; Richard Hogin acknowledges himself bail for dft.
William Samples v Humphrey Miers. Jury Robt Desha Zacheus Wilson Jos Motherall Bryant Gardner Geo Mickey Jas Wilson Robt Wynne Jas Rankin Matthew Alexander John Payton Laban Benthall Edward Hudson. Mistrial made by consent.
Deed Katey Bledsoe extx of Isaac Bledsoe decd to William Cochran 203 acres proved by William Hubart.
Appt Malachi Hereford overseer/road west fork Station Camp at John Dawsons to big east fork sd creek in place of Ezekiel Douglass.

Wednesday October 8th 1800. Present Edward Douglass James Reese John Organ David Wilson David Love Esquires.
State v Montgomery McConnell. Neglect/duty as overseer/road. Dft pleads guilty; fined one cent and pay all cost accruing.
Appt Daniel Sanders overseer/road in place of Montgomery McConnell.
State v William Francis. Peace bond, especially towards Parker Caradine.
Peter Looney P & Elisha Clary security for William Francis to keep the Peace.
p.278   State v John Young. TAB. Jury Robt Desha Jos Motherall Elisha Clary Peter Luna Nicholas Boyce Nathl Giles John Wilson Robt Patton Nathl Hughs Thos Holden Peter Dagner Wm Moorhead find dft guilty of trespass assault as charged but not guilty of battery. Dft fined six cents and pay costs.
Acct/sales of goods of William Bentley decd proved by admrs.
Motion of guardians for Isaac Abraham & Henry Bledsoe heirs & devisees of Anthony Bledsoe decd, order George Gillespie David Henry Robert Steel James Harrison & James Lauderdale divide residue of Greenfield tract of land not already appropriated between sd heirs.
Fine Isaac McNutt $5 for a contempt of the Court.
State v John Young. TAB. Found guilty of assault, dft fined 6 cents & pay costs.
State v Anthony Hogin. TAB. Dft submits; suit continued.
John Hassell records his ear mark.
Release Henry Lyon from taxes on his billard table for present year.
State v Isaac Leftwicke. Dft failed to appear; forfeits recognizance.
State v Isham A Parker. Dft fails to bring Leftwicke, forfeits recognizance.
Order Wm Hall Jas Vinson Jesse Johnson Geo D Blackmore divide Negro property of estate of William Bentley decd between heirs of decedant.
James Hennen made oath that he believes Negro Sebb & her children to be free agreeable to certificate in possession of Major Wilson; further maketh oath he believes sd Sebb to be person alluded to in sd certificate, and that he heard Capt David Love say he believed Sebb had a right to her freedom.
William Moorhead v Joseph McAdams. Covt. Jury: Robt Desha Jos Motherall Nathaniel Giles Nathl Hughs Thos Holden Richd Hogin Henry Harrison Zacheus Wilson John Gibson Thos Cocke Cornelius Herndon John Payton; mistrial made by consent.
Isaac McNutt released from his fine $5 for a contempt of the Court.

JULY 1800

Thursday October 9th 1800. Present David Wilson Edwd Douglass David Love Jas Cryer.
Joseph Davis v Spencer Glascock. Apr 1800 plf by Saml Donelson; dft by Geo Smith.
p.279   Oct 1800 jury Robert Desha Nathaniel Hughes Patk Lyon Leonard Miles John Payton George Gillespie John Gillespie Peter Dagnor John Bosley Daniel Hylton Joel Echols Richard Hogin assess plaintiffs damages $5 and costs.
Inventory/goods of Wm Cathey decd proved by administrator.
Zacheus Wilson, commr to settle with collectors, bond, James Wilson Jr security.
State v Anthony Hogin & Benjamin Kuykendall. Presentment as disturbers/Peace.
Jury: Joseph Motherall John Boyce Thomas Gillespie John Payton Joseph Burton Jesse Kirkland Robt Pearson Wm Giles Robt Patton Tandy Witcher John Deloach Danl Hylton find dfts guilty. Fined $7 each; fine mitigated to $3 each.
State v Anthony Hogin & Benjamin Kuykendall. Presentment. Recognizance $50 each for appearance; Richard Hogin dfts security recognizance $50.
Negroes/estate of William Cathey decd, except personal estate, to be sold.

Friday October 10th 1800. Present David Wilson Edward Douglass John Morgan James Cryer Jonathan Hannum Esqrs.
Deed Reuben Cage shff to Benjamin Seawell 640 acres proved by Thomas Stuart.
Deed Reuben Cage shff to Benjamin Seawell 640 acres proved by Thomas Stuart.
State v Anthony Hogin & Benjamin Kuykendall. Motion for new trial overruled.
State v Matthew Anderson. Presentment as disturber/Peace. Dfts found guilty, fined $7 each and costs therewith.
Petition of Thomas Cribbins & Armstead Rogers, scire facias issues agt Benjamin Davis & his wife Mary admrs of Abijah Millens decd to shew cause why they have not made settlement with the Court for their administration.
Jurors to Superior Court: William Maxey John Gatlin Robert Ellis James Rankin John Payton James Douglass Ezekiel Douglass.
p.280   Jurors to Jan Term: Wm Edwards Isaac Baker Wm Maxey Richd King, Jas Trousdale, Robt Anderson Jas Caruthers Patk Morrison Geo Mickey Jas Tho[binding] David Beard Jr John Sterns Henry Stout Andw Blythe Alexr Anderson John D Hannah Wm Allen Thos Reese Wm Beard Jno Gibson Eli Giles Danl McConnell Francis Locke James Graham Thos Stubblefield John Goodrum Jos Neely Jas Morrison Jas McMurry James Lauderdale Isaac Parker Edmund Browning Jesse Hainey Wm Bradshaw John Shaver Josiah Wilson.
William Philips v William Moorhead. Covt. Dft in proper person pleaded covenant performed. Jury Geo Gillespie John Gillespie John Deloach Robt Patton Richd Hogin Hezekiah Oneill Advil Atkinson James Vinson Henry Harrison Wm Giles Tandy Witcher Edmd Smith assess plfs damages $144.28.
Josiah Price v James Cotten. Debt. Apr plf by Thos Stuart; July dft by John C Hamilton. Oct 1800 jury[above except Wm Douglass for Edmund Smith] find for plf $36 debt $6.66 damages.
Ordered Peter Dagner fined $1 for rooting(?) in presence of the Court.
Sampson Williams v John Roberts. Sampson Williams recovered of Thos Morris $20 and $8.14½ costs. John Roberts garnishee had £5.6.10 Virginia money in gold two crowns 12½ cts, 35 bushels corn, and knew half dollar in hands of Mr. Grey due to dft. Roberts summoned to Court by David Shelby Clerk. Read to John Roberts 13 August in presence of Edward Hogin Senr and Archibald Hatcher. Oct 1800 dft failed to appear. Judgment against him $28.14½ & costs of scire facias.
Edward Gwin v Michael Plaster. Attachmt. Property levied on to be sold.

JANUARY 1801

p.281   Fine imposed on Anthony Hogin & Benjamin Kuykendall reduced to $3 each.
David Love v Nathaniel Parker. Debt. Plf by Thos Stuart; dft fails to appear. Judgt agt him $110 and $1.65 damages.
Thomas Cribbins v John & Ephraim Payton. Appt William Hall surveyor & Jas Wilson shooting, Jas Wilson smoaking, Archibald Marlin, Henry Bradford, James Harrison & David Love jurors to lay off a tract of 10 acres called Salt Petre Cave tract; plat to be received as testimony in suit Wm Morgan v John & Ephraim Payton.
Order Thos Donnell & James Reese settle with admrs of Henry Loving decd.
Order Thos Donnell & James Reese settle with exrs of Michael Shaver decd.
Order David Shelby released from taxes on 1936 acres listed by mistake, situated in Smith and Wilson counties.
Genl Griffith Rutherford makes oath that in 1784 or 1785 he made a location for Doctor Samuel McCorkle for land on Fountain Creek, south side of Duck River.
Court adjourns till Court in Course to meet at Town of Cairo.   David Wilson

p.282   Court of Pleas & Quarter Sessions at Cairo on first Monday in January 1801. Present James Winchester James Reese James Douglass Thomas Donnell Esquires.
Inventory of goods of Martha Johnson decd proved by admrs.
George Mickey & Jesse Hainey excused from attending as jurors for present Term.
Jurors failing to appear are fined: William Edwards William Maxwell James Caruthers Patrick Morrison Jno H Stout Jno D Hannah William Allen Thomas Reese Daniel McConnell Jos Neely Jas Morrison Jas McMurry Edmd Browning Josiah[Jonah?] Wilson.
Grand jury: Robert Anderson foreman Richard King David Beard Jr John Goodrum John Shaver Thos Stubblefield Andrew Blythe James Lauderdale James Trousdale John Gibson Eli Giles William Bradshaw James Graham.
Deed Matthew Anderson to Joseph McElwrath 57½ acres ackd.
Deed Joseph McElwrath to David Orr 60 acres ackd.
Grant admn/estate of Carleton Atkinson decd to Robert Atkinson; bond $200, Robert Laurence security.
Will of James Chapman decd proved by Charles Laurence who made oath that Thomas Campbell, another witness, subscribed his name in presence of sd Laurence.   Martha Chapman & Alexander Chapman extx & extr qualified.
Deed/gift James Lauderdale to Martha Hawkins James S Hawkins & Benjamin Hawkins daughter & sons of John Hawkins & Sarah his wife for negroes: Amy & Charlotte to Martha, Will to J S Hawkins, Harry to Benjamin, also 200 acres to be equally divided between the two boys ackd by sd James Lauderdale.
Bill/sale John Hawkins to James Lauderdale negroes Jack, Maria, Violet, Tom, Sal & Pat, also stock & household furniture ackd.
On affadavit, Elisha Cheek released from taxes in this county for present year.
Edmund Crutcher qualified as deputy sheriff under James Cage sheriff.
State v Richard Boyce[Boyer?]. Recognizance, Nicholas Boyce security.
Apprentice George Washington Mullins to John Bradley to learn hatters trade.
Deed Thomas Patton to Robert Patton 63 acres ackd.
Deed William Cage to Reuben Cage 6 acres ackd.
Deed John Sawyers to John Dobbins 320 acres proved by Wm Hall.
p.283   Deed William Cage to heirs of William Parmer decd 24 acres ackd.

JANUARY 1801

Deed William Lauderdale to James Henry & John Mills 113 acres ackd.
Deed William Stalcup to Samuel Stalcup 50 acres proved by John Patton.
Inventory/goods of Carleton Atkinson decd proved byd admr.
Acct/sales goods of David Holliday decd rendered by Sampson Williams.

Tuesday January 6th 1801. Present James Reese Benjamin Rawlings John McMurtrie and William Montgomery esquires.
    James Hart v Robert Sanders. Alias writ ordered.
    John Lancaster v Thomas Farmer. Debt. Apr 1800 plf by Benjn Seawell; dft by John C Hamilton. Jan 1801 dft in proper person confesses judgment $85.60 & costs.
    Bond Edwin Hickman to Josiah Payne proved by Benjamin John.
    Deed Thomas Harney to James Simpson 160 acres proved by James White.
    Instrument from Joyce Jones to Edward Hogin proved by John C Hamilton.
    Sion Perry v Daniel Richardson. Apr 1800 plf by Saml Donelson; dft by John C Hamilton. Jul 1800 Jury Elisha Pruett David Echols Stephen Middleton Matthew Alexander Wm Hubbard Joseph Neely Wm Neely Wm Sample Solomon Duty Henry Belote Jonathan Boone Wm Bell find for dft. Grant new trial. Jan 1801 jury Isaac Baker Wm Maxey Jas Caruthers Patk Morrison Jas Thomas Alexr Anderson Daniel McConnell Isaac Parker Josiah Wilson Edwd Hogin Hugh Elliott Geo Gillespie; plf not appearing, non suited.
    Deed Sion Perry to Robert Dobbins 466 acres proved by Henry Vinson.
    Sion Perry v Daniel Richardson. Robt Boyce plfs wit failing to answer forfeits.
p.284   William Sample v Humphrey Miers. Dft allowed to amend his plea.
    William Sample v Humphrey Miers. Jan 1800 plf by Saml Donelson; dft by B Seawell. Plf likewise, T Stuart. Jan 1801 jury[above] judgment in favour of the defendant.
    Bill/sale Samuel Nelson to Reuben Douglass negro boy Jack proved by Wm Edwards.
    Deed/gift Bernard McCarty to Humphrey McElyea eldest son of Wm McElyea a mare; to John McElyea second son of sd William a colt proved by Archibald Marlin.
    Deed William Hamilton to Thomas Perry 8 acres proved by Isaac Walton.
    Excuse Wm Edwards from attending as a juror for present term.
    Sample v Miers. Special verdict, favour of defendant.
    David Shelby exr of Wm Beakley decd v Thomas Edwards. Dec 1799 summon Thomas Edwards to court at house of William Gillespie. Jan 1800 estate of Thos Edwards p.285 attached. Apr 1800 dft in proper person ack writ. Attached property to be sold. Jan 1801 jury Isaac Baker John Gillespie James Harrison Alexr Anderson Saml Wilson Peter Looney H Michael C Dunn John Payton Josiah Wilson John Looney Joseph Bunton Wm Thompson assess plfs damages $45.05 & costs.
    Henry Williams reputed father of illegitimate child of which Anne Duger is pregnant pays fine 25 shillings equal to $3.12½; bond $500, Isaac Towell, security.
    Joel Dyer fined 25 shillings equal $3.12½
    Deed John Hamilton Senr to Thomas Perry 100 acres proved by Isaac Walton.
    Commrs apptd to appropriate residue of Greenfield land between heirs of Anthony Bledsoe decd render into Court a statement of their proceedings.
    State v John Boyd. Judgt agt John Boyd $2.65 & 1 mill for 1796 taxes & costs; order sheriff sell so much of sd John's land as will satisfy sd judgt and costs.
    State v Charles Dixon. Judgt agt Chas Dixon $11.53 for 1796 taxes [as above].
    State v Wynne Dixon. Judgt agt Wynne Dixon $6.01 8 mills 1796 taxes [as above].
    p.286   [Worded as above] agt William Metcalf, William Anderson, John Derden, Jacob Shoer, [1797 taxes]: John Dobbins, George Green, William Harrington, Daniel James, John Rains, [1798 taxes]: John Draper, Elisha Davis, George Green, Daniel

JANUARY 1801

Hunter, John Rains, William Totevine, William Whitehead, Philips heirs & Michael
p.287   Campbell, [1799 taxes]: Samuel Parker per W Jones agent, Moses Wilkerson, Joseph Woodfork, George Swingley, Samuel Marsh, Hugh Patrick, Hardy Sanders, Samuel Thornton, William Daharda, William Parker, James Woodward, Micajah Barrow, James Crockett, James Watson, William Henry per Thomas Bedford, Robert Anderson heir of
p.288   John, John Dobbins, Joseph Prior, John Blackemore, Elisha Davis, John Farland, Elias Fort, Daniel McKisock, Frederick Ward, William Harrington, William Brandon, George Green, Edward Harris, Thomas Love, Alexander McCaul, Matthew Moore,
p.289   John Shute, John White, John P Williams.

Wednesday Jan 7th 1801. Present James Winchester Thomas Donnell Isaac Walton Benj Rawlings Jonathan Hannum Edward Douglass Edward Gwin John McMurtrie Esquires.
Order James Winchester James Reese & James Clendening settle between the administrators & heirs of James Cathey deceased.
Acct/sales/goods of William Cathey decd proved by admr.
James Reese, Wm Cage, Jas Cryer, Wm Montgomery, Archd Marlin take their seats.
Order William Montgomery & Archibald Marlin settle with administrators of Abijah Millins deceased.
License Thomas Keife to keep tavern at his dwelling; Edward Douglass security.
County taxes laid [omitted].
Appointments to take lists of taxable property: Stephen Cantrill in Captain Whitsitts company. William Montgomery in Capt Kirkpatricks compy. Wm Henderson in Capt Hankins compy. Reuben Searcy in Capt Shaws compy. Edward Douglass in Capt Latimers compy. Benjn Rawlings in Capt Greens compy. James Cryer in Capt Snoddies compy. Jas Douglass in Capt Blacks company. David Wilson in Capt Vinsons compy. James Reese in Capt Neelys compy. John Morgan in Capt Loves company. Charles Donoho in Capt Carrs compy. Jonathan Hannum in Capt Haineys compy. James Hart in Capt Bradleys company. Edward Gwin in Capt William Gwins company.
Mary Jones daughter of Joyce Jones a free woman of colour bound unto Matthew Anderson until age twenty one years.
William Young orphan one year old bound apprentice to George Bush until age 21.
p.290   Account/sales of goods of Simon Totevine decd proved by admr.
Isham Jones son of Joyce Jones free woman of colour bound apprentice unto William Seawell until age twenty one.
Moses Jones son of Joyce Jones f.w.c. apprenticed unto John Cryer until age 21.
Edmund Jones son of Joyce Jones f.w.c. apprenticed to Isaac Baker till age 21.
Vina Jones daughter of Joyce Jones f.w.c. bound unto Jonathan Hannum to age 21.
Bill/sale Mary Millins to Thomas Cribbins ackd by Mary now wife of Ben Davis.
Allow Clerk for ex officio services July to July $40.
Allow Sheriff for ex officio services from July to July $35.
Appt Andrew Blythe overseer/road from Croft mills to Hugh Barrs farm.
Appt Joseph Bunton overseer/road from Hugh Barrs to top of ridge.
Appt Howell Smith overseer/road from top of ridge to Kentucky line.
Jurors to April Term: James Vinson Thomas Patton James Wilson Smkg Joseph Motherall Jesse Johnson William Neely John Goodrum James Clendening Henry Lyon Francis Weatherred Richd Parker Samuel Blythe James Steel David Echols Henry McAddin George Stubblefield Wm Parr Wm Sanders Jr John Carr Wm Lauderdale Thomas Groves Eli Stalcup Reuben Douglass James Franklin Jr James Cartwright Capt Griswold Latimer Hugh Kirkpatrick Leonard Duger Robert Wadkins Patrick Barr Smith Hansbrough Seth Mabry

JANUARY 1801

Richard Strother James Sanders John McMurry Asa Hassell.

Thursday Jan 8th 1801. Present James Winchester William Cage Edward Gwin James Hart Thomas Donnell James Reese William Montgomery Archibald Marlin Esquires.
    State v William Gibson. TAB. Prosecutor & witnesses for State failing to appear, nole prosequi entered. Prosecutor to be taxed with cost; order rescinded.
    State v Isaac Leftwicke. TAB. Nole proseque.
    State v Elijah Hendrick. TAB. Jury Isaac Baker Wm Maxey Patrick Morrison James Thomas Alexander Anderson Daniel McConnell Isaac Parker Jesse Johnson James Vinson Robert White William Wherry Thomas Bradley find dft guilty; fined 50¢ & costs.
p.291   State v Anthony Hogin. TAB. Dft pleads guilty; fined $15 & costs.
    Deed Devereux Wynne to David Dement 50 acres proved by Charles Dement.
    Deed Wm Phipps to Wm Wherry in trust for Baptist Society for half acre ackd.
    State v Joel Dyer. TAB. Dft pleads guilty; fined $2 & costs.
    Alexander Cathey son of James Cathey decd makes choice of James Graham for his guardian; bond $1000 with Griffith Cathey security.
    James Cathey son of James Cathey decd makes choice of Francis Locke for his guardian; bond $1000 with Thomas Walker security.
    State v Matthew Anderson. Disturber/Peace. Jury James Caruthers Thos Farmer Robt Patton Geo D Blackemore Michael C Dunn Robt Steel John Bayley Hugh Elliott Wm Smith Chas Elliott Wm Reed Josiah Wilson find dft guilty; fined $2 & costs.
    Appt Thomas Cribbins guardian for Philip, Mary, Susanna, Anne, & William Millens orphans of Abijah Millens decd; bond $1000, Armstead Rogers security.
    License James Woods to keep ordinary at his dwelling, Wm Henderson security.
    Order David Wilson & Thomas Donnell settle with admrs of William Bentley decd.
    Commrs apptd to settle with admrs of Abijah Millens decd render settlement.
    Commrs to divide Negro property estate of William Bentley decd render statement.
    Appt Henry Robinson constable for Capt Neelys dist; Archibald Marlin security.
    William Montgomery Esqr renders 50 shillings equal to $6.25 being fine of Isbell Stuart for having an illegitimate child.

Friday January 9th 1801. Present James Reese Wm Cage John Morgan Benjn Rawlings.
    Appt Chas Donoho & Jas Hart to make settlement with admrs of Robert Clark decd.
p.292   Deed Samuel Stalcup to John C Hamilton 50 acres proved by Isaac Baker.
    Thomas Sharp admr of Thomas Egnew decd v Isaac Hill & John Gardner. Sharp recovered agt Benjamin E Bartlett $33.81½; Bartlett came not; Hill & Gardner his special bail summoned by D Shelby Clerk/Court Apr 1800. J Cage read scire facias to John Gardner in presence of the other John Gardner and John Norris. Isaac Hill not found. Jan 1801 jury Isaac Baker Wm Maxey Jas Caruthers Patk Morrison James Thomas Chas Elliott Alexr Anderson Danl McConnell Josiah Wilson Edwd Hogin Jr Hugh Elliott Edward Hutson find for plf $48.37 & costs.
    Edmund Crutcher & Co v John Deloach. Certiorari. John Franklin constable levied on Deloach's property; execution stayed. July 1800 plfs by Samuel Donelson; dft by p.293   John C Hamilton & Boswell Johnson. Jan 1801 jury[above] find for plf.
    William Moorhead v Joseph McAdams. Covt. Plf by Samuel Donelson; dft by John C Hamilton. Jury[above] plfs damage $150.21½. Judgment overruled.
    Grand Jury dismissed.
    Deed Henry Weakfield to James Hart 71 acres ackd.

JANUARY 1801

Deed William Sanders to Henry Weakfield 71 acres proved by James Graham.
Edmund Crutcher & Co v John Deloach. Saml Harris wit behalf dft failed to appear.
Edmund Crutcher & Co v John Deloach. Dft to pay witness Robert Dolton.
Richard Hogin v Henry Harrison. Appeal. Jury Isaac Baker Wm Maxey James Caruthers Patk Morrison James Thomas Chas Elliott Alexr Anderson Danl McConnell Josiah Wilson Hugh Elliott Wm Hall Michael C Dixon assess plfs damages $22.50.
p.294   Appt James Bently constable for Capt Vinsons dist; Henry Belote security.

Saturday Jan 10th 1801. Present Jas Winchester Thos Donnell Jas Reese John Morgan.
State v Robert Pearson. appearance bond, Henry Belote security.
Richard Hogin v Henry Harrison. Appeal. New trial granted.
William Moorhead v Joseph McAdams. Judgment confirmed.
Isaac Donoho v Elijah Hendrick. TAB. Oct 1800 plf by John C Hamilton; dft by Saml Donelson. Jan 1801 jury[above except Isaac Parker & Edward Hogin Jr for Wm Hall & Michael Dixon] find defendant guilty, assess plfs damage one cent.
Henry Harrison v Jonathan Hannum. Appeal. Jury[above] plf damages $37.05 & costs.
William Thompson v John Murphey. Attachment. Oct 1800 A Hoover constable levied on Negro wench named[blank] feather bed & bedstead in possession of John Boyce. Dft by George Smith confessed judgt $100.50 & costs; property to be sold.
State v Anthony Hogin. Fine mitigated to $15.
Jonathan Hannum v Jesse Kuykendall. Dft escaped custody of sheriff.
Henry Harrison v Jonathan Hannum. Appl. New trial granted.
p.295   Laban Benthall v Anthony Hogin. TAB. Dft surrenders in discharge of his securities Richard Hogin, James Collins, & John Byrns.
State v Elijah Hendrick. Dft to pay for attendance of Peter Dagner & Moses Cummins witnesses; prosecutor Isaac Donohoo to pay all other witnesses in sd suit.
State v Joel Dyer. Dft to pay Joseph T Williams & Moses Cummons witnesses; prosecutor William Samples to pay all other witnesses in sd suit.
Laban Benthall v Anthony Hogin. TAB. Richard Hogin bail for defendant.
Additional inventory/goods of Henry Loving decd rendered by admrs.
Appt Thomas Donnell & James Reese esqrs to settle with admrs of Henry Loving.
State v William Gibson. Rescind order for taxing prosecutor with cost.
Court adjourns till Court in Course.   J Winchester

p.296   Court of Pleas & Quarter Sessions first Monday in April 1801. Present David Wilson James Winchester James Reese & Thomas Donnell esquires.
Bill/sale John Laurence to James Vinson negro man named Simon ackd.
Deed Mary Porter to Francis Fonvielle 5 acres proved by John Withers.
Commissioners report making settlement with admrs of William Bentley decd.
Deed John Morgan to Armstead H Morgan 100 acres ackd.
Deed George Stout to Robert Desha 300 acres ackd.
Grand jury: Jesse Johnson foreman, Patrick Barr, David Echols, Henry McAdin, James Vinson, Richard Parker, George Stubblefield, James Steel, James Cartwright, Eli Stalcup, James Wilson smkg, Thomas Groves, James Clendening. Constable James Bentley is appointed to attend on the Grand Jury for the present Term.

141

APRIL 1801

Commissioners report they settled with admrs of James Cathey decd.
Appt Thomas Bradley overseer/road from Bishops ferry to Second creek; hands that worked on sd road under Jonathan Badget to be divided between two overseers Badget & Bradley, and Bradley to have those living on east side of Second Creek.
Lists of Taxable property returned: Jas Reese in Capt Neelys compy; John Morgan in Capts Loves & Carrs.
Francis Weatherred excused from attending as a Juror for present term.
Deed Robert Moore to Thomas Waller 220 acres proved by Richard Waller.
Deed Charles Harryman to Thomas Waller 100 acres proved by Richard Waller.

Tuesday April 7th 1801. Present James Winchester, James Reese, John McMurtrie, Thos Donnell.
Deed James Reese to William Beard 9 acres ackd.
Appt James Hart & Charles Donoho esqrs to settle with admrs of Wm Storey decd.
Barnabas Stiner v Laurence Sigler. Attachment. 1799 Barnabas Stiner personally made oath before Thomas Masten J P that Laurence Sigler owes him $71.97¼; Sigler removed from State; shff J Cage levied on a still of 125 gallons. Apr 1801 dft came p.297   not; plf by Samuel Donelson. Jury Wm Neely John Goodrum Henry Lyon William Lauderdale Hugh Kirkpatrick Leonard Dugger Griswold Latimer Joseph Motherall Robert Wadkins Smith Hansbrough Richd Strother John McMurry find for plf $88.48.
James Hart Esqr returns list/taxable property in Capt Bradleys Company.
Appt Jas Hart & Chas Donoho Esqrs to settle with admrs of Robert Clark decd.
Deed Anne Greer to Joseph Motherall 460½ acres proved by Robert Motherall.
Deed Joseph Motherall to Anne Greer 127¾ acres ackd.
Deed William Beard to Thomas Reese 9 acres ackd.
Deed William McGee to William Hodge 252 acres proved by Alexr Anderson.
Deed William McGee to Alexander Anderson 75 acres proved by Wm Hodge.
Deed John White to Henry Belote 320 acres proved by John Bentley.
Bill/sale John Middleton to Thomas Walley negro boy Copper proved by Gadi Walley.
Jonathan Hannum Esqr returns list/taxable property in Capt Haineys District.
Deed William Reed to William Beard 4 acres 24 perches ackd.
Thomas Cribbins v John Payton. Jury[above]. Plf failed to appear. Non suit.
Thomas Masterson v William Hankins. Covt. Oct 1800 Plf by John Dickinson. Apr 1801 Jury[above] assess plfs damages to $54.85.
p.298   Deed Reuben Cage, collector/public taxes, to Edwd Giles 164½ acres ackd.
Chas Carter v Hugh Elliott & Mathew Cowan. Trespass. Oct 1800 plf by John C Hamilton; dft by Thos Stuart & Saml Donelson. Apr 1801 jury[above] non suit agt plf.
Bill/sale William Muckleyea to William Donnaldson proved by Francis Catron.
James Cryer renders list/taxable property in Capt Snoddies Company.
Commrs apptd to settle with admrs of Henry Loving decd render settlement.
Appt Thomas Parker overseer/road in place of James Morrison.
Appt John Stuart overseer/road from Second Cr to Maj Whites in place of Wm White.

Wednesday Apr 8th 1801. Present David Wilson Edward Douglass Thomas Masten William Montgomery Esquires.
Deed John Looney to Edward Sanders 240 acres proved by Abram Trigg.
Deed Shadrack Nye to George Garrett 10 acres 44 perches ackd.
Edwd Douglass esqr returns list/taxable property in Capt Latimers Company.

APRIL 1801

Redmond D Barry esqr qualified as attorney at law and is admitted to practice.
State v Richard Hogin. Trespass AB. Dft pleads guilty; fined $2 and costs.
Appoint Drury Milam constable, Edward Sanders & George Smith securities.
Appoint Elisha Pruett overseer of the road from Drakes creek at Hendersons mill to Manskers creek in place of William Hankins.
Appoint James McElroy overseer of the road from Montgomerys mill to ridge dividing Cumberland & Red rivers in place of Francis Catron.
Appoint Marlin Young Zachariah Green & Robert Moore patrollers for Capt Greens company; they are to qualify before Edward Douglass Esqr.
Rates for Cumberland River ferries [omitted].
William Montgomery esqr returns list/taxables in Capt Kirkpatricks company.
Deed Joseph McAdams to Benjamin Rawlings 100 acres proved by Edward Douglass.
William Henderson esqr renders list/taxable property in Capt Hankins company.
p.299 Ltr/atty Patrick Garvey to Howell Tatum proved by Stephen Montgomery.
Benjamin Rawlings esqr returns list of Taxable property in Capt Gwins company.
Bill/sale John Murphey to Smith Hansbrough negro wench Jude...by Wm Henderson.
State v Robert Pearson. Trespass AB. Dft pleads guilty; fined $2 and costs.
State v Pleasant Chitwood. Breach/Peace. Dft pleads guilty; fined $2 & costs.
State v Anthony Hogin. Breach/Peace. Dft pleads guilty; fined $2 and costs.
Bill/sale Elijah P Chambers to Francis Locke negro girl Jude ackd.
Deed James Hart to Jacob Slinkard 63 acres ackd.
William Smith produced license to practice as attorney at law certified by Clerk of Davidson County that he qualified in that Court; is admitted.
William Morgan v John Payton. Appt Zacheus Wilson surveyor & James Harrison David Love Jas Wilson smkg & Archibald Marlin jurors to survey 10 acres granted to John & Ephraim Payton known by name Salt Petre cave and return plat thereof.
James Hart v Robert Sanders. Jan 1801 plf by Benjn Seawell; dft came not. Apr 1801 jury Wm Neely Wm Lauderdale John McMurry Richd Strother John Goodrum Leonard Dugger Hugh Kirkpatrick Griswold Latimer Wm Parr Smith Hansbrough Geo Gillespie Robert Wadkins assess plfs damage $65.10.
Orders/sale issue agt Betsey Barrow Sherwood Barrow Matthew Barrow Henry Barrow James Barrow for taxes due thereon for 1797 & 1798.
Deed Samuel Thornton to Benjamin Mason 100 acres proved by George Mickey.
Deed Benjamin Mason to John Orr 100 acres proved by Joseph McElwrath.
Order Benjn Kuykendall & his securities Jas McKain & George Brown pay Priscilla Bloodworth $25 for maintenance of Priscilla's child of which Benjamin Kuykendall is reputed father from birth of sd child to the present time.
James Jones v William Muckleyea. Debt. William Montgomery dfts bail surrenders him; Hugh Kirkpatrick acknowledges himself bail for sd dft.
p.300 George Clark v John Young. TAB. Jan 1801 plf by John C Hamilton; dft by Saml Donelson. Apr 1801 jury[above] assess plfs damages 12½¢ and costs.
James Jones assee of David Taylor v William Muckleyea. Debt. Jan 1801 plf by John C Hamilton; dft by Saml Donelson. Apr 1801 jury[above] find for plf $216.12½.
Deed Sion Perry by John Wright his atty in fact to Richd Boyce 134 acres ackd.
David Wilson Esqr returns list/taxables in Capt Vinsons Company.
Jas Jones assee v Wm Muckleyea. Debt. Dfts bail Hugh Kirkpatrick surrenders dft.
On certificate of Wallis Harris & Edward Gwin surveyors in ascertaining limits of Sumner County ordered John Wilson be allowed $8 for services performed as marker with sd surveyors, it being for 8 days service more than heretofore mentioned.
George Clark v John Young. Jan 1801 plf by John C Hamilton; dft by Saml Donelson.

APRIL 1801

Apr 1801 jury James Sanders Wm Lauderdale Hugh Crafford Richd Strother John Goodrum Leonard Dugger Hugh Kirkpatrick Griswold Latimer John McMurry Smith Hansbrough Jos Motheral Robert Wadkins assess plfs damage $75.
Deed James Sanders to John Goodrum 200 acres ackd.
Deed James Harrison to Adam Hunter 42 acres ackd.
License Thomas Britton to keep ordinary at his dwelling, John Payton security.
Stephen Cantrill esq returns list taxable property in Capt Laurence Whitsitts co.
Deed Sion Perry and Theny his wife to Richard Boyce 134 acres ackd by John Wright their attorney in fact.
Appt Eli Stalcup constable; bond $625; Edward Gwin security.
p.301 Jurors to Superior Court: Ezekiel Douglass Robert Ellis Wm Maxey Benjamin Hudson John Douglass Jr Francis Locke James Hart.

Thursday April 9th 1801. Present David Wilson Edwd Douglass James Hart Edward Gwin.
James Maxwell v Thomas Farmer. Jan 1801 plf by Saml Donelson; dft by John C Hamilton. Jury Jas Sanders Wm Lauderdale Smith Hansbrough Richd Strothart Robert Wadkins Thos McGuire Hugh Crafford Geo McGuire Jno Gillespie Armstreet Stubblefield Wm Sanders James White assess plfs damages to $4.30. New trial granted. Dft in proper person confesseth judgt $74.93 & costs.
William Moorhead v Joseph McAdams. Debt. Jan 1801 plf by Saml Donelson. Apr 1801 plf by atty discontinues suit. Dft recovers of plf full costs expended.
Jno Payton v Geo Gillespie. Jury Jno McMurry Jos Motherall Hugh Kirkpatrick Leonard Dugger Henry Lyon Wm Lauderdale Smith Hansbrough Robert Wadkins Thomas Murry Wm Sanders Richd Strother Thos Stubblefield; plfs damages $61.36¼. New trial granted.
Philip Parchment v Sampson Williams. Jury Wm Neely Griswold Latimer William Parr John Goodrum Jas Sanders Solomon Reese Hugh Crawford Jos Neely Thomas Belew William Snoddy Edward Hutson George G Black. Mistrial by consent of parties.
John Payton v George Gillespie. John Baker witness behalf plf failed to appear; forfeits; si fa issues.
Deed James McKinsey to Benjamin Smith 43½ acres proved by William Dixon.
Micajah House records his ear mark.
Jurors to July Term: Reuben Douglass Fredk Miller Jas Frazer Henry Bunn John Payton Wm Hubbard Thos Reese Henry Harrison Nathl Gilmore Wm Robb Robt Carothers Robt Motherall Jas Trousdale Sr John Orr Wm McCorkle John Gardner Jesse Wormack Jas Wormack Reuben Cage Owen Dillard Jas Kirkpatrick Wm Alexander Arthur Axum Jas Johnson Fergus Sloan John Sterns James Watson John Byers William Morgan Jacob Browner Isaac Parker Joseph Wallace Hugh Barr John Anderson Jr James Mclin[Malin?] Andrew Blythe.
Acct/sales goods of Carlton Atkinson decd proved by admr.
p.302 James Douglass esq returns list/taxable property in Capt Blacks company.
Grand Jury dismissed.
Appt Charles Elliott overseer/road from Trousdales to main east fork of Station Camp Creek in place of Joshua Cherry.
Deeds from Jas Winchester & Wm Cage: to Robert Motherall lot 27 proved by Summers Harper. to Joseph Motherall lot 24 proved by Summers Harper. to Joseph Wilson lot 57 proved by Summers Harper. to William Dixon lots 32 & 37 proved by S Harper.
State v Richard Boyce. TAB. Dft submits; fined $3 and costs.

Friday April 10th 1801. Present Thos Donnell Jas Hart Jas Reese David Love Esqrs.

APRIL 1801

Thomas Bradley v Armstreet Stubblefield. Oct 1800 plf by Geo Smith; Apr 1801 dft by John C Hamilton. Jury Wm Neely John McMurry Leonard Dugger Hugh Kirkpatrick Robt Wadkins Richd Strother John Goodrum Smith Hansbrough Wm Lauderdale Jas White Thos Patton John L Martin assess plfs damage $100 which plf recovers.

Thomas Bradley v Armstreet Stubblefield. Bail Thomas Stubblefield surrenders dft.

Appt John Shaver overseer/road in place of Jonathan Badget.

Kupe[Keefe?] v Boyce. Dft to take deposition of Henry Ditto, Kentucky.

John Payton v George Gillespie. New trial granted.

Ezekiel Douglass v Anthony Hogin. Trespass. Plf by John C Hamilton; dft by Saml Donelson & Thos Stuart. Jury Wm Neeley John McMurry Leonard Dugger John Goodrum Smith Hansbrough Robt Wadkins Wm Lauderdale Heli Herring Joseph Wilson Geo Gillespie Malachi Hereford Richd Strother assess plfs damage to $25.

Indenture from Swen Powell emancipating a Negro ordered recorded.

p.303 Motion of David Wilson Esq; Sheriff to take Negro girl Fanny now in possession of Edward Hutson, also Negro boy James in possession of Nathaniel Parker which Negroes appear to have been free.

Laban Benthall v Anthony Hogin. TAB. Plf by John C Hamilton; dft by Samuel Donelson. Jury[above] assess plfs damages to $20.

Acct/sales & addl inventory/goods of Simon Totevine decd proved by admr.

Jonathan Hannum v Jesse Kuykendall. Dft escaped custody of shff; sheriff liable for his escape; judicial attachment ordered agt estate of defendant.

Francis Fairclaim on the demise of Peter Looney H v Baldy Badtitle alias William Gibson. With force & arms dft entered 61½ acres bounded...on Richd Strothers line .... Plf by J C Hamilton complains that Peter Looney in 1799 demised to Fairclaim afsd tract for seven years. Dft in 1799 entered sd messuage and ejected plf. Wil- p.304 liam Gibson dft failed to appear; judgt by default agt him.

Office of Sumner v John Wright. Appearance bond of Sion Perry, 9 Oct 1799, John Wright security, to prosecute agt Daniel Richardson; Sion Perry failed to prosecute & to pay charges. Scire facias to John Wright by David Shelby Clerk.

Supplemental inventory/goods of William Beakley decd rendered by executor.

Thomas Cribbins v John Payton. Plfs suit reinstated on his paying costs.

Court adjourns till Court in Course.   J Winchester

p.305 Court of Pleas & Quarter Sessions first Monday in July 1801. Present David Wilson, Thomas Donnell & John Morgan Esquires.

Release persons from tax who failed to return lists/taxable property this year.

Deed Levi Coulter to John Stroud for his service right as a soldier 640 acres proved by Marshall Stroud.

Grand Jury: Nathaniel Gilmore foreman, Hugh Barr, Jesse Womack, Jas Kirkpatrick, Robt Motheral, William Morgan, James Watson, James Wormack, John Orr, John Gardner, Frederick Miller, Jacob Browning, Thomas Reese & Henry Harrison.

Deeds ackd & proved: Isaac Braken to Albert Hendrix. Isaac Braken to Cater Hunter. Charles Dixon by atty T Dixon to George Keesee by William Loving. William Barrow by John Dawson his atty in fact to Wm McGee by James Kirkpatrick. John Williams to William Newton by Zacheus Wilson. John Williams to David Ferrell by Zacheus Wilson. John Williams to Isaac Valentine proved by Zacheus Wilson. Zacheus Wilson to

JULY 1801

David Wilson, Matthew Alexander & Joseph Wallace 2 acres.
Will of John Seawell decd proved by John Tullock a subscribing witness.
Excuse Isaac Baker James Maclin from attending as jurors for present Term.
Appt Benjamin Morgan constable for Capt Brownings company; bond $625, Marshall Stroud & James Blackemore securities.
Elizabeth Simpson formerly wife of Aaron Ready made oath that Charles Ready & William Ready are only children or legitimate offspring of sd Aaron Ready now alive that sd Aaron died possessed in fee simple of 50 acres in Sussex County Delaware called Ryans Grave about 5 miles from Broad Cr; sd Aaron died on sd acres near 22 years ago; that sd Elizabeth put a note of £5 in hands of Isaac Henry attorney to collect; note given by George Smith to sd Elizabeth in year sd Aaron died.
Anthony Sharp v Elisha Cheek. Covt. Apr 1801 plf by Thos Stuart; dft by George Smith. July 1801 dft in proper person confesses judgment $440 & costs. Plf orders execution stayed until 1 Dec 1802; Cheek agrees to pay lawful interest and costs.
p.306   County trustee to pay David Love $1.20 for tax on 640 acres 1798; sd Love having paid a double tax for sd year.
Deed John Laurence & wife Lydia to James Campbell 100 acre sproved by James Vinson.
Deed Ambrose Mauldin to James Roaney 500 acres proved by Edward Gwin.
Deed John Donohoo to David Denning 182½ acres proved by Isaac Donohoo.
James Reese esq deposits $3.12½ fine of Margaret Carr being pregnant with illegitimate child of which John Hodge distiller is reputed father.
Deed James Hawkins to John Hawkins for his undivided moiety of 3 tracts containing 759 acres in Buncum County North Carolina proved by James Lauderdale.
Deed Roderick Jenkins to Charles Elliott 107½ acres ackd.

Tuesday July 7th 1801. Present James Winchester Thomas Donnell James Hart Witheral Latimer, Esquires.
Philip Parchment v Sampson Williams. Jan 1800 order to Sheriff to bring Sampson Williams to Court at house of William Gillespie, David Shelby clerk. July 1800 plf by Benjamin Seawell. Parchment possessed Negro woman Sall of price $500; sd Philip lost the woman, found by Williams who kept her. Dft by John C Hamilton. April 1801 jury Wm Neely Griswold Latimer Wm Parr John Goodrum Jas Sanders Solomon Reese Hugh Crawford Jos Neely Thos Billens Wm Snoddy Edward Hutson Geo G Black; mistrial. July 1801 jury Reuben Douglass Henry Bunn Jas Trousdale Jr Arthur Axum Wm Alexander Jas Johnson Fergus Sloan John Payton Anthony Sharp John Scoby Henry Weakfield Wm Bell find for dft; dft recovers of plf his full costs expended. Plf obtains appeal, John p.307   Young and John Boyce his securities.
Acct/sales of goods of Martha Johnson decd proved by admr.
Sheriff brought into Court Negro girl Fanny in possession of Edward Hudson which girl appears to have been born free; she is put in possession of her mother Sibb a free woman of colour.
Deed Thomas Patton to Adam Hunter 109 acres ackd.
Bill/sale Edward Sanders to Robert Collier negro woman Celia & her child Ben proved by James Douglass.
Ephraim Payton v John Dawson. Jan 1801 plf by John C Hamilton; dft by Saml Donelson. July 1801 jury Reuben Douglass Henry Bunn James Trousdale Arthur Axum Wm Alexander Jas Johnson John Byrns Thos Edwards James Harrison Wm Douglass Thos Cribbins Fergus Sloan find for dft who recovers of plf full costs expended.

JULY 1801

Wm Seawell & Joseph Seawell exrs named in will of John Seawell decd took oath.
Thos Blackemore Chas Donohoo Jonathan Hannum Wm Montgomery John McMurtrie Wm Cage Reuben Searcy James Cryer Edwd Gwin Jas Reese Jas Douglass Benj Rawlings David Love Esquires take their seats.
Appt Joseph Wilson overseer/road in place of William Beard.
Order Shadrack Nye John Boyd William Montgomery Daniel Ogelsby Elisha Pruett Geo Campbell lay out a road from Montgomerys mill to mouth of Manskers Creek.
p.308   Order road from Richard Caveatts to Kentucky line be altered by Joseph Caveatt Saml Taylor John Hogin Richard Caveatt Jr Samuel Piper James King.
Appt David Allon constable for Capt Snoddies dist; Jas Vinson & Robt Patton sec.
Joseph Motheral records his ear mark.
Order a road from Cairo to Major Whites lane be laid off by Wm Reed Nathl Giles Henry Harrison James White Jr James Cary Peter Fisher William White Sr.
Order a road from Cairo to Major Wilsons be laid off by George D Blackemore Alexr Grayham Joseph Wilson George Someral James A Wilson William Wherry.
Order a road marked, Bledsoes lick to gap between Cumberland and Big Barren by Wm Neely Roger Gibson Jno Carr King Carr John Barr John Stone Peter Lyon John Goodrum.
Order road marked by Andrew Blythe James Brown Robert Anderson Wm Anderson Elleby Williams Isaac Stalcup Wm Gwin Jas Roney from Cairo by Deshas Gap to Kentucky line where road from Logan Court House to Cairo intersects.
Order road marked from McCorcles to Keefes lane by David Shelby Richard King William McCorcle Zachery Wilson Junr James Trousdale Senr.
Henry Harrison v Hannum. Order constable bring James Cotton into Court to give evidence behalf Jonathan Hannum.
Allow George Bush $26.60 for support of orphan William Young for one year commencing 7 January last.
Appt Samuel Elliott constable for Capt Greens company; Wm Cage & Jas Wormack sec.

Wednesday July 8th 1801. Present Edward Douglass David Wilson John Morgan Edward Gwin James Winchester.
John Payton v George Gillespie. June 1800 David Shelby ordered sheriff to bring George Gillespie to July Court to answer John Payton. Writ returned by J Cage. Plf p.309   by John C Hamilton; Payton by Saml Donelson. Apr 1801 jury John McMurry Jos Motherall Hugh Kirkpatrick Leonard Dugger Henry Lyon Wm Lauderdale Smith Hansbrough Robt Wadkins Thos Murry Wm Sanders Richard Strother Thomas Stubblefield assess plfs damage $61.66½. New trial granted. July 1801 jury Reuben Douglass Henry Bunn Alexr McKnight Jas Trousdale Arthur Axum Jas Johnson John Byrns Wm Lytle Henry Belote Jas Vinson Benjamin Mason James McKain assess plaintiffs damages to $8.33½. Dft granted appeal to Superior Court; Samuel Donelson & Thomas Stuart securities.
John Payton v George Gillespie. Robt Atkinson sitness for plf came not; forfeits.
Deed Paul Harpole to Robert Desha 127 acres 156 perches proved by Jas Winchester.
John Payton v George Gillespie. Jesse George wit for dft came not; forfeits.
Appt Edmund Crutcher collector/public taxes; Wm Cage & Edwd Douglass securities.
Appt Edmund Crutcher collector/county taxes; Wm Cage & Edwd Douglass securities.
Deed William Giles to Margaret Esspy 40 acres ackd.
Appt James Winchester & James Reese to settle with Jas Clendening as guardian for Isaac Bledsoe.
Order Vina Jones daughter of Joyce Jones free woman of colour bound unto Edward Hogin to age twenty one; sd girl was previously bound to Jonathan Hannum who agrees

JULY 1801

to release all right to sd girl.
State v Mary Davis. TAB. Recognizance Benjamin Davis & Mary Davis his wife, appearance of sd Mary at next Term to answer charge of government agt her.
p.310
Appt Matthew Cartwright overseer/road in place of John Reyley.
Appt Joshua Hadley overseer/road from Montgomerys to Dawsons in place of James Frazor.
State v Mary Davis. Peace bond. To keep peace towards Richard Hogin.
Order Priscilla Bloodworth to next Court & bring her child to be dealt with.
Philip Parchment v Sampson Williams. Appeal bond, John Young & John Boyce sec.
Ltr/atty Francis Earle to Armstreet Stubblefield authenticated by clerk of Camden County North Carolina.
Deed Wm Lytle Jr to Thos Stubblefield 37 acres 38 perches proved by Henry Lytle.
Deed Wm Lytle Jr to Woodruff Stubblefield 87 ac 84 perches proved by Henry Lytle.
Nathaniel Parker v Solomon Duty. Jury Reuben Douglass Henry Bunn James Trousdale Arthur Axum Thomas McGuire James Johnson Fergus Sloan John Payton John Byrns George McGuire James Morgan Richard Hogin; mistrial.

Thursday July 9th 1801. Present David Wilson James Winchester Edward Gwin esquires.
Henry Harrison v Jonathan Hannum. Appeal. Jury Reuben Douglass Henry Bunn James Trousdale Arthur Axum James Johnson Fergus Sloan John Payton John Byrns Reuben Cage Armstreet Stubblefield James Lyon James Blackemore; mistrial by consent of parties.
Appt John Morgan special guardian for Joshua Ramsey & Henry Ramsey heirs of Henry Ramsey decd for purpose of laying off the right of dower of widow of sd deceased.
Deed Mary Porter to George Wimbledorf 5 acres ackd.
Commissioners report settlement with administrators of William Storey deceased.
Richard Hogin v Henry Harrison. Appeal. Oct 1800 plf by Samuel Donelson; dft by John C Hamilton. Jan 1801 jury Isaac Baker Wm Maxey Jas Caruthers Patk Morrison Jas Thomas Chas Elliott Alexander Anderson Danl McConnell Josiah Wilson Hugh Elliott Wm Hall Michael C Dunn assessed plfs damage $22.50. New trial granted dft. July 1801
p.311   jury Andw Blythe Jos McCravens James Morgan Hugh Crafford Nathl Parker Jr Joshua Cherry Jos Neeley Wm White John Stamps Wm Neeley Stephen Anderson Malachi Hereford assess plfs damages $15 with costs.
Petition of Esther Ramsey widow of Henry Ramsey decd, order James Lauderdale Geo Gillespie James Harrison Francis Weatherred & John Hawkins lay off to sd widow her right of dower in real estate of decedant.
State v James Cotton. TAB. Dft submits; fined 10½¢ with costs.
State v William P Loury. Warrant for surity of Peace. Mary Davis having failed to further prosecute dft, nolle prosequi entered; dft discharged.
Bill/sale Wm Perry to James Harrison negro girl Clary proved by James Winchester.
Order Agnus Jones bring to Court a son of sd Agnus named Clinton Jones, that court may take such measures respecting sd boy as Court may deem necessary.
Bond Ananias McCoy to Robert Looney for 300 acres proved by Andrew Blythe.
Deed Samuel King to William Anderson 100 acres proved by Andrew Blythe.
Wilson & Douglass v Obediah Terrell. Allow Sheriff amend return on sd attachment.
Deed Jas Winchester & Wm Cage Jr to Richard Rapier lot 14 in Cairo ackd.
Joshua Cherry v William Sanders. Dfts plea amended.
Joshua Cherry v William Sanders. Oct 1800 plf by Benjn Seawell; dft by Geo Smith. July 1801 jury[above except Alexr McKnight Wm Anderson Wm Morgan for Hugh Crafford Joshua Cherry Wm Neeley] assess plaintiffs damages to $85.20, with costs.

JULY 1801

License Henry Lyon to keep an ordinary at his dwelling house in Cairo, bond $2500 Benjamin Seawell and Edward Gwin securities.
p.312   Order orphan boy Jarod a free boy of colour bound as apprentice to Benjamin Seawell Jr to learn art or mystery of an House Carpenter; sd Benjamin enters indenture with James Winchester senior justice for performance of covenants.
Jurors to october Term: Wm Wherry Jos Wilson John Wilson son of Sam James Micklin John Anderson Jr William Neely Jesse Johnson Jno Hamilton Jr Mattw Alexander Samuel Blythe John D Hannah George D Blackemore Alexander Graham James Sanders Wm Trigg Jr Jesse Hainey James Esspie Jno Bradley James Cary Champness Madding Wm Edwards Roger Gibson Thomas Parker Geo Gillespie Francis Weatherred Isaac Baker Solomon Barnes Wm Maxey Adam Hunter Wm Hubbard Jno Stamps Albert Holmes Jas Watson Hallery Malone Jas McMurry William Reed.

Friday July 10th. Present David Wilson James Winchester Thomas Donnell Esquires.
Ann Greer records her ear mark.
Deed Thomas Blackemore to Presley George 240 acres ackd.
Order Jas Douglass & Jas Cryer esqrs furnish Malichi Hereford with list of hands to work with him as an overseer of the road.
William Morgan v Nathaniel Giles. Debt. Apr 1801 plf by Saml Donelson; dft by Jno C Hamilton. July jury Jas Trousdale Jas Johnson Fergus Sloan John Byrns Reuben Cage Alexr McKnight Henry Belote Jas Willard Jno Payton Pleasant Chitwood Jas Vinson Jno S[T?] Martin find for plf $100 debt $5.66¾ damages, with costs.
William Morgan v Nathaniel Giles. Debt. [as above] find for plf $94.66 debt and $204 damages, with costs.
Will of John Seawell decd proved by John Brown a subscribing witness.
John Trice v Elisha Cheek. Appeal. Plf by Jno Boswell Johnson & Thos Stuart; dft by John C Hamilton. Jury Jas Trousdale Jas Johnson Fergus Sloan John Byrns Reuben Cage Wm Wilkins Jas Vinson Henry Belote Jas Willard John Payton Pleasant Chitwood
p.313   Richard Hogin find for plf $38.95½, with costs.
Release James Hays from two thirds value of mare taken up by Hays & entered with ranger which was proved to be property of a certain Gillespie.
Deed James Winchester & William Cage Jr to John Hazlet lot 6 in Cairo ackd.
John Payton v Geo Gillespie. Dft obtains appeal, Thos Stuart & Saml Donelson sec.
Joshua Cherry v Wm Sanders. Verdict of the jury confirmed.
Barnabas Stiner v Laurence Sigler. Attached property to be sold.
Commrs report they settled with guardian of Isaac Bledsoe.
Ezekiel Douglass v Anthony Metcalf. David Shelby to Sheriff of Smith County; Ezkl Douglass recovered agt Anthony Metcalf $36.13 with $8.63½ costs; $12 were paid; summon Metcalf to Sumner court in Cairo. Shff of Smith Co made known to Metcalf in presence of Moses Fisk & Grant Allin by John L Martin. July 1801 dft failed to appear; judgt agt him for $32.76½ and costs.
State v Richard Waller. Dft failed to appear; also James Carson bound in recognizance for dfts appearance forfeits.
Ephraim Payton v John Dawson. Verdict of jury confirmed.
Appt Wm Montgomery Jas Hart & Alexander Graham inspectors for ensuing election.
Appt Edwd Douglass & James Cryer to settle with admr of Simon Totevine decd.
Court adjourns till Court in Course.   David Wilson

OCTOBER 1801

p.314   Court of Pleas & Quarter Sessions, Town of Cairo, first Monday in October 1801. Present James Winchester Thomas Masten Jno Morgan David Love Jonathan Hannum. Wm Montgomery & Thos Blackemore esqrs to settle with admx of Robert Clark decd.

Luke Osburn v Thomas Millius[Millens?]. Att. Property whereon attachment was levied, 100 ac whereon dft's father lived, Drakes Cr waters, condemned for use of judgt obtained by plf for $9.50 before Thomas Masten J P; order of sale issues.

Nathaniel Parker v Solomon Duty. Dfts bail surrenders dft to sheriff's custody.

Grand jurors: Jesse Johnson foreman Joseph Wilson William Edwards William Neely Wm Reed Champness Madding George D Blackemore Jno Bradley Halery Malone John Hamilton Jr Matthew Alexander Jas McMurry Adam Hunter. Jas Bentley to attend Grand Jury.

Grant ltrs/admn on estate of Richard Gossage decd to Rachel Gossage widow of sd decd; bond $500 with William Lamburth & Champness Madding securities.

Rachel Gossage admx/Richard Gossage decd renders inventory of goods of sd decd.

Order admx of Richard Gossage decd sell personal estate of sd decd.

Bill/sale Richard & Wm Alexander to Jonathan Hannum for negroes Buk, Carter, and Fanny ackd by William Alexander.

Commissioners render settlement with admx of Robert Clark decd.

Will of James Blythe decd proved by Wm Anderson a subscribing witness who made oath that Fergus Sloan subscribed his name in presence of sd Anderson.

Grant ltrs/admn on estate of Joseph Reed decd to John Reed son of sd Joseph; bond $2000, William Ozburn & Jas Murry sec; rendered inventory of goods of sd decd.

Order admr of Joseph Reed decd expose to sale personal estate of sd decedant.

Commrs report settlement with admr of Simon Totevine decd.

State v Mary Davis. Bail for dft surrenders her; Wm Montgomery enters bail.

Deed Jas Winchester & Wm Cage to Basil Shaw lot 60, Cairo, proved by Saml Gibson.

Deed Robert Desha to Joseph Hodge 640 acres proved by William Anderson.

p.315   Deed Jas Winchester & Wm Cage to Benjamin Dickerson lot 5 in Cairo proved by Samuel Gibson.

Deed William Clark to William Draper 62½ acres proved by John Ralph.

Deed William McWhirter to John Hassell 147 acres proved by William King.

Deed William McWhirter to William King 115 acres proved by John Hassell.

Release Jno Stamps from present year tax for billiard table, not possessing same.

James Roney Eliby Williams Isaac Stalcup Jas Brown Robt Anderson Wm Anderson report they marked nighest way from Cairo to road from Logan Court House.

Appt Matthew Alexander overseer/road laid off from Cairo to road from Logan Court House, from Cairo to W Cocks field, Jas Winchester to furnish list of hands.

Appt Patrick Morrison overseer of the road from Cairo to Logan Courthouse from W Cocks field to Deshas Crk; Jas Winchester & Jno Morgan to furnish list of hands.

Appt Robert Bratney overseer/road, Cairo to Logan C H from Desha Creek below Mr Bratneys to top of ridge; Jas Winchester & Jno Morgan to furnish list of hands.

Appt John Denan overseer/road from Cairo to Logan C H from ridge and Watwoods; Reuben Searcy & Edwd Gwin esqrs to furnish sd overseer with a list of hands.

Appt Isaac Braken overseer/road from Cairo to Logan Court House between Watwoods and Ozburns; Reuben Searcy & Edward Gwin esqrs to furnish list of hands.

Appt William Osburn overseer/road from Cairo to Logan C H between Osburns & Kentucky line; Reuben Searcy & Edwd Gwin esqrs to furnish list of hands.

John Carr John Barr Wm Neely John Goodrum Peter Lyon report they laid off a road from Bledsoes lick to County line following the old road to Roger Gibsons thence to John Goodrums to Wm Harpers striking old road about John Sloans thence through flat gap past David Pursleys & John Barrs & so to County line injuring no mans farm.

OCTOBER 1801

Appt John Goodrum overseer/road from Bledsoes lick to ridge bet Rockey & Goose crks; James Winchester & John Morgan esqrs to furnish sd overseer with list/hands.
Appt William Harper overseer/road from Bledsoes lick to flat gap, the part from ridge[above] to ridge bet forks of Goose Crk; Esqrs [above] furnish list/hands.
p.316 Appt King Carr overseer/road from Bledsoes lick to flat gap from forks [above] to County line; Jas Winchester & John Morgan to furnish list of hands.
Shadrack Nye Daniel Ogelsby George Campbell John Boyd Elisha Pruett Wm Montgomery report they laid out a road from Montgomerys mill to mouth of Manskers cr from sd mills to east of Shadrack Nyes to Peter Blairs to John Boyds to Elisha Pruetts lane to mouth of creek. Appt John Boyd overseer of road; Wm Montgomery esqr to furnish sd overseer with a list of hands.
John Young v George Clark. Jan 1801 plf by Saml Donelson. Dft by John C Hamilton. Oct 1801 suit dismissed on order of parties at cost of dft; plf recovers costs.
State v Agnus Jones. Allegations set forth in scire facias are not supported by testimony; dft discharged; Matthew Anderson assumes costs.

Tuesday Octr 6th 1801. Present Jas Winchester Wm Montgomery Edward Gwin David Love.
Isaac Bledsoe son & orphan of Isaac Bledsoe decd makes choice of James Winchester esqr for his guardian; Jas Winchester is apptd guardian for Catey Bledsoe Jr; bond $5000 with David Shelby security.
Robert McConnell v Robert Clarks admx. Debt. Apr 1800 plf by Bennet Searcy; dft by Saml Donelson. Oct 1801 jury Wm Wherry John Anderson Jr Alexr Graham Wm Maxey Wm Hubbard John Stamps Albert Holmes Jas Vinson Reuben Cage Malachi Hereford Jos Steel Mark Richman find for plf $58.25; also admx has fully administered.
Will of James Blythe decd proved by Fergus Sloan.
Deed James Winchester & William Cage Jr to James A Wilson lot 12 in Cairo proved by John Hazlet.
Deed James A Wilson to John Barham lot 12 in Cairo ackd.
p.317 Deed Jas Winchester & Wm Cage to John Hazlet lot 10 in Cairo proved by Jas A Wilson.
Commrs apptd to assign to widow of Henry Ramsey decd her dower in real estate of decd report their proceedings thereon.
Deed Thomas Patton to Elmore Harris 60 acres ackd.
Deed Thomas Patton to James Duke 60 acres ackd.
Henry Harrison v Jonathan Hannum. Appeal. Jury Wm Wherry John Anderson Alexander Graham Wm Maxey Wm Hubbard John Stamps Albert Holmes Saml Blythe Richd Parker John Bailey Thomas Barnes Wm Cochran find for dft; new trial granted.
Deed William Milton to Daniel Burford 640 acres proved by Ezekiel Clampett.
Deed Elisha Clary to William Barnes 100 acres ackd.
Appoint Samuel Piper overseer/road from Kentucky line to James's blacksmith shop with hands Reuben Searcy Jas Elliott Ezekiel Norman John Perryman John Depriest Jos Cavit Anthony Sharp Elisha Hall John Hogan Daniel Taylor Edward Morgan.
William T Gardner & Co v John Standley. Wm T Gardner & Co recovered of John Standley $45.90 & $7.02½ costs; July 1799 judgt not satisfied. Summon John Standley to July Court. July 1801 return "not found," E Crutcher DS. Oct 1801 return "Not
p.318 found." Judgment against him $52.92½ & costs of suit.
License Robert Davis to keep tavern at his dwelling; Edward Sanders security.
Anthony Sharp v George Parks. Debt. Dft in proper person confesses judgt $145.60 & costs; plf stays execution 12 months provided dft pays lawful interest.

151

OCTOBER 1801

Deed Henry Turney to Edward Sanders 200 acres proved by Isaac Turney.

Robert Stothart & Co v Jacob Parks. July 1801 David Shelby orders sheriff have Jacob Parks appear before Court. Jas Lauderdale DS made known to Jacob Parks in presence of Geo Park & John Sericer. Oct 1801 dft brings into Court George Parks the principal & surrenders him to Sheriff in discharge of himself as bail.

Wed Oct 7th 1801. Present Jas Winchester Edward Douglass Wm Montgomery James Hart.

State v James White Jr. Appearance bond of Robert Pearson the prosecutor.

William Montgomery esqr deposits with Clerk $93 & ¾¢ a fine collected of Martin Whitford for profane swearing.

State v Mary Davis. TAB. Jury Wm Wherry John Anderson Jr Alexr Graham Wm Maxey Wm Hubbard John Stamps Albert Holmes Saml Blythe Heli Herring Robt Pearson Eli Stalcup p.319 Thomas Parker find dfendant guilty; fined $1 with costs.

Orphan Jonathan Bunckley bound an apprentice to James Callahan to learn art or mystery of an House carpenter.

State v Andrew Moore. TAB. Dft came not; Peter Fisher bail for dft likewise forfeits recognizance.

State v Richard Waller. Bound to appear July 1801 but came not, again fails to appear; judgt agt dft $200 with costs.

State v James Carson. James Carson bound for appearance of Richard Waller Jr to last term; sd Waller failing to appear; judgt agt Carson $100 & costs.

State v Mary Davis. TA. William B Loury prosecutor appearance bond to prosecute indictment against sd defendant.

Wm Reed Wm White Henry Harrison Jas White Jas Cary Nathaniel Giles Peter Fisher report they laid off road from Major Whites lane to Cairo crossing Bledsoes creek at Nathaniel Giles.

State v Joseph Neely Henry Harrison Samuel Gibson Rhody Philips Thomas Howell & Isaac Bledsoe. Presentment for a riot. Dfts except Thomas Howell plead guilty & submit; fines Isaac Bledsoe 12½¢, Saml Gibson 50¢, Rhody Philips 50¢, Henry Harrison $5 Joseph Neely $5; Nolle prosequi as respects Thomas Howell.

State v James White Jr. TAB. Dft pleads guilty; fined $5 with costs.

State v John Whitford. TAB. Bail for dft surrenders him to custody of sheriff.

State v John Whitford. Oct 1801 Presentment: assault on Francis Catharine during p.320 public worship in meeting house of Rev Wm McGee, signed Geo Smith CS. Witnesses Robert Latimer Jno Kirkpatrick William Mucklyea Dred Dugger John Dugger Luke Dugger Geo Kiser, Oct 5 1801 D Shelby Clk. True bill, Jesse Johnson foreman. Jury above] dft guilty of disturbing public worship but not guilty of trespass assault & battery. Dft by Saml Donelson moves arrest of judgt. Verdict of jury confirmed; dft fined $20 & costs; Dft obtains appeal to Superior Court, Saml Donelson & Jas Carson securities.

State v Richard Singleton. Peace bond towards George Evans and Jane Singleton, John H Bush and James Steel securities.

State v Mary Davis. Robbery. Dfts appearance bond with her husband Benjamin Davis in sum $200 with Thomas Cribbins & James Carson.

State v Mary Davis. TA. Mary Davis & Benjamin Davis her husband appearance bond p.321 $200, Thomas Cribbins & James Carson $100 each.

Thursday Oct 8th 1801. Present James Winchester Wm Montgomery Edward Gwin esquires.

OCTOBER 1801

State v Henry Robinson. TAB. Dft submits; fined $2 & costs.
State v Andrew Moore. TAB. Defendant released from forfeited recognizance; pleads guilty; fined $2 with costs.
State v Richard Waller. TAB. Judgment agt dft and his security James Carson; dft released from forfeiture; submits; fined 12½¢ with costs.
Malachi Hereford v Heli Herring admr of Simon Totevine decd. Covenant. Apr 1801 plf by Thos Stuart; dft by Saml Donelson. Oct 1801 jury Wm Wherry John Anderson Jr Alexr Graham Wm Maxey John Stamps Albert Holmes Thos Parker Jas Cary Nicholas Boyce Joseph Byrns Leonard Miles Tandy Witcher find issue on first two pleas for plf, and assess damge to $194.67¾; find plea of plene admt for dft.
Appt David Wilson & Thos Donnell esqrs settle with exrs of Pearce Wall decd.
Jurors to Superior Court: William Maxey Robert Shaw John Payton Jas Rankins Peter Looney H Kasper Mansker & William Bowen.
Jurors to ensuing County Court: Thos Patton James Campbell Thomas Reese John Bowman Jas Wilson shooting James Lyon Robert Desha Wm Snoddy John Weathers Thomas Willis Thomas Keeff Alexr McKnight Laurence Whitsitt Wm Harrison Moore Cotton Richard Strother Hugh Crawford Matthew Cartwright Joseph Neely Jas Morrison Nathl Parker Jr William Bradshaw Abner Spring James Lauderdale Sr Wm Anderson Jas Clendening Thomas Bradley John Norton John Sterns Patrick Barr Joshua Saxton Zachariah Wilson Jr John Norris Sr Smith Hansbrough Robert Patton.
Court adjourns one hour; met: Present James Winchester Edward Douglass James Cryer David Wilson esqrs.
Andrew Greer v William Breinberry. Edward Gwin security to plf for replevying the property attached in sd suit.
p.322 State v John Whitford. Motion in arrest of judgment argued; reasons insufficient; verdict of jury confirmed. Dft obtains appeal to Superior Court, Saml Donelson & James Carson securities.
John C Hamilton v Richard Boyce. Nicholas Boyce security for replevying property attached in said suit.
Court adjourns till Court in Course.   J Winchester

Court of Pleas & Quarter Sessions Held at Town of Cairo first Monday in January 1802. Present Thomas Donnell John Morgan James Reese esquires.
Deed William Bowen to David Carson 220 acres proved by Henry Bradford.
Deed Marshall Stroud to John Lyon 100 acres proved by John Morgan.
Deed Alexander Donelson to John Morgan & James Winchester 495 acres proved by Henry Bradford.
Grant ltrs/admn on estate of James Kelly decd to James Lauderdale; Jos Neely sec.
Acct/sales goods of Joseph Reed decd proved by admr.
Deed Thomas Stubblefield to Henry McCadin 37 ac 38 perches proved by Wm Bradshaw.
Thomas Keefe is excused from attending as juror for present term.
Grand jury: Richard Strother foreman James Lauderdale Patrick Barr Joseph Neely Jas Morrison John Norton William Bradshaw Smith Hansbrough Wm Anderson Robt Patton Thomas Patton John Bowman James Wilson shooting. James Bentley to attend jury.
p.323 Bill/sale Hugh Elliott to Isaac Baker negro man Jim, by Solomon Barnes.
Will of Edward Giles decd proved by Patrick Gibson & John B Gibson; Eli Giles one

OCTOBER 1801

of the executors therein named qualified as such.

Deed Jesse Kuykendall to Benjamin Kuykendall his proportion of 200 acres on Bledsoes creek as one of heirs at law to Benjamin Kuykendall decd proved by Jonathan Kuykendall, the quantity supposed to be 33 acres.

Appoint George Campbell constable for Capt Kirkpatricks company; bond $625, with Shadrack Nye and John McMurtry securities; took oath prescribed by law.

Deed Charles Dixon by atty in fact Tilmon Dixon to John Tucker 200 acres proved by Thomas Stuart.

Abner Spring is excused from attending as juror for present term.

Supplement inventory & account/sales goods of Simon Totevine decd proved by admr.

Deed William Lauderdale to John Mills 16 acres 136 perches ackd.

Deed George Keese to John Mills & James Henry 75 acres proved by Wm Lauderdale.

Deed Hugh Mecklin to James Mecklin 250 acres proved by Jesse Margrave.

James Sanders Esqr commissioned in peace under hand of Archibald Roane esq 14 Nov 1801 took oaths necessary for qualification, Justice of the Peace.

Deed Peter Hansbrough to Edward Sanders 255 acres proved by James Sanders.

Deed/gift Richard Hogin to daughter Elizabeth Hogin negro girl Dinah proved by David Shelby.

Tuesday January 5th 1802. Present James Reese Thomas Donnell Charles Donoho John McMurtry James Sanders Esquires.

Bond Richard Pryor to Wm Pryor 400 acres proved by James Ewing.

Henry Harrison v Jonathan Hannum. Appeal. Oct 1800 plf by Jno C Hamilton; January 1801 dft by Saml Donelson. Jury Isaac Baker Wm Maxey Jas Caruthers Patrick Morrison Jas Thomas Alexr Anderson Danl McConnell Isaac Parker Josiah Wilson Edward Hogin Jr Hugh Elliott Chas Elliott assess plfs damages $37.05. Dft granted new trial. July p.324 1801 jury Reuben Douglass Henry Bunn Jas Trousdale Arthur Axum Jas Johnson Fergus Sloan John Payton John Byrns Reuben Cage Armstreet Stubblefield Jas Lyon Jas Blackemore; mistrial. Oct 1801 jury Wm Wherry John Anderson Jr Alexr Graham Wm Maxey Wm Hubbard John Stamps Albert Holmes Samuel Blythe Richd Parker John Bailey Thos Barnes Wm Cochran found for dft. Plf granted new trial. January 1802 jury Wm Snoddy Thos Willis Lawrence Whitsitt Wm Harrison Moore Cotton Jas Clendening Robert Steel John Orr Griffith Rutherford John Hawkins George Hamilton James Orr find for dft.

Deed John Withers to Adam Hunter 35 acres 135 perches ackd.

John McMurtry esq deposits with Clerk 62½¢, half of fine on Henry Williams for breach of the Sabbath, the other half paid to the informer by sd McMurtry.

Bill/sale Charles Haynie to James A Wilson negro boy Sam proved by James Graham.

Deed James Bone to John King 228 acres proved by James King.

Deed Daniel Taylor to Edward Morgan 68 acres ackd.

Deed James Sanders to James Scott 215 acres ackd.

Will of Robert Taylor decd proved by Daniel Taylor which witness also proved that Agnist Majlohon[Masslohon?] another witness subscribed her name in the presence of sd Daniel. Robert Taylor one of the executors therein named qualified.

Deed Jas Winchester & Wm Cage to Wm Morgan lot 28 in Cairo proved by John H Bush.

John Deloach v George Young. Marlin Young bound as special bail.

Four of the commissioners apptd to purchase land for the erection of Court House, prison & stocks namely Samuel Donelson Shadrack Nye James Wilson C & Charles Donoho entered bond $2500 with John Payton & James Douglass securities.

Edward Hogin fined $2 for contempt of Court; in custody of sheriff until paid.

OCTOBER 1801

Allow Alexander Weatherspoon $31.50 for keeping an orphan female child.
p.325   Letter from Major Tilmon Dixon to Major Isaac Bledsoe respecting land business was proved by James Sanders esqr.
Edward Douglass Jas Douglass Stephen Cantrill Wm Montgomery James Cryer Witheral Latimer Thos Donnell Jas Hart Jno Morgan Archd Marlin Jona Hannum esqrs take seats.
Taxes laid [omitted].
Inventory goods of John Seawell decd proved by executors.
Appointments to take lists of taxable property: Isaac Walton in Captain Whitsitts company; Jas Sanders in Capt Montgomerys; John McMurtry in Capt Kirkpatricks; Archd Marlin in Capt Latimers; Jas Cryer in Capt Snoddys; Jas Douglass in Capt Blacks; Wm Cage in Capt Greens; Witherall Latimer in Capt Shaws; Jas Reese in Capt Neelys; Jno Morgan in Capt Brownings; David Wilson in Capt Vinsons; Thos Blackemore, Capt Haineys; Jas Hart in Capt Bradleys; Wm Seawell, Capt Barrs; Reuben Searcy, Capt Gwins.
Wm Seawell commissioned under seal of Archibald Roan 14 Novr 1801 took oaths necessary to qualify as a Justice of the Peace.
Allow Sheriff $35 for ex officio services July 1800 to July 1801.
p.326   Allow Clerk $40 for ex officio services July 1800 to July 1801.
Grant ltrs/admn on estate of Laban Benthall decd to James Cryer; bond $5000, John DeLoach and John Withers security.
Appt William Hall guardian for William Lytle Bledsoe and Katey Bledsoe orphans of Isaac Bledsoe decd; bond $5000, John Morgan security.
Order Capt William Gillespie Reuben Cage William Douglass Isaac George Jos George James Franklin Senr to lay off a road from James Franklins on Station Camp Creek to Dillards ferry on Cumberland river.
Allow John McMurtry $12 for holding three inquisitions as appears by receipt on the bodies of John Hogin John Regin and Margaret Parker.

Wednesday Jan 6th 1802. Present Edward Douglass Stephen Cantrill James Hart James Sanders Charles Donoho esquires.
State v William Lyon. Trespass Assault & battery. Dft submits; fined $1 & costs.
State v Mary Davis. Trespass assault & battery. Nolle prosequi.
State v Mary Davis. Robbery. Not within Court's jurisdiction; put off docket.
State v Pleasant Chitwood. Trespass assault & battery. Nolle prosequi.
State v Henry Robinson. Breach of Sabbath. Not in Court's jurisdiction. Quashed.
State v John Hazlet. Breach of Sabbath. Not within Court's jurisdiction. Quashed.
Arthur Cotton age 14, orphan of Thomas Cotton decd, makes choice of Arthur Cotton for his guardian; bond $5000 with Isaac Walton security.
Will of William Hamilton decd proved by Benjamin Rawlings a witness thereto.
Salley Hamilton widow of William Hamilton decd vs William Douglass an executor of sd will. Sally widow of William denies the will produced by Wm Douglass & proved by
p.327   witnesses is will of Wm Hamilton. Thos Stuart for Sally Hamilton. Jury Robt Desha Moore Cotton Thos Willis Jas Orr George D Blackmore Wm Harrison John Douglass Thos McGuire Richd Graham Stephen Ward Thos Cribbins Henry Belote find for dft that that the will of William Hamilton previously proven is his true will.
Deed David Love to Nathaniel Parker Jr 170 acres proven by Thomas Parker.
State v Edward Hogin. TAB. Dft submits; fined $5 with costs.
Appt Edward Douglass & Benjamin Rawlings esqrs to settle with executors of Robert Hobdy decd.
Reuben Cage William Douglass & Wilson Yandal executors named in will of William

OCTOBER 1801

Hamilton decd took oath necessary to qualify them as such.
   Salley Hamilton widow of Wm Hamilton decd sets forth her disclaimer to will; prays right of dower & distributive share of personal property.
   Appt Stephen Cantrill & Wm Montgomery esqrs to settle with Henry Bradford admr of Polley Fowler decd.

Thursday Jan 7th 1802. Present Jas Winchester James Reese Witheral Latimer William Seawell esquires.
   John Washington v Benjn Seawell. Jan 1801 plf by Geo Smith; dft by Thomas Stuart. Jan 1802 jury Robert Desha Moore Cotton Thomas Willis Wm Harrison Laurence Whitsitt Heli Herring Wm Snoddy Wm Cosby Alexr Graham Jno Weathers Thos Keeffe Wm Giles fail to agree; non suit entered agt plf who is liable for full costs.
   Bond Edward Hogin & Matthew Cowan to Redmond D Barry proved by Thomas Keeffe.
   Deed Martha Kuykendall to Redmond D Barry 200 acres proved by Thomas Keeffe.
   John C Hamilton v Richard Boyce. Covt. Plfs witnesses Wm P Anderson Geo M Deaderick Jos McKean failed to appear; forfeit; scire facias issue to Davidson County.
   p.328   Peter Richardson Booker esqr presented license to practice as an attorney at law; took oaths for qualification.
   Appt George D Blackmore inspector at Cairo to inspect all commodities enumerated by law, cotton excepted; bond $1000, Elkenor Echols & David Wilson securities.
   Appt Elkenor Echols inspector of cotton at his gin in Cairo; bond $1000 with George Blackmore & David Wilson securities.
   Deed James Winchester & Wm Cage to Elkenor Echols lot 92 in Cairo ackd.
   Deed Thomas Harney to Samuel Scott 214 [274?] acres proved by Robert Bratney.
   Thomas Keeffe v Christen Staley. Dft failed to appear; judgt agt him by default; the horse levied on by attachment to be sold by sheriff for use of the judgment.
   Deed John Deloach to Ephraim Payton 400 acres ackd.
   John Payton v George Gillespie. Dft Gillespie withdraws appeal with consent of John Payton; judgt of Court confirmed for principal & costs without farther costs.
   James Elder & Co v John Davidson. Scire facias. To Sheriff of Wilson County, Jas Elder & Co recovered agt John Davidson $21.90½, costs & charge of Sheriff on an execution in sd suit; $22.25 paid, leaving balance $8.58; D.Shelby Clerk, 1 Decr 1801. 28 Decr 1801 Nathl Perry D S W made known in presence of Jacob Thomas Daniel Tilny. Jan 1802 dft failed to appear; judgt agt him $8.58 & costs.
   Appt Thomas Keeffe inspector of cotton at his gin on Station Camp Creek; bond $1000, Redmond D Barry & Wm Cage securities.
   License Thomas Young Blood to keep ordinary at his dwelling in Sumner County; bond, with Alexander Graham security, and received license.
   p.329   Jurors to ensuing Court: James Vinson John Hamilton Jesse Johnson Jos Wilson George D Blackmore Thomas Cocke Joseph Motheral Joseph Wallace Zacheus Wilson John Gardner Malachi Hereford James Weathered Thomas Parker John Goodrum John Hawkins John Mills Richd Alexander James Graham King Carr Peter Lyon Mark Richmon David Henry Richard King George Hamilton David Ormond George Clark Richard Caveatt Jr Jas Braken Isaac George Lewis Crane John Deloach William Reed Jesse Womack Isreal Moore Herrin Taylor Peter Looney H Joseph Wilson Senr.
   Henry Harrison v Jonathan Hannum. Verdict in favour of dft, counsel for plf moved for new trial; which rule is discharged without argument.
   Allow John Payton $9 for settling with holders of public money.
   Allow Zacheus Wilson $6 for setting with holders of public money.

APRIL 1802

Thomas Cypert v Henry Robinson. Plf dismisses suit at cost of dft.
Allow coroner $28 for holding four inquests.
Thomas Murry one/commrs to purchase land & contract for building of court house prison & stocks entered bond $2500, George Smith & William Cage securities.
License William Henderson to keep an ordinary at his mills on Drakes Creek, bond $2500 with Patrick Gibson security and received license.
Allow Clerk $20 for recording lists of taxable property for year 1801.
Appt Alexander Graham overseer/road from Bledsoes creek to Indian creek.
Appt Archd White overseer/road Bledsoes Cr to Maj Whites in place of James White.
Jas Winchester esq deposits 2½¢ fine on Benjamin Morgan for profane swearing.
Court adjourns to meet at Cairo on the first Monday in April next. J Winchester.

p.330 Court of Pleas & Quarter Sessions held at Cairo on the first Monday in April 1802. Present James Winchester James Hart and John Morgan Esquires
Deed/gift Jeremiah Doxey to his children Thomas Doxey Stephen Hainey Doxey Jeremiah Doxey Jr, John Sandford Doxey, & Nancy Helms Doxey two negroes, stock, household furniture and farming tools &c ackd by sd Jeremiah.
Deed/gift Jeremiah Doxey to Samuel Haney Doxey 90 acres ackd.
Bill/sale Jonathan Jenkins to Laurence Whitsitt for negro girl Mary proved by Alexander Walker.
Bill/sale Geo Brisco to Laurence Whitsitt negro boy Dred proved by Alexr Walker.
Ltr/atty William Sheppard to Christopher Stump proved by Matthew Brooks.
Will of Daniel Rogers decd proved by Peter Looney & Jonathan Latimer Jr; Saml Rogers & Griswold Latimer exrs qualified & returned inventory.
Grant ltrs/admn on estate of John Standiford decd to Archibald Standford; bond $500, James Hart security.
John Bradley v John Hazlet. Bail for dft surrenders him into custody of sheriff.
John Barr commissioned in peace by Archibald Roane esqr 14 Nov 1801 took oaths & qualified as Justice of the peace and took his seat.
Acct/sales goods of Richard Gossage decd proved by admx.
Jesse Womack excused from attending as a juror for the present term.
Charles Latimer records his ear mark.
Lynde Latimer records his ear mark.
Deed Henry Lyon to Francis Weatherred 104 acres proved by Robert Dep[binding].
Grand jury Jesse Johnson foreman Joseph Wilson Sr Peter Lyon George Hamilton John Gardner Zacheus Wilson David Henry John Hawkins David Ormand James Weatherred Lewis Crane John Mills William Reed. James Bentley constable to attend Grand Jury.
Joseph Wilson James Graham Richard Cavitt Jr James Braken Isaac George John Deloach Herrin Taylor jurors apptd for present term failed to appear.
Deed Jas Winchester & Wm Cage to Oliver Smith lot in Cairo proved by Thos Wilson.
p.331 Eleven deeds from Jas Winchester & Wm Cage for town lots to Thomas Wilson.
Deed Martin Armstrong to Jona Latimer Jr 228 acres proved by Griswold Latimer.
Deed Jonathan Latimer Jr to Lynde Latimer 100 acres ackd.
Deed Jas Winchester & Wm Cage to Jesse Johnson lot 13 proved by Geo D Blackmore.
Deed Thomas Bradley to James Dickerson 119 acres proved by Nathaniel Dickison.
Deed Jeremiah Thacker to John Blackmore 50 acres proved by Henry Bradford.

APRIL 1802

Deed Willie Cherry to Robert Heaton 100 acres proved by Benjamin Seawell.
Ann Candler orphan bound to Archibald White to learn sewing, Knitting & weaving.
Orphan Samuel Turner bound to William Garrett to learn art of a taylor.
Appt Rachel Carson guardian for Honor Carson orphan of William S Carson; bond $2000 with Francis Locke and James Hart securities.
Appt John Mills guardian for James Carson orphan of William S Carson; bond $200, James Lauderdale and John Hawkins securities.
Account/sales of goods of James Kelly decd proved by administrator.
p.332 Deed Thomas Bradley to Nathl Dickison Sr 100 acres proved by Jas Dickison.
Supplementary inventory estate of Wm Cathey decd proved by administrator.
Lists of taxable property returned by James Hart esq in Capt Bradleys company; Thomas Blackmore esq in Capt Haineys Company.

Tuesday April 6th. Present James Winchester Thomas Donnell James Hart Witheral Latimer David Love William Cage William Seawell esqr.
Deed Frederick Snyder by Wm Donelson his atty in fact & James Berry to James Reed 320 acres proved by James Rolston.
Deed Frederick Snyder by Wm Donelson his atty in fact & Jeremiah Rankin to George Reed 320 acres proved by James Rolston.
Deed David Cooley to Edward Gwin 400 acres proved by Richard Cook.
David Wilson & Edward Douglass v Paul Harpole garnishee of Terrell. Garnishee swears he owed sd Obediah Terrell $317.58 at time of levying attachment.
Release Isaac George & James Braken from fines for nonattendance as jurors.
Deed Adam Tooley to James Braken 640 acres proved by Peter Walker.
Deed John Cummins to Elisha Pruitt 100 acres proved by Nicholas Boyer.
Commissioners report they settled with admrs of William S Carson decd.
Abner Bush son of Abner Bush decd who has attained age fourteen chooses John C Hamilton for his guardian.
Redmond D Barry witness in John Washington v Benjn Seawell not having proved his attendance at last term now proves same against pltf for $3.06.
Wm Cage esqr returns list/taxable property in Capt Greens company.
W Douglass, W Gillespie, Isaac George, Joseph George, R Cage report they laid off a road from James Franklins to Dillards ferry by William Douglass's to Capt Gillespies up Station Camp Creek.
David Wilson & Edward Douglass v Obediah Terrell. Attachment. July 1799 plf in proper person; proceedings stayed six months. Jan 1800 dft came not; judgt by de-
p.333 fault agt him. Oct 1801 Jno S Martin retd "not found." Jan 1802 D Shelby to Sheriff of Wilson County, Wm Wilson; attachment agt Paul Harpole garnishee; executed 27 March in presence of John Davidson & Andrew Steele by Wm Wilson S W C. Apr 1802 plfs by Jesse Wharton esq. Garnishee swears he owed Obediah Terrell $317.58; judgt agt Paul Harpole for $50.38 & costs.
Inventory/goods of Edward Giles decd rendered & proved by executor.
Deed Thomas Bradley to John Dickerson 410 acres ackd.
Deed Thomas Bradley to David Crenshaw 424 acres ackd.
Deed Robert Dobbins to Robert Taylor 57 acres proved by Leonard Dugger.
Deed Alexander Espy & John Espy to William Henderson 50 acres ackd by Alexr Espy.
Deed Robert Looney to James McKinsey 220 acres proved by Hugh Crawford.
David Wilson returns list/taxable property in Capt Vinsons company.
Appt Zachariah Green overseer/road from John Dawsons to Wm Gillespies.

APRIL 1802

Appt Reuben Cage overseer/road from Wm Gillespies to Dillards Ferry.
p.334 Appt Joseph Motherall overseer/road from James Trousdales to Maj Wilsons.
Appt Andrew Blythe overseer/road from Croft mills to Dry fork.
Appt Joseph Bunton overseer/road from dry fork of Bledsoes cr to top of ridge.
Appt Nathl Dickerson overseer/road from Second creek to Bishops ferry.
John McMurtry esq renders list/taxable property in Capt Kirkpatricks company.
State v Abraham Teal. Profane swearing. Fined 31¼¢.
Appt Elijah Simpson constable for Capt Barrs dist; King Carr security.
William Seawell esq renders list/taxable property in Capt Barrs company.
Reuben Searcy esq renders list/taxable property in Capt Gwins company.
John C Hamilton v Richard Boyce. Covt. Oct 1801 plf by Thos Stuart; dft replevied property attached & by Saml Donelson his atty pleaded covenant performed. Apr 1802 jury James Vinson John Hamilton Thomas Cocke Joseph Motherall John Goodrum Richard Alexander Mark Richman Richard King Isreal Moore Peter Luna King Carr Robert Patton assess plfs damages $97.25 with costs.
Deed Arthur Exum to Champness Madding 27½ acres proved by James Hart.
Deed Benjamin Ellis to Arthur Exum 128 acres proved by James Hart.
State v Andrew Patterson. Fornication. Dft pays his & the womans fine $6.25 and is discharged without giving bond for maintenance of the womans child.
Witherall Latimer esq renders list/taxable property in Capt Shaws company.
Inventory/personal estate of Robert Taylor decd rendered by exr Robert Taylor.
Inventory/goods & sales of Wm Hamilton decd proved by executors.
Deed Jno Purvaince to Thomas Keeffe & Redmond D Barry 100 acres proved by William Bradshaw.
p.335 Road overseers appointed: Abraham Rogers from Shelbys creek to John Hassels in place of Hugh Crawford. John Withers from Jas Trousdales to Shelbys cr in place of Solomon Barnes. Wm Hubbart from Cairo to Holstun rd near Maj Whites in place of Nathl Giles. James McKinsey from John Dawsons to foot/ridge. Benjamin Hudson from foot/ridge to Red River road in place of John Patterson. Wm Bruce from John Dawsons to William Montgomerys on Drakes creek in place of Joshua Hadley.
Appt Thos Donnell & Wm Seawell to settle with admrs of Wm S Carson.

Wednesday April 7th. Present Edward Douglass Thomas Donnell William Seawell Esqrs.
Malachi Hereford v Spencer Totevine & Joseph Westbrook. Sci Fa. Malachi Hereford recovered agt Heli Herring admr of Simon Totevine decd; sci fa from D Shelby issued agt heirs & devisees of decedant, Spencer Totevine & Joseph Westbrook. Jany 1802 E Crutcher D S retd "not found." Judgt entered. Apr 1802 dfts not appearing, judgment p.336 agt them $207.63 & costs of suit.
Grant ltrs/admn on estate of Anthony H Bledsoe decd to Catey Bledsoe; bond $1000, James Winchester security; returned inventory. Order of sale issued.
Allow John McMurtry coroner $7 for holding inquest, body of John Standiford decd.
James Winchester, Stephen Cantrill, James Reese, William Cage, Charles Donoho, John McMurtry, & John Barr esquires, take their seats.
Andrew Greer v William Brimberry. Attachment. Oct 1801 Plf by Thos Stuart. Dft by John C Hamilton. April 1802 jury[above except Heli Herring for John Goodrum] assess plfs damages $99.60, with costs.
Appt William Montgomery Entry Taker; bond $5000, Wm Sample security; took oath.
Will of John Whitworth decd proved by Isaac Lindsey Jr; no executor named; grant ltrs/admn with will annexed to Elizabeth Whitworth, bond $500, George Smith sec.

APRIL 1802

p.337 Thos Masten Benj Rawlings Wm Montgomery Isaac Walton Jas Douglass David Wilson John Morgan Archibald Marlin & James Hart esquires take their seats.
  Commrs report they settled with admr of Polley Fowler decd.
  Jury that laid off road Bledsoes Lick to Flat Gap were not qualified agreeable to law; all former orders respecting sd road discontinued. Appt George Gillespie Matthew Alexander William Reed James Clendening James Weatherred Patrick Barr Robert Desha to lay off road from Bledsoes Lick to Flat Gap.
  Lists/taxable property rendered: Isaac Walton in Capt Whitsitts company. James Douglass & James Cryer in Blacks & Snoddies companies.
  Grand Jury dismissed.
  James Hart relinquishes claim to ferry on Cumberland; released from obligation.
  John McMurtry Job Hicks John Perry James Wornock Wm Orr Orman Allon Thos Brittain to lay off a road from Kentucky rd above Thos Brittons into Holston rd to Nashville between W Nye's & Wm Montgomery's.
  Order road from Gallatin to near Wm Gillespies be laid off by Wm Gillespie Jas Cryer Geo Meeker Wm Snoddy Henry Bradford Wm Cage Nicholas Boyer & John Payton.
  State v Wright Bond. Riot. Recognizance; James Cryer & John Trice securities.
  Order James Trousdale, John Withers, Jas Wilson Curley, Joseph Motherall, Zacheus Wilson Sr, Nicholas Boyce, James Cryer lay off a road from Gallatin to Cumberland R between Station Camp & Elliotts branch.
  Order Isaac Baker, Solomon Barnes, Thomas Edwards, Wm Phipps Sr, Isreal Moore lay off road from Gallatin across Red River ridge into new road from Cairo to the old Kentucky road on this side of Big Barren near Swain Stalcups on Drakes Creek about two miles from top of Red River ridge.
p.338 Deed Benjn Kuykendall & Jonathan Kuykendall to Abraham Standley 66½ acres proved by David Wilson.
  Deed Jane Kuykendall to John Mitchell 274 acres proved by William Edwards.
  Appt Alexander Graham overseer/road Bledsoes creek to Indian creek.
  Order James Cryer esqr to furnish Charles Elliott with list of hands.

Thursday April 8th. Present Edward Douglass, Stephen Cantrill, James Sanders Esqrs.
  James Reese & James Sanders esqrs return lists/taxable property in Capt Neeleys & Capt Montgomerys companies.
  Jas Winchester Jas Hart Thos Masten Jas Reese Wm Cage Esqrs take their seats.
  Jurors to ensuing Court: Matthew Alexander Alexander Graham Joel Echols Nathaniel Gilmore Robert Bratney Robert Carothers Solomon Reese Thomas Keefe Jas S Wilson Wm Wherry James Gardner John Trousdale Alexr Cathey Daniel McConnell James Sanders G C Seth Mabry Reuben Douglass Isaac George Matthew Scobey Jas Franklin Jas Reatherford Jacob Browning John D Hannah William Allen George Gillespie John Byrns Isaac Parker Edmond Browning Saml Smith Edwd Sanders Matthew Cartwright Isaac Pearce Isaac Clark Kasper Mansker Thomas Perry Thomas Parker.
  Jurors to next Superior Court: James Frazor William Alexander G S Francis Locke Matthew Alexander Robert Desha Hugh Crafford Henry Bunn.
  George Parks v John Mansker. Motion of Mr Donelson suggesting former writ fieri facias agt dft was not retd by sheriff to whom directed; order alias writ fieri facias be issued by clerk or writ scire facias revived if necessary.
  Ltr/atty Isaac Walton to Redmond D Barry ackd.
  Wm Brimberry v Andrew Greer. Jan 1802 plf by John C Hamilton; dft by Thos Stuart. Apr 1802 jury Thos Cocke Nicholas Boyce Thos Wilson Wm Hall John Stamp James McKain

160

APRIL 1802

Wm Bradshaw Richd Boyce Marcus Sharp Reuben Pruitt John Barham Christopher Snavely; plf not supporting action, failing to appear, non suit; plf liable for costs.
p.339   David Shelby v Wm Parker. Covt. Jan 1802 plf by Thos Stuart; dft by Redmond D Barry. Apr jury Jas Vinson Jos Motherall Richd Alexander Mark Richmon Richd King Isreal Moore Peter Looney Heli Herring Thos Wilson Nichs Boyce Marcus Sharp William Bradshaw assess plfs damages $20 with costs.
Deed Oliver Smith to William Trigg Jr 300 acres proved by James Sanders.
Inventory/goods of Laban Benthall decd proved by admr.
John C Hamilton who is choosed as guardian for Abner Bush by sd Abner enters bond $1000 with John H Bush security.
Stephen Ward v Heli Herring admr of Simon Totevine decd. Covt. Jany 1802 plf by Thos Stuart. April dft by Samuel Donelson and Jesse Wharton. Jury[above except John Stamp for Heli Herring] assess plfs damages $416 & 67 cents; Court confirms verdict in favour of defendant.
Thomas Keeffe v Christen Staley. Attachment. Jan 1802 plf by Redmond D Barry; dft came not; judgt by default agt dft. Horse on which attachment levied being perishable should be sold by sheriff. Apr jury[above] assess plfs damage $98.71 & costs.
p.340   Heli Herring Admr of Simon Totevine decd v Edwd Gatlin. Trover. Jury[above except Wm Hall & Wm Neely for John Stamps & Wm Bradshaw] assess plfs damages $45; dft's atty Thomas Stuart moved for new trial; granted.
John C Hamilton v Joseph McKean. January 1802 David Shelby summons McKean from Davidson County; shff J Boyd Jr made known to McKean in presence of James Maxwell and David Dunlap. McKean failed to appear; judgment against dft $125 with costs.
John C Hamilton v George M Deaderick. Sci fa David Shelby to sheriff of Davidson County; witness Geo Deaderick failed to appear to give testimony in behalf of John C Hamilton; J Boyd Jr Shff made known to Deaderick in presence of Wiley Barrow and
p.341   Robert McConnell. Deaderick failed to appear; judgt agt him $125 and costs.
Court adjourns till Court in Course at Cairo first Monday in July. J Winchester.

Court of Pleas & Quarter Sessions at the town of Cairo first Monday in July 1802. Present James Winchester James Reese Thomas Blackemore Esquires.
Deed John Orr to John C Hamilton 100 acres ackd.
Persons who failed to make return of taxable property & polls to do so.
John McMurtry, Job Hicks, Jno Perry, James Wornock, William Orr, Orman Allen, & Thomas Britton report they laid off a road from above Thos Brittons into Holston road between W Nye and Wm Montgomery.
Appt John Perry overseer/road from Thomas Brittons into Nashville road between W Nye & Wm Montgomery Esq; Wm Montgomery to furnish list of hands to work on sd road.
Grand jury: Edward Sanders foreman, Isaac Clark Matthew Alexander Matthew Scoby, Reuben Douglass, Thos Keefe, Isaac George, Saml Smith, Solomon Reese, Jas S Wilson, Edmund Browning, William Wherry, James Franklin. Benjamin Morgan to attend jury.
Acct/sales of goods of Anthony H Bledsoe decd rendered and proved by admx.
Deeds ackd & proved: Danl McConnell to James Graham 50 ac. Charles Donoho to John Parker by John Dobyns 67 ac. Thomas Reese to John Bowan 9 ac. James Reese to John Bowman 91 ac. Robert Campbell to John Stuart 106 ac. Daniel Smith to Henry Bradford 224 ac. Daniel Smith to Henry Bradford 34 ac. Henry Bradford to Daniel Smith 32 ac.

JULY 1802

p.342 Godfrey Etheridge apprenticed to Moses Odam, sadler.
State v John Deloach. Dft files affidavit his wifes illness prevented his attendance as a juror last term; released from fine on his paying cost.
State v James Graham. Wife and a negroes illnesses prevented his attendance as a juror at last term; released from fine on his paying cost.
State v Richard Caveatt Jr. Dft files affidavit stating he was never summoned; released from fine and costs.
Avey Bloodworth & Anny Boyecan, orphans, having attained age 14, make choice of Henry Bloodworth for their guardian; bond $700, John Deloach & Heli Herring sec.
Appt John Payton, Henry Vinson, & Allen Purvis patrollers for Capt Scoby's compy.
Deed James Winchester & Wm Cage to Solomon Reese lot 9 in Cairo ackd.
Deed James Winchester & Wm Cage to Solomon Reese lot 59 in Cairo ackd.
Appt Matthew Richmond Caleb Willis & Solomon Bandy patrollers in Capt Milams company; they are to qualify before James Sanders esqr.
Allow John McMurtry coroner $7 for holding inquest on body of Wm Dennis decd.
Robt Desha Matthew Alexander Geo Gillespie Wm Reed James Weatherred Patrick Barr James Clendening report they marked a road from Bledsoes lick to flat gap.

Tuesday July 6th. Present Jas Winchester Thos Donnell James Hart Witherall Latimer.
Acct/sales of goods of John Sandiford decd rendered & proved by admr.
Deed James Rankin to Jonathan Badgett 142 acres ackd.
Edward Hogin fined $15 for contempt of Court; in custody of sheriff until paid.
p.343 Bill/sale Hallery Malone to Charles Dement negro girl Priscilla ackd.
Ltr/atty Jesse Cherry & Wm Biggs exrs of James Powell decd proved by Danl Cherry.
License James Steel to keep ordinary in Cairo, James C Wilson security.
Will of John Donoho decd proved by James Hollis & John Ferrier; John Donoho, James Reese & Archibald Marlin executors therein mentioned qualified.
Jonathan Rodgers son of Daniel Rogers decd having attained age 14 makes choice of Witherall Latimer for his guardian; Court appts Latimer guardian for Stanton Rogers another son of sd decedant; bond $1600, Griswold Latimer & Archibald Marlin sec.
Thomas Cribbins v John Payton. Plf by Saml Donelson; Oct 1800 dft by John C Hamilton. April 1801 jury Wm Neely John Goodrum Henry Lyon Wm Lauderdale Hugh Kirkpatrick Leonard Dugger Griswold Latimer Joseph Motherall Robt Wadkins Smith Hansbrough Richd Strother Jno McMurry; dft failed to appear; nonsuit; plf pays costs & suit is reinstated. July 1802 jury James Gardner John Trousdale Alexander Cathey Daniel McConnell John Byrns Wm Neely Heli Herring Jno Stamp Henry Belote Isaac Baker Hallery Malone John Deloach assess plfs damages to $62.81. Dft obtains appeal to Superior Court for Mero dist, bond $150 with Lazarus Cotton & Elkenor Echols securities.
Deed David Love to Jesse Hughes 95½ acres ackd.
Deed James Winchester to James Thomas 100 acres proved by James Odam.
Deed Gabriel Dillard to Matthew Scoby 110 acres proved by Reuben Cage.
p.344 Bill/sale Jeremiah Watson to James Williams negro girl Alea[Alex?] proved by James Watson.
Deed Charles Donoho to James Hart 12 acres ackd.
Deed John Goodrum to George Duren 46½ acres ackd.
Deed Nathl Giles to Joseph Motherall for 150 acres proved by David Wilson.
David Wilson, Edward Douglass, Thomas Masten, Reuben Searcy, Wm Montgomery, Isaac Walton, Stephen Cantrill, Jas Sanders, Wm Cage, Thos Blackemore, John McMurtry, Jas Reese, Jno Morgan, James Cryer, Jonathan Hannum, Wm Seawell, John Barr, David Love,

JULY 1802

Charles Desha, James Douglass & Archd Marlin Esqrs appear and take their seats.
Taxes for present year laid [omitted].
Thomas Edwards v Daniel Miles. Covt. Dfts bail surrenders him to sheriff.
Thomas Blackemore Esq to furnish Archd White overseer/road with list of hands.
Allow George Bush $26.66 for keeping orphan child Wm Young Jan 1802 to Jan 1803.
Deed James Sanders to James Hunt 63 acres ackd.
Deed James Sanders to William Palmer 66 acres ackd.
Appt Edmund Crutcher Sheriff for two years; bond $12500 with Edwd Douglass Isaac Baker Redmond D Barry Wm Gillespie Thos Masten securities, and took oaths.
Order Edward Hogin be taken into custody, carried to the stray pen, and there confined in the fence for half an hour for swearing in presence of Court.
Order [blank] fined $2 for contemptuous behaviour in hearing of the Court, and that he be kept in custody of the Sheriff until paid.
Deed Wm Montgomery to John Dugger 102 acres ackd.
Appt Matthew Cartwright guardian for John Beakley Sally G Beakley William Beakley Nancy Beakley Betsey Beakley orphans of William Beakley decd; bond $1000, Wm Montgomery and Isaac Clark securities.
Thomas Edwards v Daniel Miles. Covt. Edwd Hogin Sr special bail for dft.
Will of Thomas Tullock decd certified by Clerk/Court Halifax County North Carolina with certificate of chairman/Court exhibited and admitted to record.
Edmund Crutcher Sheriff bond for collection of taxes; Edward Douglass, Isaac Baker, Redmond D Barry, Wm Gillespie Thos Masten securities.
p.345 Allow Thomas Todd $30 for keeping a poor female child Morning Morrish one year commencing 18th April 1802.
Appt James A Wilson overseer/road from Cairo to near Maj Wilson; David Wilson Esq to furnish sd overseer with a list of hands.
Peter Looney Alexr Gwin Benjn Hudson Saml Jennings Griswold Latimer Wm Brigance & Jas Hamilton to lay off a road from Gallatin to intersection of Robinson County road and Kentucky road.

Wednesday July 7th 1802. Present Jas Winchester David Wilson Chas Donoho esquires.
Deed Samuel Donelson Shadrack Nye James Wilson & Charles Donoho commrs to Daniel Miles lot 15 in Gallatin ackd by Donelson, Nye, & Donoho.
Deed Samuel Donelson Shadrack Nye Chas Donoho commrs to Edmund Crutcher lot 3 in Gallatin ackd.
Thomas Cribbins v John Payton. Motion for new trial overruled; dft appeals to Superior Court; bond, Lazarus Cotton & Elkenor Echols securities.
Allow Patrick Gibson constable $25 for expences attending execution of two negro criminals property of Jeremiah Watson.
State v Wright Bond. Rioting & profane swearing. Dft by John C Hamilton moves bill/presentment be quashed; sustained by argument and quashed.
State v Terry Williams. Rioting & profane swearing. Also quashed.
State v Jesse Womack. Profane swearing; Dft submits; fined 31¼¢ which dft pays.
State v Wm Brassil. Dft fails to appear; scire facias issues.
State v Barnet Butler. Dft fails to bring Wm Brassil; scire facias issues.
Thomas Keefe v Christen Staley. Order property whereon attachment levied be sold.
p.346 State v Edward Hogin. Sd Edwd Hogin to be taken into custody of sheriff and confined in fence of stray pen for one hour for contempt of Court.
State v Richard Waller Jr. TAB. Bond of Drury Milam prosecutor, and Elisha

JULY 1802

Pruett to appear and give testimony against defendant.
Matthew Scoby one of the Grand Jury is absent on account of indisposition.
State v Richard Waller. TAB. Appearance bonds of Drury Milam prosecutor; Elisha Pruitt to give testimony.
William Morgan v John Payton. John Robinson a witness for plf failed to appear.
William Morgan v John Payton. Plf by Saml Donelson. Oct 1800 dft by John C Hamilton. July 1802 Jury George Gillespie David Orman Robt Patton Thomas Farmer John Orr John Hamilton John Gardner Elisha Pruitt Armstead Rogers Robt Ellis Wm Millikin Jos Steel assess plfs damages $56.65 with costs. Dft obtains appeal to Superior Court; his atty Thos Stuart files reasons; bond with John C Hamilton & Lazarus Cotton sec.
Zaccheus Wilson apptd County Trustee in place of James Reese resigned; bond $2000 with Matthew Alexander security.
Moses Morrish bound to William Winchester to learn the cabbinet trade.
Catey Morrish & Newburn Morrish are bound unto William Hall until full age.
Nelley Morrish bound unto James Harrison until full age.
Inventory/goods of John Donoho decd proved by John Donoho & Archd Marlin exrs.
p.347   Personal estate of John Donoho decd to be exposed to sale by the executors.
Appoint Wm Hubbard overseer/road Cairo to near Maj Whites in place of Nathaniel Giles; James Reese to furnish list of hands to work with sd overseer.
Deed James Winchester & Wm Cage lot 25 to Pleasant Chitwood ackd.
Order [blank] released from fine $2 for contempt of the Court.

Thursday July 8th 1802. Present: James Sanders, Thomas Donnell, Jonathan Hannum, Isaac Walton, Archibald Marlin, esquires.
State v Richard Hogin. TAB. Appearance bond of Henry Gambell, prosecutor.
State v Richard Hogin. TAB. Appearance bond of Malachi Hereford, prosecutor.
Jonathan Hannum v Jesse Kuykendall. Jan 1801 plf by Thos Stuart; dft by John C Hamilton. July 1801 E Crutcher D S found nothing to be attached. July 1801 E Crutcher D S levied on dfts part of 200 acres on Bledsoes creek. Jan 1802 dft came not; judgt by default. Jul 1802 jury James Gardner John Trousdale Alexr Cathey Danl McConnell George Gillespie Henry Belote Jesse Womack Heli Herring Malachi Hereford Henry Pitt Henry Bloodworth Wm Trigg assess plfs damage $45.72 with costs; attached land to be sold for use of the judgment.
David Gillespie v Ephm Payton. Deposition of Lazarus Cotton to be taken for dft.
p.348   John Bond v Edward Hogin. TAB. January 1802 plf by Saml Donelson. July 1802 jury Jas Gardner Jno Trousdale Alexander Cathey Daniel McConnell Geo Gillespie Heli Herring James Clendening Joseph Neely Halery Malone Jesse Wormack Henry Bloodworth John Orr assess plfs damage $35, with costs.
William Morgan v John Payton. Dft obtains appeal to Superior Court for Mero Dist; bond $200 John C Hamilton and Lazarus Cotton securities.
Jonathan Hannum v Jesse Kuykendall. Property whereon the judicial attachment was levied, being dfts undivided share of 200 acres on Bledsoe Creek, to be sold.
John Bond v Edward Hogin. TAB. Order dft pay Jesse Womack Halery Malone John Deloach Thos Keefe & Wm Moore; plf pay all other witnesses in said suit.
Benjamin John v Matthew Kincannon. Attacht. Jan 1801 plf by Jesse Wharton; property attached insufficient to answer plfs demand. Apr 1801 E Crutcher D S returns: Perkins not found; no property of deft to levy on. Sci fa agt Daniel Perkins, garnishee, Williamson County. Apr 1802 dft came not; judgt by default agt dft. July 1802 jury James Gardner John Trousdale Alexr Cathy Daniel McConnell George Gilles-

JULY 1802

pie John Payton Henry Belote William Moore Saml Morrison Robert Patton John Reeves Terry Turner find plfs damages $960. Property levied on, 640 acres on Second creek, condemned for use of judgment; order of sale issues.

p.349 State v Edward Hogin. Trespass assault. Dft submits; fined $1.50; kept in custody of sheriff until same is paid with costs.

John Hamilton v John Houdeshall. Attachment. Oct 1801 plf by Geo Smith; Apr 1802 dft came not; judgt by default. Jul 1802 jury Jas Gardner Jno Trousdale Alexr Cathey Daniel McConnell Geo Gillespie Jno Orr Malachi Hereford John Payton Joseph Neely William Trigg Jesse Womack Saml Morrison assess plfs damages $850 with costs; order attached property be sold for use of judgment.

Grand Jury dismissed.

Allow Benjn Morgan $5 for arresting & taking to district jail Jeremiah Watson.

Jurors to Oct Term: John Shannon John Hogan Thomas Hamilton Jr Robert Anderson Wm Bell Thos Patton Alexr Graham Thomas Cocke Jas Carothers Jas Odam Wm Edwards Joshua Cherry Wm Phipps Sr Edwd Williams John Wilson Jos Wallace Saml Piper Jno Hogan Edwd Morgan Hugh Kirkpatrick John Garrison Peter Blair Bryant Gardner Richard Jones Laurence Whitsitt James Cary Wm Reed Jesse Hainey James Rutherford Thomas Perry Gasper Mansker Isaac Pearce John Withers Samuel Wilson George D Blackemore John Roberts.

David Wilson and James Cryer esqrs to compleat a settlement made in part with the administrator of Simon Totevine decd.

David Wilson and James Cryer esqrs to make settlement with David Shelby as exr of William Beakley decd.

State v Richard Hogin. TAB. Appearance bond of Henry Gambell, prosecutor.

Fine of $15 agt Edward Hogin for contempt of Court is remitted.

Sumner v William Osburn. Wm Brimberry failed to prosecute suit against Andw Greer and has not paid costs & charges thereof. Wm Osburn, Brimberrys security, summoned.

p.350 Edmund Crutcher D S made sci fa known in presence of Nathl Simmons & Josiah Wells. Jul 1802 dft came not; judgment by default for costs of suit Wm Brimberry v Andw Greer $7.47½ and costs.

On petition of Wm Gillespie, order Wm Cage Geo Meeker & Jas Cryer assess value of an acre opposite to where Gillespie intends to build a mill.

Geo Meeker James Cryer H Bradford Nicholas Boyce John Payton report they marked a road from Gallatin to a ford on main east fork Station Camp creek between Dr Barrys and the Nashville road thence to McKnights horse mill to William Gillespies.

Appt John Payton overseer/road from Gallatin to east of McKnights horse mill; James Cryer esqr to furnish list of hands.

Bond of Edmund Crutcher as collector of taxes, George Smith & Saml Donelson sec.

Court adjourns till Court in Course to meet at the house of James Trousdale in the Town of Gallatin first Monday in October next.   Edwd Douglass

p.351 Court of Pleas & Quarter Sessions at house of James Trousdale in Gallatin, October 1802. Present David Wilson James Winchester David Love Esquires.

Deed Hugh Elliott to Thomas Curry 250 acres proved by James Cryer.

Richard Jones is excused from attending as a juror for present erm.

Grand Jury: Thos Patton foreman Saml Piper Bryant Gardner Laurence Whitsitt John Garrison John Roberts Wm Bell Edward Williams John Withers Jos Wallace Wm Edwards

OCTOBER 1802

John Hogin Thomas Hambleton. Henry Vinson constable to attend Grand Jury.

Hugh Kirkpatrick, Peter Blair, Alexr Graham, Thomas Perry are excused from attending as jurors for the present Term.

Appt Wright Barnes constable for Capt Blacks district; bond $625, Isaac Baker & Solomon Barnes securities.

Will of Hugh Elliott decd proved by Charles Elliott who also made oath that testator signed will in presence of the other subscribing witness.

Deed Moses Owen to James Stephenson 200 acres in Iredell co North Carolina ackd.

Appt Isaac Walton guardian for Franky Hamilton orphan of William Hamilton decd, bond $2000, John C Hamilton security.

Thomas Edwards v Daniel Miles. Covt. Edward Hogin surrenders dft to Court.

Sally Reed & James Reed make choice of their brother Joseph Reed as guardian; bond $1000 with Reuben Searcy and James Roney securities.

James Ross et al v John Harriss. Detinue. Joseph Neely & William Reed surrender dft, who is ordered into custody of the sheriff.

William & Will Trigg v Drury Milam. Judgt behalf sd Triggs agt Drury Milam & his securities George Smith & Edward Sanders for $51.48, the amount of judgment with interest recovered by sd Triggs agt Isaac Peirce received and unaccounted for by sd Milam as constable.

Deed John Summers to John Rhoads junior 106 acres proved by Frederick Lassiter.

Deed Thomas Donoho to Thomas Parker 100 acres proved by Edward Donoho.

p.352 Deed/release Isaac Houdeshall to John Hamilton for sd Houdeshalls share in two tracts of land one of 440 acres the other of 200 acres proved by David Shelby.

Deed William Lytle Junr to Wm Bradshaw Senr 100 acres proved by Henry Lyon.

Deed John Denning to James Roaney 120 acres proved by Isaac Stalcup.

Deed Ambrose Maulden to Isaac Stalcup 140 acres proved by James Roney.

Articles/agreement Anthony Hogin & Redmond D Barry proved by James McKain.

Writ of Habeus Corpus issues to jailer of Nashville gaol to bring Henry alias Absolam Morris to this Court to receive sentence agt him for petit larceny.

Order William Cage esqr furnish Reuben Cage overseer with a list of hands.

John Wood v Atkinson & Laurence. Dfts bail surrenders him to custody of sheriff.

License David Wilson esqr to keep tavern at his dwelling, Nathaniel Gilmore sec.

Bill/sale William Alexander to Silas Alexander negro woman Zelpha, Blacksmith tools, horse & filly, &c, acknowledged.

Deeds ackd & proved: William Alexander to Silas Alexander. Jas McCarrell to Thos Keefe by David Shelby. Jas McCarrell to Thos Keefe & Redmond D Barry by David Shelby. Edwd Gwin to Robt Shy by John Gwin. Thos Hamilton to Robt Hamilton by Jas Frazor. James Cage late shff to Thomas Graves by Jos Seawell. Samuel Donelson Shadrack Nye James Wilson & Charles Donoho to Wm Garret lot #5 in Gallatin by Will Trigg Jr.

Appt Joseph Reed guardian for Samuel Reed; bond $500, John Reed security.

Pleasant Boyce bound to Frederick Miller to learn the farming business.

Commrs report they settled with David Shelby as exr of William Beakley decd.

p.353 Appt David Campbell overseer/road from KY line to Thompsons place in place of Samuel Piper; Major Sharp and Mr Searcys hands Joseph Caveatt John Perryman and Ezekiel Norman work on sd road.

Jurors to Superior Court: Griffith Rutherford Matthew Alexander George Gillespie James Clendening William Neely George D Blackemore Thomas Donnell.

Tuesday Octr 5th. Present Wm Montgomery Jas Cryer John McMurtry Witheral Latimer.

OCTOBER 1802

Deed Richard Hogin to George G Black 80 acres 20 perches proved by James Cryer.
Bill/sale John Dobbins to Isaac Baker for 2 negroes, Milley & Abraham, proved by Alexander Dobbins.
Deed Hallery Malone to Patrick Barr 120 acres ackd.
David Gillespie v Ephraim Payton. Jury Geo D Blackemore Isaac Pierce Joshua Cherry Edwd Sanders John Deloach Thos Howell John Bond Chas Reese John Harris, Blair Harris, Thos Keefe Thos Farmer; mistrial.
Articles/agreement Jane Kuykendall & Redmond D Barry proved by Wright Bond.
William Snoddy v Anthony Sydnor. Covt. July 1802 plf by Thos Stuart; dft by John C Hamilton. This Term plf dismissed his suit; each party pays his own atty & costs.
John Den lessee of David Love v James Ashlock. Ejectment. Plf David Love in proper person dismissed his suit. Dft recovers of plf his costs.
James Ross et al v Eli Herrell. Dfts bail Joseph Neely & Wm Reed surrender dft.
Ltr/atty David Barry to Wm Hall proved by Henry Lyon.
Deed John Hassell to John Hassell Wormington 50 acres proved by Jesse Hassell.
Bill/sale W Dennis to Jeremiah Watson, negro man Powell proved by James Watson.
Bill/sale Jeremiah Watson to Joseph Hodge negro man Powell ackd.
Two ltrs/atty one from Moses Watson to Urbone Frazor, other from Mary Frazor Nancy Hewitt Rigdon Pitts Rhoda Watson to sd Urbone Frazor authenticated by cer-
p.354 tificate of John Taylor a judge of North Carolina under seal of sd state with signatures of the governor & his private secretary certifying sd Taylor was judge as afsd; ltrs/atty thereupon admitted.
Grant admn/estate of Moses Stuart decd to James Ball; bond $500 with David Henry and William Seawell securities.
Heli Herring admr of Simon Totevine decd v Edward Gatlin. Trover. Jul 1801 plf by Sam Donelson; dft by Thos Stuart. Jury Jas Vinson Jos Motheral Richd Alexander Mark Richmon Richard King Isreal Moore Peter Looney Thos Wilson Nichs Boyce Marcus Sharp Wm Hall Wm Neely assessed plfs damages $45. Dft granted new trial. Oct 1802 jury Wm Reed Reuben Douglass Eli Giles Jas C Wilson John Woods Alexr McKnight Thomas Groves Wm Brigance Smith Hansbrough Robt Trousdale Jno Lyon Chas Dement assess plfs damage to $56.50. Dft obtains appeal to Superior Court, Richd Hogin & Geo Micky security.
Motion of Solomon Sholders one of legatees of John Edwards decd with approbation of Charles Dement one of guardians for the minor legatees of sd decedant who ackd notification from sd Solomon of his intention to move the Court for order to divide real estate of sd decd between legatees, order that James Odam Gabriel Black Solomon Barnes Isaac Baker & Thomas Howell to divide sd real estate.
Appt Isaac Stalcup overseer/road lately laid off from Gallatin to KY road near Swain Stalcups from top/ridge to sd road; Reuben Searcy to furnish list of hands.
Franky Benthall & Mary Benthall make choice of James Cryer for their guardian, at same time Susannah Benthall under age 14 also present in Court, sd Court appts James Cryer her guardian; bond $1000, Wm Montgomery security.
p.355 Appt William Cage & Jas Cryer to settle with admr of Martha Johnson decd.
Inventory of goods of Moses Stuart decd rendered & proved by admr; ordered sold.
Deed William Surry to Bright Herrin 640 acres proved by William Osburn.
Deed John Baker to Thomas Hobdy 514 acres proved by James Braken.
Deed Benjamin Seawell to Joshua Rice 640 acres ackd.
John McMurtry esqr deposits 31½¢ fine of William Williams for profane swearing.
John Mills v Nathl Giles. Debt. Dfts bail surrenders him; Mark Rickmon enters himself bail in place of Seawell.
Bill/sale Richard Hogin to Elizabeth Hogin negro woman Clo ackd.

OCTOBER 1802

Deed James Cage late shff to Benjamin Seawell 640 acres proved by Joseph Seawell.
Order John Grant oversee road from Drakes Cr to 20 mile tree on upper road from Gallatin to Nashville vice Shadrack Nye.
Order Alexr Gwin oversee from head of Drakes creek to KY rd vice Robt Hambleton.
Isaac Baker Solomon Barnes Thomas Edwards Wm Phipps Isreal Moore report they laid off a road from Gallatin to Swain Stalcups passing between Jas Douglasses & Charles Dements, & crossing Red River ridge near the head of Craffords Creek.
Appt Isaac Baker overseer/road [above]; James Cryer Esq to furnish list of hands.

Wednesday Oct 6th. Present Witheral Latimer Jonathan Hannum William Seawell Esqrs.
Micajah Barrow v Thomas Farmer. Debt. Apr 1802 plf by Thos Stuart; dft by John C Hamilton. Oct 1802 dft in proper person confessed judgt $243.10 & costs.
p.356 State v Richard Hogin. TAB. Dft submits; fined $5, mitigated to $1 & costs.
State v Richard Hogin. TAB. Dft submits; fined $5, mitigated to $1 with costs.
Deed Nathan Barnes to Philip Kiser 90 acres proved by Hugh McBride.
Bill/sale Jno Bonds Jr to Anthony Hogin negro girl Sarah proved by Redmd D Barry.
Appt James Hart Charles Donoho & William Seawell divide Negroes of estate of Wm S Carson decd & assign to each heir their proportion.
Tandy Witcher v John Deloach. Trover. Jul 1801 plf by Redmond D Barry; dft by Geo Smith. Oct 1802 plf in proper person dismisses suit; each party pays half costs.
State v Joseph Wilson. Neglect as overseer of road. Dft submits; fined 25¢; paid.
John Deloach v George Young. Case. Jan 1802 plf by Saml Donelson. Apr 1802 dft by Thomas Stuart. Oct 1802 plf dismissed suit; each party pays half costs.
Deed Saml Donelson Shadrack Nye James Wilson & Charles Donoho to Isaac Lane lot 14 in Gallatin proved by Will Trigg.
Deed Andrew Boyd to heirs of William Conner: James Sterrit, Lewis, William, Jno & Peggy Conner 320 acres proved by Griswold Latimer.
Deed Andrew Boyd to heirs of William Conner: James Steret, Lewis William John and Peggy Conner 320 acres proved by Griswold Latimer.
Deed James Cage late sheriff to William Montgomery 500 acres ackd.
Heli Herring admr of Simon Totevine decd v Edward Gatlin. Trover. Dft obtains appeal to Superior Court; bond $500, Richard Hogin & George Michie securities.
p.357 Deed Joel Holland to Thomas Willis 120 acres proved by Josiah Howell.
Deed Saml Donelson, Shadrack Nye, James Wilson, Charles Donoho commrs to James Cage & Saml P Black lot 2 proved by Edmund Crutcher.
Jno C Hamilton v Elisha Pruett. Ap 1802 plf by Jno Overton; dft by Jesse Wharton. Oct 1802 jury Joshua Cherry Hallery Malone Robert Patton William Sample John Hazlet Richd Harrell John Baley Wm Moore Thos Willis Wright Bond Wm Reed John Barrow find for dft; plf by Thos Stuart atty moved for new trial; overruled. Dft recovers costs of suit; plf obtained appeal to Superior Court; Redmond D Barry & George Smith sec.
Power/atty Frederick Harget exr of Wm Dennis decd to Nicholas A Bray certified by John Louis Taylor a judge of North Carolina, signature of governor of NC; admitted.
Appt John Bowman overseer/road Cairo to Croft mills in place of Joseph Wilson; James Reese esqr to furnish sd overseer with a list of hands.
John Wood v Robt C Atkinson & Robert Laurence. James Vinson special bail for dft.
George Brown proprietor of a cotton in Cairo; bond $1000, Richard Brown security.
Appt Moses Cummins overseer/road in place of John Hassell from Hassells to where fountain head path crosses road.
Appt John Hogin overseer/road from where fountain head path crosses Red River

OCTOBER 1802

road to Richd Cavitts, hands of Richd Cavit, Wm King, Jas King, Nathl King, Joseph Bigs, Alexr Weatherspoon, Daniel Taylor, Edwd Morgan, Richard Cavitt, John Cavitt.
Orphan William Williams bound unto Samuel Piper.
Deed William Hogan to John Hogin Jr 415 acres proved by William Williams.
p.358 License Henry Lyon to keep tavern at his dwelling in Gallatin, bond $2500 with George Brown and Elisha Pruitt securities.
Deed Benjamin Rawlings to Thomas Joiner 216 acres proved by Edward Douglass.
Deed Benjamin Rawlings to Thomas Joiner 100 acres proved by Edward Douglass.
State v Richard Waller. TAB. Dft submits; fined $20; fine mitigated to $10; dft to be kept in custody of the sheriff until paid with costs.
Deed Marshall Stroud to Mark & Nathan Rickmon 340 acres ackd.
State v James Callahan. TAB. Dft submits; fined $5 & kept in custody till paid.
State v Richard Waller. Peace bond. Waller's bond $500; Isaac Pierce $250 condition Waller keep peace especially towards Elisha Pruett.
Sheriff enters protest against insufficiency of the Jail.

Thursday October 7th. Present David Wilson Wm Montgomery James Cryer Stephen Cantrill James Sanders James Winchester John Morgan Esquires.
Stephen Ward v Spencer Totevine & Joseph Westbrook. Apr 1802 Ward recovered agt Heli Herring admr of Simon Totevine $416.67 & $21.59 costs of suit. Sci fa from D Shelby C S C issues agt heirs & devisees of decedant: Spencer Totevine Joseph West-
p.359 brook heirs. July 1802 E Crutcher returns "not found." Oct 1802 Jos Westbrook not found; made known to Spencer Totevine. Oct 1802 dfts failed to appear; judgt agt them $438.26 and costs.
State v Richard Hogin. TAB. Dfts fine mitigated from $5 to $1.
State v Richard Hogin. TAB. Dfts fine mitigated from $5 to $1.
James Vinson v John Hazlet. Appeal. July 1802 plf by Redmond D Barry; dft by Thos Stuart. Oct 1802 jury Will Trigg Wm Reed Isaac Peirce James Askew John Burrow Jack Reeves Wm Milliken Robt McRunnalls Alexr McKnight Moses Tinsley John Mansker Nathan Richmon assess plfs damage $1 with costs.
Grant ltrs/admn on estate of James Lyon decd to Henry Lyon; bond $3000, Thomas Mastin and John Bailey securities.
Deed James Odam & Thomas Edwards to Alexr Rasco William Maxey & William Newton trustees one acre from James Odam and the use of a spring from Thomas Edwards ackd.
Appt John Goodrum overseer/road Bledsoes lick to ridge bet Rockey Cr & Goose Cr; James Reese esqr to furnish sd overseer with a list of hands.
Appt William Harper overseer/road from Bledsoes lick to flat gap; William Seawell to furnish sd overseer with a list of hands.
Appt William Carr overseer/road from ridge bet west & middle forks Goose creek to flat gap; William Seawell to furnish sd overseer with a list of hands.
Betsey Vinson v John Dawson. Apr 1802 plf by John C Hamilton; dft by Jesse Wharp.360 ton. Oct 1802 suit dismissed by plfs atty; dft recovers full costs.
State v Henry Morris. Petit larceny. Apr 1800 dft found guilty; dft escaped before judgt & sentence awarded; apprehended by warrant from James Winchester esqr & committed to jail. Henry Morris to be taken to the public whipping post by the Sheriff and there receive 39 lashes well laid on his bare back.
Court adjourns one hour. Present James Winchester Stephen Cantrill James Sanders.
Deed Daniel Miles to John Josey lot 15 in Gallatin ackd.
Deed James Sanders to Moses Tinsley 164 acres ackd.

OCTOBER 1802

Deed John Josey to James McKinsey lot 15 in Gallatin ackd.
William Leech v Thomas Edwards. Debt. Apr 1802 plf by George Smith. Jul 1802 dft came not; judgt by default agt him. Oct 1802 jury Wm Reed Will Trigg Jno Wood Alexr McKnight Philip Pain Leonard Miles Henry Fiser Jas C Wilson Jack Reeves Wm Millikin John Josey James Alexander find for plf $84.23¾, with costs.
Thomas Edwards v Daniel Miles. Covt. Jul 1802 plf by John C Hamilton; dft by Redmond D Barry & Thos Stuart. Oct 1802 plf dismissed his suit, each party being present, assuming to pay their own attorney & half of all other costs.

Friday Oct 8th 1802. Present James Winchester Stephen Cantrill James Sanders Esqrs.
p.361 Henry Lyon admr of James Lyon decd took oath prescribed by law.
Fanning Jones assee of Hardin v Redmond D Barry. Debt. Jury William Trigg Joseph Seawell John B Craighead Jas Desha Henry Lyon John Hutchings John Burrough John McConnell John Johns Anthony Sydner Michael Mitchell Jack Reeves find for plf $153.03 debt $37.74 damages. New trial granted, dft paying costs of this term.
Deed Edmund Crutcher sheriff to John Hamilton Junr undivided share of John Houdeshall in two tracts, one 440 ac, other 200 ac, being one third part of each, ackd.
George Parks v Jno Mansker. Sci fa. Alias scire facias from D Shelby CSC to shff: George Parks at Oct 1800 recovered agt John Mansker $30.60 with costs; John Mansker hath failed to render the monies. John Mansker to appear before justices of County Court to be held at house of Jas Trousdale in Gallatin. Executed by Thos Masten DS. Dft failed to appear; judgt agt him with costs.
John Hamilton v Elisha Pruett. Judgment of jury confirmed. Plf obtained appeal; Redmond D Barry & George Smith his securities.
Licensed David Hughes to keep ordinary at his dwelling in Gallatin; with James
p.362 Cryer his security.
Marshall Stroud v Mark Rickmon & Nathan Rickmon. Jul 1802 dft by Thos Stuart. Oct 1802 Redmond D Barry for plf. Jury Joshua Cherry William Trigg John B Craighead Jas Desha Henry Lyon John Burrough John McConnell Jno Johns Jack Reeves James Trousdale Heli Herring Wm Reed assess plfs damages $292.87½, with costs.
Jarret Feet(Seet?) v Alexander McKnight. Debt. Jul 1802 plf by Jesse Wharton; dft by Geo Smith. Jury Joshua Cherry Will Trigg John B Craighead James Desha Henry Lyon Jno Burrow Jno McConnell Jno Johns Jack Reeves James Trousdale Heli Herring Wm Reed find for plf $54 debt $1.70 damages, with costs.
Willshear Bandy v Robert Hogin. Attachment. Constable Drury Milam attached on one horse; property insufficient. Attached on mare & colt. Dft failed to appear; judgt by default; attached property condemned to sale by sheriff for use of judgment.
James Ross & others v Eli Herrell. John Stamps and Benjamin Morgan the defendants special bail.
James Ross & others v John Harris. [as above]
James Ross & others v Benjamin Tarbox for Patsey & Betsey Harriss. [as above]
p.363 License Jas Cryer to keep tavern at his dwelling, Gallatin, Will Trigg sec.
Thomas Masten appeared in Court & qualified as a Deputy Sheriff.
Allow Patrick Gipson $12 for expence in arresting & guarding Henry Morris to the district jail and bringing Morris back to this Court.
Bond of Edmund Crutcher sheriff for collection of County Taxes, Thomas Masten & Will Trigg securities.
Nicholas Boyce v Robert Moore & William Moore. Debt. Plf by John C Hamilton; dfts not appearing, judgt by default agt them.

OCTOBER 1802

Lists of taxable property and polls to be taken: Charles Donoho in Capt Bradleys company. Wm Seawell in Capt Mills company. Thomas Blackmore in Capt Whites. James Reese in Capt Neelys. David Wilson in Capt Vinsons. Thomas Donnell in Capt Blacks. Benjamin Rawlings in Capt Scobeys. James Sanders in Capt Milams. Isaac Walton in Capt Whitsitts company. Witherall Latimer in Capt Shaws company. Reuben Searcy in Capt Gwins. James Cryer in Capt Snoddies company. William Montgomery in Capt Bruces company. David Love in Capt Brownings. Edward Douglass in Capt Latimers company.

Jurors to Jan term: Jesse Hainey, Edward Bradley, Geo Stubblefield, Capt Wm Sanders, James Cary, Arthur Exum, Patrick Barr, James McMurry, Wm Allon, Jno Gillespie, Jacob Browning, Nathl Parker, George McGuire, Hugh Carothers, Joseph Hodge, Zacheus Wilson Junr, Richard King, Samuel Smith, Jonathan Pierce, Wm Montgomery Sr, William Frazor, Henry Bunn, Kasper Mansker, Elisha Pruett, Anthony Sharp, Richard Cavitt, Griswold Latimer, Peter Looney P, Isreal Moore, James Wilson Curley, James Trousdale, Adam Hunter, John Orr, William Douglass, Charles Dement, Robert Bratney.

Appt Martin Cooper & Robt Steel Junr patrollers for Captain Brownings company, to qualify before John Morgan Esqr.

p.364 Appt Geo Brown, John McConnell & Robt Trousdale patrollers for Capt Vinsons company; to qualify before James Cryer Esqr.

Appt Wright Bond Richard Anderson & John Willard patrollers for Captain Snoddies company, to qualify before James Cryer Esqr.

Appt Francis Weatherred John Cloe & Isaac Bledsoe of Anthony patrollers for Capt Neeleys company; to qualify before John Morgan Esqr.

Appt John Goodrum William Reed & Jas Rankins patrollers for Capt Whites company; to qualify before Jonathan Hannum Esqr.

Appt Matthew Richmond Isaac Peirce & Russell Wyer patrollers for Captain Milams Company; to qualify before James Sanders Esqr.

Appt Wm Hubbard overseer/road from Cairo to end of Major Whites lane; James Reese Esqr to furnish sd overseer with a list of hands.

Court adjourns till Court in Course to meet at Cairo at the house of James Steel on first Monday of January next.   David Wilson

p.365 Court of Pleas & Quarter Sessions, first Monday, January 1803. Present Edwd Douglass Reuben Searcy Stephen Cantrill Isaac Walton William Montgomery James Sanders John McMurtry James Reese Thos Donnell James Cryer Thos Blackemore John Morgan Witherall Latimer Esquires.

Grand Jury: Richd Cavitt foreman, Jno Orr, Richd King, Jas Trousdale, Jos Hodge, Hugh Carothers, Zachs Wilson Jr, Jesse Hainey, James C Wilson, Jacob Browning, Chas Dement, James Cary, William Allon. Constable Patrick Gibson to attend grand jury.

Court adjourned till tomorrow to meet at house of James Trousdale in Gallatin.

Tuesday Jan 4th. At house of James Trousdale in Gallatin. Present Edwd Douglass Wm Montgomery Jas Sanders Thos Donnell Reuben Searcy Witherall Latimer Esquires.

Deed Alexander McKee to Richard Fausit 200 acres ackd.
Deed Joseph Latimer to Robert Guthrie 150 acres proved by Witheral Latimer.
Parry W Humphreys presented license as attorney; qualified.

JANUARY 1803

Anthony Sharp is excused for attending as a juror.
Thomas Gore v Reuben Searcy. Witherall Latimer special bail for defendant.
Reuben Searcy & Charles Donoho rendered lists of taxable property by them taken.
Ltr/atty Ebenezer Rees to James Winchester proved by John Brabston.
Isaac Walton returns list of taxable property in Whitsitts company.
Thomas Gore v Reuben Searcy. Bail surrenders defendant.
Appt John Douglass constable for Capt Scobeys district; bond $625 with William Douglass & Thomas Gregory securities.
Grant ltrs/admn on estate of Stephen Brown decd to John Rhoads; bond $200 with Isaac Walton security, and took oath prescribed by law.
Isaac Walton, David Wilson, Stephen Cantrill, Charles Donoho, James Reese, James Douglass, David Love, Wm Seawell, Jno Barr, Thos Blackemore esqrs take their seats.
Ltr/atty John Smith to Wm Douglass proved by John Douglass.
Will of Wm Cochran decd proved by Robert Bruce & Benjn Hubbard; William Hubbard & John Cochran, two of executors therein named, qualified.
p.366 Deed Hugh Bradshaw to James Suddarth 170 acres proved by James Weatherred; also an assignment of sd deed from Suddarth to William Weatherred also proved by sd James Weatherred.
David Love esqr returns list/taxable property in Capt Brownings company.
County Contingent Tax laid [omitted].
Inventory/goods of Stephen Brown decd proved by admr of sd decedant.
Personal estate of Stephen Brown decd to be exposed to sale by administrator.
Deed James Hays to George Michie 289½ acres ackd.
Arthur Exum is excused from attending as a juror for present term.
Appt Thomas Parker overseer/road in place of William Irwin from Bledsoes lick to Fort Blount.
Allow Charles Donoho to turn road to cross the creek near his house.
Allow John Sullivan to turn road through his plantation not exceeding 80 poles, provided he opens another road at his own expence & agreeable to law.
Order Wm Gwin John Seriker James Braken William Osburn Joseph Caveat Norman Peak Ely Stalcup Jas Roany Senr to mark a road from Kentucky line to where Bright Herron now resides thence into Nashville road at Richard Cavitts, also a road from Aaron Neals mill toward Nashville as far as jurisdiction of this court extends.
David Wilson & Witherall Latimer esqrs return lists of taxable property by them taken for present year in Capt Vinsons and Capt Shaws companys.
Appt Robert Patton constable for Capt Vinsons company; bond $625 with David Allon and Thomas Patton securities.
Allow Sheriff $40 for ex officio services from 1 July 1801 until 1 July 1802.
Allow Clerk $40 for ex officio services from 1 July 1801 until 1 July 1802.
State v Reuben White. TAB. Dft submits; fined $1 and costs.
Bill/sale Jno Burney to Anthony Sharp for three Negroes Jenny Lydia & Rosse ackd.
Isaac Walton who is proprietor of a cotton gin entered bond $1000 for complying with requisitions of law, Edward Williams security.
p.367 Deed William Robb Sr to Robert Robb 213 acres proved by William Robb Junr.
Bill/sale David Wilson to Thomas Youngblood Negro man Waters ackd.
Bill/sale Theopholus Bass to Thomas Youngblood Negro woman Fanny ackd.
Appt James Odam Gabriel Black Solomon Barns Isaac Baker & Thomas Howell to divide Negro property, estate of John Edwards decd between heirs of sd decedant.
On petition of Mark Richmon guardian for three of heirs of Wm Storey decd, order Wm Seawell John Mills George Keesee John Trousdale & William Lauderdale commrs and

JANUARY 1803

Alexander Cathey surveyor divide real estate of sd Wm Storey decd and assign to the widow her dowry in real estate.

Order a tax laid to defray expense arising from purchase of land and erecting public buildings thereon [omitted].

Order patrollers heretofore apptd & qualified be exempted from payment of taxes.

Instrument of writing signed by Seth Mabry proved by sd Mabry.

Order Wm Montgomery Edward Sanders Robert Davis Elisha Pruett Jas C Wilson James Trousdale and Isaac Clark mark a road from Gallatin to William Gillespies.

Allow Major William Hall to move road through his plantation at his own expense.

Edward Douglass esqr returns list/taxable property in Capt Latimers company.

Wednesday Jan 5th. Present James Sanders Charles Donoho & Witherall Latimer Esqrs.

Deed Christopher Cooper to Alanson Trigg 200 acres ackd.

Thomas Keiffe v Thomas Barrott. George Michie dfts bail for dft to replevy property attached in sd suit.

James McKain v Elisha Pruett. Samuel Donelson dfts bail [as above].

Thomas Blackemore esqr returns list/taxable property in Whites compy.

p.368 William Bishop v John Reeves. Debt. Jul 1802 plf by Thos Stuart; dft by Geo Smith. Jan 1803 jury: Edward Bradley Geo Stubblefield Patrick Barr Jas McMurry John Gillespie Wm Montgomery Nathaniel Parker Geo McGuire Peter Luna Isreal Moore Elisha Pruett Samuel Smith find for plf $67.89 and his costs.

Commr apptd to divide Negroes of estate of Wm S Carson report division made.

Benjamin Rawlings esqr returns list of taxable property in Capt Scobeys company.

Gasper Mansker is discharged from attending as a juror this term.

William Morgan v John Robinson. Jul 1802 Sci fa by David Shelby CSC. In suit Wm Morgan agt John Payton, John Robinson to give testimony in behalf plf but came not; order Robinson appear at Court at house of James Trousdale in Gallatin in Oct. Not found by Thos Martin D S. Oct 1802 alias Scire facias issued; dft not found. Judgt p.369 agt dft by default $125, also costs.

Bill/sale Lewis Wilkinson to James Sanders negro girl Dorcas, certificate of the Clerk of Buckingham County, Virginia, and county seal certifying acknowledgment by sd Wilkinson at Buckingham Court 9 March 1802.

Appt Wm Montgomery & Jno McMurtry esqrs settle with executors of Robt Hobdy decd.

Deed James Franklin Sr to James Franklin Jr 132 acres proved by John Franklin.

Deed James Franklin Sr to John Franklin 132 acres proved by James Franklin Jr.

Samuel Donelson v John Comar. Oct 1802 plf by Jesse Wharton; dft not appearing, judgt by default agt him. Jan 1802 jury Edwd Bradley Geo Stubblefield Patk Barr Jno Gillespie Nathl Parker Wm Montgomery Peter Luna Isreal Moore Elisha Pruett Samuel Smith Robert Bratney George McGuire ascertain plfs damages 1¢, and his costs.

Inventory/goods of William Cochran decd proved by executors.

Deed Charles Carter to William Hall 86 acres proved by Mathew Anderson.

Appt Nicholas Boyce overseer/road in place of Malachi Hereford, from middle fork Station Camp to Dawsons Creek.

Josiah Howell v John B Johnson. Debt. Oct 1802 plf by John C Hamilton; dft by Geo p.370 Smith. Jan 1803 jury[above] assess plfs damages $122.98 & costs.

William Sample v John G Hall. Att. Issue order/sale town lot in Gallatin whereon attachment was laid to satisfy judgt recovered by plf before Thos Blackemore Esqr.

Appt Thomas Murry overseer/road in place of John Shaver, the road from Bledsoes lick to Bishops ferry, from sd lick to second creek.

JANUARY 1803

Order Isaac Baker Thos Howell Solomon Barns James Odam & George G Black appraise Negroes of estate of John Edwards decd and divide sd Negroes amongst heirs.
Deed Samuel Donelson Shadrack Nye James Wilson & Chas Donoho conmrs to Wm Sample lot 13 in Gallatin proved by Will Trigg.
William Sanders is excused from attending as a juror for present term.
Grand Jury dismissed.
John Josey v Richard Hogin. TAB. Oct 1802 plf by Samuel Donelson; Jan 1803 plf dismisses suit, dft agreeing to pay costs.
William Seawell Esqr renders list/taxable property & polls in Capt Mills compy.

Thursday Jan 6th. Present Edward Douglass Stephen Cantrill and William Montgomery.
Wm Montgomery Esqr returned tax list for Capt Bruces company.
Inventory/goods of John Whitworth decd proved by the administratrix.
John Miller v Robert Trousdale & David Orr. Oct 1802 plf by Thomas Stuart; dft by Jno C Hamilton & Jno B Johnson. Jan 1803 jury Edwd Bradley Geo Stubblefield Patrick Barr John Gillespie Geo McGuire Isreal Moore Wm Trigg Jas Desha Jos Seawell William
p.371 Bradshaw Robt Bratney Henry Bradford assess plfs damages $348.80 & costs.
Thomas Donnell esqr renders list/taxable property taken by him.
John McMurtry apptd Coroner; bond $2500, George Campbell security.
Appraisement of negroes, estate of John Edwards decd; division among heirs.
Deed John Gwin to James Denny 100 acres ackd.
Deed William McGready to Samuel Wilson Sr 320 acres ackd.
John Whitford v Josias & John Bullock. Dfts to take depositions of Ezekiel Able & Benjamin Spencer in the Spanish Dominions.
James Ross & others v John Harris. De po issues for plfs to South Carolina & Georgia; also de po for dft in Georgia.
James Ross & others v Eli Herrell. [worded as above]
John Mills v Nathaniel Giles. Debt. Oct 1802 plf by Thomas Stuart; dft by George Smith. Jan 1803 jury Edwd Bradley Geo Stubblefield Patrick Barr Jno Gillespie Nathl Parker Geo McGuire Jas McMurry Isreal Moore Robt Bratney Wm Douglass Will Trigg Jas Desha assess plfs damage to $5.50 and his costs.
James Sanders Esqr renders list/taxable property in Capt Milams company.
James Ross & others v Ben Tarbor for Patsey & Betsey Harris. De po issues for plfs to South Carolina and Georgia; also for dfts to State of Georgia.
Jurors to April Term: Kasper Mansker Thos Perry Wm Bowen Wm Frazor William Dorris Henry Bunn Joshua Hadley John Dawson Zachariah Green James Franklin Rhodam Rawlings Lewis Crane Henry Bradford Edward Sanders Joshua Cherry John Weathers Jos McElwrath Thos Howell Jno Wilson son of Saml Elmore Harris Adam Hunter Joseph Williams Robert
p.372 Shaw Wm Brigance Moore Stevenson Jno White Jas Clendening Wm Reed Jas Lauderdale Seth Mabry Jno Dickison Wm Parr Wm Gillespie Jno Mills Jno Garrett Alexander Cathey.
John Whitford v Josias & John Bullock. Plf to take deposition of Wm Spencer.
Moses Tinsley v William Weatherred. De po issues for plf to State of Virginia.
Deed Saml Donelson Shadrack Nye Jas Wilson & Chas Donoho commrs to L[binding] Latimer lots 23 & 24 in Gallatin proved by Wm Quisenberry.
James Cryer Esqr renders list/taxable property taken by him.
Deed Isreal Moore to James Wallace Harris 50 acres ackd.
William Bishop v John Reeves. Debt. Motion for new trial is overruled.
John C Hamilton v John Rhoads. Debt. Jan 1803 dft filed declaration; dft not

APRIL 1803

appearing, judgment against defendant $125.25. Plf to recover, with costs.
License Thomas Keefe to keep tavern at his dwelling, John B Johnson security.
Clerk to receive all tax lists which have not been returned to present term.
Court adjourns till Court in course to be holden in Gallatin at house of James
Cryer Esqr.   Edwd Douglass

p.373 Court of Pleas & Quarter Sessions, house of James Cryer in Gallatin, first
Monday in April 1803. Present James Winchester Thomas Donnell John McMurtry Esqrs.
Order persons who failed to make return of lists of taxable property & polls for
present year released from double tax for such failure on making return this term.
Account/sales of goods of Wm Hamilton decd proved by Wm Douglass & Reuben Cage.
Ltr/atty Alexander Mairs to Hugh Mairs with certificates of clerk & presiding
magistrate of Montgomery County Virginia with seal of sd county; ordered recorded.
Deeds ackd & proved: Jesse Womack to Joel Brown by Rhodam Rawlings. David Beard
Sr to Jas Kirkpatrick. Jno Bailey to Michael Thomas by Littleton Duty. John Patterson to James Hollis by Archd Marlin. James Winchester & David Wilson to Robt Goudy.
Hugh Mairs to Wm McClure by Jno Gwin. Jas Winchester & David Wilson to Jas Macklin.
Peter Flemming to Joseph McRannolds by Thos Anderson. Edward Hogin to Jesse Joiner.
Isaac Towell to Thos Joiner. Jas Montgomery to Robt Boyles by Jas Haw. Edwd Harris
to Stephen Montgomery by Geo Anderson. Robert Green to Jas Barrow & his wife Molly
proved by John Bowen.
Matthew Cartwright v Isaac & Joseph Clark. Debt. Henry Bradford & Edward Sanders
additional bail with the other bail heretofore taken by the sheriff.
Deed/gift Thomas Hamilton Sr to Thomas Hamilton & Robert Hamilton 50 acres proved
by John Hale.
Moore Stevenson excused from attending as a juror the present term.
Bill/sale Jesse Joiner to Edwd Hogin four negroes: Jack, Anna, Cula, Fanny ackd.
p.374 Will of John Anderson decd proved by Wm Bell & James Farr. Robert & William
Anderson executors therein named qualified as such.
Account/sales of goods of William Cochran decd proved by executors of sd decd.
John McMurtry coroner allowed $7.25 for holding inquest over body of negro woman
Mary property of John Burrow.
Appt Henry Harrison overseer/road in place of John Stuart.
Appt Peter Looney H overseer/road in place of James McKinsey.
Nicholas Boyce v Samuel Bryant. Plf in proper person dismissed suit at cost of
dft who in proper person assumes same.
Grand Jury: Henry Bradford foreman, Lewis Crane, Wm Frazor, Rhodam Rawlings, John
Wilson, Joshua Cherry, William Reed, Joseph McElwrath, John White, Thos Perry, Adam
Hunter, Edward Sanders, James Clendening.
Acct/sales goods of Hugh Elliott decd proved by executors of sd deceased.
Will of Laurence Thompson decd proved by Thomas Simpson a subscribing witness
thereto; there being no executors named, ltrs/admn with will annexed granted to
Catharine Thompson; bond $3000, Thomas Thompson & John Thompson securities.
John Dickison excused from attending as a juror for present term.
License Thomas Britten to keep ordinary at his dwelling; Thomas Simpson security.
License Robert Davis to keep tavern at his dwelling; James Sanders security.

APRIL 1803

Will of John McManamey decd proved by Charles Park & George Wooddril & Abraham King subscribing witnesses; Thomas Murry & William Mann, executors, qualified.
Allow John Turner to erect mill on Rocky crk below where road from Bledsoes lick to flat Gap crosses crk. James Hunt of land opposite proposed mill agrees to sustain all damages to sd Hunts land in consequence of erecting a dam for sd mill.
p.375 Fanning Jones assignee of Hardin vs Redmond D Barry. Debt. Jul 1802 plf by Jesse Wharton; dft by Thos Stuart. Oct 1802 jury Wm Trigg Jos Seawell Jno B Craighead Jas Desha Henry Lyon John Hutchings Jno Burrow Jno McConnell Jno Johns Anthy Sydner Michl Mitchell Jack Reeves found $153.03 debt & $37.74 damages. New trial awarded dft. Jan 1803 jury Kasper Mansker Wm Bowen Henry Bunn Jno Weathers Elmore Harris Robert Shaw William Brigance John Mills James Lauderdale Seth Mabry Thomas Howell William Parr say dft owes $146.75 and damages $46.75, and costs.
Andrew Greer v Edward Gwin. Andrew Greer at Apr 1802 recovered agt Wm Brimberry $99.60 and $22.73 & 8 mills. Edward Gwin was dfts bail for replevying attached property, which property he has failed to deliver as also failed to surrender dft to prison. David Shelby CSC summons Edwd Gwin. Thos Mastin DS returns "Not found."
p.376 Alias scire facias issued. Dft by John C Hamilton. Apr 1803 jury[above] say dft hath not surrendered principal. Plf recovers $122.33 & 8 mills & his costs.
Deed Thomas Masten collector to William Cartwright 640 acres ackd.
Deed Saml Donelson Shadk Nye Jas Wilson Chas Donoho commrs to Thomas Keefe lot 11 in Gallatin proved by John Hutchings.

Tuesday April 5th. Present Edward Douglass Stephen Cantrill Thomas Donnell Jas Hart James Sanders Esquires.
Deed Reuben Cage late sheriff to Redmond D Barry 606 acres ackd.
Deed Redmond D Barry to john Biggs 640 acres ackd.
Inventory/goods of John Anderson decd rendered by Doctor Donnell.
Grant admn on estate of George Simmerell decd to George D Blackmore & Nathaniel Thompson; bond $1000, John White & Peter Lyon securities; order/sale issued.
Thomas Jamison v James Gardner. Debt. Oct 1802 plf by John C Hamilton. Dft by
p.377 Jesse Wharton. Apr 1803 Jury [above except Joseph Wallace for Wm Parr]. Plaintiff recovers $104.50 debt & damages, with costs of suit.
Thomas Jamison v James Gardner. Debt. Oct 1802 plf by John C Hamilton; dft by Jesse Wharton. Apr 1803 dft in proper person confesses judgment $104.32 & costs.
Thomas Jamison v James Gardner. Debt. Dft in proper person confesses judgment for
p.378 for $104.27 & costs.
Deed Sterling Brewer to Jonathan Wallis 50 acres proved by Edwd Gwin.
Deed Sterling Brewer to Richard Bradley 200 acres proved by Isaac Braken.
Deed David Wilson to Jesse Johnson 8¾ acres ackd.
Deed Samuel Graham to Clarissa Graham 200 acres proved by Henry Lyon.
Deed Samuel Graham to Jane McCorcle 200 acres proved by Henry Lyon.
Appt Jesse Hainey gdn for children of sd Jesse namely Elijah, Judah, William, Betsey, George & Jesse Hainey; bond $500 with James Hart security.
Bill/sale John Cooper to Isaac Towell four negroes proved by Robert Watkins.
Deed Micajah Barrow to Alton Purvis 140 acres proved by John Payton.
Deed James Franklin to John Norris 7 acres ackd.
James Ross et al v Eli Herrell. Detinue. Bail for dft John Stamps & Benjn Morgan surrender dft; John Caffery & Blake Rutland special bail for sd dft.
Deed Arthur Exum to Joseph Exum 100 acres ackd.

APRIL 1803

Deed Arthur Exum to William Exum 100 acres ackd.
Appt Jas Winchester & Jas Reese esqrs to settle with admx of Anthony H Bledsoe.
Deed James A Wilson to Exum Johnson lot 12 in Cairo ackd.
Bill/sale James Blackemore to James Williams negro woman Mime and negro girl Kandis proved by Thomas Blackemore.

p.379   State v Redmond D Barry. TAB. Dft submits; fined $1 & costs.
Samuel Smithson admr of Isaac Etheridge decd v William Sanders. Jan 1803 plf by Jno C Hamilton & Thos Stuart; dft by Jesse Wharton & Saml Donelson. Apr Jury Kasper Mansker Wm Bowen Henry Bunn John Weathers Elmore Harris Jos Wallace Robt Shaw James Lauderdale Sr Thomas Howell Seth Mabry James Franklin Wm Parr. Plf recovers agt dft damages and costs. Dft by Jesse Wharton obtains appeal to Superior Court; bond $500 with James Sanders & John C Henderson securities.
James Ross et al v John Harris. Detinue. Dfts bail John Stamps & Benjamin Morgan surrender dft; John Caffery & Blake Rutland special bail.
James Ross et al v Benj Tarbor for Patsey & Betsey Harris. Detinue. Dft special bail John Caffery & Blake Rutland in place of John Stamps & Benjamin Morgan.
Deed Samuel donelson Shadrack Nye James Wilson Charles Donoho commrs to James McKain lot 9 in Gallatin proved by Wm M Quisenberry.
James McKain v Daniel Miles. Covt. Dfts bail surrenders him to sheriff.
James Franklin is excused from attending as a juror for present term.
Jurors to next Superior Court: Peter Luna P, Griffith Rutherford, John Payton, Robert Shaw, Charles Donoho, Matthew Alexander, James McMurry.
John Turner who obtained order for erecting mill on Rockey Crk enters bond with Trisha Turner security $5000.

p.380   Wednesday April 6th. Present Edward Douglass Stephen Cantrill James Cryer.
James Ross & others v Eli Hrrell. Detinue. Plf to take depositions of witnesses in South Carolina & Georgia. Dft to take depositions of witnesses in Georgia.
Andrew Jackson & Co v Joseph Moore. Jury[above except Zachariah Green & Robert Desha for Jas Franklin & Wm Parr]. Plf recovers agt dft; plf obtains appeal, bond $500 with Samuel Donelson & Jesse Wharton securities.
Deed/mortgage Thomas Cocke to Robert Desha 640 acres proved by James Winchester.
Moses Tinsley v William Weatherred. Plf to take despositions of Thomas & Isaac Tinsley, Amherst County, VA; give 30 days notice to John Weatherred agent for dft.
Deed/gift William Cage to his daughters Betsey & Patsey Cage two negroes, one to each daughter: to Betsey, Negro Rose; to Patsey, Negro Sarah, ackd.
Commrs report real estate of Wm Storey decd divided; widow's dowry assigned.
Bill/sale James Ferrell to James Winchester and William Cage for horses cattle household furniture farming tools &c proved by Thos Wilson.
Wilson Yandall v James White Jr. Plf by John C Hamilton; dft by Geo Smith. Jury Kasper Mansker Wm Bowen Henry Bunn Jno Weathers Elmore Harris Jos Wallace Robt Shaw Jas Lauderdale Seth Mabry Zachariah Green Hallery malone Wm Douglass. Plf recovers agt dft damages $25 and his costs about his suit expended.

p.381   Deed William Allison to David Shelby 200 acres proved by William Snoddy.
Deed Nathaniel Giles to Robert Bruce 150 acres proved by William Hubbard.
Deed John C Hamilton to Josiah Perry 213½ acres ackd.
Benjamin Bashaw v Alexander McKee. Debt. Jan 1803 plf by John C Hamilton; dft by Thos Stuart. Apr 1803 jury Wm Parr Thos Howell Jno Payton Nichs Boyer Alexr Cathey Robt Ellis Wm Brigance Ambrose Porter Heli Herring Wm Maxey Richard Bradley Robert

APRIL 1803

Laurence. Plf recovers agt dft $74.09 & 5 mills debt & damages, and his costs.

Henry Lyon v James Suddarth. Attachment. Dec 1801 Edmd Crutcher DS levied on 170 ac in Bradshaws bent adj river opposite Bartin & Spring crks. Jan 1802 12-mo stay. Jan 1803 plf by Jno C Hamilton. Dft came not. Apr 1803 jury Wm Parr Thos Howell Jno Payton Nichs Boyce Alexr Cathey Robt Ellis Wm Brigance Ambrose Porter Heli Herring Wm Maxey Richd Bradley Robt Laurence ascertain plfs damages $118.36 and costs.

p.382 Theophilus Bass v Jack Reeves. Jan 1803 plf by John C Hamilton. April 1803 referees John Allcorn Allen Purvis Henry Belote Henry Bradford assign $26.87 to Theophilus Bass and plaintiff pays costs of suit.

Motion of John Hamilton, appt Alexr Graham James Wilson Sr Adam Hunter John Withers & Robert Motherall to divide two tracts, on one of which sd Hamilton now lives, between claimants of sd land held as tenants in common, assign to John Hamilton two thirds of each tract agreeable to his claim published in Nashville Gazette.

Henry Lyon v James Suddarth. Order 170 acres in Bradshaws bent whereon attachment was levied be condemned and order of sale to issue.

John Wood v Atkinson & Laurence. De po issues for dfts to State of Kentucky.

Deed Miller Sawyer to Henry W Lawson 274 acres proved by Armstreet Stubblefield.

Deed Samuel Donelson Shadrack Nye & James Wilson commissioenrs to John C Hamilton lots 2, 12 & 8 in Gallatin proved by Wm Quisenberry.

Deed commrs[above] to Andw Jackson & Co lot 4 Gallatin proved by Wm Quisenberry.

Jury/view on road from Aaron Neils mill toward Nashville report they viewed from Richd Caveatts by where Bright Herren lived to Kentucky line, also to Aaron Neills mills; road from Nashville to Aaron Neals mills most eligible. John Shannon oversee from Nashville road to tee marked WG; Thomas Groves Jr overseer from Sharps crk to Drakes crk, Jno Moody to oversee from Drakes crk to Sulpher lick near Jas Brackens, and Thomas Hobdy to oversee from Sulpher lick by Robert Sheys to state line. Given

p.383 under hands of James Bracken Ely Stalcup William Gwin John Sereker William Osburn Norman Peak James Roaney.

Order John Shannon overseer/road; Witherall Latimer to furnish list of hands.

Order Thomas Groves overseer/road; Edward Gwin to furnish list of hands.

Order John Moody overseer/road; Edward Gwin to furnish list of hands.

Order Thomas Hobdy overseer/road; Edward Gwin to furnish list of hands.

Report of Wm Montgomery Edward Saunders Robert Davis Elisha Pruett James C Wilson Jas Trousdale Isaac Clark: marked a road from Gallatin to Capt Gillespies beginning at Judge Jacksons gin near Gallatin, west on Paytons line, by corner of Dr D Barrys plantation, between Matthew Anderson Sr two plantations, to Paytons cotton field to Ephraim Paytons spring to Capt Gilespies lane.

Order Capt Wm Gillespie oversee road from Gallatin to sd Gillespie's, James Cryer esqr to furnish sd overseer with a list of hands.

Appt Edward Sanders overseer/road in place of Capt Gillespie from Drakes crk to Station Camp.

Thursday April 7th. Present James Sanders Isaac Walton Edward Gwin James Winchester James Douglass Esquires.

Andrew Jackson & Co v Joseph Moore. Appeal withdrawn by consent of parties; new trial granted to the plaintiff.

Samuel Smithson admr of Isaac Etheridge decd v William Sanders. Dft obtains appeal, bond $500 with James Sanders & Jno C Henderson securities.

p.384 John Shaddock v Reuben White. TAB. Jan 1803 plf by Jno C Hamilton; dft by

APRIL 1803

Saml Donelson. Apr 1803 jury Kasper Mansker William Bowen Henry Bunn John Weathers Elmore Harris Joseph Wallace James Lauderdale Thomas Howell Seth Mabry Rees Porter John Payton Zachariah Green find dft guilty of the tresspass assault & battery and assess plfs damage to $1.50 and his costs.

James Turner and Mary Turner by their atty-in-fact James Winchester file petition to draw from admx of Benjamin Miers decd their share of personal estate of decedent. Subpoena issues agt Euridice Miers admx directing proceedings.

Nathaniel Kuykendall v Smith Hansbrough. Appeal. Plf by John C Hamilton, dft by Samuel Donelson. Jury Kasper Mansker Henry Bunn John Weathers Elmore Harris Joseph Wallace James Lauderdale Thos Howell Joshua Hadley Alexander Cathey Zachariah Green Elisha Pruett John Payton find for plf $44.88, with costs.

Appoint Henry Lyon guardian for Patience Lyon & James Lyon orphans of James Lyon decd; Henry Lyon's bond $3000 with Redmond D Barry & John C Hamilton securities.

Order sheriff summon jurors Thos Edwards, Jas Odam, Wm Maxey, Isaac Baker, Solomon Barns, Chas Dement, Thos Howell, J Laurence, David Dement, Wright Barns, Eusibius Stone, Thos Marquis to assess damages sustained by Robert Ellis in consequence of a road being cleared through his enclosures.

James McKain v Daniel Miles. Covt. Former bail for dft surrendered him to sheriff & Thomas Mastin & Joshua Hadley are bail for dft in place of former bail.

Thomas Patton v James Morrison. Debt. Plf by Jno C Hamilton; dft failing to appear, judgt by default for $120.

Jurors to July term: Wm Beard, Nathl Parker, Wm Sanders Sr, Thos Murry, Saml Gibson, Armstead Rogers, Hugh Crawford, Moore Cotton, Wm Moore, Reuben Douglass, Griswold Latimer, Jas Wilson Curley, Jas Wilson Smky, Richard Strother, Samuel Stuart, Robert Marshall, Hugh McGee, Mathew Alexander, Thomas Parker, Henry Belote, Bryant Gardner, Joel Childers, John Perry, Saml Smith, Isaac Pearce, Elisha Pruett, Peter
p.385 Looney P, Jesse Joiner, Richard King, James Rankin, Josiah Giles, Abraham Hassell, Robert Steel Sr, Hallery Malone, Joseph Scoby, John Denning.

Appt Edwd Gwin Esq in place of Reuben Searcy to furnish Isaac Stalcup overseer with a list of hands.

Order David Wilson & James Cryer esqrs settle with Edward Hogin Jr admr of Simon Keykendall decd.

Order capias issue agt overseer or overseers of road which Grand Jury presented.

Allow Clerk $40 for recording lists of taxable property and other trouble concerning the taxable property for the year 1802.

Court adjourns till court in course to meet at house of James Cryer in Gallatin on the first Monday in July next.   J Winchester

P.386 Court of Sumner County at house of James Cryer in Gallatin, first Monday of July 1803. Present David Wilson Thomas Donnell John Morgan Esquires.
Deed Andrew Boyd to Moses Young 272 acres proved by Josiah E Giles.
Hutchins G Burton esqr presented license to practice as atty at law; admitted.
Deed Thomas Masten collector to Euridice Miers 228 acres ackd.
Deed/gift Wm Snoddy to his daughter Rebeccah Snoddy negro Suck, horse, bed, ackd.
Deed John C Hamilton to Wm Alderson 100 acres proved by John Orr.
Deed Thos Waller to Jonathan Pearis[Peans?] 100 acres proved by John Moore.

JULY 1803

Deed Alexander Espey to Samuel Shannon 79½ acres proved by Jonathan Pea[binding].
Deed Samuel Shannon to John Moore 79½ acres proved by Jonathan Peairs.
Robert Coleman esq presented his license to practice as an atty at law; admitted.
Grand Jury: Richard Strother foreman, Matthew Alexander, James Rankin, William Moore, Joseph Scoby, Isaac Pearce, Griswold Latimer, Peter Looney P, Hallery Malone Hugh McGee, Elisha Pruett, Jesse Joiner, Armstead Rogers.
Robert Patton is nominated constable to attend the Grand Jury this term.
Acct/sales goods of Stephen Brown decd proved by administrator of sd deceased.
Deed Edwd Hoge and Susanna his wife to Moses Hoge for their undivided half under James Hoges will, land within the survey made by Thomas Buck, also their undivided fifth of 207 acres in Frederick County, Virginia, ackd by Edwd Hoge & wife Susanna.
Grant ltrs/admn on estate of James Whitesides decd to James A Whitesides & George Cathey; bond $2000, David Beard, James McGee, Alexander Dobbins, & John White sec.
Grant ltrs/admn on estate of Reuben White decd to his widow Ann White; bond $2000, Thomas Perry & Thomas Mastin securities.
James Trousdale ackd deed/gift to his son Robert Trousdale 120 acres.
Deed James Trousdale to John C Hamilton 41 acres ackd.
Bill/sale John Reeves to John Payton for waggon & hind geer & bay horse proved by Joseph Reeves.
p.387 Deed Matthew Anderson to Stephen Anderson 164 acres 95 perches ackd.
Deed Isaac Baker to David Dement lots 14 & 15 in Gallatin ackd.
Inventory/goods of Laurence Thompson decd proved by administratrix of decedent.
Appt Willis Whitfield overseer/road in place of Richard Jones.
Appt Orman Allon, John Rhoads, and Bryant Gardner patrollers for Capt Whitsitts company, to qualify before Stephen Cantrill esquire.
Inventory/goods of Reuben White decd proved by admx.
James Haw released from taxes on one free poll and 472½ acres, it appearing sd Haw stands charged twice for same on tax list for present year.
William Wyer released from taxes on 160 acres two free polls and one black poll for present year, sd Wyers taxable property was returned twice for present year.
Receipt from Samuel Donelson as guardian for orphans of Thomas Egnew decd to Thomas Sharp admr of sd estate for $1321.44 amount of estate of sd decedant ackd.
Inventory/goods of John McManimy decd proved by William Mann an executor.
William Whitesides & Elizabeth Whitesides orphans of James Whitesides decd having attained age fourteen make choice of William McGee & John White for their guardians, Wm McGee for Wm Whitesides, John White for Elizabeth Whitesides; Court appts sd Wm McGee & John White jointly as guardians for Polly Whitesides & John Whitesides other orphans of sd decd. Bond: Wm McGee $1000 with Adam McGee and John White securities; John White $1000 with Wm McGee & Adam McGee securities; Wm McGee & John White joint gdns $2000 with Adam McGee & Adam Beard securities.
State v Joseph Price. Forfeiture of recognizance. Dft acknowledges he is guilty of TAB for which he was bound to appear & answer; fined $1 & costs.
Order John Morgan esqr furnish Thomas Parker overseer/road with a list of hands.
p.388 Inventory/goods of James Whitesides decd rendered & proved by admrs.
Allow George Bush $26.76 for keeping minor orphan William Young from 1 July 1802 to same date present year, same to be payable out of the poor tax.
Release Benjamin McNeese from double tax, 640 acres for 1802, to pay single tax.
Deed Reuben Cage to Thomas Crassnor 100 acres ackd.
State v Nicholas Boyce. Neglect as overseer/road. Dft submits; Court of opinion that order/appointment was not sufficiently expressive in pointing out the hands

JULY 1803

who were to work with sd overseer; dft discharged without paying costs.
Petition of John Hamilton, claim to two thirds of 540 acres and two thirds of 200 acres; order James Wilson S, Alexander Graham, Robert Motheral, Adam Hunter, & John Withers divide sd tracts between petitioner and other claimants.
Deed Margaret Venus by James Lackey her atty in fact to Wm Hail, 465 acres proved by Wilson Cage.
Deed John Hassell Senr to William King 97 acres proved by Jesse Hassell.
Marshall Stroud v John Lyon. Debt. Oct 1802 plf by Redmond D Barry; dft by Thomas Stuart. July 1803 dft in proper person confesses judgment for $64.80 & costs.
State v James McKinsey. Neglect as overseer/road. Dft submits. Discharged.
p.389 Stothart & Bell v William McCurdy. Debt. Plfs plea amended from debt $53.37 to $56.37½ agreeable to the writing obligatory on which the suit was granted.
Abraham Hassell records his ear mark.

Tuesday July 8th. Present James Winchester Witherall Latimer Reuben Searcy Esqrs.
Patsey Angel orphan of John Angel decd makes choice of Jesse Hainey for her guardian, she having attained age fourteen; bond $3000, Champness Maddery security.
Deed Saml Donelson Shadk Nye & Jas Wilson commrs to Wm Sample lot 19 in Gallatin.
Deed Thomas Parker to Samuel Wooton 25 acres proved by John Parker.
David Gillespie v Ephraim Payton. Jury Hugh Crawford Moore Cotton Reuben Douglass James A Wilson Henry Belote Saml Smith Richard King Abraham Hassell Robert Steel Wm Beard Samuel Stuart Samuel Gibson assess plfs damages $40.
Acct/sales goods of George Simmerall decd proved by admrs.
Deed Henry Robinson & Margaret Robinson to John Hazlet 50 acres proved by James Robinson, also transfer from Will Bradshaw to sd John Hazlet of sd Bradshaws right & title to sd tract proved by John Cryer.
Deed James Robinson to Jno Hazlet 20 acres ackd; also transfer from Will Bradshaw to sd John Hazlet of sd Bradshaws right & title proved by John Cryer.
Deed Commissioners[above] to Wm Henderson lot 22 in Gallatin proved by John Lyon.
Acct/sales estate of Anthony H Bledsoe decd proved by administratrix.
Commrs apptd to settle with admx of Anthony H Bledsoe decd rendered settlement.
Deed Commrs[above] to Jinkin Whiteside lot 3 in Gallatin proved by Wm Carson.
p.390 David Gillespie v Ephraim Payton. Marlin Young a witness summoned behalf plf failing to appear, order sd Marlin Young be fined.
David Gillespie v Ephraim Payton. James Bodine, witness behalf plf[as above].
Deed Willie Cherry to James Moore 200 acres ackd.
Deed Commrs[above] to Zachariah Green lot 8 in Gallatin.
John McMurtry Jas Reese Edward Douglass David Wilson Isaac Walton James Douglass William Seawell Edwd Gwin James Hart Thos Donnell Wm Cage esqrs take their seats.
Instrument of writing Sampson Bridgers to Wm Bridgers proved by Brittain Drake.
Instrument of writing Edmond Bridgers to Wm Bridgers proved by Sampson Bridgers.
Ltr/atty William Bridgers to Reddick Bridgers proved by Brittain Drake.
Allow Joel Hart $10 quarterly out of the poor tax for maintaining John Peet who has thrown himself upon the parish by reason of old age & infirmity.
Allow Thomas Todd $30 out of the poor tax for maintaining an orphan child Morning Morrish for one year commencing 18th April last.
Appt Isaac Towell overseer/road from Col Hendersons to Montgomery mills in place of Matthew Cartwright with same hands.
Apprentice orphan John Parsons to Rolls Perry to learn art of a house carpenter.

JULY 1803

Appt John Shannon overseer/road from Aaron Onealls mill to tree marked WG about ¼ mile west of where Robinson road intersects Kentucky road to Maxfields creek, and Witheral Latimer esqr to furnish him with a list of hands.

John Sigler v Edward Gwin John Gwin & William Gwin. Debt. Plf by John C Hamilton; defendants confess judgment $63.92 & costs.

p.391 Appt Joseph Caveatt overseer/road from Aaron ONealls mill from Maxfields creek to Sharps creek; Reuben Searcy esqr to furnish list of hands.

Allow sheriff $40 for ex officio services, 1 July 1802 to same date this year.

Allow clerk $40 for ex officio services, 1 July 1802 to same date this year.

Bill/sale Nathaniel Parker Sr to Richard Parker cattle waggon team &c ackd.

Bill/sale Nathaniel Parker Sr to Isaac Parker negroes horses cows calves ackd.

Bill/sale Nathaniel Parker Sr to Nathl Parker Jr negroes Shadrack & Seal ackd.

Bill/sale Nathaniel Parker Sr to Aaron Parker negroes horses cows calves ackd.

Bill/sale Nathaniel Parker Sr to Robert Parker negroes horses cows calves ackd.

Wednesday 6th July. Present James Douglass Reuben Searcy William Seawell Esqrs.

Henry Belote records his ear mark.

John Bradley v John Hazlet. Dft by Thos Stuart. July 1803 Dft in proper person; plf by atty dismisses suit; dft pays full costs of suit.

John Whitford v Josias Bullock & John H Bullock. Oct 1802 plf by Thomas Stuart; dft by Saml Donelson. July 1803 jury Nathl Parker Hugh Crawford Moore Cotton Reuben Douglass Jas S Wilson Jas C Wilson Thos Parker Henry Belote Saml Smith Richard King p.392 Abraham Hassell Robt Steel assess plfs damages $113.45 with costs.

John Whitford v Josias[Jonas?] Bullock & John H Bullock. John Bullard witness behalf dfts not appearing, sd John Bullard is fined $125.

Ltr/atty William Barrow to John Dawson proved by John Franklin.

Deed Zachariah Green to William Sample lot 8 in Gallatin proved by Ivy Bradford.

Deed/gift William Phipps to William Phipps Junr 84 acres ackd.

Deed Saml Donelson Shadrack Nye & James Wilson to James Douglass lots 12 13 21 22 in Gallatin proved by John Lyon.

Deed Thomas Masten collector to Thomas Groves 640 acres ackd.

James Ross & others v John Harris. Detinue. Oct 1802 plfs by Thos Stuart; dft by John C Hamilton. July 1803 jury Saml Gibson Wm Beard Saml Stuart Josiah Giles Joel Childers Bryant Gardner Thos Keefe Jno Dawson John Stuart Jno Orr Robt Laurence Josiah Wills; mistrial; plfs dismiss suit; dft recovers agt plfs full costs expended.

Deed Seth Mabry to Joseph McKean 100 acres ackd.

Grand Jury dismissed.

Lynd Latimer records his ear mark.

Thursday 7th July. Present James Winchester Edward Douglass Witherall Latimer Thos Donnell, Esquires.

James Ross & others v Eli Herrill. Detinue. Oct 1802 plfs by Thos Stuart; dft by John C Hamilton. July 1803 jury Reuben Douglass Mattw Cartwright Moore Cotton Hugh p.393 Crawford Abraham Hassell John Wilson Jno Ogelsby Jas S Wilson Tandy Witcher Theopholus Bass Jas Anderson Hallery Malone; non suit; dft recovers full costs.

Reuben Cage an exr of William Hamilton decd renounced his executorship.

Edward Douglass deposits with clerk 31½¢ collected of Joseph Phipps by warrant issued upon a presentment of the Grand Jury for profane swearing.

JULY 1803

Inventory/goods of Thomas Tullock decd proved by Benjn Seawell one of trustees.
Deed/gift John Coleman to Rebeccah Clayton Turman proved by Isaac Turman.
Deed Saml Donelson Shadk Nye Jas Wilson commissioners to Wm Montgomery Jr lot 14 in Gallatin proved by John Lyon.
Deed commrs[above] to David Shelby six lots in Gallatin proved by John Lyon.
James Ross & others v Benjamin Tarbor for Patsey and Betsey Harris. Detinue. Oct 1802 plf by Thomas Stuart; dfts by John C Hamilton. July 1803 plfs enter non suit; dfts recover agt plfs full costs of said suit in that behalf expended.
John Harrison v Mark Rickmon & James Sanders. Judgt by default at last term set aside; dfts pay all costs.
James Anderson assee of Alexr Eason v Henry Lyon & Francis Weatherred. Debt. Jan 1803 plf by John C Hamilton; dfts by Thomas Stuart. July 1803 jury Reuben Douglass Moore Cotton Hugh Crawford Robt Steel Abrm Hassell Nathl Parker Jas C Wilson Saml p.394 Smith Samuel Stuart Thomas Murry William Beard Josiah Giles find for plf $133.66; and costs.
Rescind order releasing John Dawson from double tax on 1172 acres one free poll & seven black polls for 1802.
John Wood v Robert C Atkinson & Robert Laurence. Oct 1802 plf by Saml Donelson & Jesse Wharton; dft by Thos Stuart & Wm Smith at which term Robert C Atkinson one of dfts afsd ackd service of writ. July 1803 plf orders suit dismissed.
Andrew Jackson & Co v Joseph Moore. Jan 1803 plf by S Donelson; at sd term plf thrice called but failed to appear; judgt by default agt him; Apr 1803 jury: Kasper Mansker Wm Bowen Henry Bunn John Withers Elmore Harris Joseph Wallace Robt Shaw Jas Lauderdale Thos Howell Seth Mabry Zachariah Green Robt Desha find plfs damages 1¢. Plfs by atty obtained new trial. July 1803 jury Reuben Douglass Moore Cotton Hugh Crawford Robert Steel Abraham Hassell Nathaniel Parker James C Wilson Samuel Smith Samuel Stuart Thos Murry Wm Beard Thos Parker find plfs damages $73.12. And costs.
John Wood and Mary Wood petition to draw from administrator of Carlton Atkinson decd their share of personal estate of decedent; summons agt Robt C Atkinson admr.
William Dixon v Edmund Smith. Att. Plf obtained judgt agt dft for $18.50 before Isaac Walton esquire; attachment levied on 2 lots in Cairo, lot 31 to be sold.
p.395 John Burnly v Jack Reeves. Att. Burnly recovered before Edwd Douglass esqr judgt agt Reeves for $47 incl costs; levied on 50 acres, to be sold.
Wilson Cage v William Dobbins. Scire facias. Wilson Cage at July 1800 recovered agt Wm Dobbins $810.14½; Apr 1801 order sale issued directing sheriff of Wilson County to sell 320 acres previously condemned by Court. Sci fa from D Shelby: Wm Dobbins to appear before Sumner Court at house of James Cryer in Gallatin. Dobbins not found by Shff Thos Masten. Alias scire facias issued; not found in this county by Sheriff Thomas Mastin.

Friday July 8th. Present Edward Douglass William Montgomery James Cryer Esqrs.
p.396 Release Matthew Cartwright from taxes on 200 acres one free poll two black polls for 1802, having been charged twice.
John Boyce v William Snoddy. Appeal. Apr 1803 plf by Samuel Donelson & Redmond D Barry; dft by Jesse Wharton. July Jury Nathl Parker Hugh Crawford Moore Cotton Jas C Wilson Jas S Wilson Thos Parker Saml Smith Robt Steel Moses Tinsley James Turner Terry Turner Abram Hassell find for dft; dft recovers agt plf his full costs.
Deed Matthew Cartwright to David Dement lot 13 in Gallatin ackd.
Theopholus Bass v John Ogelsby. Jury Nathl Parker Hugh Crawford Moore Cotton Jas

JULY 1803

C Wilson Thos Parker Saml Smith Robt Steel Moses Tinsley Jas Turner Terry Turner Abraham Hassell John Payton find for plf $47.50; new trial granted.

John Wood & Mary Wood v Robert C Atkinson. Petition for share of estate of Carlton Atkinson decd; dedimus protestatum issues behalf dft to Logan County, KY.

Moses Tinsley v William Weatherred. Depositions of witnesses behalf plf in Virginia; also behalf dft witnesses residing in Virginia.

Jaramah Claypole v John Boyce. Apr 1803 plf by Jno C Hamilton; dft by Saml Donelson & Thos Stuart pleaded covenant performed. Jul 1803 jury Saml Wilson Wm Beard Matw Cartwright Richd King Jno Weathered Mark Rickmon Reuben Douglass Thos Barrott Jno Woods Danl Trigg Jno Mitchell Hardy Bloodworth assess plfs damage $236.52. And costs. Dft appeals to Superior Court; Wm Moore & Henry Lyon securities.

p.397 Jaramah Claypole v John Boyce. Debt. Apr 1803 plf by Jno C Hamilton; dft by Saml Donelson & Thos Stuart. Jul 1803. Non suit. Dft recovers agt plf.

Saturday July 9th. Present Isaac Walton, James Douglass, James Cryer, Esquires.

Wm Douglass Reuben Cage & Wilson Yandall exrs of Wm Hamilton decd v John Payton. Debt. Jury Robt Steel Jas S Wilson Jno Orr Isaac Clark Robt Trousdale Benjn Jolly Danl Trigg Benjn Morgan Jos Seawell Jas Blackemore Jno Weatherred Chas Harris find for plf his debt $108.30, but that the late Wm Hamilton decd was indebted to dft a greater sum, obligation date 5th Oct 1795; therefore find plea in favour of dft. Plf granted a new trial.

Appt Nicholas Boyce Charles Elliott Thomas Farmer Joseph McElwrath David Orr William Moore Jno Gardner Jno B Johnson Malachi Hereford James Odam Peter Looney Zachariah Green Elmore Harris & Richard Bradley to assess damages sustained by Redmond D Barry in consequence of a road laid off from Gallatin to Capt Gillespies passing through sd Barry's enclosures.

York v Isaac Pearce. TAB&c. Depositions to be taken behalf plf in Fayette County, Pennsylvania.

Stothart & Bell v William McCurdy. Debt. Plf by Dickinson; dft failing to appear, judgt by default agt him. Plfs recover agt dft $56.37½, damages, and costs.

James Boyce v Jack Reeves. Dft failing to appear, judgt by default agt him.

Bradford & Crutcher v Jack Reeves. [as above]

p.398 Jurors to october term: King Carr, James Lauderdale Jr, John Mills, John Trousdale, John Gillespie Junr, Champ Madding, John Rutherford, John Goodrum, James Weatherred, Isaac Bledsoe of Anthony, Joseph Hodge, William Reed, James McMurry, Jno Anderson, Robert Bratney, William Anderson (Cas), James A Wilson, Thomas Howell, James Carothers, John Mitchell, Dr[?] Thomas Edwards Sr, Lawrence Whitsitt, Edward Jones, Wm Frazor, Elisha Green, James McKain, John Smith [Mad?], Isaac Lain, John Kirkpatrick, George Michie, John Hamilton, William Harrison, William Edwards, George G Black, Peter Looney H, Rhodam Rawlings, Joshua Hadley.

Thomas Hart v Thomas Farmer. Debt. Apr 1803 plf by Thos Stuart; dft by Jno C Hamilton & Redmond D Barry. Jul 1803 jury Richd King Mark Richmon John Payton Abraham Hassell Wm Wright Hugh Crawford Moore Cotton Jesse Deloach Thos Parker Nathl Parker Alexr McKnight Marlin Young say dft has paid debt; dft recovers agt plf his costs.

Redmond D Barry v John Deloach. Debt. Apr 1803 plf by Parry W Humphreys; dft by John B Johnson says he paid debt to R D Barry or William Nash on day it became due; further pleads a sett off agt sd Barry of a like sum. Thomas Stuart for plf. July 1803 jury Robert Steel John Orr Isaac Clark Matthew Cartwright Isaac Lain James S Wilson James C Wilson Chas Harris Thos Keefe Benjn Morgan Thos Farmer Daniel Trigg

OCTOBER 1803

say dft has not paid debt $366 or any part thereof; further that dft is entitled to no set off; find for plf his debt, damages, and costs.

Appt Nathaniel Parker Jr constable for Capt Brownings district; bond $625 with Thomas Parker and Robert Steel securities, and took oath.

David Gillespie v John Payton. Att. New trial is awarded.

Appt Henry Bradford, James Wilson Curley, & Jno Mills judges to ensuing election.

Redmond D Barry v John Deloach. Debt. Dft granted appeal to Superior Court; bond $800 with Ruffin Deloach and Jesse Deloach securities.

p.399 Thomas Keefe v Redmond D Barry. Apr 1803 plf by Jno C Hamilton; dft by Thos Stuart. July cause refered to Thos Stuart & Boswell Johnson, they to name an umpire if necessary; their award to be judgt of Court. After making sd rule, parties in proper person come to Court; plf acknowledges full satisfaction of demands agt dft & dismisses suit & agrees to pay costs.

Thomas Keefe v Redmond D Barry. TAB. [as above].

Court adjourns till court in course to meet at house of James Cryer in Gallatin.

J Winchester

p.400 House of James Cryer in Gallatin, first Monday in October 1803. Present James Winchester, James Douglass, John McMurtry & William Cage Esqrs.

Court adjourns to meet in quarter of hour in the Court-house with the permission of the undertaker of the Court-house, same not yet being in a situation to be received by the commissioners from him. Court met, same members as before.

Deed David Dement to Solomon Barnes 50 acres proved by Isaac Baker.

Deed George Michie to Redmond Dillon Barry 290 acres ackd.

Release Edward Jones from present year taxes on 250 acres, 1 free poll, & 1 black poll, sd Jones being twice returned.

Bill/sale Richard Graham to Elizabeth Graham proved by James A Wilson.

Will of William Galbreath decd proved by Nimrod Browning and John Stevenson; John Galbreath executor therein named qualified.

Grant ltrs/admn to Parismus Tillery on estate of Nathaniel Woolsey decd; his bond $300 with John Franklin and Rhodam Rawlings securities.

Deeds ackd & proved: James Murray to Levi Hall by Thomas Polley. Samuel Donelson Shadrack Nye Jas Wilson & Charles Donoho to Matthew Cartwright by John Lyon. Samuel Donelson Shadk Nye Jas Wilson Chas Donoho to Matthew Cartwright by Will Trigg. John Dawson to Thos Pulley by Moses Comings. Saml Donelson Shadk Nye Jas Wilson Charles Donoho to Stephen Cantrill ackd.

Allow George Campbell $2 for services as constable in taking Robert S Slaughter a prisoner to district jail.

Excuse John Mills & Champ Madding from attending as jurors for present term.

Ltr/atty Hugh Parks to William Roark proved by Edward Gwin.

Grand Jury: George Michie foreman, William Edwards, King Carr, James Weatherred, William Frazor, Isaac Lain, Laurence Whitsitt, Jno Trousdale, John Gillespie, James Lauderdale, Isaac Bledsoe, William Harrison, John Smith. Eli Stalcup, constable.

State v Pleasant Chitwood. TAB. Appearance bond Wm Snoddy, witness behalf State.

Acct/sales goods of Reuben White decd proved by admx.

p.401 Deed Moses Tinsley to John Turner 164 acres proved by Terisha Turner.

OCTOBER 1803

Deed Samuel Gregg to William Rice 120 acres proved by Peter Looney.
Deed Saml Donelson Shadk Nye Jas Wilson Chas Donoho commrs to James Odam lot 28 in Gallatin ackd by sd commissioners.
Deed David White to Antony Swet 30 acres proved by George Wooddell.
John Franklin reputed father of an illegitimate child of Elizabeth Clary pays his fine $3.12½; enters bond for maintenance of child, $500 with John Mills security.
William Black & Co v William Giles & Josiah Giles. Debt. Plfs by Jno C Hamilton; dfts confessed judgt $103. Plfs recover debt; three months stay of execution.
State v Stephen Hall. P.L. Appearance bond of Ely Stalcup, prosecutor.
Appt Arthur Hicks constable for Capt Gwins district; bond $625, John Dinning sec.
Appt David Wilson and James Cryer esqrs to make settlement with admr of Simon Kuykendall decd.
Appt Thomas Donnell & William Montgomery esqrs to make settlement with guardians of orphans of Henry Lovin decd.
State v Stephen Hall. P Larceny. Christopher Stubbins witness on behalf the State appearance bond.
State v Pleasant Chitwood. T.A. Ambrose Porter, wit for state, appearance bond.
State v John Franklin. Peace bonds of John Franklin & William Cage, the condition that John Franklin keep peace towards Shadrack Nye until next Court.
Release from Wm McWhirter to Ephraim Payton proved by John Payton.
Appt Wright Barnes constable for Capt Lains company; bond $625, Isaac Baker and Solomon Barnes securities.
State v John Lafferty. Dft was bound to keep peace towards Abraham Ellis; dft and
p.402   Ellis give testimony; dft pays costs; discharged.

Tuesday Oct 4th. Present Reuben Searcy, John McMurtry, John Barr, Esquires.
John Clark & Rachel Stalcup alias Clark make oath that James Turmen Jr is eldest son & heir of James Turmen who died about eight years ago in Jefferson then in the Territory of US south of River Ohio but now Tennessee; sd James Turmen Jr is now of lawful age and resides in Smith County.
Deed Commrs[above] to John Trice five lots in Gallatin proved by Edmund Crutcher.
Deed Commrs[above] to Robert Trousdale lots 9 and 10 in Gallatin ackd.
Deed Commrs[above] to Peter Looney lot 20 in Gallatin ackd.
Deed Commrs[above] to John McConnell lot 15 in Gallatin ackd.
Release John Barns from tax on 200 acres 1 free poll, taxed twice in same year.
State v David Ferrell. P.L. Bond of Joshua Cherry, witness behalf state.
State v David Ferrell. P.L. Bonds of Geo G Black & Jos Phipps, wit behalf state.
Deed William Kennedy to Orman Allon 26½ acres ackd.
Bond of William Kennedy, proprietor of a cotton ginn, $1000 with Orman Allon sec.
William Douglass & Cage exrs of Wm Hamilton decd v Reuben Searcy. Appeal. April 1803 plf by Jesse Wharton & Jno C Hamilton; dft by Redmond D Barry & Thomas Stuart. Oct 1803 jury Joseph Hodge Jas McMurry Wm Anderson Thos Howell Thomas Edwards Geo G Black Peter Looney H Rhodam Rawlings Joshua Hadley George D Blackmore John Hamilton John Mills find for plfs $5, with costs.
Robert Bates v William Douglass. Appeal. Jury Jos Hodge James McMurry Wm Anderson Thos Howell Thos Edwards Jas Trousdale Peter Looney H Rhodam Rawlings Joshua Hadley George D Blackmore Jno Hamilton find for plf $13; rule to shew cause for new trial.
p.403   State v David Ferrell. P.L. Bond of John Withers, wit for state.
Appt Alexander Cathey guardian for Matthew B Cathey & Thomas D Cathey orphans of

OCTOBER 1803

William Cathey decd; bond $3000 with James Sanders security.
Report of commrs to divide two tracts, property of Henry Houdeshall decd between John Hamilton the petitioner and other claimants for sd land.
Appt James Douglass & John Barr esqrs to make settlement with Alexander Cathey as admr of William Cathey decd.
State v Stephen Hall. P.L. Bond of William Sample and James McKinsey for the appearance of Stephen Hall.
Appt Wm Seawell Chas Donoho James Hart Richd Alexander & Hallery Malone to divide negro estate of William Cathey decd between heirs of decedant.
Will of James Gardner decd proved by Benjamin Seawell who made oath that Susannah Seawell & Wilson Yandall the other subscribing witnesses subscribed in his presence and that testator was in perfect memory at execution of will. John Sloan one of the executors named in sd will qualified as such.
Order exr of James Gardner decd sell personal estate not disposed of by will.
Inventory of James Gardner decd proved by executor of sd decd.
Appt John Orr constable for Capt Vinsons company; bond $625, George Michie sec.
Report of commissioners appointed to settle with admr of Wm Cathey decd.

Wednesday Oct 5th. Present Edwd Douglass, Stephen Cantrill, John Barr, Esquires.
Inventory of goods of William Galbreath decd proved by executor of sd decd.
State v Robert Moore. TAB. Appearance bond of Arthur Hankins, prosecutor.
State v Pleasant Chitwood. TAB. Appearance bond of Richard Powell, prosecutor.
p.404   Jurors to Superior Court for Mero District: John Payton, James McMurry, Wm Gillespie, Robt Ellis, Jas Lauderdale Jr, Nicholas Boyce, Richard Strother.
Order Benjn Seawell, Wm Seawell esqr, James Simpson, John Carr, John Barr divide personal estate of Wm Galbreath decd between legatees agreeable to will of decd.
Commrs who divided estate of Henry Houdeshall decd between claimants are allowed $9; surveyor allowed legal fee for his services three days amounting to $7.50.
State v Pleasant Chitwood. TAB. Jury Joseph Hodge Jas McMurry Wm Anderson Thomas Howell Thos Edwards Geo G Black Peter Looney H Rhodam Rawlings Joshua Hadley Geo D Blackemore Jas Gambling John Mills find dft guilty of trespass assault & battery as charged; fine $5, remain in custody until paid with costs; fine mitigated to $1.
Acct/sales & supplement inventory/goods of John Donoho decd returned by Archibald Marlin one of the executors of sd decd.
Deed Henry Lyon to James Bentley 170 acres proved by John Morgan.
Deed William Bradshaw to James Bentley 170 acres proved by John H Bush.
State v Pleasant Chitwood. TAB. Appearance bond of Richard Powell for himself and wife Partheny to give evidence in behalf of State agt Chitwood.
State v Robert Moore. TAB. Appearance bond of Robt Moore, Redmond D Barry sec.
Nuncupative will of Avis[?] Bloodworth decd committed to writing 6 August 1803 proved by William Douglass whose name is subscribed as a witness.
State v Stephen Hall. Petit Larceny. Jury Jos Hodges Jas McMurry Wm Anderson Thos Howell Thomas Edwards Geo G Black Rhodam Rawlings Joshua Hadley George D Blackemore Thos Billen Isaac Baker James Vinson find dft guilty of feloniously carrying away a pair of womens leather slippers as charged. Dft is to be taken by Sheriff to public
p.405   whipping post and there receive fifteen lashes with a switch on his bare back well laid on and remain in custody until he pay the costs.
State v Robert Moore. TAB. Appearance bond of John Mansker, prosecutor; Anna Pearce and big Betsey Pearce to give testimony behalf state agt sd Moore.

OCTOBER 1803

Obligation James Powers to Henry Guthrie proved by Daniel Wilburn.

Allow John Gibson, constable $6.75 for expense in taking John Reed alias Shaw to district jail who was committed thereto by Jno Morgan & Jas Winchester esquires.

Deed Saml Donelson Shadrack Nye James Wilson Charles Donoho commissioners to Benjamin Rawlings lot 1 in Gallatin proved by Edmund Crutcher.

Lists of taxable property & polls to be taken: Stephen Cantrill in Capt Whitsitts company. Jno McMurtry in Capt Bruce's company. James Sanders in Capt Sanders compy. Archibald Marlin in Capt Latimers. William Cage in Capt Scoby's. James Douglass in Capt Lains. Witherall Latimer in Capt McKees. Edward Gwin in Capt Gwins. Jas Cryer in Capt Boyces. David Wilson in Capt Vinsons. James Winchester in Capt Alexanders. John Morgan in Capt Brownings. Thomas Blackemore in Capt Whites. James Hart in Capt Bradleys. John Barr in Capt Mills.

p.406

Edward Douglass deposits with Clerk $3.12½ collected of Elizabeth Clary for having an illegitimate child.

Deed James Trousdale to John C Hamilton 29 acres ackd.

John Wyles v William Sample. TAB. Plf by Jno C Hamilton; suit dismissed; dft recovers agt plf his costs.

Thursday Oct 6th. Present Thomas Donnell Edward Gwin William Seawell Esquires.

Deed John C Hamilton to Peter Looney 50 acres ackd.

Allow John Stephenson $22.83 being two thirds value after deducting expences for entering stray horse entered by Wm Penny which was property of sd John Stephenson and was appraised by John Bailey & Henry McKinny to $35.

State v Robert Moore. TAB. Dft pleads guilty; fined $5 and remain in custody of sheriff until paid with costs.

John Harrison v Mark Rickmon & James Sanders. April 1803 by Redmond D Barry; dft not appearing, judgt by default. Jul 1803 judgt set aside on motion of dft counsel Thomas Stuart with paying costs. Oct 1803 plf in proper person dismissed suit; dft recovers against plaintiff his costs.

State v Joseph Motherall. Neglect of duty as overseer/road. Motherall has never been furnished with a list of hands; dft discharged.

State v Robert Moore. TAB. Jury Jos Hodge Jas McMurry Wm Anderson Thomas Edwards Geo G Black Peter Looney Rhodam Rawlings Thos Howell Jno Mills Jas Orr Isaac Clark find dft not guilty. Prosecutor Arthur Hankins to pay costs.

David Cochran one of exrs of will of Wm Cochran decd took oath prescribed by law.

State v James McKain. TAB. Appearance bonds. Thomas Barrott, prosecutor; Lemon Holland to give testimony in behalf of the State.

p.407

Samuel Donelson & others commissioners in trust for Sumner County v John C Hamilton. Debt. Dft confesses judgt $187.75 and costs; execution stayed six months.

State v James McKain. TAB. Appearance bond of Henry Bloodworth to give testimony in behalf of the state.

State vs James McKain. TAB. Appearance bond of James McKain.

Edward Douglass esqr deposits 31½¢ fine of Nicholas Boyce for profane swearing.

Bond James Lyon & Henry Lyon to Wm Read proved by William Cage.

State v James McKain. TAB. Dft pleads guilty; fined $1 and costs.

State v William Hutchinson. Warrant issued agt dft for selling half pint whiskey quashed; dft pays his own costs.

State v William Hutchinson. [same as above]

State v William Hutchinson. [same as above]

188

OCTOBER 1803

State v Wm Hutchinson. Court adjudge proceedings of the Justice be quashed, dft pay his own costs in said cause.
Order David Wilson Esqr furnish Wm McKorcle with list/hands to work under him as overseer of the road.
State v Pleasant Chitwood. TAB. Dft fined $5; fine mitigated to $1 & costs.
Order sheriff notify Henry Lyon to appear at Court this term either to relinquish admn granted him on estate of James Lyon decd & also his guardianship for heirs of sd decedant or give new security in both cases.
On petition of John C Hamilton & Redmond D Barry, order shff to notify Henry Lyon to appear this term either to relinquish guardianship for heirs of James Lyon decd or give new security for sd guardianship agreeable to prayer of petitioners.
Appt Wm Rice constable for Capt Latimers dist; Peter Looney security.
p.408   Edward Gwin v William Brimberry. Motion of Edwd Gwin, judgt behalf Gwin agt Brimberry $129.38 3/10. Order execution issue agt Brimberry for amount of judgment.

Friday Oct 7th 1803. Present Thos Donnell Jas Sanders Edwd Gwin Isaac Walton Esqrs.
Release Robert Taylor from 1802 taxes on 520 acres in Captain Bruce's company, it being more land than he possesses.
John Depriest v James Trousdale. July 1802 plf by Redmond D Barry; dft by John C Hamilton. Oct 1803 plf dismisses his suit and assumes costs except dfts atty fee.
Redmond D Barry v John Deloach. Apr 1803 plf by Thos Stuart; dft by John B Johnson. Oct 1803 jury Jos Hodge Jas McMurry Wm Anderson Peter Looney Rhodam Rawlings Jno Mills Joshua Hadley Jas McKain Thos Edwards Geo D Blackmore Matthew Cartwright Jno Bonds find for dft. Dft recovers of plf full costs expended.
Redmond D Barry v John Deloach. Bail for dft surrenders him.
Wright Barns takes oath & qualifies as constable for Capt Lains company.
State v David Ferrell. Petit Larceny. Jury Jos Hodge Jas McMurry Wm Anderson Peter Looney Rhodam Rawlings Joshua Hadley James McKain Geo D Blackmore Matthew Cartwright Solomon Barns Thos Howell Jno Hamilton find dft guilty of feloniously taking a mans saddle. Sd David to be taken by shff to public whipping post, there receive five lashes well laid on his bare back; then remain in custody of the sheriff until the costs are paid.
Tandy Witcher v John Deloach. Apr 1803 David Allon levied on Bede and Dorcas two negro girls property of John Deloach. Plf by Thos Stuart; Dft by Jno B Johnson. Oct 1803 cause refered to James Sanders William Trigg & Jno Payton. Award Tandy Witcher
p.409 $380 & costs. Stay of execution except costs until first July next.

Saturday Oct 8th. Present Edwd Douglass Thos Donnell Edwd Gwin Jas Douglass Esqrs.
Jurors to Jan term: George Keesee David Henry Jno Cathey James Ball John Brown Sr Richard Carr Mark Rickmon John Tucker GC Jno Gwin Jesse Shean William Braken Reuben Douglass James Franklin Senr Jno Gardner Griswold Latimer John Hassell Moore Cotton John Cotton James Brigance Sr Matthew Cartwright Jas Clendening Wm Gwin Wm Neely Wm Brazel Samuel Beard David Beard Jr James Mecklin Robert Anderson William Bell James Carothers Jas S Wilson Jas Vinson Richd King Lewis Crane Smith Hansbrough Jas Lane.
James Trousdale v Elia Herrell John Harris & Benjamin Tarvor. Debt. Plf by Jesse Wharton; dfts not appearing, judgt by default agt them, $110 and costs.
State v David Ferrell. PL. Motion for new trial overruled; sheriff to take dft to public whipping post to receive five lashes' dft then remain in custody &c.

OCTOBER 1803

James McKain v Daniel Miles. Covt. Bail surrenders dft to custody of sheriff.
Jackson & Co v Joseph Moore. Direct alias Feiri facias to shff Wilson County.
Bradford & Crutcher v Jack Reeves. Atta. Jul 1803 Constable David Allen executed on 50 acres Station Camp cr. Plf by Jno C Hamilton. Dft not appearing, judgt by default. Oct 1803 judgt $147.33 with costs; attached property except one bay horse to be sold; sd horse claimed by John Payton.
Appt Thos Donnell & Jas Douglass esqrs to settle with admr of Benjn Miers decd.
p.410 Josias & John H Bullock v John Bullard. Scire Facias. John Bullard summoned as witness behalf Josias Bullock & John H Bullock in John Whitford's suit agt them. John Bullard failed to appear; fined $125. Bullard to appear at next court in Gallatin at house of Jas Cryer & shew cause why he could not appear. Executed by Thos Masten DS Aug 1803. Dft not appearing, plf recovers agt him, with costs.
Appt James McKain constable for Capt Scoby's company; bond $625, Nicholas Boyce & Thomas Keefe securities, and took oath prescribed by law.
James Boyce v Jack Reeves. Plf by atty enters release agt one horse levied on.
James Boyce v Jack Reeves. Covt. July 1803 Thomas Masten DS reports he levied on land and horse mill; levied on horse in hand of Wm Galespie. Dft failing to appear, judgt by default agt him. Oct 1803 jury Wright Barns Solomon Sholders Thos Edwards Thos Keefe Jas C Wilson Isaac Lain James Orr Jacob Willis Humphrey Moses Jno Stuart Joshua Cherry Christopher Stubbins assess plfs damages $142. Also costs.
Saml Donelson & others commrs in trust for Sumner Co v George D Blackmore. Debt. Plfs by Jno C Hamilton; dft not appearing, judgt by default $59.38 & costs.
Saml Donelson[worded as above] judgt agt Geo D Blackmore $114.67½ & costs.
Saml Donelson[as above] judgt by default agt Jas Steel $104.25 & costs.
p.411 Appt Joshua Cherry overseer/road in place of John Withers from Gallatin to Shelbys Creek; James Douglass esqr to furnish him a list of hands.
George Michie v John Trice. Slander. Depositions for both sides to be taken.
John L Young v David Hughes. Debt. Plf by Jno C Hamilton; dft came not; final judgt agt dft $82.40 and costs.
Saml Donelson & others commrs in trust for Sumner Co v Thomas Edwards and Edward Williams. Debt. Plfs by Jno C Hamilton; Thos Edwards confesses judgt $142.28; Edwd Williams came not; judgt final by default agt him. Plfs recover with costs.
Appt James Cryer esqr Jailer for Sumner County.
Appt John C Hamilton overseer/road to James C Wilson; hands in Gallatin to work.
James McKain v Daniel Miles. Covt. Thos Edwards & Adonijah Edwards special bail.
Appt Henry Lyon guardian for Patience Lyon & James Lyon orphans of Jas Lyon decd; bond $4000 with Jno Withers Thomas Edwards John Trice Nicholas Boyce & Robert Moore securities; bond received in lieu of bond heretofore given by sd Henry Lyon as guardian to sd children with Redmond D Barry & John C Hamilton securities.
Court adjourns till court in course.   James Douglass

p.412 Court of Pleas & Quarter Sessions at Court house in Gallatin, third Monday of March 1804. Present: James Winchester Edward Douglass Thomas Donnell Witherall Latimer John Morgan Esquires.
Deed John Kennedy & George Parks to Robert Hamilton 75 ac proved by Jacob Parks.
Deed William Perry to John Perry 100 acres proved by Isaac Baker.

MARCH 1804

Deed Reuben Cage to William Kirk 107 acres ackd.
Will of Michael Ozbrooks decd proved by Edward Gwin and Richard Smith. Ruth Ozbrooks extx & John Gwin exr qualified by taking oath prescribed by law.
Deed James Winchester to Edwin Perry 160 acres ackd.
Will of Robert Marshall decd proved by Isreal Moore & David Davis. Christana Marshal extx & William Marshall exr qualified by taking oath.
Deed Redmond D Barry to Swen Stalcup 100 acres ackd.
Deed Thomas Marquis to Stephen Stone 107 acres proved by Francis Fonvielle.
Deed Elisha Bernard to Samuel Higgason 320 acres proved by James Williams.
Deed/gift Thomas King to his son Moses King personal property ackd.
Appt Jesse Hainey overseer/road from James Whites in place of Harry Harrison.
Appt John Carr overseer in place of William Carr.
Appt James Braken overseer/road at head of dry fork of Bledsoes Creek.
Grand jury: Robert Anderson foreman, Reuben Douglass, Wm Bracken, John Cotton, Saml Beard, William Brasil, David Beard Jr, James Brigance Sr, Lewis Crane, Smith Hansbrough, John Gardner, Richard Carr, William Gwin, John Hassell, James Carothers. William Rice constable is appointed to attend grand jury.
Deed Alexander Youree to Francis Youree 320 acres proved by Patrick Youree.
Bill/sale Alexr Youree to Francis Youree personal property proved by Patk Youree.
Deed Alexander Chapman to William Harper 91½ acres proved by John Harper.
Deed David White to James White 19 acres proved by William White.
Moses Tinsley v Mary Hunt. Josiah Giles dfts special bail in place of John Hunt.
Will of Thomas Todd decd proved by James Bentley; Henry Belote exr qualified, and sd executor returned an inventory of the estate and proved same.
Deed Nathan Edwards & Thomas Edwards to Alexander Rasco 100 acres ackd.
p.413 Deed Alexander Rasco to Nathan Edwards 100 acres ackd.
Deed John Rutherford to David Ventress 3½ acres proved by Esay Ventress.
William Christmass v Browning Williams. Dfts bail John H Bush surrenders dft.
Anthony Sharp v George Parks. Scire facias issues behalf plf to revive judgment heretofore obtained by sd plf v sd dft.
State v Edward Hogin. TAB. Recognizance of Isaac House, prosecutor.
Thomas J Overton esqr presents license to practice as attorney at law; qualified.
Grant David Ventress leave to erect mill on east fk Goose Crk above junction with west fork sd crk; bond $500, James Martin security.
Appoint Edward Douglass presiding magistrate of the Court of Sumner County.
State v Edward Hogin. TAB. Dft recognizance, William Snoddy security.
John Sevier governor commissioned Matthew Alexander Nicholas Boyce William Trigg justices of the peace for Sumner; take oaths and qualify.
State v James Howard. TAB. Dft submits; fined $1 and pay same with costs.
State v Edward Hogin. TAB. Dft submits; fined $1; remains in custody of sheriff until fine is paid with costs.
Allow constable George Campbell $2 for expence in taking Benjamin Kuykendall a prisoner to the district jail.
Appt Thomas Barrott overseer/road from John Dawsons to big east fork of Station Camp creek; Nicholas Boyce esqr to furnish sd overseer with a list of hands.
Appt Jesse Johnson overseer/road Cairo to Croft mills; Matthew Alexander esqr to furnish sd overseer with a list of hands.
Appt Capt James White overseer/road Bledsoes crk to late Major Whites plantation; James Winchester esqr to furnish sd overseer with a list of hands.
Orphan William Clary apprenticed to George Logan to learn the farming business.

MARCH 1804

p.414   Appt Lemuel Stubblefield constable for Capt Bradleys district; bond $625 with Champ Madin security & took oath prescribed by law.
Deed William Walton to Isaac Walton 60 acres proved by Allen Mathis.
Deed John Perry to Isaac Walton 379 acres ackd.
Will of Nathaniel Gilmore deceased proved by Matthew Alexander & Zacheus Wilson subscribing witnesses; James Wilson & Zacheus Wilson sons of Samuel Wilson qualified as executors.
Will of David Wilson decd proved by Zacheus Wilson & James S Wilson subscribing witnesses; William Wilson & Zacheus Wilson sons of sd decd, executors, qualified.
Deed David Ferrell to John C Hamilton 100 acres proved by John Orr.
Bill/sale John Mitchell to John C Hamilton negro man Solomon proved by John Orr.
Deed James McKnight the elder to Joseph Reeves 20 acres proved by George Michie.
Deed Charles Dixon by his atty in fact Tilman Dixon to Rachel Carson 50 acres proved by John Mills.
Deed Rhodam Rawlings to Benjamin Roaney lot 6 in Gallatin proved by James Desha.
Deed Robert Patterson to John Cotton 100 acres proved by Moore Cotton.
Bill/sale James A Wilson to John Cotton negro boy Sam ackd.
Deed William Cartwright to William Henderson 296 acres proved by Daniel Smith.
Deed Thomas Masten collector to Thomas Edwards 150 acres ackd.
Deed John Hamilton Senr to Thomas Perry 100 acres proved by Isaac Walton.
Deed Saml Donelson Shadk Nye Jas Wilson Chas Donoho commrs to Thomas Edwards lots in Gallatin Nos 6 10 11 12 proved by Will Trigg.
Deed[commrs above] to Isaac Baker lots 14 & 15 in Gallatin proved by Will Trigg.
Deed Thomas Hobdy to William Boyles 514 acres proved by Edward Gwin.
Deed Edward Hogin to Redmond D Barry 150 acres proved by Thomas Keefe.
Deed Thomas Masten collector to Thomas Edwards 160 acres ackd.
Inventory/goods & acct/sales goods of Nathaniel Woolsey decd proved by admr.
Deed Isaac Baker & his wife Molley to Joseph Whitely 399 acres in Russell county Virginia ackd by sd Isaac & Molley his wife.
Deed William Gwin to Edward Williams 200 acres proved by Edward Gwin.
Deed Wm Mitchell to Benjamin Roney lots 11 & 12 in Gallatin proved by Jas Roney.
Inventory/goods of David Wilson decd proved by executors of sd deceased.

p.415   Appt Jacob Parks constable for Capt Shaws district; bond $625 with Robert Hamilton security.
Inventory/goods of James Lyon decd proved by Henry Lyon the administrator.
Deed[commrs above] to Wm Black & Co lot 2 in Gallatin proved by Edmd Crutcher.
Appt Andrew Hoover constable for Capt Sanders district; Smith Hansbrough sec.
Appt Ely Stalcup constable for Capt Gwins dist; Thomas Groves security.
Appt John Pavatt constable for Capt Bruces dist; bond $625 with Wm Montgomery & George Campbell securities.
Appt William Henry constable for Capt Mills dist; David Henry security.
John Bowan esqr presented license to practice as attorney at law; took oaths for qualification and is admitted.
George Brisco v Reuben Scott. Debt. Dfts bail surrenders him to sheriff.
George Brisco v Reuben Scott. Debt. Dfts bail surrenders him to sheriff.
Commissioners appointed to settle with admx of Benjamin Miers decd make report.
Appt Thomas Howell overseer/road Shelbys crk to John Hassells in place of Abraham Rogers.
Permit Bennett Henderson esqr to appear as atty at law during present Term.
John Motherall v Alexander McKee. Plf obtained sundry judgts agt dft before a

MARCH 1804

magistrate, executions issued, levied on 440 acres, to be sold to satisfy judgt.
Thomas Perry v Alexander McKee. [Worded as above]
Kasper Mansker v Alexander McKee. [Worded as above]
p.416   Jessey Eatherly v Alexander McKee. Plf obtained judgt agt dft before a magistrate for $49.99 with 50¢ costs; execution issued & levied on 440 acres including plantation of dft; land condemned to be sold to satisfy judgment.
William Bowen v Alexander McKee. Plf obtained judgt agt dft before a magistrate for $43.89 with 50¢ costs; execution issued; levied on 440 acres[as above].
Exr or admr of William McWhirter decd v Alexr McKee. Plf obtained two judgments agt dft before a magistrate for $72.68½ with $1 costs[as above].
Deed/lease Samuel Donelson to Andrew Hoover 100 acres ackd.

Tuesday March 20th. Present Jas Winchester Jas Douglass Witheral Latimer Wm Seawell Edwd Gwin Thos Donnell Jno Barr Thos Blackemore Jas Hart David Love Wm Trigg Esqrs.
Washington S Hannum Esqr presented license to practice as an attorney; qualified.
Jurors to Superior Court: Robert Carothers, Zacheus Wilson son of Samuel, William Sanders, Richard Bradley, Patrick Barr, George Keesee[Kusee?].
Will of Benjamin Roney decd proved by James Harten & Jas Roney Sr; Isaac Stalcup & Richard Cope exrs qualified by taking the oath prescribed by law.
Appt Theophilus Allen overseer/road in place of Isaac Baker.
Appt James Cryer & William Trigg esqrs to settle with Edward Hogin Junr admr of Simon Kuykendall decd.
On motion of David Love esqr, order John Morgan James Clendening and Patrick Barr be commrs to ascertain the boundaries of land belonging to sd Love on Bledsoes crk.
p.417   Edward Jones v Isaiah Hammond. Debt. John Jones dfts special bail.
Deed Samuel Meek to William Robb 512 acres proved by William Turnbull.
Edward Douglass John McMurtry William Montgomery William Cage James Cryer Charles Donoho Jas Sanders Jno Morgan Chas Donoho Nicholas Boyce Stephen Cantrill Archibald Marlin Isaac Walton esqrs appear and take their seats.
State v David Ferrell. PL. John Harris bound to prosecute in behalf of the state.
Bill/sale Henry Lyon to Joseph McKean negro man Sam ackd.
Joseph McCravens elected commissioner of the revenue for Sumner.
Appoint James Douglass register for Sumner County in place of David Wilson decd.
Deed James Winchester to William McGready 150 acres ackd.
Acct/sales goods of James Gardner decd proved by executor.
Bond Sampson Williams to Joseph Motherall proved by Thomas Murry.
Bond Noah Sugg to David Davis proved by Thomas Murry.
Appoint James Douglass & Thomas Donnell to make settlement with admr of Carlton Atkinson decd.
George Houch orphan bound to John Stuart to learn art & mystery of a wheelright.
License Richard Taylor to keep ordinary at his dwelling in the county; bond $2500 with Alexander Graham security.
License John Orr to keep ordinary at his dwelling in Gallatin; bond $2500 with John C Hamilton & Will Trigg securities.
William Tait & William Stothart v Redmond D Barry. Debt. Apr 1803 plfs by Bennet Searcy. March 1804 dft in proper person confesses judgt $222.60¾ with interest.
p.418   Plfs also recover their costs. Execution to be stayed two months.
Jackson & Hutchings v Thomas Barrott. Debt. Richard Hogin special bail for dft.
John Hutchings v Thomas Barrott. Covt. Richard Hogin special bail for dft.

MARCH 1804

Deed Benjamin Towler to Thomas Potter 260 acres proved by Elijah Parker.
Sion Perry v Robert Boyce. Si fa. Jan 1801 David Shelby orders sheriff to summon Robert Boyce who was to give testimony in behalf plf suit Sion Perry v Daniel Richardson but failed to appear. Apr 1801 alias sci fa issued. Jul 1801 dft not found by E Crutcher shff. Dft by John C Hamilton & Thos Stuart. Jul 1802 dft by Thos Stuart says he was citizen of Kentucky when subpoena was served; had to return to his family in Garrard County 180 miles from this court. Said he attended at trial but p.419 Sion Perry never called upon him to give testimony in sd cause. Robert Boyce believes plea to be true. Plf by Saml Donelson. March 1804 dfts plea sustained, dft recovers of plf his full costs expended.
Henry Bloodworth renders inventory/property of Avy Bloodworth and Anny Boyscan wards of sd guardian and duly proved same.
Appt Wm Cage & Jas Cryer esqrs to settle with Henry Bloodworth as gdn of Avy Bloodworth & Anny Boyecan and report such settlement to this Court.
Lucy Dugger orphan girl bound to John Dugger to learn art or mystery of a weaver.
Commrs apptd to divide negro estate of Wm Cathey decd report such division.
Present Edward Douglass Isaac Walton & John Barr Esqrs.
George Brisco v Reuben Scott. Debt. Jul 1803 plf by Jno C Hamilton; dft by Thomas Stuart. March 1804 jury Geo Kusee David Henry John Cathey Jas Ball Mark Richmon Jno Tucker Jas Franklin Griswold Latimer Moore Cotton Jas Clendening Wm Bell Jas Vinson say dft paid debt; dft in proper person assumes cost of suit.
George Brisco v Reuben Scott. Debt. Jul 1803 [as above].
p.420 Thomas Keefe v Thomas Barrott. Nov 1802 on judicial attachment shff levied on negro woman Tine. Plf by John C Hamilton; dft by Redmond D Barry. March 1804 dft confesses judgment for $57.18½ & costs.
William Christmass v Browning Williams. Plf by Redmond D Barry; dft confesses judgt $63.50 with costs.
Matthew Cartwright v Isaac Clark and Joseph Clark. Debt. Apr 1803 plf by Samuel Donelson; dft by Thomas Stuart. Mar 1804 defendants in proper person confess judgment $167.50 & costs.
Deed/lease & release Edward Gwin to Capt James Campbell 1000 acres ackd.
Order William Exum Geo Stubblefield Champness Madding David Crenshaw Jno Dickison Arthur Exum to lay off a road from the house of William Parr on Cumberland river to Squire Harts mill on Goose creek.
Deed James Trousdale to John C Hamilton 27 acres proved by James Trousdale Junr.
Zacheus Baker v Alexander McKee. Plf recovered judgt agt dft before a magistrate for $38.78; execution issued; levied on 100 acres incl inprovements; to be sold.
Christopher Stump & Co v Alexander McKee. Plfs recovered sundry judgts agt dft before a magistrate to $53.77 with $2 costs; levied on 440 acres on which McKee lives; land condemned to be sold to satisfy judgment.
p.421 Commrs apptd to settle with admr of Carlton Atkinson decd make report.
Deed Thomas Murry to James Williams 7 acres ackd.
Appt Moore Cotton guardian for Noah Cotton; bond $2000 with Isaac Walton and John Cotton securities for faithful performance of his guardianship.
Order James Vinson James Wilson(smkg) James Wilson Senr Thos Patton Jacob Houdeshall lay off a road from Gallatin to Matthew Browns ferry on Cumberland river.
Appt Joseph Pitt guardian to minor Polley Pitt dau of sd Joseph; bond $1000 with Henry Pitt & Henry Bloodworth securities.
Jurors to June session: Henry Bradford, Joseph Clark, Jesse Joiner, Jno Anderson, Thos Edwards, Wallace Harris, Isreal Moore, Alexander Cathey, Danl Sanders, Richard

MARCH 1804

Alexander, Hugh Carothers, Isaac Lain, James Hambleton, Edwd Morgan, Henry Belote, Jas Robinson, Kasper Mansker, Laurence Whitsitt, Elisha Pruett, David Pursley, Edward Maxey, Edward Cage, Peter Lemmon, Thomas Bradley, Isaac Braken, James Frazor, Jno Dugger, William Bruce, James Gamblin, William King, Alexr Kirkpatrick, George G Blackemore, Alexr Graham, Thomas Gregory, Reuben Cage, Jeremiah Doxey, James Franklin, Nathan Edwards, Richard Hogin.

March 21st 1804. Present Edward Douglass Isaac Walton James Douglass esquires.
Excused George Kusee from attending as a juror this term.
Present Isaac Walton, John Barr, Will Trigg esqrs.
Robert Stothart v James Cage. Jury David Henry, John Cathey, Mark Rickmon, John Tucker, James Franklin, Moore Cotton, William Bell, James Vinson, James S Wilson, William Neeley, James Clendening, James Lain assess plfs damages to $103.42.
Bond of James Douglass apptd Register, $2500, with John C Hamilton and Will Trigg securities, and for collection & payment of taxes on grants and deeds, $500 with sd Hamilton and Trigg securities, and took the qualifying oaths.
William Reed v Henry Lyon. David Shelby commands Sheriff to bring Henry Lyon to
p.422   court to answer William Reed in plea of covenant broken. Plf by Washington Hannum: Henry Lyon hath not conveyed to Wm Reed 450 acres originally granted to Wm Morrison of Kentucky. Dft in proper person confesses judgment for $2000 and costs.
William Reed v Henry Lyon admr of James Lyon decd. Covt. David Shelby issued sci fa for shff to bring Henry Lyon to court. Dft confesses judgt $2000 & costs.
John Overton v heirs & devisees of David Allison. Sci fa. Apr 1800 judgt recov-
p.423   ered by plf; $174.06½ remains unpaid. David Shelby orders sheriff to summon heirs & devisees of David Allison to Court. March 1804 E Crutcher sheriff returned "Not found." Plf recovers agt dfts and costs.
License Henry Lyon to keep ordinary at his house in Gallatin, Richd Taylor sec.
Inventory/personal estate of Nathaniel Gilmer decd proved by executors.
Allow John McMurtry coroner $7.25 for inquest on body of Everett Garrett decd.
Order exrs of Nathaniel Gilmer decd to expose personal property to sale.
Ltr/atty William Wortham of Sumner County to his brother Thomas Wortham of Pittsylvania county Virginia for obtaining a legacy left by one of his ancestors formerly resident in Caroline County Virginia ackd by William Wortham.
Deed Samuel Donelson Shadrack Nye and James Wilson commrs to Joshua Bradley lot 7 in Gallatin proved by John Lyon.
Grand Jury dismissed and certificates granted them for their attendance.
State v Pleasant Chitwood. TAB. James McKinsey, security, surrenders dft; dft bound in recognizance, also James Orr & John B Johnson for appearance at this term.
Theophilus Bass v John Ogelsby. Jan 1803 plf by John C Hamilton; Apr 1803 dft by Thos Stuart. Jul 1803 jury Nathaniel Parker Hugh Crawford Moore Cotton Jas C Wilson Thomas Parker Saml Smith Robt Steel Moses Tinsley James Turner Terry Turner Abraham
p.424   Hassell John Payton assess plfs damages $47.50. New trial granted dft. Mar 1804 parties in proper person; plf dismissed suit & dft assumes costs.
Appt Terisha Turner overseer/road Bledsoes lick to ridge in place of Jno Goodrum.
Nichs Boyce & Mattw Alexander esqrs report they settled with Henry Bloodworth as guardian for Avi Bloodworth and Anny Boyecan.
Edwd Douglass esqr deposits with Clerk 31½¢ fine of Wm Moore for profane swearing on a presentment of the Grand Jury.
Deed Commrs[above] to William Rice lot 16 in Gallatin proved by John Lyon.

195

MARCH 1804

Present James Cryer, Isaac Walton, James Douglass.
Moses Tinsley v William Weatherred. Jan 1803 plf by Jno C Hamilton; dft by Thomas Stuart. Mar 1804 jury Theophilus Allon James Steel George Brown Nathan Edwards Jno Weathers Wm Douglass John D Hannah Jas Orr Dempsey Moore Jno Gwin Jas Ball Griswold Latimer find for dft. Plf granted new trial. Plf in proper person and dft by John Weatherred his agent come into Court; plf orders his suit dismissed, & pays his own costs; agent assumes to pay dfts costs.
License Isaac Turman to keep ordinary at his dwelling house in Gallatin, bond $2500, James Trousdale security.
On petition of Wm Bloodworth, order Jno Orr James Orr Ruffin Deloach Heli Herring Richd Powell divide negro estate of Avi Bloodworth & Anny Boyecan between surviving claimants of sd estate.
Bill/sale James Cryer John Orr John Cotton Allon Cotton James Strother to Moore Cotton negro boy Reuben proved by Edward Wormington.
Appt David Allen constable for Capt Boyces district; bond $625 with John B Johnson and Robert Patton securities, and took oath.
Commrs report they settled with guardian of Avi Bloodworth & Anny Boyecan.

p.425 Thursday March 22d. Present Thomas Donnell Isaac Walton William Trigg Esqrs.
Robert Stothart v James Cage. New trial is granted.
Hardy Bloodworth v Henry Morris. John Looney witness behalf plf failed to appear; scire facias issues against him.
Hardy Bloodworth v Henry Morris. Jury James Franklin Jas Clendening Jas Vinson Wm Bell Jas S Wilson Jas Lain William Neely Moore Cotton Mark Rickmon David Henry John Cathey John Tucker; plf not appearing, non suit entered against him.
William Douglass Reuben Cage Wilson Yandall exrs of William Hamilton decd v John Payton. Debt. April 1803 plfs by Jesse Wharton. July 1803 dft by Parry W Humphreys. Jury Robt Steel Jas S Wilson Jno Orr Isaac Clark Robt Trousdale Benjamin Jolly Danl Trigg Benjn Morgan Jos Seawell Jas Blackemore Jno Weatherred Charles Harris say dft has not paid debt, but that late Wm Hamilton was indebted to sd dft a greater sum, plea of sett off in favour of dft. New trial granted. March 1804 jury Jas Franklin Jas Clendening James Vinson Wm Bell James Lain Samuel P Black Wm Neely Moore Cotton Mark Rickmon David Henry John Cathey John Tucker find dft has not paid debt $108.30 and find no sett off, and assess plfs damages to $9.06. Dft is granted an appeal to the Superior Court, bond $500, with Nicholas Boyce & John C Hamilton securities.
Deed Bright Herring to Zaddock Bernard 640 acres proved by Luke Bernard.
Will of John Buntin decd proved by Patrk Barr & Nancy Barr subscribing witnesses; William & Joseph Buntin exrs qualified by taking the oath prescribed by law.
p.426 Will of Everard Garrett proved by George Chapman and Job Hicks.
Deed Everard Garrett to John Garrett 100 acres proved by Job Hicks.
Kasper Mansker v John Mansker. Sci fa. Apr 1803 David Shelby CSC orders shff Thos Masten summon John Mansker to answer Kasper Mansker who obtained judgt at Apr term 1800. Oct 1803 dft by Thos Stuart & Jno C Hamilton pleaded payment. March 1804 dft came not; plf recovers of dft $25.40½ & costs.
York v Isaac Pearce. TAB. Deposition of Lydia Waller to be taken; Joseph Dorris agent for York.
Enos Hannah v Drury Milam. Dfts bail Smith Hansbrough & Andrew Hoover.
Present Edward Douglass Thomas Donnell & James Cryer. William Gillespie overseer v David Shelby. Appeal. Jury Jas Ball Jas S Wilson Jno Gwin Griswold Latimer Jno B

MARCH 1804

Craighead Adonijah Edwards Francis Eury Adam Hunter Lewis West Thomas Campbell Laurence Whitsitt Isaac Barr. Mistrial.
    Allow William Sanders to erect a mill on west fk Goose Crk half mile above where upper road from Bledsoes crk to Fort Blount crosses. William Sanders agrees to pay damages sustained by persons owning land contiguous to where mill will be erected in consequence of overflowing land of such persons.
    Ltr/atty William Right & wife Nancy Right to James Espey proved by Robert Patton.
    Commrs apptd to divide negro estate of Ava Bloodworth & Anny Boyecan make report.
    John D Hanna v James Blackemore & Thos Blackemore. Debt. Plf by Jno C Hamilton; James Blackemore one of dfts in proper person confesses judgt $402.66 with interest; Plf recovers agt sd dft.

p.427   Friday March 23d. Present Edward Douglass James Winchester Wm Trigg Esqrs.
    Thomas Leech v James Orr & James Trousdale. Debt. Jul 1803 plf by Jno C Hamilton; dfts by Thos Stuart. Dfts confess judgt. Plf recovers against defendants.
    John Young v James Hannah. Sci fa. David Shelby CSC to Shff. John Young recovered agt James Hannah but balance of $31.52½ unpaid. Thos Masten DS made sci fa known to James Hannah. Mar 1804 dft failed to appear. Plf to recover agt dft.
    Amos Bailey v Elijah P Chambers. SCi fa. David Shelby CSC to Shff. Jan 1800 Amos Bailey recovered agt dft $25.20 & costs. Thomas Masten made known to Chambers. Mar 1804 dft failed to appear; plf recovers against defendant.
p.428   John Sommerville v Clement Hall. Debt. Jul 1803 plf by Bennet Searcy; dft by John Dickison[& Dickinson]. Plaintiff by Jesse Wharton. This term defendant by his atty confesseth judgment $180.88 & cost.
p.429   Nathaniel McCreary v Shadrack Dunn. Oct 1803 plf by Jesse Wharton; dft by Wm Smith. Mar 1804 plf dismisses suit; Elisha Prewitt assumes $1.50 and plfs atty assumes balance of costs except attornies fees which parties pay respectively.
    George Washington Lent Marr v Samuel Donelson. Debt. Jul 1803 plf by Thos Stuart; dft by Jesse Wharton. Mar 1804 dfts atty confesseth judgment, interest, costs.
    James Gowen v Isaac Baker. TAB. Depositions of John W Crunk & wife Milley & John McCarton to be taken.
    Deed William Snoddy to John C Hamilton 100 acres ackd.
    Deed/gift Robert Patton to Wm Patton mare & 2 yr old colt ackd.
    Joel Dyer junr v Nathaniel Dickerson junr & Nathaniel Dickerson Senr. Debt. Oct 1803 plf by Jesse Wharton; dft by John C Hamilton. Mar 1804 jury Jas Franklin Jas Clendening James Vinson Wm Bell Jas S Wilson James Lain Wm Neely Moore Cotton Mark Rickmon David Henry John Cathey John Tucker. Plf recovers his debt and costs.
    Joel Holland v Thomas Willis & James Cryer. Debt. Oct 1803 plf by Jno C Hamilton;
p.430   dft by Parry W Humphreys. Mar 1804 dfts atty confesses judgt $317.62 with interest and costs. Execution stayd till first of May next.
    Joel Holland v Thomas Willis & James Cryer. Debt. Oct 1803 plf by Jno C Hamilton; dft by Parry W Humphreys. Mar 1804 dfts by atty confess judgt $111.72 & costs.
    Deed James Winchester to Jesse Hainey 164 acres ackd.
    Jesse Hainey records his ear mark.
    Joseph McKean v George Michie. Debt. Oct 1803 plf by Jno C Hamilton; dft by Redmond D Barry. Mar 1804 dft by atty confesses judgt $96.80 & costs.
    State v Pleasant Chitwood. TAB. Dft pleads guilty; fine $5 & committed till paid.
    Samuel Donelson & others commrs in trust for Sumner County v George G Black. Debt. Oct 1803 plf by Jno C Hamilton; dft by Parry W Humphreys. Mar 1804 dft by

MARCH 1804

atty confesses judgt $57.28 & costs.
　Edward Douglass v William Hankins. Debt. Oct 1803 plf by Jno C Hamilton; dft by Wm Smith. Mar 1804 dft by atty confesses judgt $38 & costs. Stay/exn one month.
　John Rickmon v Redmond D Barry. Trover. Jury James Franklin Jas Clendening James Vinson Wm Bell Jas S Wilson Jas Lain William Neeley Moore Cotton Mark Rickmon David
p.431　Henry John Cathey John Tucker. Mistrial.
　Deed Jonathan Wallis to Richard Bradley 50 acres proved by Thomas Bradley.
　Matthew Moss who stands charged as father of an illegitimate child of Priscilla Bloodworth enters bond for maintenance of sd child with Ruffin Deloach and James Cryer securities and pays fine also the womans, amounting to fine $6.25.
　Appt Nathaniel Thompson overseer/road in place of Alexander Graham from Bledsoes crk to Ashers crk; Matthew Alexander esqr to furnish overseer list of hands.
　Order records of Registers office late in the possession of David Wilson late register be delivered to James Douglass present register.
　William Douglass Reuben Cage & Wilson Yandall exrs of William Hamilton dec v John Payton. Debt. Motion for new trial overruled. Dft obtains appeal to Superior Court, bond $500 with Nicholas Boyce & John C Hamilton securities.
　Hardy Bloodworth v Henry Morris. Nonsuit set aside and suit reinstated.
　John Wilcocks v Andrew Hoover. Debt. Oct 1803 plf by Redmond D Barry; dft by Thos Stuart. Mar 1804 jury Jas Bell Jno Gwin Griswold Latimer Jas Brigance Jas Orr Thos Howell Thos Willis Theophilus Allen Thos Dement David Dement Jno Payton Robt Trousdale. Dft recovers agt plf his full costs expended. Plf granted appeal to Superior
p.432　Court; bond $500, Wm Hankins John Wright & Theophilus Allen securities.

　Saturday March 24th. Present James Winchester Wm Trigg Matthew Alexander Esqrs.
　Redmond D Barry records his ear mark.
　Appt Peter Rogers [blank] Coplin & Jas Winters patrollers for Capt Sanders Company; they they are to qualify before James Sanders esquire.
　Hennen & Dickson v Thomas Edwards. Debt. Oct 1803 plf by Jno Dickinson; dft by Parry W Humphreys. Mar 1804 dft by atty confesses judgt $51.70 & costs.
　Andrew Moody v Thos Bradley. Appeal. Plf not appearing is nonsuited; reinstated.
　William Caffry v John Hazlet. Appeal. Dft by Thomas Stuart & Jno C Hamilton; plf not appearing is nonsuited. Dft recovers agt plf his costs.
　On motion of Redmond D Barry, order Jas Cryer Esqr Zacheus Wilson Jas Wilson Wm Snoddy Jas Franklin Jno Gardner Jas Desha Peter Looney Capt Charles Elliott Edward Sanders Jno Norris & Jeremiah Doxey ascertain damages sustained by Redmond D Barry John C Hamilton & John Payton by road from Gallatin to Gillespie's passing through their enclosures.
　Shadk Nye & Danl Ogelsby exrs will of Everard Garrett decd take oath to qualify.
　Edward Williams v John Josey. Debt. Plf by Jno C Hamilton; dft not appearing, plf recovers $141.87 & his costs.
　Robert Bates v William Douglass. Appeal. Apr 1803 plf by Geo Smith; dft by Jesse Wharton. Oct 1803 jury Jos Hodge James McMurry Wm Anderson Thos Howell Thos Edwards Jas Trousdale Peter Luna H Rhodam Rawlings Joshua Hadley Geo D Blackemore John Ham-
p.433　ilton Jno Mills found for plf $13. Mar 1804 motion for new trial overruled.
　Appt James Braken overseer/road in place of Howell Smith.
　Appt John Gwin overseer/road to Jas Brackens in place of John Moody.
　Elisha Prewitt v John Mitchell. Plf by Wm Smith; dft by Hutchins G Burton confesses judgt $157.74 & costs. Execution stayed nine months.

JUNE 1804

Isaac House v Edward Hogin. TAB. Writ amended by inserting "with force & arms."
Appt Thomas Kiefe overseer/road in place of William McCorcle with same hands.
Appt Jas Alexander Capt John Cloe Henry Warren & Levi Hughes patrollers for Capt Alexanders district; to qualify before Matthew Alexander esqr.
Appt James Vinson Capt Abraham Trigg Isaac Furman & George Brown patrollers for Capt Vinsons district; to qualify before William Trigg esquire.
State v David Ferrell. Dft not appearing, forfeits recognizance; sci fa issues.
State v John C Hamilton. Dft called to bring David Ferrell as he was bound to do by recognizance, but failing so to do, forfeits; scire facias issues.
Appt Thos Donnell & Wm Trigg esqr to settle with gdns for heirs of Henry Loving.
Court adjourns till Court in course.   J Winchester

p.434   Court of Pleas & Quarter sessions, Courthouse in Gallatin, third Monday in June. Present Jas Winchester Thos Donnell Wm Cage David Love Mattw Alexander Esqrs.
Grand Jury: Henry Bradford foreman Joseph Clark Thomas Edwards James Frazor James Robertson Elisha Pruett Kasper Mansker Jesse Joiner Henry Belote Jno Dugger Richard Hogin Isaac Lain Wallace Harris John Anderson Isreal Moore. David Allon constable.
Bill/sale Moses Echols to Henry Belote negro &c proved by Jeremiah Belote.
Bennet Henderson Esqr produced license to practice as attorney; admitted.
State v John Ruyle. TAB. Recognizance, Ezekiel Young to prosecute behalf state.
Inventory/goods of Robert Marshall decd proved by John Marshall an executor.
State v Jno Kennedy. TAB. Recognizance, Thomas Britton to prosecute behalf state.
Deed James Trousdale to David & Thomas Dement 2 acres 29 perches ackd.
Order Wm Seawell esqr furnish Terisha Turner overseer with list of hands.
Appt John Mills overseer/road to Tuckers crk; Wm Seawell to furnish list/hands.
Appt James Ball junr overseer/road Tuckers crk; Wm Seawell to furnish list/hands.
Deed James Kuykendall to James Winchester & William Cage 30 acres 133 perches proved by Joel Echols Junr.
Deed Robert Trousdale to David Dement lot 9 in Gallatin ackd.
Excuse Thomas Gregory from attending as a juror this term.
Deed Samuel Donelson Shadrack Nye & James Wilson to John Brigance lot 24 in Gallatin proved by John Lyon.
Deed Redmond D Barry to William P Anderson in trust for John Smith 1280 acres in two tracts ackd by sd Redmond D Barry.
Deed/gift Judah Bradley to Edward Bradley negro boy Zack proved by Wm Bradshaw.
Inventory/goods of Benjamin Roney decd proved by exrs.
Deed David Watson to Joseph Hodge lot 4 in Gallatin ackd.
John Stuard v Thomas Farmer. Debt. John Josey, security, surrenders dft.
Deed James Trousdale to David Watson 1 acre ackd.
p.435   John McConnell v John Cloar. Debt. Dft in proper person confesses judgt to plf $110 & interest & costs. Execution stayed six months by plf.
Deed Samuel Donelson Shadk Nye Jas Wilson commrs to David Watson lot 4 proved by Edmund Crutcher.
Grant ltrs/admn on estate of William Brigance decd to Elizabeth Brigance & James Brigance Jr; bond $2000, John Josey John Donoho John Brigance James Gamblin securities; took prescribed oath, rendered inventory & proved same.

JUNE 1804

Will of Alexander Anderson decd proved by James Brien; Pheby Anderson extx & Wm & Thomas Anderson exrs qualified by taking prescribed oath.

Grant ltrs/admn on estate of Hezekiah J Gardner decd to William Lauderdale & John Mills; bond $3000, Charles Donoho & Zachariah Green securities; took oath, rendered inventory, duly proved by William Lauderdale.

Deed Samuel Piper to George White 65 acres ackd.

Thomas Gregory records his ear mark.

Permit admx & admr of William Brigance to sell personal estate of decedant.

Permit admrs of Hezekiah J Gardner decd to sell personal estate of sd deceased except Negroes.

Deed Samuel Donelson Shadrack Nye James Wilson Charles Donoho commissioners to Wm Trigg lot 1 in Gallatin proved by James Cage.

Deed Wm Phipps Jr to Isaac Lean[Sean?] 25 acres proved by Wm Phipps Sr.

Deed Wm Lauderdale to David Killough 86 acres ackd.

Deed Daniel Taylor to Ralph Vienst 132 acres ackd.

Deed Commrs[above] to James Steele lot 10 in Gallatin proved by Will Trigg Junr.

Deed Wm Snoddy to Geo G Black 42¼ acres proved by Will Trigg Junr.

Deed William Robb Senr to Joseph Robb 245 acres proved by Robert Robb.

Inventory/goods of John Bunton decd proved by executors.

License Elisha Prewitt to keep ordinary at his dwelling house, bond $2500, George Smith & William Moore securities.

Deed/gift Daniel Smith to Mary Donelson the use of eight Negroes: Ike Anthony Hannah Sarah Jacque Agg Levi Tom proved by David Shelby.

p.436 Report of the jury apptd to lay off a road from Gallatin to Brown's ferry: begin at first cross street above Courthouse to Charles Lawrences, thence with old road to ferry. James S Wilson Jas Vinson Jas Wilson Jacob Houdeshalt Thomas Patton.

Codicil to will of Robert Marshall decd proved by Isreal Moore Sr & Isreal Moore Jr subscribing witnesses; will was proved at last term.

Petition of Stephen Stone, a tenant in coparcenary with other heirs of Henry Loving decd, namely Polly & Betsy Loving, praying partition of the land of the estate: 210 acres near Maj Wilson. Appt James Wilson S, James A Wilson, Alexander Graham, John Hamilton, and James Vinson a commission for the purpose; report to next Court.

Deposition of Henry Gambell taken by commrs appointed to ascertain boundaries of David Loves land on Bledsoes crk, & proceedings of sd commrs are ordered recorded.

Tuesday June 19th. Present Edward Douglass William Trigg Nicholas Boyce James Winchester Thomas Blackemore Chas Donoho James Douglass Ben Rawlings Edwd Gwin Thomas Donnell Archibald Marlin William Seawell James Hart Isaac Walton Witheral Latimer.

Deed Robert Hays to Kasper Mansker 180 acres proved by Thomas Harney.

Deed Wm Martin to Jas Winchester & Wm Cage Jr 440 acres proved by Jesse Cage.

Deed Patrick Garvey to James McKain 640 acres proved by Stephen Montgomery.

Deed Edmund Crutcher sheriff to John Motherall 440 acres ackd.

Bill/sale John Harrison to James Hart negro girl Doll proved by Francis Locke.

Deed Francis Locke to James Hart 160½ acres ackd.

Deed John Stroud to Marshall Stroud 640 acres authenticated by judicial proceeding of Superior Court of Hillsbrough district, North Carolina, & is admitted.

Acct/sales goods of Nathaniel Gilmer decd proved by executors.

Order Jas Wilson C, Joseph Motheral, Hugh Carothers, James Desha, John Weathers, Wm Gwin, and Joseph Bunton lay off a road intersecting Nashville to Lexington road

JUNE 1804

near James Brakens.
Appt William Dorris overseer/road from Drakes crk in place of Alexander McKee.
Deed William Roark to Adam Turner 107 acres ackd.
p.437   Appt Thomas Masten sheriff for two years, former sheriff having resigned; bond $12,500, James Sanders George Smith Kasper Mansker Henry Bradford securities.
Polley Hunt by her next friend John Hunt v Moses Tinsley. Controversy referred to award of William Seawell Esq James Harrison William Neely.
Inventory/goods of Alexander Anderson decd proved by Thomas Anderson one of exrs.
Supplement inventory/goods of Nathaniel Gilmer decd proved by executors.
Jurors to Superior Court: James S Wilson, James Vinson, Peter Looney H, Griswold Latimer, Zacheus Wilson son of David, & Jonathan Pearce.
Grant ltrs/admn on estate of John Wilson decd to James C Wilson & Joseph Steele; bond $2000 with James S Wilson security.
Robert Stothart v James Cage. Apr 1802 plf by Thomas Stuart; dft by John Overton. Mar 1804 jury David Henry John Cathey Mark Rickmon John Tucker James Franklin Moore Cotton William Bell Jas Vinson Jas S Wilson William Neely Jas Clendening James Lain assess plfs damages at $103.42. New trial granted. June 1804 jury Edwd Maxey Peter Simmons Jas Gamblin William King Alexr Kirkpatrick George D Blackemore Alexr Graham Jeremiah Doxey Jas Franklin Nathan Edwards Alexr Cathey Richard Alexander find dft not guilty. Dft recovers agt plf his costs. Plf obtains appeal to Superior Court; bond $500 with Thomas Stuart & William Smith securities.
Deed Thomas Willis to James Douglass 120 acres proved by Vines L Collins.
p.438   Taxes laid [omitted]
Deed James Trousdale to Samuel Donelson Shadrack Nye James Wilson (Curley) son of Samuel Wilson Charles Donoho Thomas Murry, commissioners in trust for the county of Sumner, ackd by James Trousdale for 42 acres including the Town of Gallatin.
Joseph McKean v David Love. Debt. Joseph McKain by Jno C Hamilton. Dft in proper person confesses judgt $59.20 debt 47¢ damages; plf to recover, also his costs.
Thomas Masten sheriff & collector of taxes enters bond $3000 with George Smith and James Sanders securities, and took the oath prescribed by law.
Thomas Masten sheriff & collector of taxes enters bond $2000 with George Smith Henry Bradford James Sanders & Kasper Mansker securities, and takes oath.
Cage & Black v Robert Moore. Att. Wm Moore, Dempsey Moore and Ruffin Deloach bail for deft replevies the property attached in said suit.
Joseph McKean v Robt Moore. Att. Wm Moore Dempsey Moore & Ruffin Deloach acknowledge themselves bail for dft & replevy property attached in sd suit.
Order Edward Hogin & John McWilliams confined in stocks for riotting in Court.
Jurors to Sept term: James Harrison Joel Echols William Beard Jas Weatherred Jno Hawkins Wm Bunton Richd King Jas A Wilson Robt Carothers James Simpson Jno Sloan Wm Carr Wm Orr Richd Jones Willis Whitfield Daniel Melton Richd Bradley Eliby Williams Goldsberry Sanders Abner Spring Henry Young Wm Bruce Francis Catron Jas McKey James Franklin Rhodam Rawlings Allen Purvis Wm Wier Michl Black Saml Smith John Dickinson David Crenshaw Geo Stubblefield Jas Odam Adam Hunter Charles Elliott Joseph Summers Boston Martin Joshua Hadley.
p.439   Champness Madding David Crenshaw Geo Stubblefield Wm Exum report they laid off a road from Wm Parrs house on Cumberland river to Harts mill on Goose creek.
Petition of Jas Winchester guardian to Isaac Bledsoe praying court order appointing commrs to divide 640 acres Bledsoe creek held by sd Isaac Bledsoe & his brother Lytle Bledsoe heirs of Anthony H Bledsoe decd. Order Matthew Alexander Esqr George D Blackmore William Neely James Reese Thomas Cocke apptd for purpose afsd.

JUNE 1804

William Betts v Drury Milam. Plf Betts by atty moves for judgt against Milam and his securities as constable.

Wednesday June 20th. Present Thomas Donnell Edward Gwin James Sanders Esquires.
Jno Hanks Jr v Heli Herring admr of Simon Totevine decd. Covt. Oct 1802 Jno Hanks by Jno C Hamilton. Simon Totevine sold to John Hanks 200 acres in Robertson County between Bartons creek & Johnsons crk beginning at Stephen Wards, corner north along Dicksons. Plf saith 200 acres were taken from plf by a prior right of [blank] Hick. Covt hath not been kept. Dft by Jesse Wharton. Jury Edward Maxey Peter Lemmons Wil-
p.440 liam King Jas Franklin Nathan Edwards Alexr Kirkpatrick Richd Alexander Hugh Carothers Edwd Cage Laurence Whitsitt Jas Hamilton Thomas Patton assess plfs damage $200 and his costs.

Deed Saml Donelson Shadrack Nye Jas Wilson Charles Donoho to Jno Barham lot 21 in Gallatin ackd by three last named commissioners.

Appt Wm Parr overseer/road from Parrs house to Harts mill; James Hart to furnish sd overseer with a list of hands to work on sd road.

Deed William King to Thomas Smith 148 acres proved by Samuel Piper.

Inventory/goods of Everard Garrett decd proved by executors.

Deed Griffith Rutherford to Griffith W Rutherford 320 acres ackd.

Thomas Gore v Reuben Searcy. Detinue. Searcy unjustily detains a Negro woman Nell price $350 & boy named Harry worth $250 and boy named Sam worth $200. Oct 1802 Thos Gore by Jno C Hamilton. Reuben Searcy by Thos Stuart. June 1804 jury[above except Alexander Cathey for Thomas Patton] find dft does detain negroes.

Commrs apptd to settle with admr of Simon Kuykendall decd report.

Deed James Trousdale to Ephrain Wells one acre ackd.
p.441 Patsey Weathers bound unto John Weathers until age eighteen.

State v Richard Hogan. TAB. Grand jury presentment. Richard Hogin, laborer, with force & arms beat & wounded John Dawson. Hogin pleads guilty; fined $5 and costs.

Order Wm Trigg & Jas Cryer esqrs complete settlement with admr of Simon Totevine.

Present Edwd Douglass Jas Hart Wm Seawell Wm Cage Jas Douglass Matthew Alexander Stephen Cantrill Will Trigg Benjamin Rawlings Archibald Marlin Esquires.

Tax laid [omitted].

Allow Clerk $40 for ex officio services from 1 July 1803 to 1 July 1804.

Allow sheriff $40 for ex officio services 1 July 1803 to 1 July 1804.

Order that the public buildings of Sumner--courthouse, prison, and stocks--be received from commissioners, pursuant to requisition of act of assembly.

Joseph McCravins commr/revenue renders alphabetical list of taxable property and polls for year 1804, to be entered of record by the Clerk of the Court.

Allow Susanna Todd payable out of the poor tax $30 for keeping orphan child Mourning Morrish for one year commencing 18th April last.

James McKain v Daniel Miles. Covt. Dfts bail surrender dft to custody of sheriff.

Order key of courthouse door lock be delivered to William Trigg esqr.

Commissioners allowed for services & expences in contracting for building of courthouse prison & stocks $352.25.

Joseph McCravins commr/revenue allowed $250 for services for present year.

Grand jury dismissed.

Joseph McKean v Wm Sanders. Debt. Dft in proper person confesses judgt $5.27½.
p.442 James Blackburn v Armstreat Stubblefield. Covt. April 1803 Blackburn by Wm Smith. Armstreat to sell 320 ac Roring Riv entered for heirs of Thomas Fenton where

JUNE 1804

James now lives, which deed Armstreat hath not made. Dft by John C Hamilton. Dft in proper person; plf dismisses suit agt dft who assumes costs.
State v John C Hamilton. Sci fa. Jan 1804 Hamilton entered recognizance $50 for appearance of David Ferrell at County Court; charge Petit larceny. David did not appear; recognizance forfeited. State recovers against John C Hamilton.

Thursday June 21st. Present Stephen Cantril James Sanders Matthew Alexander Esqrs.
Deed Elkam Echols & Joel Echols to James White & Saml Conn lot 92 in Cairo ackd.
State v John Rule. TAB. Appearance bond of Ezekiel Young, prosecutor.
p.443 James McKain v Daniel Miles. Covt. Adonijah Edwards bail for dft.
Account/sale goods of Wm Cochran decd proved by Wm Hubbart one of the executors.
David Pursley excused from attending as juror to present term.
Deed George D Blackmore to Richard M Hannum 100 acres ackd.
William Sample v John Trice. Appeal. Jury Alexr Graham Richard Alexander Wm King Hugh Carothers Jeremiah Doxey Alexr Kirkpatrick Alexr Cathey Edwd Maxey Edward Cage Nathan Edwards James Hamilton Peter Lemmon. Dft recovers agt plf his costs.
York v Pearce. TAB. Depositions of witnesses in Fayette County, Pennsylvania, to be taken, behalf of the plaintiff.
Deed Thomas Masten collector to Joshua Rice 640 acres ackd.
John Trice v George Michie. Certiorari. Dft in proper person confesses $10 and costs; plf recovers agt dft.
Present Edward Gwin Archibald Marlin & Will Trigg Esqrs.
John Trice v John Stuart. Slander. Jury George D Blackmore Richd Alexander James Gamblin Hugh Carothers Nathan Edwards Edwd Cage Peter Lemmon Edwd Maxey Alexr Kirkpatrick Jeremiah Doxey Jas Hamilton James Franklin; assess plfs damages to 1¢. New trial is granted to defendant.
John Trice v John Stuart. Slander. Thomas Kiefe, witness behalf dft, failed to appear; scire facias issues. John Stuart releases Thomas Kiefe from forfeiture.
Lemmuel Rogers v Benoni Hassel. Appeal. Plf in proper person dismisses suit each party pays half costs except attornies which is paid for plf.
Geo Michie v John Trice. Trespass. Oct 1803 Michie by John B Johnson: that Trice maliciously said George had run away from Virginia. Dft by Jno C Hamilton. Jun 1804 plf dismisses suit at dfts cost except plfs attorneys fee.

p.444 Friday June 22d. Present Thomas Donnell Isaac Walton William Trigg, Esqrs.
John Richmond v Redmond D Barry & Joseph Biggs. Trespass with force & arms. Oct 1803 Richmond by Jno C Hamilton: dfts illegally imprisoned plf for ten hours. Dfts by Thos Stuart. June 1804 jury: Jas Gamblin Alexr Kirkpatrick Jas Hamilton Wm King Edwd Cage Peter Lemmon Alexr Graham Edwd Maxey Lawrence Whitsitt Alexr Cathey Jeremiah Doxey James Franklin find dft not guilty. Dfts recover agt plf costs of suit.
William Hutchinson v Edward Gwin. Slander. Oct 1803 Hutchinson by John C Hamilton claims Gwin in hearing of worthy citizens said Hutchison "stole my bacon out of my boat & I can prove it." Dft by Redmond D Barry. June 1804 jury Richd Alexander Hugh Carothers Matthew Moss John Weathers Chedle Harris Thos Cocke Allen Purvis Anthony
p.445 Sharp Ezekiel Norman David Campbell William Snoddy Ambrose Porter say dft is not guilty. Dft recovers of plf his costs of suit.
Petition of William Winchester stating impracticability of performing covenants specified in indenture whereby orphan boy Moses Morrish was bound apprentice to sd

JUNE 1804

William to learn art of cabinet maker by reason of a defect of genius to acquire sd art. Release Wm Winchester from the obligation thereof. Bind sd Moses Morrish an apprentice to James Winchester to learn art of a miller.

James Hamilton is excused from attending as a juror for present term.

William Snoddy v Pleasant Chitwood. Trespass. Snoddy by Parry W Humphreys: July 1803 Chitwood with swords staves sticks & fists did beat wound & gauge Jim, a negro boy property of plf. Dft by Jno C Hamilton. Jury Jas Gamblin Alexander Graham Alexr Kirkpatrick Wm King Edwd Cage Peter Lemmon Jas Franklin Edward Maxey Lawrence Whitsitt Alexander Cathey Jeremiah Doxey Nathan Edwards find dft guilty. Plf recovers damages $500 & costs.

William Snoddy v Pleasant Chitwood. Trespass. Nicholas Boyce bail for the plf in place of Ambrose Porter who is released therefrom.

Anthony Sharp v George Parks. Sci Fa. Oct 1801 sci fa from David Shelby CSC Anthy Sharp recovered in suit agt Geo Parks $145.60 with costs; execution yet to be made. Thos Masten DS made sci fa known to dft April 1804. June 1804 Dft failed to appear; plf recovers.

p.446   Jonathan Hannum v Jesse Kuykendall. Sci. fa. Oct 1803 David Shelby C.S.C. to shff, judgt for Hannum agt Kuykendall yet unsatisfied. E Crutcher shff reports dft not found. Jun 1804 Dft not appearing, plf recovers; attached property to be sold.

John Mansker v Robt Moore. Deposition of James Hannah to be taken behalf plf.

James Gowen v Isaac Baker. TAB. Deposition of Thomas Elliott of Kentucky to be taken in behalf of the defendant.

Saturday June 23d. Present Edward Douglass Thomas Donnell John McMurtry Matthew Alexander William Trigg Esquires.

Deed John Barham to Isaac Turman lot 21 in Gallatin proved by Henry Lyon.

Authorise Thomas Donnell and William Trigg esquires to contract for enclosing a stray pen with post & rail fencing fifty feet square on public land in Gallatin.

Appt Robt Patton overseer/road Gallatin to Browns ferry to Capt Vinsons; James Winchester & Matthew Alexander to furnish sd overseer with lists of hands.

p.447   Appt James Campbell overseer from Capt Vinsons to Gallatin on road to Browns ferry; James Winchester & Matthew Alexander to furnish list of hands.

Daniel Smith v John H Bush & Joshua Hadley. Debt. Dfts attached to answer Daniel Smith assignee of Benjamin Rawlings $129.50 damage $30. Danl Smith by Thos Stuart. Dfts not appearing, plf recovers his debt, damage, and costs.

John Trice v John Stuart. Slander. New trial granted.

Appt Nathaniel Thompson overseer/road Indian Crk to Bledsoes Crk; Matthew Alexander Esquire to furnish sd overseer with a list of hands.

Deed Isaac Turman to Washington S Hannum lot 21 in Gallatin proved by Jas Desha.

Commrs apptd to settle with gdns of heirs of Henry Loving decd render settlement.

Samuel Donelson and others in Trust for Sumner County v Theophilus Allen and John Brigance. Debt. Dfts attached to answer Samuel Donelson Shadk Nye James Wilson Chas Donoho & Thos Murry commrs. Commrs by John C Hamilton. Dfts by Thomas Stuart. June p.448   1804 dfts not appearing, plfs recover with interest.

Order Wm Edwards Hugh Crawford Peter Looney H Richd King Joseph Motherall Isaac Lane Shadk Nye Richd Taylor Thos Patton Adam Hunter Jas Frazor Jas Wilson S jurors to assess damages sustained by John C Hamilton Redmond D Barry & Jno Payton by road from Gallatin to Gillespie's passing through their enclosures.

James Winchester James Cryer James Douglass Esqrs appear & take their seats.

JUNE 1804

Rescind order making allowance to commissioner/revenue, it being improper to make such allowance before he completes the business of his office.
Appt James C Wilson overseer/road in place of John C Hamilton resigned.
Present Edward Douglass Matthew Alexander & Will Trigg Esqrs.
James Turner & Mary Turner v Euridice Myers admx of Benjamin Myers decd. Apr 1803 petition of James & Mary Turner for distributive share of intestates estate against Euridice Myers admx Benjn Myers: Mary wife of Jas Turner daughter of Benjamin Myers & wife Euridice Myers; Benjn died 1796 leaving wife Euridice, son Humphrey Myers, p.449 dau Milley now married to Wright Barns, dau Betsy now married to Wm Phips, sons Thomas Myers & Miles Myers, & dau Patsey Myers. Oct 1797 Euridice made return of sales of sd estate to Court $1467.14 of which distributive share your petitioner is $183.39 2½ mills. J Winchester attorney in fact. Oct 1803 dft Euridice Myers answered: her husband died on his way from North Carolina to Tennessee; she was constrained to dispose of 40 weight of feathers and a cross cut saw for provisions for support of family; all money she expended was laid out protecting real estate of heirs for whom she was apptd guardian. The suit in equity was upon best advice and not until an ejectment had been brought to turn her out of possession. Euridice herXmark Myers. Test D Shelby. June 1804. Court orders plf recover agt dft $63.48½ p.450 their distributive share and their costs of suit in this behalf expended.
Appt Jas Trousdale Jr John Orr & George Brown patrolers in bounds of Capt Vinsons district; to qualify before James Winchester or William Trigg esquires.
John & Mary Woods v Robert C Atkinson. Cause continued. Depositions of Wm Douglass Wm Gillespie & Wm Duff are to be taken at house of Wm Gillespie behalf plfs.
Appt David Dennen & Jas Bracken overseers/road ridge to Kentucky line; Edwd Gwin to furnish list of hands and divide distance of sd road between overseers.
John Trice v George Michie. TAB. March 1804 John Trice by Jno C Hamilton: George did beat, wound and ill treat plf. Dft by Redmond D Barry. June 1804 plf dismisses suit at dfts costs.
Stogdal Wilson by Richard Wilson next friend v Alexander Eury. Jul 1803 Stogdal Wilson by Richd Wilson next friend writ agt Alexr Eury to Court at house of James Cryer in Gallatin. Stogdal under age 21 plea of trespass for slanderous words damaging to Stogdal Wilson. Dft not found. Judicial attachment levied by shff on 320 acres & one corn crib two cows two sows two feather beds; plf by Thos Stuart. p.451 Francis Eury claimed the property attached whereupon plf by atty denied property; judicial attachment awarded which was returned to this term by sheriff "no goods to be found but them that was attached by a former attachment." Plf by atty afsd dismisses suit on George Brown assuming costs which he now pays.
Court adjourns till Court in Course.   Edwd Douglass

p.452 Court of Pleas & Quarter Sessions, first Monday in September 1804. Present James Winchester, James Hart, & Matthew Alexander, Esquires.
Deed Thomas Murry to David Echols 20 acres proved by Abner Spring.
Deed Thomas Murry to Abner Spring 40 acres proved by David Echols.
Commrs apptd last term to divide 640 acres between Isaac M Bledsoe & Lytle Bledsoe tenants in coparceny report in writing their proceedings.
Thomas Donnell esqr deposits with Clerk 62½¢ the fine collected of Grandison

SEPTEMBER 1804

Catlet for profane swearing.
 James McElroy is excused from attending as a juror this term for reasons offered.
 Appt William Wherry overseer/road in place of James A Wilson from Cairo to above Major Wilsons.
 Deed James Winchester & Wm Cage Jr to George Brown Sr & George Brown Jr lot in Cairo proved by Jesse Cage.
 Grand jury: Joshua Hadley foreman, Abner Spring, Richd Jones, William Orr, James Weatherred, Eliby Williams, Richard King, Francis Catron, Richard Bradley, James A Wilson, Henry Young, George Stubblefield, Goldsberry Sanders, Jno Sloan, Jno Dickerson. Patrick Gibson constable sworn to attend them.
 Deed Isaac Philips to John Smith 274 acres proved by Moses Smith.
 Acct/sales goods of Hezekiah J Gardner decd proved by admrs.
 John Angel orphan age sixteen and upwards makes choice of Henry D Parmer for his guardian; bond $2000 with Jesse Hainey security.
 Deed Tilmon Dixon to Armstead Rogers 114 acres proved by William Rogers.
 William Williams orphan apprenticed to John Pewatt until apprentice arrives at full age.
 George Cummins v John C Henderson & William Henderson. John C Henderson & Wm Henderson attached to answer George Cummins on plea of Trespass. Jun 1804 George Cummins by Geo Smith; note not paid. Dfts by Bennet H Henderson pleaded payment & sett off. Sept 1804 Court orders cause dismissed on written order of plf. p.453
 Hugh Campbell v Nathaniel Parker Senr. Covt. Oct 1803 Hugh Campbell by Jno C Hamilton. Mar 1804 dft by Thomas Stuart. Sept 1804 plf dismisses suit; dft pays costs.
 Order Thomas Donnell & James Cryer esqrs to complete settlement made in part with admr of Simon Totevine decd.
 Deed Charles Carter to Nicholas Boyce 326 acres proved by Jacob Thompson.
 Deed John P Wiggins heir at law of Henry Wiggins to John McGuire 391½ acres proved by Shadrack Nye.
 Deed John Hall to James Harrison 150 acres ackd.
 Appt Dudley Pain overseer/road, Aaron Neels mill toward Nashville in place of Jos Cavett from Sharps crk to Maxwells crk; Witherall Latimer to furnish list of hands.
 Deed Thomas Crossner to John Mitchell 100 acres proved by Reuben Douglass.
 Deed Benjamin Rawlings to Reuben Douglass 100 acres proved by Wm H Douglass.
 State v James McKinsey. John Stringer dft bail surrenders sd dft to sheriff.
 George Logan v James Hunt. Cause referred to Jas Winchester Wm Seawell Jno Morgan James Clendening & William Neely. Their award to be judgment of the Court.
 Supplementary inventory goods of Hezekiah J Gardner decd proved by admrs.
 Inventory/goods of John Wilson decd rendered & proved by Jas C Wilson an admr.
 p.454 Andrew Moody v Thomas Bradley. Appl. Plf dismissed suit; plfs costs assumed by Edward Gwin in proper person.

Tuesday Sept 18th. Present Jas Winchester, Thomas Donnell, Matthew Alexander Esqrs.
 Will Trigg Jr v Wm Douglass. Covt. June 1804 Will Trigg Jr by Hutchings G Burton. Wm Douglass & John Lafferty to pay Will Trigg Junr in merchantable cotton to be dedelivered at either of the gins in Gallatin or at James or Edward Sanders gin; cotton not delivered. Dft by Jesse Wharton pleads covenant performed. Sep 1804 parties in proper person; plf dismissed suit; plf pays costs except dfts atty fee.
 Reuben Searcy v Eli Stalcup. Jun '04 Sci fa David Shelby clk. Shf Thos Masten notified Eli Stalcup. Sep 1804 dft in proper person; plf by Thos Stuart dismiss suit.

SEPTEMBER 1804

p.455　Deed James McKinsey to Jeremiah Mitchell 220 acres proved by Allen Purvis.
Deed Robert Hays to James Wornak 220 acres proved by William Orr.
Deed Anne Greer to Joseph Motherall 640 acres proved by John Dougan.
Deed/release Isaac George, Joseph George, Rebekah George, Jesse George to David George 100 acres ackd.
Present James Winchester Isaac Walton Matthew Alexander Esqrs.
Hardy Bloodworth v Henry Morris. Judicial attachment of Morris's property to answer Hardy Bloodworth assignee of Jas King on trespass. July 1803 Hardy Bloodworth by John Dickinson. June 1801 Henry contracted to build for James a house 16' x 20' of good hewn logs, two plank floors & two doors. Sd note assigned to Bloodworth for value recd. Henry did not build the house. J C Hamilton for dft. Mar 1804 nonsuit.
p.456　Oct 1803 nonsuit set aside. Sept 1804 jury Jas Harrison Joel Eckols William Beard John Hawkins Wm Bunton Jas Simpson Wm Karr Jas Franklin Rhodam Rawlings Allen Purvis Wm Wier Saml Smith assess plfs damages to $50. Plf recovers agt dft damages and costs of suit.
Deed/release Isaac George Rebekah George David George Jesse George to Joseph George 100 acres ackd.
Deed William Donnell to Hugh Kirkpatrick 220 acres proved by Wm McG[binding].
Deed/release Joseph George David George Rebekah George Jesse George to Isaac George 40 acres ackd.
Deed Samuel Donelson Shadrack Nye Jas Wilson Chas Donoho commissioners to Stephen Conger lot 20 in Gallatin proved by John C Hamilton.
Deed Robert Carothers to James Carothers 100 acres ackd.
Deed Robert Carothers to Hugh Carothers 100 acres ackd.
Deed William Gillespie to John Butler 196½ acres in Lincoln formerly but now Mercer County, Kentucky, proved by Redmond D Barry.
Will of Robert Motherall decd proved by John Dougan; Anne Greer extx named appeared in Court and qualified.
Deed William Dillard to Gabrael Dillard 100 acres proved by Wilson Cage.
John Trice v John Stuart. Stuart attached to answer Trice of plea of Trespass for slanderous words spoken to his damage. Jul 1803 Trice by Jno C Hamilton. Trice said Stuart "killed my steer & eat him." June 1804 Dft by Thomas Stuart. Jury George D
p.457　Blackmore Richd Alexander Jas Gamblin Hugh Carothers Nathan Edwards Edward Cage Peter Lemmon Edwd Maxey Alexander Kirkpatrick Jeremiah Doxey Jas Hamilton Jas Franklin find dft guilty. New trial granted. Sept 1804 jury Adam Hunter Jas Odam Boston Martin Jos Summers Wm Maxey Robert Laurence Cornelius Tinsley Zacheus Wilson James Wornak Lewis Crane John Barnes Abraham Hollingsworth say dft is not guilty; plfs motion for new trial overruled. Dft recovers agt plf his costs of suit.
Commrs apptd to divide real estate of Henry Loving decd between heirs report.
Appt Thos Donnell & John Morgan Esqrs to settle with admr of Moses Stuart decd.
Deed Ambrose Porter to William Phipps 26¼ acres proved by Isaac Lane.
Deed David Love to William Seawell 184 acres proved by Peter Fisher.
Deed David Love to Peter Fisher 186 acres proved by William Seawell.
Deed Patrick Gibson to Elias Morrison 124½ acres proved by James Winchester.
Daniel Smith assee v John Trice. Debt. Sept 1804 David Shelby CSC issued writ agt Trice, endorsed by Sheriff Thomas Masten. Dft confesses judgt $116 debt, $4.93 interest. Plf recovers; plf stays execution until first January next.
William Leech v Thomas Edwards. Debt. Scire facias issues agt dft to revive judgt heretofore obtained by sd plf agt sd dft.
Deed William Bradshaw to Alexander Youree 320 acres proved by Francis Youree.

SEPTEMBER 1804

p.458   Anthony Sharp Esqr commissioned in peace date 4 August 1804 under seal and hand of Gov John Sevier appears and takes oaths of office.

John Trice v John Stuart. Wm Sample summoned as witness behalf the dft failed to appear; scire facias issues. John Stuart discharges Sample from forfeiture.

State v James McKinsey. Dft bound to appear to answer breach of peace by threatening the life of his wife Patsey; Court discharged dft on his paying all costs.

Appt Thomas Howell overseer/road from Gallatin to Shelbys crk in place of Joshua Cherry; James Douglass esqr to funish overseer with a list of hands.

Appt William Crawford overseer/road from Shelbys crk to John Hassells in place of Thomas Howell; James Douglass esqr to furnish overseer with list of hands.

Supplementary inventory/goods of Robert Marshall decd proved by Wm Marshall exr.

Wednesday September 19th. Present Isaac Walton William Seawell Witherall Latimer John McMurtry Esqrs.

Deed Enos Hannah to James Sanders 250 acres proved by John Hutchings.

Deed Joseph Waller to James Sanders 104 acres proved by Robert Mitchell.

Deed James Houston to Richard Cope 640 acres proved by James Roney.

John Stuart Senr v Thomas Farmer. Debt. Edward Douglass & Joshua Hadley bail for dft in place of John Dawson former bail who is hereby released.

Grant ltrs/admn on estate of Samuel Donelson decd to Andrew Jackson; bond $10,000 with Jas Winchester Jas Sanders Wm Moore Jno Morgan securities; retd inventory.

State v John Kennedy. TAB. June 1804 Grand Jurors by Thomas Stuart present John Kennedy, gunsmith, at house of Thomas Brittan beat & wounded sd Brittan. Sept 1804 dft pleads guilty; fined $1 and costs.

p.459   Order admr of Samuel Donelson decd sell personal estate of decedant.

State v John Ruyle. TAB. June 1804 Ruyle indicted by grand jurors by Thos Stuart: Rule, yeoman, at house of Elisha Prewit beat and wounded Ezekiel Young. Dft pleads guilty; fined one cent and pay costs.

Appt Jeremiah Belote constable for Capt Alexanders militia company; bond $625 with Henky Belote & Joel Eckols securities, and took the oaths prescribed by law.

Appt Cornelius Tinsley constable for Capt Lanes militia company; bond $625 with Elmore Harris & Joshua Hadley securities, and took the oaths.

State v Isaac Pearce. Appearance bond to answer threatening life & person of John Young; dft discharged on his paying all costs.

State v Jesse Dawson. TAB. Dawson indicted: with swords staves sticks & fists did assault John Marlow. H G Burton C S. Dft pleads guilty; fined $1 & costs.

Allow coroner $7.25 for inquest on dead negro Dinah, property of Rhodam Rawlings.

Appt Jas Douglass & Thos Donnell Esqrs to settle with extrs of Hugh Elliott decd, also with guardian for heirs of Pearce Wall decd.

Appt John McMurtry coroner for two years; bond $2500, Wm Carr & Samuel Smith sec.

p.460   John & Mary Woods v Robert C Atkinson. Jul 1803 plfs by atty Redmond D Barry petition agt Atkinson; plfs entitled to distributive share/estate of Carlton Atkinson from admr. Carlton Atkinson died leaving daughters Elizabeth, Sarah, & Mary & one son the sd Robert. Elizabeth married Jno Gardner; Sarah married Thomas Anderson, Mary married petitioner Jno Wood. Jan 1801 Robert obtained ltrs/admn on estate of Carlton, retd inventory & acct/sales. Robert has not accounted for money & other goods. Jun 1804 dft by Thos Stuart. Sept 1804 dft states that debts due by Carlton p.461   amounted to more than his estate is able to pay; not yet paid and estate is exhausted; test David Shelby Clf. Parties in proper person. John Woods orders suit

SEPTEMBER 1804

agt dft dismissed; dft pays clerks & shffs fees.

Henry Lyon v John Trice. Case concerning a black horse traded from Trice to Lyon referred to determination of Nicholas Boyce John Morgan & Saml P Black. Arbitrators say horse of value $100. Plf recovers of dft $100 & costs.

Power/atty William Bowen to John H Bowen proved by Wm R Bowen & H Russell.

William Trigg v George Michie. Debt. David Shelby, Clerk, summons Michie. Dft in
p.462 proper person confesses judgt to plf $106. Plf stays execution nine months.

Jno Lafferty v Abraham Ellis. Trespass. Oct 1803 Jno Lafferty by Redmond D Barry: cause was referred to the award of Wm Montgomery Jno Garrott Wm Douglass Robt Davis award to plf $100, but dft has not paid. Dft by Jno C Hamilton. June 1804 jury: Jas
p.463 Harrison Joel Eckols William Beard William Bunton William Carr Rhodam Rawlings Wm Wier Samuel Smith Bosten Martin Jas Odam Joseph Summers Asa Hassell assess plfs damages to 8½¢. Plf recovers damages & costs.

Samuel Donelson & others commrs in trust for Sumner County v James Douglass & Wm Montgomery. Debt. Oct 1803 Commrs by John C Hamilton. Dft by Thos Stuart. Sep 1804 plfs, except Samuel Donelson decd, recover of dfts $140.26 & costs.

William Sample v Christopher Stubbins. Mar 1804 plf by Thos Stuart; dft by John C Hamilton. Suit submitted to determination of James McKain John Payton & Jno H Bush.
p.464 Verdict: Christopher indebted to William Sample $51. And costs.

Betsey Turner bound to Euridice Miers to age eighteen.

License Robert B Mitchell to keep tavern at his dwelling in Gallatin, bond $2500, Will Trigg security.

Katy Bledsoe Senr v Henry Warren Levi Hughes & John Gibson. Trespass with force & arms. Plf by John C Hamilton and by directions of Isaac Bledsoe to her atty, suit is by him dismissed. Plf pays costs of suit.

Thursday 20th September. Present Edward Douglass, Matthew Alexander, Anthony Sharp.

Order Isham Uzal oversee/road to Elisha Cheeks in place of David Campbell.

John Young v John W Crunk. Appeal. Debt under $10. Judgt by James Sanders Esqr for plf $5.35 debt 75¢ costs. Dft appealed giving Andrew Hoover for security. Sept 1804 parties in proper person; plf dismisses suit; dft assumes costs except plfs atty.

Grant ltrs/admn on estate of George Seawell decd to Joseph Seawell; bond $1000 with Wm Seawell security & took oath.

Deed Manoah Taylor to Jacob Bernard 316 acres proved by Elisha Bernard.

Deed Richard Hogin to Matthew Moss 66 acres ackd.

Allow Archibald Donoho $43 for enclosing stray pen in Gallatin.

Allow Wm Rice $166 & ¼¢, two thirds appraisement of stray yearling bull taken up by John Hogin & proved to be property of sd Rice.
p.465 Stephen Mitchell bound apprentice to Thomas Moss to learn art & mystery of a wheelwright.

Deed Thomas Waller to Enos Hannah 100 acres proved by Vachel Stephens.

Ltr/atty Peter Moseley to Edward Sanders to transact business in Virginia proved by James Sanders a subscribing witness.

Jurors to next term: Wm Anderson carp, Andrew Blythe, Robert Robb, Jno Hamilton, Eli Giles, Richd Cavitt, John Biggs, Thomas Moss, Thomas Groves Sr, Albert Hendrix, Cader Hunter, Wm Harper, Richard Carr, John Trousdale, John Thurman, Albert Holmes, Smith Hansbrough, George Smith, Robt Davis, Thomas Joiner, Wm Montgomery Jr, Philip Kiser, Peter Looney H, George Gillespie, Isaac George, John Gardner, Wm Anderson B, Robt Desha, Joseph Wallace, Jas Rankin, Thos Murry, John Shaver, Champness Madding,

SEPTEMBER 1804

Jas Graham, Daniel McConnell, Wm Snoddy, Thomas Kiefe, Joseph McElwrath, David Orr.
James Gowen v Isaac Baker. TAB. Jury Wm Bunton Boston Martin Saml Smith Wm Wier Jos Summers Jas S Wilson Wm McCall Wm Carr Joel Eckols Wm Beard Allon Purvis David Campbell. Mistrial.

Friday September 21st. Present Edward Douglass Thomas Donnell James Sanders Esqrs.
Henry Bradford v Richard A Odin. Debt. Sheriff levied on two old coats four pair overalls pair legings. Plf by Jesse Wharton. Dft not appearing, judgt agt dft for $88.40 with interest & costs.
p.466   Winchester & Cage v Benjamin Morgan. Sheriff levied on two waistcoats 1 pr overalls and dfts share of 320 acres on Bledsoes creek. Plfs by Jesse Wharton. Dft came not. Attached property to be sold.
Winchester & Cage v Henry Harrison. Dft not appearing, judgt by default. Court of inquiry next term to be executed.
Appt John C Hamilton & Washington L[S?] Hannum inspectors of election to be held in November for president & vice president.
Peter Bennett v Reuben Searcy. Debt. Dft replevies property levied on by giving Elisha Cheek bail in sd suit.
Joseph McKean v Benjamin Morgan. McKean obtained judgment before a single justice agt Morgan for $43.25. No personal property found; levied on Morgan's undivided share of 320 acres on Bledsoes crk; order sheriff to sell for use of judgment.
p.367   Giles Cook v Elisha Cheek. Jun 1804 Giles by Jno C Hamilton: Oct 1802 Cheek owed Giles $95 for teaching school 10 months at Elisha's request, who would furnish Giles with boarding during the term. Giles taught for ten months. Cheek by Parry W Humphreys. Jury Boston Martin, Saml Smith, Jas Odam, Rhodam Rawlings, Jos Summers, Jas Smothers, Wm Beard, Wm Wier, Wm Bunton, Jas Harrison, Joel Eckols, Allen Purvis find for dft. Dft recovers agt plf his costs of defense.
Order James Cryer esqr furnish Thomas Kiefe, overseer, with list of hands to work that part of the road for which sd Kiefe was appointed overseer.
Samuel Donelson Shadk Nye Jas Wilson Chas Donoho Thomas Murry commrs in trust for Sumner County v John Brigance & Theophilus Allen. Oct 1803 plfs by Jno C Hamilton: Dfts owe $60 and damage $50. Dfts by Thomas Stuart pleaded payment. Saml Donelson's
p.468   death suggested. Dfts confess judgt; interest amounts to $65.98.
Saml Donelson & others commrs v Joseph Phipps & David Allen. Debt. Plfs by John C Hamilton, Mar 1804: dfts owe $48 since Oct 1802. Jun 1804 dfts by Redmond D Barry. Plfs confess judgment; plaintiffs recover agt dfts debt, interest and costs.
p.469   Power/atty Effy Curry to William Marshall to transact business in South Carolina acknowledged by sd Effi Curry.
Jackson & Hutchings v James McKinsey. Debt. Mar 1804 plfs by Jno C Hamilton. Dft by Redmond D Barry confesses judgt. Plf recovers debt & interest $106.42½ & costs.
Joseph Neely assee v Jas Lauderdale. Jos Neely assignee of Roger Gibson. Mar 1804
p.470   Plf by John C Hamilton. Dft by Thomas Stuart saith on 26 Apr 1803 he paid Roger Gibson the whole sum. Dft confesses judgt; plf recovers $86.99 & costs.
John Hutchings v Thos Barrott. Covt. Mar 1804 plf by Jno C Hamilton; Barrott owes $110 to be paid in good cotton at market price. Jun 1804 Dft by Jno B Johnson. Sept 1804 dft confesses judgt; plf recovers $113.06 & costs of suit.
Allen Purvis impannelled in cause Jas Gowen agt Isaac Baker fined $5 for being absent after the hour of adjournment to this day in contempt of court.
p.471   Jackson & Hutchings v John C Henderson. Jun 1804 plf by Jno C Hamilton. Dft

SEPTEMBER 1804

by Bennet H Henderson acknowledges plfs actions. Plfs recover $103.70¼ & costs.

Jas Watwood v Burwell Thompson. Debt. Jun 1804 Watwood by Jno C Hamilton: Thompp.472 son with Saml Thompson entered debt but have not paid. Dft by Jno H Bowen. Sep 1804 dft confesseth judgment. Plf recovers $128.12 & costs.

Saml Donelson Shadk Nye Jas Wilson Chas Donoho Thos Murry others commrs v George Cummins. Oct 1803 commrs by Jno C Hamilton. Dft by Parry W Humphreys. Sep 1804 dft confesseth judgment; plfs recover $83.56 & costs.

Martin H Wickliff assee of Stothart & Bell v Reuben Searcy. Debt. Mar 1804 plf by p.473 Washington L Hannum. Dft by Thos Stuart. Sep 1804 dft confesseth; plaintiff recovers $128.69 and his costs of suit.

Richard Rapier v James Steele. Debt. Mar 1804 Plf by Thos Stuart. Dft by Parry W Humphreys. Sept 1804 plf recovers $55.98 and his costs of suit.

p.474 Samuel Gregg v William Rice & Peter Looney. Debt. Mar 1804 Gregg by Jno C Hamilton. Dfts by [blank] Wharton. Plf recovers $110.47 & costs.

Samuel Gregg v Wm Rice & Peter Looney. Debt. Mar 1804 Gregg by John C Hamilton. p.475 Dft by Wharton. Sep 1804 plf recovers $375.30 and his costs.

Hardy Bloodworth v John Looney. Sci Fa issued by David Shelby CSC Mar 1804. Shff Lee Sullivan returned "not found but the defendant is said to be gone to the Illinois." Plf by Jesse Wharton; dft in proper person. Sept 1804 plf dismissed suit; defendant assumes payment of costs.

Bustart & Easton v Alambee Williams. Debt. Jun 1804 plfs by Jno Dickinson. Dft by p.476 Redmond D Barry. Plfs recover $56.02 & costs.

John Hoover v William Hankins. Debt. Jun 1804 Jno Hoover by Thomas Stuart. Dft by Redmond D Barry. Plf recovers $79.81 & his costs of suit.

Joseph McKean v Robert Trousdale. Debt. June 1804 plf by John C Hamilton. Dft by p.477 Hutchings G Burton. Sep 1804 plf recovers of dft $61.94 & costs.

William Maxey & James Douglass guardians to the heirs of Henry Loving decd v John Josy & Henry Vinson. Debt. June 1804 plfs by Jno C Hamilton. Dfts by Redmond D Barry. Sept 1804 plf recovers $91.62 & their costs of suit.

James Roney v Isaac Bledsoe. Debt. Jun 1804 plf by Jno C Hamilton: dft with Benjamin Morgan signed obligation. Dft by Thos Stuart. Plf recovers $145.60 & costs.

p.478 Allen Hill assee of Thos Watson v John Mitchell. Debt. Jun 1804 plf by Jesse Wharton. Dft by Hutchings G Burton. Plf recovers agt dft $287.35 & costs.

Josiah Wells v James McKain. Debt. Jun 1804 plf by John C Hamilton. Dft by John H p.479 Bowen. Plf recovers agt dft $69.90 & costs.

Cage & Black v Robert Moore. Jun 1804 plfs obtained attachment agt estate of Robt Moore; shff levied on two stud horses and town lot. Property replevied by Wm Moore Dempsey Moore & Ruffin Deloach bail for dft; dft by Hutchings G Burton. Sept 1804 plaintiffs recover agt dft their debt $116.42 & costs of suit.

James D Reeves by next friend Joseph Reeves v Josephus H Conn. TAB. Jas D Reeves under age 21 by John B Johnson: dft beat James so that his life was despaired of. Dft in proper person. Plf orders suit dismissed at dfts cost.

p.480 Absalom Richardson v James McKain. Debt. Mar 1804 plf by R D Barry. Dft by Jno C Hamilton. Plf recovers agt dft $58.48 & his costs of suit.

James Steele v James Perry. Debt. Plf obtained attachment agt Jas Perry's estate; Constable Patrick Gibson levied on chest, joiners tools, wearing apparel. Plf by P W Humphreys: Jas Perry & John H Bush have not paid obligation. Jas Perry came not; plf recovers agt dft $58.50 and his costs of suit.

p.481 Jackson & Hutchings v Thomas Barrott. Debt. Mar 1804 plf by Jno C Hamilton. Dft by Jno B Johnson. Plf recovers agt dft $224.78½ and costs of suit.

DECEMBER 1804

Ezekiel Young v John Ruyle. TAB. Plf in proper person dismisses suit; defendant agrees to pay costs.

Saturday September 22d. Present Thomas Donnell James Cryer James Sanders, Esqrs.
James McKain v Daniel Miles. Award set aside, suit to be tried at next term.
Order Clerk issue executions behalf State in every cause where judgment has been given for or in behalf of the State against any defendant or defendants.
Abner Gilmer son of Nathl Gilmer decd chose George D Blackemore for his guardian; bond $500 with Thomas Parker security.
p.482 Joseph McKean v Edward Kelly. Plf obtained two judgments before single magistrate; officer levied on dfts share of crop of corn & cotton now growing on David Allen's farm; crop condemned for use of judgment.
Allow David Shelby $6.66¾, the value of yearling property of Shelby taken up as a stray by Henry Bloodworth.
Court adjourned.   Jas Sanders

p.483   Court of Pleas & Quarter Sessions, third Monday in December 1804. Present James Winchester Isaac Walton John Morgan Matthew Alexander Esquires.
Shadrack Nye Samuel Donelson James Wilson Charles Donoho Thomas Murry commrs in trust for Sumner County v George Smith. Plfs dismiss suit; dft by Thomas Masten agrees to pay costs.
John Marlow v Jesse Dawson. TAB. Sep 1804 Marlow by Jno C Hamilton: Jesse beat wounded & ill treated Marlow. Dft by Redmond D Barry. Dec 1804 parties in proper person; plf dismissed suit; dft assumes costs.
William Reeves by next friend Edmund Reeves v Andw Philips. TAB. Wm Reeves under age 21 by John B Johnson. Dft in proper person. Plf dismissed suit at dfts cost.
Grand Jury: Richd Cavitt foreman Joseph McElwrath John Biggs Eli Giles John Gardner Thomas Groves Senr Peter Looney H William Anderson James Rankins John Hamilton Joseph Wallace Albert Hendrix David Orr Thos Kiefe Wm Harper. Wm Rice constable.
Deed Joseph Neely to Richard M Hannum 259 acres ackd.
p.484   Deed Wm McCorcle to James Trousdale 120 acres proved by Robert Trousdale.
Deed Archibald White to James White 90 acres proved by John Lauton.
Deed James Trousdale to John Tompkins one acre ackd.
Grant Ltrs/admn on estate of Ephraim Wells decd to Joseph Hodge; bond $500 with Richd King security. Admr rendered inventory. Sale of personal estate permitted.
Benjamin Foreman v Robert Combs. Debt. Combs owes £90.6 North Carolina money, value $180.60. Plf by attorney Hutchings G Burton dismisses suit, pays costs.
Grant ltrs/admn on estate of Bryant Gardner decd to Isaac Walton & John Gardner; bond $5000, James McKain & Lewis Crane securities; returned inventory.
Order admrs of Bryant Gardner decd sell personal estate except Negroes.
Grant ltrs/admn on estate of Stephen Herd decd to James L[S?] Armstrong; bond $500 with Thomas Watson & Robert B Mitchell securities.
Appt John Rork overseer/road from Bledsoes lick to flat gap; James Winchester Esqr to furnish him with a list of hands.
Will of William Brown decd proved by Elisha Cheek; Arthur Exum one of executors

DECEMBER 1804

qualified as such.
  Deed James Winchester to Jesse Hainey & James White Junr 20 acres ackd.
  Deed Tilmon Dixon to John Moore 300 acres proved by James Sanders.
  Deed Wm L[S?] Alexander to Richard Alexander 320 acres proved by Redmond D Barry.
  Deed William Morrison to William Reed 450 acres proved by William Duty.
  p.485 Bill/sale Charles Rork to William Mann household furniture farm implements horse cow hogs ackd by sd Charles Rork.
  Bill/sale Charles Rork to Barnet Rork copper still & worm ackd.
  Deed Jacob Slinkard to Alexander Cathey 2nd 63 acres proved by William Cathey.
  John Harmon v Elisha Myers & Christly Catron. Debt. Former bail for Elisha Myers surrenders him; Myers brings Solomon Sholders, acknowledges himself special bail.
  John Cathey v Andy Hamilton. Debt. Oct 1804 E Crutcher DS levied on 160 acres. Plf by John C Hamilton; dft by Jas Hart. Plf dismisses suit; dft to pay costs.
  Champness Madding v Henry Harrison & Robert White. Debt. Plf in proper person dismisses suit; plaintiff pays costs of sd suit.
  James Brown & Alexander Brown orphans of William Brown decd chose Arthur Exum for their guardian. Order Arthur Exum gdn for James & Alexr Brown as for John & William Brown brothers & minor orphans of sd decedant. Bond $2000, Thomas Murry security.
  Appt Lazarus Cotton constable for Capt Edward Bradleys militia company district; bond $625 with James Graham & George G Black securities.
  Appt Isaac Pearce constable for Capt Sanders militia company district; bond $625 with John Kennedy & Laurence Whitsitt securities.
  p.486 Nathaniel W Williams Esq having produced license to practice as atty at law certified by Clerk of Mero Dist Court, takes oaths and is admitted in this court.
  Thomas Hobdy v William Ogles. Thomas Hobdy obtained two judgments and executions before magistrate Edward Gwin. Order condemned land be sold to satisfy judgments.
  John Willbanks v William Ogels. Plf obtained judgt & execution from magistrate Edward Gwin. Order condemned land sold to satisfy judgment.
  Deed Isaac M Bledsoe to William Cage Junr 320 acres proved by Joseph Neely.
  Deed James Winchester to John Morgan for undivided half 154 acres ackd by sd Jas.
  Order Charles Donoho & James Hart esqrs complete the settlement made in part with admrs of estate of William S Carson decd.
  Appt John Shaver overseer/road from Bledsoes Lick to Rockey Creek; Thomas Blackemore Esqr to furnish sd overseer with a list of hands.
  Appt Jesse Hainey overseer/road Rockey creek to Second Creek; Thomas Blackemore to furnish sd overseer with a list of hands.

Tuesday December 18th 1804. Present Isaac Walton Charles Donoho & Witheral Latimer.
  Deed Francis Sanders to Launsford Pitts 200 acres proved by James Sanders.
  Deed Robert Trousdale to John Pankey lot 10 in Gallatin proved by James Brown.
  Grant ltrs/admn on estate of Elizabeth Kennedy decd to John Cathey; bond $1000 with James A Wilson & Joseph Sloan securities.
  p.487 Acct/sales goods of William Brigance decd proved by James Brigance admr.
  Deed James Hunt to George Logan 111 acres ackd.
  Deed Thomas Masten Collector/direct Tax to Jesse Wharton & Henry Bradford 640 acres ackd by sd Masten.
  George Logan v James Hunt. Covt. Both in proper person; plf dismisses his suit; plf pays costs of sd suit.
  Addl inventory/goods of George Summeral decd proved by Nathaniel Thompson admr.

DECEMBER 1804

Order Robert White & Robert F N Smith esqrs be admitted as attornies.

Bill/sale Francis Cornpery[Compery?] to Thomas Keife household furniture farming tools & stock proved by John Bond; also assignment from Keife to George Humphreys also proved by sd John Bond.

Deed Shadrack Nye Jas Wilson & Chas Donoho commrs in trust for Sumner County to Isaac Lain lot 8 in Gallatin ackd by sd commissioners.

Deed Peter Looney to Joseph Scoby 61½ acres ackd by sd Peter.

Deed David Brigance to Joseph Scoby 40 acres proved by James Strother.

Samuel K Blythe v Robert Moore. Att. Dempsey Moore & Reuben Searcy special bail for deft replevy attached property.

Reuben Searcy summoned as garnishee upon an execution agt Giles Cook v Elisha Cheek for costs of a suit. Searcy indebted to Cook $15; exn issues agt him.

Bill/sale James Bentley to Wm Bradshaw negro man Cherry proved by John Reed.

Stephen Wilson orphan of John Wilson decd chose James S Wilson for guardian; bond $500 with Thomas Patton security.

Bond Will Sanders to John Brigance to convey by deed in fee simple 114 acres being half of 228 acres originally granted to John Marsh proved by David Shelby.

p.488 Deed David Love to Littleton Duty 200 acres ackd.

Henry Bradford v Samuel Caldwell & Elizabeth McReynolds admrs of Robt McReynolds deceased. James C Wilson garnishee says he has $5.25, owes to admr of Robt McReynolds at least $200 whenever monies due from sale/lots in Gallatin are paid.

Henry Bradford v Richard A Odin. Att. Property whereon attachment levied-- 2 old coats four pair overalls pr of legings-- condemned to be sold for use of judgment.

Petter Bennett v Reuben Searcy. Att. Elisha Cheek bail for replevying attached property surrenders defendant; Smith Hansbrough special bail for dft.

William Trigg assee of Christopher Stubbins v Edmund Collins. Plf obtained judgt; house & lot condemned for use of judgt; to be sold.

Deed Anthony Garnes to William Crawford 48 acres proved by James Brigance.

Deed Reuben Cage late sheriff to William Bruce 70 acres ackd.

Deed Thomas Hickmon to William Bruce 21 acres proved by Thomas Stuart.

Deed Shadrack Nye Jas C Wilson Chas Donoho commrs in trust for Sumner County to Andrew Jackson & John Hutchings lot 5 in Gallatin proved by Edwd Roberts.

John Giles records his ear mark.

Deed Samuel Donelson Shadk Nye Jas Wilson Chas Donoho commrs in trust for Sumner County to George D Blackmore lots 4 & 14 in Gallatin ackd.

Order Griffith Rutherford Thos Patton & Jno Hamilton appraise personal estate of John Wilson decd & divide same amongst heirs.

Supplementary inventory estate of Saml Donelson decd; acct/sales proved by admr.

Bill/sale David Love to William Bradshaw negro girl Ann ackd by sd David.

Order Isaac Donoho orphan boy bound apprentice to James Simpson to learn art or mystery of tanning & currying leather.

p.489 Asa Hassell reputed father of illegitimate child of which Sarah Cougher is now pregnant enters bond $500 for maintenance of sd child, Jesse Hassell security; also pays fine $3.12½ and sd Sarah Coughers fine $3.12½ to Clerk of Court.

Jurors to Superior Court: Thomas Perry William Snoddy James Lauderdale Sr George Stubblefield John McMurry William Axum.

Jurors to next County Court: Jeremiah Mitchell James Vinson David Stuart William Sanders Thomas Anderson Frederick Miller Allen Purvis Thos Britton Adam Hunter Jas McDowell James Braken Senr Samuel C Gipson King Carr Abel Brannen Isaac Baker John McKee John Payton Thomas Parker John Sterns Jesse Johnson James Clendening William

DECEMBER 1804

Edwards Josiah Giles Jas Hunt Robert Gutrey Robt Hamilton Jno Bowman Elisha Prewitt Hallery Malone David Beard William Bunton James Brown James Johnson Robert Taylor Christopher Catron William Frazor William McClure Joshua Bradley James Mecklin.
 Moses King by Thomas King next friend v James Asbey. Sep 1804 plf by John C Hamilton. Asby found King's horses and though requested hath not delived horses to sd Moses. Dft by Thos Stuart. Dec 1804 parties in proper person; Thomas King dismissed suit and agrees to pay costs.

Wednesday Dec 19. Present Jas Winchester Isaac Walton Witheral Latimer Wm Seawell.
 Deed John C Hamilton to Jenkin Whiteside lot 8 in Gallatin ackd.
 Deed Zaddock Bernard to Jacob Bernard 320 acres ackd.
 p.490   State v David Ferrell. March 1804 recognizance of David Ferrell before James Cryer Esqr, charge petit larceny. David came not; David Shelby CSC orders sheriff summon David. Sept 1804 alias scire facias issued. Sd David now called & not appearing, State recovers agt sd David Ferrell.
 James Gowen v Isaac Baker. TAB. March 1804 James Gowen by John C Hamilton. Isaac with force & arms imprisoned James 15 days. Dft by W L Hannum: plf a slave who is incapacitated by law from bringing suit. Plf by Hamilton: plf is not nor has been a p.491   slave. Sept 1804 jury made mistrial. Dec jury: Andw Blythe Richd Carr Robt Robb Thos Joiner Geo Gillespie Isaac George William Bruce Wm Snoddy Jas Graham John Shaver Smith Hansbrough Jas A Wilson say plf is a free man; assess plfs damage 6½¢.
 Winchester & Cage v Robert Hall. Attachment. James Winchester one of plfs orders their suit dismissed & agrees to pay cost of suit.
 Inventory/goods of Stephen Herd decd rendered by Hutchings G Burton.
 Grant leave to admr to sell personal estate of Stephen Herd.
 Deed George Brown to James Winchester & Wm Cage 5 acres proved by Richard Brown.
 John Ziegler orphan boy bound apprentice to Thomas Shackleford to learn trade of bricklaying.
 Appt John W Crunk constable for Capt Whitsitts militia company district; bond $625 with Elisha Prewitt & Nicholas Boyce securities.
 John Withers v George G Black. Withers says Black with force & arms assaulted beat and got with child Betty Withers daughter of sd John Withers an infant and servant of sd John Withers, whereby sd John lost the service of sd Betty. Plf dismissed suit; dft pays all costs.
 Deed James Trousdale to John Stamps 120 acres ackd.
 p.492   Henry D Allen v Corban Hall. Trespass. Sept 1804 plf by Jno C Hamilton: Aug 1803 plf swapd horses with Corban but horse plf received was unsound. Dft by Thomas Stuart. Dec 1804 parties in proper person; plf dismissed suit at dfts costs.

Thursday Dec 20th. Present Edward Douglass Thomas Blackemore John McMurtry Esqrs.
 Deed John C Hamilton to McNutt Findley & Co lots 2 & 12 in Gallatin ackd.
 Polley Hunt by next friend John Hunt v Moses Tinsley. Deposition of Wm Giles of Cairo to be taken in behalf of the petitioner.
 Moses Tinsley v Polley Hunt. Deposition of William Giles of Cairo to be taken on behalf of the defendant.
 Joseph McKean v Robert Moore. Attachment. May 1804 E Crutcher Shff levied on stud p.493   horse. Was L Hannum atty for plf. Attached property replevied by Wm Moore Demsey Moore and Ruffin Deloach bail for dft; dft by Jno C Hamilton. Dec 1804 jury

DECEMBER 1804

Andw Blythe Richd Carr Thos Joiner Robt Robb Geo Gillespie Wm Snoddy Jas Graham Jno Shaver Smith Hansbrough Isaac George Jno Harrison Robert Laurence. Plf recovers agt dft $189.94; execution stayed till 20th March next.

Release Henry Box from two thirds of the appraisement of cow and calf taken up as strays by sd Henry, appraised to six dollars.

James Douglass esqr deposited 31¼¢, fine of James Blackemore for profane swearing collected on a presentment of the Grand Jury.

Permit Thomas Blackemore to build a mill on Rockey Creek on 250 acres Blackemore purchased of James White, where south boundary of said land crosses said creek.

Edward Douglass Esqr deposited 31¼¢, fine of John Burrow for profane swearing collected on a presentment of the Grand Jury.

State v William Ogels. Dft bound in recognizance before Edward Douglass Esqr; stands charged with breaking custody, also with killing and abusing the stock of
p.494   Aaron Butler. Sd William appeared; no prosecutor. Dft discharged.

David Love v John Payton. Trespass. Oct 1803 Love by Redmond D Barry. Dft by John C Hamilton. Dec 1804 jury[above]. Plf recovers damages $120 and costs. Dft obtains appeal to Superior Court, bond $500, John C Hamilton & Robert Laurence securities.

Henry Fuller v John W Crunk. Fuller obtained judgt before Benjn Rawlings Esqr agt John W Crunk for $4.86 & costs. Wm Montgomery & Jno McMurtry justices ordered Clerk
p.495   to issue writs. Sept 1804 Edward Douglass & Joshua Hadley arbitrators. Dec 1804 judgt set aside. Jury[above] find Crunk indebted.

Friday Decr 21st. Present Edwd Douglass Thos Blackemore Thos Donnell James Sanders.

Cage & Black assees v Edmund Collins. James Cage & Samuel P Black trading as Cage & Black as assignees of Isaac Hogin, obtained exn agt Edmund Collins for $47.50 and costs. Levied on land where Collins lives in Gallatin on northwest square fronting Jackson & Hutchings gin. House & land condemned for use of judgt, to be sold.

Thomas Cribbins v John Jones & Edward Jones. Trespass. June 1804 Cribbins by Redmond D Barry says Joneses complained agt plf to Jas Sanders Esqr who issued warrant causing plfs arrest & confinement for 6 days, cost $100 to get himself discharged.
p.496   Dfts by Wm Smith. Dec 1804 jury[above except Thos Edwards Sr & Thos Edwards Jr for Thos Joiner & Wm Snoddy] assess plfs damages to $40 & costs.

George Harrison v Terisha Turner. Deposition of John Bird of Logan County, Kentucky, to be taken on behalf of the plaintiff.

Mary Benthall by next friend James Cryer v Robert Patton. TAB. March 1804 plf by Jno C Hamilton. Decr 1804 dft by Redmond D Barry. Jury[above] find dft guilty of trespass, assault, & battery, assess plfs damages to 12½¢. Dft files for arrest of judgment: 1st, after issue joined, plf Mary Benthal married Webb Bloodworth. 2nd, Court cannot render judgt in consequence of coverture. 3d dft liable again. Reasons insufficient, and plf recovers against dft her damages afsd and her costs of suit.

Deed James Sanders to John Turner 300 acres ackd.
p.497   Deed of Elisha Deford for manumission of negro man Matthew, certified copy from Queen Ann's County, Maryland, admitted to record.

Deed Allen Jones to Josiah Payne 533½ acres proved by Arthur Turner.

John C Henderson v Andrew Jackson. TAB. Anthony Winston Sr summoned as witness behalf plf not appearing, Henderson recovers agt Winston; scire facias issues.

John C Henderson v Andrew Jackson. TAB. March 1804 Henderson by John C Hamilton. Jackson, a judge of Superior Court, on 13 Feb 1804 beat, wounded & ill treated plf. Dft by Thos Stuart & Jesse Wharton. Dec 1804 jury Geo Gillespie Andw Blythe Robert

DECEMBER 1804

Robb Richd Carr Jno Shaver Isaac George Thos Farmer Thos Edwards Sr Thos Edwards Jr Jno Harrison Jas Graham Robt Laurence find dft guilty; assess plfs damages $100 and costs. Dft obtains appeal to Superior Court; bond $500 with Thomas Stuart and Jesse Wharton securities.
    Appt William Henderson & Jas Sanders inspectors of Tobacco at James Sanders warehouse; bond $3000, with Edward Douglass & Thomas Masten securities.
    Bill/sale Abner H H Bush to Nathaniel Edwards for negro girl six years old named Rachel ackd.
    Appt George D Blackemore and Thomas Gregory inspectors of tobacco at Cairo; bond $3000 with Edward Douglass and William Edwards securities.
p.498   Pleasant Chitwood v William Snoddy. Covt. Plf by Jno C Hamilton: 31 March 1803 agreement that Chitwood would attend Snoddy's plantation, Snoddy to furnish 2 blacks & 2 whites 3 horses 3 plows, and Snoddy to give Chitwood 3rd & 4th of all that is made. Snoddy did not furnish four hands. Dec 1804 dft by Parry W Humphreys. Parties in proper person; plf dismissed suit, each party pays own costs.
    Wm Snoddy v Pleasant Chitwood. Covt. Agreement[above], also to go equal shares in field belonging to Mr Shelby. Dft by John C Hamilton & John B Johnson. Parties in p.499   proper person; plf dismissed suit; each pays his own costs.
    Pleasant Chitwood v William Snoddy. Parties in proper person; plf dismisses suit.
    Winchester & Cage v Edwin Perry. Plfs Jas Winchester & Wm Cage obtained agt Edwin Perry two judgments; constable levied on 160 acres joining Wm Cochran & James Aspey near Bledsoes Crk belonging to Edwin Perry; to be sold to satisfy judgment.
    Appt Thomas Donnell & James Cryer esqrs to complete settlement made in part with admr of Simon Totevine decd and make report to next Court.
    Appt Robert Combs overseer/road from Gallatin to ridge between Cumberland & Red River in place of Theophilus Allen with same hands.

Saturday Dec 22d. Present Edward Douglass James Sanders Thomas Blackemore Esquires.
    Joseph House v Isreal Miles. Detinue. Plea that Miles was to render House a silver watch value of $25. Plf not appearing, non suit entered, dft recovers agt plf.
    James Gwin v Robert Hains. Debt. Plf by Thomas Stuart. Dft not appearing; plf rep.500   covers against defendant $150 debt $11.06¼ interest & also his costs.
    Jas Gwin v Robt Hains. Debt. Plf recovers $50, $5.18¼ interest, also his costs.
    Sheriff appts William H Douglass as deputy sheriff; approved by Court.
    Enos Hannah v Drury Milam. Plf obtained judgt before James Sanders Esq agt Drury Milam for $10.75. Dft on petition from William Montgomery & James Cryer, justices, requiring Clerk enable Milam to have relief provided in such cases. Dec 1804 plf by Jesse Wharton; dft by Parry W Humphreys & Wash Hannum. Court dismisses certiorari; p.501   plf recovers agt dft $10.75 & costs of court.
    John D Hannah v James Blackemore. Debt. Mar 1804 judgt confessed by dft. Dec 1804 parties direct judgment be set aside & annulled.
    John D Hanna v Thomas Blackemore. Debt. Plf recovers agt dft $426.76 & his costs.
    Thomas Blackemore v James Blackemore & John Thompson. John D Hannah recovered agt Thomas Blackemore $426.76 on a bill single given by James Blackemore & Jno Thompson & Thos Blackemore on which bill Jas & Jno were principals, and Thomas was security, sd sum being paid by sd Thomas Blackemore in satisfaction of sd judgment to sd John D Hannah. Thomas Blackemore recovers agt dfts $426.76 & his costs.
p.502   Robert Laurence v John Boyce. Plf to take deposition of James McKinsey.
    Lists of taxable property to be taken: Stephen Cantrill Esqr in Capt Whitsitts

MARCH 1805

company. Jas Sanders in Capt Sanders company. Wm Montgomery in Capt Bruces compy. Archibald Marlin in Capt Latimers compy. Witheral Latimer in Capt Shaws. Edwd Gwin in Capt Gwins. Jas Cryer in Capt Wills. Jas Douglass in Capt Lains. Mattw Alexander in Capt Vinsons. Jno Morgan in Capt Brownings. Wm Seawell in Capt Mills. Jas Winchester in Capt Alexanders. Thos Blackemore in Capt Whites. Jas Hart in Capt Bradleys. Wm Cage in Capt Scobeys.

James Douglass esqr deposited 31½¢, a fine collected of James Norris on a presentment of the Grand Jury for profane swearing.

John Payton v Ephraim Payton. Dft not appearing, judgt by default agt dft.

Appt Wm Snoddy overseer/road in place of Thos Barrott from west fork Station Camp creek at Dawsons old place to the big east fork of sd creek.

Order James Reese late county trustee be allowed $4, two thirds of appraisement of a stray cow taken up by Henry Box who was this term released from payment.

Court adjourned till Court in Course.   Edwd Douglass

p.503 Court of Pleas & Quarter Sessions held at Court house in Gallatin on third Monday 1805. Present James Winchester William Montgomery Matthew Alexander Esqrs.

Deed Francis Fonvielle to Stephen Stone 65 acres ackd.

Deed James Roney to Micajah House 128 acres proved by Alexander Rasco.

Deed Richard Cope to Alexander Rasco 225 acres proved by Micajah House.

Grand Jury: William Edwards foreman, King Carr, Jas Vinson, Jno Sterns, Frederick Miller, John Payton, Thos Britton, Robt Hamilton, Jas Mecklin, Adam Hunter, Christley Catron, James Brown, Robt Gutrey, Jas Hunt, Wm McClure. Eli Stalcup constable.

Henry Miller records his ear mark.

John Miller records his ear mark.

Deed Thomas Cocke to Robert Desha 640 acres proved by James Winchester.

Inventory/sales & supplementary inventory; goods of Elizabeth Kennedy decd proved by administrator.

Deed Henry Harrison to Henry Lyon 101 acres proved by John Morgan.

Appt John Barr admr/estate of John Galbraith decd; bond $500, John Carr and Silas Alexander securities.

Commrs apptd to appraise estate of John Wilson decd rendered appraisement.

Heli Herring records his ear mark.

Appt Thomas Blackemore and Jonathan Hannum to settle with James Williams guardian for orphans of John Neely decd.

Deed James Byrns by John Byrns, atty-in-fact, to Abraham Byrd 380 acres proved by John Hawkins.

Deed John Payton to Samuel Harris 30 acres proved by Allen Purvis.

Deed John Payton to Samuel Harris 61 acres proved by Allen Purvis.

Deed Joseph McKean to Thomas Kiefe 100 acres proved by John Trice.

Present Anthony Sharp Matthew Alexander & Edward Gwin Esqrs.

George Duty records his ear mark and brand.

Solomon Duty records his ear mark.

Joseph Clark records his ear mark.

p.504 Deed Thomas Masten sheriff to William Beard for Jesse Kuykendall's undivided share of 200 acres estimated at 33½ acres ackd.

MARCH 1805

Deed John Trousdale to Hallery Malone 165 acres proved by Silas Alexander.
Bill/sale Hallery Malone to John Trousdale for four negroes Dennis Peggy Pleasant and Real ackd.
Appt John Douglass constable for Capt Scobeys district; bond $625, Matthew Scobey and William Douglass securities and took oaths for qualification.
Appt William Bell overseer/road through Gallatin from James C Wilsons to lower road in place of Joseph Motherall.
Commrs apptd to finish settlement with admr/Simon Totevine decd render statement.
Appt Green B Orr constable for Capt Vinsons district in place of John Mitchell, resigned; bond $625 with John Orr & Wm Alderson securities, took oaths.
Edward Douglass Esqr rendered following bonds by him taken as chairman of Sumner Court, of inspectors of cotton: William Edwards with James Cage and Samuel P Black securities. James Sanders with James Howard and Thomas Masten sec. Edward Sanders with Will Henderson & Daniel Smith sec. William Henderson with Daniel Smith & Will Cunningham sec. David Dement with Josephus H Conn & Robert Trousdale sec. Richard Brown with Geo Brown & Saml Conn sec. William Gillespie with Wm Cage & Wm Douglass sec. White & Conn with George Brown and Richard Brown sec. Thomas Kiefe with John Trice & Henry Darr[Dan?] securities, each payable with penalty of $5000.
Inventory/goods of William Brown decd proved by executor.
Appt Elizabeth Brigance guardian for Robert Brigance & Peggy Brigance, orphans of William Brigance decd; bond $1000 with Moore Stevenson & James Brigance securities.
Appt William Montgomery esqr guardian for Jane Egnew George Egnew Elender Egnew & Jesse Egnew orphans of Thomas Egnew decd; bond $3000, with James Frazor and Robert Taylor securities.
Appt George S Brigance guardian for Vilet Brigance & Betsey Brigance orphans of William Brigance decd; bond $1000 with Levi Hall and James Brigance securities.
Richard Brown, orphan of William Brown decd, makes choice of Arthur Exum for his guardian who is apptd such by court; bond $500 with Lazarus Cotten security.
Will of William Bowen decd proved by Hendley Russell. John Henry Bowen an executor qualified by taking the oath.
p.505 Deed Richard Hogin & Matthew Moss to Allen Purvis 400 acres & 100 perches proved by James Cryer.
Deed Rencher McDaniel to Edward Gwin 640 acres ackd.
Deed John Morgan & James Winchester to James Watson 369¾ acres ackd.
Orphan William Jones bound an apprentice to Joseph Clark until age 21.
Deed William Stephens & Joshua Stephens to John Bonds Junr 300 acres in Nash County North Carolina ackd by sd William & Joshua Stephens.
Supplementary inventory/goods of Simon Totevine decd rendered by admr.
Lists of taxable property & polls returned by commrs for Capt Alexanders company, Capt Lyons company, Capt Watsons co, Capt Whites co, Capt Bradleys co, Capt Whitsitts company, Capt Vinsons co, Capt Shaws co, Capt Gwins co, Capt Scobys company.
John Richmond v Redmond D Barry. March 1804 Plf by Jno C Hamilton: in 1802 plf's horse lost; in 1803 came to hands of dft who has kept horse. Mar 1805 plf by atty orders suit dismissed, each party pays his own atty & witnesses, & dft pays costs.
p.506 Edward Jones v Isaiah Hammond. Debt. Mar 1804 plf by Wm Smith. Dft by Redmond D Barry. Mar 1805 plf orders cause dismissed at dft's cost.
David Watson v James Trousdale Jr. TAB. Sept 1804 plf by John C Hamilton: August 1804 dft wounded plf. Mar 1805 plf orders suit dismissed, costs paid by parties.
Winchester & Cage v Thomas W Waters. Debt. Dec 1804 James Winchester & Wm Cage Jr p.507 trading as Winchester & Cage by atty W L Hannum. Dft by Jno C Hamilton can-

MARCH 1805

not deny plfs action. Plfs recover $1026.16¼ agt dft. Exn stayed till 16 July next.
Winchester & Cage v Thomas W Waters & Robert Hall. [As above]. Plfs recover agt
p.508   dft $113.08 & costs; execution stayed till 16 July next.
 Order suit of David Gillespie against Ephraim Payton be revived in name of James
Wills admr of sd Gillespie whose death was suggested to Court.

Tuesday March 19th. Present John Morgan Edward Gwin Matthew Alexander Esqrs.
 Appt James Steel overseer/road Cairo to Croft mills in place of Jesse Johnson;
Matthew Alexander esqr to furnish said overseer with a list of hands.
 Appt Lazarus Cotten overseer/road in place of James Sanders.
 Appt John Hamilton overseer/road from Harts ferry instead of Francis Locke.
 Appt Alexr Cathey Junr overseer/road from west Goose cr by Richard Brittons;
Charles Donoho Esqr to furnish said overseer with a list of hands.
 Deed Edward Gwin to John Orr 200 acres ackd.
 Appt James Winchester & William Montgomery to settle with Andrew Jackson esqr as
administrator of Samuel Donelson decd.
 Deed Zacheus Wilson to James A Wilson 16 acres 35 perches ackd by sd Zacheus.
 James Wills admr of David Gillespie decd v Ephraim Payton. Robert C Atkinson
Marlin Young & James Bodine witnesses behalf plf not appearing, judgment agt each
for $125, scire facias to issue against them respectively.
 James Wills admr of David Gillespie decd v Ephraim Payton. Jan 1801 David Gillespie then plf by Saml Donelson; dft by Thomas Stuart & Jno C Hamilton. Jul 1803 jury
Hugh Crawford Moore Cotten Reuben Douglass James S Wilson Henry Belote Samuel Smith
Richd King Abraham Hassell Robert Steel Wm Beard Saml Stuart Samuel Gibson say plfs
p.509   damage $40; verdict set aside & new trial granted. Oct 1803 death of plf is
suggested.   Jun 1804 scire facias agt Jas Wills admr of David Gillespie decd to Da-
vidson County but not found. Mar 1805 jury Jeremiah Mitchell Thos Anderson Jas Mc-
Dowell Allen Purvis Jas Clendening Jno Bowman Hallery Malone David Beard Wm Bunton
Wm Frazor Robert Taylor Isaac Baker find for dft. Dft recovers agt plf costs of de-
fence to be levied in hands of sd administrator of goods & chattels of sd deceased.
 Deed John Garrison to John Pavatt 133 acres proved by Shadrack Nye.
 Appt Thos Donnell & Mattw Alexander settle with Jas Ball admr/Moses Stuart decd.
 Appt Jas Winchester & Mattw Alexander settle with admrs/Henry Houdeshall decd.
 James Cathey orphan of James Cathey decd chooses Thomas Walker for his guardian;
bond $1000 with James Hart, security.
 Samuel King v Joseph Norman. TAB. Plaintiff in proper person dismisses his suit
at the cost of William Jones who assumes the same in open court.
 Deed Elisha Clary to Jarrett Seatte[Scatle?] 50 acres ackd.
 Deed Willey Cherry atty in fact for exrs of James Powers decd to John Garrison
for 365 acres ackd by sd Cherry.
 Order Charles Donoho & James Hart esqrs complete settlement with admrs of William
S Carson decd.
 Deed Robert Taylor to Elisha Bernard 320 acres proved by Jacob Bernard.
 Acct/sales personal estate of Moses Stuart decd proved by admr of sd decd.
 Deed Adam Harpole to Christly Catron 100 acres proved by Hugh Kirkpatrick.
 Commissioners render to Court their settlement with admr of Moses Stuart decd.
p.510   James McKain v Danl Miles. Covt. Oct 1802 plf by Jno C Hamilton: 1801 cove-
nant to build McKain a house 34 x 22 of hewed logs, 2 stories high, McCain to fur-
nish nails sufficient for a roof & floor, vituals & lodging for sd Miles when work-

MARCH 1805

ing, sd building to be finished in six months; house not completed. March 1805 jury Jeremiah Mitchell Thos Anderson Jas McDowell Allen Purvis Jas Clendening Jno Bowman Hallery Malone David Beard Wm Bunton Wm Frazor Robt Taylor Isaac Baker say dft hath not kept his covenant; assess plfs damages to $10. Plf recovers $10 & costs.

State v Joseph Wilson Moses Wilson Rauls Perry Chestley Jackson. By oath of Wm Edwards foreman & 14 other good men make presentment [omitted] fined 50¢ & costs.

p.511   Bill/sale Thomas Cartwright to Moore Cotten negro boy Harry proved by Hugh Findley.

Bill/sale John Bond to William Bradshaw negro boy Phill proved by Samuel McMurry.

Acct/sales goods of Bryant Gardner decd proved by admr.

Richard Boyce v Samuel Murphy. Dfts bail Smith Hansbrough surrenders dft.

John Withrow v Samuel Murphy. Dfts bail Smith Hansbrough surrenders dft.

Appt Matthew Alexander & Thos Donnell esqrs to settle with admrs/Jno Wilson decd.

Ltr/attorney Abagail McCray & John Smith extx & extr of Lemuel Cotton decd to Jas Cryer empowering Cryer to execute a deed to land vested in sd Cotton at time of his death, certificate of Cato West governor of Mississippi Territory pro tem, certifying Zachariah Kirkland before whom sd ltr/atty was ackd was an acting justice/peace for Jefferson County in sd Territory.

Deed William Willoughby to John Cage 640 acres proved by Moses Pinkston.

Deed John Donohow to William Gwin 128 acres 104 perches ackd by sd Jno Donohow.

Deed Samuel Donelson Shadrack Nye James Wilson Chas Donoho commrs in trust for Sumner County to Henry Lyon lots 1 & 7 in Gallatin proved by Will Trigg.

Deed John Goodrum to James Turner 100 acres ackd.

Polley Hunt by her next friend John Hunt v Moses Tinsley. Jury[above except John Carr & James Johnson for Hallery Malone & Isaac Baker] find dft guilty of speaking & publishing scandalous & defamatory words as charged; assess plfs damages to $250.

John Boyce v Robert Laurence. Debt. Dec 1804 plf by Redmond D Barry; Mar 1805 plf p.512   dismisses suit; plf pays costs of suit.

William Sample v Roger Gibson. Debt. Plf dismisses suit; dft assumes costs.

Henry Belote assignee of Edmund Barker v Thomas Keefe. Covt. Parties in proper person; dft confesseth judgt $161.32; execution stayed until 19 September next.

Deed Abba McCray & John Smith extx & extr will of Lemuel Cotton decd by James Cryer atty in fact to John Franklin 125 acres ackd by sd James Cryer.

Deed Henry Lyon to John Trice & Thomas Keefe lots 1 & 7 in Gallatin ackd.

Jurors to next County Court: Richd Hannum John Stamps James Reese Elias Morrison Littleton Joiner Wm Henderson Junr James Garrett Joseph Hodge Patk Barr Wm Gwin Jno McMurrey Thos Hamilton Thos Groves Junr Jas Roney Gumry McConnell Thos Stubblefield Jno Irwin John Kerr Joseph Robb Richard Taylor Zacheus Wilson D James Wilson Joseph Motherall Joel Hart Richard Bradley Elijah Anthony Joel Childress David Stuart John Ruyle Joseph Scoby Moore Cotton Richd Strother Elmore Harris Richard Bradley Edward Bradley William Dickison William Reed Henry Palmer William Hale.

James Cryer v John Trice. Debt. Dft confesseth judgt to plf $124.59 & costs.

p.513   Moore Cotton v Lazarus Cotton. Debt. Plf recovers agt dft $79.38 & costs.

James Cryer v Lazarus Cotton. Debt. Plf recovers agt dft $157.16½ & costs.

Deed/release David Shelby to Hugh Crawford 70 acres ackd.

Wednesday March 20th. Present James Winchester Isaac Walton Thomas Blackemore Matthew Alexander Esqrs.

Appt Wm White overseer/road from Capt Jesse Haineys to Second Creek; Jonathan

MARCH 1805

Hannum Esqr to furnish sd overseer with a list of hands.
Appt Whitehead Joiner overseer/road from Dawsons now Rawlings to Drakes Creek in stead of William Bruce with same hands.
John Blair v John Gwin. Debt. Plf recovers agt dft $83.66 & his costs.
p.514   Deed John Trice to Henry Lyon lots 16 & 17 in Gallatin ackd.
Bill/sale Benjamin Jolly to James Cryer negro boy James proved by Will Trigg.
Deed Samuel Donelson Shadk Nye Jas Wilson Chas Donoho commrs in trust for Sumner County to Isaac Clark lot 2 in Gallatin proved by Will Trigg Jr.
Appt Jesse Deloach constable, Capt Walls militia district in place of David Allen who resigned this day; bond $625 with Ruffin Deloach & Robert Patton securities.
Deed Isaac Clark to John & Robert Allen lot 2 in Gallatin proved by Saml P Black.
Deed James Trousdale to Will Trigg Jr one acre ackd.
Lists/taxable property & polls in Capt Scobys company & Capt Shaws company rendered by William Cage & Witheral Latimer esqrs.
Deed William Snoddy to James Cryer 56 acres 88 perches ackd.
Bill/sale Benjamin Jolly to Josiah Wells four negroes Nutt Charles Delsee & Kennedy & three feather beds proved by John Pickering.
John Trice v Nathaniel Simmons. Cause refered to Will Trigg Josephus H Conn James Desha. Referees deliver award: Simmons to pay $60 & cost.
Bill/sale Wm L Armstrong to John Cavett negro man Bob proved by Michael Cavitt.
Bill/sale Wm L Armstrong to John Cavett household furniture farming utensils and crop proved by Michael Cavett.
John C Henderson v Andrew Jackson admr of Samuel Donelson decd. Deposition of Lilburn Henderson to be taken on behalf plf.
John Withrow v Samuel Murphey. Deposition of Richd Boyce to be taken in Kentucky.
Appt Thomas Parker oversee/road from Deshas ford on Bledsoes Creek to Second Creek; John Morgan Esqr to furnish overseer with list of hands.
p.515   Bill/sale Adam Hunter to David Shelby negro woman & two children named Nance Will & Dine ackd.
Wm Black & Co v John Mitchell. Plf obtained an attachment against estate of John Mitchell for $76.95¼; Wm H Douglass shff levied on two negro wenches 1 kettle. Jan 3d 1805 levied on negro girl Lucinda. James Desha one of plfs orders his suit dismissed; dft assumes costs.
Peasley & White v Arthur Exum. Debt. Plfs Thos Pasley & Jas White by Josephus H Conn dismiss suit and pay costs.
Thomas Watson v Richard Waller & Richard Waller. Debt. Plf by Robt F N Smith dismisses suit; dfts pay costs of sd suit.
John Kennedy v John Mitchell & Enos Hannah. Shff Thomas Masten summons Hutchins Burton Esqr garnishee. Sd Hutchings G Burton dismissed suit at dfts costs.
p.516   Francis Murphy v Nicholas Boyce. Plf by Hutchings G Burton his attorney dismissed suit and paid sheriffs fees and clerks fees to each respectively.
William Carson v Samuel Caldwell & Elizabeth McReynolds admrs of Robert McReynolds decd. Wm Carson obtained attachment agt estate of Robert McReynolds decd; summoned Jas C Wilson Shadrack Nye & Chas Donoho as garnishees, executed by Wm H Douglass. Plf by Jesse Wharton dismisses suit and pays costs arising thereon.
Redmond D Barry v Seth Mabry. Plf in proper person dismissed suit, pays costs.
John Andrews v Redmond D Barry. Debt. Redmond Dillon Barry summoned; plf by John B Johnson his atty dismissed suit; each party paying half costs.
Order sheriff to hold inquest on Joseph Wilson of whom it is suggested he is in a state of lunacy.

MARCH 1805

Thursday March 21st 1805. Present Thos Donnell Witheral Latimer Mattw Alexander.
Deed James White to Henry Lyon 21¾ acres proved by John Lyon.
Order suit of Richard Searcy against John C Henderson be revived in names of the representatives of sd Richd Searcy whose death was heretofore suggested to Court.
p.517 Representatives of Richard Searcy decd v John C Henderson. Appeal. Mar 1804 Judgt given agt dft for debt under $10 by Wm Cage esqr. Plf by Jno C Hamilton; dft in proper person. Mar 1805 representatives of Richd Searcy not appearing, non suit entered; dft recovers agt them his costs of suit.
John Den on demise of Maxwell Sharp v Uridice Myers. Ejectment. Jan 1798 John Den agt Richard Fen. Maxwell Sharp on 9 Decr 1797 demised to John Den 228 acres on Station Camp adj Capt Winchester corner, Richd Hogins line, Capt Winchesters line. Fen p.518 with force & arms entered afsd land to damage of John Den; Samuel Donelson for plf. 19 Mar 1798 Richard Fen to Uradice Miers, to appear by attorney at Court at Capt Wm Gillespies or suffer judgt by default. Apr 1798 Sheriff R Cage summoned Uradice Miers, the tenant in possession in suit in room of Rd Fen, by Isaac McNutt her attorney. Summons by David Shelby, Clerk, to Uridice served by Thos Masten D.S. Mar 1804 Euridice Miers by Thos Stuart & Jno C Hamilton. Plf by John H Bowen. March 1805 jury Jeremiah Mitchell Thos Anderson Jas McDowell Jas Bracken Allen Purvis Jas Clendening Hallery Malone David Beard Wm Bunton James Johnson Robt Taylor Wm Frazor find dft not guilty of trespass. Plf granted appeal to Superior Court of Mero Dist, bond $500 with John H Bowen and Parry W Humphreys securities.
p.519 David Love v Nicholas Boyce. Debt. Sep 1804 plf by Jno C Hamilton: Nicholas and James Boyce owe $210. Mar 1805 plf recovers agt dft; exn stayed till June next.
Letter/attorney Thomas Sanders to James Sanders proved by Edward Sanders.
Verbal will of Aaron Parker decd exhibited; the next of kin must be advertised thereof. Sheriff to make known to John Parker, Thomas Parker, Richard Parker, Isaac Parker, Nathaniel Parker, Robert Parker, Elizabeth Calyar & Mary Thompson the heirs of sd decedent to appear at next Court.
State v Henry Morris. Mar 1804 Robt Anderson foreman of Grand Jury informed of an orphan boy John Zeigler about 12 or 13 years old under care of Joshua Morris whose character is infamous; process issue agt Joshua alias Henry alias Absalom Morris to bring boy to Court. Sd orphan was apprenticed; dft discharged but pay costs.
p.520 Nicholas Boyce v Thomas Barrott. Plf by Redmond D Barry dismissed suit; dft assumes costs.
James Cryer esqr returns list/taxable property in Capt Wills company.

Friday March 22d. Present Edward Douglass James Sanders John McMurtry Esquires.
Order judgt agt John Mitchell constable & Saml Donelsons admr (sd Donelson being sd constables security) for $17.50 amt of an exn behalf state agt Jas McKinsey for profane swearing which amt collected by Mitchell but not accounted for. Also scire facias agt Andrew Jackson admr of said Samuel Donelson decd.
Order sheriff to procure a lock for public stray pen, also to forbid persons from tying horses to outside of stray pen which is likely to be injured.
John Mansker v Robert Moore. Mar 1804 plf by Thos Stuart. Dft by John C Hamilton.
p.521 Mar 1805 jury[above] find dft not guilty; dft recovers agt plf his costs.
William Henderson v Richard Waller Sr & Richard Waller Jr. Debt. Plf dismissed suit at defendants cost, costs assumed by James Sanders Esqr.
Archibald Marlin returns list/taxable property & polls in Capt Latimers company.
Bond of Wm Trigg Sr as Inspector/Cotton, Will Trigg Jr & Jas Sanders securities

223

MARCH 1805

returned into Court by Edward Douglass Esqr.

George Harrison v Terisha Turner. Jury Jeremiah Mitchel Thomas Anderson James McDowell Jas Bracken Allen Purvis James Clendening David Beard Wm Bunton Jas Johnson Robt Taylor Wm Frazor Thos Edwards; juror withdrawn and cause continued.

John Quarles v George Michie. Debt. Mar 1804 plf by John C Hamilton. Dft by Redmond D Barry. Plf recovers $53.41 and his costs of suit.

p.522 Deed Richard Boyce & John Boyce to George Trumbo 134 acres proved by John Pickering.

Lists/taxable property & polls taken by Jas Cryer & Jas Douglass in Capt Wills & Capt Lains militia districts were delivered to Court.

Stothart & Bell v Samuel Caldwell admr of Robert McReynolds decd. Mar 1804 David Shelby summons dft; E Crutcher Shff. Apr 1804 Plfs by John Dickison; dft by Jno C Hamilton. Mar 1805 jury[above except Hallery Malone for Thos Edwards]. Plfs recover $64.34 and their costs.

Thomas Keife v George Michie. Debt. Jun 1804 Thos Keife, assignee of Jno Deloach, by John B Johnson his atty. Sep 1804 dft by Redmond D Barry. Mar 1804 jury[above].

p.523 Defendant recovers against plaintiff his costs of defence.

Acct/sales personal estate of Stephen Heard decd proved by admr.

William Wyer v James L Armstrong admr of Stephen Heard decd. Appeal. Suit refered to Daniel Smith Henry Bradford & Saml P Black whose award to be judgment of Court.

John Coffee v John W Crunk. Appeal. Jun 1804 judgment by Jas Sanders esqr agt dft for $28.50. Plf by Thomas Stuart; dft by John C Hamilton. Mar 1805 jury[above] find for plf $27.86 & costs.

Bond Joseph Hendrick late of Wilson County decd to Obed Hendricks for title to 640 acres in Sumner three miles from Bledsoes lick adj heirs of Wm Prewitt on South & John Blackemore on west, proved by George Michie a subscribing witness.

Assignment of land warrant 200 acres John Fisher James Fisher and King Fisher to Thomas Murray proved by William Hall.

Bill/sale Polley Harrison to Thomas Howell for household furniture, two cows and yearlings proved by Nathan Edwards.

p.524 Isaac House v Edward Hogin. TAB. Mar 1804 plf by Thomas Stuart: Hogin with force & arms beat and ill treated House. G Smith for plf. Dft by John C Hamilton. Mar 1805 plf orders suit dismissed; dft pays Court costs.

Reddick Bridgers v Web Bloodworth. TAB. June 1804 plf by John C Hamilton: Webb maimed Redick by biting off his nose. Dft by John B Johnson. Jury[above except John Bowman for Allen Purvis] find dft guilty; plaintiffs damage 10¢ and costs of suit.

p.525 Robert Laurence v John Boyce. Dft to take deposition of William Lobb.

James Stuard v Thomas Farmer. Debt. June 1804 James Steward by atty J C Hamilton. Dft by Redmond D Barry. Mar 1805 jury William Trigg Jas Desha Elias Browning James Brigance Allen Purvis Alexr McKnight Richard Cope Abraham Ellis Jas Simpson William Edwards Thomas Edwards Jas Roney say dft has paid debt except $377.57 not paid. Plf recovers debt, damages, and his costs of suit.

William Brigance son of William Brigance decd makes choice of John Brigance for guardian; bond $1000 with Levi Hall and James Brigance securities.

Licence James Trousdale to keep ordinary at his dwelling in Gallatin; bond $2500 with Richard Taylor security.

Licence Richard Taylor to keep ordinary at his dwelling in Sumner County; bond $2500 with James Trousdale security.

William Maxey & James Douglass guardians for heirs of Henry Loving decd v Matthew
p.526 Brown & Robert Patton. Debt. Sep 1804 plfs by John C Hamilton. Dfts by Thos

MARCH 1805

Stuart. Mar 1805 dfts confess judgt. Plfs recover debt & interest $73.77 & costs.
Thomas Keefe v David Orman. Jun 1804 plf by John B Johnson. Mar 1805 dft by Jesse Wharton relinquishes plea. Plf recovers $48.00½ & costs of suit.
Heli Herring v Jesse Deloach & Henry Bloodworth. Debt. Sept 1804 plf by Thos Stu-
p.527 art. Dfts by John B Johnson relinquish plea. Plf recovers $68.59 & costs.
William Ogle v Christopher Stubbins. Plf by Thomas Stuart dismisses suit.

Saturday March 23d. Present Edward Douglass James Sanders Edward Gwin Thos Donnell.
John McAdam v Richard Cope. Covt. Jun 1804 plf by John C Hamilton: Richard was to make warranty deed to McAdam for 200 acres on Drakes Crk of Barren R adj Jas Roneys
p.528 tract. Dft by Redmd D Barry pleads tender & refusal. Mar 1805 jury Jeremiah Mitchell Thomas Anderson Jas McDowell Hallery Malone Jas Clendening David Beard Wm Bunton Jas Johnson Robt Taylor Wm Frazor Jno Bowman Elias Browning say dft has kept covenant. Plf obtains appeal to Superior Court, Elisha Cheek & John C Hamilton sec.
Deed Richard Waller Sr to James Sanders 136 acres proved by Wm Pittman.
Court designates prison bounds: David Shelbys corner adj Main St & public square then north to corner of Trousdales lot south across Main st to include the spring east to Demsey Moore thence to beginning.
William Douglass v Thomas Keife. Justices Thos Donnell & Jas Cryer grant Keifes petition for wits/certiorari & supersidias; plf dismissed suit at his own cost.
Robert Harris v Solomon Shoulders. Sep 1804 plf by Jno C Hamilton: swap of horses but Robt found horse unsound. Dft by Wharton. Mar 1805 suit dismissed.
p.529 James Sanders renders list/taxable property & polls in Capt Sanders dist.
Appt John Wiley constable in Capt Vinsons company, bond $625 with Thomas Edwards & Ruffin Deloach securities.
Henry Belote v Edwin Perry. Property levied on is to be sold for use of judgment.
Robert Bruice v Edwin Perry. Acreage levied on is to be sold for use of judgment.
Report of jury to inquire in lunacy of Joseph Wilson: is & has been for some time in a state of lunacy; James Wilson apptd guardian; bond $2000, Henry Bets and Griswold Latimer securities.
Appt Jno Gatlin overseer/road from Dawsons now Rawlings in place of Peter Looney.
Polley Hunt by next friend John Hunt v Moses Tinsley. Continued.
Thos Willis Solomon Sholders & others petition to draw from William Edwards admr of John Edwards decd their distributive share of personal estate; order writ issue in behalf petitioners against sd administrator.
John Boyce v George Trumbo. Debt. Plf by Jesse Wharton: 6 Aug 1803 obligation by
p.530 George to pay John $467. Mar 1805 dft came not. Plf recovers agt dft.
Redmond D Barry v John Deloach. Barry recovered judgt agt Deloach at July 1803 term; Deloach obtained appeal to Superior Court but failed to submit transcript; David Shelby orders Sheriff to cause Deloach to appear at Courthouse Dec next to show cause if any why execution ought not issue against his goods.
Isaac Walton assee v Robt Laurence Nicholas Boyce & James McKain. Debt. Dec 1804 Isaac Walton assignee of John Boyce by atty John C Hamilton: Isaac Walton assignee of Burrell J Thompson assignee of John Boyce. Mar 1805 defendants not appearing,
p.531 plf recovers agt dfts his debt & interest $161.22½ & costs of suit.
John H Bush v Parismus Tillery admr of Nathaniel Woolsey decd. Mar 1804 Bush by John C Hamilton: John at instance of Nathl bestowed healing & curing of divers diseases & maladies, medicines & other necessary things, & promised to pay sd John
p.532 as physician. Dft by Parry W Humphreys says Nathaniel did not assume upon

MARCH 1805

himself as John Bush complains. Parties by attys dismiss suit.
Samuel K Blythe v Robert Moore. Septr 1804 plf obtained attachment agt estate of Robt Moore, sum $52.50; attachment retd to Septr 1804 Term endorsed: Attached 18th Sep 1804 in hands of Saml Blithe one acct book by me Patrick Gibson. Insufficiency of property being suggested by plf, judicial attachment awarded with rule to summon Wm Douglass, Andrew Blythe, Thos Donnell & Robert Roble garnishees which attachment issued & was returned by sheriff to Dec Court 1804 endorsed levied on one town lott in Gallatin E Crutcher. Whereupon sd Saml K Blythe by Jesse Wharton filed declaration upon: Dec 1804 Saml K Blythe by atty complains of Robert Moore in custody of a plea of covenant broken. Sd Robt Moore Jan 1804 made obligation subscribed with his hand, sealed with his seal, & to Court now shewn, which obligation is also signed & sealed by plf. Sd writing obligated Robt Moore bound to pay to Saml $80 to be paid 1 September next, in consideration of which Saml bound himself to keep a stud horse named Trimmer six months which horse belonged to deft for the above $80 and the plf plaitniff was to have the season of six mares in addition; plf was to keep horse in good order for mares, & was to take the eighty dollars upon such men that put mares to Trimmer. If there would not mares sufficient put to the horse Trimmer to pay the $80, Robert bound himself to pay $80 himself. Plf says he kept sd horse Trimmer for 6 months as agreed; there were not mares put to sd horse sufficient to pay the $80; Plf in fact says that deft altho often requested hath not kept his covenant as afsd made, that is to say Robert hath not paid the afsd $80 nor any part thereof, wherefore plf says he is injured to amount $100 and therefore he sues. Wharton atty for plf. Dft by Hutchings G Burton: attached property replevied, covenant performed.
Mar 1805 plf in proper person dismissed suit; plff pays costs of sd suit.
p.533 Appt Edmund Reeves overseer/road from Capt Gillespie to Thos Keife; Nicholas Boyce esqr to furnish sd overseer with a list of hands.
Court adjourned until Court in Course. Thos Donnell Mattw Alexander Nichs Boyce.

Court of Pleas & quarter Sessions, third Monday in June. Present James Winchester, Witheral Latimer, & Matthew Alexander Esquires.
Grand Jury: Richd M Hannum foreman, Littleton Joiner, Joseph Robb, Henry Palmer, Joseph Motheral, Richd Bradley, David Stuart, Joel Hart, Edwd Bradly, Joseph Hodge, Thos Stubblefield, Jas Garrett, Moore Cotton, John McMurry, John Carr. Green B Orr, constable, to attend them.
Those who failed to return taxable property & polls released from double tax.
Excuse Jas Roney & John Ruyle from attending as jurors for present term.
Deed John Hamilton to David Orman 120 acres ackd.
Deed Nathaniel Dickerson Sr to Robert Hanes 100 acres proved by Wm Parr.
Deed Tilmon Dixon to John Comar 100 acres proved by Hutchings G Burton.
Deed Tilmon Dixon to Ezekiel Philips 100 acres proved by Hutchings G Burton.
Deed Isaac Lane to George G Black lot 8 in Gallatin ackd.
Deed George G Black to Samuel Barr 80 acres 70 perches ackd.
Bill/sale Elisha Freeman to Robert Parker 4 horses ackd.
Appt William Neely guardian for James Neely & Alexander Neely orphans of John Neely decd. Wm Neely bond $1000, with Richard M Hannum & William Reed securities.
Report/Commrs apptd to settle with former guardians for James & Alexander Neely.

JUNE 1805

Deed Alexander McCulloch to Alexander Dobbins 600 acres proved by Robert Dobbins.
Deed William Dixon to James McKinsey 112 acres proved by James Reasons.
p.534   Deed Elisha Clary to Robert Davis 100 acres acknowledged.
Appt John Hawkins overseer/road in place of Terisha Turner.
Present James Winchester James Douglass Witheral Latimer Nicholas Boyce Esqrs.
Zachariah Betts v Jesse Harrison. Trespass. Oct 1803 plf by Redmond D Barry: Debt and hire of Negro man Davs to work in Zachariah's tan yard. Dft by John C Hamilton.
p.535   Jury Elias Morrison Wm Henderson Jr Patk Barr Wm Gwin Thomas Hamilton Montgomery McConnell John Irwin Richd Taylor Zacheus Wilson James Wilson Elijah Anthony Joseph Scoby. Defendant recovers against plaintiff his costs of defence.
Inventory/goods of John Galbraith decd proved by admr.
Nathaniel Giles v Robt Bruce. Appeal. Giles obtained judgt agt Bruce for $10.87½ from which dft appeals. Plf orders suit dismissed; dft assumes costs.
John Lauderdale records his stock ear mark.
Appt John Dickerson overseer/road to Parrs ferry in place of Nathaniel Dickerson.
Joshua Bowdin fined $5 for contempt/Court; stands committed until paid.
Hugh McGee v Lewis West. Oct 1804 McGee obtained attachment against estate of Lewis West; executed on one pide cow one yellow steer 4 yearlings 7 acres/corn one medley colt one stack/hay property of Lewis West executed by Jno Mitchel constable. Mar 1805 McGee by Redmond D Barry: dispute over a horse. Mar 1805 plf dismissed his suit at sd plaintiffs costs.
Deed John P Wiggins to David Love 108 acres 107 perches proved by Shadrack Nye.

Tuesday June 18th. Present James Winchester John Barr Matthew Alexander Esquires.
Fine of Joshua Bowden rescinded; Joshua released from confinement.
p.536   Joel Hart records his stock ear mark.
James Winchester rendered bond of Priscilla Burket with Roger Gibson & Henry Harrison securities $200, for maintenance of bastard child of which Priscilla has been delivered, together with her fine $6.25.
James Winchester rendered bond taken of Susannah Burket with Roger Gibson & Henry Harrison securities, $200, for the maintenance of a bastard child of which Susannah has lately been delivered, together with her fine $6.25.
Winchester & Cage v Henry Harrison. Aug 1804 Constable Patrick Gibson levied on a gelding, old negro Cate, feather beds & furniture, pair cart wheels, livestock. Jun 1805 plfs dismiss suit at plfs costs paid in full.
Robt Patton v David Allen. Appeal. Plf no further prosecutes; dft recovers costs.
Grant ltrs/admn on estate of Thomas Gaither decd to John Goodrum; bond $1000 with John Turner & George D[binding] securities.
Overseers/roads apptd: Edward Maxey in place of John Carr. John Orr in place of James Wilson. John Seriker in place of John Shannon.
Appt Ernest Watson John McMurry and Isaac Bledsoe patrollers for Capt W[binding]s company, & they are to qualify before John Morgan Esqr.
Bill/sale Lazarus Cotton to Grant Allen negro man James proved by James Hart.
p.537   Moses Tinsley v Mary Hunt. Jury Thos Hamilton Wm Gwin Elias Morrison, Zacheus Wilson Wm Henderson Jr John Irwin James Wilson Elijah Anthony Jos Scoby Richard Strother Patrick Barr Joel Childress find defendant guilty; plfs damage $100.
Joseph McKain v Henry Lyon. Debt. Plf by William Bradshaw. Dft in proper person. By consent, order by Court that suit be dismissed at equal cost of each party.
Deed Henry Lyon to William Duty 122¾ acres proved by William Hall.

JUNE 1805

Elmore Douglass v Ezekiel Douglass. Ejectmt. Awaits decision by Court of Equity.
Deed Joel Brown to James Brown 145 acres proved by John Brown.
Deed William Palmer to George Duren 33 acres proved by James Hunt.
John Murphy v John Payne. Cause submitted to determination of Nicholas Boyce and George Blackemore.
Deed Anne Loftin & Henry Loftin to Amy & Sucky Todd 90 acres proved by Jeremiah Belote.
Deed Anne Loftin & Henry Loftin to Henry Belote 250 acres proved by Jeremiah Belote.
Jas Winchester & Mattw Alexander esqrs to settle with admrs of George Simral dec.
Appt Thomas Donnell & Jno Morgan Esqrs to settle with exrs of John Anderson decd.
Deed John Hogin Jr to Samuel Briley 200 acres ackd.
Appt John Caveatt overseer/road in place of John Hogin, resigned.
Deed William Montgomery to Robert Taylor 200 acres ackd.
Deed John Cage to James Carr 159 acres ackd.
Deed Edward Cage to John Carr 230 acres ackd.
p.538   Fine Wm Wilkins $1 for contempt/Court; fine immediately paid.
Jurors to next Superior Court: John Mills, George Martin, Richard Carr, John Gillespie, John Gatlin, James Wilson smk.
Fine Wm Wilkins $2 for contempt/Court; confined until same is paid with costs.
Appt Wm White overseer/road; Jonathan Hannum Esqr to furnish list/hands.
Present: Jas Winchester Matthew Alexander Anthony Sharp Isaac Walton Jas Sanders Jas Hart Nichs Boyce Stephen Cantrill Witheral Latimer Thos Blackemore Jas Douglass Jonathan Hannum Edward Gwin James Cryer Esquires.
Allow Frederick Miller $20 for keeping orphan child Thomas Smith one year.
Allow Mrs Susannah Todd $20 for keeping orphan Morning Morrish one year.
Jurors to next County Court: Geo D Blackemore George Brown Solomon Reese Wm Hall Robt Steel Sr Woodruff Stubblefield Edward Cage Wm Eubanks Jno Miller Jno McConnell John Cathey James Sanders Arthur Exum Jas Roney Jr Moses Cummins James Reese Kasper Mansker Thos Murry Wm Duty Cornelius Herndon Edwd Williams Wm Boyles John Moody Geo Smith Michl Black Jno Mitchell Robt Mitchell Robt Williamson Richd Cavett Sr Thomas Kiefe Chas Elliott Richd Jones Isaac Baker Wm Edwards Thos Howell Solomon Sholders Francis Catron William Dorris DC James Gar[binding].
Appt James Trousdale Jas Desha Chas E[binding] Jas Trousdale Jr & Richard Bradley to review road near John C Hamiltons plantation.
Appropriate $20 to purchase two blank record books.
Allow sheriff $40 for ex officio services for one year preceding this date.
Allow Clerk $40 for ex officio services for one year preceding this date.
Winchester & Cage v Ephraim Alexander. Lot levied on to be sold for use of judgt.
Winchester & Cage v Samuel Scott. Land adj Rhody Philips near head of Bledsoes Creek to be sold for the use of judgment.
Appt Jas Hart & Jno Barr Esqrs to settle with John Sloan exr of Jas Gardner decd.
Release Wm Wilkins from confinement, he having paid fine of $2 for contempt afsd.
p.539   David Love v Littleton Duty. Covt. Plf dismissed suit.
David Love v Littleton Duty. Attacht. Suit dismissed.
William Wyer v James S[L?] Armstrong admr of Stephen Herd decd. Appeal. Cause to determination of Daniel Smith Henry Bradford Samuel P Black who are of opinion that Armstrong withdraw his appeal and each pay his own costs.

JUNE 1805

Wednesday June 19th. Present Stephen Cantril Isaac Walton Witheral Latimer William Cage James Hart and Matthew Alexander Esquires.

Bill/sale Fanny Sanders to Lunsford Pitts negroes Pegg Ryal & Rachel proved by Edmund Crutcher.

Bill/sale Lunsford Pitts to Fanny Sanders two negroes Sucky & Willis proved by Edmund Crutcher.

Deed Washington Lee Hannum & Patsey his wife to Richard M Hannum lot 21 in Gallatin proved by Jonathan Hannum.

Cage & Black v Seth Mabry. Trespass. Sept 1804 James Cage & Saml P Black trading p.540 under firm of Cage & Black, by John C Hamilton their attorney. Dft by Thos Stuart. Jun 1805 dft in proper person cannot deny plfs action; plf recovers agt dft $53 & their costs of suit. Execution stayed until 19th December.

John C Henderson v Anthony Winston. Plf scire facias to Wilson Co; dft not found by G Hallum, Wilson county sheriff. Suit dismissed at dfts costs.

p.541 Jno Trice v Giles Cook. Deposition of Reuben Norman behalf dft to be taken. Appt Alexr Gwin overseer/road to first fork of Red River.

Deed William Smothers to William Dorris 65 acres proved by James Hamilton.

Private settlement made between Andrew Jackson admr/estate of Samuel Donelson & William Montgomery guardian/heirs of Thomas Egnew decd.

Deed George Hauser by Thomas Johnson atty in fact, to Isham Uzzell 640 acres proved by Elisha Cheek.

State v Benjamin Ingram. TAB. Mar 1805 Wm Edwards foreman & others presented Benjamin Ingram assaulted David Benton with fists & sticks. Ingram saith he is guilty; fined $1 and pay costs of prosecution.

State v Griffith W Rutherford. TAB. Jun 1805 Richard M Hannum foreman & others present Rutherford for assault on James Hart Esqr. H G Burton C.S. Rutherford saith he is guilty; fined $30 and costs.

p.542 Noncupative will of John Headon decd subscribed by Fanny Gibson & Wilson Yandell is proved by sd Fanny Gibson & Wilson Yandell.

Deed James Trousdale to Joseph Reeves 2 acres ackd.

Deed William Sanders to James Sanders 123½ acres proved by Alexander Cathey.

Present Jas Winchester Edward Douglass Thos Donnell Jno Morgan Anthy Sharp Edward Gwin Isaac Walton Stephen Cantrill Wm Cage Wm Montgomery Thomas Blackemore Jonathan H[binding] James Douglass.

William Suiter allowed $50 pr Ann for keeping & clothing Jno Putt a pauper during his life, first year commenced third Monday in June last.

George Harrison v Terisha Turner. Deposition of John Byrd of Logan Co, Kentucky, to be taken, benefit plaintiff.

Supplementary inventory/goods of Samuel Donelson decd proved by admr.

Allow Commissioner of revenue for 1804 $100 for his services.

Tax laid for present year [omitted].

Tax for upport of the poor laid [omitted].

Tax for procuring a standard of weights & measures laid [omitted].

Polley Hunt by next friend John Hunt v Moses Tinsley. 1803 plf by Jno C Hamilton; dft attached for false scandalous & malicious words, damage $5000. Dft by Redmond D Barry. Mar 1805 jury [binding] Mitchell Allen Purvis Robt Taylor David Beard James McDowell Wm Frazor Wm Bunton Thos Anderson Jno Carr Jno Bowman Jas Clendening Jas Johnson find dft guilty; plfs damages $250. Bill/exceptions, cause continued. June 1805 cause dismissed; each party pays own costs.

p.543 Moses Tinsley v Mary Hunt. Plf by Redmond D Barry. Dft by Jno C Hamilton.

JUNE 1805

Jury Thos Hamilton Wm Gwin Elias Morrison Zacheus Wilson [cut off] Henderson Jr Jno Irwin Jas Wilson Elijah Anthony Joseph Scoby Richd Strother Pat Barr Joel Childress find dft guilty; assess plfs damage to $100. Suit dismissed, parties pay own costs.

Appt Drury Milam Vachel Stephens Peter Rogers & Thos Kirkham patrollers for Capt Sanders Company, they are to qualify before James Sanders Esqr.

Appt Jesse Hainey William Duty Henry D Palmer patrollers for Capt W[cut off] company; to qualify before Thomas Blackemore Esqr.

State v Griffith W Rutherford. Peace bond $500. Dft ackd debt to W[cut off]; Thos Patton his security, to keep peace especially toward James Hart esqr.

Robert Laurence v John Boyce. Trespass. 1804 plf by Jno C Hamilton. Dec 1803 Dft stated to plf that Nicholas Boyce purchased at shff sale property of Jack Reeves. Jack Reves had not legal title to sd land; transferred by Jack to his brother Joseph p.544 Reeves. [Margin & binding obliterate much of this page.] Deft by Redmond D Barry. Jury John Stamps Patk Barr John Irwin Joel Childress Elijah Anthony Richard Taylor E Harrison Montgomery McConnell Wm Gwin James A Wilson Wm Dickison William Ree[binding] assess plfs damages to $347. Plf recovers damages and costs.

Orphans named William Lowry & Reuben Lowry apprenticed to Christ[binding] until age twenty one to learn business of farming.

Thursday June 20th. Present Jas Winchester Thos Donnell Wm Montgomery Ed[binding].

Bill/sale John Mitchell to William Pittman negro boy Sam ackd.

Wilson Cage v Jacob Slinkard. Covt. Plf in proper person orders suit dismissed.

Appt Jas Winchester & Archibald Marlin esqrs settle with Edward Douglass guardian for William Price orphan of William Price decd.

Deed John Grant by Robert Hays, atty in fact, to John Morgan 320 acres proved by John H Bush.

Samuel Woods v William Gillespie. Debt. Woods by Thos Stuart at March Term. Dft by Why[binding]. Jun 1805 parties in proper person dismiss cause.

p.545 Appt John Pavatt[Paratt?] overseer/road from Drakes creek in place of John Garrett, resigned.

Theophilus Bass v Samuel Piper. Mar 1804 plf by John C Hamilton; dft by Parry W Humphreys. Apr 1803 Jas Simpson at Gallatin offered for sale negro man Tom as property of John Barrow; whilst Simpson was crying sd fellow and before he was bid off, sd Saml Piper as agent of sd John Burrows did falsely affirm sd negro fellow to be sound and healthy. Theophilus bid $360 and being highest bidder, Jas Simpson struck off sd fellow to plf & money then & there paid to Saml Piper. Plf says fellow was sickly & infirm, dft fraudently cheated plf. Jury Wm Hale Richd Strother Jos Scoby Elmore Harris Zacheus Wilson Richard T Bradley Wm Henderson William Faulk Abraham Hollingsworth Hugh Crawford John Mitchel Henry Belote; dft recovers agt plf.

John C Henderson v Andw Jackson admr/estate of Saml Donelson decd. Samuel Donelson was attached to answer complaint of Jno C Henderson, debt $500. June 1804 Henderson by B H Henderson. [bottom of page obliterated]. Dft by Wm Smith. Sept 1804 p.546 death of dft suggested; scire facias issues agt Andrew Jackson admr/estate of decd. Jun 1805 jury John Stamps John Irwin Wm Dickerson Wm Reed Richd Taylor Jno Payton Abraham Hollingsworth Elias Morrison Wm Gwin Jos Scoby Richd Strother Jas A Wilson. Plf recovers agt dft $169.10 to be levied on goods of decd.

Commrs apptd to settle with Edward Douglass esqr as guardian of William Price orphan of William Price decd report settlement in writing.

William Payton v Allen Purvis. Dft to take deposition of Wm Kennedy of KY or VA.

JUNE 1805

John Young v Isaac Pearce Jr. Appeal. Dft confessed judgt before Benjamin Rawlings & James Sanders esqrs for $6 [bottom of page obliterated.]. June 1805 plf p.547 by Thos Stuart & Redmond D Barry; dft by Nathl W Williams. Jury Jno Henderson Jno Mitchel Abraham Trigg Wm Henderson Jr Elijah Anthony Thomas Edwards Ambrose Porter Henry Hoover Jno Brigance Hugh Crawford Richd T Bradley Jas Hale find for plf $32.52 with costs.

James Cryer v John Mitchell. Jas Cryer obtained attachmt agt estate of Jno Mitchel for $105.62; Dec 1804 shff levied on negro woman Cate. June 1805 suit dismissed.

Martin Armstrong v Jabus Fisher. Plf by Nathl W Williams orders suit dismissed.

Sherrard Williams v John Ogels. TAB. Plf in proper person dismissed suit.

James Wills admr/estate of David Gillespie decd v Marlin Young. Plf by Jesse Wharton dismissed suit; dft assumes cost.

Jackson & Hutchings v James Orr. [bottom of page obliterated].

p.548 Friday June 21st. Present Edwd Douglass Thos Donnell Arch Marlin Edwd Gwin.

Thomas Masten sheriff & Collector with Edward Douglass & Josephus H Conn, securities entered bond $3000 for collection & payment of county Taxes for present year.

John Young records his stock mark, also personal mark, a bite out of the right ear done by John W Crunk.

Andrew Hoover v Archibald Donoho. Appeal. Sept 1804 dft appealed plfs judgment obtained before a justice/peace. Plf by Thomas Stuart; dft by Jesse Wharton. Jury Richd Taylor Wm Henderson Montgomery McConnell Wm Reed Elijah Anthony Joseph Scoby Elias Morrison Richard Strother William Gwin William Dickinson James A Wilson John Irwin. Plf recovers agt dft $2.37½ and his costs of suit.

Thomas Weatherred v Moses Tinsley & Barnet Rork. Debt. June 1804 plf by John C Hamilton. Dft by Thos Stuart. Plf recovers agt dft debt and interest and costs.

p.549 Earnest Watson v Marshall Stroud. Att. Mark Rickman & Nathan Rickman garnishees. Garnishees carried judgt agt them into Court/equity.

Petter Bennett v Reuben Searcy. Debt. Sep 1804 plf by Hutchings G Burton: Searcys property attached. Dft by Thos Stuart. Jun 1805 jury Richd Taylor William Henderson Montgomery McConnell Wm Reed Elijah Anthony Jos Scoby Elias Morrison Richd Strother Wm Gwin Wm Dickerson Jas A Wilson Jno Irwin. Plf recovers $62 debt & costs of suit.

Thomas Barnes v Thomas Edwards. 1804 plf by Jno C Hamilton. Dft by Thomas Stuart. p.550 Jury Richd Taylor William Henderson Montgomery McConnell William Reed Elijah Anthony Joseph Scoby Elias Morrison Richard Strother Wm Gwin Wm Dickerson Jas A Wilson John Irwin. Plaintiff recovers against defendant damages $25 and costs.

Edmund Crutcher v Thomas W Waters. Attachment by Jas Douglass JP; Thomas W Waters hath removed or is about to remove out of county; his estate to be attached. G B Orr levied on 2 barrels[binding], mare, Negro boys Robt, David, Anthony, girl Lucy, &[binding]. Plf by Jno C Hamilton. Dft not appearing, Edmd Crutcher recovers agt sd p.551 Thomas $1494.98 the balance of debt with interest; execution against dft.

John Coffee & Co v Burwell J Thompson & Jarvis Deal. Debt. Plfs by Jesse Wharton dismiss suit.

Bill/sale John McCarty to John Ruyle household furniture farming tools stock & crop now growing proved by Roger Reese.

Francis Fairclaim lessee of Thomas Edwards v John Cloud. Ejectmt. Suit continued.

Deed William Robb to John Irwin 150 acres proved by Eli Giles.

William Padfield assignee &c v John Stewart. Debt. William Padfield assignee of Benjamin McClendon by Nathaniel W Williams. Defendant not appearing, plf recovers

JUNE 1805

his debt and interest $102.96 & costs of suit.

p.552 Elias Browing v William Edwards. Dec 1804 Browning by Hutchings G Burton: concerns superintendance of farm & cotton gin of dft; plf to manage farm & gin; dft to furnish hands. June 1805 dft by John C Hamilton. Jury Elias Morrison John Irwin [binding] Wilson William Dickerson Wm Gwin Montgomery McConnell Jas A Wilson Joseph Scoby [binding] Anthony Richard Strother Richd Taylor Wm Reed. Plf recovers agt dft p.553 damage & costs. Dft obtains appeal, John Withers & Saml P Black securities.

Elias Browing v William Edwards. Thomas Edwards Jr witness for[obliterated] not appearing, forfeits according to act of assembly.

Robert Searcy v Burwell J Thompson. Debt. Sep 1804 Searcy by John Dickinson. Deft by John H Bowen. Jury Wm Hale Richd T Br[obliterated] Abraham Hollingsworth John C Henderson Lewis Crane Abraham Ellis Isaac Lindsey Robert D[obliterated] James Desha William Henderson Hugh McGee Elmore Harris. Plf recovers agt dft $78.80 & costs.

Cage & Black v John Withers. Debt. Sep 1804 Jas Cage & Saml P Black merchants by atty Jno C Hamilton. Dft in proper person cannot deny plfs action [bottom of this page obliterated].

p.554 Daniel Dunham assee v Thomas Edwards Adonijah Edwards Edward Bradley. Debt. Suit continued on affidavit of dft Thomas Edwards.

Abraham Ellis v John Lafferty. Appeal. Dec 1804 plf obtained judgt before a JP. Mar 1805 plf by Jno C Hamilton; dft by Redmd D Barry. Jury Wm H[binding] Richard T Bradley James A Wilson Elias Morrison John Irwin Elijah Anthony Wm Henderson James Desha Montgomery McConnell Joseph Scoby Zaccheus Wilson Elmore Harris. Plf recovers agt dft $19.50 with costs. Dft appeals, Redmond D Barry & Edward Gwin securities.

William Cook v John Young. Dft in proper person; plf by atty dismissed suit.

Herbert Hood v John Young. Dft in proper person; parties dismiss suit.

Deed Alexander Rasco to James Duke 100 acres proved by Thomas Howell.

John Donoho James Reese Archibald Marlin exrs of John Donoho decd v James McKinp.555 sey & John Josey. Dft by Redmond D Barry cannot gainsay plfs action. Plfs recover agt dfts $92.35 debt with interest & costs.

Thomas Kessee v James Davidson. Debt. Sep 1804 plf by Redmond D Barry. Dft by Jno C Hamilton cannot deny plfs action. Plf recovers debt & interest $106 & costs.

Joseph McKain v Seth Mabry. Debt. Plf by Wm Bradshaw dimissed suit at his costs.

Saturday June 22d. Present Edward Douglass Thomas Donnell Edward Gwin Esquires.
p.556 Henry Bradford v Samuel Caldwell & Elizabeth McReynolds. Dfts not appearing, judgt by default agt them; writ/enquiry be executed at next Term.

Motion of Elizabeth Brigance relict of William Brigance decd, order commrs Griswold Latimer Peter Looney H Archibald Marlin Reuben Douglass & Wm Edwards to lay off her right of dower in sd estate.

Abraham Ellis v Jno Lafferty. Appeal. Dft obtains appeal to Superior Court; bond $500 with Redmond D Barry & Edward Gwin securities.

Appt James S Wilson James A Wilson John Hamilton James Vinson & Alexander Graham commissioners to divide & allot real estate of Henry Loving decd to heirs of decd.

Appt Wm Dorris overseer/road up Drakes creek in place of Jas McElroy resigned.

John C Henderson v Andrew Jackson admr of Samuel Donelson decd. Parties by attornies, plf relinquishing interest mentioned in special verdict; plf recovers agt dft $169.10 to be levied of goods of sd decd, and costs.

Francis Fairclaim lessee of Thomas Edwards v John Cloud. Ejectment. Richard [obliterated] to survey premises and return plat of survey to next Court.

JUNE 1805

John Coffee & Co v John W Crunk. Appl. Scire facias agt security of Crunk.

Francis Fairclaim lessee of John Cage v Joseph Sloan. Ejectment. Order James Frazer Richard Carr James Clendening & Joseph McElwrath view with Richard Taylor surveyor to survey land in dispute.

Order Redmond D Barry have license to erect a mill on East fork Station Camp cr on land he bought of George Michie about 200 yards from road from Gallatin.

Edward Gwin v Joshua Rice. Trespass. Plf by Redmond D Barry dismissed suit.

Appt Daniel Smith special guardian for heirs of Samuel Donelson decd for purpose of defending further prosecution of a suit John C Henderson v admr of decedant.

Joseph McKain v Roger Gibson. Debt. Wm Bradshaw, bail, brings dft Gibson; John Withers special bail.

John Ezell v Sampson Bridgers. TAB. Plf by John C Hamilton dismissed suit.

p.557 Appt Wm Faulk John Mitchell & Willey Lassiter patrollers for Capt S[obliterated] company, they are to qualify before Benjamin Rawlings esquire.

Elizabeth & James Brigance admrs of William Brigance decd v Anthony Hogin & Rich Hogin. Debt. Plf moves to amend writ in sd cause which is permitted.

William Kavanaugh v Joseph Neeley. Debt. Plf by John C Hamilton. Suit dismissed by plf at sd plaintiffs costs.

Admrs of William Brigance decd v Anthony Hogin & Richard Hogin. Dfts file plea in abatement which on argument is overruled.

Order suits on docket to this Term which have not been continued already be continued to next Court.

Order James Douglass & Nicholas Boyce esqrs make settlement with D Shelby as acting guardian for Abraham Bledsoe, which settlement they return into Court.

Appt Rhodam Rawlings James Franklin Peter Looney P Zachariah Green John Franklin William Gillespie Jeremiah Doxey Ruffin Deloach Matthew Scoby Henry Bloodworth Thomas Bloodworth & Hardy Hunt assess damages sustained by John Payton sustained on account of road from Gallatin to Gillespies passing through his enclosures.

Greenberry Orr resigns his appointment as Constable for Capt Vinsons company.

Court adjourned till Court in Course.   Edward Douglass

INDEX

--, Abner 2
--, Abraham 17 18
--, Adam 17
--, Alexander 11
--, Benjamin 1
--, Charles 7
--, Christopher 16
--, Edward 18
--, Hugh 30
--, Isaac 4
--, Isaiah 1
--, James 1 5 8 18
--, John 1 6 7 13 16
--, Joseph 5 7 14
--, Josiah 17
--, Obediah 5
--, Philip 1
--, Richard 17
--, Thomas 1 16
--, William 1 6 8 10 12
--, Zachariah 2 12
--, Zebulon 2
ABLE, Ezekiel 67 174
Abraham 167
ACHOLS, Joel 54 56 57 Moses 81
ADAM, James 8 73
ADAMS, David 89 109 111 Thomas 90 99
AFLICK, John 70
Agg 134 200
Aggy 63
AGIN, John 16 30
AGNEW, Thomas 18
ALDERSON, William 179 219
Alea 162
Alex 162
ALEXANDER, Asaph 97 Captain 188 199 208 218 219 Daniel 89 90 93 131 132 Ebenezer 78 92 Ephraim 133 228 George 54 101 James 3 4 50 170 199 Mathew/Matthew 9 10 14 26 28 32 33 43 45 53 54 63 66 85 87 90 91 95 96 99 105 109 124 128 130-32 135 138 146 149 150 160 162 164 166 177 179 180 191 192 195 198 199 201 202-7 209 212 218 220 221 223 226-29 Richard 82 87 90 94 118 124 131 150 156 159 161 167 187 195 201-3 207 213 Silas 118 166 218 219 Stephen 59 Watris 75 William 68 76 82 84-88 90 114 120 144 146 150 160 166 213
ALLCORN, John 94 101 108 126 178

ALLEN, David 190 196 210 212 222 227 Grant 98 103 114 227 Henry 215 John 222 Nathan 75 116 Ormand 61 161 Rhody 36 63 Robert 222 Samuel 61 114 Theophilus 193 198 204 210 217 William 123 136 137 160
ALLEY, Thomas 6
ALLIN,Grant 149 Osman 61 Rhody 65
ALLISON David 39 99 117 125 195 Henry 63 William 177
ALLON, David 81 147 172 189 199 Grant 110 118 Nathan 79 O 52 Orman 68 77 102 109 117 121 160 180 186 Osman 52 54 Rhody/Rody 34 37-39 41 64 67 Theophilus 50 78 79 82 112 113 196 William 104 171
ALLOR/ALTON Rhdy/Rhody 32 38 41
AMBROSE, Isreal 95 96 118
AMHERST COUNTY, VIRGINIA 177
Amy 137
ANDERSON, Alexander 62 115 136 138 140-42 148 154 200 201 Daniel 54 100 119 George 175 James 182 183 Jane 97 John 74 87 89 97 132 139 144 149 151-54 175 176 184 194 199 228 Matthew 6 35 36 41 42 52 54 90 121-23 126-28 136 137 139 140 151 173 178 180 Pheby 200 Richard 100 171 Robert 76 79 97 123 132 136 137 139 147 150 165 175 189 191 223 Sarah 208 Stephen 25 77 82 93 97 148 180 Thomas 175 200 201 208 214 220 221 223-25 229 Uriah 2 4 7 10 12 14-16 21 25 42 44 65 74 76 81 100 William 31 51 52 74 76 86-88 98 103 105 107 113 117 118 122 128 129 133 138 147 148 150 153 156 175 184 186-89 198-200 209 212 -- 13 14
ANDREWS, John 100 222
ANGEL, John 181 206 Patsey 181
Ann 214
Anna 175
Annis 36
Anthony 79 200 231
ANTHONY, Elijah 221 227 230 231 232
ARCHER, Thomas 59 67
ARMSTEAD, Addison 98
ARMSTRONG, Andrew 54 112 120 131 James 51 59 60 61 212 224 228 John 68 Martin 68 117 157 231 William 38 39 41 51 60 61 77 114 115 222
ARNET/ARNETT, Nathan 65 120
ARRINGTON, Charles 2 William 96
ARRINGTONS CREEK 11 22 26 32 33

234

INDEX

ASBEY, James 215
ASBY, William 51
ASHERS CREEK 108 198
ASHLOCK, James 167
ASKEW, James 169
ASKINS, Mrs 31
ASPEY, James 217
ASTEN/ASTIN, William 100 119
ATKINSON, Advil 136 Carlton/Carleton 73 137 138 144 183 184 193 194 208 Elizabeth 208 Mary 208 Robt 137 147 168 183 184 205 208 220 Sarah 208 -- 166 178
ATMORE, William 80 87
AUST, Frederick 101
AVERETT, John 50
AXUM, Arthur 144 146-48 154 William 214
B--, Robert 6
BACKER, James 95 101 106
BADGET/BADGETT, Jonathan 142 145 162
BADTITLE, Baldy 145
BAILEY, Amos 121 197 John 101 151 154 169 175 188 Thomas 34
BAILON/BAILOR, Samuel 45
BAILS, Jesse 100 105
BAIRD, David 75 Joseph 97 103 William 97 103
BAKER, Isaac 22 108 118 120 121 128 130 132 136 138-41 146 148 149 153 154 160 162 163 166-68 172 174 179 180 185-87 190 192 193 197 204 210 214 215 220 221 228 James 72 86 107 108 John 22 76 79 80 89 144 167 Molley 192 Zacheus 194
BALCH, Amos 38 39 43 49 50 53
BALDWIN, Joshua 5 13 Sarah 13 William 2 5 7 8 17 23
BALEN, James 83 93
BALEY, John 168
BALL, James 167 189 194 196 199 220
BALOW, James 93
BALY, John 24
BANDY, Solomon 162 Wilcher 129 Willshear 170
BANKLERS, John 58
BANKS, Richard 93 101 104
BANT, William 65
BARCKLEY/BARCKLY, John 33 60
BARCLAY, James 120 John 120
BARHAM, John 151 161 202 204
BARKER, Edmund 221
BARKLEY, John 59 78

BARNES/BARNS, Frederick 18 22 James 22 John 50 53 85 186 207 Jorden 78 Joseph 31 50 53 74 98 Nathan 121 168 Milley 205 Selah 50 Solomon 73 74 76 77 79 96 99-102 113 114 116 124 149 153 159 160 166 167 168 172 174 179 185 186 189 Thomas 151 154 William 151 Wright 166 179 186 189 190 205
BARNET, -- 31 34
BARNETT, Robert 48 70 100
BARR, Captain 155 159 Hugh 90 139 144 145 Isaac 197 John 105 128 147 150 157 159 162 172 186-88 193-95 218 227 228 Nancy 196 Patrick 99 113 118 120 139 141 153 160 162 167 171 173 174 193 196 221 227 230 Samuel 226
BARROTT, Thomas 173 184 188 191 193 194 210 211 218 223
BARROW, Betsey 100 101 119 143 Henry 100 101 119 143 James 100 101 119 143 175 John 168 230 Matthew 100 101 119 143 Micajah 58 132 139 168 176 Molly 175 Robert 70 76 77 113 114 116 Ruffin 125 Sherwood 100 101 119 143 Wiley 161 William 70 83 89 145 182 Willie 65
BARRY, D 178 David 167 Dr 165 Redmond 111 112 116-18 132 143 156 158-61 163 166-70 176 177 179 181 183-94 197-99 203-5 207-13 216 219 221-25 227 229-33
BARTLET, John 12 22 24 William 19
BARTLETT, Benjamin 115 140
BARTLEY, John 9
BARTON, Samuel 42 52 54 58 76 77 82 86 89 92 94 95 98 103 108 119 Gabriel 103 Joseph 103 Samuel 105 115 123 124 Samuel 105 115 123 124 -- 43 51 52 creek 89 104 109 115 116 202
BARYE, George 101
BASHAW, Benjamin 70 177
BASS, Job 76 98 108 Theophilus/ Theopholus 172 178 182 183 195 230
BATES, Robert 75 186 198
BATTS, Frederick 61
BAUL, William 65
BAYES, John 43
BAYLEY, John 140
BEADLE, William 44
BEAKLEY, Betsey 163 John 163 Nancy 163 Sally 163 William 105 108 109 121 125 138 145 165 166

INDEX

BEARD, Adam 28 114 180 David 2-7 9-11 14 19 21 23 27-31 36 37 41 42 56 58 59 64-66 68 69 83 87 89 103 114 126 136 137 175 180 189 191 215 220 221 223-25 229 Hannah 94 Joseph 14 19 94 97 Samuel 189 191 William 10 22 30 37 40 63 64 68 82 85 90 94 121 136 142 147 179 182 183 184 201 207 209 210 218 220
BEASLEY, Ephraim 114 Isham 115 John 118
BEASON, James 63 John 71
BECK, John 71
BECKLEY, William 120
BEDDLE, William 44
Bede 189
BEDFORD, Thomas 132 139
BEDFORD COUNTY, VIRGINIA 114
BEDGEGOOD, Malachi 65
BEESON, John 67
BELEW, Thomas 144
BELL, Captain 76 James 198 Robert 2 7 9 11 17 20 24 26 30 35 36 40 42 43 53 56 80 Samuel 18 26 Simon 93 William 69 72 75 89 128 131 132 138 146 165 175 189 194-98 201 219 -- 181 184 211 224
BELLEN, Page 27
BELLEW, -- 81
BELOTE, Henry 109 116 126 129 131-33 138 141 142 147 149 155 162 164 165 178 179 181 182 191 195 199 208 220 221 225 228 230 Jeremiah 199 208 228
BELOW, James 93
Ben 146
BENNETT, Peter/Petter 210 214 231
BENS CREEK 7 11
BENTHALL, Charlotte 76 89 Daniel 70 76 Elizabeth 76 89 Enos 84 Frances 89 Francis 76 Franky 167 Joseph 79 82 86 Laban 68 70 84 123 126 134 135 141 145 155 161 Mary 70 76 84 89 167 216 Rhody 84 Susannah 76 89 167 William 68 74 76 79 82 84 86 89 110
BENTLEY, James 129 132 141 150 153 157 187 191 214 John 132 142 William 129 131 132 135 140
BENTLY, James 141
BENTON, David 229
BERKLEY, John 37 39 82 116 117
BERNARD, Elisha 75 112 191 209 220 Jacob 209 215 Luke 196 Zaddock 196 215
BERRY, James 30 158

BERRYMAN, Jesse 132
BESON, John 52 71 77 85 88 97
BETS, Henry 225
BETTS, William 202 Zachariah 40 82 227
BIDDLE, William 45 -- 46
BIG, Joseph 169
BIGGS, John 176 209 212 Joseph 203 William 162
BILLEN/BILLENS, Captain 101 James 86 90 100 101 116 Leonard 132 Page 25 31 37 Thomas 2 55 146 187
BILLEW, James 82 85
BILLINGSLY, James 66
BIRD, Abraham 14 15 23 24 27 30 31 Alexander 115 Francis 42 44 54 John 216 Shadrick 64 William 17 20 25-27 30 37
BISHOP, Joseph 80 102 103 104 110 116 William 173 174 ferry 124 142 159 173
BLACK, Agnus 58 Captain 139 144 155 166 171 Gabriel 32 60 64 72 74 79 84 86 105 106 109-11 115 128 167 172 George 84 97 116 118 119 123 129 130 144 146 167 174 184 186-88 197 200 213 215 226 Michael 78 201 228 Samuel 168 196 209 216 219 222 224 228 229 232 Susannah 36 William 58 61 67 93 186 192 222 -- 201 211
BLACKBURN, Benjamin 100 James 100 202 William 96
BLACKEMORE/BLACKIMORE,/BLACKMORE, G 20 George 5 6 10-12 14 20-22 27-29 31 33-35 39 45 53 55 58 59 61 63 64 66 70 76 78 85 92 95 108 109 123 129 130 135 140 147 149 150 155-57 165-67 176 186 187 189 190 195 198 201 203 207 212 214 217 228 James 91 97 146 148 154 177 184 196 197 216 217 John 92 108 132 139 157 224 Thomas 39 40 65 67 68 82 89-91 93 94 97 99 102 103 105 108 109 112 113 116 121 122 124 125 127 130 147 149 150 155 158 161-63 171-73 177 188 193 197 200 213 215-18 221 228-30 William 5 14 70
BLACK'S COMPANY 160
BLACKWELL, Joel 80 95
BLAIR, Andrew 66 John 66 222 Peter 68 70 151 165 166
BLAKES, George 43
BLALOCK, Charles 85 90 91 107 108 115 117 118
BLEDSOE, A 4 Abraham 11 44 45 52 67 69 135 233 Anthony 2-8 11 14 15 29 36 41

INDEX

44 47 48 52 53 55-57 61 62 65-67 69 117 122 129 135 138 159 161 171 177 181 184 201 Catey 86 151 159 Catharine 35 54 65 Henry 11 44-46 52 69 135 Isaac 1-16 18 20 21 28-33 35 36 38 42 44-46 49 50 52- 55 65 66 69 86 135 147 149 151 152 155 171 184 185 201 205 209 211 213 227 Katey 134 135 155 Katharine 63 Katy 46 209 Lytle 201 205 Major 1 2 Mary 11 14 Polley/Polly 11 44 45 52 66 67 69 111 113 Prudence 11 44 45 129 Prudy 69 Sally 86 Thomas 11 46 48 50 54 55 63 67 68 William 155 -- 1 4 100 119 creek 1 51 63 65 66 74 75 78-81 88 89 98 101 108-11 116 121 129 131 152 154 157 159 160 164 191 193 197 198 200 201 204 210 217 222 228 lick 19 26 29 66 71 98 103 108-10 124 147 150 151 160 162 169 172 173 176 195 212 213 224
BLEDSOESBOROUGH 93 94 98 101 104 108
BLOOD, Thomas 156
BLOODWORTH, Ava/Avey/Avi/Avis/Avy 162 187 194-97 Hardy 184 196 198 207 211 Henry 50 112 113 119 123 133 162 164 188 194 195 212 225 233 Milley 78 Priscilla 121 143 148 198 Thomas 82 123 233 Web/Webb 216 224 Wm 82 196
BLOUNT, John 132 William 18 21 24 39 48 49 59 117
BLUME, Jacob 110
BLYTHE, Ander/Andrew 49 50 56 73 76 77 81 84 101 103 105 106 110 115 118 120 123 124 136 137 139 144 147 148 159 209 215 216 226 James 35 77 85 150 151 Samuel 139 149 151 152 154 214 226 -- 81
BOALS, David 92 James 92
Bob 117 222
BODINE, James 69 181 220
BODLEY, Thomas 85
BOLES, John 4
BOLIE, John 4
BOLLEW, James 97
BOND, John 70 164 167 214 221 Joshua 92 William 16 Wright 160 163 167 168 171
BONDS, John 168 189 219
BONE, James 5 6 11 13 18 19 21 28 43 154 Susannah 21
BOOKER, Peter 156 William 134
BOON/BOONE, Jonathan 138 Isaiah 69 105 Jonathan 105 131
BORNS, Jonathan 99
BOROUGH, John 125
BOSLEY, James 10 14 John 55 136 Christian 83 100
BOSTON, John 81
BOSWELL, George 99
BOWAN/BOWEN, John 161 175 192 209 211 219 223 232 William 1 3 4 6-8 13 14 22 27 28 31 35 36 38 42 45 47 49 56 57 65 68 70 83 86 100 123 126-28 153 174 176 177 179 183 193 209 219
BOWDEN/BOWDIN, Joshua 227
BOWER, Reason 20 22 23 25 38 39 43 44 52
BOWERMAN, Jacob 100
BOWMAN, Andrew 75 110 John 153 161 168 215 220 221 224 225 229 Joseph 99 Robert 70 76 82 98 Thomas 94 98 111 115-18 William 2 8 11 13 14 16 25 29 49 63
BOWYER, Reason 17 32 37 40 41 43 -- 16
BOX, Henry 216 218 Robert 71 Stephen 73
BOYCE, Captain 188 196 James 184 190 223 John 122 127 128 132 136 141 146 148 183 184 217 221 224 225 230 Nicholas 71 97 100 101 117-19 135 137 153 160 161 165 167 170 173 175 177 178 180 184 187 188 190 191 193 195 196 198 200 204 206 209 215 222 223 225-28 230 233 Pleasant 166 Richard 100 115 118 131 137 143 144 153 156 159 161 221 222 224 Robert 100 101 112 138 194 -- 145
BOYD, Andrew 54 168 179 J 161 John 20 29 30 62-65 68 70 101 109 122 138 147 151 Robert 96 William 68 105
BOYECAN/BOYSCAN, Anny 162 194-197
BOYER, John 127 Nicholas 122 158 160 Richard 119 137
BOYLES, Robert 175 William 192 228
BRABSTON, John 172
BRACKEN, James 178 198 205 223 224 William 191
BRADEN, Alexander 41 42 78 87
BRADFORD, H 99 165 Harris 92 Henry 38- 40 42 55 60 62 63 68 70 74 76 81 90 97 99 122 135 137 153 156 157 160 161 174 175 178 185 194 199 201 210 213 214 224 228 232 Ivy 182 Major 64 -- 184 190
BRADLEY, Captain 90 92 93 99 122 125 131 139 142 155 158 171 188 192 218 219 Edward 84 85 105 133 134 171 173 174

INDEX

199 213 221 232 George 100 James 74 78 97 101 116-18 121 123 133 John 108 116 127 137 149 150 157 182 Joshua 195 215 Judah 199 Richd 91 103 176-78 184 193 198 201 206 221 226 228 230 231 232 Thos 69 103 108 110 127 132 133 140 142 145 153 157 158 195 198 206 compy 134
BRADLY, Edward 226 James 109
BRADSHAW, Hugh 95 127 172 J 127 William 127 136 137 153 159 161 166 174 181 187 199 207 214 221 227 232 233 bent 178
BRAKEN, Isaac 98 107 109-11 115 145 150 176 195 James 115 156-58 167 172 191 198 201 214 William 189
BRALON, Charles 44 Mary 44
BRALY, John 132
BRANDON, William 100 132 139
BRANNEN, Abel 214
BRASIL/BRASSIL, William 163 191
BRATCHER, Isaac 101
BRATNEY, Charles 80 Robert 68 89 103 150 156 160 171 173 174 184
BRATTON/BRATON, Charles 44 47 64 74 James 103 Mary 44 74
BRAY, Nicholas 168
BRAZEL/BRAZIL, William 19 28 77 133 189
BREAZEALE, H 117
BREDEN/BREDON, Alexander 44 60 65
BREINBERRY, William 153
BREVARD, John 103 Zebulon 85 126
BREWER, Sterling 176
BRIDGERS, Edmond 181 Reddick 181 224 Sampson 181 283 William 181
BRIEN, James 200
BRIGANCE, Betsey 219 D 38 David 13 14 16 20 24-26 30 34 37 46 56 61 65 98 214 Elizabeth 199 219 232 233 George 122 219 James 17 46 51 54 58 60 95 100 101 105 106 109 110 115 116 127 189 191 198 199 213 214 219 224 233 John 3 13 105 111 199 204 210 214 224 231 Peggy 219 Robert 2 6 12 16 17 20 21 23 25 27 28 30 31 33 46 48 51 219 Stuart 19 105 129 Vilet 219 William 13 16 17 20 21 23 25-28 33 42-46 49 51 53 61 62 71-73 79 80 84 96 101 107 109 111 113 115 121 163 167 174 176 177 178 199 200 213 219 224 232 233 -- 14
BRIGANER, David 14 48 John 12 Stuart 19
BRIGHAM, David 2 James 5 John 1 2 5 9

Robert 5 6 7 16 William 5 7 8 10
BRILEY, Samuel 228
BRIMBERRY, William 159 160 165 176 189
BRISCO, George 91 157 192 194
BRITTAIN/BRITTON, Richard 86 89 90 93 94 127 220 Thomas 43 51 52 65 90 91 144 160 161 175 199 208 214 218
BRODERICK, -- 93
BROOKS, Matthew 101 119 157 William 40 82
BROTHERS, John 100
BROUGH, Richard 40 -- 31
BROWN, Alexander 213 Edmund 118 George 41 54 56 79 98 120 121 125 130 133 143 168 169 171 196 199 205 206 215 219 228 James 102 113 128 147 150 213 215 218 228 Joel 175 228 John 61 68 90 93 101 103 104 115 117 149 189 213 228 Lewis 35 Matthew 62 78 92 115 194 224 Richard 168 215 219 Stephen 81 94-96 172 180 William 96 98 120 128 212 213 219
BROWNEN, Jacob 144
BROWNING, Captain 146 155 171 172 185 188 218 Constable 114 Edmond/Edmund 136 137 160 161 Elias 224 225 232 Jacob 145 160 171 Nimrod 185 Richard 108 mill 104 ferry 200 204
BRUCE, Captain 171 174 188 189 192 218 Robert 172 177 227 William 55 62 77 84 114 159 195 201 214 215 222
BRUFF, Richard 29
BRUICE, Robert 225
BRYAN, James 66
BRYANCE, David 16 17 21 30 115 James 111 114 John 5 12 18 35 64 Robert 19 30 William 35 70 71 76 111 112 113
BRYANT, Samuel 175 William 67
BUCHANAN, Archibald 35 James 98
BUCHANNON, Archibald 16 17 54 71 74 James 40 51 52 54 56 Samuel 101
BUCKINGHAM COUNTY, VIRGINIA 123 173
BUCK, Thomas 180
BUCKLY, John 29
BUCKNELL, William 6
Buk 98 150
BULLARD, John 182 190
BULLOCK, John 174 182 190 Jonas 182 Josias 174 182 190
BUNCKLEY, Jonathan 152
BUNCUM COUNTY, NORTH CAROLINA 146

INDEX

BUNN, Henry 70 75 77 78 97 104 109 110 111 114 115 121 144 146 147 148 154 160 171 174 176 177 179 183
BUNTIN, John 196 Joseph 196 William 196
BUNTON, John 120 200 Joseph 120-23 138 139 William 201 207 209 210 215 220 221 223 224 225 229
BURFORD, Daniel 101 102 151
BURGES/BURGESS, John 29 33 45 51
BURK, William 89
BURKET, Priscilla 227 Susannah 227
BURNEY, John 172
BURNLY, John 183
BURROUGH, John 170
BURROW, John 169 170 175 176 216
BURROWS, John 230
BURTON, H 208 229 Hutchings/Hutchins 179 198 206 211 212 215 222 226 231 232 Jean 66 Joseph 118 136 William 66
BUSH, Abner 1 2 158 161 217 Elinder 2 George 139 147 163 180 John 105 152 154 161 187 191 209 211 225 226 230
BUSHNELL, Eusebius 13 17 104 Ezra 104
BUSTART, -- 211
BUTLER, Aaron 216 Barnet 163 John 15 16 17 19 29 30 38 51 207
BUTTON, Thomas 58
BUYET, Jonathan 124
BYERS, John 144
BYRD, Abraham 218 John 229 Thomas 59 William 59
BYRNS, James 218 John 117 141 146 147 148 149 154 160 162 218 Joseph 153
BYRUM, James 111 116 118 John 112
C--, Lewis 13
CADRY, John 43
CAFFERY, John 66 86 113 131 176 177
CAFFRY, William 198
CAGE, Betsey 177 Edward 195 202-4 207 228 J 112 113 118 122 127 128 129 132 140 142 147 James 70 120 123 124 130 137 166 168 195 196 200 201 216 219 229 232 Jesse 200 206 John 221 228 233 Patsey 177 R 73 101 110 111 117 131 158 223 Reuben 23 31 45 49 53 61 63 66 68-70 76 80 84 87 89 90 98 100 101 104 107 108 110 114 115 120 122 128 129 132 133 135-37 142 144 148 149 151 154 155 159 162 166 175 176 180 182 184 191 195 196 198 214 William 15 16 18 23 25 27 28 31 34 36 38-40 44-48 50-52 56 57 60 61 63-70 72 73 75-80 82-85 87 88 90-93 96-101 103 105-8 111 119 122 123 125-27 130-34 137 139 140 144 147-51 154-60 162 164-67 177 181 183 185 186 188 193 194 199 200 202 206 213 215 217-19 222 223 229 Wilson 16 18 22 23 41 43 56 60 64 69 82 86 92 94 101 105 110 116 129 131 134 181 183 207 230 -- 186 201 210 211 215 216 220 227 228
CAILER, Charles 5
CAILY, James 29
CAIR, King 32 Richard 22 24
CALDWELL, David 78 115 Samuel 214 222 224 232
CALLAHAN, James 152 169
CALLEN, John 23
CALYAR, Elizabeth 223
CAMBELL, James 22 Robert 21
CAMDEN COUNTY, NORTH CAROLINA 148
CAMPBELL, Charles 50 51 David 166 203 209 210 George 120 147 151 154 174 185 191 192 Hugh 206 James 24 37 50 146 153 194 204 John 1 3 Joshua 2 5 7 13 17 29 32 Michael 68 69 123 139 Robert 39 43 47 59 123 161 Samuel 1 3 Thomas 131 137 197 William 85
CANADY, -- 109
Candass 63
CANDLER, Ann 158
CANNON, David 116
CANTREL/CANTRELL, Stephen 9 17 20 24 26 35 43 45 46 47 50 119
CANTRIL/CANTRILL, Captain 35 36 40 59 68 69 82 90 96 99 122 Stephen 10 24 26 30 31 39 40 42-52 55-57 59-67 71 76 82 85 91 93 94 96 98 99 103 104 108 109 112 139 144 155 156 159 160 162 169-72 174 176 177 180 185 187 188 193 202 203 217 228 229 -- 30
CAPLINGER, John 115
CARADINE, Parker 135
CARITHERS, Robert 63 91
CARLY, James 29
CARNAHAN, Andrew 66
Caroline 65
CAROLINE COUNTY, VIRGINIA 195
CAROTHERS, Hugh 171 195 200 202 203 207 James 165 184 189 191 207 Robert 76 144 160 193 201 207

INDEX

CARR, Captain 92 99 122 126 139 142
James 228 John 20 37 71 86 89 90 123
128 139 147 150 187 191 218 221 226-29
King 4-6 10 13 14 25 26 44 45 47 55 58
62 67 147 151 156 159 184 185 214 218
Margaret 146 Richard 2 3 7 8 10 14 15
20 21 114 189 191 209 215-17 228 233
Sarah 35 William 77 86 89 105 132 169
191 201 208 209 210
CARRELL, Demse 99
CARROTHERS, Samuel 105
CARSON, David 80 87 153 Honor 158 James
46 55 56 60 67 97 149 152 153 158
Rachel 124 133 158 192 William 124 131
133 158 159 168 173 213 220 222
ferry 56 60
Carter 150
CARTER, Charles 2 3 6-11 13 16 17 22 23
25 27-29 31 33-35 37 38 40-44 46 48 49
51 52 56 58-61 70-73 79 80 84 142 173
206 Jesse 82 87 John 89
CARTON, James 45
CARTWRIGHT, James 110 111 142 144 107
108 139 141 Justinian 12 21 23 28 29
31-33 Matthew 65 70-73 83 84 96 97 113
114 148 153 160 163 175 181-85 189 194
Robert 31 Thomas 221 William 52 79 80
176 192 -- 31 99
CARTY, -- 7
CARUTHERS, Hugh 133 James 87 118 121-
23 128 136-38 140 141 148 154 Robert
62 64 79 81 95 96 118 120 126 -- 81
CARY, James 124 130 147 149 152 153 165
171
CASWELL COUNTY, NORTH CAROLINA 134
Cate 227 231
CATHARINE, Francis 152
CATHEY/CATHY, Alexander 90 128 134 140
160 162 164 165 173 174 177-79 186 187
194 201-4 213 220 229 Alice 134 Elizabeth 134 George 112 180 Griffith 140
James 134 139 140 142 220 John 85 92
123-25 128 134 189 194-98 201 213 228
Matthew 186 Thomas 186 William 85 93
120 127 128 134 136 139 158 187 194 213
CATLET, Grandison 206
CATRON, Christly 93 213 218 220 Chris-
topher 215 Francis 63 64 70 73 74 76 77
97-100 102 142 143 201 206 228
CAVEATT, John 228 Joseph 101 102 123

147 166 172 182 Michael 24 25 30 33 65
83 92 114 Moses 92 Richard 2 3 11 24
26-29 32 37 40 41 61 65 73 77 86 92 101
106 111 114 118 119 147 156 162 178 ---
-- 61
CAVETT/CAVETTE, John 222 Joseph 206
Michael 222 Richard 51 65 106 228
CAVIT/CAVITT, John 169 Joseph 68 151
Michael 14 30 31 68 70 222 Richard 4 6
7 11 18 37 39 56 60 68 157 169 171 172
209 212 -- 75
Celia 146
CHAMBERS, Elijah 40 42 43 49 51 56 62
67 68 96 98 103 121 132 143 197 Elisha
37 39 Henry 103 Patton 51
CHANDLER, George 75 Mary 75
Timothy 77 82 97
CHAPMAN, Alexander 137 191 George 196
James 120 137 Martha 137
Charity 116
Charles 85 222
CHARLESTON, SOUTH CAROLINA 104
Charlotte 123 137
CHASE, Samuel 49
CHATHAM COUNTY, NORTH CAROLINA 126
CHEEK, Elisha 131 137 146 149 209 210
212 214 225 229
Cherry 214
CHERRY, Daniel 162 Jesse 162 Joshua
95 118 121 124 144 148 149 165 167 168
170 174 175 186 190 208 Wilie/Willie/
Willey 89 92 115 158 181 220
CHILDERS, Joel 179 182 Sarah 23
CHILDRESS, Joel 221 227 230
CHITWOOD, Pleasant 143 149 155 164 185-
87 189 195 197 204 217
Chloe 75
CHLOE, John 98
CHRISTIAN, Thomas 37
CHRISTMASS, Thomas 23 24 31 William
114-16 119 191 194
CLACK, Andw 108 120 George 114 120 John
108 Richd 108 Robt 108 116 120 Wm 108
CLAIRY, Elisha 110-13 John 103-7 110
115 William 105 107
CLAMPETT, Ezekiel 151
CLAP, Adam 20-22 33 39 41 47 53 61
CLARK, Andrew 108 114 118 125 131
George 114 118 125 131 143 151 156
Isaac 160 163 173 175 178 184 188 194

INDEX

196 222 James 132 John 108 186 Joseph 84 175 194 199 218 219 Mary 114 Rachel 134 186 Richard 104 107 108 114 Robert 108 116 120 134 140 142 150 151 Thomas 39 41 43-45 William 84 108 150
Clary 148
CLARY, Elisha 5 7 8 13 14 20 22 36-38 43 45 46 58 76 78 79 84 104 107 109-11 113 115 135 151 220 227 Elizabeth 186 188 John 101 William 2 4 5 7 8 76 77 80 191 -- 5
CLASS, Adam 38
CLAYPOLE, Jaramah 184
CLENDENING, James 3-5 10 20 21 23 28 29 32 33 37 40-47 51 52 54 56 58 59 65-67 69 74 75 78 81 92 105 107 108 110-13 118 120 127-29 139 141 147 153 154 160 162 164 166 174 175 189 193-98 201 206 214 220 221 223-35 229 233 branch 93
CLOAR, John 199
Clo 167
Cloe 65
CLOE, John 171 199
CLOUD, John 231 232
CLOYD, David 54 56 58 60 115 Ezekiel 54 56 58
COCHRAN, David 92 188 John 172 William 109 113 116 135 151 154 172 173 175 188 203 217
COCK, Robert 107 W 150
COCKE, Thomas 85 90 113 120 123 133 135 156 159 160 165 177 201 203 218
COFFEE, John 224 231 233 Joshua 66
COGLIN, James 126
COLEMAN, John 183 Robert 180
COLLIER, Isaac 63 Robert 63 75 96 97 112 116 121 126 146
COLLINS, Edmund 214 216 James 98 103 116 121 141 Vines 201
COMAR, John 173 226
COMBS, Robert 212 217
Comfort 63
COMINGS, Moses 185
COMPERY, Francis 214
COMYN, James 122 124
CONDRY, William 109
CONGER, Stephen 133 207
CONN, Josephus 211 219 222 231 Samuel 203 219 -- 219
CONNER, John 168 Lewis 168 Peggy 168

William 168
CONROD, Nicholas 5 45
CONWAY, Miles 123
CONYER/CONYERS, Thos 16 25-27 57 93 103
COOK/COOKE, Giles 210 214 229 James 4 John 99 Richard 90 116 125 126 158 Thomas 118 William 232
COOLEY, David 158
COOPER, Benjamin 58 61 62 66-68 71 96 105 107 110 Christopher 58 65 67-69 73 74 76 77 83-88 96 97 110 173 David 20 21 James 84 John 20 21 96 102 104 176 Martin 171 William 11 12 -- 102
COPE, Richard 193 208 218 224 225
COPLIN, -- 198
Copper 142
CORDRY, John 40
CORNPERY, Francis 214
COSBY, James 52 William 69 72 156
COTHERN, John 96
COTTEN, James 136 Lazarus 219 220 Moore 220 221
COTTON, Allon 196 Arthur 155 James 68 71 95 121 147 148 John 11 13-17 20-22 25 53 60 67 72 73 75 77 97 109 113 189 191 192 194 196 Lazarus 15 17 19 28 37 38 44 46-48 51 53 55 60 61 68 75 79 83 87 88 91 95 100 101 111 113 116 117 119 162-64 213 221 227 Lemuel 108 221 Moor/Moore 62 65 70 77 81 87 109 153-156 179 181-84 189 192 194-98 201 221 226 Noah 194 Patsey 60 Polly 60 Samuel 96 103 Sarah 60 Thomas 40 45 46 48-51 58 61 62 64 77 155 -- 24
COUGHER, Sarah 214
COULTER, Levi 145
COVENANT, John 94
COWAN, Mathew/Matthew 51 84 117 126 127 129 132 133 142 156
COWENY/COWINS, Margaret 76
COWPER, William 120
COX, Edward 41 Lewis 78
CRABTREE, James 31 58 122 Joseph 42 44 51 53 55 91 96 99 Wm 12 45 46 54 61 85
CRADDOCK, John 91
CRADY, David 4 5
CRAFFORD, Hugh 93-98 101 105 106 115 124 133 144 148 160 Wm 36 37 creek 168
CRAIGHEAD, John 170 176 197
CRANE, Lewis 2 4-6 10-12 18 19 26 27 30

INDEX

31 39 40 58 65 76-78 83-88 90 91 98 101
102 110 113 114 127 156 157 174 175 189
191 207 212 232   -- 11 39
CRAVENS/CRAVINS, John 2 5 6 8 21-23
CRAWFORD, Hugh 2 3 5 7-9 11 16 17 20
25-30 34 36 40-42 44 47 48 51-55 58 60
61 65 67 70 73 76 79 82 83 86 90 93 105
106 110 111 118 133 144 146 153 158 159
179 181-84 195 204 220 221 230 231
John 104 107 Samuel 78 William 208 214
CRENSHAW, David 158 194 201
CRIBBINS, Thomas 16 25-27 50 60 61 71
74-77 80 83 97 113 136 137 139 140 142
145 146 152 155 162 163 216 William 16
CROCKETT, James 132 139
CROFT MILL 7 65 73 75 80 109 118 120
121 124 139 159 168 191 220
CROMWILL, Alexander 18
CROP, Samuel 62
CROSS, Saml 62 85 Zachariah 12 19 -- 5
CROSSNER, Thomas 206
CRUNK, John 4 197 209 215 216 224 231
233 Milley 197
CURRY, Effy 210
CRUTCHER, Anthony 36 40-44 68 130 133
E 151 159 164 194 195 204 213 215 224
Edmund 103 112 120 137 140 141 147 163
165 168 170 178 186 188 192 199 200 229
231 Hugh 75   -- 184 190
CRYER, James 70 79 81 82 84 86 89 91 92
97 98 109-11 115 120-24 126 127 130 133
134 136 139 142 147 149 153 155 160 162
165-71 174 175 177-79 183-86 188 190
193 194 196-98 202 204-6 210 212 215-19
221-25 228 231 John 97 120 139 181
CUATY, Augustin 112
CUBBINS(CRIBBINS?), Thomas 14 15 50 75
76 -- 77
Cuff 5
Cula 175
CUMMINS, George 73 74 85 86 109 206 211
John 60 63 99 100 158 Moses 115 118
131-33 141 168 228 Thomas 97 104 -- 51
CUNNINGHAM, Will 219
CURICA, John 76
CURL, William 70 77
CURLEY/CURLY, James 12 28 29 49 134 160
-- 7
CURRY, Thomas 165
CURTIS, Thomas 108

CYPERT, Thomas 157
D--, George 227
Dagner/Dagnor, Peter 126 127 135 136
141
DAHARDA, William 139
DALE, Joshua 54
DAMRIL, Joseph 22
Dan 55
DAN, Henry 219
Daniel 71 117
DANIEL, William 67 134
DARHADA, William 132
Darkes/Darkess 89 121
DARR, Henry 219
DAUGHETY, James 117 132 135
David 98 231
DAVIDSON, James 232 John 110 156 158
DAVIDSON COUNTY 7 36 50 52 58 63 78 109
120 143 156 161 220
DAVIES, Arthur 70
DAVIS, Andrew 9 Arthur 79 Benjamin 119
125 136 139 148 152 David 191 193 Elisha 85 123 132 138 139 Frederick 93 94
99 James 99 Joseph 136 Mary 125 136 139
148 150 152 155 Nicholas 66 75 Robert
108 151 173 175 178 209 227 Thomas 38
William 16 22   -- 82
DAVISON, John 109
Davs 227
DAVYSON, John 116
DAWSON, Jesse 208 212 John 19 21 24 26-
29 32 34 36-39 42 44 49 51 52 54 55 58
60 62 63 65 67 70 73 75 76 79 80 90 91
95 97 101 102 107 111 113 115-18 120
130 133 135 145 146 149 158 159 169 174
182 183 185 191 202 208 -- 148 218 222
225 creek 173
DEACON, James 72
DEADERICK, George 77 86 117 156 161
John 77
DEAL, Jarvis 231
DEAN, Robert 86
DEBOW, Frederick 93
DEFORD, Elisha 216
DELAWARE (state) 146
Delce 63
Deley 98
DELOACH, Jesse 184 185 222 225 John 30
50 51 62 69 75 83 86 87 88 90 111 116
117 119 123 126-28 130-32 136 140 141

INDEX

154-57 162 164 167 168 184 185 189 224 225 Ruffin 25-31 34 36-39 41 42 44 45 50 58 115 116 185 196 198 201 211 215 222 225 233
Delsee 222
Demarcus 104
DEMENT, Charles 29 35 38 39 41 49 51 55 56 57 60 63 64 71-74 85 87 90 92 101 103-7 110 113 115 118 121-23 125 140 162 167 168 171 179 David 140 179 180 183 185 198 199 219 Thomas 198 199
Demon 63
DEN, John 99 167 223
DENAN, John 150
DENEHEW, John 111
DENING, John 130
DENISON, Gideon 92
DENNEN, David 205 John 114
DENNING, David 146 John 123 166 179
Dennis 219
DENNIS, W 167 William 162 168
DENNY, James 174
DENTON, Thomas 21
DEP--, Robert 157
DEPRIEST, John 151 189
DERDEN, John 122 138
DESHA, Charles 163 James 57 65 170 174 176 192 198 200 204 222 224 228 232 John 1 Joseph 7 8 11-14 16-18 25 30 40 Robert 1-4 7 9 11 14-16 20-22 29 31 37 39 40 48 52 53 55 57 59 60 62 65 70 75 79 83 84 113 118 120 121 123-25 127 133-36 147 153 155 156 160 162 177 183 209 218 -- 81 creek 19 79 ford 222 fork 1 gap 147 station 7
DEVER, Alexander 2 3 7 14-16 18 John 60
Dick 126
DICKER, George 49
DICKERSON, Benjamin 150 James 157 John 158 206 227 Nathaniel 159 197 226 227 William 230-32
DICKESON, Ben 8 9
DICKIN/DICKINS, Jeremiah 79 93
DICKINSON, John 130 142 197 198 201 207 211 232 William 231 -- 184
DICKISON, Ben 10 James 158 John 174 175 194 197 224 Joseph 6 Nathaniel 157 158 William 221 230
DICKSON, John 100 Joseph 14 William 71 -- 198 202

DILLARD, Gabrael/Gabriel 162 207 Joel 71 76 77 John 78 Mr 73 Owan/Owen 76 77 83 85-88 96 97 133 144 William 27 31-34 39 41 70-72 207 Zachariah 73 ferry 155 158 159
DILLON, Edward 100 119
Dina/Dinah 98 154 208
Dine 222
DINNING, John 186
DITTO, Henry 145
DIX, James 90
DIXON, Betsey 59 116 120 Charles 54 112 122 130 134 138 145 154 192 Elizabeth 57 59 120 Henry 51 Joseph 2 4 5 7-10 12 16 17 28-30 57 59 120 Michael 141 T 78 93 145 Tilmon 50 51 54 74 78 82 84 90 93 97-99 101 103 104 111-13 130 134 154 155 192 206 213 226 William 103 123 128 144 183 227 Wynn 50 69 122 Wynne 138 creek 65 66 78 81 83 86 89 98 100 104 116 springs 75 82 90 93 129
DOBBINS, Alexander 84 167 180 227 John 31-33 122 126 132 137-39 167 Robert 75 77 85 86 88 114 131 138 158 227 William 13 20 27 32 34 41 50 52 57 60 61 63 66-68 72 73 75 76 86 94 101 110 122 129 131 134 183
DOBYNS, John 161
DOCTOR, -- 9
DOHERTIE, James 71-74 80 82 83 86 91 93 95-97 101 105 107 109
DOHERTY, J 50 67 James 35 44 56 59 62 66 69 76 Mr 69
DOIL, Thomas 19
DOLERHIDE, Aquilla 87
Doll 65 92 200
DOLTON, Robert 141
DONALD, Thomas 35 61
DONELSON, Alexander 153 John 32 49 124 Mary 200 Mr 160 Robert 49 62 Samuel 47 48 65 66 74-76 78 79 83 84 86-88 93-98 100 103-7 109-13 115-17 119-25 127 128 131-34 136 138 140-49 151-54 159 161-68 173 174 176-82 184-86 188 190 192-95 197 199-202 204 207-12 214 220-23 229 230 232 233 Stockley/Stockly 92 95 107 117 William 34 158
DONELY, William 25 26 27
DONIHO, Thomas 76
DONIHOO, Charles 72 John 76 103

243

INDEX

DONNALDSON, William 142
DONNELL, Doctor 176 George 59 John 98 Thomas 37 41 42 47 48 50-54 56-62 67-70 72-74 77-79 82-84 87 89-91 98 99 102 104-8 110 111 113 115 116 119 120 122 128-30 132 133 137 139-42 144-46 149 153-55 158 159 162 164 166 171 174-76 179 181 182 186 188-90 193 196 199 200 202-8 210 212 216 217 220 221 223 225 226 228-32 William 53 81 101 207
DONOHO, Archibald 209 231 Charles 85 90 91 93 98 99 103 105 108 110 114 115 122 125 129 134 139 140 142 147 154 155 159 161 162 163 166 168 171-74 176 177 185-88 192 193 200-4 207 210-14 220-22 Edward 90 166 Isaac 104 110 111 130 141 146 214 John 96 97 103-8 110 146 162 164 187 199 232 Patrick 85 107 108 Thomas 78 79 81 85 90 93 166 William 133 -- 81 mill 76 78 93
DONOHOW, John 221
Dorcas 173 189
DORRIS, Isaac 70 John 78 Joseph 196 Samuel 70 William 174 201 228 229 232
DOUGAN, James 37 40 John 207 Robert 44 45 62-64
DOUGHERTY, Henry 81 James 54 Robert 43 -- 45
DOUGIN, James 43 Robert 67
DOUGLASS, Captain 1 3 4 6 8 11 Colonel 64 E 4 Edward 1 5-9 11 13-24 26-28 30-55 57 59 61 63-69 71 72 74 75 77 80 82-88 91 92 95 96 98 99 102-9 111 113 114 116-18 121 122 124 127 128 130-32 135 136 139 142-44 147 149 152 153 155 158-60 162 163 165 169 171 173-77 181-83 187-91 193-98 200 202 204 205 208-10 215-19 223-25 229-33 Elmore 1-7 9-15 17 19 21 23 25 27 29 31 35 36 40 47 51 52 65 68 87 89 90 93 98 101 103 104 108-10 112 115 116 228 Ezekiel 2 3 5 7 8 10 16 19 22 23 26 32 33 35-39 41-43 45-47 49-53 55-58 60 61 63 64 66 67 70 73-75 83 84 87 88 94 95 97 98 100 101 110-13 119 121 125 126 132 133 135 136 144 145 149 228 J 69 James 1 2 5 7 8 10 11 15 16 18 24 26 29 36-38 45 47 49-52 54 55 57 60 61 63-69 72 73 75 77-79 81-85 91 93 95-101 104 107-9 111-13 115-18 120 122 124 130 136 137 139 144 146 147 149 154 155 160 163 168 172 178 181 182 184 185 187-90 193 195 196 198 200-2 204 208 209 211 216 218 224 227-29 231 233 John 102 144 155 172 219 Margaret 68 Martin 81 102 109 Reuben 2 5 8 10 11 13 14 17 18 22 23 27 28 31 33 34 37-39 42 43 47 52 56 57 59 65 70 72 73 75 79 80 87 95 96 104 113-20 123 135 138 139 144 146-48 154 160 161 167 179 181-83 189 191 206 220 232 Sarah 35 70 72 77 103 W 127 158 William 27 34 37 38 40 47 49 50 53 56 58 60 65 67 70 72-74 83 84 115 123 127-29 131 136 146 155 158 171 172 174 175 177 184 186 187 196 198 205 206 209 217 219 222 225 226 -- 6 17 55 148
DOXEY, Jeremiah 61 80 85 114 123 157 195 198 201 203 204 207 233 John 157 Nancy 157 Stephen 157 Thomas 157
DRAKE, Brittain 181 creek 64 68 80 81 91 103 109 143 150 157 159 160 168 178 201 222 225 230 232
DRAPER, John 122 138 Thomas 81 84 86 88 100 115 132 William 108 150
Dred 157
DREW, Newit 108
DUFF, William 205
DUGER, Anne 138 Leonard 139
DUGGAN, Robert 83
DUGGER, Dred 152 John 152 163 194 195 199 Leonard 143-45 147 158 162 Lucy 194 Luke 152
Duke 92
DUNGWORTH, Charles 89
DUNHAM, Daniel 232
DUNIHOO, Charles 69 70 John 60-62 73 75 92 Patrick 65 Thomas 75
DUNLAP, David 161
DUNN, Michael 138 140 148 Shadrack 197
DUNOHO, Charles 90
DUREN, George 162 228
DUTY, George 218 Littleton 175 214 228 Solomon 131 138 148 150 218 William 213 227 228 230
DYAL, Jenny 13
DYER, Joel 101 105 110 111 113-16 133 134 138 140 141 197
DYSART, James 134
E--, Charles 228 Thomas 6
EARLE, Francis 148
EASON, Alexander 183

INDEX

EASON, Alexander 183
EASTON, -- 211
EATHERLY, Jessey 193
EATON, Charles 123 John 126
Ebe 97
ECHOLS, Alkenah 70 Caner/Canu 109 David 125 130-32 138 139 141 205 Elkam 203 Elkenor 156 162 163 Joel 25 32 41 98 123 127 128 136 160 199 201 203 John 125 Moses 71 80 89 109 119 122 199
ECKOLS, David 128 Joel 108 109 133 207-210 Moses 123 124
EDGAR, John 100 103
EDMANSTON, Robert 36
EDMUNSTON, David 126 Robert 90
EDWARDS, Adonijah 93 94 108 126 127 129 190 197 203 232 Amelia 92 Benjamin 85 Clarissa 85 Elisha 121 126 Frederick 80 87 101 105 James 130 John 52 54 56 60 85 86 92 115 167 172 174 225 Milly 85 Nathan 79 85 108 191 195 196 201-4 207 224 Nathaniel 217 Thomas 20 24 33-36 38 39 44 49-53 55 57 60 61 63-65 70 74 79 83 84 86 94 101 102 105 107 113 126-129 133 138 146 160 163 166 168-70 179 184 186-92 194 198 199 207 216 217 224 225 231 232 Williams 14 15 17 20-23 27 28 32 34 37 38 41 42 44-47 52 54-56 60 61 65 67 73 74 76-78 85 92-94 101 102 105 115 116 127 129 133 136-38 149 150 160 165 184 204 215 217-19 221 224 225 228 229 232
Edy 130
EGNEW, Elender 219 George 121 219 Jane 219 Jenny 121 Jesse 121 219 Nelley 121 Robert 79 Thomas 4 10 18 19 22 23 26 27 32 35 56 58 60 64 65 68 120 121 140 180 219 229 -- 84-86 88 115 132
ELDER, James 98 110 156
ELLIOTT, Charles 89 108 140 141 144 146 148 154 160 166 184 198 201 228 George 48 Hugh 30 48 51 52 65 67 68 75-77 79 84 87 91 138 140-42 148 153 154 165 166 175 208 James 151 John 17 48 Samuel 95 102 107 108 147 Simon 29 35 37 53 75 78 Tebiah 48 Thomas 204 branch 160
ELLIS, Abraham 134 186 209 224 232 Benjamin 81 94 98 159 James 81 Robert 24 25 27 38 53 62 71 75-77 79 80 83 85-88 91 94 95 110 112 119 127-29 131 132 136 144 164 177-79 187 Simon 30 41 87 William 55
Ephraim 121
ERVIN, John 7
ESPEY/ESPY Alexander 84 158 180 James 31 87 96 113 127 197 John 84 158 Robert 10 29 30 43 84
ESSPIE, James 149
ESSPY, James 21 99 100-2 118 120 121 125 Margaret 147 Robert 11 12 16 50 54 63 71 75
ESTELL, Benjamin 43
Esther 63 85 121
ESTILL, Benjamin 51 52 Wallace/Wallis 74 84 90
ETHERIDGE, Godfrey 162 Isaac 177 178
EUBANK, Joseph 54
EUBANKS, William 228
EURY, Alexander 205 Francis 197 205
EVANS, George 152 Joseph 46 Thomas 54
EWING, Alexander 64 Elijah 25 James 22 23 25 26 28 154 Robert 24 50 122
EXUM, Arthur 78 85 93 126 127 159 171 172 176 177 194 212 213 219 222 228 Joseph 176 William 129 177 194 201
EZELL, John 233
F--, Captain 10
FAIR, Ephraim 8 16 35 67 James 14 27 61 Samuel 30 35 37 -- 7
FAIRCLAIM, Francis 145 231-33
FALKNER, William 101 119
Fan 75
FANNING, Joseph 87 88
Fanny 145 146 150 172 175
FARLAND, John 132 139
FARMER, Stephen 92 Thomas 101 103 105-7 110 115 126 130 132 138 140 144 164 167 168 184 199 208 217 224
FARR, Ephraim 17 44 68 76 77 80 117 James 27 40 47 50 59 61 76 77 175 Jane 124 Jennet 77 Samuel 50 William 92
FARRIER, John 73 100 Prudence 32
FAULK, William 230 233
FAUSIT, Richard 171
FAVAS, Elisha 67
FAYETTE COUNTY, PENNSYLVANIA 184 203
Feeb 110
FEET, Jarret 170
FELAND, James 110 116
FELTS, Archibald 64 101

INDEX

FEN, Richard 223
FENNER, Richard 54 71 Robert 114 115 119 135
FENTON, Thomas 202
FERGUSON, Joshua 12
FERRELL David 145 186 189 192 193 199 203 215 James 114 123 177
FERRIER, John 74 103 107 122 162
FIGUERES, Major 104
FIGURES, Matthew 92
FIKE, Malachi 126
FINDLEY, Samuel 5 97 -- 215
FISER, Henry 170
FISHER, Archibald 9-11 14 34 36 37 62 92 Jabus 29 120 121 123 126 131 231 James 224 John 75 224 Joshua 75 King 224 Peter 14 34 59 147 152 207 William 65 -- 31
FISK, Moses 149
FLEMING/FLEMMING, John 81 Joseph 81 Peter 50 175 Samuel 70 81
FLENER/FLENOR, Adam 16 19
FLETCHER, William 97
FLIN, Ebenezer 130
FLINER/FLINOR, Adam 18 25
FLYNNS CREEK 122
FONVIELLE/FONVILL, Francis 75 78 80 81 82 97 129 191 218
FORDNER, Francis 24
FOREMAN, Benjamin 212
FORK, William 89
FORKAID, S 59
FORRESTER, Charles 133 Robert 128
FORT, Elias 132 139 William 54 130 Blount 56 57 59 65 66 68 74 75 77 78 81 87 100 172 197
Fosey 65
FOSSIT, Richard 73 74 76 77
FOSTER, Alexander 81 Anthony 77 Robert 81 96 John 81 Richard 79 William 120
FOWLAR, Benjamin 90
FOWLER, Polley 99 102 112 156 160
FRANCIS, William 135
Frank 85
FRANKLIN, James 1-3 5-8 11 13 19 22 23 25 28 31 33 38 41 42 46 51 53 56-58 65 68 70 73 75 78 79 82 83 97 127 134 139 155 158 160 161 173 174 176 177 189 194 195-98 201-4 207 233 John 67 100 103 108 109 131 140 173 182 185 186 221 233

FRANKLIN COUNTY, N C 54 71 112
FRANKLIN COUNTY, VIRGINIA 114
FRAZ--, Captain 14
FRAZER, Captain 22 31 35 36 43 James 2 3 33 38 53 55 113 118 144 233 William 2 35 -- 30
FRAZIER, Captain 16 19 James 5 6 9 13 17 20-22 25 27 38 41 William 5 9 10 13 14 15 65
FRAZOR, Capt 28 45 47 Daniel 78 James 5 20 26 27 31 38 39 45 46 49 53 54 64 70 78 90 93 114 115 120 121 124 125 128 148 160 166 195 199 204 219 Mary 167 Urbone 167
FRAZUR, Captain 48 William 25 27 31 35 38 43 46 53 76 77 107 108 131 171 174 175 184 185 215 220 221 223-25 229
FREDERICK COUNTY, VIRGINIA 180
FREEMAN, Elisha 226
FRY, Basil/Bazel 3 4 5 8 19 James 53 Thomas 35 William 39
FRYAT/FRYATT, Nancy 36 107 Peggy 36 Polly 36 Robert 37 57 Thomas 113
FRYIT, Nancy 37 Peggy 37 Polly 37
FUGATE, James 64
FULLER, Henry 216
FUNKHAUSER/FUNKOUSER/FUNKHOWER, Christopher 13 15 16 25 31 41 42 54
FURMAN, Isaac 199
FURNEY, Peter 14
GADRAY, James 101 119
GAITHER, Thomas 227
GALASPIE, William 106
GALBRAITH, John 218 227
GALBREATH, John 185 William 63 65 66 185 187
GALESPIE, William 102 107 190
GALLASPIE, John 88 George 90 91 100 William 89 91 96 97 101 106
GALLISPIE, George 123
GAMBELL, Bradley 78 Edmund 60 Henry 81 164 165 200 John 106 107
GAMBLIN, James 195 199 201 203 204 207
GAMBLING, James 120 187
GAMBOL, Edmund 98
GAR--, James 228
GARDNER, Bryant 76 134 135 165 179 180 182 212 221 Elizabeth 208 Hezekiah 200 206 James 160 162 164 165 176 187 193 228 John 60 66 79 87 105 108 114 122

INDEX

123 130 133 140 144 145 156 157 164 184 189 191 198 208 209 212 William 112 151
GARN, Anthony 96
GARNER, Anthony 109 Bryan 72
GARNES, Anthony 214
GARRARD COUNTY, KENTUCKY 194
GARRET/GARRET, Everard 101 196 198 202 Everett 195 George 98 142 Jacob 127 James 221 226 John 174 196 230 William 98 158 166
GARRETT COUNTY, KENTUCKY 113
GARRISON, John 79 80 81 165 220 Mary 70
GARROTT, John 209
GARVEY, Patrick 143 200
GATLIN, Edward 161 167 168 John 76 85 96 136 225 228
GATLING, John 65 96 George 65
GEORGE, David 207 Isaac 109-13 115 155-58 160 161 207 209 215-17 Jesse 147 207 Joseph 130 155 158 207 Presley 149 Rebekah 207 Thomas 93 101 103 104 108 115
GEORGIA(State) 107 174 177
GERARD, Charles 89
GIBBONS, James 101 119
GIBSON, Fanny 229 John 118 133 135-37 153 188 209 Joseph 110 Patrick 89 98 120 121 125 153 157 163 171 206 207 211 226 227 Roger 61 62 64 71 84 94 98 106 124 127 128 147 149 150 210 221 227 233 Sally 86 Samuel 133 150 152 179 182 220 William 60 64 107 111 116 118 120 140 141 145
GIFFIN, John 96
GILASPIE, William 108
GILBERT, Samuel 66
GILES, Edward 142 153 158 Eli 131 134 136 137 153 167 209 212 231 Elizabeth 125 John 214 Josiah 179 182 183 186 191 215 Nathaniel 110 111 121 125 128 130 131 135 147 149 152 159 162 164 167 174 177 227 William 136 147 156 186 215
GILESPIE, Captain 178 John 121 William 113 117 123
GILLASPIE, Captain 63 73 75 John 79 83 88 William 60 62 70 71 73-78 80 83 87 108-10 119
GILLESPIE, Capt 158 178 184 226 David 164 167 181 185 220 231 George 124 127 135 136 138 143-45 147-49 156 160 162 164-66 209 215 226 John 136 138 144 171 173 174 184 185 228 Thomas 136 W 158 William 128 132 138 146 155 158-60 163 165 173 174 178 187 196 205 207 219 223 230 233 -- 149 198 204
GILMER, Abner 212 Nathaniel 195 200 201 212
GILMORE, Nathaniel 71 83 87 89 121 125 144 145 160 166 192
GINNE/GINNEY 68 130
GIPSON, Patrick 170 Roger 70 Samuel 214 -- 81
GIVINS, Samuel 119
GLASCOCK, Spencer 136
GLASGOW, Cornelius 65 70 102 109
GODFREY, James 89 92
GOFF, Andrew 108
GOLAGHER, John 71 74
GOLSTON, John 91
GOOD, William 65
GOODRUM, John 136 137 139 142-47 150 151 156 159 162 169 171 184 195 221 227
GORDON, Alexander 122 123 John 60 122 Richard 89 Susannah 89
GORE, Thomas 172 202
GOSSAGE, Rachel 150 Richard 150 157
GOUDY, John 130 Robert 175
GOWEN, James 197 204 210 215 Grace 65
GRAGG, Samuel 65 108
GRAHAM, Alexander 82 87 106 117 118 120 124 125 149 151-54 156 157 160 165 166 178 181 193 195 198 200 201 203 204 232 Clarissa 176 Elizabeth 127 185 James 79 82 83 92 97 136 137 140 141 154 156 157 161 162 210 213 215-17 Jane 92 Richard 92 106 125 127 155 185 Samuel 176
GRANT, John 81 168 230
GRAVES, Francis 81 83 85 89 90 Thomas 166
GRAY, Mr 122 Samuel 85 89 93 William 93 98 104 -- 104
GRAYHAM, Alexander 147
GREEN, Andrew 86 89 90 93 Captain 128 134 139 143 147 155 158 Elisha 184 George 122 123 132 138 139 Isaac 82 Robert 78 175 William 61 63 65 67 76 77 85 Zachariah 60 65 67 69 79 80 86 87 89 101 105 106 107 110 113 114 115 143 158 174 177 179 181 182 183 184 200 233

INDEX

GREEN COUNTY 64
GREEN TOWN, KENTUCKY 123
GREENAWAY, John 132
GREENFIELD, Will 83 -- 135 138
GREER, Andrew 133 153 159 160 165 176
Ann 149 Anne 142 207
GREGG, Samuel 186 211
GREGORY, Thomas 172 195 199 200 217
GREY, Mr 136
GRISHAM, Harris 77 93
GROVES, Thomas 139 141 167 178 182 192 209 212 221 -- 114
GUN, Andrew 107 108
GUTHRIE, Henry 188 Robert 171
GUTREY, Robert 215 218
Guy 123
GUYS, Isaac 107
GWIN, Alexander 65 68 77 78 89 97 163 168 229 Captain 122 126 143 155 159 171 186 188 192 218 219 Edward 61 62 65 68 70 71 76 78-81 83 84 90 91 96 103 105 115 116 118 119 121-24 126-28 130 131 136 139 140 143 144 146 147 149-53 158 166 176 178 179 181 182 185 188 189 191-94 202 203 205 213 218-20 225 228 229 231-33 James 61 62 64-66 68 69 71 72 74 76 79 83 84 86 89-91 103 105 108-10 115 200 206 217 John 71 76 79 108 109 166 174 175 182 189 191 196 198 222 William 123 128 139 147 172 178 182 189 191 192 200 221 227 230 231 232
H---, Jonathan 229
HACKETT, John 117
HADLEY, Joshua 66 76 90 94 96 100-2 105 113 114 123 131 133 148 159 174 179 184 186 187 189 198 201 204 206 208 216
HAIL, John 123 William 181
HAINEY, Betsey 176 Captain 122 131 139 142 155 158 Elijah 176 George 176 Jesse 70 89 121 136 137 149 165 171 176 181 191 197 206 213 221 230 Judah 176 William 176
HAINS, Robert 217
HAIR, James 121
HALE, James 231 John 175 William 221 230 232
HALIFAX COUNTY, NORTH CAROLINA 163
HALIFAX COUNTY, VIRGINIA 81
HALL, Absolam 103 Clement 197 Corban 215 Dolly 93 Edmund 63 74 75 79 80 93 96 Elisha 151 Francis 74 86 87 James 95 John 63 106 108 173 206 Levi 185 219 224 Robert 63 106 108 215 220 Stephen 186 187 William 63 64 66 70 75 87 88 90 92 94 103 105 106 108 110 115 117 124 129 134 135 137 141 148 155 160 161 164 167 173 224 227 228
HAMBLETON, Jas 195 Robt 168 Thomas 166
HAMILTON, Andrew 115 Andy 213 Bob 95 Captain 69 82 93 99 114 122 Franky 166 George 117 124 154 156 157 Hance 62 J 207 James 73 74 107 108 163 202-4 207 229 John 59-61 67 71 79 82 87 93-96 99 100 102-6 110-19 121 122 125-28 130-34 136 138 140-51 153 154 156 158-70 173 174 176-90 192-97 199-207 209-17 219 220 223-33 Robert 61 72 74 87 95 96 103 128 166 175 190 192 215 218 Salley/Sally 155 156 Thomas 60-62 68 76 77 118-20 165 166 175 221 227 230 William 122 138 155 156 159 166 175 182 184 186 196 198 station 68 race path 68
HAMMOND, Isaiah 193 219 William 91 105 Hampton 63
HANES, Robert 226
HANEY, Jesse 118
HANKINS, Arthur 61 99 100 103 110 111 118 120 127 187 188 Captain 95 106 122 125 129 139 143 Richard 129 William 63-65 68 70 91 95 97 99 100 101 103-05 107 -09 112 119 120 124 126 134 142 143 198 211 mill 65 68 71 72 97 99 103 109 121
HANKS, John 202
HANNA, John 197
Hannah 80 83 200
HANNAH, Eneas 116 126 Enos 128 196 208 209 217 222 James 61 79 86 116 128 197 204 John 108 113 131 134 136 137 149 160 196 217 Jonathan 63 65 77 79 98 118 124 125 128-31 136 139 141 142 145 147 150 151 154-56 162 164 168 171 204 218 222 226 228 229 Joseph 101 Patsey 229 Richard 203 212 221 226 229 W 215 219 Washington 193 195 204 210 211 215 217 229
HANSBERRY, Smith 118
HANSBROUGH, Captain 60 64 66 69 70 75 76 80 82 87 95 99 Peter 90 154 Smith 62 65 77 79 80 120 123 126 130 139 142-45 147 153 162 167 179 189 191 192 196 209

INDEX

214 215 216 221
HARDIMAN, Thomas 98
HARDIN, Abraham 83 88   -- 170 176
HARDIN COUNTY, KENTUCKY 121
HARDY, Charles 70 Jonathan 70
HARGET, Frederick 168
HARGIS, John 81
HARMAN/HARMON, John 213 Richard 92 101 119 Thomas 78 92
HARNEY, Selby 100 119 122 Thomas 101 114 119 122 138 156 200   -- 100 119
HARPER, John 191 Summers 144 William 150 151 169 191 209 212
HARPOLE, Adam 88 220 Captain 92 99 105 108 George 89 John 61 68 70 71 78 89 93 101 104 115 Martin 89 93 99 Paul 84 85 98 133 147 158 Solomon 101 103 104 106 110 Thomas 89   -- 103
HARPOOL, Adam 76 John 62 Solomon 68
HARRALL, Eneas 127
HARRELL, Enos 126 Nathan 113 Richd 168
HARRIMAN, Charles 79 83 106 118
HARRINGTON, Charles 126 William 91 101 122 132 138 139
HARRIS/HARRISS, Betsey 170 174 177 183 Blair 167 Charles 184 196 Chedle 203 Edward 91 132 139 175 Elmore 151 174 176 177 179 183 184 208 221 230 232 James 174 John 166 167 170 174 177 182 189 193 Patsey 170 174 177 183 Phebe 74 Robert 225 Samuel 62 75 83 84 123 141 218 Thomas 76 80 83 85 87 101 119 Tyre 86 Wallace 194 199 Wallis 143
HARRISON, E 230 George 216 224 229 Harry 191 Henry 62 91 107 110 130 131 133-36 141 144 145 147 148 151 152 154 156 175 210 213 218 227 James 61 62 70 71 73-77 79 82 83 86 92 94 97 99 100 102 103 105-7 109 111 112 115 128-31 133 135 137 138 143 144 146 148 164 201 206 207 209 210 Jesse 227 John 72 183 188 200 216 217 Joseph 116 118 120 Nathaniel 70 92 118 Polley 224 William 95 153-56 184 185
Harry 137 202 221
HARRYMAN, Charles 142
HART, J 115 James 76 85 89 90 92 93 105 107 115 125 128 130 131 134 138-140 142 -144 146 149 152 155 157-60 162 168 176 181 187 188 193 200 202 205 213 218 220

227 228-30 Joel 181 221 226 227 Squire 194 Thomas 184 ferry 90 93 129 220 mill 129 201 202
HARTEN, James 193
HASSEL/HASSELL, Abraham/Abram 92 179 181-84 195 220 Asa 92 140 209 214 Benoni 203 Jesse 92 167 181 214 John 92 96-98 118 135 150 159 167 168 181 189 191 192 208
HATCH, Edmund 118 121 125
HATCHER, Archibald 79 136
HAUSER, George 229
HAW, James 121 175 180
HAWKINS, Benjamin 137 Borden/Burden 102 125 James 104 137 146 John 101 102 104 107 108 123 124 126 137 146 148 154 156 158 201 207 218 227 Martha 137 Sarah 137
HAWKINS COUNTY, 78
HAYNES, John 68
HAY, William 132
HAYNIE, Charles 154 William 93 95 99 105 117 125
HAYS, Charles 85 Elijah 111-13 James 62 69 70 72 74 95 172 John 72 81 92 104 Robert 65 78 81 96 200 207 230 Samuel 61 96 William 122
HAZLET, John 149 151 155 157 168 169 181 182 198
HEAD, William 122
HEADON, John 229
HEARD, Stephen 224
HEATON, Enoch 109 Robert 92 158
HEDGCOCK, Elijah 76 100
HELLEN/HELLIN James 95 123 Mary 84 107
HENDERSON, B 230 Bennett 192 199 206 211 Colonel 181 John 123 134 177 178 206 210 222 223 229-33 Lilburn 222 Robert 119 William 100 103 109 120 126 127 129 130 134 139 140 143 157 158 181 192 206 217 219 221 223 227 230-32   -- 230 mill 143
HENDRICK/HENDRICKS Elijah 80 133 140 141 Jeremiah 80 81 92 99 Joseph 65 71 74 78 81 83 224 Obed/Obediah 80 81 92 99 125 224
HENDRIX, Albert 145 209 212
HENNEN, James 135   -- 198
HENRY, David 134 135 156 157 167 189 192 194-98 201 Isaac 146 James 68 138

INDEX

154 Lemuel 130 Will 132 William 139 192
HENSLY, Harman 77
HERD, Stephen 212 215 228
HEREFORD, Jesse 134 Malachi 103 114 118 134 135 145 148 149 151 153 156 159 164 165 173 184
HERNDON, Cornelius 124 130 133 135 228 Jo 68 Joseph 116 128
HERRALL/HERRELL, Eli 167 170 174 176 177 Elia 189 Eneas 126 Nathan 113
HERREN/HERRIN/HERRON, Bright 114 122 123 167 172 178
HERRILL, Eli 182
HERRING, Bright 196 Heli 130 145 152 153 156 159 161 162 164 167-70 177 178 196 202 218 225
HESSION, Arthur 75 -- 81
HEWITT, Josiah 91 Nancy 167
HIBBITS, James 100 103
HICK, -- 202
HICKERSON/HICKESON, John 6 10 13
HICKISON, Isaac 48 John 2 12 15 16 19 23 27 28 33 42 48 Mrs 33 28 48 Patsey 23 Tabitha 48 William 48 -- 9 17 81 branch 93
HICKMAN/HICKMON, Edwin 10 24 138 Thomas 44 99 105 121 214
HICKS, Arthur 186 Benjamin 65 Henry 37 Joab 81 Job 63 65 79 80 160 161 196 John 1 2 22 23 Nancey/Nancy 4 6
HICKSON, Captain 6
HIGGASON, Samuel 191
HIGGS, Jacob 55 97 98
HIKISON, John 16
HILL, Allen 211 Green 54 Henry 76 77 97 Isaac 140
HILLSBROUGH DISTRICT, NC 200
HINDS, John 85
HINSON, Peggy 72
HOBDY, Robert 70 77 78 173 Telitha 70 Thomas 167 178 192 213
HODGE/HODGES, James 89 John 117 146 Joseph 167 171 184 186-89 198 199 212 221 226 William 142
HODGKISS, Edward 48
HOFFLER, Thomas 89
HOGAN, Arthur 121 E 6 Edward 14 44 John 58 63 151 165 Richard 5 7 9 12 23 25 35 42 53 55 56 60 73 William 57 169
HOGE, Edward 180 James 180 Moses 180 Susanna 180 William 88
HOGIN, Anthony 132 133 135-37 140 141 143 145 166 168 233 Arthur 93 119 Edward 2-5 11 13 15 17 24 30 31 34 38 47 51 52 58 66 72 76 77 85 86 88 92 102 104 112 123 126 132 136 138 140 141 147 154-56 162-66 175 179 191-93 199 201 224 Elizabeth 154 167 Isaac 216 John 147 155 166 168 209 228 Rebecca 92 Richard 2-5 9 10 12 13 16 20 22 26 31 32 34 35 37 38 41-46 51 56 62 72 73 76 77 82 83 86-88 94 97 102 105 112 123-25 134-36 141 143 148 149 154 164 165 167-69 174 193 195 199 202 209 219 223 233 Robert 63 65 66 78 122 123 170
HOLAMAN, Daniel 47
HOLDEN, Thomas 135
HOLDMAN, Daniel 47 51
HOLLAND, Joel 79 85 168 197 Lemon 188
HOLLEY, Nathaniel 30
HOLLIDAY, David 106 138 Sarah 106
HOLLIDY, Benjamin 74
HOLLINGSWORTH, Abraham 207 230 232
HOLLINSHEAD, Francis 85
HOLLIS, James 162 175
HOLLY, Nathaniel 34
HOLMES, Albert 82 149 151-54 209
HOLSTON 24 41 42
HOOD, Herbert 232
HOOVER, A 141 Andrew 66 67 79 80 91 100 110 120 126 127 192 193 196 198 209 231 Henry 58 231 John 211
HOPKINS, James 111 Joseph 55
HORTON, Willis 72
HOUCH, George 193
HOUDESHALL/HOUDESHELL, Henry 7-9 25 27 35 37 39 187 220 Isaac 166 Isbel 35 Jacob 53 68 76 80 81 194 John 165 170
HOUDESHALT, Jacob 200
HOURT, Jacob 100
HOUSE, Isaac 191 199 224 Joseph 217 Micajah 124 144 218
HOUST, Jacob 100 119
HOUSTON, James 101 208 William 99
HOW, James 23
HOWARD, James 191 219
HOWEL/HOWELL, Edward 64 121 Fanny 115 Frances 64 123 Josiah 63 65 66 70 79 93 94 112 168 173 Philip 79 80 82 83 97 Thomas 63 73 74 77 117 121 152 167

INDEX

172 174 176-79 183 184 186-89 192 198 208 224 228 232 William 121
HUBART, William 98 135
HUBBARD, Benjamin 172 Captain 19 22 25 31 William 97 113 128 130-32 138 144 149 151 152 154 164 171 172 177 Zebulon 1 2 13 14 18 20-22 24 -- 20 26 30
HUBBART, William 125 127 159 203
HUBERT, William 96 109 116 121
HUDDLESTON, Henry 72 73 132
HUDSON, Benjamin 144 159 163 Chamblin 91 Edward 73 79 82 86 94-96 99 120 121 135 146
HUGHES, David 6 12 13 16 28 33 39 170 190 Davis 39 Jesse 8 13 35 162 John 15 16 23 30 Levi 199 209 Nathaniel 123 124 135 136 Rowland 33
HUGHETT, William 80 87
HUMPHREYS, George 214 Parry 171 184 196-98 204 210 211 217 223 225 230
HUNT, Hardy 133 233 James 163 176 206 213 215 218 228 John 191 201 215 221 225 229 Mary 191 227 229 Polley 201 215 221 225 229
HUNTER, Adam 101 103 104 128 133 144 146 149 150 154 171 174 175 178 181 197 201 204 207 214 218 222 Cader/Cater 145 209 Daniel 123 139 Josiah 61 Mary 10
HURT, John 39
HUSE, John 22
HUSTON, James 65 William 94
HUTCHINGS, John 170 176 193 208 210 214 -- 193 210 211 216 231
HUTCHINS, Thomas 65
HUTCHINSON, William 188 189 203
HUTSON, Chamberlain 52 63 64 Edward 72 73 140 144 145 146
HYDE, Henry 54 100 101
HYLTON, Daniel 123 132 136
HYNES, John 32
Ike 200
ILLINOIS 211
IMPSON, Caleb 122
INGLES, John 68
INGLISH, Thomas 6
INGRAM, Benjamin 229
IREDELL COUNTY, NC 120 166
IRELAND, David 68
IRWIN, John 37 45 51 95 105 133 221 227 230-32 William 54 172

Isaac 63 130
ISBELL, Thomas 90 94
Jack 92 137 138 175
JACKSON, Andrew 8-10 12-14 17 22 23 25 27 29 31 34-36 38-45 48 49 52-55 59 60 62 72 74 75 98 117 177 178 183 208 214 216 220 222 223 229 230 232 Chestley 221 Judge 178 Nathan 132 Samuel 115 -- 47 52 190 193 210 211 216 231
Jacob 89
Jacque 200
James 81 145 222 227
JAMES, Daniel 56 122 138 Dragon 80 Jim 80 blacksmith shop 151
JAMISON, Thomas 6 176
Jarod 149
JEFFERSON COUNTY, MISSISSIPPI 221
JEFFREYS, Mildred 134 Thomas 134
JEFFERIES, John 54
JENKINS, Jacob 114 Jonathan 157 Roderick 92 98 102 146
JENNINGS, Edmund 5 9 Samuel 163 Thomas 27 creek 60
Jenny 172
JETT, James 59
Jim 65 92 153 204
JIMASON, Thomas 3 9 10 12 16 17 30 31 36 37 41-44 50 54 55 57 58 60-62 66 70 71 75 79 82 87 89 90 93 97 William 80 87
JINKINS, Roderick 58 65 71 81 98
JINNINGS, Edmund 65 81 83 85 86 87 89 93 Edward 81 Henry 40 Joshua 40
Job 44
JOHN, Benjamin 138 164
JOHNS, John 170 176
JOHNSON, Boswell 140 185 Exum 177 James 144 146-49 154 215 221 223-25 229 Jesse 132 133 135 139-41 149 150 152 156 157 176 191 214 220 John 126 130 149 173-75 184 189 195 196 203 210-12 217 222 224 225 Martha 133 135 137 146 167 Thomas 229 -- 7 creek 202
JOHNSTON, Boswell 123 James 70 100 101 103 Jesse 125 John 16-18 21 32 46 50 Robert 37 39 54 62 82 101 110 114 119 Thomas 17 105
JOINER, Jesse 175 194 Littleton 221 226 Thos 169 175 209 215 216 Whitehd 85 222
JOLLY, Benjamin 184 196 222

INDEX

JONES, Agnus 25 66 67 148 151 Allen/Allon 80 87 216 Ambrose 47 Clinton 148 Dianah 34 36 Edmund 139 Edward 19 40 43 47 61-63 71 103 109 184 185 193 216 219 Elizabeth 38 60 83 113 Fanning 170 176 Hardy 89 Isham 139 James 91 97 106 110 143 John 13 83 193 216 Jos 20 Joseph 24 Joyce 127 128 138 139 147 Lazarus 130 Mary 139 Moses 139 R 34 Richard 13 22 23 45 46 58 59 60-62 65 73 74 87 89-91 165 180 201 206 228 Robert 16-19 25 27 37 38 41 43-45 70 86 92 101 102 106 111 115 126 128 Stephen 23 Thomas 3 Vina 139 147 W 132 139 William 25 34-36 38 219 220 Willis 93 101 104 bluff 55
JOSEY/JOSY, John 61 79 84 90 96 100 103 107 109 115 116 128 130 169 170 174 198 199 211 232
Juda 65 71
Jude 99 143
Kandis 177
KARR, William 207 -- 17
KASPERS CREEK 7 12 16 26
KAVANAUGH, Benjamin 108 William 233
KEEFE, Thomas 153 160 161 163 164 166 167 175 176 182 184 185 190 192 194 221 225 -- 145 146
KEEFF/KEEFFE, Thomas 153 156 159 161
KEESEE, George 145 154 172 189 193
KEIFE/KEIFFE, Thomas 139 173 214 224 225 226
KEITH, James 6 Reuben 6
KELLEY, Nathaniel 43
KELLY, Dennis 71 Edward 212 James 90 96 99 153 158
KENDRICK, Jane 4 6
KENEDAY, William 31
Kennedy 222
KENNEDY, Abraham 90 Crusy 108 Dempsey 79 82 Dennis 92 Elizabeth 213 218 John 64 190 199 208 213 222 William 34 37 38 42 44 45 49 60 64 67 77 93 102 109 186 230 -- 100
KENNY, Thomas 12
Kent 65
KENTUCKY 12 20 23 24 37 43 45 51 52 55 67 71 74 81 85 92 95 96 113 114 121 123 126 145 178 194 204 205 207 216 222 229 230
KERLIN, Peter 43 51 52

KERR, Captain 93 James 65 John 93 129 221
KERRS, Philip 97
KESSEE, Thomas 232
KEYKENDALL, Simon 179
KIDD, John 94
KIEFE, Thos 199 203 210 212 218 219 228
KILGORE, Charles 46 103 113 Johnston 46 Thomas 1 2 5 8 12 13 22 23 46 54 -- 7 14
KILLOUGH, David 200
KILTY, John 49
KIMBERLIN, Michael 74
KINCANNON, Matthew 70 101 134 164
KINDRICK/KINDRICKS, John 18 Thomas 18
KING, Abraham 176 Captain 35 36 43 47 48 57 59 64 123 David 114 James 147 154 169 207 John 154 Moses 191 215 Nathaniel 169 Richard 33 35 37 38 45 46 51 56 63 73 74 84 123 126 128 129 136 137 147 156 159 161 167 171 179 181 182 184 189 201 204 206 212 220 Robert 32 41 48 Samuel 49 59 87 103 107 148 220 Thomas 191 215 William 68 92 98 150 169 181 195 201-4
KINNY, Thomas 13
KIRBY, Pleasant 109 Richard 100
KIRK, William 191
KIRKHAM, Thomas 230
KIRKLAND, Jesse 136 Zachariah 221
KIRKPATRICK, Alexander 195 201-4 207 Captain 127 139 143 154 155 159 Hugh 139 142-45 147 162 165 166 207 220 James 120 128 133 144 145 175 John 152 184
KISER, George 152 P 99 Philip 47 85 86 168 209
Kit 121
KITCHEN/KITCHING, James 59 80 87
KITTREL, Isam 101 119
Kity 109
KNIGHT, Murfree 120
KNOWLTON, Joshua 93
KNOX, John 50 62 68 120 Robert 57
KNOX COUNTY 117
KUKENDALL, Captain 3 11 Simon 3
KUPE, -- 145
KUSEE, George 193 194 195
KUYKENDALL, Adam 15 16 21 23 25 31 41 Benjamin 1 3 4 6-8 10 13 14 21 23-25 27

INDEX

29 40 48 72 87 88 94 121 129 131 136 137 143 154 160 191
KUYKENDALL, Captain 1 2 James 40 199 Jane 48 55 62 89 90 94 121 131 160 167 Jean 131 Jesse 40 72 141 145 154 164 204 218 Jinny 48 John 2 4 8 9 11 12 16-19 25 32 35 40 48 Jonathan 40 82 94 154 160 Joseph 1 2 4 5 8-14 16-18 20 21 25 28-35 39 41 June 23 Lewis 40 131 Martha 92 156 Matthew 2 4-6 10 12 13 15 21 25 30-33 39 41 42 44 46 50 51 54 Mrs 25 44 Nathaniel 179 Peter 3 Robert 40 S 6 Simon 2-13 18 19 22-26 32 35 39 40 43 45 48 50-53 57 60 72 75 82 92 94 102 104 106 113 186 193 202   -- 1 7 15 17 81 company 1
KYSER, Peter
L--, Abraham 8
LACEY/LACY, Amos 93 116 119 123 129 130 Hopkins 15 17 19 21 Thomas 119 129 130
LACKEY, James 181
LAFFERTY, John 186 206 209 232
LAFORCARD, John 60
LAIN, Captain 186 188 189 218 224 David 86 88 Isaac 83 91 95 184 185 190 195 199 214 James 83 195-98 201
LAMBERT, Aaron 89 Avery 89
LAMBURTH, William 150
LANCASTER, John 36 126 138
LAND, Peter 20
LANDERS, Abraham 50 57 58 61 Jacob 9
LANDRY, Isaac 41
LANE, Captain 208 David 73 74 83 88 113 114 125 Isaac 94-96 107 128 129 168 204 207 226 James 84 189
LARIMORE, Thomas 30
LASH, Nathaniel 110
LASSITER, Frederick 166 Willey 233
LATHAM, John 5
LATIMER, Captain 139 142 155 171 173 188 189 218 223 Charles 35 38 43 44 58 71 96 157 Griswold 42-45 47 64 71 77 90 91 94 107 108 118 123 124 139 142-44 146 157 162 163 168 171 179 180 189 194 196 198 201 225 232 Hannah 71 79 109 Jonathan 33 37 41 42 71 73 157 Joseph 25 27 28 33 38 89 171 Lynde 157 182 Mr 36 Nathaniel 25 27 28 42 43 45 47 71 74 78 79 83 109 Robert 49 51 71 73 76 114 116 152 Wetherall 45 William 71 79 109

Witheral 50 61-69 71 72 76-80 82-84 89 93-95 98 99 101 104 109 110 112 115 116 120-23 125 126 130 131 146 155 156 158 159 162 166 168 171-73 178 181 182 188 190 193 200 206 208 213 215 218 222 223 226-29
LATIMORE, Jonathan 37
LAUDERDALE, James 43 48 68 71 93 101-3 113 114 117 119 121 126 135-37 146 148 152 153 158 174 176 177 179 183-85 187 210 214 John 114 128 130 227 Sarah 102 William 58 68 71 83 87 125 138 139 142-45 147 154 162 172 200
LAURANCE, Lemuel 28
LAURENCE, Adam 7 11 20 21 29 31 33 37 56 62 Charles 137 George 62 101 J 179 John 22 23 25 37 41 42 44 45 47 57 62 82 120 141 146 Lemuel 92 Lydia 146 Robert 137 168 178 182 183 207 216 217 221 224 225 230   -- 166 178
LAUTON, John 212
LAWRENCE, Charles 200
LAWSON, Henry 178
LEACH, Thomas 62 William 62 115
LEAN, Isaac 200
LEATHERDALE, James 37 William 37
LEE, James 101 119
LEECH, Thomas 197 William 170 207
LEEPER, George 32
LEFORKARD, -- 60
LEFOUARD, John 60
LEFTWICKE, Isaac 135 140
LEMAR, William 25
LEMASTER, Thomas 5 8 9
LEMMON/LEMON/LEMONS, Peter 37 60 73 74 78 96 100-2 195 202 203 204 207 Samuel 94 Simon 59
Levi 200
Lewis 110
LEWIS, Archibald 86 Jacob 81 James 116 Seth 54 58 64 65-67 69 73 82 83 86 87 94-96 98 99 102 105-7 111 113 116 117 119 William 36 90   -- 56 60
LEXINGTON DISTRICT, KENTUCKY 85
LILLEY, Robert 114
LIMMON, Samuel 99
LIN--, Israel 6
LINCOLN COUNTY, KENTUCKY 20 24 67 207
LINDSEY, Ezekiel 58-61 76 79 87 88 Isaac 1 3-5 7 10-14 21 22 25 26 31 40

INDEX

58 62 68 82 87 88 159 232 -- 88
LINTON, Isaac 29 Silas 29
LLOYD, Thomas 114
LOBB, William 224
Lock 75
LOCKE, Francis 98 129 131 136 140 143 144 158 160 200 220 Matthew 106
LOFTIN, Anne 228 Henry 228
LOGAN, George 130 191 206 213
LOGAN COUNTY, KENTUCKY 55 95 126 147 150 184 216 229
London 79
LONG, Laniford 54 Nicholas 4 Samford 54
LOONEY/LUNA, Captain 36 37 46 48 57 59 64 67 82 87 92 99 Daniel 127 David 7 8 40 55 61 68 71 127 John 79 81 138 142 196 211 Peter 1-15 17-19 23 25-31 34 37 -39 42-46 48-50 52 55 58 60-62 65 67 71 73-77 80 85-90 92 93 101-3 114 116 120 121 123-25 127 134 135 138 145 153 156 157 159 161 163 167 171 173 175 177 179 180 184 186-89 198 201 204 209 211 212 214 225 232 233 Robert 2-7 9 11 12 14 20-22 24 25 28 30 31 37 39 41 43 45 47 53-55 58 76 84 87 88 90 96 107 117 118 148 158 -- 6
LOONIE, Captain 31 47 69
LOONY, Peter 33 51
LOURY, William 148 152
LOVE, Captain 95 106 114 122 126 139 142 Charles 86 David 96 99 101 102 117 120 122 125 126 129 130 134-37 143 144 146 147 150 151 155 158 162 165 167 171 172 193 199-01 207 214 216 223 227 228 John 100 119 Josiah 9-20 22 23 25 27 31 34 Thomas 132 139
LOVIN, Henry 78 186
LOVING, Betsy 200 Edward 32 129 Elizabeth 32 79 Henry 48 59 65 76 77 79 82 84 132 137 141 142 199 200 204 207 211 224 232 Mary 79 Polly 200 Walter 79 William 32 79 145
LOW, Elenor 46
LOWEL, Isaac 2 5 17 27
LOWRY, Reuben 230 William 230
LOWTHAR/LOWTHER, William 68 84
LOYD, Lijah 71 Samuel 71
Lucinda 222
LUCK, William 43
Lucy 41 65 81 231

LUNA, Captain 35 43 48 77 85 103 105 108 122
LUSK, William 34
Lydia 172
LYNN, Adam 9 Captain 1 2 James 2 5 7 12-14 17 56-59 -- 51 57 district 1
LYON, Henry 62 67-69 71-73 81 86 87 90 91 98 100 109 110 119 125 129 130 135 139 142 144 147 149 157 162 166 167 169 170 176 178 179 183 184 187-90 192 193 195 204 209 218 221-23 227 James 69 70 72 73 95 98 101 106 129 131 134 148 153 154 169 170 179 188 189 190 192 195 John 62 72 96-98 153 167 181-83 185 195 199 223 Patience 179 190 Patrick 136 Peter 62 63 65 96 147 150 156 157 176 William 75 155 -- 68 72
LYONS, Captain 219 Henry 65 66 John 107 James 64 Peter 134
LYTLE, Archibald 61 Henry 148 William 59 121 147 148 166
M--, Captain 14
MABRY, Mr 123 Seth 104 115 118 119 123 128 129 133 139 160 173 174 176 177 179 182 183 222 229 232
MACKLIN, James 102 103 175
MACLIN, Archibald 75 James 146
MADDEN, Champ 70 90
MADDERY, Champness 181
MADDING/MADING, Champness 79 94 98 101 149 150 159 184 185 194 201 209 213
MADDISON lick 9 creek 11 63
MADDISON COUNTY, KENTUCKY 52
MADIN, Champ 192
MAGNESS, John 66 Jonathan 65
MAIRS, Alexr 175 Hugh 101 119 175 Wm 95
MAIRY, Thomas 85
MAJLOHON, Agnist 154
MALIN, James 144
MALLARD, Joseph 134
MALONE, Caty 99 Hallery/Hillory 90 99 121 149 150 162 164 167 168 177 179 180 182 187 215 219-21 223 224 225 Lewis 28 50 Thomas 125
MANGLE, Daniel 86
MANN, William 176 180 213
MANNING, John 95 102
MANRY, Elizabeth 28
MANSCO/MANSCOE, George 1 John 93 -- 2
MANSKER, Gasper 118 165 173 George 1 5

INDEX

6-9 12 13 17 19 21-25 127 128 Jane 4 8
John 104 119 128 129 131 134 160 169
170 187 196 204 223 Kasper 70 80 107
120 128 153 160 171 174 176 177 179 183
193 195 196 199-01 228 -- 9 creek 64
67 91 95 102 143 147
MANY, Thomas 85
MARCHBANKS, William 106 110
MARGRAVE, Jesse 154
Maria 137
MARLEY, Robert 81
MARLIN, Archibald 90 93 95-97 101 105-7
113-15 121 122 130 137-40 143 155 160
162-64 175 187 188 193 200 202 203 218
223 230-32
MARLOW, John 208 212
MARQUIS, Thomas 179 191
MARR, George 197
Marriam 81
MARSH, John 214 Samuel 101 115 132 139
MARSHAL/MARSHALL, Christana 191 Dixon
70 80 87 John 51 75 199 Robert 179 191
199 200 208 William 191 208 210
MARTIN, Archibald 61 73 76 77 110
Bostic/Bostick 28 30 51 Bosten/Boston
52 79 80 201 207 209 210 Captain 10 D
29 Francis 72 73 George 5 12 14 19 25
31-33 50 95 228 James 191 Jane 52 John
90 132 145 149 158 Major 29 Reuben 88
121 Thomas 2 3 5 9 15 21 97 173 William 66 72 110 114 118 120 200 -- 68
creek 118
Mary 92 135 157 175
MARYLAND (state) 49 216
MASON, Benjamin 143 147 James 85 Samuel
8 9 10 12
MASON COUNTY, KENTUCKY 123
MASON TOWN 31
MASSLOHON, Agnist 154
MASTEN/MASTIN, Archibald 39 44 45 Jenny
55 Major 46 Thomas 35 36 42 44 45 47 48
60 61 64 67-72 74 75 77 79 80 82-89 91
95 98 99 101-3 106 108 109 112 113 118
120-22 125 126 130 132 142 150 160 162
163 169 170 176 179 180 182 183 190 192
196 197 201 203 204 206 207 212 213
217-19 222 223 231 --6
MASTERSON, Chas 121 Thomas 91 110 142
MASTON, Thomas 60
MATCALF, Anthony 53 60 63 Edwd 53 William 122
MATHIS, Allen 192
Matthew 216
MATTHEWS, Mussenden 31 62
MAULDIN/MAULDING, Ambrose 50 68 146 166
MAXCEY, James 89
MAXEY, Betsey 72 Edward 32 40 195 201-4
207 227 Elizabeth 32 Jesse 14 15 32
Walter 40 82 116 William 32 37 38 40 48
77 79 80 99 106 112 116 117 121 127 136
138 140 141 144 148 149 151-54 169 177-
79 207 211 224
MAXFIELD CREEK 182
MAXWELL, James 8 9 144 161 William 1 2
6 7 10 11 14 24-26 31 32 35-37 137
-- 9 creek 206
MAYES, John 74 75 77 97 98 115 117-119
MAYS, John 72 73 76 131 132
McADAM/McADAMS, John 225 Joseph 61 62
89 94 98 100 101 106 107 114 121 123
126-29 131 135 140 141 143 144 Saml 98
William 19 21 23 27 30 40 46 96 97 114
McADDIN/McADIN, Henry 139 141
McBEE, Elias 9 Silas 18-21 24 25 34 37-
39 45 48
McBRIDE, Captain 95 122 Hugh 168 Samuel
93 103
McCADIN, Henry 153
McCAFFERTY, James 91
McCAIN, James 220
McCALL, William 210
McCALLESTER, James 22 37
McCANN, Nathaniel 71
McCARRELL, James 48 166
McCARTON, John 197
McCARTY, Bernard 138 John 61 62 71 231
McCASLAND, Andrew 76 77
McCAUL, Alexander 132 139
McCAULY, John 24
McCLAIN, William 81
McCLELAN, Andrew 58
McCLENDON, Benjamin 231
McCLURE, William 175 215 218
McCOLGIN, James 18 36
McCOLLISTER, James 21 22 24
McCONNELL, Daniel 92 136-38 140 141 148
154 160-62 164 165 210 Gumry 221 John
170 171 176 186 199 228 Montgomery 70
81 84 92 93 134 135 227 230-32 Robert
151 161 -- 81

INDEX

McCORCLE/McCORKLE, Jane 176 Robert 100 119 Samuel 137 William 71 74 83 84 123 128 144 147 199 212 -- 147
McCORMACK, George 65 Matthew 30 82
McCOWAN, Alexander 12
McCOY, Ananias 85 148
McCRAVENS/McCRAVINS, Joseph 148 193 202
McCRAY, Abagail 221 Abba 221
McCREARY, Nathaniel 197
McCUISTON, James 100
McCULLOCH, Alexr 227 Benjamin 101 119
McCUMSEY, John 27
McCURDY, William 181 184
McD--, James 13
McDANIEL, John 91 Rencher 130 219
McDANOLD, James 42-44 Magness 123 William 22 24 46 52 56 96
McDONOLD, William 94
McDOWELL, James 214 220 221 223-25 229
McELROY, James 143 206 232
McELWRATH, Captain 14 16 19 22 30 35 37 43 45 47 Joseph 70-73 78 83 84 107 117 122 126 135 137 143 174 175 184 210 212 233 -- 23 25
McELYEA, Humphrey 138 John 138 Wm 138
McFARLAND, Daniel 94 98 John 40 43 45
McG--, William 207
McGARY, Hugh 12 17
McGAVOCK, Jas 23 Randal 87 Randolph 57
McGEE, Adam 180 Hugh 62 130 179 180 227 232 James 180 John 103 William 59 62 142 145 152 180
McGLOUGHLIN, Joseph 114
McGOODEN/McGOODIN, Daniel 9 11 22
McGREADY, William 98 128 174 193
McGUFFEE, Henry 6
McGUIRE, George 144 148 171 173 174 John 206 Thomas 144 148 155
McKAIN, Captain 14 16 19 22 James 1-4 6-8 10-17 20-23 25 27 28 31 34 36-38 40-46 49 51 52 55 57 58 64 65 75 86 89 90 94 98 104 109-11 114 115 119 121 130 133 143 147 160 166 173 177 179 184 188 -90 200 203 209 211 212 220 225 Jane 39 52 Joseph 201 227 232 233 -- 7-9 11 12 14 17 23 30 creek 11
McKEAN, Joseph 156 161 182 193 197 201 202 210-12 215 218
McKEE, Alexander 59 65 67 80 95 131 171 177 192-94 201 Capt 188 Jno 214 William 59 63
McKELWRATH, Captain 10 49
McKENNY, Henry 115
McKESICK, Daniel 101 119
McKEY, James 201
McKINNEY/McKENNY, Elijah 70 84 Henry 71 75 93 94 98 100 106 111 115-18 188 James 66
McKINSEY, James 72-75 79 80 83 91 93 103 122 123 126 128 130 144 158 159 170 175 181 187 195 206-8 210 217 223 227 232 Patsey 208
McKISICK/McKISOCK, Daniel 132 139
McKLIN, James 87
McKNIGHT, Alexander 98 147-49 153 167 169 170 184 224 James 90 131 192 horse mill 165
McKORCLE/McCORKLE, Wm 70 72 126 189
McLENDON, Ann 85
McLIN, James 101 144 William 42
McMANAMEY/McMANIMY, John 176 180
McMANN, William 84
McMILLEN, Alexander 92
McMURREY, John 221
McMURRY, Charles 97-102 David 107 113 James 101 102 136 137 149 150 173 174 177 184 186-89 198 John 140 142-45 147 162 171 214 226 227 Samuel 221
McMURTREE/McMURTRIE, John 120-23 138 139 142 147
McMURTREY/McMURTRY, John 63 65 67 70-72 79 87 102 120 122 127 130 154 155 159 160-62 166 167 171 173-75 181 185 186 188 193 195 204 208 215 216 223
McNAIR, Benjamin 122 James 34
McNAIRY, Andrew 58 62 John 10 125
McNEELY, Pheba/Phebe 14 16 18 William 1 5 6 14-18 35 36 58
McNEESE, Benjamin 180
McNIGHT, James 81
McNUT/McNUTT, Isaac 56 61 66 69 71-73 76 77 88 92 93 96 99 100 103 105 110-12 116-20 126 129 131 135 223 -- 215
McPHERSON, Ivy 31
McRANNOLDS, Joseph 175
McREYNOLDS, Elizabeth 214 222 232 Robt 214 222 224
McRUNNALLS, Robert 169
McWHARTON, George 24
McWHIRTER, George 8 23-25 43 William 46

256

INDEX

48 93 104 115 116 150 186 193
McWILLIAMS, John 201
MEARS, Benjn 80 81 85 Humphry 81 Uridice 81 85
MECKLIN, Hugh 154 James 74 154 189 215 218
MEEK, Samuel 134 193
MEEKER, George 160 165
MEEKLY, Betsey 77
MEIRS, Humphrey 115 118 Uridice 99 104
MELONE, Hallery 62 81 Henry 65 67 Lewis 27 29 32 57 59 Lydia 27 27 33 Mrs 29
MELTON, Daniel 133 201
MENEES, Benjamin 130
MERCER, Nancy 33 Spencer 62 71
MERCER COUNTY, KENTUCKY 37 71 74 207
MERRITT, Stephen 126
METCALF, Anthony 60 103 113 115 121 125 126 149 William 138
MICHIE, George 168 172 173 184 185 187 190 192 197 203 205 209 224 233
MICHY, George 101
MICKEY/MICKY, George 102 105 116 119 123 124 126 130 134-37 143 167
MICKLIN, James 149
MIDDLETON, John 142 Stephen 128 130 131 132 138
MIERS, Benjamin 93 179 190 192 Euridice 179 209 Humphrey 93 109 111-13 116 135 138 Miles 93 Patsey 93 Thomas 93 Uridice/Uradice 93 223 -- 138
MILAM, Captain 162 171 174 Drury 84 97 118 122 123 126-28 143 163 164 166 170 196 202 217 230
MILBURN, David 8
MILES, Daniel 107 163 166 169 170 177 179 190 202 203 212 220 Isreal 217 John 92 Leonard 136 153 170
MILLENS, Abijah 102 113 119 132 136 140 Anne 140 Crotia 113 Mary 140 Philip 140 Susanna 140 Thomas 113 150 William 140
MILLER, Frederick 90 93-96 110 115 130 144 145 166 214 218 228 Henry 218 John 79 174 218 228 Randall 90 Wm 22 24
Milley 167
MILLIGAN, William 132
MILLIKIN, William 164 169 170
MILLINS, Abijah 80 86 125 139
MILLIS, Abijah 50
MILLIUS, Thomas 150

MILLS, Captain 171 174 188 192 218 John 68 89 96 98 103 107 117-19 128 154 156-58 167 172 174 176 184-89 192 198-200 228
MILLUS, Abijah 97
Milly 65
MILTON, william 151
Mime 177
MINER, Margaret 127
MINOR, Daniel 71 Dr 5 Hannah 71 John 3 4 9 Margaret 55 71 William 10
MIRES, Dicy 77 Benjamin 61 77 78 79
MISSISSIPPI TERRITORY 221
MITCHEL/MITCHELL, Elijah 68 Jeremiah 207 214 220 221 223-25 Michael 170 176 John 78 92 160 184 192 198 206 211 219 222 223 227 228 230 231 233 Richard 78 132 Robert 208 209 212 228 Samuel 78 82 132 Stephen 209 William 192 -- 229
Molly 98
MONGLES GAP 90
MONTGOMERIES MILL 65 72 76
MONTGOMERY, Alexander 3-5 10 13 25 28-31 52 Captain 155 160 Esther 50 James 53 55 70 78 87 89 175 Robert 11 12 16 19 50 Stephen 1 123 132 143 175 200 William 1-3 23 24 26 27 37 38 42 44 45 50 52 58 65 68 70-76 78-80 83 85 86 91 94 97 98 106 112 113 116-18 120 126 128-30 132 133 138-40 142 143 147 149-52 155 156 159-63 166-69 171 173 174 178 183 186 192 193 209 216-20 228-30 --16 21 72 148 mill 97 99 143 147 181
MONTGOMERY COUNTY, VIRGINIA 175
MOODY, Andrew 198 206 John 178 198 228
MOONEY, Patrick 52
MOORE, Andrew 72 152 153 Charles 78 David 125 Demcy 90 Demsey 215 225 Dempsey 196 201 211 214 Edward 70 Francis 54 Isreal 49 50 55 63 66 67 78 95 96 156 159-61 167 168 171 173 174 191 194 199 200 James 63 181 John 50 54 58 78 82 179 180 213 Joseph 128 177 178 183 190 Matthew 132 139 Moses 79 83 106 118 Robert 50 52-54 78 142 143 170 187 188 190 201 204 211 214 215 223 226 Samuel 54 58 96 William 59 67 164 165 168 170 179 180 184 195 200 201 208 211 215
MOORHEAD/MOORHED, William 94 131 135 136 140 141 144

INDEX

MORE, John 79
MORGAN, Armistead/Armstead 33 36 Benijah 118 Benjamin 146 157 161 165 170 176 184 196 210 211 Captain 3 4 16 19 22 23 35 36 43 47 48 57 59 64 Charles 1-4 Edward 151 154 165 169 195 Isaac 63 James 109 110 112 115 116 148 Jeremiah 35 56 70 71 John 1 6-8 10 14 15 19 24 33 36 41 51 53 55 56 62 63 65 70 71 75 76 79-81 85 90 91 95 99-101 106 107 112 113 117 118 123-30 136 139-42 145 147 148 150 151 153 155 157 160 162 169 171 179 180 187 188 190 193 206-9 212 213 218-20 222 227-30 Joseph 2 9 11 16 17 35 Susanna 134 William 56 59 65 75 79 81 87 92 98 103 109-11 116 118 120 125 137 143-45 148 149 154 164 173
MORRIS, Absolam 166 223 Henry 62 86 127 128 133 166 169 170 196 198 207 223 Joshua 223 Thomas 104 122 136
MORRISH, Cathey 164 Morning 163 181 228 Moses 164 203 204 Mourning 202 Nelley 164 Newburn 164
MORRISON, Elenor 130 Elias 89 207 221 227 230-32 James 69 81 84 92 96 99 101 115 118 120 121 125-28 130 133 136 137 142 153 179 John 18 Patrick 62 136-38 140 141 148 150 154 Samuel 165 William 51 56 87 89 101 102 213
MORROW, James 100 119 John 100 119
MOSBY, Samuel 31
MOSELEY, Peter 209
Moses 92 98
MOSES, Humphrey 190
MOSIER, Adam 41
MOSS, Matthew 198 203 209 219 Thos 209
MOTHERAL/MOTHERALL, John 74 192 200 Joseph 12 48 85 101 105 107 108 115 133-36 139 142 144 147 156 159-62 167 188 193 200 204 207 219 221 226 Robert 12 113 123-25 142 144 145 178 181 207
MOUNTFLORENCE, J 23 James 4-7 12 14 21 25 30 34 41 71 73 74 99 112 119-21 -- 38
MOYARS, Captain 30
MUCKLEYEA, William 91 97 106 109-11 115 142 143 152
MULHERIN, James 100
MULLINS, George 137

MUNGLE, Daniel 74 78 87 88 90 93 105 -- 81 gap 93 100 116
MURFREE, Hardy 28 56 63
MURPHEY, John 119 127 132 141 143 Saml 222
MURPHY, Francis 222 John 58 59 66 69 72 79-81 88 90 97 98 100 101 109 111 113 116 117 228 Samuel 221
MURRAY/MURRY, Captain 82 91 92 99 James 150 185 Thomas 6 10 13 55 79 90 95 96 103 104 114 121 123 126 127 144 147 157 173 176 179 183 193 194 201 204 205 209-13 224 228 William 101
MYARS, Ben 81 Philip 25-27 Uridice 81
MYERS, Benjamin 205 Betsy 205 Elisha 213 Euridice 205 Humphrey 205 Miles 205 Milley 205 Patsey 205 Thomas 205 Uridice 223
MYRS, John 54
Nan 75
Nance 222
Nancy 68
Nan 87
Nanny 44
NASH, William 34 184
NASH COUNTY, NORTH CAROLINA 219
NEAL, Aaron 172 178
Ned 82
NEEL, Aaron 206 Charles 6
NEELEY, Captain 99 107 160 171 Joseph 94 118 120 148 233 William 106 120 123 124 148 195 198
NEELY, Alexander 3 6 7 9 10 13 20 23 57 63 66 67 226 Captain 122 129 139 140 142 155 171 James 57 226 John 18 36 43 50 51 53 57 66 70 74 218 226 Joseph 63 66 131 136-38 144 146 152 153 164 165-67 210 212 213 Margaret 20 23 Massey 50 57 William 14 20 29 36 37 40-42 44-46 49 50 55 60 62 63 66 69 78 103 121 125 128 131 138 139 142-47 149 150 161 162 166 167 189 196 197 201 206 226
NEIL, Aaron 178
Nell 202
NELSON, Margaret 33 Robt 43 48 Saml 138
NELSON COUNTY, KENTUCKY 12 23 45 52
NETTLES, John 41
NEVELL, George 48
NEVELLS, Martin 88 -- 88
NEVILLE/NEVILLS, William 88 -- 88

INDEX

NEWBY, Henry 85 Tomson 85
NEWTON, William 18 30 41 44 48 58 78 145 169
NICHOLS/NICHOLLS, John 115 Thomas 46
NICHOLSON, Elijah 97
Nick 98
NOLEN/NOLIN, William 85-88 99
NORFIELD, James 28
NORFLEET, Cordall 89
NORMAN, Ezekiel 114 123 151 166 203 Joseph 220 Reuben 229
NORRIS, Ezekiel 1-4 6 8-12 21 22 25 28 32 61 George 83 95 James 87 218 John 1 3-10 12 13 16 17 35 45 46 65 75 90 93-96 140 153 176 198 William 79 88 95
NORTH CAROLINA 54 58 66 71 72 82 102 111 112 125 126 134 146 148 166 167 168 200 205 212 219
NORTON, John 153 Sally 89
NOWLIN, William 83 86
Nutt 222
NUTY, Joseph 92
NYE, Shadrack/Shadrick 86 89 93 98 100 103-5 118 120 124 128 142 147 151 154 163 166 168 174 176-78 181-83 185 186 188 192 195 198-02 204 206 207 210-12 214 220-22 227 W 160 161
OARR, William 16 17
ODAM, James 4 19 22 23 36 38 39 43 46 49 50-52 63 65 74 76 77 79 82 83 96 97 105 113 116-18 162 165 167 169 172 174 179 184 186 201 207 209 210 Elizabeth 65 John 46 Moses 162
ODIN, Richard 210 214
OGELS, John 231 William 213 216
OGELSBIE/OGILSBY, Elisha 3 5 7 9 10 12 13 16 17 20 21 24-30 38 39 41 42 54 58 59 60 65 70 71 77 86 89 Daniel 57 123-25 147 151 198 John 182 183 195
OGLE/OGLES, William 213 225
OHIO COUNTY, VIRGINIA 119
ONEAL/ONEALL/ONEEL, Aaron 182 Hezekiah 74 Jonathan 19 21 Thomas 59 -- 82
ONEILL, Hezekiah 63 83 106 110 112 117 121 123 124 136
ORE, William 53
ORGAN, John 32 135
ORMAN, David 164 225 226 Jane 117 William 117
ORMAND/ORMOND, David 156 157

ORR, D 112 David 92 105 137 174 184 210 212 G 231 Green 219 226 Greenberry 233 James 123 124 154 155 188 190 195-98 231 John 86 117 135 143-45 154 161 164 165 171 179 182 184 187 192 193 196 205 219 220 227 Robert 75 William 25 28 51 59 90 91 160 161 201 206 207
OSBORN/OSBURN, Luke 150 William 114 150 165 167 172 178
OVERFIELD, Paul 39 40
OVERTON, John 9 10 13 15 17 19-21 23 27 29 34 37 40 42-45 48 50 52 55 56 58-60 62 92 95 99 104 117 125 168 195 201 Thomas 66 71 191 -- 51
OWEN, Moses 166
OWINGS, Thomas 134
OZBROOKS, Michael 191 Ruth 191
OZBURN, William 150
PACK, Bartimus 62
PADFIELD, William 231
PAGE, Jesse 129 Robert 103 112
PAIN, Dudley 206 George 11 Matthew 29 Philip 170
PALMER, Henry 221 226 230 Wm 163 228
PANKEY, John 66 67 77 85 88 93-96 99 105 107 110 116 120 213 Joseph 99 118
PARATT, John 230
PARCHMENT, Philip 144 146 148
PARK, Charles 176 George 152
PARKER, Aaron 182 223 Elijah 194 George 92 Isaac 101 115 136 138 140 141 144 154 160 182 223 Isham 76 78 84 135 Jacob 96 John 161 181 223 Margaret 155 Mary 36 37 44 62 Nathaniel 61-63 65-67 69 70 72 76 82 87 90 92 96 97 99 115 117 137 145 148 150 153 155 171 173 174 179 182-85 195 206 223 Richard 133 139 141 151 154 182 223 Robert 182 223 226 Samuel 132 139 Thomas 65 66 69 72 87 89 90 92 101 107 109-12 116 121 129 131 142 149 152 153 155 156 160 166 172 179-85 195 212 214 222 223 William 92 125 132 139 161 -- 72
PARKES/PARKS, George 74 91 95 114 119 125 128 134 151 152 160 190 191 Hugh 185 Jacob 74 82 91 114 119 131 152 190 192 Sarah 134
PARMER, Daniel 110 Henry 206 John 110 Thomas 109 Wm 12 47 58 65 69 70 71 73 74 76 90 93-97 103 110 124 137 Wilson 110

INDEX

PARR, Henry 126 William 69 88 90 103 108 110 113 116 124 139 143 144 146 174 176-78 194 201 202 226 -- 103 ferry 227
PARSONS, Harrison 55 57 60 James 111 John 181
PASLEY, Thomas 222
Pat 137
PATE, Anthony 88 100 114 Howell 132 Joel 79 82 100 132 John 114
PATONS CREEK 106
PATRICK, Hugh 132 139
Patsey 121
PATTERSON, Andrew 61 100 101 159 John 31 39 81 93 94 97 159 175 Robert 60 192 Samuel 92
PATTON, Isaac 54 70 Robert 132 133 135-37 140 147 159 164 165 168 172 180 196 197 204 216 222 224 227 Thomas 1 7-10 20 24 34-36 38 40 41 43 46 49 54 55 57 60 63 64 66 70-72 76 91 93 113-15 123 124 133 137 139 145 146 151 153 165 172 179 194 200 202 204 214 230 William 197
PAVATT, John 192 220 230
PAYNE, George 31 40 41 John 228 Joseph 43 51 52 Josiah 138 216 Matthew 31 89
PAYTON, Elizabeth 38 Ephraim 1-4 6-14 16 19 22-27 31 34 38 41 44 52-56 60 63 66 68 69 75 76 79 80 83 85 87 91 93 106 107 109 110 112 115-17 122 130 137 143 146 149 156 164 167 178 181 186 218 220 John 2 5-9 24 34 38 42 44 45 50 57 58 60 63 65 67 70 71 75-77 85-88 91 93 97 100-2 106-10 112 113 115-19 122-24 127 135-38 142-49 153 154 156 160 162-65 173 176-80 184-87 189 195 196 198 204 209 214 216 218 230 233 Peggy 52 Robert 20 57 Thomas 27 29 33 38 41 William 230 -- 5 17 77 178 creek 63 73 81 82 93 100 116
PEA--, Jonathan 180
PEAIRS, Jonathan 180
PEAK, Norman 172 178
PEANS, Jonathan 179
PEARCE, Anna 187 Betsey 187 Isaac 21 24 30-32 37 40 46 52 56 61-63 71-73 78 82 83 91 97 105 160 165 179 180 184 196 208 213 231 Jonathan 32 47 54 106 201 Robert 105 127 128 William 59 -- 51 203
PEARIS, Isaac 79 Jonathan 179
PEARSON, Robert 87 136 141 143 152

PEASLEY, -- 222
PECK, Norman 115
PEET, John 181
Peg/Pegg/Peggy 66 219 229
PEIRCE, Isaac 166 169 171
PENDLETON, Giddeon 61
PENELTON, Isaac 10
PENNINGTON, Jacob 49
PENNSYLVANIA 92 184 203
PENNY, Lushy 48 William 33 48 79 92 98 120 124 129 131 188
PENRICE, Joseph 81
PERKINS, Daniel 164 Nicholas 134
PERRY, Aaron 15 105 Burrell 114 116-18 121 126 128 Edwin 98 105 191 217 225 George 62 James 211 John 40 51 52 59 65 70-73 87 89 160 161 179 190 192 Josiah 89 177 Nathaniel 114 156 Rauls 221 Robert 90 Rolls 181 Sion 13 19 21 25-28 31 32 34 38 40 42-44 49-51 54 55 60-62 66 70 72 73 76 77 79 82 83 88 97 100 101 103-7 109-11 115 117 131 133 138 143-45 194 Theny 144 Thomas 39 46 57 67 68 70 76 102 109 122 123 125 138 160 165 166 174 175 180 192 193 214 William 87 89 148 190 -- 14
PERRYMAN, John 151 166
PETEGREW/PETIGREW, Charles 83 122
Peter(slave) 75 80 83 84 98
PETERS, Stephen 75
PEWATT, John 206
PEYTON, Ephraim 14 Joseph 89
PHARR, Ephraim 9
PHIFER, Caleb 71
PHILADELPHIA, PENNSYLVANIA 92
PHILIPS, Andrew 212 Ezekiel 226 Isaac 114 206 John 110 111 116 Man/Mann 17 92 P 68 69 Philip 68 69 Rhody 152 228 William 131 136 -- 123 139
Philis/Phillis 66 69
Phill 221
PHIPPS/PHIPS, Betsy 205 Joseph 182 186 210 William 83 94 140 160 165 168 182 200 205 207
PICKEREL, Jacob 80
PICKERING, John 222 224
PIERCE, Isaac 167 169 Jonathan 171 Robert 105
PINKSTON, Moses 221
PIPER, Alexander 89 Morgan 114 Samuel

INDEX

89 104 114 115 147 151 165 166 169 200 202 230
PIPKIN, Philip 61
PITT, Henry 95 164 194 Joseph 194 Polley 194
PITTMAN, William 225 230
PITTS, Launsford 213 Lunsford 229 Rigdon 167
PITTSYLVANIA COUNTY, VIRGINIA 195
PLASTER, Michael 124 131 136
Plato 65
Pleasant 219
PLUNKET/PLUNKIT, John 71 88 93-96 99 100 William 112
POE, Terry 86
POLK, William 119
Poll 92
POLLEY, Thomas 185
PORTER, Ambrose 74 83 88 127 177 178 186 203 204 207 231 John 100 Mary 74 129 148 Rees 179 William 100 101 117
POTTER, Thomas 194
POTS/POTTS, Henry 42 44 62 Thomas 42
Powell(slave) 167
POWELL, James 162 Partheny 187 Richard 187 196 Swen 145
POWERS, James 92 188 220
PREWITT, Elisha 197 198 200 208 215 William 224
PRICE, Joseph 180 Josiah 136 William 1 2 9 11 16 18 110 230
PRIMER, William 27
PRIOR, Joseph 132 139 William 114
Priscilla(slave) 75 162
PROVINCE, John 5
PRUETT/PRUIT, Elisha 107 108 118 128 130-32 138 143 147 151 158 164 168-71 173 178-80 195 199 Joseph 115 Reuben 129 131 161 Sinclair 64
PRYOR, John 22 54 Joseph 59 Morning 101 Richard 59 154 William 20 51 56 85 154 -- 24
PULLEY, Thomas 185
PURSLEY, David 150 195 203
PURTLE, George 89
PURVIANCE/PURVAINCE, John 115 120 159
PURVIS, Allen/Allon/Alton 162 176 178 201 203 207 210 214 218-21 223 224 229 230
PURVOINCE, David 35 50 Jinny 51 John 33 34 35 50 51
PURVOINER/PURVOYNER, David 31 John 33
PUTT, John 229
QUARLES, John 224 William 49
QUARTER, William 34
QUEEN ANN'S COUNTY, MARYLAND 216
QUISENBERRY/QUISENBURY, John 73 74 96 97 105 William 109 175 177 178 Rachael/Rachel(slave) 44 92 103 217 229
RAILEY, John 87
RAINEY, Benjamin 92 William 92
RAINS, John 122 123 138 139
Ralf/Ralp(slave) 65
RALPH, John 150
RAMSEY, Esther 148 Henry 2 15 17 20 148 151 Hetty 15 Joshua 148
RANKEN/RANKINS James 90 92 94 98 116 127 134-36 153 162 171 179 180 209 Jeremiah 158
RAPIER, Richard 148 211
RASCO, Alexander 56 57 66 169 191 218 232 Jesse 47 William 47 66
RATCLIFF, Henry 68
RATHER, James 89
RAWLINGS, Benjamin 128-30 138-40 143 147 155 160 169 171 173 188 200 202 204 206 216 231 233 Rhodam 174 175 184-89 192 198 201 207-10 233 -- 222 225
RAY, Ezekiel 72 95 101 106 William 66
RAYFORD, John 101 119 Morris 101 119
REA, William 120
READ, William 126 188
READY, Aaron 146 Charles 72 75 96 98 146 William 146
Real(slave) 219
REASONS, James 227 John 74
REE--, William 230
REECE, William 121
REED, Archibald 103 Captain 64 69 72 73 82 85 90 94 95 George 158 James 158 166 John 150 166 188 214 Joseph 150 153 166 Robert 108 Sally 166 Samuel 166 William 28 46 56 58 63-66 70 75 83-87 94 106 109 116 123 125 127-29 131-33 140 142 147 149 150 152 156 157 160 162 165-71 174 175 184 195 213 221 226 230-32
REEDY, Charles 133
REES, Ebenezer 172
REESE, Captain 78 120 Charles 12 13 30 54 107 110 167 James 9 11 14 17 20 21

261

INDEX

27-29 33 53 55-63 65-69 72 77-79 81 82
84 85 87 90-96 98-100 104 106-9 111 112
116-18 120-25 128-35 137-42 144 146 147
153-56 159-62 164 168 169 171 172 177
181 201 218 221 228 232 Roger 231 Solomon 73 78 126 134 144 146 160 161 162
228 Thomas 76 77 109 133 136 137 142
144 145 153 161
REEVES, Edmund 212 226 George 122 Jack
169 170 176 178 183 184 190 230 James
211 John 165 173 174 180 Joseph 180 192
211 229 230 William 212
REGIN, John 155
REGLOUR, Howard 49
Reuben(slave) 196
REYLEY, John 148
RHODES, James 128
Rhody 92
RICE, Elisha 59 75 83 Joel 16 59 75 83
John 59 75 83 Joshua 167 202 233 Nathan
59 75 83 William 59 83 186 189 191 195
209 211 212
RICHARDS, William 71 75 76
RICHARDSON, Absalom 211 Daniel 91 100
113 131 133 138 145 194
RICHESON, Joseph 48
RICHMAN/RICHMON, Mark 120 151 156 159
161 167 172 194 Nathan 120 169
RICHMOND, James 124 125 130 John 203
219 Matthew 162 171
RICKMON, John 198 Mark 126 127 134 167
170 183 184 188 189 195-98 201 231
Rickmon 170 231
RIDLEY, George 2 7 8 11 Wm 47 50 58 62
RIGHT, James 6 51 Nancy 197 Stephen
19 William 197 -- 5
RILEY, John 71
ROADS, James 86
ROAN/ROANE, Archibald 154 155 157 Wm 13
ROANEY/ROANY, Benjamin 192 James 146
166 172 178
ROARK, William 65 101 102 116-18 120
121 185 201
ROBB, Joseph 200 221 226 Robert 172 200
209 215 216   Wm 65 144 172 193 200 231
Robert(slave) 231
ROBERTS, Edward 214 James 38 40 46 65
74 John 2 5 10 11 13 37-39 48-50 65 78
85 97 99 104 117 118 121 122 136 165
-- 11

ROBERTSON, Alexander 17 Henry 17 18 27
96 140 James 111 117 121 199 John 33
100 101 105 116 117 121
ROBERTSON COUNTY 202
ROBINSON, Alexander 20 21 24 Elijah 10
Elizabeth 39 Henry 17 19-21 25 27 37 39
91 153 155 157 181 James 6 181 195 John
7 8 37 91 105 107 164 173 Margaret 181
Margery 8 Mary 24 63 Richard 39 Robert
51 road 182
ROBLE, Robert 226
RODGERS, Jonathan 162
ROGAN, Hugh 6 47 53 55 59 61 62
ROGERS, Abraham 35 45 46 62 65 67 159
192 Anthony 54 58 86 Armstead 71 73-75
80 87 89 97 99 136 140 164 179 180 206
Daniel 33 41 65 67 69 74 156 162 Elizabeth 35 Jeremiah 46 55 Lemmuel 203 Peter 198 230 Samuel 157 Stanton 162 William 206
ROHRER, David 106
ROLLINGS, Rhodeham 88
ROLLS, Elisha 19 Silas 93
ROLSTON, James 158
RONEY, Benjamin 192 193 199 James 147
150 166 192 193 208 211 218 221 224-26
228
ROOF, Nicholas 68
ROPER, William 78
RORK, Barnet 213 231 Chas 213 John 212
Rose(slave) 54 81 92 98 177
ROSER, Jonathan 52
ROSES, William 59
Ross 89
ROSS, Geo 92 96 99 117 Jno 17 19 Wm 66
Rosse (slave) 172
ROWLES, Silas 98
ROWLEY, Silas 108
ROWLIN, Milley 114
ROWLINGS, Benjamin 92 106 113 114 120
122 123 Rhoadham/Rhodam 76-78 86-88 98
101-3 118 120
ROYAL/ROYALL, Hardy 85 101 Rachel 85
RUDDLE, Cornelius 100
RULE, Catharine 15 Henry 2 3 5 9 15 Jno
10 15 18 19 25-27 37 53 203 208
RUSSELL, H 209 Hendley 219 John 75 114
115 118 Joseph 124 134
RUSSELL COUNTY, VIRGINIA 64 192
RUTHAGE, Sarah 63

INDEX

RUTHERFORD, Elizabeth 31 Griffith 35 36 47 59 72 79 94 98 103 115 137 154 166 177 202 214 229 230 Henry 94 John 49 67 78 94-96 103 123 132 184 191
RUTLAND, Patsey 111
RUYLE, Henry 102 John 26 27 47 63 102 199 208 212 221 226 231 Peter 102
Ryal(slave) 229
RYANS GRAVE 146
S--, William 7
SADLER, Henry 96 100-2 111 116 John 24 31 41 53 70 79 83 84 92 95 William 62 135 -- 31 102
Sal/Sall 60 64 89 125 137 146
Sam 62 115 154 192 193 202 230
Sampho 65
SAMPLE, William 98 113 114 123 126 131 135 138 141 159 168 173 174 181 182 187 188 203 208 209 221 -- 138
SAMUEL, Anthony 101
SANDERS, Abraham 10 14-16 18 20 21 26 35 39 41-43 45-48 50 53 54 56-59 61-65 68 74 76 Captain 188 192 198 213 218 225 230 Daniel 135 194 Edward 142 143 146 151 152 154 160 161 166 167 173-175 178 198 206 209 219 223 Fanny 229 Francis 213 Goldsberry 201 206 Hardy 91 92 94 97 132 139 Jacob 8 13 31 33 42 45 50 James 1 40 43 48 50 51 55 60 75 79 82 86 90 91 97 98 103 106 109 121 123 128 133 134 140 144 146 149 154 155 160-64 169-71 173-78 183 187-89 193 198 201-3 206 208-10 212 213 216-20 223-25 228-31 Jane 104 Jenny 91 115 120 Robert 138 143 Thomas 123 223 W 78 William 12 51 63 69 74 75 83 85 87-90 93 94 97 98 104 113 115 120 133 134 139 141 144 147-49 171 174 177-79 193 197 202 214 229 -- 9 ferry 103 109 121
SANDIFORD, John 162
Sandy(slave) 65
Sarah(slave) 81 168 177 200
SAUNDERS, Edward 178 Jane 97 Jenny 97 William 70
SAVELY, John 70 78 126 128
SAWYER/SAWYERS, John 137 Miller 178
SAXTON, Joshua 153
SCATLE, Jarrett 220
SCHEEN, Jesse 87
Scipio 65

SCOBEY/SCOBY, Captain 162 171-73 188 190 218 219 222 David 35 36 39 42 44 53 59 Esther 39 42 John 146 Joseph 179 180 214 221 227 230-32 Matthew 64 92 103 123 160 161 162 164 219 233 Mrs 53
SCOT/SCOTT, Jacob 35 James 154 John 20 32 72 74 78 101 119 Joshua 16 19 22 31 34 41 42 44 48 56 60 72 79 85 124 Reuben 192 194 Richard 68 72 Samuel 156 228 William 125
SCUDDER, Nathaniel 105 110
SEAMON, Peter 72
SEAN, Isaac 200
SEARCY, Bennett 8 19 29 31 36 38 42 43 48 49 54 55 57-60 65 68 69 72 73 76 77 97 100 110 111 121 151 193 197 John 1 Reuben 1 99 114 115 120 122-24 130 131 139 147 150 151 155 159 162 166 167 171 172 179 181 182 186 202 206 210 211 214 231 Richard 1 223 Robert 42 78 232 - -- 166
SEATTE, Jarrett 220
SEAWELL, Benjamin 98 107 111 112 114 119 120 123 127 128 131 132 136 138 143 146 148 149 156 158 167 168 183 187 George 209 John 133 146 147 149 155 Joseph 147 166 168 170 174 176 184 196 209 Mr 116 Susannah 187 Thomas 89 104 William 139 147 155 156 158 159 162 167 -69 171 172 174 181 182 187 188 193 199-02 206-9 215 218
Sebb 135
SEET, Jarrett 170
SEFOCARD, John 60
SELLEY, Robert 114
SERAKER/SEREKER/SERICER/SERIKER/SEROKER /SERRICA, John 54 68 73 77 152 172 178 227
SETGRAVES, Joseph 13
SETTLE, Edward 88 90
SEVIER, John 82 85 120 124-126 191 208
SH--, Robert 11
SHACKLEFORD, Thomas 215
SHACKLER, Philip 15 36 37 73 106
SHADDOCK, John 178
SHANNON, David 21 59 John 165 178 182 227 Joseph 21 Michael 54 68 123 124 Robt 30 56 124 Michael 25 Samuel 93 180
SHARP, Anthony 12 15-22 24-27 29-32 37 39 47-51 56 57 59 60 62 63 65 73 74 81

INDEX

87 103 109 114 123 146 151 171 172 191 203 204 208 209 218 228 229 Major 65 73 102 166 Marcus 161 167 Margaret 56 60 Maxwell 68 99 223 Robert 19 30 34 84 Thomas 13 60 64 68 84-86 88 115 132 140 180 Sharps creek 178 182 206
SHAVER, Catey 133 Catharine 35 John 30 75 136 137 145 173 209 213 215 216 217 Michael 31-35 39 137
SHAW, Basil 99 114 Captain 14 16 125 139 155 159 171 172 192 218 219 222 Hance 125 James 19 20 23 John 188 Joseph 116 Robert 11 18 21-24 29-33 42 44-46 49-51 54 55 61 62 83 84 91 94 96 97 114 153 174 176 177 183 William 29 45
SHEAN/SHEEN, Jesse 81 114 189
SHEFFER, Michael 7
SHEIBLY, George 79 80
SHELBY, Catharine 38 D 28 49 60 63 88 110 117 122 127 132 140 152 156 158 159 169 170 205 233 David 1 2 5 6 10 13-16 18 23 29 31 33 36-38 40-46 48-55 59 61 63 64 66-69 71 73 81 83 89 92 94 98-100 103 108-13 116 122 124-27 134-38 145-47 149 151 152 154 161 165 166 173 176 177 183 194-97 200 204 206-9 211 212 214 215 221-25 Isaac 32 39 51 59 John 48 51 59 -- 217 Shelby creek 118 124 159 190 192 208
SHELBYVILLE, KENTUCKY 92
SHELTON, David 92 John 87 92 103 104 William 52 -- 98
SHEPPARD, Benjamin 89 James 19 John 101 119 William 157
SHEREL, Samuel 109
SHEY, Robert 178
SHOAT, Jesse 119 Valentine/Volentine 14 15 25-27 45 46 50 53-55 58 61 73 74 130
SHOER, Jacob 122 138
SHOLDERS, Solomon 167 190 213 225 228
SHORES, Jacob 93
SHOULDERS, Solomon 225
SHOUT, Jesse 101
SHUTE, John 132 139 Robert 79 Thomas 75
SHY, Robert 166
Sibb 146
Sid 110
SIGLER, John 182 Laurence 142 149
SIMMERALL/SIMMERELL, George 176 181

SIMMONS, Nathaniel 165 222 Peter 201
Simon (slave) 68 99 141
SIMON, Peter 59 60 99
SIMPSON, Caleb 126 Elijah 159 Elizabeth 146 James 94 134 138 187 201 207 214 224 230 Levise 29 Thomas 10-13 19 21 24 26 31 32 35 38 41 43 45 47 51 52 56 65 70 76 79 86 89 123 175
SIMRAL, George 228
SINGLETON, Jane 152 Richard 152
SIRNEY, John 69
SIZEMORE, William 121
SKINNER, Henry 65 66 Jonathan 45 52 Joseph 117 Josiah 114 Wiley 112 113
SLADE, William 66
SLAUGHTER, Robert 185
SLINKARD, Jacob 143 213 230
SLOAN, Fergus 75 96 99-02 128 129 144 146 148-51 154 John 150 187 201 206 228 Joseph 213 233
SLOO, -- 93
SLOP/SLOSS John 62 89 131 134
SMITH, Amos 25 27 28 Benjamin 16-18 78 80 87 144 Buton 24 C 2 Col 8 Daniel 1-11 13-15 17 29 32 40 41 43 47 48 52 54 55 60 62 70 86 103 109 120 134 161 192 200 204 207 219 224 228 233 Drury 84 Edmund 112 123 136 183 G 224 George 74 75 80 83 84 86-89 94-96 99-02 105 107 113 116 124 126-29 132 136 141 143 145 146 148 152 156 157 159 165 166 168-70 173 174 177 200 201 206 209 212 228 Howell 124 139 198 James 111 113 John 100 114 119 172 184 185 199 206 221 Moses 206 Obediah 31 Oliver 101 119 157 161 Pleasant 94 Richard 191 194 Robert 214 222 Samuel 160 161 171 173 179 181-84 195 201 207-10 220 Sarah 39 Thomas 16 17 21 26-30 32 34 38-40 45 46 50-52 54 58 101 114 119 130 202 228 William 75 96 99 100 101-3 110 123 124 127 140 143 183 197 198 201 202 216 219 230 -- 17 Smith fork 64
SMITH COUNTY 130 137 149 186
SMITHSON, Samuel 177 178
SMOTHERS, James 68 70 210 William 63 65 66 72 86 229
SN--, William 8
SNAVELY, Christopher 161
SNODDIE, Captain 57 59 62 64 69 77 73

INDEX

82 85 96 99 107 108 122 139 142 147 171
SNODDIES COMPANY 160
SNODDY, Andrew 97 Captain 113 124 155 Rebeccah 179 Samuel 72 74 84 William 2 4-6 9 11 14-17 24 26 31 32 34 35 38 41 43-45 47 50 53-57 61 62 65 67 71 82 83 90 92 97 108 111-13 116 121 125-27 144 146 153 154 156 160 167 177 179 183 185 191 197 198 200 203 204 210 214-18 222
SNOWDEN, James 61 96
SNYDER, Frederick 158 Solomon 192
SOMERAL, George 147
SOMMERVILLE, John 197
SOUTH CAROLINA 104 174 177 210
SPANISH TERRITORY, 106 174
SPENCER, Able 174 Benjamin 174 Elizabeth 50 59 99 103 Ezekiel 174 T 58 71 Thomas 1 19 20 22 23 28-30 32 34 42 43 47 48 51 52 56 57 59 61-63 81 84 William 47 48 50 51 54 58 59 71 74 78 115 174 -- 51 57 Spencers creek 103
SPRADLING, Jesse 124
SPRING, Abner 153 154 201 205 206 Simon 29 131
SPURGIN, John 27
SPURLOCK, John 6 William 6
STAIR, William 8
STAJNER, Henry 88
STALCUP, Eli/Ely 114 139 141 144 152 172 178 185 186 192 206 218 Isaac 101 118 147 150 166 167 179 193 Rachel 186 Samuel 84 138 140 Swain 160 167 168 Swen 191 William 65 84 101 108 114 120 138 -- 98
STALEY, Christen 156 161 163
STAMP/STAMPS, John 86 96 99 148-54 160-62 170 176 177 215 221 230
STANDFORD, Archibald 157
STANDIFORD, John 157 159
STANDLEY/STANDLY, Abraham 160 John 112 151 Jonathan 69 William 51 55 56 60 63 87 90 111
STANWELL, William 54
STARKEY, Jesse 114
STARR, William 3 4 8 9 11 -- 6
STAYNER, William 93
STAZNER, Henry 88
STEEL, Andrew 9 12-14 23 26 57 64 65 89 98 104 George 90 James 25 27 36 40 49

54 81 84 90 107 114 133 135 139 141 152 162 171 190 196 220 John 1 5 7 9 13 14 16 18 19 25 27 28 31 33 36 Joseph 38 39 50 52 56 58 90 151 164 Mary 54 Rebecca 54 Robert 12 16 30 34 36 37 47 52 54 59-61 65 70 75 79 80 84 87-90 95 121 124 125 134 135 140 154 171 179 181-85 195 196 220 228 W 26 William 97 118 120 -- 16
STEELE, Andw 158 Jas 200 211 Joseph 201 Stephen(slave) 90
STEPHEN/STEPHENS, Elizabeth 103 Joshua 219 Moore 42 Vachel 209 230 Wm 219
STEPHENSON, Captain 99 David 107 James 166 John 188 Moor/Moore 27 31 33 43 46 50 52 58 92 98
STERN/STERNS, John 50 73 76 80 90 96 97 99 120 123 124 127 136 144 153 214 218
STERET/STERRIT, James 168
STEUART, Thomas 63
STEVENSON, Captain 77 82 87 91 104 107 122 John 128 185 Moor/Moore 54 65 67 73 74 76-78 103 107 113 114 118 127 174 175 219 Moses 25
STEWARD, James 224
STEWART, John 231
STILL, Jeremiah 109 115
STINER, Barnabas 142 149
STOFZ, John 110
STOKES, Thomas 71 72
STONE, Eusibius 179 John 147 Stephen 191 200 218 William 89 Stones river 60
STOREY/STORY, Ann 120 134 Elizabeth 134 James 134 Sarah 134 William 120 125 134 142 148 172 173 177
STOTHART, Robert 109 113 117 119 125 128 152 195 196 201 William 193 -- 181 184 211 224
STOUT, George 85 120 Henry 136 John 137 Polley 107
STRADER, Conrod 25 45 47 56 58
STRAIN, Anne 64 Betsy 37 Thomas 25-27 30 38 43 45 47 48 50
STRINGER, John 206
STRINGFIELD, James 104 William 82
STROTHART, Richard 144
STROTHER, James 99 196 214 Richard 25 29 31 33 75 78 105 106 111 140 142-45 147 153 162 179 180 187 221 227 230-232
STROUD, John 145 200 Marshall 134 145

INDEX

146 153 169 170 181 200 231
STUARD, James 224 John 199
STUART, David 58 91 130 214 221 226
  Isbell 140 James 114 118 121-23 132
  John 102 121 125 134 142 161 175 182
  190 193 203 204 207 208 Moses 167 207
  220 Robert 13 95 Samuel 73 75 98 130
  179 181-83 220 T 138 Thomas 61 65 72
  74 88 101 105 111-13 117-19 122 128 130
  134 136 142 145-47 149 153-56 159-61
  164 167-70 173 174 176 177 181-86 188
  189 194-98 201-11 214-17 220 223-25
  229-31
STUBBINS, Christopher 186 190 209 214
  225
STUBBLEFIELD, Armstead 103 Armstreat
  202 Armstreet 95 96 103 114 133 144
  145 148 154 178 George 139 141 171 173
  174 194 201 206 214 Lemuel 192 Thomas
  78 103 105 114 136 137 144 145 147 148
  153 221 226 Woodruff 148 228
STUMP, Christopher 157 194
Suck/Sucky 75 179 229
SUDDARTH, James 172 178
Sue 65
SUG, Andrew 35
SUGG, George 31 Noah 51 55 56 60 193
SUITER, Ann 229 Benjamin 114 William
  114 229
SULLIVAN, John 172 Lee 71 211 William
  71 102
SULLIVAN COUNTY 38
SUMMERAL, George 213
SUMMERS, George 71 Jesse 1 3 John 166
  Joseph 63 64 68 80 201 207 209 210 Mary
  80 Summers branch 114
SUMNER, Jesse 5 7 Jethro 6 8 9 11-13
  41 -- 6 8
SURRY, William 167
SUSSEX COUNTY, DELAWARE 146
SUTTON, John 2 3 5 8 17 19 21 22 31 34
  41 Richard 45 52   -- 1
SWEARINGON, William 115
SWEAT, Isaac 68
SWEETMAN, Michael 91 96 97 111
SWET/SWETT, Abram 90 Antony 186 Isaac
  62
SWINGLEY, George 132 139
SYDNER/SYDNOR, Anthony 167 170 176
Sylva(slave) 104

SYNN, James 56-59
TAIT, John 71 81 88 90 William 111 193
TARBOR, Benjamin 174 177 183
TARBOX, Benjamin 170
TARIAS, Elisha 67
TARVOR, Benjamin 189
TATE, John 58 60 97 98 William 9
TATUM, Howel/Howell 10 13 16 19 21-23
  34 36 38 39 42 44 54 55 58 59 99 108
  112 114 128 143 James 99
TAUNT, Jesse 101
TAYLOR, Daniel 74 107 114 123 151 154
  169 200 David 143 Elisha 128 Herren/
  Herrin 114 156 157 James 44 John 167
  168 Joseph 30 Manoah/Menoa 123 209
  Perigan 55 74 85 Polly 84 Richard 193
  195 204 221 224 227 230-33 Robert 89
  114 154 158 159 189 215 219-21 223-25
  228 229 Samuel 147 -- 91 97 110
TEAGUE, Moses 132
TEAL, Abraham 159
TEMPLE, Turner 130
TENESON, Joseph 115
TENNESSEE COUNTY 22 43 59
TENNING, Laurence 90
TENNON, Hugh 32 John 56 Sibella 68
TERRELL, Garland 52 James 114 Obediah 1
  8 14 29 31 34 85 148 158
THACKER, Jeremiah 82 157 Larken/Larkin
  82 84 108
THERMOND, John 114
THO--, James 136
THOMAS, Jacob 49 50 56 61 62 71 83 84
  103 104 115 156 James 50 138 140 141
  148 154 162 Michael 175 Richard 37 54
  William 33 38 39 41 43 45 46 63 64 70
  87 91 103 124
THOMPSON, Azariah 19 24 25 30-33 36 38
  39 42 43 46 47 57 58 61 75 Burrell 225
  Burwell 211 231 232 Catharin 57 Cath-
  arine 175 Caty 57 Charles 117 Ezra 30
  Jacob 115 206 Jason 24 32 36 40 90 John
  29 175 217 Joseph 3 57 Katy 39 Laurence
  2 3 9-11 13-17 19 21 28 30 57 87 175
  180 Mary 223 Nathaniel 126 133 176
  198 204 213 Samuel 108 211 Sarah 57
  Thomas 2 3 45 46 57 175 William 2 6
  138 141 -- 166
THOMSON, Charles 108
THORNTON, Joel 82 87 Samuel 63 72-74

INDEX

132 139 143
THURMAN, John 209
Tiblen 98
TILLERY, Parismus 185 225
TILNY, Daniel 156
Tine/Tiner 65 194
TINNAN, Hugh 29
TINNING, John 105 Laurence 93-95 102 109 Thomas 102 109
TINNON, Hugh 24 38 39 44 50 52 53 56 John 45 46 50 53 56 Laurence 109 Sibella 50 Thomas 109
TINSLEY, Cornelius 74 207 208 Isaac 177 Moses 169 174 177 183-85 191 195 196 201 215 221 225 227 229 231 Thomas 177
TITTLE, George 79 80
Todd 110
TODD, Amy 228 Sucky 228 Susanna 202 Susannah 228 Thomas 163 181 191
TOLWINE, William 22
Tom 48 81 118 137 200 230
TOMPKINS, John 212
Tomtom 135
Toney/Tony 65 121
TOOLEY, Adam 108 117 118 158 James 118
TOPP, John 31
TOTEVINE, Simon 91 107 109 112 114 126 130 134 139 145 149 150 153 154 159 161 165 167-69 202 206 217 219 Spencer 159 169 William 14 16 21 97 109 111 114 117 123 139
TOTEWINE, Isaac 75
TOTWINE, Simon 97 William 20
TOWEL/TOWELL, Isaac 27 31 34 38 42-45 54 59 60 61 64 76 79 82 83 87 97 105 123 124 126-28 138 175 176 181
TOWLER, Benjamin 194
TRAMMELL, Nicholas 31 Philip/Phillip 2-5 10 11 18 21 22 28 30 31 39 41 43 45 50 -- 11
TRAVERS, Thomas 73
TRAVES/TRAVIS, Thomas 56 69 72 73 -- 68
TRICE, John 149 160 186 190 203-5 207-9 218 219 221 222 229
TRIGG, Abraham 199 231 Abram 142 Alancon/Alenson 51 87 173 Daniel 120 184 196 William 94 103 109 113 114 120 125 128 133 149 161 164-66 168-70 174 176 185 189 191-93 195-200 202-6 209 214 221-24

TRIPPLET, John 74 76
TROUSDALE, James 105 108 111 127 134 136 137 144 146-49 154 159 160 165 170 171 173 178 180 186 188 189 194 196-99 201 202 205 212 215 219 222 224 228 229 John 108 130 133 160 162 164 165 172 184 185 209 219 Mr 118 Robert 167 171 174 180 184 186 196 198 199 211-13 219 -- 124 144 225
TROUSDELL, Captain 65 75 James 58 63 65 67 98 106 107 John 98
TROY, John 132
TRUETT/TRUITT, Elijah 84 Henry 84
TRUMBO, George 224 225
TUCKER, John 117 154 189 194-98 201
TUCKERS CREEK 199
TUGGLE, John 92
TULLOCK, John 146 Thomas 163 183
TURMAN, Isaac 183 196 204 Rebeccah 183
TURMEN/TURMON, James 6 186
TURNBULL, William 21 193
TURNER, Adam 79 201 Arthur 216 Betsey 209 Edward 18 Elizabeth 18 Frederick 108 James 179 183 184 195 205 221 John 89 176 177 185 216 227 Mary 76 179 205 Samuel 158 Terisha 185 195 199 216 224 227 229 Terry 165 183 184 195 Trisha 177
TURNEY, Henry 50 81 85 152 Isaac 152 Michael 50 78 P 78 93 Peter 15 16 27 31 32 34 35 37-39 41 44 45 49-51 54 55 57 58 62 63 66 68 71 74 76 78 79 81-83 85 86 90 93 97 100-3 105 109 110 113 119 129 130 -- 17
TURNING, Laurence 87
UZAL/UZZELL, Isham 209 229
VALENTINE, Isaac 145
VANSEL, Edmund 6
VEAL, John 60 74
VENTRESS, David 191 Esay 191 Lovick 66
VENTURA, David 81
VENUS, Margaret 181
VIENST, Ralph 200
VINCENT, Henry 22 23 James 20 21 44
VININGHAM, Thomas 15
VINSON, Betsey 169 Captain 90 92 99 104 105 122 128 139 141 143 155 158 171 172 187 188 199 204 205 218 219 225 233 Henry 23 27-29 33 35 41 42 44-47 49 50 56 62 64 71 91 104 107 111 126 131 138

INDEX

162 166 196 211 James 20 21 25 27-29 33 37 43-45 49 51 56 61 62 71 84 92 97 99 111 112 116 120 123 126-30 133 135 136 139-41 146 147 149 151 156 159 161 167-69 187 189 194 195 197-201 214 218 232 Violet/Violett(slave) 103 137
Virgil 85
VIRGINIA(state) 11 20 25 26 32 33 40 44 45 54 64 67 79 92 96 102 104 114 119 122 123 136 173 174 175 177 180 184 192 195 203 209 230
W--, Captain 227 230
WADKINS, Robert 78 139 142-45 147 162
WALKER, Abraham 62 Alexander 157 David 95 George 37 55 John 47 56 70 82 95 101 Peter 158 Thomas 52-55 58 79 85-87 90 99 100 140 220 William 56
WALL, Captain 222 Hugh 98 111 Pearce/Pierce 13-15 18 25-28 32 33 38 48 53 58 61 68 91 95 105 111 153 208 Simon 98 111 -- 17
WALLACE, James 119 Jonathan 114 Joseph 13 15 17 22 24 27 30 32-34 41 44 47 53 55 62 63 70-73 77 119 123 124 129 131 133 144 146 156 165 176 177 179 183 209 212 Miles 62 -- 13
WALLER, Joseph 18 25 26 36 37 45 47 56 78 208 Lydia 196 Richard 21 35 56 70-73 78 79 142 149 152 153 163 164 169 222 223 225 Thomas 35 38 42 44 56 61 76-78 83 142 179 209 -- 14
WALLEY, Gadi 142 Thomas 142
WALLIS, Jonathan 176 198
WALTON, Captain 3 Isaac 2 5-7 11 18-20 24 26 27 32 33 42 52-55 58 59 61 62 64 67 68 72 76 77 80-82 86 87 89-91 103 104 107 109 111 121 122 126-28 132 138 139 155 160 162 164 166 171 172 178 181 183 184 189 192-96 200 203 207 208 212 213 215 221 225 228 229 William 1 10 11 14-17 27 43 53 81 86 91 103 104 108 120 192 ferry 94 98 108
WARD, Frederick 90 105 109 132 139 John 93 101 104 Michael 88 Polly 86 Stephen 91 97 155 161 169 202
WARDLAW, Hugh 103
WARE, Charlotte 75
WARREN, Henry 199 209
WARRNOCK, James 70
WASHINGTON, John 156 158

Waters(slave) 172
WATERS, Thomas 219 220 231 William 115
WATKINS, David 52 Robert 176 -- 101 119
WATSON, Capt 219 David 199 219 Elizabeth 121 Earnest/Ernest 227 231 James 79 86 90 94 101 107 113 116-20 132 139 144 145 149 162 167 219 Jeremiah 75 79 80 90 121 128 162 163 165 167 Josiah 86 100 119 Moses 167 Nicodemus 75 80 Rhoda 167 Thomas 73 211 212 222
WATWOOD, James 211 -- 150
WEAKFIELD, Henry 140 141 146
WEAKLEY, Robert 47 89 121
WEATHERED/WEATHERRED, Francis 129 130 139 142 148 149 157 171 183 James 72 98 113 114 116 117 128 129 156 160 162 172 184 185 201 206 John 177 184 196 Polley 116 117 129 Thomas 231 William 172 174 177 184 196
WEATHERLY, Joseph 97
WEATHERS, John 13 28 29 30 33 35 36 38 65 153 156 174 176 177 179 196 200 202 203 Patsey 202
WEATHERSPOON, Alexander 155 169 Joseph 114
WEBSTER, Henry 70 74 Randal 97
WEIR, Bazaleel 100 101 William 100 101
WELHAM, John 56
WELLS, Ephraim 202 212 Josiah 165 211 222
WEST, Cato 221 Isaac 101 John 74 92 Leonard 16 19 Lewis 197 227 Simon 31
WESTBROOK, Joseph 159 169
WETHERED, Francis 101
WHARTON, Jesse 90 104 117 158 161 164 168-70 173 176 177 183 186 189 196-98 202 206 210 211 213 216 217 222 225 226 231 -- 211 225
WHEATON, Charles 58 Daniel 51
WHERRY, Thomas 133 William 78 97 123 124 133 140 147 149 152-54 160 161 206
WHITE, Andrew 117 Ann 180 Archibald 64 92 100 105 157 158 163 212 Captain 171 188 218 219 David 51 52 66 69 79 83 186 191 George 200 H 117 James 19 22 24 28 29 33 35 37 39 44 47 55 63 64 68 79 87 89 102 103 106 108 121 126 130 138 144 145 147 152 157 177 191 203 212 213 216 222 223 John 14 16 17 28-30 44 62-65 67 68 79 87-89 132 139 142 174-76 180

268

INDEX

Joshua 90 Major 64 91 98 121 125 142 147 152 157 159 164 171 191 Mary 74 80 Meady 70 Reuben 172 178 180 185 Robert 75 92 102 103 131 140 213 214 Samuel 68 74 80 85 89 103 118 Thomas 10 11 60 William 31 65 75 78 90 91 94 95 98 99 125 130 131 134 142 147 148 152 191 221 228 -- 219 company 173
WHITEHEAD, William 123 139
WHITELY, Joseph 192
WHITESIDE/WHITESIDES, Jenkin/Jinkin 181 215 Elizabeth 180 James 180 John 180 Polly 180 William 180
WHITFIELD, Bryan 100 James 76 Willis 63 65 73 74 180 201
WHITFORD, John 152 153 174 182 190 Martin 152
WHITSETT James 24 32 Jno 14 17 28 31 32
WHITSITT, Captain 126 139 155 160 171 180 188 215 217 219 James 38 40 43 56 70-72 75 83 89 90 John 19 33 35 36 38 39 42 46 47 49 50 58 59 64 Laurence/Lawrence 59 90 91 128 133 144 153 154 156 157 165 184 185 195 197 202 203 204 213 William 43 -- 172
WHITTS, James 87
WHITWORTH, Elizabeth 159 John 159 174
WICKLIFF, Martin 211
WIER, Bazaleel 100 Russell 129 William 19 70 83 84 119 125 127 201 207 209 210
WIGGINS, Henry 34 44 51 206 Jno 206 227
WIL--, John 9
WILBURN, Daniel 78 100 101 188
WILCOCKS, John 94 96 198
WILEY, John 225
WILKERSON, Moses 132 139
WILKES COUNTY, GEORGIA 107
WILKESON, James 21 22
WILKINS, William 149 228
WILKINSON, Jesse 75 Lewis 173
WILKISON, James 12 18
Will 65 137 222
WILLARD, James 149 John 171
WILLBANKS, John 213
WILLIAMS, Alambee 211 B 49 Benjamin 17-19 21 26 31 33 44 48 Browning 191 194 Captain 82 92 93 99 Edward 29 31 32 38 47 53 59 61 113 118 165 172 190 192 198 228 Eliby/Elleby 147 150 201 206 Henry 138 154 James 130 162 177 191 194 218 Jesse 74 John 17-19 22 23 28 29 31 33-36 40-42 44-46 48 49 51 52 55 56 58 63 65 73 74 78 93 97 107 123 124 132 139 145 Joseph 88 131 141 174 Nathaniel 213 231 Oliver 89 Robert 59 S 20 Sampson 7 8 20 32 34 36 39 47 59 65 66 68 78 81 83 86 99 100 104 106 110 122 124 136 138 144 146 148 193 Sherrard 231 Terry 163 Thomas 20 21 70 Turner 23 William 76 167 169 206
WILLIAMSON, John 43 46 50 54 Robert 228 Thomas 47 49 51 54 61 62 71 72 77 115
WILLIAMSON COUNTY 164
WILLINGHAM, -- 5
Willis 229
WILLIS, Caleb 65 162 Francis 97 108 114 Jacob 190 John 116 Mary 108 Richard 65 114 121 Thomas 65 97 125 153-56 168 197 198 201 225
WILLOUGHBY, William 221
WILLS, Captain 218 223 224 George 9 James 42 220 231 Josiah 182 William 38 45 46
WILSON, Aaron 92 Captain 10 11 69 73 82 Curley 81 David 2 3 5-10 13-21 23-26 28-30 32-49 51-59 61-67 69-76 78 82 84-96 98 99 102-4 106-8 110-13 115 116 118 119 122-31 133-37 139-47 149 153 155 156 158 160 162 163 165 166 169 171 172 175 176 179 181 186 188 189 192 193 198 201 Ebenezer 56 57 109 George 93 108 James 1 2 5-11 13 14 16 17 21 23 24 27 32 34 35 38 39 44 45 47 49-52 54-60 63-65 67 68 70-75 78-81 83 85 86 89 91 92 94 101 103 105-7 109 110 114-16 118 121 123 124 126-28 134-37 139 141 143 147 151 153 154 160-63 166-68 170 171 173 174 176-79 181-86 188-90 192 194-202 204-7 210-15 219-22 225 227 228 230-32 Joel 132 John 4 6 7 9 13-15 18 26-33 35 38 48-51 56 58 63-65 67 70 76-78 93 135 143 149 165 174 175 182 201 206 214 218 221 Jonah 137 Joseph 22 24 76-78 97 108 121 128 129 144 145 147 149 150 156 157 168 221 222 225 Josiah 136-38 140 141 148 154 Major 7 9 11 14 29 63 64 73 75 135 147 159 163 200 206 Moses 132 221 Richard 205 Robert 38 43 45 46 55 63 64 73 76 79 87 90 91 93 95 96 108 121 134 Samuel 26 32 34 36 42 44 58 63 74 92

269

INDEX

115 132 138 149 165 174 184 192 193 201
Stephen 214 Stogdal 205 Thomas 98 157
160 161 167 177 William 2 7 9 15 24 25
32 33 37 38 45 47-49 51 52 59 61-65 71
75 79 85 89 101 107 158 192 Z 127 Zach
83 Zachariah 153 Zachery 147 Zacheus 25
27 32 36 38 39 42 53 58 61 71 75 85 91
118 120 133-36 143 145 156 157 160 164
171 192 193 198 207 220 221 227 230 232
-- 14 16 148 232
WILSON COUNTY 137 156 158 183 190 224 229
WILWOOD, George 57
WIMBELDORF, George 65 148
WINCHESTER, Captain 2 3 223 David 48 49
59 Elizabeth 48 General 79 George 1-4 6
7 11 14 18-24 28 29 31-36 38 40-44 49
50 53 55 J 66 141 145 James 7 10 18 25
31 40 48-50 53-55 57 59 61-66 68 72 74
77-88 92 98-03 106-9 111-13 117-33 137
139-42 144 146-54 156-65 169 170 172
175 177-79 181 182 185 188 190 191 193
197-201 204-8 212 213 215 217-21 226-30
Lydia 48 Richard 48 49 Stephen 48 49
William 48 49 164 203 204 -- 210 215
220 227 228 mill 1
WINHAM, Stephen 116
Winny 55 86
WINSTON, Anthony 216 229
WINTERS, James 198 Welham 38
WITCHER, Tandy 136 153 168 182 189
WITHERS, Betty 215 John 39 43 51 57 63
67 74 83 84 89 91 103 105 106 111 121
129 134 154 155 159 160 165 178 181 183
186 190 215 232 233
WITHERSPOON, Alexander 62 68
WITHIN, John 56
WITHROW, John 221 222
WOLWOOD, George 30 38 57 60
WOMACK, James 78 96 Jesse 68 71 101 102
122 145 156 157 163-65 175
WOOD, John 68 82 114 166 168 170 178
183 184 Mary 183 184
WOODARD, Daniel 61 James 132 Noah 115
Simm 27 Simon 47 56 Thomas 27 33 47
WOODDELL, George 186
WOODDRIL, George 176
WOODFORK, Joseph 132 139
WOODRAM, Jacob 70
WOODS, James 140 John 167 184 205 208

Mary 205 208 Samuel 230 William 100
WOODWARD, James 139
WOODWERT, Henry 19
WOOLSEY, Nathaniel 185 192 225
WOOTON, Samuel 181
WORLDLY, William 36
WORMACK, James 144 145 147 Jesse 144 164
WORMINGTON, Edward 196 John 167
WORNAK, James 207
WORNOCK, James 72 75 76 79 83 84 160 161
WORTHAM, Thomas 195 William 195
WOTWOOD, George 38 39 51-53 55 60 62 85 114
WRIGHT, Ann 115 Elizabeth 115 James 66
90 115 116 118 121 John 74 76 90 100
115-17 119 128 129 143-45 198 Stephen
18 60 William 184
WYER, Bazaleel 64 107 121 122 Russell
128 131 171 Susannah 42 William 13-15
21 23 31 38-42 44 45 49 50 71-73 110
115-18 121 180 224 228
WYLES, John 188
WYLLS, John 128
WYN, William 14 17
WYNHAM, Obediah 125 Stephen 124 125
WYNN/WYNNE, Devereux 93 94 111 116 140
George 93 113 114 118 James 12 John 90
116 Robert 104 111-13 127 135
WYSS, John 53
YANDAL/YANDALL, Wilson 155 177 184 187
196 198 229
YATES, James 5 6 12-14 18 20-22 31 32
46 53 61 62 Thomas 32 51
York 63
YORK, -- 184 196 203
YOUNG, Abraham 38 39 41 43-46 49 51 53
56 Abram 43 Adam 70 Captain 35 37 43 45
47 48 57 59 Daniel 45 Elizabeth 106
Ezekiel 199 203 208 212 George 154 168
Henry 201 206 John 13 14 17-20 30 31 33
35 37 39 42-46 50 54 55 57 59 61 62 68
78 101 102 104 116 120 122 124 126-28
131 132 135 143 146 148 150 190 197 208
209 231 232 Lydia 39 Marlin 108 143 154
181 184 220 231 Moses 179 William 13 14
16-18 31 39 78 81 106 110 114 129 139
147 163 180 -- 44 46
YOUNGBLOOD, Thomas 156 172

INDEX

YOUREE, Alexander 191 207 Francis 191 207 Patrick 191
Zack 199
ZEIGLER, Betsey 129 Christina 32 33 37 Elizabeth 37 Hannah 37 129 Jacob 22 32 33 37 43 77 78 129 John 37 129 223 Laurence 79 80 Mary 37 Polley 129
Zelpha(slave) 166
ZIEGLER, John 215

SUMNER COUNTY, TENNESSEE,

COUNTY COURT MINUTES
June 1808 – March 1810

Abstracted by Carol Wells

JUNE 1808

p.1   Sumner County Court June Sessions 1808. Thursday morning June 16th. Present the worshipful Isaac Walton, James Cryer, and James C Wilson Esquires.
  William Douglass v Andrew Jackson & John Hutchings. Jury Thomas Donnell, Joseph Clark, Jesse Joiner, Jeremiah Belote, Samuel Stuart, William Phipps Junr, David Beard Senr, George Reed, Henry Bledsoe, Henry Pitt, Henry Vinson, James Franklin. Plf recovers agt dfts damages $114.06 and his costs of suit.
p.2 John Crawley who was summoned to appear this day as witness for Jackson & Hutchings came not; fined $125 unless sufficient cause be shewn at next Court.
  Commission apptd last term to divide real estate of Abraham Rogers decd between devisees render statement of such division.
  John Lafferty summoned to appear this day as witness for Jackson & Hutchings came not; fined $125 unless sufficient cause be shewn at next Court.
  Account of sales of property of Abraham Hassell decd rendered by Moore Stephenson an admr.
  John Morgan resigns as Justice/peace.
  Appt Cornelius Thomas overseer/road from Hendersons mill up Drakes Creek in place of James Reed, resigned.
p.3 William Rentfro v Josiah Wells. Detinue. Sheriff levied on a small horse of dfts; James Cryer & James McKain special bail for dft; attached property replevied.
  Edmund Crutcher v Samuel P Black. No declaration by plf; nonsuit; Plf by John C Hamilton moves court to set aside the nonsuit.
  Edmund Crutcher v Samuel P Black. [Worded as above]
  Grand jury dismissed.
  On petition of Nancy Wells relict of Ephraim Wells decd, order sheriff summon twelve freeholders to lay off to her one third part of one acre adjoining lots of David Walton & Samuel P Black near Gallatin for her dower.

p.4 June 17th 1808. Present James Cryer, Nicholas Boyce & James C Wilson.
  James Cryer v Matthew Moss. Debt. Parties in proper person; dft confesseth judgment $140.42 with interest after deducting a credit of $100. Plf recovers agt dft sd sum $140.42 and also his costs of suit.
  James Wheeler v John Young. Trespass assault & battery. Jury Jesse Joiner Samuel Stuart Joseph Clark Thomas Donnell Thomas Dement David Beard Senr George Reed Goldsby Thurman Henry Bledsoe Henry Vinson Henry Pitt James Franklin. Plf recovers agt dft his damages $10 and costs of suit.
p.5 On motion of Nathaniel Parker, stop proceedings of judgt obtained by Rivers[?] Hodge vs sd Parker before Edward Gwin for $23; rehearing at next Court.
  Daniel Holeman summoned here this day as witness for John Young ads James Wheeler came not; fine $125 unless sufficient cause be shewn at next Court.
  Thomas Haynes summoned here this day [worded as above]
  Gideon Rayne summoned here this day [worded as above]
  Abram Young Senr summoned here this day [worded as above]
  Robert Brown summoned here this day [worded as above]
p.6 Deed Archibald Marlin late sheriff to Thomas May 640 acres ackd.
  Charles Donoho summoned here this day as a witness for James Wheeler v John Young came not. Fined $125 unless sufficient cause be shewn at next Court.
  Appt Thomas Rawlings constable for Capt Sanders company, Rhodam Rawlings Josephus H Conn & Redmond D Barry securities.
  William White v Robert Collier. Trespass. Plf to take deposition of Stephen Sherock of Bertie County No Carolina.

JUNE 1808

Saturday June 18th 1808. Present William Montgomery James Cryer & James C Wilson.
p.7   Deed Montgomery McConnell & Danl McConnell to Jno McConnell 125 acres ackd.
   Present James C Wilson Wm Montgomery Sion Hunt.
   James Lauderdale v James Hart. Debt. Jury Jeremiah Belote Jesse Joiner Joseph Clark Henry Bledsoe Robert Simpson Samuel Stewart Thomas Donnell David Beard Senr George Reed Henry Pitt Henry Vinson Jas Franklin. Dft recovers agt plf his costs of defence in this behalf expended.
   Edward Cage v William Mann. Appeal. Ordered by Court that plf not be taxed with costs of attendance of more than four witnesses for deft, to wit Thomas Murry Owen Rosh[]?] John Bradshaw & Stephen Jackson.
   William Campbell v George Brown. TAB. Plf by John Stewart no further prosecutes; pays his attorney & witnesses; dft by Mattw Alexander pays all other costs.
p.8   Present Wm Montgomery James C Wilson Sion Hunt Esqrs.
   Elizabeth Davis v Benjamin Smith. Jury[above]. Juror Henry Bledsoe is withdrawn; jury discharged from rendering a verdict.
   Jackson & Hutchings v John Lafferty. Sci fa. Dft in proper person swears he was unable to attend as witness; dft released from judgt agt him at last term.

Monday June 20th 1808. Present James Winchester John McMurtry Benjamin Rawlings.
p.9   Bill/sale John Trousdale to John Nichols four negroes: man Dennis, female Peggy two children of sd Peggy, proved by Thomas Farmer a subscribing witness.
   Elizabeth Davis v Benjamin Smith. Plfs declaration amended so that sd declaration may read Ephraim Payton instead of John Payton.
   Present James Cryer James C Wilson Sion Hunt. Elizabeth DaviS v Benjamin Smith. Covenant. Plf maketh oath that when she gave her atty Red D Barry directions respecting persons whose lands interfered with hers she bought from deft she told her atty it was John Peytons preemption that interfered through mistake not knowing any thing of Ephraim Payton. Sworn Elizabeth Davis. Test D Shelby Clk.
   Elizabeth Davis v Benjn Smith. John Payton maketh oath that since commence-
p.10   ment of this suit he heard Richd Smith agent for dft say he intended to purchase the land subject of this suit from William Peyton, son of Ephraim Peyton Declaration amended to read "who derives under Ephraim Peyton & Lazarus Cotton." Signed by James Cryer, Sion Hunt, James C Wilson.
   Bill/sale Henry Young to James Winchester mulatto girl Dicy ackd.
p.11   Appt John Shaw[?] overseer/road from Bledsoes lick to Bishops ferry; Thomas Blakemore esqr to furnish sd overseer with a list of hands.
   Deed James Roney to Jesse Dawson, lott #6 in southwest square of Gallatin proved by John C Hamilton.
   Deed Jesse Dawson to John Hutchings lot #6 in southwest square of Gallatin proved by James S Rawlings.
   Polly Wynn orphan of John Wynn decd made choice of John Dickison as her guardian; bond $3000, Thomas Blakemore & John Harris securities.
   Issue ltrs/admn on estate of John Trice decd to Patsey Trice relict; bond $5000, John Cavett & Thomas Keife securities.
p.12   State v Thomas Ritter. TAB. Dft saith he is guilty; fine 12½¢ & costs.
   Allow Thomas Ritten[Ritter?] $15 for supporting John Putt a pauper 5 mos.
   Allow Jesse Spradlin $16.66¾ for supporting John Putt a pauper four months.
   Assign John Putt a pauper to Jesse Spradlin for support for one year.
   Appt Miche Looney overseer/road in place of Reuben Douglass resigned.
   Present Wm Montgomery John McMurtry & Mat Alexander Esqrs. James Trousdale

2

JUNE 1808

Jr v John Stamps. Sci fa. Jury John Withers Richd Smith John Spradlin Josias B Mallary Joshua Hadley John Payton John Cavett Ebsworth Baynes Thomas T Rawlings John Mitchell John Gardner. Mistrial.
p.13 James Trousdale v John Stamps. Sci fa. Permit dft further to plead.
    State v Ebsworth Baynes. Recog. forfeited. Ebsworth released from forfeiture of recognizance. Sd Ebsworth with John Baynes & Thomas Cruthers his securities acknowledge bond to Justices $500 condition the maintenance of bastard child of which Elizabeth Night has lately been delivered whereof sd Baynes stands charged with being the reputed father.

Tuesday June 21st 1808. Present John McMurtry, Thomas Masten, Edward Gwin.
    John Hunt v William Giles. Sci fa. Grant plf execution agt dft for $14.24½ & his costs of prosecuting this suit.
p.14 Present James Douglass Isaac Walton John McMurtry. Silas Jernigan v Josiah Wells. Appeal. Jury Richard Smith Josias B Mallery James Sanders Hugh Gurley John Withers Isaac Baker Jas Hale John G Mitchel Wm Sanders John Cavett Jesse Sheen John Spradlin. Plf recovers agt dft damages $14 and his costs.
    Edward Hudson v Nathaniel Hunt. Sci fa. Plf by John G Bowen. Dft not appearing, plf recovers agt dft $8.07 & costs.
    Acct/sales of goods of Samuel Armstrong decd rendered by Abel Brandon exr.
    Appt James Winchester & William Seawell Esqrs to examine & settle the accounts of Abel Brandon exr of Samuel Armstrong decd.
p.15 Appt Wm Trigg & Mattw Alexander to examine and settle accounts of guardians for heirs of Henry Loving decd.
    Appt John Gillespie guardian to Margaret Armstrong Zenos Armstrong Knox Armstrong & Samuel Armstrong orphans of Samuel Armstrong decd; bond $3000 with George Gillespie and Abel Brandon his securities.
    William Douglass v Andrew Jackson & John Hutchings. Dfts obtain appeal to Superior Court; bond with John Withers and John Bosley securities.
    Deed Matthew Brown to Robert Patton 343 acres ackd by sd Brown.
    Deed Lazarus Cotton to Armstreat Stubblefield 560 acres proved by Tilman Stubblefield & Jonathan White subscribing witnesses.
    Robert Laurence v Nicholas Boyce. Covt. Plf no further prosecutes; each party pays his own costs.
p.16 Present Isaac Walton, Jas Douglass & John McMurtry. Benjamin Bashaw v Larken Bradford. TAB. Jury Jas Franklin Jesse Joiner Henry Bledsoe David Beard Henry Pitt George Reid Thomas Donnell Henry Vinson Samuel Watson John Jones Tilmon Stubblefield Clement Stubblefield assess plfs damages to $83.83½.
    John Webb an orphan age eighteen years apprenticed to Joshua Draper until age twenty one years to learn art & mystery of a blacksmith. Joshua Draper entered indenture with John McMurtry chairman pro tem.
    Jurors to next county court: John Rutherford William Wherry Thomas Anderson Wm F McNutt Thomas Dement Samuel Conn James Steele George Smith Thomas Preston Edward Sanders Edmond Turpin Samuel Dorris Robert Hamilton William Duty John Jones John Sternes John Hawkins Joseph Hodge Edwd Sanderson Reuben Douglass Isaac George
p.17 John Franklin John Carr John Mills Wm Sanders Sr William Alexander Sr John McAdams Jacob Barnett Allen Groves Robert Williamson Elisha Prewitt Thomas Britton Thomas Joiner Robert Taylor Philip Kiser William Edwards.
    Sheriff to summon Thos Rawlings & Solomon Shoulders constables to next Ct.
    Preent Edwd Douglass Jas Douglass Isaac Walton Esqrs. Nicholas Boyce v

JUNE 1808

Michael Murphey. Jury Jeremiah Belote Jesse Joiner Joseph Clark John Withers Jesse Sheen Jesse Coker Henry Bledsoe Geo Reed Thomas Donnell Henry Pitt Henry Vinson Jas Franklin. Mistrial by consent of parties.

John Jones & Kenedy Owen v Robert B Mitchel. Dft relinquishes his pleas. Plf recovers agt dft damages $128.52 and costs.

p.18 Howard Douglass qualified as Deputy Sheriff.

Fine William Kirkpatrick $2 for not attending as a juror when summoned.

Thomas Cahoon v David Campbell. Debt. Plf dismisses suit, recovers agt dft his costs.

Edward Douglass delivers a performance bond by him taken in his name as chairman of Thomas M Dement with Charles Dement & Robert Ellis his securities, as inspector of cotton, $5000. Also a like bond of William Brooks as inspector of cotton with affidavits of Thomas Dement & William Brooks.

p.19 John & William Allen v Henry Betote. Sci fa. Plfs by John C Hamilton; Dft not appearing, plf granted exn agt dft for $88.34.

Wednesday June 22d 1808. Present James Winchester James Cryer & Isaac Walton esqrs.

State v John G Mitchell. Sci fa. Dft by John C Hamilton. Dft released from forfeiture of recognizance.

Stay proceedings of three judgments obtained by Deaderick & Sittler agt John Mitchell before John McMurtry Esqr for about $112 returnable to next Court.

Deed Jesse Haynie to Henry Young 136[126?] acres ackd by sd Haynie.

p.20 Quit claim between Wm Pittman & Tabitha Pittman of one part and John R Eaton for negroes Obedience and Lucy proved by James Sanders.

Isaac Walton & John Gardner admrs of Bryant Gardner decd v James Kirkham & James Kirkham. Debt. Plfs recover balance of debt $100, $16.58 damages & costs.

Deed George Brown to John Bentley, lot 69 in High Street, Cairo, proved by James Winchester and James Bentley.

Deed Robert Trousdale to McNutt Findley & Co 4½ acres ackd.

p.21 Inventory/sales of goods of John Josey decd rendered by admr.

James Richmond v Elisha Prewitt. Debt. Dft to take depo of Lemuel Prewitt.

Edmund Crutcher v Samuel P Black. Nonsuit overruled; plf recovers costs.

Edmund Crutcher v Samuel P Black. [as above]

Isaac Walton & John Gardner admrs of Bryant Gardner decd v James Kirkham & James Kirkham. Debt. Dfts obtain appeal to Superior Court; bond, with William Payton & Thomas Kirkham securities.

p.22 Deed Archibald Marlin late sheriff to Abram Trigg, house & lot 21 on Franklin Street in Gallatin ackd by sd Marlin.

Bill/sale Archibald Marlin late sheriff to Francis Sanders three negroes household furniture horses & cattle ackd by sd Marlin.

William Granger v John McClure. Motion to dismiss certiorari sustained; plf recovers agt dft his costs.

John Lafferty failing to attend as a witness in suit Wm Douglass v Andrew Jackson & John Hutchings in behalf of dfts, exhibits affidavit; released from forfeiture on his paying costs. Costs paid.

Thursday June 23d 1808. Present James Sanders Isaac Walton & James C Wilson Esqrs.

p.23 License Thomas Keife to keep tavern in Gallatin, James Berry & John Stewart his securities; bond $2500.

William Black James Desha & Sampson Williams v Josiah Giles. Sci fa. Grant

4

SEPTEMBER 1808

plf execution agt dft for $204.15½ debt, interest $8.37½ and costs.
  John Den lessee of Thomas Farmer v John Keen. Ejectment. Dec 1807 non suit was entered agt plf. Motion of Redmond D Barry atty for dft.
p.24 Francis Weatherred v William H Ramsey. Cer. Plf by John C Hamilton. Plaintiff recovers against defendant $17 and costs.
  William Lyon v Jas Blackmore. Plf recovers agt dft damages $84.80 & costs.
  Deed Redmond D Barry to Joseph Cavitt, 274 acres ackd.
Court adjourned until Court in Course. Jas Sanders Isaac Walton Jas C Wilson.

p.25 Court of pleas & quarter Sessions. Second Monday, September 1808. Present James Winchester James Cryer James C Wilson esqrs.
  Felix Grundy is admitted to practice as an atty at law; took oaths.
  Deed John Giles to Mourning Winn 96 acres proved by William Giles and Wm F Purvians.
  Deed/relinquishment Elizabeth Giles to Mourning Winn of her title to 96 acres conveyed by deed dated with date of relinquishment between John Giles and sd Mourning Winn was proved by William Giles and William F Purvians.
  Bill/sale Sampson Murdock to John Bearding negro girl Judith proved by Humphrey Bate & Bartholomew Stovall.
  Deed Elisabeth Davis to John G Mitchel 40 acres proved by John Gardner & Thomas House.
p.26 Deed James Kirkham to John Peyton 83½ acres proved by Joseph Clark & John Bysor[?].
  Deed John Peyton to John Bysor 83½ acres acknowledged.
  Deed George Brown to George D Blackmore half acre lot in Cairo ackd.
  Deed Tilmon Dixon to Jonathan Purse 140 acres ackd.
  Deed George Brown to Francis Youree 150 acres ackd.
  Deed John Pendergrast to John Hodge half lot #5 in Gallatin ackd.
  Lease Stephen Cantrill to Perrin Smith 15 acres to 25 Decr 1809 ackd.
p.27 Commrs apptd last Term to divide land between Nathan Rickmon and heirs of Mark Rickmon render division of sd land between sd persons in writing.
  Deed Thomas Keefe & Redmond D Barry to Ephraim Cates 201 acres ackd.
  Deed John Beakley to John Prendergast lots 19 & 20 in Gallatin ackd.
  Deed Wm Brown to George Brown 50 acres proved by James Steele & John Brown.
  Deed George Brown to William Beard 50 acres ackd.
  Deed Richard Rapier to Jesse Johnson lot 14 in Cairo ackd.
  Deed Alexander Dobbins to Robert Dobbins 162½ acres ackd.
p.28 James Clanton[Claxton?] vs John Bailey & John Pritchell. Joseph Lauderdale one of securities, surrenders dft Bailey; William Sanders will pay the debt & damages if John Bailey is convicted, and surrenders himself.
  Deed David Beard Senr to Alexander Dobbins Senr 30 acres proved by Robert Dobbins and Carson Dobbins.
  Deed/gift Alexander Dobbins to Carson Dobbins 227½ acres ackd.
  Deed Henry Bradford & Daniel Smith to James W Harris 320 acres ackd.
  Appt Andrew Blythe overseer/road from Croft mills to William McMu[binding] in place of Benjamin Tarver resigned.

SEPTEMBER 1808

      Deed Jesse Johnson to William Wherry Junr lot 13 in Cairo ackd.
p.29   Grand jury: George Smith foreman, William Duty, William F McNutt, John Jones, Robert Williamson, William Edwards, Thomas Dement, John Sternes, John McAdam John Rutherford William Wherry Samuel Conn William Sanders Senr, Edward Sanders.
      Appt Solomon Shoulders constable to attend Grand Jury this Term.
      Appt Robert Marshall overseer/road in place of Lewis Johnson resigned.
      Grant ltrs/admn on estate of William Phipps Junr decd to Humphrey Meirs; Humphrey Miers bond $1000 with Isaac Baker security.
      Allow admr/estate of Wm Phipps Jr to expose goods & chattels to sale.
      Appt Elisha Green constable in Capt Bridgers district, Redmond Barry and Michael Green his securities.
p.30   Apprentice orphan Andrew Melton age twelve unto Thomas McGuire to age 21; James Winchester chmn enters indenture with Thomas McGuire.
      Orphan Peggy McClung age eight apprenticed to George Duty to age 18; Duty enters indenture with chairman James Winchester.
      Letter/attorney from John Knott of Bertie County North Carolina to Humphrey Bate dated 25 August 1807 acknowledged by John Knott before Cornelius Ryan a Justice/peace of Bertie County and certified by actg Clerk/Court of sd county, also certificate of Geo Outlaw J P certifying that Joseph Blount was actg Clk of Bertie County Court. Solo Cherry Jr endorsed on sd power/atty which is ordered registered.
p.31   James Winchester & William Seawell esqrs apptd last term to settle with Abel Brandon exr of Samuel Armstrong decd render statement; ordered recorded.
      Philip Kean & Edmund Turpin jurors released from further attendance.

Tuesday Sept 18th 1808. Present Jas Winchester John McMurtry & John Barr esquires.
      Deed John Cathey to William Cathey 90 acres 30 poles proved by Alexander Cathey Junr and William Cathey.
      Bill/sale William Brinkley & Thomas Brinkley to John C Hamilton negro boy Blackman proved by Josephus H Conn & Edmund Green.
      Deed William Hogan to John Caldwell 225 acres dated 25 Septr 1800 proved by Samuel Gattis.
      Appt Robert Bruce overseer/road near Capt Haneys in place of George Brown removed and James Winchester esqr to furnish list of hands for sd overseer.
p.32   Robert Desha Senr v Nicholas Boyce. Debt. Dft by atty cannot deny plfs declaration. Plf recovers agt dft $700 debt, $57.70 damages, and his costs of suit.
      Robert Patterson v John Lafferty. Debt. Jury Reuben Douglass Thos Britton Wm Kennon John Hawkins John Carr Robert Hamilton Seth Mabry Rhodam Rowlings Isaac George James Claxton Thomas Joiner Joshua Cherry. Plf recovers agt dft debt & damages $137.29 and his costs about his suit in this behalf expended.
p.33   James Watkins v Stephen Montgomery & Edwd Hoge. Debt. Jury[above]. Plf recovers agt dft debt and damages $553.96 & also his costs of suit.
      James White & Samuel Conn v James Steele. Debt. Jury[above]. Plf recovers
p.34   agt dft debt & damages $175.92 and also his costs of suit.
      William F McNutt Findley & Co v John Spooner. Debt. Lewis Johnson and Walter Loving securities for the defendant.
      Thomas Deaderick & Isaac Settler v John Lafferty. Jury[above except David Stuart for John Hawkins]. Plf recovers agt dft debt & damages $93.52 & costs.
p.35   Stephen Pitt assee &c v James McKain. Debt. Jury[above]. Plf recovers agt dft debt & damages $110.31½ and also his costs about his suit expended.
      Thomas Parker v Robert White. Debt. Jury[above]. Plf recovers agt dft

SEPTEMBER 1808

balance of debt together with damages $66.99 and also his costs of suit.
p.36   Nicholas Boyce v Allen Purvis. Debt. Jury[above]. Plf recovers agt dft debt
& damages $95.99 and also his costs about his suit expended.
     Garland McAllaster v John Payton & William Payton. Debt. Jury[above].
p.37   Plf recovers agt dfts debt & damages $204.41 and his costs of suit.
     William W. Whitaker v James McKain. Debt. Jury[above]. Plf recovers agt dft
debt & damages $110.50½ and also his costs about his suit in this behalf expended.
     Isaac Bledsoe v Thomas Parker. Debt. Order Richard Brown be made a defendant jointly with Thomas Parker. William Edwards special bail for sd Brown.
p.38   Present Jas Winchester John McMurtry Jas C Wilson John Ball. William
Gillespie v John Wood. Covt. Jury[above]. Plf recovers agt dft his damages & costs.
     Bill/sale Marmaduke Kimbrough to William Duty negro girl Dove proved by
George Duty and Henry Young.
     Deed William A Covington to Jesse Moore 8 acres proved by James Douglass
and Jacob Mays.
     Deed Isaac Lane to William A Covington 8 acres ackd by Isaac Lane.
p.39   Grant ltrs/admn on estate of John C Henderson to Ednis Henderson relict of
sd decd; Ednis Henderson bond $3000 with William Trigg Francis Sanders Bennett H
Henderson & Edward Sanders her securities, and took oath as prescribed by law.
     Present the worshipful James Winchester John McMurtry James C Wilson James
Cryer Will Trigg Thomas Blakemore William Seawell Matthew Alexander William Montgomery Joshua Rice James Hart Sion Hunt esqrs.
     Order David Beard Jr & Samuel Beard be apptd guardians to minor orphans
Robert Allen Sarah Allen Sophia Allen Charity Allen Anna Allen children of Orman
Allen decd. Bond of David & Samuel Beard $2000, Henry Neill & Alexr Dobbins secys.
     Wm Rentfro v Josiah Wells. Detinue. Depositions of Isaac Gregory Kesiah
Gregory Mary Shelton & Nancy Baker residents of So Carolina to be taken behalf dft.
     Bill/sale Andrew Hoover Senr to Henry Hoover for household furniture cattle
horses dated 29th August 1808 ackd by sd Andrew Hoover.
p.40   Deed John Biggs to Isaac Hudson 140 acres ackd.
     Deed John Biggs to Drury Hudson 317 acres ackd.
     Appt Solomon Sholders constable in Capt Bakers district; James Cryer and
Isaac Baker his securities; took oath as prescribed by law.
     Deed Hugh Wall to Elmore Harris one acre two poles land proved by Joseph W
Withers and John Withers.
     On motion W Thomas Stuart ordered that James Hennen be apptd special
guardian for Jep[Jes?][end of the name is lost in the binding].
     Appoint Thomas Blackemore George D Blackemore Joel Eckols Senr Thomas Murry
Henry Gambell Wm Edwards Junr Samuel Conn William Hubert and John Bentley a jury to
to view and straighten the road near Captain Haynies from where sd road crosses the
road from Croft mills to Belotes ferry to somewhere between Bledsoes Creek and
Cairo, having regard to convenience of a bridge proposed to cross sd creek.
p.41   On petition of John Barr Esq, appt Capt John Carr Wm Carr John Miller Robert
Mafit David Pursley Andw McPetters Robert Shaw Robert Simpson & King Carr to review
road from Bledsoes lick to flat Gap and make alterations when it passes through sd
Barrs land for benefit of sd Barr avoiding inconvenience or injury and make report.
     Excuse jurors James Steel Elisha Prewitt & William Alexander from further
attendance to this Term.
     Thomas Young orphan now age nine years six months bound apprentice to Summers Harper until age twenty one to learn the art and mystery of a stone mason or

SEPTEMBER 1808

brick layer; indentures acknowledged by the Chairman and sd Summers.
Appt George D Blackmore inspector/Tobacco at Cairo, James Cryer and David Shelby his securities; bond $3000; took oath prescribed by law.
p.42   Appoint John Johnson an inspector of Tobacco at Cairo in place of Thomas Gregory who appears from proof exhibited to be rendered incapable of discharging the duties enjoined by law by reason of age & infirmity. John Johnson's securities George Smith Edward Sanders.
On motion of Thomas Stuart esq order Doctor James Hennon of Nashville be apptd special guardian for Jesse Wilkerson for defending a suit brought by William Terrel Lewis against sd Jesse Wilkerson.
George Smith foreman and others, sworn a Grand Jury, deliver indictment agt Elisha Keen for assault & battery, one against Ashlin Keen, and one against Pamelia Collins for like offences; true bill.
David Bundy v Armstead Stubblefield & Tilmon Stubblefield. David Bundy obtained execution from Chas Donoho J/P agt estate of Armstead Stubblefield and Tilmon Stubblefield to satisfy judgt $34.62½ and costs; return endorsed No personal
p.43   property to be found, levied on 114 acres on Goose Creek by Lemuel Stubblefield constable. Property condemned; order to sell to satisfy judgment.
Andrew Allison v Armstead Stubblefield. Andw Allison obtained exn from Jas Hart J/P agt estate of Armstead Stubblefield to satisfy judgt $13.83½ & costs. Return: levied on 114 acres; Leml Stubblefield constable. Condemned, to be sold.
Robert Cotton v Armstead Stubblefield. Robert Cotton obtained exn from Jas Hart J/P...$46.12½[as above]
p.44   David Bundy v Armstead Stubblefield & Tilmon Stubblefield. David Bundy obtained exn from Chas Donoho J/P...to satisfy judgment $19.75 & costs [as above]
p.45   James Richmond v Elisha Prewitt. Debt. Plf no further prosecutes; dft pays costs and plaintiff's cost of suit.

Wednesday Sept 14th 1808. Present the Worshipful James Winchester Matthew Alexander James C Wilson, Esqrs.
Robert McKinley v James McKain. Jury Reuben Douglass Isaac George Thomas Joiner Thomas Britton David Stuart Jesse Shien Nicholas Stone William White Elmore Harris Ambrose Porter Demcey Moore Robert Simpson. Dft recovers agt plf his costs about his defence in this behalf expended; plf pays all other costs.
p.46   Robert McKinley v James McKain. George Anderson witness in behalf deft came not. Fined $125 unless cause of disability be shewn to next Court.
Commissioners apptd to divide real estate of William Brigance decd delivered a written statement of the division.
Jury to lay out a road make report; same is rejected. Order another jury to lay a road as ordered from Gallatin to State line crossing ridge at head of Little Trammell. Appt John Payton James Frazor Joseph McElwrath William Edwards Senr Hugh Crawford Peter Luna H & Wm Douglass to mark & lay out sd road.
Receive report of jury apptd at March Term last to alter road down Drakes Creek by Montgomerys Mills between Henry Bunns & George Reeds.
p.47   Joseph Scobey proved his right to a stray heifer taken up and posted by William Edwards, appraised at $3.75; half to be paid to Scobey.
Present Stephen Cantrill James Cryer & James C Wilson. Francis Comperry v Thomas Keefe. Jury John Hawkins Robert Hamilton John Carr Samuel Cluny Wm Woodall Loftain Cage Wm McCall John Gardner Jeremiah Bower Samuel Watson William Gillespie Elisha Miers. Defendant recovers against plaintiff his costs of defence.

SEPTEMBER 1808

James & Robert Desha v John Trice Dempsey Moore & Robert Moore. Sheriff returned scire facias agt Patsey Trice admr of John Trice to revive suit against sd admx; she is made a defendant jointly with the other defendants.
p.48   John & Robert Allen v George Michie. Debt. Dft in proper person saith plfs declaration is in every thing expressly true. Plfs recover $81.79, $273 damages & their costs; stay of execution for six months.
    Deed Ambrose Porter to Nicholas Stone 26 acres ackd.
    Deed Ambrose Porter to Walter Loving 21½ 7 20 poles ackd.
    Deed Cornelius Thomas to Henry Bradford 31¾ acres ackd.
    Deed Thomas Masten late sheriff to Hugh Barr 640 acres ackd.
p.49   On petition of Armstreat Stubblefield order James Hart esqr to send to Court all papers in a suit wherein judgt was rendered by sd Jas Hart behalf Robert Cotten agt petitioner; proceedings suspended until a rehearing of this matter be held.
    John Gourley v Robert Simpson. Trespass with force. Refered to John Barr Esq King Carr Henry Belote & James Vinson for final determination.
    Hugh Gourley v Robert Simpson. Trespass with force. [as above]
    Order a jury to lay off the dower of Catey Haw relict of James Haw decd: Sheriff to summon Henry Bunn Joseph Clark Jesse Joiner Wm Montgomery Isaac Fowell Wm Wier Robert Wadkins George Reed James Reed Wm Draper Thos Joyner Shadrack Nye.

Thursday Septr 15th 1808. Present Jas Winchester Stephen Cantrill Mattw Alexander.
p.50   Deed John Starnes to George Cooper 105 acres 27 poles ackd.
    John Burnley v Thomas Masten. Jury Leonard Reed Benjamin Duvall Richd Moore Jeremiah Bowers James Mills Richard Smith Isaac Lindsy John Hawkins John Carr Isaac George Thomas Britton Thos Joiner. Dft recovers agt plf his costs of suit.
    Deed Thomas Dement & Charles Dement to Samuel K Blythe Richard King & Richard Blythe one acre 32 poles ackd.
    Allow Wm Penny $6 being the money paid by Thos Stubblefield for a stray steer taken up by Stubblefield legally proved the property of sd William Penny.
    In consequence of an asthematic disease which he has long laboured under besides senses of hearing and seeing being much decayed, Thos Masten J.P. resigns.
p.51   Bill/sale James Hargrove to John Hargrove: 5 negroes Lucy Tony Cherry Bob Judy proved by William Davis and John Davis.
    Bill/sale James Hargrove to John Hargrove: horse cows household furniture &c proved by William Davis and John Davis.
    Grand Jury dismissed.
    Deed Ephraim Payton by John Payton agent, to John Gardner 25 acres ackd.
    Francis Comperry v George Tillmon. Sci fa. Plf by John C Hamilton; dft in proper person. Plf no further prosecutes. Dft releases half his allowance as a witness in suit Comperry v Keefe & pays costs of sci fa. Cause dismissed.
    Francis Comperry v John Tillmon. Sci fa. [as above]
p.52   William White v Robert Collier. Trespass &c. Dft recovers agt plf.
    Jackson & Hutchings v Redmond D Barry. Appl. Plfs no further prosecute. Each party pays their own costs.
    Deed James Winchester & Wm Cage Jr to Lemuel T Turner lot 5 in Cairo ackd.
    Deed Jas Winchester & Wm Cage Jr to Lemuel T Turner lot 90 in Cairo ackd.
p.53   John Willard v Joseph Reeves. Jury Reuben Douglass Robt Hamilton Thos Howell Wm Harper Stephen Chambless Isaac Clark Benjn Tarver William Payton Wm Maxey Jacob Fuller Thos Kirkham John Payton. Plf recovers damages $89.62½ & costs.
    Present Wm Trigg James C Wilson Wm Bracken. John Murphy v Michael Murphy.

SEPTEMBER 1808

Jury[above]. Plf recovers agt dft damages $100 besides costs.
p.54 Hugh Gourley v Robert Simpson. Trespass. Dft agrees plaintiff has sustained damages by overrun $3; each party pays his own costs.
   John Gourley v Robert Simpson. Trespass. Parties in proper person agree to dismiss suit, each paying his own costs.
   Appt Wm Seawell & Matthew Alexander esqrs to settle with John Starns as guardian for Robert Steel George Steel & Joseph Steel orphans of James Steel decd.
   Appt Wm Montgomery & Wm Trigg esqrs to examine and settle the accounts of executors of Nathaniel Gilmore decd.
   Ruffin Deloach v Theophilus Allen. Ruffin Deloach obtained exn from Will Trigg J/P agt goods of Theophilus Allen to satisfy $12.98 debt 93¼¢ costs. Levied
p.55 on 2 lots in Gallatin between Mrs Trice & Wm Trigg the property of Theophilus Allen; lots condemned for use of sd judgment; order of sale issues.
   William Maxey v Theophilus Allen. Wm Maxey obtained exn from Jas Douglass J/P agt property of Theophilus Allen to satisfy judgmt $33.25 principal & 31¼¢ costs. Levied on two lots in Gallatin Nos. 23 & 25; order of sale issues.
   Will & A Trigg v Theophilus Allen. Will & A Trigg obtained exn from Edwd Douglass J/P to satisfy judgt $20.43 debt & 93¼¢ costs; order of sale issues.
p.56 Dempsey Moore v Isham Usell. Referred to determination of Archibald Marlin William Bracken James Gwin[Givin?] & James McKain.
   George Smith foreman & others of Grand Jury indict Wm Wallace a true bill.

Friday September 16th 1808. Present Jas Winchester Jas Cryer Will Trigg esqrs.
   James Brown v John Tompkins. Order prosecution bail released from costs of sd suit; whereupon Thomas Stuart Redmond D Barry John C Hamilton & Bennett H Henderson undertake in case plaintiff fails to prosecute.
p.57 Present Jas Winchester Stephen Cantrill Jas Cryer. James Brown v John Tompkins. Jury John Hawkins Reuben Douglass John Carr Thomas Joiner Isaac George Thomas Britton Wm Dodson Dempsey Moore Wm Kirkpatrick Porter Allen Robert Simpson Wm Bruce. Plf recovers agt dft damages & costs. Dft botains appeal to Superior Court with John Jones and James Barry his securities.
   Motion of Edniss Henderson by her atty, order she be made dft as administrator of John C Henderson in the suit of James White & Joseephus H Conn v John C Henderson by certiorari, death of sd John C Henderson having been suggested by plf.
p.58 Present Jas Winchester Stephen Cantrill Wm Bracken. James White & Jos H Conn v Edness Henderson admr of John C Henderson decd. Jury Robt Hamilton William Kennon John Edwards Thomas Howell Wm Payton Wm Buckner Peter F Jefferson Willie Lassiter Adam Crump Richard Smith John Withers Robert Moore cannot agree. Mistrial.
   William Pendergrass v Laurence Owen. Sci fa. Jury Isaac George John Carr Thos Britton Thos Joiner Wm Payton Edmd Bridges Wm Harper Jas Sanders Danl Sanders Wm Bell Jas Stewart Ephraim Cates. Plf awarded execution agt dft $125 & costs.
p.59 Present Jas Winchester Will Trigg Wm Bracken esqrs. William Buckner v Edward Hogin. Jury[above] cannot agree. Mistrial.
   Robert Desha v Nicholas Boyce. Debt. Plf obtained judgt this term agt dft $757.20 & costs. Dft obtains appeal to Superior Court, Benjamin Rawlings and John Withers his securities.
   Present Jas Cryer Will Trigg Jas C Wilson. Andrew Jackson & John Hutchings v Benjamin Rawlings. Jury Richd Smith Isaac Clark Jesse Joiner Goldsberry Thurman Smith Hansbrough Peter F Jefferson John Baynes Wm Dodson Wm Buckner Willie Lassi-
p.60 ter Wm Bruce John Pendergrass say dft kept covenant. Dft recovers agt plf.

10

SEPTEMBER 1808

Plf obtains appeal to Superior Court, Jinkin Whitesides & Felix Grundy securities.
David Stafford v John Josey. TAB. Suit abated by reason of death of dft; plaintiff pays costs of said suit.
Archibald Marlin late sheriff who was summoned as a garnishee in behalf of James Stuard at instance of Thomas Farmer v John Givin[Gwin?] declares on execution issued in favour of sd Farmer for $160.12 principal. Marlin recd of Gwin $137.89 of above exn, that previous to his garnishment he paid unto Farmer $65, and after deducting cost there remained in his hand $60.45½.
Commrs apptd to settle with exrs of Nathaniel Gilmore decd make return.

Saturday 17th September 1808. Present William Montgomery Jas Douglass Jas C Wilson.
Deed/gift John Josey to his daughter Sarah two negroes Rachel & Coalrain dated 12 February 1805 proved by Ruffin Deloach.
p.61 Appt Jas Cryer & Will Trigg esqrs to settle with exrs of Hugh Elliott decd.
Appropriate $7.25 for repairs to jail.
Order Jas Cryer & Wm Trigg esqrs settle accts of admr of Edwd Howell decd.

Monday 19th Septr 1808. Present Stephen Cantrill John McMurtry Matthew Alexander.
State v Josiah B Mallery. Recognizance. James Shaw prosecutor. Dfdt to keep the peace; Mallery pays half costs of recognizance.
White & Josephus H Conn v Theophilus Allen. White & Josephus H Conn obtained exn from Matthew Alexander J/P agt sd Theophilus to satisfy a judgt $31.75 debt and 93¼¢ costs. Levied on 2 lots between Mrs Trice & Sgn Trigg; Francis Youree
p.62 constable. Lots condemned for use of sd judgment; order of sale issues.
White & Josephus H Conn v Theo. Allen. Debt $40.38 & 93½¢ costs[as above]
Elizabeth Davis v Benjamin Smith. Covt. Jury Reuben Douglass Thos Britton Thos Joiner Isaac George Wm McMunn John Felligin Jas Shaw Porter Allen Robt Patton Moore Cotton Jesse Dawson Geo Trumbo. Plf recovers agt dft damages & costs.
p.63 Jeremiah Deal assee v Patton Anderson & John C Hamilton. Sci fa. Dfts not appearing; plf granted executiona gt dfts for $173 debt, interest $8.40 & costs.

Tuesday 20th Sept 1808. Present Edward Douglass Stephen Cantrill James Douglass.
John Jones & Co v Theophilus Allen. John Jones & Co obtained exn from Will Trigg Jr J/P agt Theophilus Allen to satisfy judgt $13.29 debt & 93¼¢. Levied on land whereon sd Allen now lives J Tomkins. Land Condemned and to be sold.
Deed John Trice to Thomas Keefe lots 9 & 10 in Gallatin proved by Jno Orr.
p.64 Stephen Pitt assee v James McKain. Debt. Defendant obtains appeal to Superior Court, John Jones & Redmond D Barry securities.
William W Whitaker v James McKain. Debt. [as above]
Present Edwd Douglass Stephen Cantrill Jas Douglass Wm Trigg Jr. John Mills v William Sanders. Jury Reuben Douglass Wm Harper Edward Turpin Isaac Clark Thomas Britton Dempsey Moore Thomas Joiner Isaac George Jacob Thompson Adam Crump Robert Hamilton John Goodrum. Plfs damages by reason on nonperformance $189.72 & costs. Dft obtains appeal to Superior Court, Edward Sanders & Thomas Anderson securities.
p.65 Deed William Edwards Senr to William Edwards Junr 320 acres ackd.
Bill/sale Wm Edwards Sr to Wm Edwards Jr two negro boys Terry & Jim ackd.
By consent of Thomas Keefe & Ephraim C Davidson pertaining to suits: two appeals wherein Keefe is plf & Davidson dft, one suit covenant, Davidson v Keefe, also Keefe v Davidson, referred to determination of James Cryer William F McNutt Henry Belote James S Wilson Will Trigg; award made at house of Keefe in Gallatin.

SEPTEMBER 1808

    Deed William Kirk to Ephraim Trumbo 100 acres proved by George Trumbo and Robert Laurence.
    Deed William Hall Sheriff to John Carr 370 acres ackd.
    Deed James Trousdale to Matthew Neale two acres eight poles ackd.
p.66   Appoint Cornelius Herndon Goolsby Sanders & James Carey appraisers to value property in Capt James Blackmore's company.

Wednesday September 21st 1808. Present Edwd Douglass Stephen Cantrill Jas Douglass.
    Present Stephen Cantrill Jas Cryer Mattw Alexander. Richard Pendergrass v James Kirkham. Jury Wm Kinnon Thos Richey Ashley Stanfield Jonathan Trousdale David Stuart Thos Anderson Wm Boyer James McKinsey John Payton Jeremiah Doxey Jr Clement McDaniel Zacheus Wilson assess plfs damages $3.12½. Plf recovers afsd sum & costs.
    William Edwards v James Cage & Saml P Black. Depositions of John F Gray & John Taylor of New Orleans to be taken by Benjamin Morgan & Maunsel M White.
p.67   Present Edward Douglass James Cryer James C Wilson. Nicholas Boyce v Michael Murphey. Jury Thos Britton Isaac George Thos Joiner Robt Trousdale Robt Hamilton Robt Lytle Wm McMunn Jonathan Trousdale Elisha Forrest Isaac Forrest Jas Brown Richd Smith assess plfs damages to $78.50. Plf recovers also his costs of suit.
    Wilson Cage v Nicholas Boyce. Debt. John Mitchel & John Goodrum defendants securities.
    Andrew Hoover v John Lafferty. Appeal. Jury[above]. Plf by atty orders nonsuit. Dft recovers agt plf his costs of defence.
p.68   Present Edward Douglass James C Wilson Mattw Alexander. John Orr v Clement McDaniel. Appeal. Jury[above] find for plf $20.85 & costs.
    Robert Patterson v John Lafferty. Debt. Defendant obtains appeal to the Superior Court, Thomas Kirkham and John Payton his securities.
    Garland McAllister v John Payton & William Payton. Debt. Dfts obtain appeal to Superior Court, Nicholas Boyce & John Lafferty securities.
p.69   Dempsey Moore v Matthew Moss. Sci fa. Dft not appearing, plf granted execution against dft $100.32 debt & damages & $8.50 costs of writ and costs of suit.
    John Pankey v Matthew Neal & James Vinson. Plaintiff no further prosecutes. Defendants recover against plaintiff their costs of defence.
    Andrew Jackson & John Hutchings v Micajah Viverett. Defendant not appearing plintiffs are granted execution against defendant for $125 and their costs.
    Andrew Jackson & John Hutchings v James Odam. Plaintiffs by Thomas Stuart no further prosecute. Defendant recovers his costs of defence.
p.70   Order Jas Winchester & Jas C Wilson to settle with exrs of James Blair decd.
    Commrs to settle with gdns for heirs of Henry Loving decd render statement.

Thursday Sept 22d 1808. Present Edward Douglass Benjamin Rawlings Will Trigg esqrs.
    Benjamin Rawlings v John Dawson. Trespass. Jury Thomas Britton Thos Joiner John Jones Isaac George Robt Hamilton Robt Trousdale Thomas F Cheeddle Edmd Collins Robert Patton Henry Hart Robert Looney Richard Holliway find dft not guilty.
    Allow James Turner constable $5.50 for conveying Joseph Wright from Gallatin to Edward Gwins esqr, sd prisoner being charged with horse stealing.
p.71   Present Edwd Douglass Isaac Walton Jas C Wilson. Alexander Kirkpatrick v Reuben Searcy. Covt. Jury Zacheus Wilson Charles Henderson John Banes Jacob Fuller Elesworth Baynes Swen Stalcup Elisha Forrest Webb Bloodworth Thomas Howell Jacob Thompson Jas Howard Reuben Douglass say defendant has not kept his covenant. Plf recovers agt dft damages $1710 and his costs.

SEPTEMBER 1808

  Will & A Trigg assees v Thomas Keefe. Debt. Defendant came not; plaintiffs recover against defendant $68.50 debt $2.30 damages and their costs.
  Deed James Brigance & William Brigance to George Dempsey 33 7/9 acres ackd.
  John Jones v Thomas Keefe. Debt. Defendant not appearing, plf recovers agt dft $354.37 debt, 70¢ damages and his costs of suit.

p.72 Present Edward Douglass Isaac Walton Jas C Wilson. Alexander McMillin v James Claxton. TAB. Jury Thos Britton Thos Joiner Isaac George Robt Hamilton Robert Trousdale Thos F Cheedle Edmund Collins Robt Patton Henry Hart Robert Looney Richd Holloway Harrison Hendrick assess plfs damages $25. Plf recovers agt dft.

  Jurors to next Superior Court: Stephen Cantrill Senr Edward Douglass James Douglass John Withers Solomon Shoulders Nathan Edwards Zacheus Wilson son of David Porter Allen.

  Jurors to next County Court: Kasper Mansker John Perry Jonathan Pearce John Ruyle Henry Bunn Robt Wadkins Robt Shaw George Martin Isaac Stalcup Griswold Latimer Peter Looney James Wilson Smo, John Peyton Senr William Beard William Edwards Junr(B Creek) Joseph Wilson John Swancy William Alexander Junr Elisha Ogelsby Bartholomew Stovall Jesse Hainey John Shaner James Blackemore William Kennon Stephen Stone John Anderson John White William Ball Joseph Wallace William Haughton John Byrn Samuel Blythe Joseph McElwrath John Pendergast John Chapman (planter) William McKing[Wm M King?]

p.73 John Murphey v Michael Murphey. Dft obtains appeal to Superior Court, Sampson Williams and Thomas Keife his securities.

  Edward Douglass James Douglass Jas C Wilson esqrs. Kitty Twopence v Thomas Howell. TAB. Jury Andrew Robertson John Banes Elesworth Banes James Claxton Jacob Thompson Jas Trousdale Reuben Douglass Joshua Cherry Saml Clenny Jesse Hollis Swain Stalcup Webb Bloodworth find dft guilty. Plf recovers damages $10 and costs.

  Commrs Jas Cryer & Isaac Walton apptd to settle with exrs of Orman Allen decd return statement of such settlement.

  John Nichols v Daniel Twigg. Atta. Dft came not; plf recovers damages by occasion of dfts nonperformance.

  Andrew Jackson & John Hutchings v John A Cathey. Debt. Plfs by Thos Stuart no further prosecute; plaintiffs pay costs of sd suit.

p.74 Andrew Jackson & John Hutchings v Lazarus Cotton. Debt. Plfs by Thos Stuart no further prosecute; plaintiffs pay costs of said suit.

Friday Sept 23d 1808. Present Edward Douglass Isaac Walton James Douglass esqrs.

  Jas Winchester & Wm Cage v Robert Hall surviving partner of Waters & Hall. Debt. Dft came not; plfs recover agt dft $234.79 debt, $25.07 damages, and costs.

  William H Douglass v Ezekiel Norman. Sci fa. Defendant not appearing, plf granted execution against goods &c of dft for $26.72 and costs of suit.

p.75 Edward Hogin v Matthew Alexander. Sci fa. Defendant not appearing, plaintiff granted execution against defendant's goods &c for $16.23 and costs of suit.

  John Tomkins v James Franklin. Sci fa. Dft not appearing, plf granted exn agt goods &c of dft for $28.62 and costs of suit.

  John C Hamilton v Isaac M Bledsoe. Judgt obtained this term by Jeremiah Dial assee v Patton Anderson & John C Hamilton as special bail for Isaac M Bledsoe. John C Hamilton to recover agt Isaac M Bledsoe $95 the part of the judgt afsd paid by sd Hamilton as appears by the sheriffs receipt now shewn to Court, also costs.

  John Jones & Laurence Owen v Richard Holloway. Debt. Dft not appearing, plf
p.76 recovers agt dft $92.25 debt $2.26 damages and also their costs.

SEPTEMBER 1808

John Payton & William Payton v Mattw Anderson. Green Williford witness for Mattw Anderson ads John Payton & Wm Payton failing to appear, is fined $125 to use of Mattw Anderson unless sufficient cause of disability be shewn at next Court.

Deed Reuben Cage late sheriff to James Davis 2091 acres ackd.

Apprentice John Rosber orphan age fifteen to Samuel K Blythe to learn the nailers business.

Will of John Trice decd proved by John Orr a subscribing witness. Patsey Trice executrix named in will qualified as such.

Deaderick & Settler v John Mitchel. Certiorari. Cert dismissed; plaintiffs recover agt dft their costs.

p.77 Deaderick & Settler v John Mitchel. Certiorari dismissed; plfs recover agt dft their costs. Writ/procedendum issues to justice who rendered judgt to proceed.

Deaderick & Settler v John Mitchel[as above]

Allow Thomas Rawlings constable $11 for attendance this Term.

Appt Ruffin Deloach guardian to Betsey Anderson Polley Anderson & Alfred Anderson orphans of Miles Anderson decd; David Green & Michael Green securities for Deloach in penalty of $1000 conditioned as the law directs.

Elisha Prewitt v Jno Latimer. Plf not appearing is nonsuited; dft recovers.

p.78 Hugh Loving v John Askew. Certiorari. Motion to dismiss made by plfs atty; plf recovers agt dft his costs in this behalf expended; dft pays all other costs.

Hugh Loving v John Askew. [as above]
Hugh Loving v John Askew. [as above]
Hugh Loving v John Askew. [as above]
p.79 Hugh Loving v John Askew. [as above]

Elisha Forrest v John Askew. Cert. Writ of procedandum issues to justice who rendered judgment to proceed thereon.

Order James Cryer admr goods & chattels of Laban Benthall decd to sell a negro man belonging to the estate of sd decd. Order rescinded.

Allow James Clendening & John Peyton $12 each for services as commissioners settling with collectors and treasurers.

James White & Samuel Coun v James Steele. Debt. Plfs obtain judgt for $125.92. Dft obtains appeal to Superior Court, Henry Belote & Wm Steele securities.

p.80 Deed James McKinsey to Allen Purvis 112 acres ackd

Deed Nicholas Boyer to Allen Purvis ackd.

Deed Solomon Reese to Isreal Miles lot 59 in Cairo proved by Jesse Johnson and Thomas Cocke.

Order Wm Trigg & Jas C Wilson examine & settle accts of admr Porter Allen of estate of Sherod Allen decd.

John Jones & Kennedy Owens assees v William Ozburn. Debt. Dft not appearing plfs recover agt dft $90 debt $3.04½ damages and their costs.

Order apptg a jury to lay out a road from Gallatin to Kentucky road near Joel Brakins be revived.

Saturday Sept 24th 1808. Present James Douglass James Cryer Will Trigg esquires.
p.81 George Johnson v Drury Nobb[Noble?]. Covt. Plf not appearing, dft recovers agt plaintiff his costs about his defence expended.

George Brown Jr & John Bently v John Giles. Sci fa. Dft not appearing, plfs have execution agt goods &c of dft for $31.82 and costs.

Timothy Demumbro, witness summoned to prove execution of a deed from Martin Armstrong to Alexander McMillin for 640 acres, failing to appear, is fined $200

DECEMBER 1808

unless sufficient cause of his disability be shewn at next court.
James Johnson, witness[as above]
p.82   James Winchester & William Cage v Robert Hall surviving partner of the firm of Waters & Hall. Attached property condemned for use of the judgment; order of sale issues to sell same to satisfy judgment.
Elizabeth Davis v Benjamin Smith. Covt. Plf obtained judgt agt dft for $40 & costs, dft is granted a writ of error. Benjamin Smith's bond $500 with Richard Smith William Payton Bennett H Henderson & John C Hamilton his securities.
Lewis Lane v David Stafford. Sci fa. Plf not appearing, dft recovers agt plf his costs of defence.
Richard Pendergrass v James Kirkham. Plf recovers agt Thomas May security for dft for obtaining a writ of certiorari, damages assessed by jury, also costs.
p.83   Permit Zacheus Wilson one of executors of Richard Taylor decd to sell one still belonging to the estate, and make return of such sale to next Court.
William Trigg & James Cryer esqrs to examine & settle with admr of Abram Hassell decd and make report thereof to next Court.
The Court adjourned until Court in Course.   James Cryer Will Trigg Jas Douglass

p.84 Court of pleas & quarter Sessions held at Court house in Gallatin second Monday in December 1808. Present James Winchester John McMurtry Matthew Alexander.
Deed James Byrns to John Byrns 130 acres ackd.
Bill/sale Charles Dement to Moore Cotton negro man Glases proved by John Cotton & Stephen Pitt.
Grand Jury: Peter Looney foreman, Joseph McElwrath John White Jonathan Pearce William Edwards Junr William Ball William Alexander John Byrns John Pendergrast George Martin Wm Beard John Anderson Joseph Wilson. Elisha Green constable.
Deed Charles Brigance to Stephen Pitt 43 acres proved by Robert Strother and James Brigance.
Deed William Crawford to Hugh Crawford 48 acres proven by Hugh Findley and John Crawford.
p.85   McNutt Findley & Co v John Spooner. Debt. Bail surrenders dft. William Maxey & Nicholas Stone special bail.
Deed Jas Reed to Moore Cotton 47 acres proved by Jno Cotton & Hugh Findley.
Bill/sale Thomas Campbell to Thomas Edwards Junr two negro boys Laurence & London proved by William Edwards.
On motion of Robert Hall admr of James White Junr decd, order James Cryer & Wm Seawell esqrs examine and settle with sd admr.
Deed Thomas Potter to James Williams 260 acres proved by Edmund Taylor & Nathaniel M Taylor.
Deed James Walker to Humphrey Bate 90 acres proved by Robert Moore & Ebenezer Slaughter.
Bill/sale Jacob Garrison to William Bowles negro girl Milly proved by William Bracken.
p.86   Order Jas Cryer & Wm Seawell esqrs settle with executors of Wm Cochran decd.
John Avent v John Hamilton. Appeal. Suit referred to Genl James Winchester & Wm Trigg esqrs whose award to be made the judgment of the Court.

15

DECEMBER 1808

Grant ltrs/admn on estate of William Brown decd to Nancy Brown & William Dorris; bond $2000 with Leonard Brown and John Pavatt securities, & took oath.

Deed Nicholas Boyer[Boyce?] to James Leath 25 acres proved by Peter Leath & Arisck Thomas.

Isaac Pavatt charged with being reputed father of a bastard child of which Frances Ruyle has lately been delivered and who was bound to appear this Term, pays his fine of $3.12½, and the father of Frances also pays a like fine. Isaac Pavatt enters bond $500 with Henry Ruyle security for support of sd child.

p.87   Permit admrs of William Brown decd to sell personal estate of sd decd.

On motion of Wm M King order Hugh Crawford Moore Cotton Isaac Baker Peter Looney & Wm Edwards divide the negroes of estate of Abraham Hassell between legatees of sd decd, to wit between wife of sd Wm M King & Gennet Hassell.

Grant ltrs/admn on estate of Richard Cavett Junr to John Cavett. Bond, $500 with Wm Kirkpatrick & Jeremiah Doxey Junr securities, and took the oath of admr.

Grant ltrs/admn on estate of Willie Carrell decd to Elizabeth Carrell & Robert Gardner. Robt Gardner & Elizabeth Carrell with John Barr and John Sloan their securities entered bond $400, and took oath of admr.

On motion of admrs of Willie Carrell decd, ordered they sell the personal estate of sd decedent.

Appt Gabriel Black overseer/road from Hassells lane to Caveatts and that Archibald Marlin esqr furnish sd overseer with a list of hands.

On motion of admr of James Simpson decd, order John Barr & George Keesee esqrs settle accounts of administrator of sd decedent's estate.

p.88   On motion of exrs of Wm Cochran decd, order George D Blackmore Wm Beard Jesse Johnson Joseph Wilson & Jeremiah Betote divide estate among legatees.

Hiram Cochran & Anna Cochran orphans of Wm Cochran decd choose John Cochran for their guardian. John Cochran with Wm Hubert & Henry McAddin his securities enters bond $6000 conditioned as the law directs.

Appoint John Cochran guardian to minor orphans Rachel Cochran Sally Cochran Julia Fryatt the two former being orphans of William Cochran decd; bond $6000 with William Hubert & Henry McAddin his securities.

Appoint David Green constable in Capt Paytons district for two years; bond $625 with Michael Green and William Payton his securities.

James White & Josephus H Conn v Allen Purvis. Debt. Plaintiffs recover agt dft p.89   the balance of the debt & damages $21.48 & costs.

James White & Josephus H Conn v Allen Purvis. Debt. Plfs recover agt dft debt & damages $76.56½ also their costs.

James White & Josephus H Conn. Debt. Thomas S Rawlings bail for dft surrenders him; judgt rendered for $91.48 & costs and dft being required in execution by Jos H Conn one of the plfs, whereupon John Franklin undertakes that if sd deft does not pay sd judgment, John Franklin will do it for him.

James White & Jos H Conn v Allen Purvis. Debt. Thomas S Rawlings surrenders p.90   defendant; judgt rendered for plf for $76.56½ [worded as above]

On motion of Mr Porter merchant, one of the firm of Porter & Allison, order as Porter & Allison failed to pay tax on their store for present year and are now willing to pay same that it be received by the clerk.

McNutt Findley & Co v Thomas Keefe. McNutt Findley & Co obtained three executions from Wm Trigg Jr J/P agt goods &c of Thos Keefe to satisfy three judgmts, levied on 100 acres property of Thos Keefe adj Redmond D Barry on Camp Creek. Plfs by John C Hamilton move to have 25 acres of sd land condemned for use of the judg-

DECEMBER 1808

ments; order of sale issues to sell same to satisfy sd judgments and costs.
p.91   Report of jury apptointed to straighten the road from Cairo to Holston near Captain Haynies: from Crofts mill to Belote ferry through James Aspies land Robert Bruces land to Bledsoes creek to where bridge is building, through David Shelbys land & Genl James Winchesters land intersecting sd road near Joel Eckols lane. G D Blackmore, Joel Eckols Senr Thomas Murrey Henry Gambell John Bentley Samuel Conn.

Tuesday December 13th 1808. Present Benjamin Rawlings James C Wilson Wm Braken.
    James & Robert Desha v Patsey Trice Admn of John Trice decd & Dempsey Moore & Robert Moore. Affidavit of James Desha stating that Robert Desha Junr, witness for plfs, is sick and unable to attend; order his deposition be taken.
p.92   John Willard v James Howard garnishee of Joseph Reeves. Howard declares he has $48.60 property of Reeves which he collected when he acted as Deputy Sheriff on execution at the instance of Cage & Black agt sd Reeves being balance arising from sale of property sold in virtue of sd execution after paying costs and also the amt of a judgment obtained by James White & Jos H Conn agt sd Reeves.
    James Bustard & William Eastin v Alexander McKee. Debt.   Jury James Turner Wm Kennon Saml K Blythe John Chapman John Ruyle Thomas Anderson Robert Shaw Robert Watkins Robt Strother John Brigance Thos Dement John Spooner. Dft recovers agt plf.
    James Harrison assee v Isaac Street. Debt. Defendant cannot deny plaintiff. Plf recovers balance of debt and his costs.
p.93   Present John McMurtry James Wilson Wm Bracken. Debt. Jury[above except Jonathan Spooner for John Spooner]. Plaintiff recovers agt defendant his debt, damages $437.21½ and also his costs about his suit.
    Samuel A Bowen v Matthew Rogers. Debt. Dft cannot deny plfs declaration; plf recovers debt $77.50 damages $2.32 and also his costs of suit.
p.94   Present James Hart Geo Keesee Wm Braken Esqrs. Mourning Winn v Anthony Hogin. Debt. Jury[above except Robt Wadkins & Terisha Turner for Robt Watkins & Thos Dement]. Plf recovers agt dft balance of debt, damages & costs.
    Bill/sale John Cotton to John Mills negro boy Jack proved by James Hart.
    Mourning Winn v Anthony Hogin. Debt. Jury[above except Henry Bunn for Thos
p.95   Anderson]. Plf recovers agt dft debt, damages & costs.
    Bill/sale Henry Mitchell to Wilson Yandell negro man Buck alias Dorrell proved by Samuel P Black & Richard G Gillespie.
    Present Will Trigg Jr Jas Wilson Geo Keesee. James Howard v Loftain Cage & Wm Cage. Debt. Jury Wm Barr Wm Kennon Jno Shaver Saml K Blythe Henry Bunn Robt Shaw Jno Chapman Robert Wadkins Jno Ruyle Hugh Carothers James Charlton Jas McMurry. Plf recovers agt dfts debt & damages $481.50 and also his costs of suit.
    Mourning Winn v Wm Edwards. Debt. Jury[above]. Plf recovers agt dft debt,
p.96   damages, costs.
    Francis Weatherred v John Bailey. Debt. Jury[above except Jas Wadkins for Robt Wadkins]. Plf recovers agt dft debt & damages $103.50 & costs.
p.97   Robert Holmes v John Orr & James Alderson. Debt. Dfts confess judgt $238.05 & costs; plaintiff stays execution three months.
    Redmond D Barry v Wm Lauderdale. Dft bail John Mills surrenders dft. John Byrns special bail.
    Humphrey Warren v Hillery Malone. Debt. Jury[above]. Plf recovers agt dft
p.98   debt & damages $117.90 & costs.
    Wilson Cage v Nicholas Boyer[Boyce?]. Debt. Addition to defendant's plea.
    Bill/sale John Mills to Wilson Yandell negro boy Jim ackd.

DECEMBER 1808

Bill/sale Robert Norvell & wife Sarah Norvell to Wilson Yandell negro girl Maria proved by Samuel P Black & John Mills.
Report of commrs apptd to settle accounts of estate of James White Junr decd rendered settlement made with Robert Hall one of the admrs.
Appt Sion Hunt guardian for Polley Seawell orphan of John Seawell decd; bond $800 with Edmund Bridges his security.
Tandy P Duncan apptd inspector/tobacco at Harts ferry, John Barr & John Mills his securities; bond $3000.
p.99   Appt Zacheus Wilson son of Samuel overseer/road Gallatin to Wilsons; Will Trigg esq to furnish a list of hands.

Wednesday December 14th 1808. Present James Winchester Matthew Alexander Wm Trigg.
Andrew Blythe v Henry Young. Debt. Jury John Ruyle Robert Shaw Wm Kennon Henry Bunn John Shaver Robt Wadkins John Chapman Saml Clenny Robt McElberry Wm Bell Jeremiah Bowers Jas Charlton. Plf recovers agt dft debt & damages $128.22½ & costs.
John Orr v Allen Purvis. Debt. Jury[above]. Plf recovers agt dft debt &
p.100   damages $103.50 and also his costs by him about this suit expended.
John Denning v Robert Davis. Debt. Jury[above]. Plf recovers agt dft debt & damages $154.50 & costs. Dft obtains appeal to Superior Court, Will Trigg Junr & Daniel Jones his securities.
p.101   Isaac Bledsoe v Thomas Parker & Richd Brown. Debt. Jury[above]. Plf recovers agt dft debt & damages $1498.84½ and his costs in this behalf expended.
Deed Robert Hall to James Winchester & William Cage Junr ackd.
Edward Sanders v John Payton & William Payton. Debt. Jury[above]. Plf recovers agt dft debt & damages $463.50 & also his costs about his suit expended.
p.102   Bill/sale Moses Harding to Edward Wormington negro man Harry proved by Richard Caveatt & Asa Hassell.
Mortgage John Beakley to Matthew Cartwright. Beakley mortgages his share of 50 acres held by descent from his father William Beakley redeamable on payment of $200 by 25th Decr 1808 proved by James Newby a subscribing witness thereto.
Deed Joshua Donoho to David Love 110 acres proved by James Desha.
Wilson Cage v Nicholas Boyce. Debt. Dft confesses debt. Plf recovers agt dft debt & damages $343.53½ and also his costs about his suit expended.
Bill/sale Joseph Stevenson to John Cotton negro woman Feraby proved by Moore Cotton and Edward Wormington.
p.103   Account/sales goods of James White Junr decd rendered by Robert Hall.
Commrs apptd to settle accounts of the estate of James White Junr render statement of settlement made with Robert Hall, administrator.
Report of jury to view road crossing ridge at head of little Trammel Creek submitted and rejected.
Allow Alexander McMillan out of poor tax $40 a year for supporting a poorman named Andrew Nusum.
Order James Cryer & William Trigg esqrs to examine accounts of estate of Hugh Elliott decd.
Appt Robert Hamilton overseer/road in place of Alexander Gwin resigned.
Appt Robert Hall guardian to Mira Saint John White orphan of James White Jr decd. Bond $1000; James Winchester and William Hall his securities.
Deed Robert Hall to William Hall 32 acres ackd.
Deed Matthew Alexander to William Cage Junr ackd.
p.104   John Avent v John Hamilton. Appl. Report of arbitrators Will Trigg Jr J

18

DECEMBER 1808

Winchester to whom was refered controversy. Plf pays costs of appeal and recovers agt dft 75¢ and costs which accrued before appeal was granted.

Report/jury to lay off dower of Caty Haw relict of James Haw decd received.

Peter Looney & Grand Jurors deliver indictment agt Moses Carter for assault & battery a true bill; also indictment agt Randal Carter (both free men of colour) for like offense, a true bill.

Thursday Decr 15th 1808. Present Jas Winchester Will Trigg Jr James Sanders esqrs.

Redmond Dillon Barry v Seth Mabry. Jury Jno Ruyle, Isaac Johns, John Shaver Robt Wadkins, Henry Bunn, Robt Shaw, Wm Kennon, John Chapman, Denney[?] Moore, Isham Uzzell, Littleton Joiner, Edmund Bridges. Plf recovers agt dft damages & costs.

p.105 William Rentfro v Josiah Wells. In detinue. Plf no further prosecutes & each pays his own costs.

Robert Mickelberry inspector/tobacco at Harts ferry, bond $3000, Edward Bradley & Josephus H Conn his securities; took the oath.

Deed William Hall sheriff to Wilson Yandell 114 acres ackd.

Will & A Trigg v Robert Overstreet. Will & A Trigg obtained exn from James Cryer agt goods of Robt Overstreet to satisfy judgmt for $32.53 debt & 93¾¢ costs. Elisha Green levied on one acre adj Owen Campbell & John C Hamilton. Sd land con-
p.106 demned for use of judgmt; order of sale issues.

Deed William Montgomery to William King 500 acres ackd.

Suspend proceedings of judgment obtained by Daniel Bargsdale agt John Webb before Sion Hunt J/P for $21.25.

Deed James Trousdale to Abraham Trigg 1¼ acres 29 poles ackd.

Friday Decr 16th 1808. Present James Winchester James Sanders Edward Gwin esquires.

James & Robert Desha v Patsey Trice admr of John Trice. Allow Patsey Trice to plead fully administered so as not to delay trial.

p.107 Walter Bennett v Elijah Hendrick for debt wherein plf recovered judgt agt dft; sd Elijah surrenders himself.

James & Robert Desha v Patsey Trice admr of John Trice Demcy Moore & Robert Moore. Jury John Brown Thos Richey Jno Gwin Samuel K Blythe Robert Shaw Henry Bunn Robt Wadkins Jno Ruyle David Stewart Jno Stewart Jeremiah Bowers John Chapman. Plfs recover agt dfts damages and costs to be levied on goods of sd deceased in hands of admr and of the goods of the other defendants Demcey Moore & Robert Moore.

Appt William Douglass & Hardy Hunt inspectors/tobacco at Barrows landing. Douglass with Hardy Hunt & Edwd Gwin securities. Hunt with Wm Douglass & Henry Bunn securities, enter bond and take coath.

p.108 Present Stephen Cantrill Jas Sanders James C Wilson. James White & Josephus H Conn v Edness Henderson admx of John C Henderson. Jury James Kirkham Needham Reynolds James Claxton John Shaver James S Wilson Robert Moore Wm Ogels Zacheus Wilson Andw Hoover Peter Fisher Larken Bradford Abner Gilmore. Plaintiff recovers agt dft debt & damages $23.70 also costs about their suit expended.

William Buckner v Edward Hogin. Jury[above]. Plf recovers agt dft damages
p.109 as assessed $50 and also his costs of suit.

Deed Samuel Harris to William Bloodworth 50 acres 100 poles proved by David Hobbs and Hardy Hunt.

Acct/sales goods of John Seawell decd rendered by Wm Seawell, an exr.

David Dement v Elisha Green & William Wallace. Debt. Plf no further prosecutes; dft pays costs.

DECEMBER 1808

Saturday Decr 17th 1808. Present James Cryer Edward Gwin Will Trigg Junr esqrs.
Appoint Richard Caveatt guardian to Moses Caveatt Andrew Caveatt and James Caveatt minors; bond $500, Abraham Young his security.
Appt James McKain administrator/estate of Jesse Wells decd, the widow of sd deceased having relinquished her right to admn; bond $2500 with Josephus H Conn & Henry Wells his securities.

p.110 Deed Shadrack Nye James C Wilson & Chas Donoho surviving commrs for Sumner County to Samuel P Black, lot 4 in South East square of Gallatin ackd by Wilson, and proved by James Howard & Lunsford Pitt subscribing witnesses thereto.

William Edwards v James Cage & Saml P Black. Depositions of Benjamin Morgan & Maunsel M White to be taken on behalf of the defendants, also of John F Gray and John Taylor of New Orleans.

Francis Comperry v John Willard. Sci fa. Dft came not; Comperry granted execution agt sd Willard for $125 and costs.

Bill/sale Robert Raley to Andrew Hoover Junr household furniture proved by George Smith & Thomas Preston.

p.111 Andrew Jackson & John Hutchings v John Crawley. Sci fa. Plfs by Thomas Stuart; dft not found; plfs granted exn agt sd Crawley $125 and costs.

John Bentley & George Brown v James Hunt. Sci fa. Plfs by John C Hamilton; dft not found. Plfs granted execution agt dft for $30.29½ & costs.

Thomas Keefe v William Boles. Sci fa. Plf by Thomas Stuart; dft not found. Plf granted execution agt dft for $79.28 & costs.

p.112 William Douglass v John Parker. Sci fa. Plf by Thos Stuart; dft not found. Plf granted execution agt dft for $10.25 and costs.

Present James Cryer, Edwd Gwin, Samuel P Black. Richard Fairclaim lessee of John Goodrum v Warren Walker. Ejectment. Jury Andrew Hoover John Chapman Wm Kennedy Jno Shaver Jas S Wilson Henry Bunn Robt Laurence John Ruyle Robt Wadkins Swen Stalcup Joshua Cherry Thos Dement find dft guilty of trespass. Plf recovers against dft his term yet to come together with damages.

p.113 John Jones & Laurence Owen v Jas Steele. Henry Belote will pay dft damages.
John Jones & Co v James Steele. Att. Henry Belote will pay dfts damages.
Deed William Wilson to David Wilson 216½ acres ackd.

Monday Decr 19th 1808. Present James Cryer Edward Gwin Will Trigg Jr.
Deed Thomas May to Jesse Wells 640 acres ackd.
Inventory of goods of Jesse Wells decd rendered by James McKain admr.
State v Elisha Kean. A&B. Dft fined 1¢ and costs.
p.114 State v Ashlin Kean. A&B. Dft fined 1¢ and costs.
State v William Wallace. A&B. Jury Wm Kennon Wm Payton Jacob Thompson Isaac Sowel[?] Jas Claxton Matthew Rogers Jno Payton John Goodrum Samuel K Blythe Zacheus Wilson Peter Fisher Allen Groves. Dft fined 25¢ and pay costs of prosecution.
p.115 Administrators of John Josey decd lack funds to pay debts; order sale of negro man Isam[Jeam?].
Order admrs of Jesse Wells decd expose to sale the estate goods & chattels.

Tuesday Decr 20th 1808. Present Edward Douglass Edward Gwin Will Trigg Jr.
State v Moses Carter. A&B. Jury Jas S Wilson William Kennon Robt Shaw Robt Wadkins Jno Ruyle Danl Jones Warren Walker Joseph Weathers Ephraim Cates Robt Moore Jno Copelin Lawson Barber find dft guilty. Fined $1 and costs.
State v Randel Carter. A&B. Jury Henry Bunn Jno Chapman Wm Payton Willis

DECEMBER 1808

Dosset Jas Claxton Mattw Rogers Saml Kenedy Ruffin Deloach Saml Clenny William Wallace Church Fulcher Cornelius Findley say dft is guilty. Fined 6½¢ & costs.
p.116   George House & William House orphans of Baliss House decd choose Jas Cryer esqr for their guardian; bond $5000, Edward Sanders & John Peyton securities.

Appt James Cryer guardian for James House & Baliss House minor orphans of Baliss House decd; bond $5000, Edward Sanders and John Peyton securities.

Order Edward Douglass & Will Trigg esqrs settle with admr of estate of Baliss House and make report to next Court.

Appt Allen Purvis guardian to Clary, Miles, Allen, & John Purvis minors and children of sd Allen Purvis; sd Allen Purvis with William Payton & Matthew Anderson securities enters into bond $4000.
p.117   Edward Sanders v John Payton & Wm Payton. Debt. Plf having recovered judgmt for $463.50 & costs. Defendants obtain appeal to Superior Court, John Payton & Matthew Rogers securities.

Richard Fairclaim lessee of John Goodrum v Warren Walker. Ejectment. Plf obtained judgt agt dft for 6½¢, dft obtains appeal to Superior Court with John Mitchel & Griffith W Rutherford his securities.

John Payton & William Payton v Matthew Anderson. Certiorari. Jury James S Wilson Wm Kennon Robt Shaw Jno Ruyle Robt Patton Saml K Blythe Jos Weathers Ephraim Cates Jno Shaner[?] Robt Wadkins John Copelen Lawson Barber cannot agree; mistrial.

Wednesday December 21st 1808.
p.118   Present Benjamin Rawlings Edward Gwin Edward Douglass.

Robert B Mitchell v John Beakley. Dft not appearing, plf recovers agt dft $75 debt $1.74 damages & costs.

Zachariah Stringer v Patsey Trice extrx of John Trice decd. Sci fa. Plf by John C Hamilton. Dft not appearing though sci fa executed, plf granted execution agt goods of sd John Trice decd in hands of extx Patsey Trice for $74.97¾ and also his costs of suit.

Charles Marshal & Charles Marshal Junr v Benjamin Rawlings. Dft in proper person agrees plfs sustained damages $87.39, also their costs.
p.119   Admrs of James Blair decd agt John Johnson, court orders original writ be amended by inserting: Elizabeth & Robert adm.

Mourning Winn v William Edwards. Debt. Judgt this Term for $365.75 debt & damages $25.62 & costs agt dft, dft obtains appeal to Superior Court, Seth Mabry & Allen Purvis his securities.

Wilson Cage v Nicholas Boyce. Debt. Plf obtained judgt $327.18½ balance of debt & $16.35 damages & costs. Dft granted appeal to Superior Court, Josephus H Conn & John Payton his securities.

Redmond Dillon Barry v Seth Mabry. Plf obtained judgt agt dft $70.83 &
p.120   costs. Dft obtains appeal to Superior Court, Josephus H Conn & Thomas [Senny/Scurry/Lenny?] his securities.

John Orr v Allen Purvis. Debt. Plaintiff this term obtained judgment agt dft $100, $3.50 damages, & also costs. Defendant obtains appeal to Superior Court, John Payton & William Edwards securities.

James Bustard & William Easton v Alexander McKee. Debt. Jury's verdict for dft; plfs obtain appeal to Superior Court, Thos Stuart & Elisha Prewitt securities.

Samuel K Blythe owner of a cotton gin & press is appointed an inspector of cotton at his press; bond $5000 with Henry Bunn & Seth Mabry securities; took oath.
p.121   Bright Herring v William Surry. Dft not appearing, plf recovers agt dft;

DECEMBER 1808

damages to be inquired of at next Court.

Appt Witheral Latimer special guardian for George Wyles Jenny Wyles Samuel Wyles Margaret Wyles infant heirs of John Wyles decd for prupose of defending the suits of William Donelson agt heirs of sd John Wyles decd; further order alias sci fa issue in afsd suit agt afsd heirs of sd deceased as also such of the heirs as have attained to full age.

Joseph Park v James Kirkham. Debt. Dft made default; plf recovers agt dft $131 debt, $5.80 damages & also costs.

Deed Allen Josey to Benjamin Rawlings 108 acres proved by John Mitchel.

John & William Payton v Matthew Anderson. Cert. Deposition of John Patton of Warren County to be taken on behalf of the defendant.

p.122 Allen Matthews v Elisha Prewitt. Deposition of John Corner[Comar?] of Adams County, Mississippi Territory, to be taken for the defendant.

Nicholas Boyce v Henry Wells & Jesse Wells. Trespass. On motion of the defendants by attorney, deposition of John Fleming to be read as evidence.

Appoint Edward Gwin & Joshua Rice to settle with Micajah House as admr of James Kelly decd.

James Hood v Isaac Larue. Dft not appearing, plf recovers agt dft his damages in the declaration mentioned, to be enquired of by a jury at next Court.

Released James Cage from payment of tax on three black polls as he has only one black poll.

Deed Hugh Wall to William Crocket & Thomas Culbert 1¼ acres ackd.

p.123 Thomas Keefe v Ephraim C Davidson. Appeal. Arbitrators deliver award: dft indebted to plf $14; cost of suit equally divided between parties.

Thomas Keefe v Ephraim C Davidson. Appeal. Arbitrators deliver award: suit to be dismissed; costs equally divided between parties.

Ephraim C Davidson v Thomas Keefe. Covt. Arbitrators deliver award: suit to be dismissed; costs to be equally divided between parties.

Appt Stephen Cantrill esqr to take list of taxable property & polls in Capt Waltons militia company district for ensuing year.

[Worded as above] Wm Montgomery in Capt Montgomery's district. Will Trigg p.124 esqr in Capt McCalls district. Matthew Alexander esqr in Capt Turners dist. James Winchester esq in Capt Charltons dist. George Keesee esq in Capt Balls dist. John Barr esq in Capt Cowdens dist. Wm Seawell esq in Capt Sanders dist. Charles Donoho esq in Capt Blacks dist. William Seawell esq in Capt McMurrys dist. William Braken esq in Capt Aldersons dist. Joshua Rice in Capt Gwins dist. Edward Gwin in Capt Mitchells dist. James Douglass esq in Capt Bakers dist. Sion Hunt esq in Capt p.125 Paytons dist. Archd Marlin esq in Capt Wadkins dist. James Sanders in Capt Sanders old dist. Thomas Murry esq in Capt Blakemores dist. James Cryer esq in Capt Bridges dist.

Jurors to next Court: William Alderson, Robert Latimer, Jesse Shien, Elisha Bernard, Levy Hall Sr, Richd Caveatt, John Garrett, Laurence Whitside, George Reed, Wm Aspy, Thomas Preston, Smith Hansberry, Lewis Crane, William Douglass, Adam Hunter, Jeremiah Mitchell, Josiah Giles, James Charlton, Isaac Bledsoe, James McMurry, Thos Anderson, William McCall, Isaac Lane, William Edwards Sr, Robert White, David Pursley, Hillery Malone, Montgomery McConnell, Jos Motherall, William Bell, Abraham Trigg, John Allen, James Cage, George Gillespie Senr, Wm C Anderson, Patrick Barr.

Thomas Keefe v Ephraim C Davidson. Arbitrators deliver award: suit to be dismissed; costs to be equally divided between the parties.

Appt William Glasgow overseer/road in place of Thomas Parker resigned.

DECEMBER 1808

p.126   Caty Haw admx of James Haw decd v Cornelius Thomas. Debt. Plf recovers agt dft debt $98.25 with $4.53 damages and also her costs about her suit expended.

Thursday December 22d. Present the worshipful Will Trigg Jr esqr.
Court adjourned till tomorrow morning 10 Oclock.

Friday December 23d 1808. Present the worshipful Will Trigg Jr Esqr.
The Court adjourned till tomorrow morning 10 Oclock.

Saturday December 24th 1808. Present Matthew Alexander James C Wilson Will Trigg.
   Redmond D Barry v William Lauderdale. Plf to take deposition of James Trousdale Junr.
p.127   Bill/sale James McKinsey to John Shelby negro boy Coldwater ackd.
   John Payton & William Payton v Edward Sanders. Plf no further prosecutes; defendant recovers agt plf his costs by him about his defence expended.
   Robert B Mitchell v John Beetley. Debt. Dft not appearing, plf recovers agt dft $58.09½ debt and also his costs in this behalf expended.
   Inventory/goods of John C Henderson decd rendered by Bennet H Henderson.
   Appt James Winchester & Mattw Alexander to settle lwith executors of William Cochran decd.
   Order jury to lay off road from Gallatin to Kentucky state road near James Brackens and report to next court.
p.128   Richard Holloway v James Hunt. Richard Holloway as security for James Hunt discharged and payed off the amt of a judgment obtained by John Jones & Laurence Owen agt him at last term for $95.01 and damages $2.02½. Richd Holloway to recover agt sd James Hunt the debt, damages, & costs aforesaid & costs of this motion.
   On motion ordered that Jones & Owen recover agt Wm Boyce constable and Nicholas Boyce & James McKain his securities $38.98 the amt of a judgt which sd Jones & Owen recovered agt Daniel Rawson which sd Wm Boyce as constable collected by virtue of an exn agt sd Rawson but failed to account for to sd Jones & Owen.
   Will Trigg & Jas C Wilson esqrs settle with admrs of Sherrod Allen decd.
   Suits on dockets this term that have not been disposed of to be continued till next Court.
Court adjourned till Court in Course. Matthew Alexander Jas C Wilson Will Trigg Jr

p.129   Court of pleas & quarter sessions second Monday in March 1809. Present the worshipful James Winchester Matthew Alexander John McMurtry James C Wilson esqrs.
   Grand Jury George Gillespie foreman William McCaul Robert White William Edwards Isaac Lane Abram Trigg William C Anderson Joseph Motheral Isaac Bledsoe Robert Latimer George Reed Josiah Giles James Charlton Thomas Anderson.
   Deed Allen Purvis to Nathan Barnes 400 acres 100 perches ackd.
   Richard Cavatt Laurence Whitsitt & David Pursley jurors to this Term are excused from further attendance for reasons offered.
   Acct/sales of goods of James Simpson decd rendered by administrator.
   Nathan Edwards v Alexander Rasco & Thos Howell. Debt. John Gwin & Edwd Gwin

MARCH 1809

will pay debt should Alexander Rasco be convicted.
    Deed Fergus Sloan to William Burton 100 acres ackd.
    Deed Benjamin Hudson to James Guthrie 560 acres proved by Robert Guthrie & David Guthrie.
p.130 Deed James Godfrey to Robert Guthrey 223[333?] acres proved by Witheral Latimer & James Guthrie.
    Deed Redmond D Barry to Colson Lovel 217 acres ackd.
    Deed Jesse Spradlin to Richard Bradley 100 acres ackd.
    Deed Porter Allen to Charles Lewis 4½ acres 13 poles proved by William F McNutt and John C Hamilton.
    Deed Narcissa White to James Harrison 70 acres proved by William Hall & Samuel Conn.
    Deed John Bentley to Beverly Williams half of lot in Cairo ackd.
    Deed Alexander Province & John Province to David Green & Edmund Green 150 acres proved by James S Wilson & Elisha Green.
p.131 Deed Richard Vincent & Elisabeth Laurence 50 acres proved by William McCall & Humphrey Mires.
    Deed Hance Shaw to William Chaney 120 acres proved by William H Douglass & Anthony B Shelby.
    Deed John Cooper to George Cooper 110 acres ackd.
    John Jones v James Steele. James Barry special bail surrenders defendant whereupon Henry Belote undertakes that if James Steele should be convicted sd James Steele shall pay such damages as shall be adjudged to sd plaintiff.
    Grant ltrs/admn on estate of James Wilson decd to John Parson, the widow having relinquished her right to adm. John Parson with Joseph Wilson his securities bond $2000, Simon Wherry & Joseph Wilson his securities.
    On motion of John Parson admr of James Wilson, order to sell personal estate except negroes of sd decd; make return of amount of sales to next Court.
p.132 William Britt v Moore Stephenson. Cert. Article of agreement is produced in Court by James Sessums and is filed with the papers of said suit.
    John Walker v Alexander McKee. Debt. Dft in proper person cannot deny he owes $79.76 balance of debt, also his costs of suit.
    Edmund Bridgers v William Johnson. Attachment. Cornelius Thomas James Barry Edmund J Bailey defendant's securities.
    Deed James Gwin to John Gwin 123 acres proved by Edward Gwin & Wm Woodell.
p.133 Edmund Turpin in behalf of himself and of John Freeland, securities for Alexander McKee in suit John Walker agt Alexr McKee surrenders said McKee.
    Appoint John McAdams overseer/road in place of Jesse Reppi resigned.
    Deed James Trousdale to Joseph Hodge half acre land acknowledged.
    List/taxable property & polls in Capt Cowdens company taken by John Barr esq was returned into Court. Also in Capt Waltons company by Stephen Cantrill esq.
    Account/sales goods of Wm Brown rendered by Wm Dorris an administrator.
    Appoint Michael Green a constable in Capt McCauls district for two years; David Green & William Payton his securities, and he took the oath.
    Appoint Thomas Wilson guardian for Juliat Fryett a minor orphan in place of John Cochran heretofore apptd gdn. John Wilson & Matthew Alexander his securities.
p.134 Winchester & Cage recovered judgment before a magistrate agt James Steele for $33.22 debt 43¢ costs. Levied on Steele's house & lot in Cairo; ordered sheriff sell same to satisfy said judgment and all accruing costs.
    McNutt & Findley recovered judgt before a magistrate agt James Steele for

$43.83½ & 31¢ costs. Steele's house & lot to be sold to satisfy judgment.

Abraham Brandon recovered judgmt before a magistrate agt James Steele for $20.17 debt & 93¢ costs. Steele's house & lot to be sold to satisfy judgment.

Benjamin Brandon recovered judgmt before a magistrate agt James Steele for $9 debt & 93¢ costs. Steele's house & lot to be sold to satisfy judgment.

p.135 Abel Brandon recovered judgment before a magistrate agt James Steele for $12.15 debt & 93½¢ costs. Steele's house & lot to be sold to satisfy judgment.

Will & A Trigg recovered judgment before a magistrate agt Isaac Johns for $43.39½ & 43¾¢ costs. Levied on a house & lot on main street just above John Jones in Gallatin. Order of sale issues to sell same to satisfy sd judgment & costs.

Will & A Trigg recovered judgt before a magistrate agt Isaac Johns for $20 fourth cents costs. Sheriff to sell Johns's house and lot to satisfy judgment.

Will & A Trigg recovered judgmt before a magistrate agt Isaac Johns for $25.81¼ debt & 43¾¢ costs. Johns's house and lot to be sold to satisfy judgment.

p.136 Will & A Trigg recovered judgt before a magistrate agt Isaac Johns $43.39½ debt 43¾¢ costs. Johns's house & lot to be sold to satisfy judgment.

Robert B Mitchell recovered judgt before a magistrate agt Isaac Johns for $12.75 debt 43¾¢ costs. Johns's house & lot to be sold to satisfy judgment.

John Jones recovered judgment before a magistrate agt Isaac Johns $46.41 debt 93¾¢ costs. Johns's house & lot to be sold to satisfy judgment.

p.137 [Jno Jones recovered other debts against Isaac Johns: $48, $3.80, $46.07½.]

George Hodge recovered judgment before a magistrate agt Isaac Johns for $21.62½ debt & 43¾¢ costs. Johns's house & lot to be sold to satisfy judgment.

p.139 John Jones & Co recovered judgt before a magistrate agt Isaac Johns $31.82½ debt & $1.62½ costs. Johns's house & lot to be sold to satisfy judgment.

McNutt & Findley & Co recovered judgmt before a magistrate agt Isaac Johns for $35.37½ debt 43¾¢ costs. Johns's house & lot to be sold to satisfy judgment.

Charles D Lewis recovered judgment before a magistrate agt Samuel Clenny for $40.20 debt & 73¾¢ costs. Levied on 30 acres adjoining Redmond D Barry & Thos Keefe's land it being part of William Wallers land bought of Thomas Keefe as the
p.139 property of Saml Clenney. Order land condemned for use of sd judgment; order of sale issues to sheriff to sell same to satisfy judgment & all costs.

Thomas Keefe recovered judgment before a magistrate agt Samuel Clenney for $4.25 debt 93¾¢ costs. Clenney's land to be sold to satisfy judgment.

White & Crockett recovered judgt before a magistrate agt Samuel Clenney for $2.37½ debt 93¾¢ costs. Clenney's land to be sold to satisfy judgment.

John Mitchel recovered judgment before a magistrate agt Samuel Clenney $20 debt & 93¾ costs. Clenney's land to be sold to satisfy judgment.

p.140 Porter Allen recovered judgment before a magistrate agt Samuel Clenney $18.90 debt & 93¾¢ costs. Clenney's land to be sold to satisfy judgment.

Thomas Cribbins recovered judgment before a magistrate agt Matthew Rogers for $44.50 debt & 93¾¢ costs. Levied on 114 acres on Drakes Creek joining Joseph Clark's land he lives on said to be Matthew Rogers property. Order half of sd land be condemned for use of judgmt; sheriff to sell same to satisfy judgment & costs.

Hugh McBride admr of Solomon Ruyle decd recovered judgmt before a magistrate agt Matthew Rogers for $4.47 debt & 93¾¢ costs. Land to be sold to satisfy judgment and costs.

Will & A Trigg recovered before a magistrate two judgmts agt Stephen Baldradge for $96.87½ & costs. Levied on land where Stephen Baldradge then lived joining James Carothers. Land condemned; sheriff to sell same to satisfy judgments.

MARCH 1809

p.141 John Turner recovered judgmt before a magistrate agt Stephen Baldradge $41.37½ debt 43¼¢ costs. Baldradge's land to be sold to satisfy judgment.

Edward Bradley recovered thre judgments before a magistrate agt Armstreet Stubblefield amounting to $143.00½ & costs. Levied on 114 acres on Goose Creek; sheriff to sell same to satisfy the judgments afsd and all accruing costs.

Peter Razel recovered judgment before a magistrate agt Lewallen Phips for $22.11 debt 81¼¢ costs. Levied on 100 acres on Paytons fork of Drakes Creek joining Robt Davis that he lives on deeded from Nathan Stagner[?] to Lewallen Phipps; land to be sold to satisfy judgment and all costs accruing.

p.142 William P Bowers recovered judgment before a magistrate agt Lewallen Phips $22.12½ debt 81¼¢ costs. Land to be sold to satisfy judgment and costs.

Hugh Shaw recovered judgment before a magistrate agt Lewallen Phips $16.42 debt 81¼¢ costs. Phips's land to be sold to satisfy judgment and costs.

George Chapman recovered judgment before a magistrate agt Lewallen Phips $4.08½ & 81¼¢ costs. Phips's land to be sold to satisfy judgment and costs.

p.143 Peter Razel recovered judgment before a magistrate agt Lewallen Phips for $23.12½ & 81¼¢ costs. Phips's land to be sold to satisfy judgment and costs.

Peter Razel recovered judgment before a magistrate agt Lewallen Phips for $2 debt 81¼¢ costs. Phips's land to be sold to satisfy judgment and costs.

Thomas Harrison recovered judgment before a magistrate agt Lewallen Phips for $6 and 81¼¢ costs. Phips's land to be sold to satisfy judgment and costs.

p.144 Pursuant to law requiring an orphans court to be held at the first court of pleas & quarter sessions in each and every year; proclamation was made by the sheriff in due form that the court was now sitting for the purpose of transacting business relative to orphans and that Stephen Cantrill James Douglass William Seawell James C Wilson were nominated to settle with all guardians executors and administrators during the present term and report thereon.

Appt Abel Brandon overseer/road in place of William Burton resigned.

List/taxable property & polls in Capt McElberrys company for present year taken by George Keesee esq was rendered into Court.

Will & A Trigg recovered judgment before a magistrate agt Edward Kelly for $15.76 debt & costs. Levied on 100 acres head of Red River whereon Kelly then lived; sheriff to sell same to satisfy judgment and accruing costs.

James Barry recovered judgment before a magistrate agt Edward Kelly for $3.92 debt and 93¾¢ costs. Kelly's land to be sold to satisfy judgment & costs.

p.145 Account/sales of goods of Willie Carroll decd rendered by Robert Gardner.

Inquisition on dead body of unknown person since found to be John McKee purporting that he was drowned in attempting to ford Bledsoes creek was delivered into court by James Winchester esqr.

Tuesday March 14th 1809. Present James Winchester Isaac Walton Edward Gwin esqrs.

Juror John Allen excused from further attendance this term.

Certified copy from Washington County Virginia of will of William King decd exhibited and ordered to be recorded.

Seth Mabry owner of a cotton gin & press is appointed an inspector of cotton. Bond $5000, John B Johnson & Benjamin Seawell his securities & took oath.

Deed James Askew to Humphrey Mires 58 acres ackd.

James Desha & Robert Desha v Patsey Trice admx of John Trice Demsy Moore & Robert Moore. Levied on negro woman named Lucy; Nancy Carroll bid $210 which was highest bid but refused to pay the money; have had no time since to expose sd negro

MARCH 1809

to sale.
p.146   Present Jas Winchester Isaac Walton Jno McMurtry. Anderson Thompson &c v Patsey Trice admx of John Trice decd. Debt. Jury Edwd Bradley Edwd Sanders William Kirkpatrick Patrick Barr Hallery Malone Jeremiah Mitchell Jas McMurry John Moore Wm Jones Jesse Sheen Wm Bell Joshua Hall. Plf recovers agt dft debt & damages $103.28.

Will of Robert Patton decd proved by John Whitsitt & Shadrack Nye. Margaret Patton & Robert Patton extx & extr qualified.

John Bustard & William Easten v Silas Jernigan. Debt. Jury George Black Jno Shaver John Bailey James Rankin Edward Cage Wm Douglass Jno Franklin John Dickerson John Gardner Peter Lyon Wm Hanna Samuel Holloway. Plf recovers agt dft. Dft obtains
p.147 appeal to Superior Court, Isom Uzzell & Edwd Gwin securities.

James Rutherford v Bennett H Henderson exr of will of William Henderson decd. Debt. Jury[above]. Plf recovers agt dft debt & damages amounting to $75.16 and also his costs to be levied on goods of sd deceased.

Jarrett a free boy of colour age thirteen is bound to Robert Steele until age twenty one.
p.148   Present Edward Douglass William Montgomery Matthew Alexander Jas C Wilson. Walter Loving v John Goldston & Zacheus Wilson. Debt. Jury[above]. Plf recovers agt dft debt & damage $169.04½ and also his costs about his suit expended.

James Winchester v Benjamin Tarver. Debt. Jury Wm Wallace William Haughton Patrick Barr Wm Bell Hillery Malone Jeremiah Mitchell Lyons Latimer Thos Keefe Jas McMurry Jesse Sheen Abraham Bledsoe John Pendergrast. Plf recovers agt dft debt & damages $97.11¼ and also his costs about his suit expended.
p.149   Report of commrs apptd to divide negro property of Abraham Hassell between legatees, to wit between wife of William King and Gennet Hassell, recd & recorded.

Deed Samuel Piper to Jacob Warren & Edward Morgan trustees for the Baptist Church ackd.

Appt James Scott overseer/road in place of Goldsby Sanders resigned.

Appt Reaf Greaves overseer/road from Capt Gillespies to Keefes in place of Edmund Reeves resigned.

Deed Edward Gwin to Isaac Atkins 400 acres proved by Joshua Rice and Isaac Braken.

Appt Jesse Sheen guardian for Watson Goostra[Goortra?] a minor orphan. Bond $2000, Thomas Groves and James C Alderson his securities.

On motion of exrs of Richard Taylor decd order they sell personal estate except negroes.
p.150   Deed William Hogan to John Caldwell 225 acres proved by John McCauley having been previously proved by Samuel Gattes another subscribing witness.

James Winchester v Patsey Trice extx of John Trice. Debt. Jury Jesse Sheen Wm Bell Ephraim Payton Edmund Turpin Isreal Ambrose Wm Maxey James McMurry Jeremiah Mitchell Wm Waller Wm Haughton Hillery Malone Patrick Barr. Plf recovers agt dft debt & damages $120.05 and also his costs.

Deed John Donoho to George Croper[Crofer?] 110 acres proved by Josiah Stevenson & George G Black.

Commrs apptd to settle with admr of James Kelly decd render statement.

Deed William T Henderson to Cornelius Thomas 200 acres proved by Henry Bradford and Bennett H Henderson.
p.151   Present Jas Winchester Mathew Alexander Edd Gwin. Samuel Trotter & George Trotter v William Howard. Debt. Jury Josiah Stevenson John McKisick Hillery Malone Wm Bell Jeremiah Mitchell Joseph Scobey Saml Gibson Wm Stoval Carson Dobbins George

MARCH 1809

Elliott Archd McKesick. Plf recovers agt dft debt & damages $56.63 & costs.
Deed William Neely to Francis Weatherred 320 acres ackd.
John Copeland v Fleming G Thurmond & John Thurmond. Debt. Jury Josiah Stevenson John McKisick Hillery Malone Wm Bell Jeremiah Mitchell Joseph Scoby Samuel Gibson Wm Stoval Carson Dobbins George Elliott Archd McKesick Patrick Barr.
p.152 Plaintiff recovers agt defendant debt & damages $66.31 & his costs.
Bill/sale Francis Weatherred to Henry Bledsoe negro woman & two children Hannah Jacob & Allyeras ackd.
Bill/sale Francis Weatherred to Henry Bledsoe negro men Bob & Dick ackd.
John Copeland v John Bailey. Debt. Jury Robert Malone Wm Payton Edmund J Bailey Zacheus Wilson Chas Dement Wm Douglass Saml McMurry Robt Steele Wm Wallace Mathew Anderson Geo Chapman. Plf recovers agt dft debt & damages $210.48½ & costs.
p.153 George D Blackemore v William Johnson. Atta. Dfts security John Johnson & William Ball.
Bill/sale James Ware to Alexander Porter negro woman Nina[Vine?] ackd.
Appoint Fleming Thurmond overseer/road in place of Bartholomew Stoval resigned.
Allow Jesse Spradlin $37.50 for keeping a poor man named John Putt for nine months; pauper was consigned to sd Spradlin at June term last.
Petition of Ralph Graves, William Trigg esq is to send to present term all papers in his possession relative to a Judgment obtained by Ralph Graves v Edmund Bridgers rendered by sd William Trigg esq wherein sd Ralph appealed.
Deadrick & Sutler recovered judgment before a magistrate agt Lewalen Phips for $29.32½ & costs. Levied on 100 acres property of Lewallen Phips; sd land to be sold to satisfy sd judgment and all accruing costs.
p.154 Deed Edward Douglass to William Cage 191½ acres ackd.
Grant ltrs/admn on estate of George Duty decd to Elizabeth Duty & George Gillespie. Bond $3000, Henry Bledsoe & Solomon Duty securities.
James Neeley & Alexander Neeley orphans of John Neeley decd choose Isaac Bledsoe & George D Blackemore their guardians; bond $2000, Henry Bledsoe security.
Deed Thomas Keefe to Redmond D Barry 5 acres ackd.
Deed Ephraim Cat[binding] to Michael Green 43 acres 78 poles proven by Elisha Green & Thomas Edwards.
Deed Ephraim Cates to Elisha Green 71 acres 10 poles proven by Michael Green & Thomas Edwards.
p.155 Deed Seth Mabry to Nathan Parker & others trustees for one acre land ackd.
Report of jury apptd to lay out a road from Gallatin to end of state road on Kentucky line: starting from William Triggs & James C Wilsons corner, along the ridge, by a schoolhouse, leaving Stewarts on left, Browns gap, William Dennings, intersecting road at James Brackins plantation, from Bledsoes lick. Signed James Bracken David Denning William Denning Carson Dobbins Robert Anderson.

Wednesday March 15th 1809. Present Isaac Walton James C Wilson Will Trigg Junr.
Inventory goods of George Duty decd rendered by George Gillespie.
Matthew Alexander, Robert Robb, Elizabeth Robb, Zacheus Wilson admrs of James Blair[?] decd v John Johnson. Debt. Jury John Allen James Cage James Barry Allen Matthews Hillery Malone Patrick Barr Wm Douglass William Bell James McMurry Jesse Sheen William Kilpatrick Patton Anderson. Plaintiff recovers agt dft debt and
p.156 damages $109.15½ and also costs.
John Lafferty v Robert Rayleigh. Covt. Jury[above except Wm Kirkpatrick

MARCH 1809

for Wm Kilpatrick]. Mistrial; cause continued till next Court.
    Grand Jury delivered indictments endorsed thereon a true bill. State v William Ogels & David Flat for Petit larceny. State v Thos T Rawlings TAB. State v John Moore TAB. State v Peter F Jefferson TAB. State v Hugh Walls TAB. State v Richard King neglect of duty as overseer/road. State v Zacheus Wilson for like offence and sundry presentments.
    James White & Jos H Conn v Isam Uzzell. Plfs & dft in proper persons; dft agrees plfs have sustained damages. Plfs recover agt dft damages & costs.
p.157   Deed George Perry to Isaac Walton ten acres land ackd.
    Present Jas Winchester Isaac Walton Stephen Cantrill Jas C Wilson Mattw Alexander esqrs. Benjamin Bashaw v Larkin Bradford. TAB. Jury Edmund Hogin Thos Dement John Stuart Richd Edwards Jacob Lewis Jno Stuart Geo Woodall Peter Fisher Wm Stuart Jas Claxton Geo Steele Edmund Turpin. Dft not guilty. Plf obtains appeal to Superior Court, Jinkin Whiteside & Redmond D Barry his securities.
    Deed John Bailey & John Thurmond to Reuben D Brown 100 acres proved by William Hall & Ben Morgan.
    Present Jas Winchester James Cryer M Alexander. David Stewart v Thomas Richey. Trespass &c. Jury William Douglass William Bell Jesse Sheen Hillery Malone Patrick Barr John Stuart Richd Edwards Mourning Wynn George Chapman James Wilson John Jones Charles D Lewis find dft not guilty.
p.158   Statement of a settlement by the committee composing an orphans court with Isaac Walton & John Gardner guardians for heirs of Bryant Gardner.
    Will & A Trigg v Henry Belote & Moses King. Appeal. Plfs and Belote in proper person; Belote with assent of plfs waves appeal granted by the magistrate in the above cause; agrees that judgmt of the Justice be affirmed, & plfs recover agt defendant Belote $7 debt and $1.37½ costs and also costs of sd suit.
    State v William Ogles & David Flat. TAB. Appearance bond of Elijah Anthony the prosecutor.
    Bill/sale Elisha Green to Redmond D Barry negro man Jack ackd.
    Brown & Bentley v John Giles. Mourning Wynn garnishee of John Giles declares he owes dft nothing nor has any of dfts property.
p.159   James Winchester & William Cage v Henry Belote. Debt. Parties in proper person. Dft cannot deny he owes $140. Plfs recover agt dft debt & damages $155.75 and their costs. Plfs stay execution until next Court.

Thursday March 16th 1809. Present the worshipful Edward Gwin James C Wilson Will Trigg Junr esqrs.
    Deed Jas Winchester & William Cage Junr to Samuel Conn lot 9 in Cairo ackd.
    Mortgage Porter Allen to James Trousdale for parcel of land said to contain 4½ acres 43 poles ackd by Porter the mortgager; at same time assignment of mortgage from mortgager to Charles D Lewis endorsed on sd mortgage acknowledged by sd James Trousdale mortgager afsd.
    List of taxable property &c in Capt Paytons Co taken by Benjamin Rawlings esqr rendered into Court by sd Rawlings.
    Abraham Britton v William Cobler. Plf by Jenkin Whiteside his attorney says he intends no further to prosecute; Dft recovers agt plf his costs of defence.
p.160   William Crabtree & Wm Crutchfield exrs of Wm Thomas decd v Rhodam Allen & Walter Maxey. Debt. Plfs by atty also Maxey one of dfts; plfs agree to discontinue suit, Maxey paying costs.
    Present Jas Winchester Edwd Gwin & Ben Rawlings. Edmund Bridgers v Ebsworth

MARCH 1809

Baynes. Cer. Jury James McMurry Adam Crump John Rutherford Hilary Malone William Douglass John Johnson Lemuel T Turner Patrick Barr Joshua Claxton Jesse Skeen William Bell George Watwood. Plf recovers agt dft damages $6.50 and costs. Dft obtains new trial; cause continued till next court.

Rivers Hodge v Nathaniel Parker. Cer. Jury John Butler Joel Campbell Isaac Forrester(?) John Shever Armstead Rogers John Edwards William Payton Charles Wadkins James Elliott Jeremiah Mitchell James Campbell Needham Reynolds. Plf recovers agt dft damages 43¢ and costs about his suit expended.

p.161 William Woodall summoned as witness for Nathaniel Parker failing to appear fined $125 unless sufficient cause of disability be shewn at next Court.

William Woodall summoned as witness for Rivers Hodge failing to appear is fined $125 unless sufficient cause be shewn of his disability to next Court.

Jesse Sheen & Edward Sanderson fined $1 each for contempt/Court absenting themselves after being sworn as jurors.

James Winchester Jas Wilson Will Trigg esqr. John Nichols v Daniel Twigg. Jury James Cage James Barry Patrick Barr Wm Bell Henry Malone Wm Douglass Peter Lyon Frederick Holland Dempsey Moore James McMurry Jeremiah Mitchell Benjn Howard. Plf recovers agt dft damages $60.89 & costs. Sheriff to sell the land levied on.

p.162 Fines on Jesse Skeen & Edward Sanderson remitted on their paying costs.

John Brown v William T Henderson. Cornelius Thomas garnishee says he is not indebted to William T Henderson & has no property of sd Wm T & is not indebted to sd William T nor had any of Wm T's property at time he was summoned as garnishee.

Friday March 17th 1809. Present James C Wilson Joshua Rice and [blank].

Licence Robert B Mitchel to keep tavern at his dwelling in Gallatin, Felix Grundy & John H Bowen his securities.

Grand Jury dismissed.

Alexander McMillan v Joshua Claxton. Caveat. Plfs atty amends his caveat by inserting that Alexr McMillan also claims the land surveyed for Joshua Claxton by virtue of two entries made on military warrant #5120 for 640 acres: #12 is for 200 acres entered 1 August 1807; #2706 is for 440 acres dated 7 November 1808.

p.163 On petition of William Jones who lately married Polly Haw one of heirs of James Haw praying to appoint commissioners to divide the real estate of sd decd 326 acres on Drakes Creek between petitioner and the other heirs. Order Wm Montgomery Wm Clark Henry Bunn Jesse Joiner George Reed commrs & Shadrack Nye surveyor divide and appropriate the land.

Report of jury to alter the road from Bledsoes lick to flat lick, passing through John Barrs land, it being 80 yards further than the old way though on better ground; review made on oath March 1st 1809 before John Barr. Signed Wm Carr King Carr David Pursley Robert Maffitt Robt Shune Andrew McPeters John Miller John Carr Robert Simpson overseer of road now open for carriages.

Saturday March 18th 1809. Present Benjn Rawlings Jas C Wilson Will Trigg Jr Esqrs.

Deed Maxwell Sharp to John Hendley 131½ acres ackd.

Deed Euridice Mires to John Hendley 131½ acres proved by Leander J Sharp and John Martin.

p.164 Zacheus Wilson v Patton Anderson. Deposition of James Steele to be taken in benefit plaintiff; deposition of Jesse Yokum to be taken in benefit defendant.

Deed Nicholas Boyce to John Peyton Senr 33½ acres proved by Jacob Thompson & Sally Murphey.

MARCH 1809

Power/atty Maxwell Sharp to John H Bowen 1 Sept 1806 ackd.

Monday March 20th 1809. Present Benjamin Rawlings Will Trigg Jr Jno McMurtry Esqrs.
William Edwards v James Cage & Samuel P Black. Benjamin Morgan & Maunsel M White to take depositions of J F Gray & John Taylor of New Orleans in behalf dfts.
Appoint John McMurtry coroner pro tem until next Court.
p.165   State v Thomas T Rawlings. TAB. Jury Jacob Lewis Robert Moore John Jones Wm Douglass Patrick Barr Wm Spycer Jeremiah Mitchell Hilery Malone Jesse Skeen Wm Bell Webb Bloodworth Samuel Clenny find dft guilty of trespass assault & battery.
Supplementary inventory/sales of goods of John Josey decd proved by admr.
Joseph Barren recovered judgment before a magistrate agt Porter Allen for $10.60 debt and 93¾¢ costs. Levied on house & 4 acres adj Motheral & others on road between Gallatin & James C Wilsons; property to be sold to satisfy debt.
Will & A Trigg recovered judgment before a magistrate agt Porter Allen for
p.166 $36.11½ [worded as above]
Thomas Wood recovered judgment before a magistrate agt William A Covington & Porter Allen for $35.30 debt and 43¾¢ costs [worded as above]
State v Hugh Wall. TAB. Jury Josephus H Conn Jesse Skeen Wm Ford Robt Moore Jas McMurry Wm Douglass Jeremiah Mitchell Patrick Barr Henry Malone William Wallace Joseph Scobey Ambrose Porter find dft guilty; fined $1.50 & pay costs.
p.167   Relinquishment Samuel Gibson to William S Bledsoe of Gibsons claim & right to negro boy Nat now in possession of Catherine Bledsoe ackd by Samuel Gibson.
James Holland v William Spycer. Appeal. Parties in proper person plf no further prosecutes; defendant pays clerks fees and law tax.
Francis Comperry v John Bridgers & Edmund Bridgers. Trespass. Jury John Chapman James McMurry Wm Douglass Abram Trigg Jesse Skeen Adam Crump Saml K Blythe John Franklin Joseph Scobey Jeremiah Mitchell William Bell Samuel Gibson. Plf recovers agt dft damages $40 and his costs.
List of taxable property & polls taken in Capt Blakemores company for present year by Thomas Murry was rendered into Court by Thomas Blackemore esqr.

Tuesday March 21st 1809. Present John McMurtry Will Trigg Jr James C Wilson esqrs.
Alexander McMillan v Joshua Claxton. Caveat. Dft by Thos Stuart comes into
p.168   court and excepts to opinion of the Court.
License Matthew Neal to keep tavern at his dwelling in Gallatin, with James Trousdale & Josephus H Conn his securities.
Present John McMurtry Jas Cryer Jas C Wilson. Alexander McMillan v Joshua Claxton. Caveatt. Jury Jas Barry Jas Cage Joshua Hadley Hilary Malone Patrick Barr Jeremiah Mitchell Thos Scurry Thomas Richey Robert Ellis Edmund Turpin Jesse Skeen Demsey Moore. [Plaintiffs facts somewhat obliterated by ink blots. Questions deal with entry by Martin Armstrong deeded to plaintiff.] Peter Fishers entry under which dft claims has been removed from the land now in controversy found in affirmative. Did not the arbitrators to whom the titles of Martin Armstrong & Peter Fisher were referred for arbitration determin in favor of Armstrongs claim; found in affirmative. (Continued)
p.169   Deed Archibald Marlin late sheriff to Samuel Conn assignee of Josephus H Conn lot 8 in Gallatin ackd.
Deed Archibald Marlin late sheriff to Samuel Conn assignee of Josephus H Conn two acres ackd.
White & Jos H Conn recovered judgment before a magistrat agt James Steele

MARCH 1809

for $8 debt and 25¢ costs. Levied on house & lot in Cairo; order of sale issued.
John Mitchel recovered judgt before a magistrate agt Robert Lytle for debt $14.12½ and 93¾¢ costs. Levied on house and half acre adjoining Porter Allen and others on road from Gallatin to James C Wilson; to be sold to satisfy debt.
Deed Armstreat Stubblefield to Thomas Mason 274 acres ackd.
p.170 Elisha Green v William Wallace. TAB. Parties by attornies and in proper person; plf no further prosecutes; each party pays half costs.
Order Nancy Boyce & Archibald Marlin to admr estate of Nicholas Boyce decd; bond $15000 with Smith Hansbrough and Benjamin Rawlings their securities.
List/taxable property &c in Capt Watkins company for present year taken by Archibald Marlin esqr was rendered into Court by sd Marlin.
Appoint George Hall overseer/road in place of David Stuart resigned.
Deed Matthew Neal to Joseph Motheral one acre ackd.
Deed Anne Furr[Greer?] to John Motheral 1020 acres proved by James Furr [Green?] & Joseph Motheral.
License William Duty to keep tavern at his house, Jas McMurry his security.
Supplementary inventory/goods of Jesse Wells rendered by James McKain admr.
p.171 [Alexr McMillin v Joshua Claxton continued] Facts submitted by deft; was warrant 938 ever assigned to Martin Armstrong; affirmative, as appears by R McGavocks certificate. Dfts survey does not correspond with his entry. Was not the arbitration mentioned in plfs facts made between Martin Armstrong & Jabus Fisher; affirmative, but it appeared from evidence that Jabus Fisher was acting as legal rep of Peter Fisher. Considered by Court that no grant shall issue to sd Joshua Claxton for land caveated by sd Alexander McMillan and plf recovers agt dft his costs in this behalf expended. Dft obtains appeal to Superior Court, John Shaver & James Claxton securities.
Supplementary inventory sales of goods of John Josey rendered by Edward Douglass admr.

Wednesday March 22d 1809. Present Matthew Alexander Joshua Rice William Trigg.
On petition of Armstreat Stubblefield order writs of certiorari issue to call up proceedings of three judgments obtained by Edward Bradley agt him for $46.23 each on sd Stubblefield giving bond and security.
Appt William Henry constable for Capt McElberrys district, John Mills & Hillery Malone his securities. Sd Wm Henry took oaths for qualification.
p.172 Robert Cotton v Armstreat Stubblefield. Cer. Plf not appearing, defendant recovers agt plf his costs of defence in this behalf expended.
Michael Thomas v James Blakemore. Appeal. Jury Patrick Barr Chas D Lewis Hilary Malone Wm Bell Jeremiah Mitchel Geo Logan Armstreat Stubblefield Ambrose Porter Jesse Skeen Jno Withers Jas Claxton David Stewart. Plf recovers agt dft debt $18.33¼ and damages 72¢ and also his costs in this behalf expended.
Joshua Rice & Charles Donoho esqrs rendered lists of taxable property by them taken in Capt Greers & Capt Blacks companys. Matthew Alexander returns list of taxable property & polls by him taken for present year in Capt Turners company.
Joseph Boothe witness for James Hargrove ads Edmond Hogan failing to appear is fined unless sufficient cause of disability to attend be shewn at next Court.
p.173 Edmond Hogin v James Hargrove. Cert. Jury[above]. Plf recovers agt dft debt & damages $25.27 & his costs.
Jesse Dawson v William Gilespie. Appeal. Jury[above]. Dft recovers agt plf his costs about his defence in this behalf expended.

MARCH 1809

p.174   John Barnes v John Lafferty. Sci fa. Jury[above]. Plf recovers agt dft $14.49½ and also his costs of suit.
John Stamps v Patsey Trice extx of John Trice. Sci fa. Jury Charles D Lewis, Hilary Malone Wm Bell Geo Logan Jeremiah Mitchell Armstreat Stubblefield John Withers Jesse Skeen Ambrose Porter Jas Claxton David Stewart Patrick Barr. Plf recovers agt dft $99.72¾ debt damages & costs and also costs of this suit.
William Dodson v Clement McDaniel. Appeal. Plf not appearing, dft recovers agt the plf his costs about his defence expended.
Appt Marmaduke Kimbrough overseer/road from second creek to Rocky Creek in place of James Martin resigned.
James Douglass delivered list/taxable property & polls by him taken for present year in Capt Bakers company.
p.175   Appt John Bearding overseer/road in place of Humphrey Bates resigned from Bledsoes creek to the 9 mile post.
Bill/sale James Vinson to Balaam Barnes for household furniture date 26 Dec 1808 proved by E Cates.
Article/agreement between Michael Green Elisha Green & William Wallace stipulating division of 226 acres between them which they purchased jointly of Ruffin Deloach by which agreement Michael Greens part is 52 acres 59 poles; Elisha Greens part 96 acres 30 poles & William Wallace's part 77¼ acres ackd by parties.
Present Stephen Cantril Wm Montgomery Mattw Alexander esqrs. White & Jos H Conn v Ambrose Porter. Appl. Jury Jeremiah Mitchell Chas D Lewis Wm Wallis Edmund J Bailey Hilery Malone Wm Bell Jas Claxton Stephen Baldridge Jesse Skeen Patrick Barr James Edwards David Stewart. Plaintiffs recover agt defendant damages $20 & costs.
Inventory/goods of Nicholas Boyce decd rendered by Archibald Marlin. Order sd admr expose to sale the personal estate of sd decedent.
p.176   William Donelson v John Wyles & William Wyles heirs of full age of John Wyles decd, George Wyles Jenny Wyles Saml Wyles & Margaret Wyles infant heirs of sd decd and by Witheral Latimer their guardian. Sci fa. Dfts failing to appear, plf recovers agt dfts $85.03¾ the debt & damages and $6.90 costs.
Jacob Gardner v James Blakemore. Appl. Jury Hilary Malone Thos Howell Jno Pugh Wm Sholders Jno W Crunk Ephraim Cates Jno Jones Wm F Cheedle Elisha Prewitt Ambrose Porter Harvey R Willis Allen Purvis. Plf recovers agt dft debt & damages $19.38½ and also his costs about his suit expended.
p.177   Exonerate Wm Woodal from fine of $125 adjudged to Nathaniel Parkers use for failing to appear and give testimony in behalf of sd Parker ads Rivers Hodge.
David Shelby v Richard T Bradley. Debt. Dft not appearing, plf recovers agt dft $60 & $7.85 damages and his costs.
Deed Thomas Hobdy to Adam Hope 178 acres ackd.

Thursday March 23d 1809. Present Wm Montgomery Jas C Wilson Matthew Alexander.
Wm Hall esqr sheriff is allowed $2.88 in settlement with treasurer of West Tennessee & county trustee for taxes of 1808 on account of insolvencies.
Allow Howard Douglass deputy sheriff & collector in settlement with treasurer of West Tennessee $3.37½ & with county trustee $1.21 for insolvencies.
p.178   Allen Matthews v Elisha Prewitt. Jury Ruffin Deloach Hilary Malone Wm Bell Patk Barr Jeremiah Mitchel Wm Payton James McMurry Jesse Skeen Fredk Holland Miles Mires Thomas Keefe John Gardner. Defendant recovers agt plf his costs of defence.
Drury Walton recovered judgment agt John Harrison before a magistrate for $20.50 debt & costs. Levied on 16¼ acres on Goose Creek joining James Story.

MARCH 1809

List of taxable property & polls in Capt Lauderdales compy, also like list in Capt McMurrys compy both taken by William Seawell esqr rendered into Court. Present James Sanders Wm Montgomery Matw Alexander. James Hood v Isaac Larue. Jury Chas D Lewis Thos Scurry Jno Shaver James Claxton Wm Avent Hugh Wall Ambrose Trumbo John Brigance David Dement George Elliott Harris Avent Allen Purvis. Plf recovers against defendant damages $117.46 & costs.

p.179   Joshua Hadley v George D Blackmore. Debt. Dfts demurrer overruled; plf recovers agt dft $129.05 debt $12.88 damages & his costs.

John C Hamilton v William Edwards. Jury[above]. Plf recovers agt dft damages $161 & costs.

Henry Belote recovered three judgments before a magistrate agt James Steele for $49 each and sued executors for same. Executions levied on lot in Cairo joining John Hazlet and others. Sheriff to sell same to satisfy judgments.

p.180   James Barry v John Cavitt. Jury James Cage Archd W Overton Hilary Malone Patk Barr Jeremiah Mitchel Miles Mires Jno B Truitt William Bell Harris Avent James McMurry Geo Elliott Jesse Skeen. Plf recovers agt dft damages $37 & his costs.

James Winchester & William Cage v Jourdan Gibson. Debt. Dft not appearing, plfs recover agt dft $132.25 debt & $11.88 damages & also their costs.

Majority of Justices being present, taxes laid to contingent charges.

p.181   Jurors to next Superior Court John Withers John Payton Shadrack Nye Samuel Clenney George Smith Stephen Cantrill Jas Franklin John Gwin.

Jurors to next County Court Chas D Lewis Thos Scurry Jno Shaver Jas Claxton Wm Avent Hugh Wall Ambrose Trumbo John Brigance David Dement George Elliott Harris Avent Allen Purvis Wm Haughton Hugh Wall. This entry rescinded.

William Hall esqr sheriff & collector of taxes for 1808 reports unpaid taxes: John Caffery 640 acres Manskers Creek. Levisa Bowen 640 Manskers Cr. John Latimer 284 Manskers Cr. Wm Conners heirs, 220 acres B & Rocky Cr. James Maclin by John Maclin agent 191 acres Station Camp. Hardy Murphy 280 acres Drakes Creek

p.182   joining Benj[blank] preemption, 640 granted to Nancy Sheppard on Salt lick, 640 granted to Nancy Sheppard on Salt lick, 301 granted to Nancy Sheppard being part of 640 acres on west fork of Bledsoes Creek, this entry so far as relates to Hardy Murphy is ordered to[lost in binding]. Stephen Montgomery 640 acres Goose Cr whereon Benj Seawell lives. Samuel Marsh 640 acres middle fork D Creek, 320 Sulpher F D Creek. Mr Pyrtle 160 acres SFD Creek joining Col Martin. Benj Shepherd heirs 640 acres M Fork D Creek Henry Newby lives on it, 640 M Fork Drakes Creek John Clem living on it, 640 do Solomon Manarde[Manarcle?] living on it. Samuel Williams 140 acres Dry fork D Creek. William Hart 250 acres Goose Creek joining Wm Lauderdale on

p.183   the north. William Stalcup 91 acres Station Camp. Ordered by Court that afsd tracts or so much thereof as shall satisfy taxes costs & charges due thereon be sold; to be published agreeable to law.

Friday March 24th 1809. Present James Sanders James C Wilson William Bracken esqrs.

Thomas Parker v Roger Gibson & Jordan Gibson. Debt. Dft not appearing, plf recovers agt dft $609 debt $71.97½ damages and also his costs of suit.

Hugh Wall v Edmund Bridgers. Appeal. Jury Dempsey Moore Wm Bell Patk Barr Hilary Malone Jas McMurry Jeremiah Mitchel Wm Douglass Jno Stuart Jesse Skeen Fredk Holland Wm Kirkpatrick Miles Mires. Plf recovers agt dft $31.74 debt, 16¢ damages and also his costs about his suit in this behalf expended.

p.184   Hugh Wall v Edmund Bridgers. Appeal. Jury[above]. Plf recovers $33.17 debt, 17¢ damages, and also his costs of suit.

MARCH 1809

Robert B Mitchel v John Jones. Appeal. Jury Joshua Hadley Edwd Cage James Edwards James Elliott George Elliott William Edwards Thomas Keefe John Turner Hugh Wall Edmund Reeves Josephus H Conn Adam Crump. Plf recovers agt dft $8.87½ & costs.

Order John C Josey an orphan age 14 years 4 months be apprenticed to John B Truett to learn the art of a shoe & boot maker.

p.185 Jurors to next Court, Robt Patton James Vinson Davis King David Dement Thos Scurry Wm Bennett Junr William Dorris James Garrett Samuel Conn William Wherry Junr John Larner[Sarver?] Senr Leonard Bowen Junr Edward Sanders Robert Williamson David Stuart Adam Hunter Reuben Douglass John Mitchell(D.N) John Dickerson(GC) Wm Sanders George Stubblefield Jesse Joiner William Reed William Duty Joseph Hodge Thomas Donnell Wm Alderson Montgomery McConnell James Cary John Cryer Richard Edwards Joseph McElwrath Joseph Wallace Henry Bradford John Turner Abraham Bledsoe.

Thomas Parker v Roger Gibson & Jordan Gibson. Debt. Sheriff ordered to sell 200 acres west end of tract levied on by attachment; order rescinded.

William Pannell v John Mitchell. Depositions of Stephen Sneed Leonard Cardwell & Elijah Mitchell of Greenville County North Carolina to be taken for defendant.

James Sanders & Will Trigg esqrs render list/taxable property & polls taken by them in Capt Preston & Capt McCalls companies.

William Sanders v Redmond D Barry. Parties in proper persons. Plf no further prosecutes, defendant pays costs.

p.186 On motion of County Solicitor and on satisfactory evidence of the maltreatment of Matthew Bayne an orphan bound to John Webb, order sd apprentice be removed from John Webb and subject to be rebound to some other person.

Appoint Robert Shaw overseer/road from Station Camp Cr to the ridge in place of Moore Cotton resigned.

On motion of Sheriff, Clerk to issue executions for jailors fees agt plfs in following suits: James Trousdale v Archibald Donoho & Walter Bennet v Elijah Hendrick, for $5 in the first suit and for $2.50 in the latter, said fees being due the jailor for finding &c the defts when imprisoned.

Appt Isaac Lain overseer/road from Gallatin to Kentucky road near James Brackens from Gallatin to where sd road crosses Cairo road, and that William Trigg esqr furnish sd overseer with list of hands.

Appt Carson Dobbins overseer/road from Gallatin to Kentucky road near James Brackens from where Cairo road crosses it to two & half miles north of ridge and that Wm Bracken furnish sd overseer with a list of hands.

Appt William Denning overseer/road from Gallatin to Kentucky road near Jas Brackens from two and half miles north of the ridge to Stubbins tan yard, William Bracken esqr to furnish sd overseer with a list of hands.

Appt James Bracken Senr overseer/road from Gallatin to Kentucky road near James Brackens from Stubbins tan yard to end of Kentucky road; William Bracken esqr to furnish sd overseer with a list hands.

p.187 Will Trigg one of commrs apptd to settle with exrs of Hugh Elliott decd rendered settlement into Court.

Saturday March 25th 1809. Present James Cryer James C Wilson Will Trigg esqr.

George W Darnell v Thomas Brinkley. Sci fa. Dft not appearing, plf granted execution agt dft for $18 debt & $6.95 costs.

Andrew Jackson & John Hutchings v Thomas Blakemore. Debt. Dft not appearing, plaintiffs recover agt dft $1110 debt to be discharged by payment of $560 with

JUNE 1809

interest from 25 Decr 1808 & costs of suit.
  John C Hamilton v John Stevens. Debt. Dft not appearing, plf recovers agt dft $66 debt & costs; credit given by plf for $59.25.
p.188 Commrs apptd to settle with executors of William Cochran decd render statement of settlement.
  Report of division of estate of William Cochran decd between legatees was rendered into Court.
  James Winchester esqr delivered list/taxable property &c by him taken in Capt Charltons company for present year.
  Thomas Neelley v Wm Collins admr of John Hewell. Debt. Plf no appearing, plf nonsuited, dft recovers agt plf his costs of defence in this behalf expended.
  William Brit v Moore Stevenson. Deposition of John Philpotts of Goochland County Virginia to be taken at Eldridge's grocery store on behalf plaintiff.
  Order James Cryer & Will Trigg esqrs settle accounts with executors of Hugh Elliott decd.
  State v Thomas T Rawlings. TAB. Appearance bond of dft.
p.189 State v Thos T Rawlings. TAB. Bond of John Jones & Howard Glass securities for Thos T Rawlings.
  John Jones v Geo D Blackmore & Zacheus Wilson exrs of Richard Taylor decd. Debt. Dfts not appearing, plf recovers agt dfts $48 debt $5.92 damages and costs. Court adjourned till Court in Course. Will Trigg James C Wilson Benjn Rawlings

p.190 Second Monday in June 1809. Present the worshipfull James Winchester Will Trigg Jr Mathew Alexander Esqrs.
  Grand Jury Thomas Donnell foreman David Stuart David Dement Joseph McElwrath Richd Edwards Abraham Bledsoe Wm Wherry Senr Geo Stubblefield Davis King John Cryer William Bennett Senr John Mitchell Reuben Douglass Robert Williamson.
  Deed Hugh Parks by atty William Roark to John Harper 274 acres proved by Anthony B Shelby & Abraham Trigg.
  Deed Reuben Cage sheriff to Redmond Dillon Barry 606 acres proven by John C Hamilton & Thomas Scurry.
  Deed Edward Cage to Thomas White 194 acres ackd.
p.191 Deed Alexander Rasco to James Gwin 225 acres ackd.
  Wm Davis a juror is excused from further attendance.
  Juror Adam Hunter is excused from further attendance for present term.
  Will of Ruth Ozbrooks decd proved by William Granger & John Bradley & Edward Gwin; Wm Granger extr named in will qualified by taking oath.
  Deed William McClon[McClore?] to Edward Gwin son of John Gwin 158 acres proved by Edward Gwin & John Gwin.
  Deed Zacheus Wilson to Will & Abram Trigg 75 acres ackd.
  Inventory/goods of Ruth Ozbrooks decd rendered by William Granger extr.
  Deed Redmond D Barry to Joseph McGloughlin 100 acres ackd.
p.192 Deed Redmond D Barry to James Gwin 60 acres ackd.
  Deed Roger Gibson to Isaac Bledsoe Abraham Bledsoe & Henry Bledsoe 270 acres proven by James Winchester & Francis Weatherred.
  Deed Elijah Nicholson to Edward Gwin 274 acres proven by John Gwin &

JUNE 1809

Joseph McGloughlin.
    Power/atty Solomon Duty & Susanna Duty his wife to William Hall to collect a legacy due from estate of Joseph Whitmore to sd Susannah Duty daughter of sd Joseph Whitmore ackd.
    Bill/sale Obed Britt to Jeremiah Mitchell negro man Sam & three feather beds and two horses proved by William Bell & John Mitchell.
    Permit William Granger extr of Ruth Ozbrook decd to sell personal estate of sd decd.
    Appt Edward Sanderson overseer/road from Croft mills to Sterns ford on dry fork in place of Joseph Hodge resigned.
p.193   On motion of Moore Stevenson order Stephen Cantrill & James Cryer examine & settle administration of estate of Abraham Hassell decd and report to this Court.
    Appt Thomas Moss overseer/road in place of James Roney resigned.
    Grant ltrs/admn on estate of William McClelen decd to William Simpson & John Sloan the widow having declined administering estate; Wm Simpson & John Sloan give bond $750 with John Barr & King Carr their securities.
    On motion of Moore Stevenson acting executor of Abraham Rogers decd, order James Cryer & Stephen Cantrill esqrs settle account of admn of deceased's estate.
    Appt George Hall overseer/road in place of David Stuart resigned.
    Thomas L Harris orphan makes choice of William Hall esqr for his guardian; William Hall with John Morgan his security entered bond $1000.
    James Harrison to William Hall plat & certificate of survey made for sd Harrison 149¾ acres & 35 poles, assigned to Hall, ackd by James Harrison.
    Appt Samuel Roney overseer/road in place of William Lilly resigned.
p.194   John C Hamilton v Wm Milton & John Robertson. Debt. Jesse Sheen & James Roney bail for Wm Milton surrender dft to Court.
    Deed Nathaniel Parker Junr to Ordell Garrett 100 acres proved by William Seawell & Solomon Duty.
    Acct/sales goods of James Wilson decd proved by John Parson admr.
    Bond of William Hall sheriff & collector with John Morgan & Redd D Barry securities.
    Isaac Baker Edward Sanders & Samuel McMurry who were commissioned in the peace by the governor appear and take the oaths.
p.195   Licence James Brown to keep ordinary at his house, James Bruce Wm Bruce & Robert Williamson his securities.
    Order Daniel Smith appointed guardian for John Donelson & Andrew Donelson orphans of Samuel Donelson decd. Daniel Smith with Edward Sanders & Thomas Masten his securities entered bond $3000.
    Appt Jno W Byrn constable in Capt Lauderdale's district for two years, Jno W Byrn & Henry Bledsoe & Saml D Lauderdale his securities entered bond $625.
    Orphan James Hellon made choice of George Martin as guardian. Sd George Martin with George D Blackmore securities entered bond $1000.
    Orphan Caty Morrish who was bound to William Hall; bound by consent of Court & Wm Hall to Erben Crook until age eighteen years.
p.196   Order Neubern Morrish orphan heretofore bound to William Hall by mutual consent be bound to Erben Crook until age twenty one years to learn art & mystery of a house carpenter.
    John Smith recovered judgment before a single magistrate agt Thomas Keefe for $40 & $1 cost. Levied on Thomas Keefe's lot adjoining Samples decd in Gallatin. Sheriff to sell same to satisfy judgment and all accrued costs.

JUNE 1809

Allow County Solicitor $25 for ex officio services for preceding year.
Allow Clerk/Court $25 for recording lists/taxable property of present year & other business relating thereto.

Petition of William Jones one of heirs of James Haw decd in right of his wife Polly Jones formerly Polly Haw daughter of sd decd praying order of Court appointing commrs to divide & appropriate 320 acres on Drakes Creek of James Haw decd between him the petitioner and the other heirs on guardian for other heirs coming into Court and acknowledging receipt of legal notice from sd petitoners of p.197 his intention. Court orders Wm Montgomery Jos Clark Henry Bunn Jesse Joiner George Reed & Shadrack Nye divide & appropriate afsd land between heirs so that the petitioner may have one fifth part thereof, there being five surviving heirs.

Order Wm Seawell Matthew Alexander & Jas Winchester esqrs examine & settle accounts of admr of Robert Harris decd and make report thereof to next Court.

William Sanders & Levi Hall jurors excused from further attendance this Term, likewise Henry Bradford is excused on account of health.

Allow James Harrison half price of four stray hogs posted by Levi Hall, sd hogs being proved the property of sd Harrison.

Henry Hoover v George Smith. TAB. Plf intends no further to prosecute on dfts paying costs.

Tuesday June 13th 1809. Present Jas Winchester Stephen Cantrill Isaac Walton Edwd Gwin, esquires.

McNutt Findley & Co v John Spooner. Debt. Jury Wm Reed George Hogan Wm Allen Jas Cary Jas Vinson Montgomery McConnell Joseph Wallace Thos Seuny(?) William p.198 Duty Amos Webb John Dickinson Robert Patton cannot agree; mistrial.

Deed George Black to James Hart 20 or about half of 40 acres acres ackd.

Lemuel Prewitt v Nicholas Boyce & Elisha Prewitt, death of Nicholas Boyce suggested. Suit revived agt Nancy Boyce & Archd Marlin admrs of sd Nicholas Boyce.

Lemuel Prewitt v Nancy Boyce & Archibald Marlin admrs of goods of Nicholas Boyce decd & Elisha Prewitt. Debt. Jury George Black Jesse Shein Jonathan Spooner Christly Catron Joseph McReynolds Philip Brothers John Rowland King Carr Jacob Fuller Wm Horton John Dinning Wallace Kirkpatrick. Plaintiff recovers agt dft debt & p.199 damages $347.56½ and also costs of suit, to be levied on goods of sd decd and on goods & chattels lands & tenements of Elisha Prewitt the other defendant.

Lemuel Prewitt v Elisha Prewitt. Debt. Jury[above]. Plf recovers agt dft debt & damages $154.26 and also his costs in this behalf expended.

Bill/sale Thomas D Martin to Elisabeth Martin negro girl Mary ackd.

William Lytle v Nathaniel Dickison. Debt. Jury[above]. Plf recovers agt p.200 dft debt & damages $544.85 and also his costs of suit.

John Moore v James Green & Zachariah Green. Debt. Jury Wm Harper William Anderson Jas Barr Wm Barr Alexander Gwin Jas Odam Richard Holloway William Hale Wm Kirkpatrick Jas Edwards Silas Jernigan Stephen Pitts. Plf recovers agt dft debt & damages $203.30 & also his costs about his suit expended.

Deed Roger Gibson to James Winchester 214 acres proved by John Frazor and William Cage.

p.201 James Claxton v John Bailey & John Pritcher. Debt. Jury[above]. Plf recovers agt dft debt & damages $110.14 and also his costs of suit.

William W Carney v John Lafferty. Debt. Jury[above]. Plf recovers agt dft debt and damages $125.70½ and also his costs of suit in this behalf expended.
p.202 Nicholas Boyce v Henry Wells & Jesse Wells, death of plf suggested. Suit

38

JUNE 1809

revived in name of Nancy Boyce & Archibald Marlin admrs of sd deceased.
Nancy Boyce & Archibald Marlin admrs of Nicholas Boyce v Henry Wells & Jesse Wells. Henry Wells in proper person; order in writing of plaintiffs being produced for the dismission of above suit on dfts paying costs which is assumed in open court by sd Henry Wells. Suit dismissed; plfs recover agt Henry their costs.
Will of Jacob Archer decd proved by Simon Shurcraft & Lemuel Rogers; Jacob Archer qualified as executor.
Deed David Shelby to Reuben Cage 61½ acres ackd.
Deed John Stewart to Stephen White 106 acres proved by Richard Ball and James Stewart.
p.203 James Hart Joshua Rice Thomas Blackmore James Winchester William Seawell Isaac Walton John McMurtry Samuel McMurry William Trigg James C Wilson Isaac Baker Stephen Cantrill James Cryer James Douglass William Montgomery present.
Jacob Fuller allowed out of the poor tax $12 for maintaining Isaac McClung an orphan for three months previous to this time.
Allow Francis Youree out of poor tax $20 for maintaining William McClung an orphan for one year previous to this date.
Allow William Martin $48 for maintaining his daughter Jemima a pauper for one year commencing this date, payable quarter yearly.
Order poor tax levied: 6¼¢ each hundred acres 6¼¢ per poll 12½¢ per slave.
Allow sheriff $50 for ex officio services for 1 year preceding this date.
Allow clerk $40 for ex officio services for one year preceding this date.
Deed/gift William Cage to Jesse Cage 320 acres ackd.
Allow Jesse Spradling for maintaining John Putt a pauper $50 payable quarterly out of the poor tax for one year commencing 2d Monday in March last.
p.204 Deed William Harper to Martha Chapman 91½ acres proved by John Chapman & James Chapman.
Deed James Read to Samuel Holloway 40 acres ackd.
Power/atty Robert Dobbins to Witheral Latimer 640 acres #1648 dated 11 Feb 1809 proved by Alexander Gwin & Thomas Shaw.
Benjamin Taylor v Stephen Treble[Trebb?]. Debt. Parties in proper person. Plf recovers agt dft $173.66 and his costs.
Will of Matthew Brown decd proved by Church Fulcher; Jackson Brown one of executors named qualified by taking oath.
Bill/sale Caty Bledsoe to Clarissa Bledsoe five negroes Agg, Jess Delita, Dave, Hannah proved by William Hall and David Humphreys.
p.205 Deed James Douglass to James Cage lot 12 in Gallatin ackd.
Deed Hugh McGee to Walter Maxey 100 acres proved by Joseph Wallace and William Maxey.
Juror John Farmer excused from further attendance at this term.
Deed Jesse Moore to Isaac Lain 8 acres ackd.
Appt William Anderson blacksmith overseer/road in place of John Dobbins between McMunns on Desha Creek and the top of the ridge.
Present Mattw Alexander James C Wilson John Barr esqrs. Jonathan Peairs v Jno Payton & Wm Payton. Debt. Jury Jas Vinson Jno Dickinson Jos Wallace Ambrose Porter Wm Giles Jno Franklin Jas Cary Wm Duty Robt Patton Stephen Baldridge Montgy
p.206 McConnell Wm Reed. Plf recovers agt dfts debt & damages $127.20 & costs.
William J Harwell v William Payton & John Payton. Debt. Jury Robt Patton Wm Reed Jno Dickerson Jos Wallace Jas Vinson Montgomery McConnell Wilson Shockley Thos Scurry Ephraim Cates Jas Cary Jas Brown Jno Chapman. Plf recovers agt dfts

JUNE 1809

debt & damages $525 and also his costs about his suit in this behalf expended.

McNutt Findley & Co v Patsey Trice exx of John Trice decd. Debt. Jury above] say that the currency in pounds shillings & pence in plfs declaration is of value $123.62½ which dft owes plf; dft by atty moves to shew cause for new trial.

p.207 Appt Stephen Trible guardian for orphan Betsey Goosher; bond $500 with James Roney & John Denning his securities.

Bill/sale John Orr to James Douglass negro boy Isaac ackd.

Bill/sale John Dobbins to James Douglass negro girl Bridget ackd.

John C Hamilton v William Melton & John Robinson. Debt. Plf released James C Wilson one of the bail for John Robinson.

Appt Odell Garrett guardian for Betsey Garrett Nathan Garrett Peggy Garrett Joseph Garrett & Patty Garrett minors and children of sd Odell Garrett; sd Odell Garrett with William Hall & Isaac Bledsoe his securities entered bond $500.

John M Taylor produced licence to practice as an attorney, took oath, and is admitted to practice as such in this court.

p.208 Appt Isaac Lain William Edwards Zacheus Wilson William Bell Jas Odam John Withers Chas Elliott to review roads from Gallatin to mouth of Station Camp and from Gallatin to mouth of Elliotts branch, report distance of each, kind of land they would pass over, damages each would be to the county, & report to next court.

On petition of Edward Sanderson and others, order James Clendening Thomas Parker Hugh Rogan John Morgan Robert Steel William Anderson Patrick Barr alter road from Stamps's to Johnstons on the ridge by turning sd road east or through Sandersons plantation beginning at William Knights; report to next court.

Appt Joseph Motheral John Turner James Lane William Bell Robert Anderson Thomas Donnell James Stuart to review road from Gallatin to intersect Kentucky road near James Brackens as lies between Will Triggs meadow and Gallatin and to lay off same between sd places having regard to interest and benefit of public as well as individuals through whose land road may pass; report to next court.

Power/atty from Odell Garrett as guardian for his children named Betsey Nathan Peggy Joseph & Martha Garrett to William Hall for purpose of collecting legacy due to sd children from estate of Joseph Whitman decd late of Laurence County

p.209 South Carolina dated 13 June 1809 was ackd by sd Odell.

Order road from Smith County near head of Long creek to Kentucky line near Mr Russells be laid out by John Sullivan Cap James Trousdale George Anderson Edward Hogin Robert Simpson John Sloan; make report to next Court.

Petition of John Denning praying road be altered where it passes through a small bottom belonging to sd petitioner so that road when altered may not so materially injury sd low ground; appt Isaac Bracken Benjamin Granger James Roney Richard Cope Micajah House for purpose; report to next Court.

On petition of sundry persons to grant Jeremiah Murphy liberty to turn road from Gallatin over ridge at James Johnsons, appoint James Johnston Joseph Bunten William Bunten Fergus Sloan John Sternes George McGuire James McMurry for that purpose, sd road not to be more than 20 poles further and over equally good ground; report to next Court.

p.210 William Hall sheriff made return on transcripts of orders made at last term appointing overseers of roads: Fleming Thurmond M D Kimbrough Carson Dobbins Abel Branden James Scott John Bearding; he delivered a copy to each overseer.

Appt William Eubanks overseer/road in place of Robert Simpson.

Ashley Stanfield v John C Hamilton. Debt. Dft in proper person says he owes $107.80 debt. Plf recovers agt dft debt also costs of suit.

JUNE 1809

Wednesday June 14th 1809. Present Mathew Alexander John Barr Will Trigg esqrs.
    Fleet Howard v James Cryer & Frederick Holland. Debt. Jury John Dickason Montgomery McConnell James Cary Wm Reed Wm Duty Chas Lewis Jeremiah Doxey Joseph Wallace Robt Patton Jas Vinson Jno Edwards John Chapman. Plf recovers agt dft debt
p.211   & damages $128.43 and also his costs of suit.
    John Jones v Allen Purvis & Wm Payton. Debt. Jury[above]. Plf recovers agt dft debt & damages $389.50 and also his costs about his suit expended.
    James Cage v William Payton. Debt. Jury[above]. Plf recovers agt dft the
p.212   debt & damages $61.70 and also his costs of suit.
    William Williams v Benjamin Rawlings & Wm Montgomery. Debt. Jury[above but Jno Dickerson for John Dickason]. Plf recovers debt & damages $342.48½ & costs.
    Nathan Edwards v Alexander Rasco & Thomas Howell. Debt. Jury[above]. Plf
p.213   recovers agt dft debt & damages $667.31 and also his costs of suit.
    Edmond Bridgers v William Johnson. Debt. Jury[above but John Dickison for Jno Dickerson]. Plf recovers agt dft debt & damages $217.03 and his costs of suit.
    Deed Montgomery McConnell to Daniel McConnell 200 acres ackd.
p.214   Henry D Palmer v Francis Weatherred. Debt. Jury[above]. Plf recovers agt dft debt & damages $305.25 and also his costs.
    James Douglass v William Haughton & Moore Cotton. Debt. Jury[above]. Plf recovers agt dfts debt & damages $411 and his costs about his suit expended.
p.215   Lewis Land v Ruffin Spain. Plf no further prosecutes; dft recovers agt plf his costs about his defence in this behalf expended and all other costs.
    Present Matthew Alexander John Barr Jas C Wilson Esqrs. William Edwards v James Cage & Saml P Black. Jury Wm Reed Jno Dickerson James Cary Wm Payton Thos Scurry Wm Duty Thos Preston Robt Patton Jas Vinson Jeremiah Doxey Montgy McConnell Jos Wallace cannot agree. Mistrial; cause continued till next court.
    Acct/sales of goods of Nicholas Boyce decd rendered by Archd Marlin admr.
    Loftain Cage v Redmond D Barry. Plf in proper person intends no further to prosecute. Dft recovers agt plf his costs about defence in this behalf expended.
p.216   Appt William Edwards Jr overseer/road from Stamps to Belotes ferry between Stamps & cross road; Henry Belote former overseer continues as overseer from cross road to sd Belotes ferry; Matthew Alexander to furnish sd overseers lists of hands.

Thursday June 15th 1809. Present James Winchester Archd Marlin Will Trigg esqrs.
    Edmund Bridgers v Ebsworth Baynes. Plf not appearing, dft recovers agt plf his costs about his defence in this behalf expended; plf pays all other costs.
    Bill/sale Bennett H Henderson to William Edwards negro boy Powhatan ackd.
    John Doe lessee of Levisa Bowen v Perrin Smith. Eject. Plf by atty no further prosecutes her suit and agrees to pay half costs, dfts paying other half.
p.217   Edward Hogin v James Hargrove. Cir. Jury James Cary Wm Reed John Dickerson Jas Vinson Robt Moore Thos Scurry Wm Haughton Amos Witby Wallace Kirkpatrick Montgy McConnell Joseph Wallace Robert Patton. Plaintiff recovers agt dft $26.25 & costs.
    Power/atty Jesse Beasley to Redmond D Barry date 17 Decr 1808 proved by Hardy Pursell.
    Instrument from Redmond D Barry attorney in fact for Jesse Beasley to William P Anderson and Jenkin Whiteside a transfer of a judgment recovered by sd Beasley agt Martin Armstrong in Superior Court dated 21 February 1809 ackd.
    Deed Roger Gibson to James Winchester & William Cage 104 acres proved by Lemuel T Turner and John Frazor.
    Jonathan Trousdale v John C Hamilton. Detinue. John Brigance witness for

JUNE 1809

Jonathan Trousdale v John C Hamilton failing to appear is fined $125 unless sufficient cause of his disability to attend be shewn at next court.
p.218   Jonathan Trousdale v John C Hamilton. Detinue. Jury Wm Duty Jas Vinson Danl Shaver Henry Densberry Jacob Seaver[Scavea?] Thomas Preston Miles Mires Henry Hoover Willis Hall John Hood Benthal Vinson Joshua Cherry say dft has detained the negro as plf declares; sd negro valued $300. Dfts motion for new trial continued.

Edmund Hogin v James Hargrove. Cer. Pitt Bowers a witness for James Hargrove not appearing is fined $125 unless sufficient cause of his disability to attend be shewn at next court.

Appt William Wharton overseer/road from his house to where other overseer stops on sd road & Isaac Baker Esqr to give overseer a list of hands.

Friday June 16th 1809. Present James Cryer Isaac Baker Benjamin Rawlings esqrs.

James L Armstrong v John Mitchell. Appeal. Deposition on behalf plf to be taken of William F McNutt.
p.219   Present Ben Rawlings Will Trigg Isaac Baker. Jonathan Trousdale v Miles Mires. Jury Wm Reed Jas Carey Wm Duty Jas Vinson Jno Dickison Montgy McConnell John Goodrum Chas Lewis Edwd Cage Wm Allen Robt Patton Saml Clenny. Dft recovers agt plf his costs about his defence in this behalf expended; plf pays other costs.

William Williams v Benjamin Rawlings and William Montgomery. Debt. Plf recovered judgt agt dfts $342.48½ and costs. Dfts obtain appeal to Superior Court, John C Hamilton & Redmond D Barry their securities.

Bill/sale Roger Gibson to James Winchester 4 negroes Ralph Sell Jim and Lilia proven by Lemuel T Turner & Wm Cage.

Power/attorney William Whitted of Orange County North Carolina to Thomas Anderson of Sumner dated 6 December 1808 admitted on certificate of clerk of Orange County with seal of sd county annexed & certificate of chmn of Orange County Court.
p.220   Present James Cryer Isaac Baker Saml McMurry. Nathan Boon v James Campbell. Appeal. Jury Jas Elliott James Edwards Joshua Cherry Charles Morgan Joseph Wallace James Graham Miles Mires Mathew Anderson Allen Josy James Howard Thomas Scurry Wallace Kirkpatrick. Plf recovers agt dft debt $42.90 damages $1.40 & costs.

John & Robert Allen v Edmund Bridgers. Appeal. Jury John Franklin Wm Reed Montgy McConnell Jas Cary Jno Dickerson Wm Duty James Vinson Chas Lewis Robt Patton Jno Goodrum Saml Clenny Jesse Sheen. Plfs recover agt dft debt & damages & costs.
p.221   John & Robert Allen v Edmund Bridgers. Appeal. Jury[above]. Plf recovers agt dft debt & damages $8.05 & costs of suit.

John Furguson v Edmund Bridgers. Appeal. Jury Wallace Kirkpatrick Amos Webb Charles Morgan Demsy Moore Thos Scurry Robt Moore Ruffin Deloach Jos Wallace Wm Kirkpatrick Matthew Anderson Joshua Cherry Miles Mires cannot agree; mistrial, cause continued until next court.

Thomas Masten v John B Johnson. Sci fa. Dft confesseth judgment. Plf has execution agt dft for $45.95, costs of sci fa and his cost of suit.
p.222   Deed Redmond D Barry to William Jones 150 acres ackd.

Orphan John Perry chose Shadrack Nye for his guardian; bond $10,000 with Benjamin Rawlings and William Hall his securities.

James Barry v George D Blackmore & Zacheus Wilson exrs of Richard Taylor decd. Appeal. Jury Wm Reed Jas Cary Jas Vinson Thos Scurry Montgy McConnell Geo Chapman Chas Lewis Wm Duty Wallace Kirkpatrick Robt Patton Jno Goodrum Jos Wallace. Plf recovers agt dft debt & damages $51.12½ and his costs of suit.

Ralph Graves v Edmund Bridgers. Appl. Jury[above]. Plf recovers agt dft

JUNE 1809

p.223 $42.33 debt $2.96 damages and also his costs about his suit expended.
    James Trousdale v John & Robt Allen. Appl. Jury[above]. Plf recovers agt dft his debt & damages $36.66½. Dft moves for new trial; continued.
    Ambrose Porter v Ruffin Deloach. Debt. Plf by atty; dft in proper person confesseth judgment. Plf recovers agt dft $106.20 & costs of suit.
p.224   Ambrose Porter v Ruffin Deloach. Debt. Dft in proper person confesseth judgment. Plf recovers agt dft debt & interest $53.67 & costs.

Saturday June 17th. Present Will Trigg Jas C Wilson Saml McMurry esqrs. Adjourned.

Monday June 19th. Present James Winchester Matthew Alexander Will Trigg Jr esqrs.
    James Franklin v Chichester Howard. Trespass. Plf not appearing, is nonsuited. Dft recovers agt plf his costs of defence.
    Inventory/goods of Robert Patton decd rendered on oath by Robert Patton one of the executors of sd deceased.
p.225   State v John Moore. TAB. Dft in proper person saith he is guilty; fined $1 and costs of prosecution.
    State v Thomas T Rawlings. TAB. Dfts appearance bond for assault upon John Bryance, Wm H Douglass Richd Scott & Wm Payton his securities.
    Porter Allen v Patsey Trice admx of John Trice decd. Jury Wm Reed Montgy McConnell Thos Carey Wm Duty Jno Shaver Allen Josey Reddick Bridgers Zacheus Wilson Jas Vinson Chas Lewis Robt Patton Robt Moore. Plf recovers agt dft $17.42½ & costs.
p.226   Bill/sale Robert Nowell & Sarah Nowell to John Mills two negroes Winney & Jenny proved by James Martin & Thomas Briant.
    Power/atty Robert Alexander of Lincoln County North Carolina to Lawson Henderson of sd county relative to land therein mentioned dated 19th Apl 1809 & with testimonials thereto annexed is ordered to be recorded.
    State v Peter F Jefferson. TAB. Jury William Giles Wm Ball Joseph Wallace Thos Scurry Edmund J Bailey Wallace Kirkpatrick Saml Beard Adam Turner Jno Bridges Robt Strawth Jas Stratton Benthall Vinson find dft guilty. New trial granted dft.
    Appt Elijah Simpson guardian to Thomas Simpson orphan of James Simpson decd; bond $500 with Joseph Wallace & Robert Simpson his securities.
p.227   Present Jas Winchester John McMurtry Edwd Sanders esqrs. [Principals not named]. Jury Wm Reed Wm Duty Jas Carey Wm Gwin Jno Robertson Chas Morgan Jno Cooper Montgy McConnell Jos Wallace Hugh Gourley Robt Patton Jas Vinson who say[blank]
    Petition of Eliza Duty widow of George Duty decd praying commrs be apptd to set apart to widow sufficient support of her & family. Appt Wm Seawell esq Jno D Hannah Wm Hannah Moses Duncan for that purpose; report to this court.
    Plat & certificate/survey 100 acres made for Reuben Searcy 15th Feb 1809 with assignment of sd plat & certificate from Reuben Searcy to Wm Bracken ackd.
    John Bridgers v Robert Moore. Jury[above]. Mistrial; cause continued.
p.228   Acct/sales goods of George Duty decd proved by Geo Gillespie one of admrs; commrs apptd to assign family support for one year render statement of proceedings.
    Report/commrs to settle with admrs/estate of Jas Simpson render statement.
    Present John McMurtry Will Trigg Jas Wilson esqrs. Edmund Crutcher v Samuel P Black. Jury Wm Ball Edwd Jones Thos Scurry Joshua Hadley Jas Hargrove Ruffin Deloach Edmund Bridgers John Moore Ralph Graves Benthall Vinson Adam Crump Wm Kirkpatrick. Plf recovers agt dft damages $112 & costs of suit.
    Poor tax laid for preent year rescinded; according to General Assembly sd tax should have been laid at time other county taxes were laid.

JUNE 1809

p.229 Tuesday June 20th 1809. Present John McMurtry James Cryer Will Trigg esqrs.
On motion of admr of Wm Cathey Junr decd order James Hart & Charles Donoho esqrs settle account of administrator and make report to next court.
James Douglass & Sion Hunt esqr apptd to examine & settle account of admr of estate of Richd Cavitt Junr decd and make report to next Court.
Inventory/goods of Richd Caveatt Jr decd rendered by Wm Kirkpatrick one of securities for John Cavitt for adm of sd decedents estate.
Bill/sale John Dorris to Wm Draper for two negro females Venus & Senia proved by John Pavatt & John Ralph.
Demcy Moore v Isom Uzzell. Jury Wm Reed Montgy McConnell Jas Cary Wm Duty Chas Lewis Joshua Hadley Armstreat Stubblefield Saml Clenny Jas Vinson Jos Wallace
p.230 Isreal Barker Perrin Smith assess plfs damages to $65 & costs.
Allow John McMurtry coroner pro tem $23 for holding inquest on bodies of Becky Moody & John Murphey & for expenses for interment of sd John Murphey.
Deed Peter Luna to Zachariah Green 200 acres proved by John Hall and James Green.
Present Jno McMurtry Sion Hunt Saml McMurry. Allen Josey v Edward Douglass admr of Jno Josey decd. Jury Thos Scurry Jno Brown Peter F Jefferson Chas Lavender Wm Wallace Jno Goodrum Abraham Ellis Jno Glantan Jno King Isaac Graves John Edwards Perren Smith. Plf recovers agt dft damages $287.01 & costs to be levied on goods of sd deceased in the hands of the defendant to be administered.
p.231 Adam Crump v Hugh Wall. TAB. Jury Wm Reed Jas Carey Wm Duty Joshua Hadley Mat Armstrong Solomon Mitchell Silas Jernigan Jno Moore Whitehead Joyner Benjn P Howard Allen Josey Jos Wallace. Plf recovers agt dft damages $7.50 & costs.
John Moore v James Green & Zachariah Green. Debt. Plf obtained judgt agt dfts; dfts obtain appeal to Superior Court, Josephus H Conn & Jas Cryer securities.
Settlement by Stephen Cantrill & James Cryer esqrs with admrs of Abraham Hassell decd rendered into Court by sd commissioners.
Appt Thomas Groves constable in Capt Moores district, Allen Groves & Isaac Groves his securities, and took the oath of constable.
p.232 Present Jas Hart Isaac Baker Jas Cryer esqrs. Abraham Trigg v Patsey Trice. Jury Wm Reed Jas Carey Wm Duty Jno Harper Joshua Smith Chas Lewis Hugh Findley Jos Wallace Ephraim Cates Jas Vinson Allen Josey Richard Edwards. Plf recovers agt dft damages $60 and also his costs of suit in this behalf expended.
John Jones v James Steele. Covt. Jury[above]. Plf recovers agt dft damages $77.67½ and also his costs about his suit in this behalf expended.
p.233 John Spradlin v Jesse Sheen. Appl. Deposition of Francis Foster to be taken on behalf of the defendant.
Permit admr of Jesse Wells decd to sell negro girl Pegg and a mare.
Present Jas Hart Jas Cryer Saml McMurry. John Smith v Cornelius Thomas. Jury Joshua Hadley John Mitchell Wm Summers Thomas Scurry Jesse Skeen Edwd Bradley Ruffin Deloach Jno Hodge Jeremiah Stubblefield Robert Marshall John Bradley Willis Hall. Plf recovers agt dft damages $179.78 & his costs.
Inventory/estate of Watson Goostree an orphan was rendered on oath by Jesse Skeen guardian for sd orphan. Order of sale issued.
p.234 Isaac M Bledsoe v Henry Belote. Deposition of Deenah Steele of Mississippi Territory to be taken on behalf of defendant.

Wednesday June 21st 1809. Present Stephen Cantrill James Hart James C Wilson Will Trigg, esquires.

JUNE 1809

Appoint William Frazor overseer/road from Drakes Cr to Station Camp in place of James Frazor resigned.

Jurors to next court Bartholomew Stoval Thomas G Sanders Jno Carr Jno Lauderdale Richard Parker James Clendening James Sanders Edward Bradley Jno Thurmon Wm Allen Mourning Wynne Jas Rankins Alexander Graham Jno Irwin Jno Hamilton John Chapman David Orman Charles Lewis Richard Jones John Perry Kasper Mansker Jesse Joiner Jas Frazor Isaac Pierce William Buckener Isaac George Rhodam Rawlings Jas Brigance Sr John Cotton Nathan Edwards Solomon Barnes Edmund Bridgers Ruffin Deloach Elisha Bernard John Gwin Levi Hall

James White & Josephus H Conn v Patsey Trice extx of John Trice decd. Jury Shadrack Nye William Reed Thomas Scurry Jas Carey Jeremiah Stubblefield Joshua Hadley Charles Lewis William Duty Jesse Dawson Jas Vinson Joseph Wallace Thos Dement.
p.235 Plf recovers agt dft damages $112.74½ and their costs.

Present Stephen Cantrill James Hart Saml McMurry. John Shelby v Josephus H Conn. Jury Adam Crump Joshua Smith Garrison Stubblefield Armstreat Stubblefield James Cary Dempsey Moore Amos Webb John Mitchell Howell Ran Oran Faulk James Vinson Wallis Kirkpatrick cannot agree. Mistrial, continued to next court.

White & Josephus H Conn v Elisha Cheek. Appeal. Jury Joseph Wallace Robert Dobbins Jno Brown Henry Neill Thos Neill Thos Keife Loftain Cage Ephraim Cates Carson Dobbins Wm Duty Thomas Scurry William Reed. Plf recovers agt dft $14 & costs.
p.236 Commissioners for purchasing & laying off Gallatin: Shadrack Nye and James Wilson acting commrs, allowed $86.77 for services; James Wilson is further allowed $87.50 for further services.

Thursday June 22d 1809. Present Edward Douglass James Sanders Sion Hunt esqrs.

Inventory goods of Watson Goostree & Elizabeth Goostree orphans of Absolam Goostree decd rendered by Jesse Skien & Stephen Trible guardians for sd orphans; order of sale agreeably to law is issued; return an account to next term.

Whitehead Joiner v Isom Uzzell. Dft's bail surrender him; Josephus H Conn & Allen Groves securities.

Edward Cage v James Blackmore. Appl. Jury Wm Reed Wm Duty Thos Scurry Jas Cary Jas Vinson Geo Tarver Wm Ball Demsy Moore Thos Dement Jas Brown Jas Brigance
p.237 Jos Wallace. Plf recovers agt dft $40 debt & $1.13 damages and costs.

Micha Looney v John Tompkins. Appl. Plf not appearing, dft recovers agt plf his costs about his defence in this behalf expended.

Commrs ordered to settle with exrs of Hugh Elliott decd render settlement.

William & A Trigg recovered judgment before a magistrate agt Sterling Tinsley for $9.09 debt and $1.25 cost. Levied on 200 acres adjoining Nathan Edwards & others, the property of Sterling Tinsley; land to be sold to satisfy debt.

John & William Allen recovered judgment before a magistrate agt Sterling Tinsley for $19.30 debt & $1.25 cost. Levied[worded as above].
p.238 Motion of Josephus H Conn by his atty; deposition of James Brown of Bourboun County Kentucky to be read in evidence in suit John Shelby v sd Conn.

Hardy H Seawell orphan of John Seawell chose Sion Hunt for his guardian; bond $2000, Hardy Hunt and John Franklin his securities.

Appoint Sion Hunt guardian to Benjamin P Seawell orphan of John Seawell; bond $2000, Hardy Hunt and John Franklin his securities.

Samuel Wilson v Robert Robb & William Robb. Debt. Dfts not appearing make default. Plf recovers $100 debt and $33 damages and his costs of suit.

Deed Thomas Mastin to Daniel Smith 261[?] acres ackd.

JUNE 1809

p.239   Jonathan Peairs v John Payton & William Payton. Debt. Plf recovered judgment $127.20 & costs. Dfts obtain appeal to Superior Court, Josephus H Conn Michael Green & David Green their securities.

William J Harwell v William Payton & Jno Payton. Debt. Plf recovered judgment $525 & costs. Dfts obtain appeal to Superior Court; David Green Josephus H Conn & Michael Green their securities.

James Cage v Wm Payton. Debt. Plf recovered judgment $61.70 & costs. Dft obtained appeal, Josephus H Conn David Green Michael Green & Jno Payton securities.

Depositions of William Neely & James Morrison of Louisiana Territory to be taken behalf of Isaac M Bledsoe vs Henry Belote.

p.240   James Winchester v Roger Gibson. Debt. Dft not appearing, plf recovers agt dft $53.26½ debt $13 damages and also his costs of suit.

James Winchester & William Cage v Roger Gibson. Dft not appearing, plfs recover agt dft $270.80 balance of debt and also their costs of suit.

John Payton v James Hays. Covt. Dft not appearing, plf recovers his damages to be enquired of by a jury at next court.

Friday June 23d 1809. Present Edward Douglass James Sanders James C Wilson esqrs.

p.241   State v William Ogels. P.L. William Ogels ackd debt to State $100 and Redmond D Barry & John Orr severally $50 each to be levied of goods lands &c, condition Ogels makes personal appearance at next court.

James Hargroves in suit of Edmund Hogin v sd Hargroves obtains appeal, John Hargrove & John Mitchell his securities.

James Barry v John Cavitt. Motion of plf to enter up judgment agt dfts security for obtaining the certiorari, plf recovers agt Adam Crump the security afsd $37 the damages recovered in afsd suit, also costs of suit, execution agt sd security for damages & costs.

Court adjourns till Court in Course.   Edwd Douglass

Court of pleas & quarter Sessions, second Monday in September 1809. Present the worshipful James Winchester Matthew Alexander and Isaac Baker esquires.

Grand Jury   Charles Lewis foreman Nathan Edwards Kasper Kasper[sic] James Brigance Senr James Sanders Jesse Joiner Rhodam Rawlings David Orman Richard Jones John Lauderdale James Rankin Levi Hall Edward Bradley Isaac George.

Appoint Michael Green constable to attend Grand Jury this term.

Deed Robert White to William Duty 11¾ acres proved by Thomas G Sanders and John Harrell.

Deed Wyot Lindsey to David Tulloch ackd.

Deed John Boyd to Richard Jones 32 acres proved by Shadrack Nye and Vachel Stephens.

Deed/gift Robert Cartwright to James Rutherford 274 acres proved by Rhodam Rawlings and William Rogers.

p.243   Bill/sale Lawrence Yance to John Copeland two negroes Peter & Nancy ackd.

Deed Samuel Briley to John Hogan Junr ackd.

John Beardon v Thos Barret & Wm Snoddy. Appl. Appeal dismissed; papers in suit redelivered to plf and he recovers agt defendants his costs.

SEPTEMBER 1809

   Deed Robert Alexander by Lawson Henderson his atty in fact to heirs of Col Anthy Bledsoe proved by John Patterson one of the subscribing witnesses, 274 acres.
   Grant ltrs/admn on estate of Daniel Sanders decd to Jane Sanders relict of sd decd & James Sanders jointly; sd Jane & James took oath; bond $2000 with Hillery Malone & Edward Bradley security. Returned inventory/goods of sd deceased.
p.244 Robert B Mitchell v John Beetley. Stephen Pitt garnishee swears he had a note on James McKain for about $106 and that when collected, $36.62½ with interest was to be paid to dft Beetley, that garnishee had assumed payment of sd sum to Jacob Lewis on account of sd Beetley at least twelve months ago. Robert B Mitchell recovers agt sd garnishee $36.62½ and interest.
   Grant ltrs/admn on estate of James Hargrove decd to Amy Hargrove relict; bond $2000 with John Hargrove and John Mitchell her securities, and took oath.
   Will of James Clark decd proved by Andrew Blythe and Archa Skipper. Mary Clark, William C Anderson & Joseph Hodge, exrs named in sd will, qualified.
p.245 Allow Jacob Fuller for support of Jsu McClurg a minor pauper for three months previous the sum of $12.
   William Moody v Ashford Keen. TAB. Plf in proper person no further prosecutes; dft recovers agt plf his costs of defence.
   Appoint Vachel Stephens constable in Capt Waltons district for two years; bond $625 with Jesse Joyner and William Montgomery his securities, and took oath.
   White & Conn recovered three judgmts before a magistrate agt Robert Fleming; levied on 137 acres on Bledsoes creek. On motion of plfs by John C Hamilton their atty, land condemned for use of sd judgments & costs; order/sale issued.
p.246 Eaton Freeman recovered judgt before a magistrate agt Benoni Ferrell and Robert Fleming for $11.43 debt & 81¢ costs. Levied on 137 acres[worded as above].
   Alexander Youree recovered judgment before a magistrate agt Benoni Ferrel & Robt Fleming for $40 debt & 81¢ costs; levied on 137 acres[worded as above].
   Acct/sales goods of William McClellan decd rendered by John Sloan an admr.
   Appt Edwin Perry guardian to minor orphans George E Cater Britain Cater John Westley Cater; bond $160 with Henry Belote & Jeremiah Belote securities.
   Jury apptd to turn road Stamps to Johnsons; begin at Wm Knights, through
p.247 Edwd Sandersons plantation. Signed James Clendening Thos Parker Jno Morgan Robt Steel Wm Anderson.
   Jury apptd to turn road from where bridge was built near mouth of Bledsoes cr to head of Rock house fork of Bledsoes cr thence to state line near John Sloans render report. Signed John D Hanna Solomon Duty Joel Echols Senr James Clendening William Allen John Sloan Thomas Henson.
   Appt Isaac Bledsoe overseer/road from bridge on Bledsoes cr to state line near John Sloans between sd bridge and Greenfield; hands who work under overseers Thomas Parker Wm Edwards Robt Bruce & Henry Belote shall work under sd overseer until sd road be opened; then hands shall be assigned to their proper roads in proportion to the distance by Matthew Alexander esqr.
   Appt John D Hanna overseer/road bridge on Bledsoes cr to State line near John Sloans between Greenfield & sd Hanna's plantation; William Seawell to furnish sd overseer with list of hands.
   Appt Tarlton Boren overseer/road between John D Hanna's plantation & top of ridge; William Seawell to furnish sd overseer with list of hands.
   Appt Solomon Duty overseer/road from bridge on Bledsoes cr to state line near John Sloans; David Alseps & Wm Seawell to furnish sd overseer with list/hands.
p.248 Appt Thomas Hinson overseer/road[above] between David Alseps & state line;

SEPTEMBER 1809

William Seawell esqr to furnish a list of hands.

Tuesday September 12th 1809. Present James Winchester Mathew Alexander Isaac Baker.
Oliver B Hays, licensed attorney, is admitted to practice in this Court.
Ambrose Porter v Walter Loving. Debt. Dft not appearing makes default. Plf recovers agt dft $203.75 debt $8.12 damages and also his costs of suit.
Deed Stephen Winchester to William Winchester Senr undivided eighth part of 5000 acres proved by James Winchester & Lemuel T Turner.
p.249 Regulations to be observed in conducting Sumner County Court business. County business first day of term; state business on second Monday of term.
David Love v Thomas Keefe & Patsey Trice exrs of John Trice decd. Debt. Jury Wm Allen Jas Frazor Jno Irwin Jno Hamilton Thos G Sanders Alexr Graham Jas Lane Reuben Ross Thos Richey Jno Chapman Edmund Turpin Jas Brown assess plfs damages to $390.15; find other pleas except plea of fully admrd which they find in favour of Patsey Trice extx in favour of plf. Plf recovers agt dfts debt & damages amounting to $2124.15 to be levied of goods lands &c of Thomas Keefe and of testator when so much shall come to hands of extx Patsey Trice to be administered, and also his costs by him about his suit expended.
p.250 Will of Patrick Hamilton decd proved by William L Alexander & Thomas Donoho; John W Hamilton extr named therein appeared & took the oath of executor.
Appt Wm Montgomery & John McMurtry esqrs to settle the account of exrs of Thomas Perry decd.
Bill/sale Thomas D Martin to John Henley negro man Billy proved by Richd Scott & William A Covington.
Bill/sale Thomas Camp to William H Douglass negro woman Grace ackd.
Deed Thomas Donnell to James Williams 200 acres ackd.
Bill/sale David Kelough to Wilson Yandel negro girl Harriott proved by Richard G Gillespie and John G Thurmond.
Bill/sale Elisabeth Watson & Samuel Watson to Wilson Yandell negro girl Harriott proved by John Mills & Tandy P Duncan.
p.251 Edward Hogan v John Payton & William Payton. Debt. Jury Bartholomew Stoval John Thurmond Solomon Barnes Ruffin Deloach Mourning Wynn Joseph Bunton Geo Logan Henry Boyer Joseph McReynolds Robt Norrell David Stewart Jas Williams. Plf recovers agt dfts $157 and his costs of suit.
Inventory/goods of James Clark decd rendered by Wm Anderson & Joseph Hodge two of the executors of sd decd.
Bill/sale Moses Hardin & Edward Wormington to David Hardin negro man named Harry ackd.
Deed Robert McCorkle to Elizabeth McCorkle 140 acres ackd.
p.252 James Jackson & Washington Jackson v William Brooks. Debt. Jury Bartholomew Stoval John Thurmond Solomon Barnes Ruffin Deloach Mourning Wynn Joseph Bunton George Logan Henry Boyer Joseph McReynolds Robt Norrell David Stuart Jas Williams. Plfs recover agt dft debt & damages $72.99 & their costs of suit.
John Jones & Kennedy Owen v John B Johnson. Debt. Jury[above]. Plfs recover agt dft debt $75 & damages $7.74 and their costs of suit.
p.253 Appoint Edward Gwin and Joshua Rice esqrs to settle with administration of of estate of Richard Caveat decd.
Witnesses sworn touching validity of the will of Zacheus Wilson decd are of opinion that sd writing is not the will & testament of sd deceased.
John Henderson admr/will of Bennet Henderson decd v Obed Britt. Debt. Jury

SEPTEMBER 1809

James Frazor John Hamilton Alexr Graham Mourning Wynn Solomon Barnes Ruffin Deloach Barthw Stoval Thos G Sanders Jno Thurman John Irwin John Givin[Gwin?] Wm Allen. Plf recovers agt dft $140.01 & costs; may be discharged by payment of $128.84 & costs.
p.254   Robert Smith v Cornelius Thomas. Debt. Jury Green Williford John Shaver James Stra[binding] Peter Wynn Amos Gowen Simon Wherry John Edwards Joseph Motheral Wm McCaul Wm Robb William Bennett Noble Osburn. Plf recovers agt dft debt & damages $645.70 & also his costs of suit.

Thomas James v John Mitchell. Debt. Jury Green Williford Jno Shaver Jas Stratton Peter Wynn Amos Gowen Simeon Wherry Jno Edwards Jos Motheral Wm McCaul Wm Robb Wm Nosh[binding] Noble Osburn. Plf recovers agt dft debt & damages $76.32 and
p.255   also his costs about his suit in this behalf expended.

Grant ltrs/admn on estate of Zacheus Wilson decd to John Wilson & William Wilson, the widow of sd decd having relinquished her right to admn. Bond $8000 with Zacheus Wilson & James C Wilson their securities; took oath of admr.

Order admrs of Zacheus Wilson sell personal property agreeably to law.

Receipt from John Caveatt to Richard Caveatt Senr dated 13th Jany 1809 for $183.68 proved by Anthony Sharp a subscribing witness.

Bill/sale Alexander D Gorden to James Reed negro girl Patsey ackd.

Commrs apptd last term on petition of Wm Jones to divide a tract of 320 acres of estate of James Haw decd between petitioner & other heirs make report.
p.256   Samuel Elliott v Matthew Brown. Debt. Scire facias made known to Jackson Brown executor of Matthew Brown decd; suit is revived in name of Jackson Brown.

Wednesday Sept 18th 1809. Present James Winchester Matthew Alexander Isaac Baker.
John Cage v Richard Ball. Debt. Dft relinquishes his plea. Plf recovers agt dft debt & damages $60.46½ and also his costs about his suit expended.

John C Hamilton v William Melton & John Robertson. Debt. Jury Thomas G Sanders Mourning Winn Ruffin Deloach Jno Irwin Andrew Hoover Matthew Anderson James
p.259   McKain James Frazor Alexr Graham Solomon Barnes Joshua Smith John Thurmon. Plf recovers against defendant debt & damages $103 & costs.

Andrew Goff v Henry Lyon. Debt. Dft relinquishes his plea. Plf recovers agt dft debt & damages $60.77 and also his costs about his suit expended.

William Lytle Junr v James Vinson. Debt. Dft relinquishes his pleas. Plf
p.258   recovers agt dft debt & damages $67.14½ and his costs of suit.

James Hood v Edmond J Bailey. Debt. Jury Thomas G Sanders Mourning Wynn Ruffin Deloach John Irwin Andrew Hoover Matthew Anderson James McKain James Frazor Alexr Graham Solomon Barnes Joshua Smith John Thurmon. Plf recovers agt dft debt & damages $101.07 and also his costs about his suit expended.

Thomas Richey v Edmund Turpin. Case. Parties in proper person; plf no further prosecutes; dft pays costs.
p.259   Thomas Richey v David Stuart. Case. Edmund Turpin for the dft; plf no further prosecutes on costs being paid by dft.

Henry Belote v Catey Bledsoe. Debt. Dft relinquishes her plea. Plf recovers agt dft debt & damages $79.93 & also his costs about his suit expended.

Anne Logan v Andrew Allison. Debt. Dft relinquishes his pleas. Plf re-
p.260   covers agt dft debt & damages $132.22½ and also her costs of suit.

John Shelby v Loftain Cage. Debt. Dft relinquishes his pleas. Plf recovers agt dft debt & damages $156.10 and also his costs in this behalf expended.

Present Jas Winchester Mat Alexander Saml McMurry. James Cage v Robert B Mitchell. Debt. Jury[above]. Plf recovers agt dft debt & damages $324.32 & costs.

49

SEPTEMBER 1809

p.261 James Cage v Robert B Mitchell. Debt. Jury Thomas G Sanders Mourning Wynn Ruffin Deloach John Irwin Andrew Hoover Matthew Anderson James McKain James Frazor Alexander Graham Solomon Barnes Joshua Smith John Thurmon. Plaintiff recovers agt defendant his debt and damages $114.91 and also his costs of suit.

p.262 Thomas Wilson v Charles Elliott. Debt. Dft relinquishes his pleas. Plf recovers agt dft debt & damages $161.25 & also his costs.

Bill/sale Griffith W Rutherford to Jno Rutherford negro girl Lillane ackd.

John Bowles v William Douglass. Debt. Jury[above]. Plf recovers agt dft
p.263 debt & damages $79.53½ and also his costs.

Power/atty Reuben Searcy to his son Reuben Searcy and Francis Richardson of Clark County Kentucky 9 Sep 1809 proved by Leonard Ferrell.

Orphan Enos Benthall apprenticed to William McCall to learn art & mystery of Hatting.

Power/atty James Mebane William Mebane Robert Mebane & John Mabane(sic) to Thomas Anderson to transact land business in Tennessee dated 11 Mar 1808; having been executed in Orange County North Carolina, bearing seal of sd Court.

Bill/sale Drury Walton to Wilson Yandell negro man George proved by Robert Sanders.

Jury apptd to review road to James Brackens, the piece between Will Triggs
p.264 meadow & Gallatin report: best way is strait line from Triggs meadow by SE corner of Jas Wilsons field to strike great road from Bledsoes lick near sd Wilsons house. Signed Thomas Donnell John Turner James Lane Wm B[binding] Joseph Motherall.

Jury apptd on petition of Jeremiah Murphy to alter road from Gallatin over ridge at Jas Johnsons report; signed Jas McMurry Jas Johnson Wm Bunton Jno Starns Joseph Bunton Fergus George McGuire.

Jury apptd on petition of John Denning to alter road; leave the old road at lane running with Henry Servers line to near Drakes Creek, then to corner of Dennings fence intersecting the old road at the sd ford. Signed Isaac Bracken Benjamin Granger James Roney Richard Cope Micajah House.

Thursday September 14th 1809. Present James Douglass James Cryer Edward Sanders.

John Morris & Thos Dennington v Daniel Jones. Dft withdraws demurrer. Plfs
p.265 recovers agt dft $112.22½ damages and also their costs.

Deed Allen Purvis to John McCann 47 acres ackd.

William T Lewis v Jesse Wilkerson. Jury John Thurmond Solomon Barnes James Frazor John Irwin William Allen Alexander Graham John Hamilton John Rutherford Mourning Wynn Bartholomew Stoval Ruffin Deloach Thomas G Sanders. Plf recovers agt dft damages $42 and also his costs about his suit expended.
p.266 Henry Belote v Thomas F[T?] Rawlings. Plf no further prosecutes. Dft recovers agt plf his costs of defence in this behalf expended.

Friday September 15th 1809. Present Matthew Alexander James C Wilson Isaac Baker.

Account/sales goods of Elias Morrison decd rendered by James Stewart extr.

David Love v John Payton Senr. Jury[above except James Vinson for James Frazor. Plaintiff recovers against defendant damages $120 & costs.
p.267 Zachariah Green proved right to stray steer taken up by John C Hamilton.

Nancy Daniel orphan of Roger Daniel decd chose William Douglass for her guardian; bond $300 with Zachariah Green and James McKain securities.

Tapley P Daniel orphan of Roger Daniel [worded as above]

Nicholas Boyce v John B Johnson. Covt. Nicholas Boyce died since commence-

SEPTEMBER 1809

ment of this suit; suit revived in name of admrs, to wit Nancy Boyce & Archibald Marlin admrs of goods of Nicholas Boyce decd v John B Johnson.
p.268   Present Jas Douglass James Cryer Jas C Wilson. Nancy Boyce admx & Archibald Marlin admr/goods of Nicholas Boyce decd v John B Johnson. Jury Wm Dodson Jesse Skeen Zachariah Green Wm Cannon Henry Vinson Demcy Moore Thomas Keefe John Bridgers Isaac Forrest William Trice Jas Frazor Nathan Boon. Plf recovers agt dft damages $168.86 & costs about their suit in this behalf expended.

Report/jury to view road Gallatin to mouth of Station Camp, also from Gallatin to mouth of Elliotts branch certify road to mouth of Elliotts branch is nearest & best. Signed Isaac Lane Wm Edwards Charles Elliott Jno Withers Jas Adam.

Saturday September 16th 1809. Present James Winchester James Cryer Edward Sanders.
p.269   John Hunt v Loftain Cage. Sci fa. Dft exhibited affidavit stating he was never summoned as a witness. Dft released from fine.

George House v Thomas Richey. Covt. Jury John Thurmond Solomon Barnes Jas Frazor Wm Allen Alexr Graham John Hamilton John Jones Wm Dodson Jas Ferrell Jesse Skeen Barthw Stovall Ruffin Deloach. Plf recovers agt dft damages $228.20 & costs.

William Dodson v Clement McDaniel. Appeal. Jury[above except Thos Scurry
p.270   for Wm Dodson]. Plf recovers agt dft damages $7.02½, also his costs.

Monday September 18th 1809. Present Jas Winchester Jas C Wilson Matthew Alexander.
Deed Thomas White to Benoni Ferrell 137 acres proved by Edward Cage and Henry Mitchell.

Appoint Thomas Scurry overseer/road Station Camp to James Wilson Esqr.

State v Peter F Jefferson. TAB. Jury John Thurmond Solomon Barnes Wm Allen Jno Irwin Alexr Graham John Hamilton Bartholomew Stoval John Shaver James Frazor Henry Newby Ruffin Deloach Mourning Wynn find dft not guilty. Defendant discharged.
p.271   State v James Claxton. Peace bond. James Blakemore & John Shaver securities for dft to keep peace particularly towards Alexander McMillan.

Deed Isaac Bledsoe Abraham Bledsoe & Henry Bledsoe to Henry Steele 183 acres acknowledged in open court by the bargainers.

State v William Ogels. P.L. Appearance bond of Elijah Anthony to give evidence against sd Ogels.

Justice who took recognizance of Jacob Young failed to return it; Jacob Young by his atty is released on his paying costs of this motion.
p.272   State v Archibald Donoho. Gambling. Jury James Wilson Ashley Stanfield George Stovall Benjn Murrow John Swancy James Blakemore Robert Nowell George Redin Thomas Keefe Jeremiah Claxton Jonathan Badgett Hillary Malone find dft guilty. Dft by Redmond D Barry moves in arrest of judgment; overruled. Fined $5 & costs.

Present Edward Douglass James Winchester Benjamin Rawlings James Douglass James Cryer James Hart Thomas Blackmore James C Wilson Samuel McMurry Matthew Alexander Thomas Murry William Montgomery Joshua Rice Edward Gwin esquires.

Bill/sale William Rice constable to James Gun negro boy Tom ackd.

Bill/sale William Rice constable to William Bracken negro boy Isaac ackd.

Bill/sale William Rice constable to Jane Searcy negro woman Dilcey and negro girl child named Sarah ackd.
p.273   Deed John Cathey & Alexander Cathey to John Bressee 91 acres ackd.

Motion of James Sanders one/admrs of estate of Daniel Sanders decd, allow sale of personal estate of sd decd except negroes; return account to next court.

Amount/sales goods of Wm Bracken decd rendered by James Bracken admr.

SEPTEMBER 1809

Deed John Cathey & Alexr Cathey to Nathaniel Irwin 73 acres ackd.

Appt John Rowland overseer/road from Harts lane to county line in place of Wilson Yandell resigned; Charles Donoho & James Hart to furnish list of hands.

Allow George D Blackmore $180 for furnishing county with tobacco scales chain beam & fifteen hundred pounds weights for use of inspection at Cairo.

Allow George D Blackmore $180 for furnishing county with tobacco scales chains beam & fifteen hundred pounds weights.

p.274   Present James Douglass Jas C Wilson Saml McMurry esqr. Bright Herring v William Surry. Jury John Thurmond Solomon Barnes Wm Allen Jas Frazor Jesse Skeen Jno Irwin Jno Hamilton Alexr Graham Geo Stovall Mourning Wynn Ruffin Deloach Barthw Stovall. Plf recovers agt dft damages $500 and also his costs of suit.

Order tobacco scales &c furnished by George D Blakemore be for use of the tobacco inspection at the town of Cairo.

Wm & Jno Payton v Matthew Anderson. Motion of plf John Payton. Depositions of John Payton & John Patton to be taken; also for plaintiff, the deposition of Yelverton Payton of Kentucky to be taken.

Deed James Morrison to Thomas Leroy Harris Mary Gibson Harris heirs of Sarah Caroline Simpson decd Frances Houston Robertson, Araminta Juliet Orr, Martha Spear Harris & Elisabeth Harriot Harris heirs of Robert Harris decd for 222½ acres was proved by John White.

p.275   John Spradlin v Jesse Skeen[Sheen?]. Appeal. Jury John Thurmond Solomon Barnes Wm Allen Jas Frazor Jno Irwin Alexr Graham Jno Hamilton Loftain Cage Barthw Stovall Allen Purvis Mourning Wynn Ruffin Deloach find for dft; cause continued till next court for a new trial.

State v John Payton Junr. TAB. Dfts appearance bond, Wm Payton & David Green his securities.

State v William Payton. TAB. Dfts appearance bond, John Payton & David Green his securities.

p.276   State v William Ball. TAB. Dft saith he is guilty of trespass assault & battery; fined $5 and pay costs of prosecution.

State v William Ogels. P.L. Dfts appearance bond, Redmond D Barry & John Orr his securities.

Appt Francis Youree a constable in Capt Coo[binding] company for two years, George D Blackmore & John Hamilton his securities, and took oath.

Deed William Montgomery to Robert Dobbins, sd Montgomery's undivided right to 480 acres ackd.

p.277   Appt Tandy P Duncan inspector of tobacco at Harts ferry, John Mills and James Hart his securities, and took oath.

Appt Robert Meckelberry an inspector of tobacco at Harts ferry, James Hart & James Sanders his securities, and took oath.

George D Blackmore apptd inspector of tobacco at Cairo, Alexander Graham & John Bearden securities, and took oath.

Hillery Malone appointed an inspector of tobacco at Cairo, John Irwin and Terisha Stovall his securities, and took oath.

Order James Hart entitled to demand pay for storage at his warehouse at Harts landing, sd warehouse is sufficient for safe keeping of tobacco.

Tuesday September 19th. Present Edwd Douglass John McMurtry Saml McMurry esqrs.
p.278   Henry Lyon v Porter Allen. Appeal. Jury Mourning Wynn James Frazor John Thurmond Alexr Graham Ruffin Deloach Jno Irwin Wm Allen Jno Hamilton Solomon Barnes

SEPTEMBER 1809

William Kirkpatrick Wallace Kirkpatrick Silas Jurnigan. Plf recovers agt dft debt & damages $14.62½ and also his costs about his suit in this behalf expended.

Bazel Brown witness for James McKain v Allen Purvis not appearing, fined $125 unless sufficient cause of his disability to attend be shown at next court.

John Moore witness for James McKain v Allen Purvis not appearing is fined $125 unless sufficient cause of his disability to attend be shown at next court.

p.279   Jas McKain v Allen Purvis. Deposition of Bazel Brown & Jno Moore of Christian County Kentucky to be taken in behalf of the plaintiff.

John Jones & Lawrence Owen v James Steele. Jury Mourning Wynn James Frazor Jno Thurmond Alexr Graham Ruffin Deloach John Irwin Wm Allen John Hamilton Solomon Barnes Wm Kirkpatrick Wallace Kirkpatrick Silas Jernigan. Plfs recover against dft damages $19.31 and also their costs about their suit expended.

John Jones & Co v James Steele. Jury[above]. Plf recovers agt dft damages
p.280 $68.59½ and also their costs about their suit expended.

Deed Thomas Stubblefield to Edward Bradley 150 acres proved by Jeremiah Stubblefield & Robert Stubblefield.

William Trigg & Abraham Trigg v James Campbell. Jury[above]. Plfs recover agt dft damages $94.27½ besides their costs.
p.281   John Jones & Laurence Owen v George D Blackmore & Zacheus Wilson exrs of Richard Taylor decd. Jury[above]. Plfs recover agt dfts damages $137.53½ & costs.

Present Edwd Douglass James Sanders James Cryer Saml McMurry esqrs. John Bridgers v Robert Moore. Jury John Thurmond Solomon Barnes John Irwin Jas Frazor Alexr Graham John Hamilton Mourning Wynn Ruffin Deloach Barthw Stovall Wm Boyce John Spradling Robt Stubblefield find dft guilty, assess plfs damages $5. Dfts atty
p.282   moves for new trial; motion continued for argument till next court.

James Ferrell v Anthony Sharp & Silas Jernigan. Deposition of John J Henry to be taken in behalf of Anthony Sharp.

Jurors to next court: John Morgan William Beard Henry Bledsoe John Beardon William Wherry John Rutherford Robert Patton Thomas Anderson Abraham Trigg William Kirkpatrick John Pankey Joseph Hodge William Anderson (Capt) William Gwin Jr Wilson Yandell Robert Hanes James Sanders Cornelius Herndon George Logan James Scot Richard Bradley Norman Pike Benjamin Granger William Draper Jesse Joiner James Kirkpatrick Edmund Bridger David Orr Elmore Harris Richard T Bradley Griswold Latimer Reuben Douglass Peter Looney Joshua Hadley William Bruce Lawrence Whitsitt.

Appt Thomas Keefe overseer/road from east fork Station Camp creek to fork above Indian Creek at plantation of the late Richard Taylor.

Wednesday September 20th 1809. Present Edward Douglass Jas Sanders Jas Cryer esqrs.
p.283   Appt John Bentley overseer/road from Cairo to near Croft mills in place of Thomas Cocke resigned.

John Moore & wife v William Hall. Deposition of Nathaniel Williams & others to be taken in behalf of the defendant.

Deed James Trousdale Senr to John Shelby one acre 18 poles 6 tenths ackd.

White & Jos H Conn v Allen Purvis. Jury Wm Allen Alexr Graham Mourning Wynn Jno Hamilton Jno Irwin Jas Frazor Jno Thurmond Barthw Stovall Ruffin Deloach Adam Crump Jno Fillingin Wm Boyer. Plfs recover agt dft damages $23.30 & costs.
p.284   Edward Bradley v Armstreat Stubblefield. Jury[above except Solomon Barnes for Barthw Stovall]. Plf recovers agt dft debt & damages $48.97½ and also costs.

Deed John Young to Jacob Young 272 acres proved by John Rogers & Littleton Abernathy.

SEPTEMBER 1809

  Order Jas Winchester & Jas Douglass esqrs settle accounts of admr of estate of Baloss House decd and report to next court.
  Isaac Lain v John & Robert Allen. Appeal. Jury Wm Ball Josephus H Conn Jno Jones Jas S Wilson Thos Keefe Ephraim Cates Jas McMurry John Spradling Jno B Trousdale Joseph Alley Isaac Forrest Henry Vinson. Dft recovers agt plf his costs.
  Bill/sale Drury Walton to Wilson Yandell for a negro man George proved by William Parr.
p.285 Edward Bradley v Armstreat Stubblefield. Jury Wm Allen Alexr Graham Mourning Wynn Jno Hamilton Jno Irwin Jas Frazor Jno Thurmond Solomon Barnes Ruffin Deloach Adam Crump Jno Fellengin William Boyce find for plf $45 debt $3.82½ damages. Also his costs about his suit in this behalf expended.
  Edward Bradley v Armstreat Stubblefield. Jury[above]. Plf recovers agt dft debt & damages $29.29 and also his costs about his suit expended.
p.286 Jurors to next Superior Court Samuel McMurry Robert Ellis William Bunton Joseph Robb Benjamin Rawlings Edward Douglass Alexander Gwin James Douglass.

Thursday September 21st 1809. Present Edwd Douglass John McMurtry Samuel McMurry.
  James L Armstrong v Jno Mitchell. Appeal. Jury Jno Thurmond Solomon Barnes Jas Frazor Wm Allen Jno Irwin Edwd Cage Alexr Graham Jno Hamilton Lewis Crane Ruffin Deloach Mourning Wynn Barthw Stovall. Plaintiff recovers against defendant $43 damages assessed and also his costs.
  John Dickerson v William Parr. Matters in difference refered to determination of James Winchester & George Keesee, Charles Donoho an umpire if necessary.
p.287 Orphan Timothy Moore bound apprentice to George Hall to learn art & mystery of Farming; Edward Douglass chairman and sd George Hall entered bond.
  Allow George Blackmore $7.50 for half appraisement of a stray mare taken up & posted by William Read.
  Joel Echols relinquished his right to keep a ferry on Cumberland River half mile below Bledsoes Creek which ferry was established by this Court Jan 1799.
  John Smith v Cornelius Thomas. Jury Jno Thurmond Solomon Barnes Jas Frazor Jno Irwin Wm Allen Alexr Graham John Hamilton Austin Carpenter John Bridgers Hugh Wall Ruffin Deloach Barthw Stovall. Plf recovers agt dft damages $156 & his costs.
p.288 Redmond D Barry v Patsey Trice executrix of John Trice decd. Continued. Defendant to pay costs accruing at this term.
  John Peyton v James Hays. Jury[above]. Plf recovers agt dft damages by breach of covenant $4592.50 besides his costs.
  Jurors appointed to view road from Smith County near head of Long creek to Kentucky line near Mr Russells report that they marked road from Smith County near Kerbys powder mill to Kentucky line near Russells it being 7 or 8 miles; request Henry Butler oversee half way to Smith county & Wm Bowman oversee from thence to Smith county line. Signed John Sulivant James Cowden George Anderson Edward Hogan Robert Simpson John Sloan.
p.289 Appt Henry Butler overseer of road lately laid off from Kentucky line to a point that will divide the same into equal distances; John Barr to furnish sd overseer with a list of hands.
  Appt William Bowman overseer of half the distance of the road [above] and John Barr esqr to furnish sd overseer with a list of hands.

Friday morning September 22d 1809. Present Edward Douglass James Sanders Jas Cryer.
  John Evans v Joshua Hadley. Debt. Death of plf being suggested, order suit

SEPTEMBER 1809

revived in names of Zachariah Stull & William Williams executors of the will of sd plaintiff.

James Stuard v Archibald Marlin garnishee of Farmer. James Stuard recovers agt Archibald Marlin garnisheee of Thomas Farmer $60.44½, being sum agreeable to garnishment remaining in hands of sd garnishee which he as sheriff collected on a writ from this court at instance of sd Farmer against John Gwin and that sd Stuard also recover agt sd Marlin the costs of this motion.

p.290 James Trousdale v John & Robt Allen. Appeal. Plf by Mattw Neal his atty in fact. Plf no further prosecutes his suit and agrees to pay half costs, John Allen agreeing to pay the other half costs.

Bill/sale William Snelling to William H Douglass negro girl Susannah ackd.

Authorise Clerk/Court to issue commission in any suit pending in this Court on application of either parties provided clerk shall endorse on commission the time necessary to be given as notice to adverse party of time & place of taking depositions of witnesses named in sd commissions.

Appt Web Bloodworth overseer/road from Capt Gillespies to Gallatin in place of Matthew Anderson resigned.

Motion of Greenberry Orr one of executors of Robert Harris decd, order Jas Winchester & Matthew Alexander esqrs examine & settle accounts of administration.

Lauchlan McLean v Walter Leake admr/estate of Lain Jones decd. Debt. Dft not appearing, plf recovers agt dft $200 debt, $127 damages & his costs, of goods
p.291 of sd deceased, if he hath not so much, to be levied of goods of sd deft.

John Cage v Barney Stewart. Debt. Dft not appearing, plf recovers $677.20 debt & $3.04 damages & costs of suit.

On petition of Thomas Barrott, order writs of certiorari & supersideas issue in behalf sd Barrott to call up judgment obtained by John Beardon agt sd Barrott for $31.50 & costs; sd Barrott to give bond & security.

Henry Belote released from forfeiture by incurred by reason of failing to attend as witness in cause State v Thomas T Rawlings on his paying costs.

William Granger v Edwd Gwin & Edmd Keen. Sci fa. Plf by John C Hamilton. Plf has execution agt dfts for $12.67. Plf also recovers agt dfts his costs/suit.
p.292 John Josey v Joseph Scobey. Sci fa. Plf granted execution agt goods of dft for $8.37½ the costs in the writ and also his costs expended in suing.

Bright Herring v William Leury[Scurry?]. Property whereon attachment was levied is condemned; order of sale issues to satisfy judgment.

Saturday September 23d 1809. Present Edwd Douglass Jas Douglass Will Trigg esqrs.

Supplementary inventory/goods of Baliss House decd rendered by Allen Purvis one of the executors of sd deceased.

Jonathan Trousdale v John Brigance. Sci fa. Plf not appearing, nonsuit, and dft recovers agt plf his costs about his defence expended.

Nancy Boyce v Allen Purvis. Judgment by default set aside and dft allowed to pleas to issue.

Court adjourned till Court in Course.   Edwd Douglass

p.293 At a Court of Pleas & Quarter sessions begun & held on second Monday in

DECEMBER 1809

December 1809. Present James Winchester Matthew Alexander John McMurtry.
Grand jurors William Beard foreman Wm Wherry Richd F Bradley Abram Trigg Thos Anderson Jas Kirkpatrick Wm Gwin Junr David Orr Reuben Douglass George Logan Richard Bradley Edmund Bridgers John Pankey William Bruce.
William Rice apptd to attend the grand jury for the present term.
Norman Peak & Benjamin Granger jurors excused from further attendance.
Wilson Yandell juror excused on ground of his being a practitioner of physic.
Deed John Morgan to James Johnson for 275 acres proved by William Hall & William Barr.
Deed John Morgan to Richard Holloway 200[?] acres proved by Thomas McGuire & John [name obliterated].
Deed Isaac Bledsoe Abraham Bledsoe & Henry Bledsoe to Matthew Wilson 137 acres ackd.
p.294 Deed/gift Stephen Trible to Polly Trible Susanna Trible Milley Trible & Lucinda Trible horses cattle household furniture ackd.
Deed Ambrose Porter to Nicholas Stone 10 acres ackd.
Deed Isom Uzzell to Charles Harford 15½ acres proved by James Herring & Alexander Herring.
William Payton v Richard Pendergrass, covenant, Redmond D Barry one of the bail for dft surrenders him; defendant ordered into custody of sheriff.
Account/sales goods of Ruth Ozbrooks decd rendered by Wm Granger executor.
Assignment of plat & certificate of survey for 100 acres from Moses Gains to William Seawell ackd in open court by sd Moses Gains.
p.295 Deed Corban Hall to William Barker 200 acres proved by Archer McKinney & Josia Barker.
John & Robert Allen obtained judgment before a magistrate agt Nathaniel Dickerson for $23.19 debt & .50 costs. Lemuel Stubblefield levied on 119 acres on Cumberland River in Bradleys bent. Twenty acres of afsd tract condemned for use of sd judgment; order of sale issued to sherriff to sell same.
John Doe lessee of Stephen Winchester v William Ring. Ejectment. Motion of William Ring the tenant in possession; order Thomas Murray esqr survey sd premises.
Orphan William Wilson Osbrooks age thirteen the 6th inst bound apprentice to Daniel Parker until age twenty one; Parker & chairman entered indentures.
p.296 Nancy Osbrooks orphan age eleven in March 1810 bound unto James Gambling until age eighteen.
Account/sales of personal estate of Zacheus Wilson decd rendered by John Wilson one of the administrators of said estate.
Affidavit of John Morris proving property of a bay horse taken up & posted with the ranger by Moses Cummins to be in Anderson Cheatham; county trustee to pay Cheatham half value of sd estray.
Deed Isaac Bledsoe Abraham Bledsoe Henry Bledsoe to Doctor John Mitchell 150½ acres ackd.

Tuesday December 12th 1809. Present Jas Winchester John McMurtry John Barr esqrs.
Licence Nancy Pankey to keep ordinary at her house in Gallatin, John Stuart & Thomas Scurry her securities.
p.297 Connelly Findley surviving partner of the firm of McNutt & Findley v John Spooner. Debt. Jury Henry Bledsoe Wm Anderson Jno Rutherford Robt Patton Wm Kirkpatrick Cornelius Herndon Jesse Joiner Elmore Harris Abner Gilmore John Mitchell

DECEMBER 1809

John Moore Silas Jernigan. Plf recovers agt dft balance of debt $68.96 & his costs.
James Rankin records his stock mark.
Zachariah Stull & William Williams exrs of John Evans decd v Joshua Hadley.
Debt. Jury Wm Hale Jonathan Badgett Elijah Simpson John Jones John D Bradley Wm
Barr David Beard Robt Campbell Fergus Hall John Wilson Thomas White Robert Hayns.
p.298   Plf recovers agt dft debt & damages $2092.65½ & also their costs.
George Keesee v John Turner & John Goodrum. Debt. Jury[above]. Plf recovers
agt dfts debt & damages $529.64 & also his costs of suit.
p.299   Ephraim Drake v William Ford. Debt. Jury[above]. Plf recovers agt dft debt
& damages $72.25 & also his costs of suit.
John Page v James Blackmore and Thomas Blackmore. Debt. Jury[above]. Plf
p.300   recovers agt dft debt & damages $74.12½ and also his costs of suit.
Ann Greer[Green?] v John Payton & William Payton. Debt. Jury Griswold Latimer Cornelius Herndon Robt Dobbins Chas Lavender Jno D Bradley Wm Kirkpatrick Jesse
Joiner Jno Rutherford Elmore Harris Robt Patton Wm Anderson Wm Wiley. Plf recovers
agt dfts debt & damages $204.67 & also costs of suit.
Allow Jacob Fuller out of the poor tax $12 for keeping a poor orphan child
Jsu McClung three months previous to this date 12 Decr 1809.
p.301   James Ford v John Lafferty. Debt. Jury[above]. Plf recovers agt dft debt &
damages $98.92 and also his costs of suit.
Elihu S Hall & Washington Hall v William Gwin. Debt. Jury[above]. Plaintiff
p.303[Note that pages are misnumbered. There is no page 302].   recovers agt dft
debt & damages $196.30 & also their costs of suit.
Matthew Cartwright v Bennett H Henderson acting exr of Wm Henderson decd.
Debt. Jury John Edwards Isaac Street John Barr Thos Neel Elijah Anthony Wm McCall
David Orman Alexr Gwin Thos Ferrell Jno Chapman Jno Hodge Nicholas Stone. Plf
recovers agt dft debt & damages $530.44 & also his costs of suit.
William Lytle Junr v Edward Bradley. Debt. Jury[above]. Plaintiff recovers
p.304   agt dft debt & damages $136.25 and also his costs of suit.
David Love v John Coopper. Debt. Jury[above]. Plf recovers agt dft debt &
samages $280.18 and also his costs about his suit expended.
Grant ltrs/admn on estate of Susanna Moss decd to Herbert Avent, bond
$10,000 with Robert Patton & Elisha Green his securities; Herbert took oath/admr.
Appt Abraham Ellis constable in Capt Prestons district for two years; Ellis
took oaths, Wm Cage & Wm Gillespie his securities.
p.305   William Lytle Junr v Edward Gwin. Debt. Jury[above]. Plaintiff recovers agt
defendant his debt & damages $63.28 and also his costs.
License John Johnson to keep tavern at his dwelling in Sumner, Alexander
Graham his security.
Deed Owen Campbell to John Stuart 4 acres proved by Isaac Lane & Robert B
Mitchell.
Deed Cornelius Thomas to Reuben B Patterson two tracts, one 200 of acres,
the other of 169 acres proved by Henry Bradford and John Payton Junr.
Bill/sale Cornelius Thomas to Reuben B Patteson negros household furniture
p.306   livestock proved by Henry Bradford & John Payton Junr.
Robert Shaw recovered judgmt agt Alexr Fleming before a magistrate. Levied
on 100 acres property of Alexr Fleming lying on Arringtons fork of Red River; order
sheriff to sell same to satisfy sd judgment and all costs.
Appt John White overseer/road Stamps mill to McMons on Deshas Creek in
place of Andrew Blythe resigned.

DECEMBER 1809

Inventory/estate of Matthew Brown decd rendered by Jackson Brown executor.
Supplementary amount/sales goods of George Duty decd rendered by George Gillespie one of the administrators of sd deceased.
Order Wm Trigg esq furnish Thomas Scurry overseer/road with a list/hands.
Henry Bledsoe records his stock mark.
William Lytle Jr v Edwd Gwin. Debt. Jury Jno Edwards Isaac Street John Barr Thomas Neel Elijah Anthony Wm McCall David Orman Alexr Gwin Thos Ferrell John Chapman Jno Hodge Nichs Stone. Plf recovers agt dft debt & damages $105.45 & his costs.

p.307   Wednesday Dec 13th 1809. Present Jas Winchester William Trigg Jas C Wilson.
Samuel K Blythe & Co v Patton Anderson. Debt. Jury John Moore Wm Anderson Jesse Joiner Cornelius Herndon Henry Bledsoe Thomas Ferrell Green Williford Leonard Ferrell John Chapman Robert Patton John Rutherford Elmore Harris. Plfs recover agt dft debt & damages $125.75 and also their costs about their suit expended.

Samuel K Blythe & Co v Patton Anderson. Debt. Jury[above]. Plfs recover agt
p.308   defendant debt $120 and their costs of suit.
Robert Strother assignee v Jno Mitchel. Debt. Jury[above]. Plf recovers agt dft debt & damages $93.52½ and also his costs of suit.
John Lafferty v Robert Rayleigh. Covt. Jury[above except Wm Kirkpatrick for John Chapman] find for defendant. Dft recovers against plf his costs of defence.
p.309   Deed John C Hamilton to Will Trigg Junr & Abram Trigg one acre proved by Orran Faulk & Robert M Boyers.
Deed William Wallace to Will Trigg Jr & Abram Trigg 30½ acres proved by Orran Faulk & Robert M Boyers.
Present Jas Winchester Jas C Wilson Isaac Baker esqrs. William Edwards v James Cage & Samuel P Black. Jury Wm Alonson Jacob Thompson Matthew Armstrong Dawson Wood Silas Jernigan Saml Alley John Stewart Ephraim Cates Joseph Campbell Henry Bledsoe Jesse Joiner Wm Kirkpatrick. Mistrial. New trial at next court.
p.310   Will of William Kennedy decd proved by John Tinnen Lemuel Tinnen & Shadrack Nye. Armstrong W Kennedy & John Perry[Parry?] executors took the oath.
Deed William Haughton to Thomas Donnell 100 acres ackd.
Ltrs/admn on estate of Daniel Stuart decd granted to Andrew Buckham who took oath, bond $2000, James & Bennett H Henderson his securities.
Appt John D Bradley constable in Capt Bradleys district for two years, Richard T Bradley & Redmond D Barry his securities, and took the oaths.
Authorise executors of Alexander Anderson decd to sell negro man to meet the debts of sd estate; return account of sale to next court.
Will Trigg Jr Esqr records his stock mark.
p.311   Mistake was made by the justice returning list/taxable property Wm Cages dist by omitting eight slaves and one free poll; release Wm Cage from double tax.
Affidavit of John Garrison states cow & steer posted with the ranger by Eusebius Stone were property of sd Garrison.

Thursday Decr 14th 1809. Present Jas C Wilson Will Trigg Jr Isaac Baker esqrs.
Andrew Hoover v Vachel Stephens. Trespass. Jury James Ferrell John Rutherford Cornelius Herndon Elmore Harris Robt Patton Wm Anderson Griswold Latimer Saml Holloway Joshua Smith William Lauderdale Peter F Jefferson Abner Gilmore. Plf recovers against defendant his damages $13 and his cost.
p.312   Appoint George Cooper constable in Captain McMurrys district for two years, Wm Bunton & Samuel McMurry securities, and took the oath for qualification.

58

DECEMBER 1809

Edmund Gwin produced copy of notice to take deposition of [blank] in suit White & Jos H Conn v John Withers; made oath he delivered to Jno Withers on 8 November last the original notice; proof is sufficient to entitle plaintiffs to right of reading sd deposition on trial of sd suit.

Edmund Green produced copy of notice to John Withers requiring Withers to produce an acct furnished him by White & Jos H Conn to be exhibited in the trial of suit wherein sd White & Jos H Conn are plfs vs sd Withers which copy notice was sworn by sd Green & filed with papers of the suit.

Friday Decr 15th 1809. Present James Cryer Will Trigg Edward Sanders esquires.

John Payton v Matthew Anderson. Jury Griswold Latimer Leonard Ferrell Joshua Smith William Anderson Ephraim Cates Silas Jernigan Elmore Harris Jesse Joiner Henry Bledsoe Cornelius Herndon Dawson Wood Robert Patton find for defendant. Plf
p.313 obtains appeal to Superior Court, James McKain & John Louis securities.

Deed Charles Reese to Samuel McMurry 50 acres proved by Silas Alexander & Peter Lyon.

William Allen who was returned by sheriff as a juror for the day having refused to attend is fined for contempt $2 & costs.

John Wilson & William Wilson admrs of Zacheus Wilson decd v Patton Anderson. Jury Allen Groves John Chapman James Steel Edmund Green Porter Allen Berry Orr Elijah Simpson Josiah Giles John Rutherford Joseph Bunton Ruffin Deloach Jacob Lewis. Plaintiff recovers agt dft by reason of his not performing damages $368.33½
p.314 besides their costs.

John Payton & William Payton v Matthew Anderson. Deposition of Timothy Merrell[Merrett?] of Logan County, Kentucky, to be taken in behalf plfs; also the deposition of John Patton for sd plffs.

Saturday December 16th 1809. Present James Winchester James C Wilson Will Trigg Jr.

Jonathan Trousdale v John C Hamilton. Detinue. Jury Elmore Harris Norbert Patton Jesse Joiner Hervey R Willis William Anderson Charles Lewis John Chapman Ephraim Cates John Rutherford Cornelius Herndon Thomas Howell Joshua Smith. Plf recovers agt dft his negro if he may be found; if not $300 together with costs of suit. Dft by atty motion for new trial; argument at next Court.
p.315 John W Hamilton assee v Robert Brown. Defendant in proper person. Plaintiff recovers agt dft $250 and his costs.

Allen Josey witness for Jonathan Trousdale v John C Hamilton came not, is fined $125 unless sufficient cause of disability to attend be shewn at next court.

John Brigance a witness for Jonathan Trousdale [worded as above].

Deed John Cage to Washington C Ballard 84 acres ackd.

James Ferrell v Anthony Sharp & Silas Jernigan. Plf no further prosecutes; dft pays costs.

Monday Decr 18th. Present John McMurtry James C Wilson Samuel McMurry Esqrs.
p.316 Assignment of plat & certificate/survey made for Ephraim Herrin for 115½ acres, endorsed from Ephraim Herrin to William Smith was ackd in open court.

Will of Moses Cummins decd proved by Asa Hassell & Jesse Hassell; William Edwards Junr & John Cotton executors qualified by taking the oath.

Deed William White by Alexander A White his atty in fact, to James White & George Crockett 357 acres in Smith County proved by John Jones & Thomas Culbert.

Deed George G Black to James Jackson 100 acres proved by Hugh Crawford &

DECEMBER 1809

Josiah Stevenson.
State v William Ogles. P.L. Jury Henry Bledsoe Robt Haynes Cornelius Herndon Wm Kirkpatrick Jas Claxton Jno Rutherford Jesse Joiner John Jones Jas Stratton p.317 John Payton Wm White Elmore Harris find Ogles not guilty of larceny. Dft Ogles taxed with cost of prosecution.

Deed John Motherall to Edward Sanderson 324 acres proved by David Shelby & John B Truitt.

Appoint Heli Herring overseer/road from Elisha Cheeks to Kentucky road; Joshua Rice esqr to furnish a list of hands.

Tuesday Decr 19th. Present James Cryer Thomas Blakemore Matthew Alexander.

Deed Robert Dobbins by atty in fact Witheral Latimer to Thomas Hamilton 298 acres 132 poles proved by Robert Shaw & James Hamilton.

Deed Robert Dobbins by Witheral Latimer atty in fact to Daniel Latimer 217 acres proved by Robert Shaw & James Hamilton.

Deed Robert Dobbins by Witheral Latimer atty in fact to Robert Shaw 123 acres 64 poles proved by Daniel Latimer & James Hamilton.

p.318 Jones & Owen v William Boyce. William Boyce as constable has failed to account & pay over to sd Jones & Owen $50 the amount of judgment obtained by them agt Demcy Moore which Boyce ought to have collected by virtue of an execution on sd case. Jones & Owen recover sat sd Wm Boyce constable & Nicholas Boyce & Jas McKain his securities the sd sum of $50 and also costs of this motion.

State v Samuel Holloway. TAB. Samuel Holloway saith he is guilty of the trespass assault & battery; fined $50 and imprisoned in county jail without bail for four hours and pay costs of the prosecution.

Appt John D Bradley overseer/road from fork below Gallatin to Shelbys creek in place of James Elliott resigned.

Allow collector/taxes for 1808 the taxes on 100 acres one free poll & three slaves on account of James Clarks taxable property being returned on two lists.

p.319 State v William Payton. TAB. Indictment quashed; reason, evidence of a person of colour incompatible with laws of the government; dft pays costs.

State v John Payton. TAB. [as above]

Order James Cryer & Will Trigg Jr esqrs settle accounts of admn on estate of William Phipps decd and report to next court.

On motion of dfts by attorney in following suits: Wm Ball v Chas Lavender. Wm Ball v Thos Keefe. Wm Ball v Wm Lavender. Order depositions of James Right & Pickins Lavender of Gallatin County Kentucky be taken in behalf defts.

Lists of Taxable property &c to be taken: Wm Trigg esq in Captain McCalls Company. Stephen Cantrill esq in Capt Waltons company. William Montgomery in Capt p.320 Montgomerys company. Isaac Baker esq in Capt Bakers compy. Edward Douglass in Capt Watkins compy. Joshua Rice in Captain Moore's compy. Wm Bracken esq in Capt Alderson's compy. Archibald Marlin esq in Capt Allens compy. Matthew Alexander esq in Capt Cook's company. Jas Winchester esq in Capt Charltons compy. William Seawell esq in Capt Lauderdale's company. George Keesee esqr in Captain Mickelberrys compy. James Cryer esq in Capt Bradley's compy. Thomas Murry esq in Capt Blackmores compy. p.321 Sion Hunt esq in Captain Paytons compy. Samuel McMurry esq in Capt McMurrys compy. John Barr esq in Capt Cowdens compy. Edward Gwin esq in Capt Lewis's compy. Charles Donoho esq in Captain Blacks company.

Wednesday Decr 20th. Present James Cryer Will Trigg Jr Isaac Baker Esqrs.

DECEMBER 1809

Thomas Keefe v John C Hamilton James Desha William Covington. Jury William Kirkpatrick Henry Bledsoe Jno Moore Jesse Joiner Wm Anderson Cornelius Herndon John Rutherford Jno Jones Jno B Truett Jno Mitchell Chas Lewis John Turner. Plf recovers agt dfts $78.87 and costs in the writ and plfs costs of suit.

p.322 John Forguson assee v Edmund Bridgers. Appeal. Jury[above]. Plf recovers agt dft debt & damages $17.13½ and also his costs of suit.

Edward Cage v Thomas Blakemore. Covt. Parties in proper persons, dft agrees plf sustained damages. Plf recovers agt dft $508 and his cost of suit.

Motion of Wm Douglass admr/Frances Howell decd, order Wm Trigg & Jas C Wilson esqrs examine & settle accounts of the administration of sd decedent.

p.323 Appt Henry Bradford inspector/cotton at his press; took oath, William Gillespie and William Montgomery his securities.

John Moore & wife v William Hall. Depositions of Nathaniel Williams of Rockingham County, North Carolina, James Vaughn of Halifax County, Virginia, and Epinatus Winders of Rowan County, North Carolina, to be taken in behalf defendant.

Deed Edward Douglass to William Montgomery 80 acres ackd.

Order tax levied for purchasing weights & measures be paid by collector to James Winchester esqr.

Jurors to next court: John Hodge Jacob Gillespie John Dobbins Robert Goudy Richard Blythe Robert Robb William Barr Robert Parker Jonathan Pearce George Smith Thomas Beard Samuel Lauderdale David Clark Isaac Towell[Powell?] Henry Bunn Thomas Howell John Burns James Vinson Robert White Sr Joseph Motheral Eusebius Stone Joseph Wallace Hugh Crawford Mourning Wynn Wm Edwards(Cotton) Robert Steele Sr Joshua Hadley Peter Looney James Busby Rhodam Rawlings Elisha Clary Robert Shaw Isaac Street John Goodrum James Rankins James Clendening.

p.324 Present Jas Winchester Edwd Douglass Stephen Cantrill Wm Montgomery Isaac Baker Wm Bracken Will Trigg Jr Archd Marlin esqrs.

Motion of Saml Holloway by atty Thos Stuart, order fine of $50 on Holloway for A&B on James Roney be mitigated to 50¢, and that he pay costs of prosecution.

Bond Peter Turney to Henry Span $600 acres dated 17 August 1784 proved by Charles Elliott who deposed that both subscribing witnesses are dead and that he heard sd bond acknowledged.

Supplementary inventory/goods of Baliss House decd rendered by Thomas House of the executors.

White & Josephus Conn v John Withers. Jury Henry Bledsoe William Anderson John Rutherford Jesse Joiner Jacob Thompson Elijah Simpson Samuel Holloway Robert Haynes Nathan Boon John Moody Ephraim Cates William Lavender. Plaintiff recovers agt dft damages assessed at $37.47, and also his costs about his suit expended.

p.325 Thursday Decr 21st 1809. Present Edwd Douglass Wm Montgomery Jas C Wilson.

John Shelby v Josephus H Conn. Jury Joshua Cherry Samuel Alley Matthew Armstrong Jesse Joiner Robert Patton David Allen Elijah Simpson Thomas Barrett Robert Haynes Cornelius Herndon John Rutherford Wm Anderson. Plaintiff recovers against defendant his damages by reason of dfts not performing $125.54½ and his costs.

Power/atty William White to Alexander A White empowering sd Alexr to sell land in Smith County proved by Will Trigg Jr & David Shelby.

Whitehead Joiner v Isam Uzzell. Deposition of Joseph Kirkpatrick to be taken in behalf of the plaintiff.

p.326 Deed William Hall sheriff to Samuel Conn 37 acres ackd.

Assignment of platt & certificate for 30 acres surveyed for Loftain Cage

DECEMBER 1809

from sd Cage to James Blackemore endorsed on sd platt & certificate ackd.
Assignment of platt & certificate for 48 acres surveyed for Loftain Cage from Cage to James Blakemore endorsed on sd platt & certificate acknowledged.
Appoint James Cryer & Isaac Baker esqrs to take private examination of Rhoda Carter wife of Alexander Carter touching the execution of a deed from Alexr Carter & wife Rhoda to Redmond D Barry dated 21 December 1809.

Friday December 22d 1809. Present Edward Douglass Wm Montgomery Jas Cryer.
Release John Jones from double tax on his paying legal tax due on land.
Deed Robert Patton to Isaac Gregory 63 acres ackd.
John S[L?] Luany[Swany?] records his stock mark.

p.327 In the suits of John Jones & Laurence Owen v James Steele, John Jones & Co v James Steel, John Jones assee v James Steel, and John Jones & Lawrence Owen v George Blakemore & Zacheus Wilson exrs of Richard Taylor, in all of which suits judgmt recovered by plffs agt dfts, Henry Belote bail for defendant in afsd suits brings into court the sd James Steele; Steele ordered into custody of sheriff.

John Payton & Wm Payton v Matthew Anderson. Depositions of John Payton Senr & Yelverton Payton to be taken in benefit of plaintiffs.

James Franklin v Chichester Howard. Trespass. Deposition of Zachariah Green to be taken in benefit of plaintiff.

Bill/sale Cornelius Thomas to Benjamin Rawlings negro man Micajah proved by Henry Bradford & John Bysor.

Supplementary inventory/estate of Baliss House decd rendered by Allen Purvis one of the executors of sd deceased.

Appt William A Trice constable in Capt Dements company for two years, took oath, John Jones & William Payton his security.

p.328 Acct/sales goods of Daniel Sanders decd rendered by James Sanders.

Payton v Anderson, deposition of Kinchen Carter to be taken in benefit defendant.

Authorise Will Trigg esq to have repair done to court house at county expence, also to procure a coarse table & six chairs for upper storey of sd house.

Hugh Stephenson v William Montgomery. Debt. Plf recovers agt dft $113.08 and also his costs of suit.

John Allen v Archibald Marlin late sheriff. Dft recovers agt plf his costs.
p.329 Plf obtains appeal, William Allen & Charles Lewis securities.

John Looney v Jacob Slinkard. Plf granted execution agt dft $319 damages & $7.32½ costs and his costs of suit.

Thomas Moris v John Lafferty. Debt. Dft not appearing, plf recovers agt dft $180 and $24.30 damages for detention and also his costs of suit.

p.330 James Bracken v Samuel Richardson. Debt. Dft not appearing, plf recovers $73.50 debt and $2.20 damages for detention and also costs of suit.

James Bracken v Goalbesberry Thurman. Debt. Dft no appearing, plf recovers agt dft $73.50 debt $2.20 damages and also his costs of suit.

James Bracken v John Bailey. Debt. Dft not appearing, plf recovers agt dft $73.50 debt $2.20 damages and also his costs of suit.

Deed Alexander Carter & wife Rhoda to Redmond D Barry undivided fourth part of 200 acres proved by Abraham K Shaifer & John Allen.
p.331 Acct/sales of goods of Roger Daniel decd rendered by David Green admr.

Appt James Cryer & Sion Hunt esqrs to settle accounts of admn on estate of Roger Daniel decd.

MARCH 1810

Motion of Zacheus Wilson & Jacob Houdeshell admrs of goods of James Wilson decd v William Moore & James Steele. It appearing to court that sd William Moore & James Steele and James Wilson the deceased in his life time were joint securities for Demcy Moore in appeal from judgment of this court to Superior Court in action of debt at suit of James Williamson agt sd Demcy Moore, and also appearing to Court that judgment was recovered in sd appeal by sd James Williamson agt sd Demcy & his securities afsd, thereupon execution awarded by sd Court directed to sheriff and levied on goods of sd decd and sold to amount of $650 to satisfy sd judgment. Therefore considered sd Zacheus Wilson & Jacob Houdeshell admrs afsd recover agt sd William Moore & James Steele $433.33½, two thirds of the judgment afsd also their costs of this motion.

Saturday Decr 23d 1809. Present Edwd Douglass Will Trigg Jr & James C Wilson.
p.332 All suits on docket not already disposed of continued till next court.
    Deed Bennett H Henderson exr of William Henderson decd to Hubbard Sanders 100 acres ackd.
Court Adjourned till Court in Course.   Edwd Douglass

p.333 Court of Pleas & Quarter Sessions at the court house in Gallatin on second Monday March 1810. Present James Winchester Matthew Alexander James C Wilson.
    Deed James Johnston to John Maxwell Neisbet 75 acres ackd.
    Order Matthew Alexander esq furnish John Beardon overseer with a list of hands to work on the road with said overseer.
    Deed Redmond D Barry to Peter Lemmon 150 acres ackd.
    Deed James Williams to Thomas Jones 90 acres proved by Hillery Malone & Reuben D Brown.
    Deed Peter Lemon to Micajah House 17 acres ackd.
    Deed James Murray to John Donoho 236 acres proved by Levi Hall & Jas Hall.
p.334 Samuel Elliott v Jackson Brown exr. Debt. Jury Jacob Gillespie Henry Bunn Robert Parker James Clendening William Barr John Byrn David Clark Isaac Street Thomas Beard James Rankin Mourning Winn John Hodge say[blank]
    Assignment of a plat & certificate of survey 20 acres from John Rule to William Hammon ackd.
    Assignment of plat and certificate/survey 50 acres John Ruyle to William Smith ackd.
    Deed George G Black to Moses Cummins 100 acres proved by Levi Hall & Josiah Stevenson.
    Deed James Brigance & Hannah Brigance to George Dempsey 6½ acres proved by William Brigance & Peter Looney.
p.335 Samuel Elliott v Jackson Brown exr of Mathew Brown. Debt. Jury[above]. Plf recovers agt dft $152.34½ debt & damages to be levied on goods in hands of exr.
    William Nolin v James Sanders. Debt. Jury Thos Howell Elisha Clary Isaac Towell[Fowell?] Hugh Crawford John Goodrum Joshua Hadley Wm Edwards(cotton) John Dobbins Robt Robb Rhodam Rawlings Peter Looney Jas Busby. Plf recovers agt dft
p.336 debt & damages $61.27 and also his costs.
    Deed John Young to Joseph Caveatt 250 acres ackd.

MARCH 1810

Deed John Young to James Roney 327 acres ackd.
Robert Hamilton William Dorris Charles Lewis commissioned in the peace under seal of State 23 Novr 1809 took oaths prescribed by law.
Bill/sale Willie Lassiter to Jesse Joiner negro man David proved by George Reed & Henry Bunn.
Deed William Morgan to Nathaniel Giles 150 acres proved by Jas Winchester.

p.337 Deed George Litsinger to John Litsinger 147 acres Chester District, South Carolina, acknowledged in open court by the bargainor.
Mortgage Daniel Stewart to Redmond D Barry negro fellow Collins proved by William Hall & John Stewart.
Appt James Hart Charles Donoho & George Keesee esqrs or any two to settle with admr of estate of William Cathey deceased.
Account/sales goods of Watson Goostree and Elizabeth Goostree rendered by guardians of sd Watson and Elizabeth.
Appt Edwd Gwin & Joshua Rice esqrs to settle with Jesse Skeen and Stephen Trible guardians of Watson & Elisabeth Goostree and make report to next court.
William Kerney[Kenny?] v Loftain Cage Edwd Cage & Alfred H Douglass. Debt. Jury Thos Howell Elisha Clary Isaac Towell[Fornell?] Hugh Crawford John Goodrum Joshua Hadley Wm Edwards John Dobbins Robt Robb Rhodam Rawlings Peter Looney Jas Busby. Plf recovers agt dft debt & damages $185.26 & also his costs of suit.

p.338 David Shelby v William Ford. Debt. Jury[above]. Plf recovers agt dft debt & damages $78.66 and also his costs of suit.
Thomas Shackleford v Joseph Cavett. Debt. Jury[above]. Plf recovers agt dft debt & damages $128.50 and also his costs of suit.

p.339 Lawrence Youce[Yoner?] v Elisha Cheek. Debt. Jury[above]. Plf recovers agt dft debt & damages $367.42 & also his costs of suuit.
License David Dement to keep tavern at his dwelling in Gallatin, Adam Wallace & Jesse Skeen his securities.
Appt James Bentley constable in Capt Cooks district for two years, James Vinson and Jeremiah Belote his securities, and took the oaths.

p.340 Appt John Pavatt constable in Capt Montgomerys district for two years, Henry Bunn and Joshua Hadley his securities, and took the oaths.
Appt Thomas Jones overseer/road; George Keese esqr to furnish list/hands.
Appt Nathaniel Granger overseer/road in place of James Scott resigned.
Inventory/goods of Wm Kenedy decd rendered by Armstrong W Kennedy one of the executors of sd deceased.
Inventory/property of orphans of Bryant Gardner decd, and list of expenditures made for said orphans rendered by Isaac Walton one of the guardians.
Will of William F McNutt decd proved by James Barry & Connally Findlay; supplement naming executors thereto proved by James Barry. Thereupon Thomas McNutt and Connally Findlay the executors qualified as such.

p.341 Appt Edmund Turpin overseer/road in place of William Dorris resigned.
Commrs apptd to settle with admr of Francis Howell decd render statement of such settlement.
Stephen Cantrill esq renders list/taxable property & polls in Capt R[P?] Cantrills company.

Tuesday March 13th 1810. Present Isaac Walton Jas C Wilson Isaac Baker esqrs.
Edwd Douglass esqr renders list/taxable property & polls, Capt Edwards co.
James Franklin v Chichester Howard. Trespass. Suit submitted to determina-

64

MARCH 1810

tion of Wm Montgomery James Frazor Will Trigg Chas Lewis Jeremiah Doxey.
    Appt William Woodall constable for Capt Lerners[?] district for 2 years, Joshua Rice & John Moore his securities, and took the oaths.
p.342   Elijah Tompson & James Cowden commissioned in the peace under seal of the State 23d Novr 1809 took the oaths prescribed by law.
    George Kesee esqr rendered list/taxable property & polls in Capt McKleburys company.
    John Barr esqr renders list/taxable property & polls in Capt Cowdens.
    Bill/sale Basil Trail to Solomon Trail negro female Malinder ackd.
    Present James Winchester Isaac Walton James C Wilson Robert Hamilton Edward Douglass Geo Keesee John Barr Isaac Baker Stephen Cantrell esqrs.
    On petition of Joseph Erwin for emancipating negro Elisha property of petitioner, sd slave having rendered meritorious services to petitioner, Court are of opinion that same would be consistent with interest & policy of the State. Order sd slave emancipated and set free at the end of three years and four months from
p.343   this date 13th March 1810, sd Joseph Erwin with Felix Grundy & Nicholas Wilson his securities having entered bond $1000.
    Corban Hall v William Barker. Debt. Jury John Hodge Jacob Gillespie John Dobbins Wm Barr Thomas Beard David Clark Isaac Towell Henry Bunn John Byrn Hugh Crafford James Busby & James Clendening. Plf recovers agt dft debt & damages $82.86 & 4 mills and also his costs in this behalf expended.
p.344   Thomas Moss v William Douglass & isaac Pearce. Debt. Jury Mourning Winn Rhodam Rawlings Robt White Thos Howell Robt Robb Jas Vinson Robt Steele Isaac Street Wm Edwards Elisha Clary Robt Parker Jos Wallace. Plf recovers agt dfts debt & damages $210.50 and also his costs about his suit expended.
    Deed David Brigance & Charles Brigance to Richard Strother 85 acres 51 poles proved by Arthur Cotton & James Strother.
    George D Blackmore v William Johnson. Covt. Dft by John Johnson his atty in fact relinquishes his pleas. Plf recovers agt dft damages $71.25 and his costs.
p.345   Deed John Carr to King Carr 140 acres ackd.
    Deed Edward Gwin to William Alderson 251 acres ackd.
    Deed Ethelderd Bunn[Berson?] to William Durham 300 acres proved by William Seawell and William Hanna.
    Order Matthew Alexander esq furnish William Anderson overseer with list of hands to work on the road for which he is appointed overseer.
    Deed John Carr & Wilson Yandell to Francis Marshal 255 acres ackd.
    Deed Robert Patton to William Patton 100 acres proved by William McCall & Philip Chapman.
    Deed Hugh Stevenson to Elisha Jones 78 acres proved by John Rowland & Wilson Yandell.
p.346   Deed Richard Blythe to Andrew Blythe 77½ acres proved by Samuel K Blythe & Saml M McCorkle.
    Deed James Clendening to Nathl Parker Jr 51 acres ackd.
    Motion of exrs of Abraham Rogers decd, order Isaac Baker & James Cryer esqrs settle accounts of the administration of the estate of sd deceased.
    Deed Richard Winchester to James Winchester on undivided eighth of 5000 acres on the Cheeckasaw bluff on the Mississippi River proven by George D Blackmore & Thomas Cocke.
    James Gwin commissioned in the peace under seal of State 23d Nov 1809 took the oaths prescribed by law.

MARCH 1810

License William Duty to keep tavern at his dwelling in Sumner county, with William Parr & George Gillespie his securities.

p.347 Deed Thomas Donnell to Nathan Buckley 100 acres ackd.

Deed William Montgomery to Leonard Dugger 84 acres ackd.

Allow Jacob Fuller $12 for keeping orphan boy Jsu McClung for 3 months.

Deed David Hobbs to Isaac Forrest 40 acres 40 poles proved by David Green & Hardy Hunt.

Deed James Morrison to Thomas Leroy Harris, Mary Gibson Harris, heirs of Sarah Caroline Simpson decd, Francis Houston Robertson Araminta Juliet Orr Martha Spears Harris and Elizabeth Harriott Harris heirs of Robert Harris decd 222½ proved by James Morrison, sd deed having been heretofore proved by Joseph White the other subscribing witness to sd deed.

Appt Needham Hunter overseer/road in place of Allen Groves resigned.

p.348 Joseph Motheral v Joseph Clark. Debt. Jury Mourning Winn Rhodam Rawlings Robt White Thos Howell Robert Robb James Vinson Robt Steele Isaac Street Wm Edwards Elisha Clary Robert Parker Joseph Wallace. Plaintiff recovers against defendant his debt & damages $141.03 and also his costs about his suit expended.

Present Jas Winchester Edwd Douglass Jno McMurtry Jno Barr Edwd Gwin Jas C Wilson Jas Cryer Isaac Walton Isaac Baker Robt Hamilton William Montgomery Matthew Alexander Thomas Murry Charles Donoho Joshua Rice Will Trigg esqrs.

Tax is laid to defray contingent charges of the county, and another tax for support of the poor.

p.349 Allow John Mitchel $7 for maintaining prisoners in Jail when sd Mitchel was jailor.

Allow John Stuart, carpenter, $6.50 for repairs done to the court house.

Allow Samuel Holloway $56 for keeping certain state prisoners.

Allow Jacob Fuller $40 for supporting poor orphan child Jsu McClung one year from this date payable quarterly out of the poor tax.

Orphan Tabitha Hobdy chose her brother William Hobdy for her guardian; Hobdy with Wm Baker & Noah Cotton his securities ackd bond to justices present.

Wm Seawell esq renders list/taxable prperty & polls in Capt Lauderdales company by him taken for the present year. Also Wm Montgomery in Capt Montgomery's company, Joshua Rice in Capt Moores company.

Deed John Morgan to William Gwin 259 acres 3 rods 20 poles proved by George Cooper & John Gwin.

p.350 Deed Thomas Murry to Jonathan Hannum 42 acres ackd.

Edwd Douglass esq renders list taxable prperty & polls in Capt Edwards co.

Power/atty David Carter to Armstreat Stubblefield dated 1 March 1805 proved by Thomas Stubblefield a subscribing witness thereto.

Order indenture binding John Brown an apprentice to John Pendergrass to learn taylors trade dated 24 March 1808 be received on account of his removal out of the county and sd Pendergrass released from his covenant. Order John Brown bound apprentice to Patrick Youree to age 21 to learn art & mystery of a blacksmith.

Appt Robt White Jr overseer/road in place of Marmaduke Kimbrough resigned.

Appt Saml Holloway overseer/road from Wm Edwards to Shelleys creek.

Appt James Jackson overseer/road from William Edwards to State road.

Charles Donoho esq rendered list/taxable property & polls Capt Blacks co.

p.351 On petition of sundry persons praying a road be laid off from Cairo passing by Jesse Johnsons & John Hamiltons to join Nashville road between Andrew Buckhams & Richard Kings, order Jesse Johnson John Hamilton Henry Cook James Wilson S John

MARCH 1810

Rutherford Stephen Alexander Andrew Buckham lay off & mark sd road and make report to next Court.

    Assignment of platt & certificate/survey 20 acres made for William Martin from sd Wm Martin to Francis Marshel endorsed on sd plat & certificate was proved by the oaths of Wilson Yandell & John Carr subscribing witnesses thereto.

    On petition of sundry inhabitants for a public road from Cumberland River where Sterling Tarpley of Wilson County contemplates a ferry over sd river to Cairo, order Wm Lytle Bledsoe Isaac Street James Rankins Benjamin Morrow John S Swancy Joel Eckols & Humphrey Bates lay out sd road agreeable to petition and report to next court.

    On petition of sundry inhabitants praying a road from Gallatin to Hendricks ferry on Cumberland river running from Gallatin to Gallaspies as far as the place where the common pathway turns off to Mr Thos Keefs thence along sd pathway to upper end of Keefs lane thence through Mr McReynolds plantation to sd p.352 Hendricks ferry. Order Joseph McElwrath Thomas Anderson William Douglass Thomas Keefe Charles Elliott Richard King Boswell Johnson lay out said road and report to next Court.

    Petition of Shadrack Nye praying alteration of road for 126½ poles to begin 10 poles east of Nye's house thence parallel with present road for distance afsd. Appoint George Garrett John Garrett Danl Ogelsby Peter Blair & Philip Kiser a jury for purpose afsd and they are to report thereon to next court.

    Appt John Perry Laurence Whitsitt Robert Williamson Samuel[Lamuel?] Tennon & Josiah Perry commissioners to divide & appropriate an undivided legacy bequeathed to Pachaner Cartwright Lithey Byrn & Bethey Hobday between sd divisees.

    Appt William Rice constable for 2 years in Capt Edwards dist, Peter Looney & Rhodam Rawlings his securities.

    List of taxable property & polls in Capt Paytons company taken by Sion Hunt esq rendered into court.

    Deed Shadrack Nye James C Wilson & Charles Donoho town commissioners for Gallatin to Shadrack Nye in his individual capacity for two town lots, one #3 in the southwest square of Gallatin, the other in the north east square #18 ackd.

    The Court adjourned till tomorrow morning 9 Oclock.

[End of this microfilm]

INDEX

ABERNATHY, Littleton 53
ADAM, James 51
ADAMS COUNTY, MISSISSIPPI TERRITORY 22
ALDERSON, Captain 22 60 James 17 27
  William 22 35 65
ALEXANDER, Matthew 2 3 7-13 15 18 22-24
  27-29 32-34 36 38 39 41 43 46-51 55 56
  60 63 65 66 Robert 43 47 Silas 59
  Stephen 67 William 3 7 13 15 48
ALLEN, Anna 7 Captain 60 Charity 7
  David 61 John 4 9 22 26 28 42 43 45 54-
  56 62 Orman 7 13 Porter 10 11 13 14 24
  25 29 31 32 43 52 59 Rhodam 29 Robert 7
  9 42 43 54-56 Sarah 7 Sherod 14 Sherrod
  23 Sophia 7 Theophilus 10 11 William
  4 38 42 45 47-54 59 62
ALLEY, Joseph 54 Samuel 58 61
ALLISON, Andrew 8 49 -- 16
ALONSON, William 58
ALSEPS, David 47
AMBROSE, Isreal 27
ANDERSON, Alexander 58 Alfred 14 Betsey
  14 George 8 40 54 John 13 15 Matthew 14
  21 22 28 42 49 50 52 55 59 62 Miles 14
  Patton 11 13 28 30 58 59 Polley 14
  Robert 28 40 Thomas 3 11 12 17 22 23
  42 50 53 56 67 William 22 23 38-41 47
  48 53 56-59 61 65 -- 62
ANTHONY, Elijah 29 51 57 58
ARCHER, Jacob 39
ARMSTRONG, James 42 54 Knox 3 Margaret
  3 Martin 14 31 32 41 Matthew 44 58 61
  Samuel 3 6 Zenos 3
ARRINGTONS FORK 57
ASKEW, James 26 John 14
ASPIE, James 17
ASPY, William 22
ATKINS, Isaac 27
AVENT, Harris 34 Herbert 57 John 15 18
  William 34
BADGETT, Jonathan 51 57
BAILEY, Edmond 49 Edmund 24 28 33 43 49
  John 5 17 27 28 29 38 62
BAKER, Captain 7 22 33 60 Isaac 3 6 7
  16 37 39 42 44 46 48 49 50 58 60 61 62
  64 65 66 Nancy 7 William 66
BALDRADGE, Stephen 25 26
BALDRIDGE, Stephen 33 39
BALL, Captain 22 John 7 Richard 39 49
  William 13 15 28 43 45 52 54 60

Washington 59
BANES, Elesworth 13 John 12 13
BAPTIST CHURCH 27
BARBER, Lawson 20 21
BARGSDALE, Daniel 19
BARKER, Isreal 44 Josia 56 Wm 56 65
BARNES, Balaam 33 John 33 Nathan 23
  Solomon 45 48 49 50 51 52 53 54
BARNETT, Jacob 3
BARR, Hugh 9 James 38 John 6 16 18 22
  24 30 37 39 41 54 56 57 58 60 65 66
  Patrick 22 27-34 40 William 17 38 56
  57 61 63 65
BARREN, Joseph 31
BARRET/BARRETT/BARROTT, Thomas 46 55 61
BARROWS LANDING 19
BARRY, James 10 24 26 28 30 31 34 42 46
  64 Redmond 1 2 5 6 9-11 16 17 19 21 23
  24 25 28 29 35 36 37 41 42 46 51 52 54
  56 58 62 63 64
BASHAW, Benjamin 3 29
BATE/BATES, Humphrey 5 6 15 33 67
BAYNE, Matthew 35
BAYNES, Ebsworth 3 30 41 Elesworth 12
  John 3 10
BEAKLEY, John 5 18 21 William 18
BEARD, David 1 2 3 5 7 57 Samuel 7 43
  Thos 61 63 65 William 5 13 15 16 53 56
BEARDEN, John 52
BEARDING, John 5 33 40
BEARDON, John 46 53 55 63
BEASLEY, Jesse 41
BEETLEY, John 23 47
BELL, William 10 18 22 27-34 37 40
BELOTE, Henry 11 14 20 24 29 34 41 44
  46 47 49 50 55 62 Jeremiah 1 2 4 47 64
  ferry 7 17 41
BENNETT, Walter 19 35 William 35 36 49
BENTHALL, Enos 50 Laban 14
BENTLEY/BENTLY, James 4 64 John 4 7 14
  17 20 24 53 -- 29
BERNARD, Elisha 22 45
BERRY, James 4
BERSON, Ethelderd 65
BERTIE COUNTY, NORTH CAROLINA, 1 6
BETOTE, Henry 4 Jeremiah 16
BIGGS, John 7
BISHOPS FERRY 2
BLACK, Captain 22 32 60 66 Gabriel 16
  George 27 38 59 63 Samuel 1 4 12 17 18

INDEX

20 31 41 43 58 William 4 -- 17
BLACKEMORE, George 7 28 James 13 62
Thomas 7 31
BLACKMORE, Captain 60 G 17 George 5 8
16 34 36 37 42 52 53 54 65 James 5 12
45 57 Thomas 39 51 57
BLAIR, James 12 21 28 Peter 67
BLAKEMORE, Captain 22 31 George 52 62
James 32 33 51 62 Thomas 2 7 35 60 61
BLEDSOE, Abraham 27 35 36 51 56 Anthony
47 Catey 49 Catherine 31 Caty 39 Clarissa 39 Henry 1-4 28 36 37 51 53 56 58-
61 Isaac 7 13 18 22 23 28 36 40 44 46
47 51 56 William 31 67 creek 7 17 26
33 34 47 54 lick 2 7 28 30 50
BLOODWORTH, Web/Webb 12 13 31 55 Wm 19
BLOUNT, Joseph 6
BLYTHE, Andrew 5 18 47 57 65 Richard 9
61 65 Samuel 9 13 14 17 19-21 31 58 65
BOLES, William 20
BOND, James 18
BOON, Nathan 42 51 61
BOOTHE, Joseph 32
BOREN, Tarlton 47
BOSLEY, John 3
BOURBOUN COUNTY, KENTUCKY, 45
BOWEN, John 3 30 31 Leonard 35 Levisa
34 41 Samuel 17
BOWER, Jeremiah 8
BOWERS, Jeremiah 9 18 19 Pitt 42 Wm 26
BOWLES, John 50 William 15
BOWMAN, William 54
BOYCE, Nancy 32 38 39 51 55 Nicholas 1
3 6 7 10 12 14 16-18 21-23 30 32 33 38
39 41 50 51 60 William 23 53 54 60
BOYD, John 46
BOYER, Henry 48 Nicholas 16 17 Wm 12 53
BOYERS, Robert 58
BRACKEN, Isaac 40 50 James 23 28 35 40
50 51 62 William 9 10 15 17 34 35 43
51 60 61
BRACKIN, James 28
BRADFORD, Henry 5 9 27 35 38 57 61 62
Larken 3 19 Larkin 29
BRADLEY, Captain 58 60 Edward 19 26 27
32 44 45 46 47 53 54 57 John 36 44 57
58 60 Richard 24 33 53 56 58 bent 56
BRADSHAW, John 2
BRAKEN, Isaac 27 William 17 22
BRAKIN, Joel 14

BRANDEN, Abel 40
BRANDON, Abel 3 6 25 26 Abraham 25
Benjamin 25
BRESSEE, John 51
BRIANT, Thomas 43
BRIDGER, Captain 6 Edmund 53
BRIDGERS, Edmond 41 Edmund 24 28 29 31
34 41 42 43 45 56 61 John 31 43 51 53
54 Reddick 43
BRIDGES, Capt 22 Edmd 10 18 19 John 43
BRIGANCE, Charles 15 65 David 65 Hannah
63 James 13 15 45 46 62 John 17 34 41
55 59 William 8 13 63
BRILEY, Samuel 46
BRINKLEY, Thomas 6 35 William 6
BRIT/BRITT, Obed 37 48 William 24 36
BRITTON, Abraham 29 Thomas 3 6 8-11
BROOKS, William 4 48
BROTHERS, Philip 38
BROWN, Bazel 53 George 2 4 5 6 14 20
Jackson 39 49 58 63 James 10 12 37 39
45 48 John 5 19 30 44 45 66 Leonard 16
Matthew 3 39 49 58 63 Nancy 16 Reuben
29 63 Richard 7 18 Robert 1 59 William
5 16 24 -- 29 gap 28
BRUCE, James 37 Robert 6 17 47 William
10 37 53 56
BRYANCE, John 43
BRYANT, John 9
BUCKENER, William 45
BUCKHAM, Andrew 58 66 67
BUCKLEY, Nathan 66
BUCKNER, William 10 19
BUNN, Etheldred 65 Henry 8 9 13 17 18
19 20 21 30 38 61 63 64 65
BUNTEN, Joseph 40 William 40
BUNTON, Joseph 48 50 59 Wm 50 54 58
BURNLEY, John 9
BURNS, John 61
BURTON, William 24 26
BUSBY, James 61 63 64 65
BUSTARD, James 17 21 John 27
BUTLER, Henry 54 John 30
BYRN, John 13 37 63 65 Lithey 67
BYRNS, James 15 John 15
BYSOR, John 5 62
CAFFERY, John 34
CAGE, Edward 2 27 35 36 42 45 51 54 61
64 James 12 20 22 28 30 31 34 39 41 46
49 50 58 Jesse 39 John 49 55 59 Loftain
8 17 41 45 49 51 52 61 62 64 Reuben 14

INDEX

36 39 William 9 13 15 17 18 28 29 34 38 39 41 42 46 57 58 Wilson 12 17 18 21 -- 17 24
CAHOON, Thomas 4
CALDWELL, John 6 27
CAMP, Thomas 48
CAMPBELL, David 4 James 30 42 53 Joel 30 Joseph 58 Owen 19 57 Robert 57 Thomas 15 William 2
CANNON, William 51
CANTRELL/CANTRIL/CANTRILL, Captain 64 Stephen 5 8-13 19 22 24 26 29 33 34 37 38 39 44 45 60 61 64 65
CARDWELL, Leonard 35
CAREY, James 12 42-45 Thomas 43
CARNEY, William 38
CAROTHERS, Hugh 17 James 25
CARPENTER, Austin 54
CARR, John 3 6-10 12 30 45 65 67 King 7 30 37 38 65 William 7 30
CARRELL, Elizabeth 16 Willie 16
CARROLL, Nancy 26 Willie 26
CARTER, Alexander 62 David 66 Kinchen 62 Moses 19 30 Randal 19 Randel 20 Rhoda 62
CARTWRIGHT, Matthew 18 57 Pachaner 67 Robert 46
CARY, James 35 38 39 41 42 44 45
CATER, Britain 47 George 47 John 47
CATES, E 33 Ephraim 5 10 20 21 28 33 39 44 45 54 58 59 61
CATHEY, Alexander 6 51 52 John 6 13 51 52 William 6 44 64
CATRON, Christly 38
CAVATT, Richard 23
CAVEAT/CAVEATT, Andrew 20 James 20 John 49 Joseph 63 Moses 20 Richard 18 20 22 44 48 49 -- 16
CAVETT, Jno 2 3 16 Joseph 64 Richard 16
CAVITT, John 34 44 46 Joseph 5 Richd 44
CHAMBLESS, Stephen 9
CHANEY, William 24
CHAPMAN, George 26 28 29 42 James 39 John 13 17-20 31 39 41 45 48 57 58 59 Martha 39 Philip 65
CHARLTON, Capt 22 36 60 Jas 17 18 22 23
CHEATHAM, Anderson 56
CHEEDDLE/CHEEDLE, Thos 12 13 William 33
CHEEK, Elisha 45 60 64
CHERRY, Joshua 6 13 20 42 61 Solo 6

CHESTER COUNTY, SOUTH CAROLINA, 64
CHRISTIAN COUNTY, KENTUCKY, 53
CLANTON, James 5
CLARK, David 61 63 65 Isaac 9 10 11 James 47 48 60 Joseph 1 2 4 5 9 25 38 66 Mary 47
CLARK COUNTY, KENTUCKY, 50
CLARY, Elisha 61 63 64 65 66
CLAXTON, James 5 6 13 19 20 21 29 32 33 34 38 51 60 Jeremiah 51 Joshua 30 31 32
CLEM, John 34
CLENDENING, James 14 40 45 47 61 63 65
CLENNEY, Samuel 25 34
CLENNY, Samuel 13 18 21 25 31 42 44
CLUNY, Samuel 8
COBLER, William 29
COCHRAN, Anna 16 Hiram 16 John 16 24 Rachel 16 Sally 16 William 15 16 23 36
COCKE, Thomas 14 53 65
COKER, Jesse 4
COLLIER, Robert 1 9
COLLINS, Edmund 12 13 Pamelia 8 Wm 36
COMAR, John 22
COMPERRY, Francis 8 9 20 31
CONN, Josephus 1 6 10 11 16 17 19-21 29 31 33 35 44-46 53 54 59 61 Samuel 3 6 7 17 24 29 31 35 61 White 11 31 33 45 53 59 61 -- 47
CONNER, William 34
COOK, Captain 60 64 Henry 66
COOPER, George 9 24 58 66 John 24 43
COOPPER, John 57
COPE, Richard 40 50
COPELAND, John 28 46
COPELEN/COPELIN, John 20 21
CORNER, John 22
COTTEN, Robert 9
COTTON, Arthur 65 John 15 17 18 45 59 Lazarus 2 3 13 Moore 11 15 16 18 35 41 Noah 66 Robert 8 32
COUN, Samuel 14
COVINGTON, William 7 31 48 61
COWDEN, Captain 22 24 60 65 James 54 65
CRABTREE, William 29
CRAFFORD, Hugh 65
CRANE, Lewis 22 54
CRAWFORD, Hugh 8 15 16 59 61 63 64 John 15 William 15
CRAWLEY, John 1 20
CRIBBINS, Thomas 25

INDEX

CROCKET/CROCKETT, Geo 59 Wm 22 -- 25
CROFER, George 27
CROFT MILLS 5 7 17 37 53
CROOK, Erben 37
CROPER, George 27
CRUMP, Adam 10 11 30 31 35 43-46 53 54
CRUNK, John 33
CRUTCHER, Edmund 1 4 43
CRUTCHFIELD, William 29
CRUTHERS, Thomas 3
CRYER, James 1 2 4 5 7 8 10-15 18-22 29 31 35-37 39 41 42 44 50 51 53 54 59 60 62 65 66 John 35 36
CULBERT, Thomas 22 59
CUMMINS, Moses 56 59 63
DANIEL, Nancy 50 Roger 50 62 Tapley 50
DARNELL, George 35
DAVIDSON, Ephraim 11 22
DAVIS, Elizabeth 2 5 11 15 James 14 John 9 Robert 18 26 William 9 36
DAWSON, Jesse 2 11 32 45 John 12
DEADERICK, Thomas 6 -- 4 14
DEADRICK, -- 28
DEAL, Jeremiah 11
DELOACH, Ruffin 10 11 14 21 33 42-45 48-54 59
DEMENT, Captain 62 Charles 4 9 15 28 David 19 34 35 36 64 Thomas 1 3 4 6 9 17 20 29 45
DEMPSEY, George 13 63
DEMUMBRO, Timothy 14
DEN, John 5
DENNING, David 28 Jno 18 40 50 Wm 28 35
DENNINGTON, Thomas 50
DENSBERRY, Henry 42
DESHA, James 4 9 17 18 19 26 61 Robert 6 9 10 17 19 26 creek 39 57
DIAL, Jeremiah 13
DICKASON, John 41
DICKERSON, John 27 35 39 41 42 54 Nathaniel 56
DICKINSON, John 38 39
DICKISON, John 2 41 42 Nathaniel 38
DINNING, John 38
DIXON, Tilmon 5
DOBBINS, Alexander 5 7 Carson 5 27 28 35 40 45 John 39 40 61 63 64 65 Robert 5 39 45 52 57 60
DODSON, William 10 33 51
DOE, John 41 56

DONELSON, Andrew 37 John 37 Samuel 37 William 22 33
DONNELL, Thos 1-4 35 36 40 48 50 58 66
DONOHO, Archibald 35 51 Charles 1 8 32 44 52 54 60 64 66 67 John 27 63 Joshua 18 Thomas 48
DORRIS, John 44 Samuel 3 Wm 16 24 35 64
DOSSET, Willis 21
DOUGLASS, Alfred 64 Edward 3 4 10-13 20 21 27 28 32 44-46 51-55 60-66 Howard 4 33 James 3 7 10-15 22 26 33 39-41 44 50 -52 54 55 Reuben 2 3 6 8-13 35 36 53 56 William 1 3 4 8 13 19 20 22 24 27-31 34 43 48 50 55 61 65 67
DOXEY, Jeremiah 12 16 41 65
DRAKE, Ephraim 57 creek 1 8 25 26 30 34 38 45 50
DRAPER, Joshua 3 William 9 44 53
DUGGER, Leonard 66
DUNCAN, Moses 43 Tandy 18 48 52
DURHAM, William 65
DUTY, Eliza 43 Elizabeth 28 George 6 7 28 43 58 Solomon 28 37 47 Susanna 37 William 3 6 7 32 35 38 39 41-46 66
DUVALL, Benjamin 9
EASTEN/EASTIN/EASTON, William 17 21 27
EATON, John 4
ECHOLS/ECKOLS, Joel 7 17 47 54 67
EDWARDS, Capt 64 66 67 James 33 35 38 42 John 10 30 41 44 49 57 58 Nathan 13 23 41 45 46 Richard 29 35 36 44 Thomas 15 28 William 3 6-8 11-13 15-17 20-23 31 34 35 40 41 47 51 58 59 61 63-66
ELDRIDGE GROCERY STORE 36
ELLIOTT, Charles 40 50 51 61 67 George 28 34 35 Hugh 11 18 35 36 45 James 30 35 42 60 Samuel 49 63 branch 40 51
ELLIS, Abraham 44 57 Robert 4 31 54
ERWIN, Joseph 65
EUBANKS, William 40
EVANS, John 54 57
FAIRCLAIM, Richard 20 21
FARMER, John 39 Thomas 2 5 11 55
FAULK, Oran/Orran 45 58
FELLENGIN/FELLIGIN, John 11 54
FERRELL, Benoni 47 51 James 51 53 58 59 Leonard 50 58 59 Thomas 57 58
FILLINGIN, John 53
FINDLAY, Connally 64
FINDLEY, Connelly 56 Cornelius 21 Hugh

INDEX

15 44 McNutt 15 16 -- 4 6 24 25 38 50
FISHER, Jabus 32 Peter 19 20 29 31 32
FLAT, David 29
FLEMING, Alexander 57 John 22 Robert 47
FORD, James 57 William 31 57 64
FORGUSON, John 61
FORNELL, Isaac 64
FORREST, Elisha 12 14 Isaac 12 51 54 66
FORRESTER, Isaac 30
FOSTER, Francis 44
POWELL, Isaac 9 61 63
FRANKLIN, James 1-4 13 34 43 62 64 John 3 16 27 31 39 42   street 4
FRAZOR, James 8 45 48-54 65   John 38 41 William 45
FREE BLACKS: Elisha 65   Jarrett 27
FREELAND, John 24
FREEMAN, Eaton 47
FRYATT, Julia 16
FRYETT, Juliat 24
FULCHER, Church 21 39
FULLER, Jacob 9 12 38 39 47 57 66
FURGUSON, John 42
FURR, Anne 32   James 32
GAINS, Moses 56
GALLATIN COUNTY, KENTUCKY, 60
GAMBELL, Henry 7 17
GAMBLING, James 56
GARDNER, Bryant 4 29 64   Jacob 33   John 3 4 5 8 9 27 29   Robert 16 26
GARRETT, Betsey 40   George 67   James 35   John 22 67   Joseph 40   Martha 40   Nathan 40   Odell 40   Ordell 37   Patty 40   Peggy 40
GARRISON, Jacob 15   John 58
GATTES/GATTIS, Samuel 6 27
GEORGE, Isaac 6 8-13 45 46
GIBSON, Jordan 34 35   Jourdan 34   Roger 34 35 36 38 41 42 46   Samuel 27 28 31
GILES, Elizabeth 5 John 5 14 29 Josiah 4 22 23 59   Nathl 64 William 3 5 39 43
GILESPIE, William 32
GILLESPIE, Captain 27 55 George 3 22 23 28 43 58 66   Jacob 61 63 65   John 3   Richard 17 48   William 7 8 57 61
GILMORE, Abner 19 56 58 Nathaniel 10 11
GIVIN, James 10   John 11 49
GLANTON, John 44
GLASGOW, William 22 23
GLASS, Howard 36
GODFREY, James 24

GOFF, Andrew 49
GOLDSTON, John 27
GOOCHLAND COUNTY, VIRGINIA, 36
GOODRUM, John 11 12 20 21 42 44 57 61 63 64
GOORTRA, Watson 27
GOOSHER, Betsey 40
GOOSTRA, Watson 27
GOOSTREE, Absolam 45 Elizabeth 45 64   Watson 44 45 64
GORDEN, Alexander 49
GOUDY, Robert 61
GOURLEY, Hugh 9 10 43   John 9 10
GOWEN, Amos 49
GRAHAM, Alexr 45 48-54 57   James 42
GRANGER, Benjamin 40 50 53 56   Nathaniel 64   William 4 36 37 55 56
GRAVES, Isaac 44   Ralph 28 42 43
GRAY, J 31   John 12 20
GREAVES, Reaf 27
GREEN, Ann 57   David 14 16 24 46 52 62 66   Edmund 6 24 59 Elisha 6 15 19 24 28 29 32 33 57 James 32 38 44 Michael 6 14 16 24 28 33 46 Zachariah 38 44 50 51 62
GREENFIELD, -- 47
GREENVILLE, NORTH CAROLINA, 35
GREER, Ann 57   Anne 32   Captain 32
GREGORY, Isaac 7 62   Kesiah 7   Thomas 8
GROVES, Allen 3 20 44 45 59 66   Isaac 44   Thomas 27 44
GRUNDY, Felix 5 11 30 65
GUN, James 51
GUTHREY, Robert 24
GUTHRIE, David 24   James 24   Robert 24
GWIN, Alexander 18 38 39 54 57 58 Capt 22 Edmund 59 Edward 1 3 12 19-24 26 27 29 36 38 48 51 55 57 58 60 64 66 James 10 24 36 65   John 11 19 23 24 34 36 45 49 55 66   William 43 53 56 57 66
HADLEY, Joshua 3 31 34 35 43 44 45 53 54 57 61 63 64
HAINEY, Jesse 13
HALE, James 3   William 38 57
HALIFAX COUNTY, VIRGINIA, 61
HALL, Corban 56 65 Elihu 57 Fergus 57 George 32 37 54 James 63 John 44 Joshua 27   Levi 38 45 46 63 Levy 22 Robt 13 15 18   Washington 57   Wm 12 18 19 24 29 33 34 37 39 40 42 53 56 61 64 Willis 42 44
HAMILTON, James 60 John 1 2 4-6 9-11 13

INDEX

15 16 18-21 24 34 36 37 40-42 45 47-55 58 59 61 66 Patrick 48 Robert 3 6 8-13 18 64-66 Thomas 60
HAMMON, William 63
HANES, Robert 53
HANEY, Captain 6
HANNA, John 47 William 27 65
HANNAH, John 43 William 43
HANNUM, Jonathan 66
HANSBERRY, Smith 22
HANSBROUGH, Smith 10 32
HARDIN, David 48 Moses 48
HARDING, Moses 18
HARFORD, Charles 56
HARGROVE, Amy 47 James 9 32 41 42 43 46 47 John 9 46 47
HARPER, John 36 44 Summers 7 William 9 10 11 38 39
HARRELL, John 46
HARRIS, Elisabeth 52 Elizabeth 66 Elmore 7 8 53 56-60 James 5 John 2 Martha 52 66 Mary 52 66 Robert 38 52 55 66 Samuel 19 Thomas 37 52 66
HARRISON, James 17 24 37 38 John 33 Thomas 26
HART, Henry 12 13 James 2 7 8 9 17 38 39 44 45 51 52 64 William 34 -- 52 ferry 18 19 52
HARWELL, William 39 46
HASSELL, Abraham 1 16 27 37 44 Abram 15 Asa 18 59 Gennet 16 27 Jesse 59 lane 16
HAUGHTON, William 13 27 34 41 58
HAW, Catey 9 Caty 19 23 James 9 19 23 30 38 49 Polly 30 38
HAWKINS, John 3 6 8 9 10
HAYNES, Robert 60 61 Thomas 1
HAYNIE, Captain 7 17 Jesse 4
HAYNS, Robert 57
HAYS, James 46 54 Oliver 48
HAZLET, John 34
HELLON, James 37
HENDERSON, Bennett 7 10 15 23 27 41 48 57 58 63 Charles 12 Edness 19 Ednis 7 Edniss 10 James 58 John 7 10 19 23 48 Lawson 43 47 William 27 30 57 63 mill 1
HENDLEY, John 30
HENDRICK, Elijah 19 35 Harrison 13 ferry 67
HENLEY, John 48
HENNEN/HENNON, James 7 8

HENRY, John 53 William 32
HENSON, Thomas 47
HERNDON, Cornelius 12 53 56-61
HERRIN, Ephraim 59
HERRING, Alexander 56 Bright 21 52 55 Heli 60 James 56
HEWELL, John 36
HINSON, Thomas 47
HOBBS, David 19 66
HOBDAY, Bethey 67
HOBDY, Tabitha 66 Thomas 33 William 66
HODGE, George 25 John 5 44 57 58 61 63 65 Joseph 3 24 35 37 47 48 53 Rivers 1 30 33
HOGAN, Edmond 32 Edward 48 54 George 38 John 46 William 6 27
HOGE, Edward 6
HOGIN, Anthony 17 Edmon/Edmund 29 32 42 46 Edward 10 13 19 40 41
HOLEMAN, Daniel 1
HOLLAND, Frederick 30 33 34 41 James 31
HOLLIS, Jesse 13
HOLLIWAY, Richard 12
HOLLOWAY, Richard 13 23 38 56 Samuel 27 39 58 60 61 66
HOLMES, Robert 17
HOOD, James 22 34 49 John 42
HOOVER, Andrew 7 12 19 20 49 50 58 Henry 7 38 42
HOPE, Adam 33
HORTON, William 38
HOUDESHELL, Jacob 63
HOUSE, Baliss 21 55 61 62 Baloss 54 George 21 51 James 21 Micajah 22 40 50 63 Thomas 5 61 William 21
HOWARD, Benjamin 30 44 Chichester 43 62 64 Fleet 41 Jas 12 17 20 42 William 27
HOWELL, Edward 11 Frances/Francis 61 64 Thomas 9 10 12 13 23 33 41 59 61 63-66
HUBERT, William 7 16
HUDSON, Benjamin 24 Drury 7 Edward 3 Isaac 7
HUMPHREYS, David 39
HUNT, Hardy 19 45 66 James 20 23 John 3 51 Nathaniel 3 Sion 2 7 18 19 22 44 45 60 62 67
HUNTER, Adam 22 35 36 Needham 66
HUTCHINGS, John 1-4 10 12 13 20 35 -- 1 2 9
IRWIN, John 45 48-54 Nathaniel 52

INDEX

JACKSON, Andrew 1 3 4 10 12 13 20 35 James 48 59 66 Stephen 2 Washington 48 -- 1 2 9
JAMES, Thomas 49
JEFFERSON, Peter 10 29 43 44 51 58
JERNIGAN, Silas 3 27 38 44 53 57 58 59
JOHNS, Isaac 19 25
JOHNSON, Boswell 67 George 14 James 15 40 50 56 66 Jesse 5 6 14 16 66 John 8 21 26 28 30 42 48 50 51 57 65 Lewis 6 William 24 28 41 65 -- 47
JOHNSTON, James 40 65 -- 40
JOINER, Jesse 1-4 9 10 30 35 38 45 46 53 56-61 64 Littleton 19 Thomas 3 6 8-13 Whitehead 45 61
JONES, Daniel 18 20 50 Edward 43 Elisha 65 John 3 4 6 10-14 20 23-25 29 31 33 35 36 41 44 48 51 53 54 57 59-62 Lain 55 Polly 38 Richard 45 46 Thomas 63 64 William 27 30 38 42 49 -- 23 60
JOSEY, Allen 22 43 44 59 John 4 11 20 31 32 35 44 55 Sarah 11
JOSY, Allen 42
JOYNER, Jesse 47 Thomas 9 Whitehead 44
JURNIGAN, Silas 53
KEAN, Ashlin 20 Philip 6
KEEF, Thomas 67
KEEFE, Thos 5 8 11 13 16 20 22 25 27 28 33 35 37 48 51 53 54 60 61 67 -- 9 27
KEEN, Ashford 47 Ashlin 8 Edmd 55 Elisha 8 John 5
KEESEE, George 16 17 22 26 54 57 60 64 65
KEIFE, Thomas 2 4 13 45
KELLY, Edward 26 James 22 27
KELOUGH, David 48
KENEDY, Samuel 21 William 64
KENNEDY, Armstrong 58 64 William 20 58
KENNON, William 6 10 13 17-21
KENNY, William 64
KENTUCKY 45 50 52 53 59 60
KERBY, -- 54
KERNEY, William 64
KESEE, George 65
KILPATRICK, William 28 29
KIMBROUGH, M 40 Marmaduke 7 33 66
KING, Davis 35 36 John 44 Richard 9 29 66 67 William 13 16 19 26 27
KINNON, William 12
KIRK, William 12

KIRKHAM, James 4 5 12 15 19 22 Thomas 4 9 12
KIRKPATRICK, Alexander 12 James 53 56 Joseph 61 Wallace 38 41-43 53 Wallis 45 William 4 10 16 27 28 34 38 42 43 44 53 56 57 58 60 61
KISER, Philip 3 67
KNIGHT, William 40 47
KNOTT, John 6
LAFFERTY, John 1 2 4 6 12 28 33 38 57 58 62
LAIN, Isaac 35 39 40 54
LAND, Lewis 41
LANE, Isaac 7 22 23 51 57 James 40 48 50 Lewis 15
LARNER, John 35
LARUE, Isaac 22 34
LASSITER, Willie 10 64
LATIMER, Daniel 60 Griswold 13 53 57 58 59 John 14 34 Lyons 27 Robert 22 23 Witheral 22 24 33 39 60
LAUDERDALE, Captain 34 37 60 66 James 2 John 45 46 Joseph 5 Samuel 37 61 William 17 23 34 58
LAURENCE, Elisabeth 24 Robert 3 12 20
LAURENCE COUNTY, SOUTH CAROLINA, 40
LAVENDER, Charles 44 57 60 Pickins 60 William 60 61
LEAKE, Walter 55
LEATH, James 16 Peter 16
LEMMON/LEMON, Peter 63
LENNY, Thomas 21
LEURY, William 55
LERNERS, Captain 65
LEWIS, Captain 60 Charles 24 25 29 32-34 41-46 59 61 62 64 65 Jacob 29 31 47 59 William 8 50
LILLY, William 37
LINCOLN COUNTY, NORTH CAROLINA, 43
LINDSEY/LINDSY, Isaac 9 Wyot 46
LITSINGER, George 64 John 64
LOGAN, Anne 49 George 32 33 48 53 56
LOGAN COUNTY, KENTUCKY, 59
LOONEY, John 62 Micha 45 Miche 2 Peter 13 15 16 19 53 61 63 64 67 Robert 12 13
LOUIS, John 59
LOUISIANA TERRITORY 46
LOVE, David 18 48 50 57
LOVEL, Colson 24
LOVING, Henry 3 12 Hugh 14 Walter 6 9

INDEX

27 48
LUANY, John 62
LUNA, Peter 8 44
LYON, Henry 49 52 Peter 27 30 59 William 5
LYTLE, Robert 12 32 William 38 49 57 58
MABANE, John 50
MABRY, Seth 6 19 21 26 28
MACLIN, James 34 John 34
MAFIT/MAFFITT, Robert 7 30
MALLARY/MALLERY, Josiah 11 Josias 3
MALONE, Hallery 27 Henry 30 Hilary/Hillery 17 22 27-34 47 51 52 63 Robert 28
MANARDE, Solomon 34
MANARCLE, Solomon 34
MANN, William 2
MANSKER, Kasper 13 45 46 creek 34
MARLIN, Archibald 1 4 10 11 16 22 31-33 38 39 41 51 55 60-62
MARSH, Samuel 34
MARSHAL, Charles 21
MARSHALL, Robert 6 44
MARSHEL, Francis 67
MARTIN, Colonel 34 Elisabeth 38 George 13 15 37 James 33 43 Jemima 39 John 30 Thomas 38 48 William 39 67
MASON, Thomas 32
MASTEN/MASTIN, Thomas 3 9 37 42 45
MATTHEWS, Allen 22 28 33
MAXEY, Walter 29 39 William 9 10 15 27 39
MAY, Thomas 1 15 20
MAYS, Jacob 7
McADAM/McADAMS, John 3 6 24
McADDIN, Henry 16
McALLASTER/McALLISTER, Garland 7 12
McBRIDE, Hugh 25
McCALL, Captain 22 35 60 William 8 22 24 50 57 58 65
McCANN, John 50
McCAUL, Captain 24 William 23 49
McCAULEY, John 27
McCLELEN, William 37
McCLELLAN, William 47
McCLON, William 36
McCLORE, William 36
McClung, Isaac 39 Jsu 57 66 Peggy 6 William 39
McCLURE, John 4

McCLURG, Jsu 47
McCONNELL, Daniel 2 41 John 2 Montgomery 2 22 35 38 39 41-44
McCORKLE, Elizabeth 48 Robt 48 Saml 65
McDANIEL, Clement 12 33 51
McELBERRY, Captain 26 32 Robert 18
McELWRATH, Joseph 8 13 35 36 67
McGAVOCK, R 32
McGEE, Hugh 39
McGLOUGHLIN, Joseph 36 37
McGUIRE, Fergus 50 George 40 Thos 6 56
McKAIN, James 1 6-8 10 11 20 23 32 47 49 50 53 59 60
McKEE, Alexander 17 21 24 John 26
McKESICK, Archibald 28
McKING, William 13
McKINLEY, Robert 8
McKINSEY, James 12 14 23
McKISICK, John 27 28
McKLEBURY, Captain 65
McLEAN, Lauchlan 55
McMILLAN, Alexander 18 30 31 32 51
McMILLIN, Alexander 13 14 32
McMON, -- 57
McMU--, William 5
McMUNN, William 11 12 -- 39
McMURRY, Captain 22 34 58 60 James 17 22 27 28 30-34 40 50 54 Samuel 28 37 39 42 43 45 59 51-54 58 59 60
McMURTRY, John 2-4 6 7 11 15 17 23 27 31 39 43 44 48 52 54 56 59 66
McNUTT, Thomas 64 William 3 6 11 24 42 64 -- 4 16 24 25 38 40 56
McPETERS/McPETTERS, Andrew 7 30
McREYNOLDS, Joseph 38 48 -- 67
MEBANE, James 50 Robert 50 William 50
MECKELBERRY, Robert 52
MEIRS, Humphrey 6
MELTON, Andrew 6 William 40 49
MERRELL, Timothy 59
MERRETT, Timothy 59
MICHIE, George 9
MICKELBERRY, Captain 60 Robert 19
MIERS, Elisha 8
MILES, Isreal 14
MILLER, John 7 30
MILLS, James 9 John 3 11 17 18 32 43 48 52
MILTON, William 37
MIRES, Euridice 30 Humphrey 24 26 Miles

INDEX

33 34 42
MISSISSIPPI TERRITORY 22 44
MITCHEL/MITCHELL, Captain 22 Elijah 35
Henry 17 51 Jeremiah 22 27 28 30-34 37
John 3-5 12 14 21 25 32 35-37 42 44-47
49 54 56 58 61 66 Robert 4 21 23 25 30
35 47 49 50 57 Solomon 44
MONTGOMERY, Captain 22 60 64 66 Stephen
6 34 William 2 7 9-11 19 27 30 33 34 38
39 41 42 47 48 51 52 60-62 65 66 mill 8
MOODY, Becky 44 John 61 William 47
MOORE, Captain 44 60 66 Demcey 8 Demcy
19 44 51 60 63 Dempsey 9-12 17 30 34 45
Demsey 31 Demsy 26 42 45 Denney 19
Jesse 7 39 John 27 29 38 43 44 53 57 58
61 65 Richard 9 Robert 9 10 15 17 19 20
26 31 41 42 43 53 Timothy 54 William 63
MORGAN, Benjamin 12 20 29 31 Charles 42
43 Edward 27 John 1 37 40 47 53 56 66
William 64
MORIS, Thomas 62
MORRIS, John 50 56
MORRISH, Caty 37 Neubern 37
MORRISON, Elias 50 James 46 52 66
MORROW, Benjamin 67
MOSS, Mattw 1 12 Susanna 57 Thos 37 65
MOTHERAL, John 32 Joseph 23 32 40 49 61
66 -- 31
MOTHERALL, John 60 Joseph 22 50
MURDOCK, Sampson 5
MURPHEY, John 13 44 Michael 4 12 13
Sally 30
MURPHY, Hardy 34 Jeremiah 40 50 John
9 Michael 9
MURRAY/MURREY, James 63 Thomas 17 56
MURROW, Benjamin 51
MURRY, Thomas 2 7 22 31 51 60 66
NASHVILLE 8
NEAL/NEALE, Matthew 12 31 32 55
NEEL, Thomas 57 58
NEELEY, Alexander 28 James 28 John 28
NEELLEY, Thomas 36
NEELY, William 28 46
NEILL, Henry 7 45 Thomas 45
NEISBET, John 63
NEW ORLEANS 12 20 31
NEWBY, Henry 34 51 James 18
NICHOLS, John 2 13 30
NICHOLSON, Elijah 36
NIGHT, Elizabeth 3

NOBB, Drury 14
NOBLE, Drury 14
NOLIN, William 63
NORMAN, Ezekiel 13
NORRELL, Robert 48
NORTH CAROLINA 1 6 35 42 43 50 61
NORVELL, Robert 18 Sarah 18
NOSH--, William 49
NOWELL, Robert 43 51 Sarah 43
NUSUM, Andrew 18
NYE, Shadrack 9 20 27 30 34 38 42 45 46
58 67
ODAM, James 12 38 40
OGELS, William 19 29 46 51 52
OGELSBY, Daniel 67 Elisha 13
OGLES, William 29 60
ORANGE COUNTY, NORTH CAROLINA, 42 50
ORMAN, David 45 46 57 58
ORR, Araminta 52 66 Berry 59 David 53
56 Greenberry 55 John 11 12 14 17 18
21 40 46 52
OSBROOKS, Nancy 56 William 56
OSBURN, Noble 49
OUTLAW, George 6
OVERSTREET, Robert 19
OVERTON, Archibald 34
OWEN, Kenedy/Kennedy 4 48 Laurence/Law-
rence 10 13 20 23 53 62 -- 23 60
OWENS, Kennedy 14
OZBROOK/OZBROOKS, Ruth 36 37 56
OZBURN, William 14
PAGE, John 57
PALMER, Henry 41
PANKEY, John 12 53 56 Nancy 56
PANNELL, William 35
PARK, Joseph 22
PARKER, Danl 56 Jno 20 Nathan 28 Nathl
1 30 33 37 65 Richard 45 Robert 61 63
65 66 Thomas 6 7 18 22 23 34 35 40 47
PARKS, Hugh 36
PARR, William 54 66
PARRY, John 58
PARSON, John 24 37
PATTERSON, John 47 Reuben 57 Robt 6 12
PATTESON, Reuben 57
PATTON, John 22 52 59 Margaret 27
Norbert 59 Robert 3 11-13 21 27 35 38
39 41-43 53 56-59 61 62 65 William 65
PAVATT, Isaac 16 John 16 44 64
PAYTON, Captain 16 22 29 60 67 Ephraim

INDEX

2 9 27 John 2 3 7-9 12 14 18 20-23 34 39 46 48 50 52 57 59 60 62 William 4 7 9 10 12 14-16 18 20-24 28 30 33 39 41 43 46 48 52 56 57 59 60 62 Yelverton 52 62 -- 62 fork 26
PEAIRS, Jonathan 39 46
PEAK, Norman 56
PEARCE, Isaac 65 Jonathan 13 15 61
PENDERGAST, John 13
PENDERGRASS, John 10 66 Richard 12 15 56 William 10
PENDERGRAST, John 5 15 27
PENNY, William 9
PERRY, Edwin 47 George 29 John 13 42 58 67 Josiah 67 Thomas 48
PEYTON, Ephraim 2 John 2 5 13 14 21 30 54 William 2
PHILPOTTS, John 36
PHIPS, Lewalen/Lewallen 26 28
PHIPPS, William 1 6 60
PIERCE, Isaac 45
PIKE, Norman 53
PIPER, Samuel 27
PITT, Henry 1 2 3 4 Lunsford 20 Stephen 6 11 15 47
PITTMAN, Tabitha 4 William 4
PITTS, Stephen 38
PORTER, Alexander 28 Ambrose 8 9 31 32 33 39 43 48 56 -- 16
POTTER, Thomas 15
PRENDERGAST, John 5
PRESTON, Captain 35 57 Thomas 3 20 22 41 42
PREWITT, Elisha 3 4 7 8 14 21 22 33 38 Lemuel 4 38
PRITCHELL, John 5
PRITCHER, John 38
PROVINCE, Alexander 24 John 24
PUGH, John 33
PURSE, Jonathan 5
PURSELL, Hardy 41
PURSLEY, David 7 22 23 30
PURVIANS, William 5
PURVIS, Allen 7 14 16 18 21 23 33 34 41 50 52 53 55 62 Clary 21 Jno 21 Miles 21
PUTT, John 2 28 39
PYRTLE, -- 34
RALEY, Robert 20
RALPH, John 44
RAMSEY, William 5

RAN, Howell 45
RANKINS, James 45 61 63 67
RAPIER, Richard 5
RASCO, Alexander 23 24 36 41
RAWLINGS, Benjamin 2 10 12 17 21 22 29-32 36 41 42 51 54 62 James 2 Rhodam 1 45 46 61 63-67 Thomas 1 3 14 16 29 31 36 43 50 55
RAWSON, Daniel 23
RAYLEIGH, Robert 28 58
RAYNE, Gideon 1
RAZEL, Peter 26
READ, James 39 William 54
REDIN, George 51
REED, George 1 2 4 8 9 22 23 30 38 64 James 1 9 15 49 Leonard 9 William 35 38 39 41-45
REESE, Charles 59 Solomon 14
REEVES, Edmund 27 35 Joseph 9 17
REID, George 3
RENTFRO, William 1 7 19
REPPI, Jesse 24
REYNOLDS Needham 19 30
RICE, Joshua 7 22 27 30 32 39 48 51 60 64 65 66 William 51 56 67
RICHARDSON, Francis 50 Samuel 62
RICHEY, Thomas 12 19 29 31 48 49 51
RICHMOND, James 4 8
RICKMON, Mark 5 Nathan 5
RIGHT, James 60
RING, William 56
RITTEN, Thomas 2
RITTER, Thomas 2
ROARK, William 36
ROBB, Elizabeth 28 Joseph 54 Robert 28 45 61 63 64 65 66 William 45 49
ROBERTSON, Andrew 13 Francis 52 66 John 37 43 49
ROBINSON, John 40
ROCKINGHAM COUNTY, NORTH CAROLINA, 61
ROGAN, Hugh 40
ROGERS, Abraham 1 37 65 Armstead 30 John 53 Lemuel 39 Matthew 17 20 21 25 William 46
RONEY, James 2 37 40 50 61 64 Samuel 37
ROSBER, John 14
ROSH, Owen 2
ROSS, Reuben 48
ROWAN COUNTY, NORTH CAROLINA, 61
ROWLAND, John 38 52 65

INDEX

ROWLINGS, Rhodam 6
RULE, John 63
RUSSELL, -- 40 54
RUTHERFORD, Griffith 21 50 James 27 46 John 3 6 30 50 53 56 57 58 59 60 61 67
RUYLE, Frances 16 Henry 16 John 13 17 18 19 20 21 63 Solomon 25
RYAN, Cornelius 6
SAMPLE, -- 37
SANDERS, Captain 22 Daniel 10 47 51 62 Edward 3 6-8 11 18 21 23 27 35 37 43 50 51 59 Francis 4 Goolsby 12 Hubbard 63 James 3-5 10 19 22 34 35 45-47 51-54 62 63 Jane 47 Robert 50 Thomas 45 46 48 49 50 William 3 5 6 11 35 38 company 1
SANDERSON, Edward 3 30 37 40 47 60
SARVER, John 35
SCAVEA, Jacob 42
SCOBEY/SCOBY, Joseph 8 27 28 31 55
SCOT/SCOTT, James 27 40 53 64 Richard 43 48
SCURRY, Thomas 21 31 34-36 39 41 42 44 45 51 55 56 58
SEARCY, Jane 51 Reuben 12 43 50
SEAVER, Jacob 42
SEAWELL, Benjn 26 34 45 Hardy 45 John 18 19 45 Polley 18 William 3 6 7 10 15 19 22 26 34 37-39 43 47 48 56 60 65 66
SENNY, Thomas 21
SERVERS, Henry 50
SESSUMS, James 24
SETTLER, Isaac 6 -- 14
SEUNY, Thomas 38
SHACKLEFORD, Thomas 64
SHAIFER, Abraham 62
SHANER, John 13 21
SHARP, Anthony 49 53 59 Leander 30 Maxwell 30 31
SHAVER, Daniel 42 John 17 18 19 20 27 32 34 43 49 51
SHAW, Hance 24 Hugh 26 James 11 John 2 Robert 7 13 17 18 19 20 21 35 57 60 61 Thomas 39
SHEEN, Jesse 3 4 27-30 37 42 44 52
SHEIN, Jesse 38
SHELBY, Anthony 24 36 D 2 David 8 17 33 39 60 61 64 John 23 45 49 53 61 crk 60
SHELLEYS CREEK 66
SHELTON, Mary 7
SHEPHERD/SHEPPARD, Benjamin 34 Nancy 34

SHEROCK, Stephen 1
SHEVER, John 30
SHIEN, Jesse 8 22
SHOCKLEY, Wilson 39
SHOLDERS, Solomon 7 William 33
SHOULDERS, Solomon 3 6 13
SHUNE, Robert 30
SHURCRAFT, Simon 39
SIMPSON, Elijah 43 57 59 61 James 16 23 43 Robert 2 7-10 30 40 43 54 Sarah 52 66 Thomas 43 William 37
SITTLER, -- 4
SKEEN, Jesse 30-34 44 51 52 64
SKIEN, Jesse 45
SKIPPER, Archa 47
SLAUGHTER, Ebenezer 15
SLAVES: Agg 39, Allyeras 28, Billy 48, Blackman 6, Bob 9 28, Bridget 40, Buck 17, Cherry 9, Coalrain 11, Coldwater 23, Collins 64, Dave 39, David 64, Dennis 2, Delita 39, Dick 28, Dicy 2, Dilcey 51, Dorrell 17, Dove 7, Feraby 18, George 50 54, Glases 15, Grace 48, Hannah 28 39, Harriott 48, Harry 18 48, Isaac 40 51, Isam 20, Jack 17 29, Jacob 28, Jarrett 27, Jean 20, Jenny 43, Jess 39, Jim 11 17 42, Judith 5, Judy 9, Laurence 15, Lilia 42, Lillane 50, London 15, Lucy 4 9 26, Malinder 65, Maria 18, Mary 38, Micajah 62, Milly 15, Nancy 46, Nat 31, Nina 28, Obedience 4, Patsey 49, Pegg 44, Peggy 2, Peter 46, Powhatan 41, Rachel 11, Ralph 42, Sam 37, Sarah 51, Sell 42, Senia 44, Susannah 55, Terry 11, Tom 51, Tony 9, Venus 44, Vine 28, Winney 43
SLINKARD, Jacob 62
SLOAN, Fergus 24 40 John 16 37 40 47 54
SMITH, Benjamin 2 11 15 Daniel 5 37 45 George 3 6 8 10 20 34 38 61 John 37 44 54 Joshua 44 45 49 50 58 59 Perrin 5 41 44 Richard 2 3 9 10 12 15 Robert 49 William 59 63   county 40 54 59 61
SNEED, Stephen 35
SNELLING, William 55
SNODDY, William 46
SOUTH CAROLINA 7 40 64
SOWEL, Isaac 20
SPAIN, Ruffin 41
SPOONER, John 6 17 38 56 Jonathan 17 38

INDEX

SPAN, Henry 61
SPRADLIN, Jesse 2 24 28 John 3 44 52
SPRADLING, Jesse 39 John 53 54
SPYCER, William 31
STAFFORD, David 11 15
STAGNER, Nathan 26
STALCUP, Isaac 13 Swain 13 Swen 12 20 William 34
STAMPS, John 3 33 -- 40 41 47 57
STANFIELD, Ashley 12 40 51
STARNES/STARNS, John 9 10 50
STEEL, George 10 James 7 10 31 59 62 Joseph 10 Robert 10 40 47
STEELE, Deenah 44 George 29 Henry 51 James 3 5 6 14 20 24 25 30 34 44 53 62 63 Robert 27 28 61 65 66 William 14
STEPHENS, Vachel 46 47 58
STEPHENSON, Hugh 62 Moore 1 24
STERNES, John 3 6 40
STERNS FORD 37
STEVENS, John 36
STEVENSON, Hugh 65 Josiah 27 Joseph 18 Josiah 27 28 60 63 Moore 36 37
STEWART, Barney 55 Daniel 64 David 19 29 32 33 48 James 10 39 50 John 2 4 19 39 58 64 Samuel 2 -- 28
STONE, Eusebius 58 61 Nicholas 8 9 15 56 57 58 Stephen 13
STORY, James 33
STOVAL/STOVALL, Bartholomew 5 13 28 45 48-54 Geo 51 52 Terisha 52 Wm 27 28
STRATTON, James 43 49 60
STRAWTH, Robert 43
STREET, Isaac 17 57 58 61 63 65 66 67
STRINGER, Zachariah 21
STROTHER, Jas 65 Richd 65 Robt 15 17 58
STUARD, James 11 55
STUART, Daniel 58 David 6 8 12 32 35-37 48 49 Jas 40 John 29 34 56 57 66 Saml 1 Thos 7 8 10 12 13 20 21 31 61 W 7 Wm 29
STUBBINS TAN YARD 35
STUBBLEFIELD, Armstead 8 Armstreat/ Armstreet 3 9 26 32 33 44 45 53 54 66 Clement 3 Garrison 45 George 35 36 Jeremiah 44 45 53 Lemuel 8 56 Robert 53 Thomas 9 53 66 Tilman/Tilmon 3 8
STULL, Zachariah 55 57
SULIVANT, John 54
SULLIVAN, John 40
SUMMERS, William 44

SURRY, William 21 52
SUTLER, -- 28
SWANCY, John 13 51 67
SWANY, John 62
TARPLEY, Sterling 67
TARVER, Benjamin 5 9 27 George 45
TAYLOR, Benjamin 39 Edmund 15 John 12 20 31 40 Nathaniel 15 Richard 15 27 36 42 53 62 Robert 3
TENNON, Lamuel/Samuel 67
THOMAS, Arisck 16 Cornelius 1 9 23 24 27 30 44 49 54 57 62 Michael 32 Wm 29
THOMPSON, Anderson 27 Jacob 11 12 13 20 30 58 61
THURMAN, Goalesberry/Goldsberry/Goldsby 1 10 62 John 49
THURMON, John 45 49 50
THURMOND, Fleming 28 40 John 28 29 48 50 51 52 53 54
TILLMON, George 9 John 9
TINNEN, John 58 Lemuel 58
TINSLEY, Sterling 45
TOMKINS, J 11 John 13
TOMPKINS, John 10 45
TOMPSON, Elijah 65
TOWELL, Isaac 61 63 64 65
TRAIL, Basil 65 Solomon 65
TRAMMEL CREEK 18
TREBB/TREBLE, Stephen 39
TRIBLE, Lucinda 56 Milley 56 Polly 56 Stephen 40 45 56 64 Susanna 56
TRICE, John 2 9 11 14 17 19 21 26 27 33 40 43 45 48 54 Mrs 10 11 Patsey 2 9 14 17 19 21 26 27 33 40 43-45 48 54 William 51 62
TRIGG, A 10 13 19 25 26 29 31 45 Abraham 19 22 36 44 53 Abram 4 23 31 56 58 William 3 7 9-23 25 26 28-32 35 36 39- 45 50 53 55 58-63 65 66 -- 11
TROTTER, George 27 Samuel 27
TROUSDALE, James 2 3 12 13 19 23 24 29 31 35 40 43 53 55 John 2 54 Jonathan 12 41 42 55 59 Robert 4 12 13
TRUETT/TRUITT, John 34 35 60 61
TRUMBO, Ambrose 34 Ephraim 12 Geo 11 12
TULLOCH, David 46
TURNER, Adam 43 Captain 22 32 James 12 17 John 26 35 40 50 57 61 Lemuel 9 30 41 42 48 Terisha 17
TURNEY, Peter 61

79

INDEX

TURPIN, Edmond/Edmund 3 6 24 27 29 31 48 49 64 Edward 11
TWIGG, Daniel 13 30
TWOPENCE, Kitty 13
USELL, Isham 10
UZZELL, Isam 29 61 Isham 19 27 Ison 44 45 56
VAUGHN, James 61
VINCENT, Richard 24
VINSON, Benthal 42 43 Henry 1-4 51 54 Jas 12 33 35 38 39 41-45 49 50 61 64-66
VIRGINIA [state] 26 36 61
VIVERETT, Micajah 12
WADKINS, Captain 22 Charles 30 James 17 Robert 9 13 17 18 19 20 21
WALKER, James 15 John 24 Warren 20 21
WALL, Hugh 7 22 31 34 35 44 54
WALLACE, Adam 64 Jos 13 35 38 39 41-45 61 65 66 Wm 10 19-21 27 28 31-33 44 58
WALLER, William 25 27
WALLIS, William 33
WALLS, Hugh 29
WALTON, Capt 22 24 47 60 David 1 Drury 33 50 54 Isaac 1 3-5 12 13 26-29 38 39 64-66
WARE, James 28
WARREN, Humphrey 17 Jacob 27
WARREN COUNTY 22
WASHINGTON COUNTY, VIRGINIA, 26
WATERS, -- 13 15
WATKINS, Capt 32 60 James 6 Robert 17
WATSON, Elisabeth 48 Samuel 3 8 48
WATWOOD, George 30
WEATHERRED, Francis 5 17 28 36 41
WEATHERS, Joseph 20 21
WEBB, Amos 38 42 45 John 3 19 35
WELLS, Ephm 1 Hry 20 22 38 39 Jesse 20 22 32 38 39 44 Josiah 1 3 7 19 Nancy 1
WHARTON, William 42
WHEELER, James 1
WHERRY, Simeon/Simon 24 49 William 3 6 35 36 53 56
WHITAKER, William 7 11
WHITE, Alexr 59 61 Jas 6 10 14-19 29 45 59 Jno 13 15 52 57 Jonathan 3 Joseph 66 Maunsel 12 20 31 Mira 18 Narcissa 24 Robt 6 22 23 46 61 65 66 Stephen 39 Ths 36 51 57 Wm 1 8 9 59 60 61 -- 25 47
WHITESIDE, Jenkin 29 41
WHITESIDES, Jinkin 11 29
WHITMAN, Joseph 40
WHITMORE, Joseph 37
WHITSIDE, Laurence 22
WHITSITT, John 27 Laurence/Lawrence 23 53 67
WHITTED, William 42
WIER, William 9
WILEY, William 57
WILKERSON, Jesse 8 50
WILLARD, John 9 17 20
WILLIAMS, Beverly 24 James 15 48 63 Nathaniel 53 61 Sampson 4 13 Samuel 34 William 41 42 55 57
WILLIAMSON, Jas 63 Robt 3 6 35-37 67
WILLIFORD, Green 14 49 58
WILLIS, Harvey 33 Hervey 59
WILSON, David 13 20 James 1 2 4 5 7-14 17 19-21 23 24 26-37 39-41 43-46 49-52 54 58 59 61 63-67 John 24 49 56 57 59 Joseph 13 15 16 24 Matthew 56 Nicholas 65 Samuel 18 45 Thomas 24 50 William 20 49 59 Zacheus 12 13 15 18-20 27-30 36 40 42 43 48 49 53 56 59 62 63
WILSON COUNTY 67
WINCHESTER, James 2-10 12 13 15 17-19 22 23 26 27 29 30 34 36 38 39 41-43 46 48 49 51 54-56 58-61 63-66 Richard 65 Stephen 48 56 William 48 -- 24
WINDERS, Epinatus 61
WINN, Mourning 5 17 21 49 63 65 66
WITBY, Amos 41
WITHERS, John 3 4 7 10 13 32-34 40 51 59 61 Joseph 7
WOOD, Dawson 58 59 John 7 Thomas 31
WOODAL/WOODALL/WOODELL, George 29 William 8 24 30 33 65
WORMINGTON, Edward 18 48
WRIGHT, Joseph 12
WYLES, Geo 22 33 Jenny 22 33 Jno 22 33 Margaret 22 33 Saml 22 33 William 33
WYNN/WYNNE, Jno 2 Mourning 29 45 48-54 61 Peter 49 Polly 2
YANCE, Lawrence 46
YANDEL/YANDELL, Wilson 17-19 48 50 52-54 56 65 67
YOKUM, Jesse 30
YONER, lAWRENCE 64
YOUNG, Abraham 20 Abram 1 Henry 2 4 7 18 Jacob 51 53 John 1 53 63 64 Thos 7
YOUREE, Francis 5 11 39 52 Patrick 66

Other Heritage Books by Carol Wells:

Abstracts of Giles County, Tennessee: County Court Minutes, 1813-1816 and Circuit Court Minutes, 1810-1816

CD: Tennessee, Volume 1

Davidson County, Tennessee County Court Minutes, Volume 1, 1783-1792

Davidson County, Tennessee County Court Minutes, Volume 2, 1792-1799

Davidson County, Tennessee County Court Minutes, Volume 3, 1799-1803

Dickson County, Tennessee County and Circuit Court Minutes, 1816-1828 and Witness Docket

Edgefield County, South Carolina Probate Records, Boxes One through Three Packages 1-106

Edgefield County, South Carolina Probate Records, Boxes Four through Six Packages 107-218

Edgefield County, South Carolina: Deed Books 13, 14 and 15

Edgefield County, South Carolina: Deed Books 16, 17 and 18

Edgefield County, South Carolina: Deed Books 19, 20, 21 and 22

Edgefield County, South Carolina: Deed Books 23, 24, 25 and 26

Edgefield County, South Carolina: Deed Books 27, 28 and 29

Edgefield County, South Carolina: Deed Books 30 and 31

Edgefield County, South Carolina: Deed Books 32 and 33

Edgefield County, South Carolina: Deed Books 34 and 35

Edgefield County, South Carolina: Deed Books 36, 37 and 38

Edgefield County, South Carolina: Deed Books 39 and 40

Edgefield County, South Carolina: Deed Book 41

Edgefield County, South Carolina: Deed Books 42 and 43, 1826-1829

Genealogical Abstracts of Edgefield, South Carolina Equity Court Records

Natchez Postscripts, 1781-1798

Rhea County, Tennessee Tax Lists, 1832-1834, and County Court Minutes Volume D: 1829-1834

Robertson County, Tennessee Court Minutes, 1796-1807

Sumner County, Tennessee Court Minutes, 1787-1805 and 1808-1810

Williamson County, Tennessee County Court Minutes, July 1812-October 1815

Williamson County, Tennessee County Court Minutes, May 1806-April 1812

www.ingramcontent.com/pod-product-compliance
Lightning Source LLC
Chambersburg PA
CBHW072133220426
43664CB00013B/2229